D1738702

Cultures of the Future

World Anthropology

General Editor

SOL TAX

Patrons

CLAUDE LÉVI-STRAUSS
MARGARET MEAD

LAILA SHUKRY EL HAMAMSY
M. N. SRINIVAS

MOUTON PUBLISHERS · THE HAGUE · PARIS
DISTRIBUTED IN THE USA AND CANADA BY ALDINE, CHICAGO

Cultures of the Future

Editors

MAGOROH MARUYAMA
ARTHUR M. HARKINS

MOUTON PUBLISHERS · THE HAGUE · PARIS
DISTRIBUTED IN THE USA AND CANADA BY ALDINE, CHICAGO

General Editor's Preface

Like the proverbial man from Mars, at a time when space exploration was still fictional, "looking backward" from a time far in the future has been a literary device to achieve perspective on the condition of humankind. The present book broaches seriously the problem of how anthropology can add some part of our species' future to the empirical studies of our 3-million-year past. The book itself points to a transition from a past in which the scholars of the Western industralized world spoke for the species to a future in which participation comes from all concerned. It is appropriate that the occasion of the change should be an unusual world congress of anthropologists.

Like most contemporary sciences, anthropology is a product of the European tradition. Some argue that it is a product of colonialism, with one small and self-interested part of the species dominating the study of the whole. If we are to understand the species, our science needs substantial input from scholars who represent a variety of the world's cultures. It was a deliberate purpose of the IXth International Congress of Anthropological and Ethnological Sciences to provide impetus in this direction. The *World Anthropology* volumes, therefore, offer a first glimpse of a human science in which members from all societies have played an active role. Each of the books is designed to be self-contained; each is an attempt to update its particular sector of scientific knowledge and is written by specialists from all parts of the world. Each volume should be read and reviewed individually as a separate volume on its own given subject. The set as a whole will indicate what changes are in store for anthropology as scholars from the developing countries join in studying the species of which we are all a part.

The IXth Congress was planned from the beginning not only to include as many of the scholars from every part of the world as possible, but also with a view toward the eventual publication of the papers in high-quality volumes. At previous Congresses scholars were invited to bring papers which were then read out loud. They were necessarily limited in length, many were only summarized; there was little time for discussion; and the sparse discussion could only be in one language. The IXth Congress was an experiment aimed at changing this. Papers were written with the intention of exchanging them before the Congress, particularly in extensive pre-Congress sessions; they were not intended to be read aloud at the Congress, that time being devoted to discussions — discussions which were simultaneously and professionally translated into five languages. The method for eliciting the papers was structured to make as representative a sample as was allowable when scholarly creativity — hence self-selection — was critically important. Scholars were asked both to propose papers of their own and to suggest topics for sessions of the Congress which they might edit into volumes. All were then informed of the suggestions and encouraged to rethink their own papers and the topics. The process, therefore, was a continuous one of feedback and exchange and it has continued to be so even after the Congress. The some two thousand papers comprising *World Anthropology* certainly then offer a substantial sample of world anthropology. It has been said that anthropology is at a turning point; if this is so, these volumes will be the historical direction-markers.

As might have been foreseen in the first post-colonial generation, the large majority of the Congress papers (82 percent) are the work of scholars identified with the industrialized world which fathered our traditional discipline and the institution of the Congress itself: Eastern Europe (15 percent); Western Europe (16 percent); North America (47 percent); Japan, South Africa, Australia, and New Zealand (4 percent). Only 18 percent of the papers are from developing areas: Africa (4 percent); Asia-Oceania (9 percent); Latin America (5 percent). Aside from the substantial representation from the U.S.S.R. and the nations of Eastern Europe, a significant difference between this corpus of written material and that of other Congresses is the addition of the large proportion of contributions from Africa, Asia, and Latin America. "Only 18 percent" is two to four times as great a proportion as that of other Congresses; moreover, 18 percent of 2,000 papers is 360 papers, 10 times the number of "Third World" papers presented at previous Congresses. In fact, these 360 papers are more than the total of *all* published after last International Congress of Anthropological and Ethnological Sciences which was held in the United States (Philadelphia, 1956).

The significance of the increase is not simply quantitative. The input of scholars from areas which have until recently been no more than subject matter for anthropology represents both feedback and also long-awaited theoretical contributions from the perspectives of very different cultural, social, and historical traditions. Many who attended the IXth Congress were convinced that anthropology would not be the same in the future. The fact that the next Congress (India, 1978) will be our first in the "Third World" many be symbolic of the change. Meanwhile, sober consideration of the present set of books will show how much, and just where and how, our discipline is being re-volutionized.

Although the present volume is unique, readers will find of interest other books in the series which, in describing the familiar past and present, deal with widely varying cultures, unfamiliar cultural forms, extra-mundane phenomena, and especially anthropological theory which is timeless. For those who find future models interesting precisely because they provide keys to understanding mankind's threatening social problems, the *World Anthropology* series provides a rich variety of books on human nature, on interpersonal and intergroup and international relations, on education and on problems of population, nutrition, drug abuse, alcoholism, etc. in worldwide perspective.

Chicago, Illinois   SOL TAX
January 19, 1978

Foreword

ALVIN TOFFLER

The general crisis of industrialism that now crackles across the face of the planet like some vast cultural thunderstorm forces each of us to confront time in a new way. Throughout the world, scholars and intelligent laymen are realizing that the future can no longer be taken for granted. One reflection of this growing concern with tomorrow is the development of what has come to be known as "cultural futuristics."

Wherever techno-cultural change is slow, a knowledge of past and present makes reasonably accurate expectations about the future possible. A cross-section of one generation provides a fair basis for sketching the cross-section of the next. As change accelerates, however, present and future diverge, and conscious adaptation requires a sharpened sense of the differences between the two; it requires a higher level of future-consciousness.

So long as industrial society was still growing, so long as it continued to provide a "progressive" model for the nonindustrial cultures, the problem of the future was simplified. Hundreds of millions of people in the diverse cultures of Africa, Asia and Latin America, were encouraged by emissaries from the rich nations, and by their own Western-educated elites, to picture their future in terms of the industrial past. History was a temporal staircase with fixed landings, and one could eliminate poverty and provide decent standards of health and education only by hopping upward, one step at a time, through each of the so-called "stages of growth." Success in ascending this staircase would result in "modernization" — i.e. transmutation of the existing "under-developed" culture into a full-fledged, "developed" industrial culture. The metaphor of the factory dominated all thinking about the future in academic and governmental circles.

Today, as one crisis after another rips through the industrial nations themselves, as fantastic technological breakthroughs puncture their traditional boundaries and make one institution after another obsolete, it is clear that the industrial world system is itself undergoing a profound transformative process. A new civilization is in birth, a new cultural ecology is taking form, and both groups of cultures —industrial and nonindustrial — are poised on the edge of something radically new and unfamiliar, a world game, as it were, for which the rules are still to be discovered.

In this situation, it is no longer sensible for the nonindustrial cultures to picture their own future in industrial terms. And it is absurd for those of us who were reared in the industrial system to assume its indefinite perpetuation. In both sectors, we desperately need new, alternative images of the future — visionary explorations of the possible, systematic investigation of the probable, and moral evaluation of the preferable.

The power of such images in influencing the future is inestimable, and it is precisely here that anthropology has much to offer. Forecasts, predictions, prophesies, even literary utopias, all tend to be highly simplistic in their representation of future states of reality. Economists, with their input-output models and national income statistics serve up ghastly, one-sided images of society. Systems engineers, technologists, planners, for all their insistence on the necessity for holistic thinking, tend to produce simpleminded schematics when they begin talking about the future. Novelists, poets and visionaries tend to be ignorant of the potential impacts of science and technology.

The generation of worthwhile images of the future — images from which we can learn and which can guide our decisions in the present — requires a degree of roundedness and cultural sensitivity that anthropology, at its best, brings with it. We need to explore our possibilities, not merely with respect to economic trends and technological breakthroughs, but with respect to deeply buried cultural forms and assumptions. How can we, will we, should we deal with time, space, structure, scale, and the other elementals of human experience? How do our deeply hidden assumptions about these elementals constrain or liberate our images of the future? Anthropologists are not insensitive to these issues, and while projecting forward in time may still be an unfamiliar exercise for most of them, they come to it with useful equipment.

Anthropology has taught all of us the lessons of cultural relativity, but, unfortunately, the lesson has not yet been fully learned at home. Anthropology today is still primarily based on the theories of European and North American scholars. Steeped in the culture of industrialism, these experts bring with them baggage in the form of unquestioned assumptions, models, and metaphors that fix boundaries to their imagination. Thus, it seems taken for granted that anthropologists from Western industrial cultures ought to study "simpler" nonindustrial cultures. It seldom occurs to most of us that the reverse may be even more necessary. It seems taken for granted that nonindustrial cultures are going to fade away and become industrialized. It seldom occurs to most of us that industrialism, itself, is in even greater danger of nonsurvival.

Today, as industrialism reaches its historical climax, and a new culture begins to make its appearance, we need alternative images of tomorrow based on the principle of diversity. For cultural heterogeneity is not a luxury but a critically essential adaptive mechanism for the species. The world must not belong to, and cannot survive as, a monoculture.

Once we begin to generate a profusion of rounded, multidimensional futural images, we shall make possible wholly new lines of human development that have been, until now, foreclosed to us. For these reasons, work in the field of cultural futures is more than an academic exercise. It is a survival activity — a crucial function at a moment when the human species is beginning to reappraise its long-term goals as a species. Cultural futuristics helps guarantee that there will be a future, not merely for the rich and powerful, but for all the world's people.

ALVIN TOFFLER

Table of Contents

Introduction

MAGOROH MARUYAMA

For two decades now, a young discipline devoted to the study of the future has been in formation. It has come to be called "futuristics," usually, and occasionally by some other name like "futurology." Initially, its main focus was on technological and economic forecasting. More recently, however, trend analysis of social and cultural change, mainly within the United States and other industrialized countries, has been added. The emphasis, in both technoeconomic and sociocultural studies, has begun to shift from forecasting to the examination of alternatives. In spite of its rapid development, futuristics still remains basically ethnocentric. It mainly expresses the views of futurists in industrialized countries.

To remedy this ethnocentrism in the study of the future, a session on "The Future of the Human Species seen by the Entire Species" was undertaken at the IXth International Congress of Anthropological and Ethnological Sciences in 1973, and a special effort was made to obtain contributions from the developing countries.

The Congress occurred at a time which was very propitious for such an effort. Futuristics needed input directly from the developing coun-

The editors wish to thank the following copyright holders for their permission to use the works indicated below:

American Anthropological Association: "Contribution of anthropology to the science of the future" by Margaret Mead; "Futuristics and the imaging capacity of the West" by Elise Boulding; "Toward human futuristics" by Magoroh Maruyama; "Population and environment" by Steven Polgar; "The prehistory of *Homo sapiens*" by James Gifford; "Past and future culture change" by Robert McKnight; "Toward polyocular anthropology" by Sue-Ellen Jacobs; and "The anthropology of the future as an academic discipline" by Roger Wescott.

The Viking Press: "Ways of perceiving oneself in urban planning interaction" by Edmund N. Bacon, © 1974 by Edmund N. Bacon in *Design of cities* by Edmund N. Bacon, in its enlarged 1974 edition, the Viking Press.

tries as well as from the discipline of anthropology in general; anthropology, in turn, needed greater exposure to futuristics as well as stimulus in its transition from being a white-dominated field to being a multiracial discipline.

The study of the future as it is currently practiced in the industrialized countries has two main components: a descriptive component and a goal-generating component. The latter is becoming increasingly important for two reasons. First, there is a growing realization among people in the industrialized countries that they are heading for catastrophe and will drag the whole world with them unless something is done to avoid it. Second, there is a realization that catastrophe cannot be avoided unless changes are made in the philosophy of life which had never been questioned before. This entails two sets of considerations. First, some action must be taken, and action requires goals. Second, the assumptions and implicit goals of life which had been taken for granted as "truth" must be reexamined.

Generating goals for action involves the risk of ethnocentrism if cross-cultural input is not provided. Furthermore, examination of hidden assumptions and implicit goals is facilitated by such input.

Cultural futuristics was included in the annual meeting of the American Anthropological Association for the first time in 1970, and only a small number of anthropologists have participated in it so far. The participants in the early symposia were all North Americans or were from Japan or the industrialized countries of Europe.

The discipline of anthropology is at present in a stage of fundamental transition, from a period in which white anthropologists with a Western epistemological framework studied nonwhite cultures, to a period in which nonwhite anthropologists with non-Western epistemological frameworks will bring unprecedented enrichment to the science. The result will be polyocular anthropology, in which cross-subjective comparisons between research projects based on different epistemologies will ensure greater relevance than ethnocentric insistence on measurability and "objectivity" based on the paradigm of eighteenth-century physics. A culture, white or nonwhite, can be studied by endogenous researchers with an endogenous epistemology as well as by exogenous researchers from other cultures. Needless to say, the future of the whole world must be studied by researchers from different cultures. The session on "The Future of the Human Species seen by the Entire Species" at the IXth International Congress of Anthropological and Ethnological Sciences provided a needed direct input from the Third World.

During the organizing work for the session, we had many adventures and surprises. A brief description of some of these will perhaps enhance an understanding of our session and of this volume. Shortly after the task of organizing the IXth International Congress of Anthropological and Ethnological Sciences was entrusted to Sol Tax, he suggested to Arthur Harkins and myself that a session on the future ought to be included in it. That was in 1970, when Arthur Harkins and I, as coorganizers, had just completed our first Cultural Futurology Symposium at the American Anthropological Association annual meeting. The ICAES was still three years ahead. Meanwhile, Arthur Harkins and I had organized or attended a number of anthropological and sociological futuristics symposia and conferences in the U.S.A. and abroad and had become keenly aware of the lack of input from the Third World.

Consequently, with Sol Tax's support, we decided to concentrate our efforts on obtaining panelists from the Third World for our ICAES session. We tried a novel approach to recruitment. We wanted to contact endogenous anthropologists in countries which are usually underrepresented in international congresses. We wanted to avoid the usual method of using the chains of professional acquaintances for recruitment because of our suspicion that this would produce undue overrepresentation of Westernized anthropologists. We had no satisfactory method to follow, and under the constraints of time and budget we tried the following. There was a two-day ICAES preparatory meeting in Chicago in October 1972, and a file of subscribers to several international social science journals was available there. During coffee breaks, Arthur Harkins and I went through the file and picked out 100 non-European names in relatively poor countries. We wrote letters to these 100 persons. We received fifteen responses. After extensive correspondence, seven of them wrote papers for the Congress. Four of these papers were reassigned to other sessions of the Congress because of their topics. The remaining papers were incorporated in our session. These were papers by Samir Ghabbour, Lalitha Gunawardena, and T. K. Moulik. Furthermore, from the few thousand papers and abstracts submitted to the ICAES headquarters, we also selected Kivuto Ndeti's and Chudi Nwa-chil's papers for inclusion. We were to have a pre-Congress research session in Oshkosh, Wisconsin, during the week preceding the Congress. Sol Tax was optimistic about the possibilities of funding the participants' travel, either from American or foreign funding sources.

When I arrived in Oshkosh, I was shocked to find that nobody on our panel had showed up except Chudi Nwa-chil. No one else had been able to obtain travel funds beyond a subsistence allowance for their stay in Chicago, which Sol Tax had promised *if* the participants could get travel funds from other sources. During the Congress week in Chicago, I frantically selected new panel members from among those who could come. Fortunately there were several who had articulate ideas relevant to our session. They were: Ajato Amos, Sory Camara, Samir Ghosh, and Beatrice Medicine and they joined Chudi Nwa-chil on our panel. Furthermore, Alvin Toffler, who had previously agreed to write a foreword for our volume, was able to fly from New York to participate in the session. The session itself turned out to be a success. In fact, we went on beyond the time allocated and had to continue our discussions in another room. These discussions are reproduced in this volume. In addition, Sory Camara wrote a paper based on his contribution during the session. This paper is also included.

We had a further surprise three weeks after the ICAES, when our original panel members who had been unable to come to Chicago turned up in Frascati, Italy, for another conference. I had previously given their names to Dr. Eleonora Masini of the Istituto Ricerche Applicate Documentazione e Studi, organizer of the Frascati Conference, and this conference was able to pay their travel expenses to Italy. They were Samir Ghabbour, Lalitha Gunawardena, T. K. Moulik and Kivuto Ndeti. We set aside one and a half hours while in Frascati and held our "Chicago session" in Italy. The discussions which took place at that session are also reproduced in this volume.

The field of cultural futuristics is only eight years old, and many of the readers of this volume are probably not familiar with it. It is not yet an "established" field; its foundations have yet to be firmed up, and it is open to new developments. For this reason, it seemed useful to include selected papers from several previous cultural futuristics symposia in this volume. As stated earlier, the ICAES session was intended to remedy the ethnocentrism of other symposia, in which the participants were mainly Americans. Therefore, inclusion of some selected papers from those symposia in the present volume is appropriate in indicating what the ICAES session was complementary to.

It is important, for example, to appreciate Camara's African conceptualization in contrast to Gifford's American formulation. Camara sees heterogeneity as the very basis of biological and social processes. Heterogeneity makes symbiosis possible, and the living world consists of interaction and harmony among heterogeneous elements. Positive combinations of diversity are the source of life and are indispensable. On the other hand Gifford's thinking, like several other Euro-American* authors' chapters in this book, stems from a homogenistic philosophy even though it often appears to be heterogenistic on the surface. According to Gifford, a global agreement must first set the boundaries of cultural and individual variability; then heterogeneity is *allowed* within the boundaries. Heterogeneous cultural units develop independently without necessarily needing one another's cultural

---

* Europeans and North Americans of European origin.

differences. For Gifford, heterogeneity is useful mainly as a means to discover empirically what is the best. He assumes that the "best" way can be found if experiments with many different ways are made, and that the populations with unsuccessful ways will eventually adopt the successful way. Another crucial point is that Camara sees the living world as horizontally interactive and morphogenetic, while Gifford's version consists of vertical relations. For Camara, nonhierarchical interactions between heterogeneous elements generate mutual benefit, new patterns, new wisdom, and further heterogenization. On the other hand, Gifford's concept is to let each individual or each group "do his own thing" *separately* as long as each individual or group stays vertically "meshed" and "integrated" with the supranational imperatives.

Euro-Americans tend to oscillate between two sides of the same coin: Aristotelian logic. One side of the coin is homogenism and hierarchism; the other side is individualism and the ethics of noninterference. Some non-Western cultures, such as Islamic and Hindu cultures, are also homogenistic and hierarchical. But many of the Third World cultures have a wider range of alternatives in their heterogenistic, nonhierarchical, mutualistic and interactive philosophies. As Camara points out, similarity causes competition and conflict while heterogeneity generates harmony. Euro-Americans believe the opposite and advocate unity by similarity. Many Westerners are unaware of this distinction. If you, the readers, keep this basic distinction in mind, you will be amazed to see what you have not noticed before, not only in this volume but also in other volumes of *World Anthropology*.

Section I of this volume consists of three papers outlining the anthropological study of the future. Section II presents some Western views on what our thinking ought to be for the future of the world. Section III presents Third World views, including some of the papers written for the Chicago Session and transcriptions of the discussions which took place in Chicago and Frascati. Section IV consists of papers dealing with conceptualizations of the future in various cultures as seen by American anthropologists. Section V deals with a number of aspects of current social and cultural change in the United States. Section VI contains papers dealing with changes in professional paradigms in anthropology, policy making, and planning. Section VII discusses education for the future. Section VIII contains papers presenting cultural alternatives in the form of imaginary future cultures, which were the basis of discussions at the "Symposium on Cultural Alternatives" held at the 1973 meeting of the American Anthropological Association. This symposium of 1973 was an experimental one and revealed the extent and the limitations of anthropologists' imaginativeness regarding future cultural alternatives. The symposium came about in the following way. The symposia on cultural futuristics in 1970, 1971, and 1972 were based on papers solicited through professional media and personal contacts. After these three symposia, Arthur Harkins and I felt that we needed new blood, and we came up with the idea of holding a contest for papers dealing with cultural alternatives for a society of the size of the U.S.A. In January 1973 we advertized the contest in the Newsletter of the American Anthropological Association and announced a cash award of $300 each for the three most interesting papers. We expected to be overwhelmed by entries. However, there were only seven, of which four were chosen for the AAA symposium. In September we announced the availability of these papers and solicited comments on them, again in the Newsletter of the American Anthropological Association. We received only one comment. This came from H. L. Lefferts who quite rightly pointed out the culture-boundedness of the perspectives of the contest papers. His comments are included in Section VIII. Finally, we have included as an appendix some excerpts from the discussions which took place at the 1970 symposium which marked the beginning of cultural futuristics.

Cultural futuristics is a new branch both of anthropology and of futuristics. This volume is among the first publications in the field to be available in the general book market. It announces a new, very different sort of baby. We hope you will contribute to its growth by sending us your ideas, criticisms, and suggestions.

The contents of this volume are arranged mainly by topic, in a sequence which makes logical sense while disregarding the chronological order in which they were written. The papers included represent diverse but complementary views. This diversity is the strength of the volume, and as editors we have made efforts to emphasize complementary diversity rather than to follow the usual editorial policy of homogenizing the contents and standardizing format and length. Many American publications aim at spoon-feeding predigested, homogenized food to the reader. We chose to depart from this practice and serve some vitalizing raw meat.

The Future as a New Dimension of Anthropology

The Contribution of Anthropology to the Science of the Future

MARGARET MEAD

Anthropology has to this date made very meager contributions to man's developing concern with the future. It may therefore be useful to suggest some of the distinctive contributions which anthropologists could be prepared to make. This is an area of scarce manpower, and I suggest that it will be uneconomical for anthropologists to attempt to supply techniques, insights, or energy for action which can be provided by other disciplines.

We may consider the contributions of anthropology to the field of human sciences as: (1) history which gives us a better grasp of the processes of change in the past, including the nature of man himself (in such controversies as those spearheaded by Lorenz or Ashley Montagu), the nature of change, and the historical background for today's world; (2) a comparative critique of the nature of man, his innate characteristics, his capacity to learn and to change, which will correct the culture-bound theories of those behavioral science disciplines developed within Western cultures; (3) new theories generated by intensive research in small, relatively closed societies where intergenerational relationships can be closely examined; (4) a source of new designs for living for the extensive worldwide culture building which is needed in today's interconnected planetary system. This list of possibilities is not exhaustive, rather it is presented as a basis for further discussion.

Methodologically, anthropology (including archaeology, linguistics, cantometrics, etc.) has three special contributions to make: (1) data on very, very long runs, which can lay the basis for necessary allowances for changes of scale in innovation; (2) a disciplinary habit of dealing with wholes — whole tribes, whole villages, whole cultures, the whole of the culture — which is an excellent preparation for dealing with the whole planet; (3) a disciplinary practice of working with living people, without a break between the collection of the raw data — by interviewing, observing, and participating — and the final analysis. This practice is useful in counteracting the treatment of men of the future as either statistics or science fiction monsters. With the familiarity that anthropologists have with the ways individuals express the entirety of their culture, they should be able to specify the gaps in prediction whenever the information on the projected future is inadequate.

The requirements for a science of the future in turn may be described as follows: (1) responsibility; the creation of the same kind of responsible relationship as that now held by a specialist in the cultural sequences of the American Southwest, present knowledge of Neanderthal man, the specialist in the Renaissance in Italy or Ming pottery. It would seem possible to demand the same meticulous attention to the known, and responsible avowal of the unknown, as we ask of a first-rate archaeologist, ethnographer, or historian. No speculation about the future should be advanced without a competent knowledge of what may in fact be competently predicted. (Examples: the appalling presentation of the probable use of fossil fuel in the rest of the twentieth century, presented at the AAAS centennial meeting in 1948 (American Association for the Advancement of Science 1950); predictions about the use of gasoline and natural gas which do not take into account the consequences of the exploitation of the present technology, in pollution, risk, etc.) Speculation should be separated from hard data; (2) a disciplined allowance for the extent to which the whole system of human cultures is subject to feedbacks and unpredictable incursions of innovation, concatenations of events, and the dependence of this planet on wider cosmic systems; (3) a careful recognition of the importance of self-fulfilling prophecy and the way in which all predictions about the future, if circulated and given credence, become actual factors in the shape the future will take, contributions to despair, hope, carelessness, inertia or effort, as the case may be; (4) a scrutiny of all planning as a component in the future of the particular system to which the planning is directed. (Here the ethics adopted by the Society for Applied Anthropology in 1952 can be invoked — responsibility for the longest time perspective and the greatest spread of any innovation or consciously induced change which can be foreseen by the innovator.)

To these I would add one further, more controversial but important requirement — a search for a balance between conscious and unconscious purpose, with the hope that neither too much planning, in itself inevitably somewhat linear, nor too much institutionalization of affectively linked behaviors will occur (see Bateson 1972).

It will be important to recognize the different levels of possible participation of anthropologists in the science of the future, as for example, in the problem of world population control: (1) provision of carefully collected materials on fertility control in well-studied small societies or sectors of larger societies; (2) provision of comparative material on the interaction of such cultural factors as sex preference, age of marriage, fear of loss of virility, status of the elders, within closely comparable cultures; (3) the study of attempts at population control as part of the cultural systems within historical cultures; (4) the attempt to build a worldwide ethic suitable for rich and poor and all races, religions, and ideologies; (5) the integration of the effects of modern medicine and social responses with the demand for population control, and the changing roles of men and women in the future.

If each of these levels (1–5) of scale of enquiry were to be consciously related to the problem of world population in the future, it would not be necessary for those anthropologists and archaeologists who prefer to work at the micro scale, to be personally involved in world problems, but they would work with a sense of responsibility for the way in which their results could contribute to the whole.

It is an old practice of the field ethnographer and the archaeologist to bear in mind the needs and interests of many specialists far beyond their own fields of enquiry, and also to recognize their responsibility to a future when the material which they are collecting or studying will be forever gone beyond recall. It should not, therefore, be difficult to include in the working inventory for field research, ways of tagging information which is specifically important for certain problems which are at present part of the scope of predicting and planning for the future.

Anthropologists have traditionally dealt with materials of such complexity that any attempt to reduce them to a few variables has been frustrating, if not downright misleading. The possibility of shifting to far more delicate methods of measurement, and to the sophisticated use of a great number of variables should be rapidly included in our methods of field collection, and our analysis of our materials. There can be no science of the future without the use of the computer — with the term computer taken in the widest sense — especially for simulation.

At present, urban planners, who necessarily build for the future and bind the future, are making, explicitly or implicitly, assumptions about human capacities to stand crowding, to live among strangers, to move out and away as far as technology renders possible. One device for the integration of anthropological research into the science of the future is through an active concern with the design of the new emerging urban systems, for which we have as yet no name and which will involve not only entirely unprecedented combinations of open space and building but unprecedented opportunities for human development.

It is possible that the greatest contribution that anthropology can make will be to keep men's imaginations open, as they tend to let the predictable hardware coerce the form of the software.

REFERENCES

AMERICAN ASSOCIATION FOR THE ADVANCEMENT OF SCIENCE
   1950   *Centennial: collected papers presented at the centennial celebration, Washington, D.C., September 13–17, 1948.* Washington, D.C.: American Association for the Advancement of Science.
BATESON, MARY CATHERINE
   1972   *Our own metaphor: a personal account of a conference on the effects of purpose on human adaptation.* New York: Knopf.

Futuristics and the Imaging Capacity of the West

ELISE BOULDING

THE THEORY OF THE IMAGE OF THE FUTURE

With professional futurists crowding to the microphone to announce the outlines of the future, it is of some interest to examine today's futurology in the light of the work of one of the first post-World-War-Two futurologists, Fred Polak. When he sat down at his desk in The Hague to write *The image of the future*[1] in 1951, he felt driven by a sense of extreme urgency to point out to his colleagues in the West that their visioning capacity was becoming seriously impaired. Many great European thinkers had suffered, gone underground, or died, and he himself emerged from years of continuous hiding as a Jew in the Netherlands determined to show that young men could still dream dreams.

At a time when the next meal was the major preoccupation of most Europeans, he was calling people to look to the far horizon, to imagine the totally other. He saw the Spenglerian gloom which was settling on Europe as essentially a disease of the imagination and became totally preoccupied with the self-fulfilling qualities of expectations of disaster. His book was written as a documentation of the role of images of the future in the development of Western civilization, tracing input from Sumerian, Hellenic, and Judeo-Christian sources. Then having shown how the heights of the Renaissance, the Enlightenment, and the early industrial era had been achieved through continuous daring breaches of time, he turned angrily to the present and held up the mirror to present-ridden, mid-century man, clinging desperately to today for fear of what tomorrow would bring.

---

[1] The 1961 two-volume edition of Polak is the source of quotations in this paper.

He was angry because he saw his contemporaries failing to exercise a capacity which they still had but might soon lose through disuse. Failure to work with the imagination to create other and better futures would lead to endless projections of present trends and a petty unfolding of technological possibilities which would in the end leave man crippled.

Fred Polak's concept of the image of the future and its dynamic shaping action on the social present deals with a rather different dimension of man's imaging capacity than does most current futurism. Social planning, blueprinting, and the technological fix are not what Polak had in mind. Social prediction based on extrapolation of existing trends or predicted breakthroughs are not what he meant either. In Polak's view, the ideal type of the image of the future has two elements: (1) eschatological and (2) utopian. The eschatological or transcendent is the element which enables the visionary to breach the bonds of the cultural present and mentally encompass the possibility of a totally other type of society, not dependent on what human beings are capable of realizing. While transcendence refers to the super-natural dimension, there is a theoretically unspecified interaction be-tween the known and the conviction concerning the eventually attaina-ble imagined other.

The "totally other" is, in fact, not conceivable by man, but this term (an exact translation of the Dutch) is used without modification be-cause it emphasizes the notion of discontinuity as a key aspect of dynamic social change. Kenneth Boulding's discussion of expecting the unexpected (1966), points up the dilemma underlying the concept of discontinuity (see also Drucker 1968). It is clear, however, that a society with an eschatological outlook, one which conceives the possi-bility, even the desirability, of drastic social change, is very different from one that seeks familiar tomorrows.

The second element in the ideal-type image of the future is the humanistic utopian, or immanent, element which designates men as the copartners with nature (or God) in the shaping of the other in the here-and-now. Polak suggests that the Judaic image of the future was an ideal embodiment of these twin elements. The Judaic conception of "the covenant," a unique bonding between man and the supernatural,[2] held man responsible for creating the new Zion out of the dusty materials of the planet Earth. Paradise was to be nowhere but here. But man had instructions and he had to listen carefully to get them right. If he didn't listen, the deal was off — the covenant broken. It was

---

[2]   The supernatural, which is referred to in several different ways by Polak, may in general be thought of as a kind of governor of the total ecosystem of the earth, standing outside that system even while partaking of it.

the character of the instructions that set a handful of nomads apart from their fellow tribes in Syriac-Palestine.

This delicately balanced conception of the relationship between immanence and transcendence, man and the supernatural, has never lasted for long, though it has reappeared from time to time in the history of the West. The pendulum has swung back and forth. Either God was taking care of everything and man had but to go along with it (St. Augustine) or everything was up to man and he'd better get with it (Comte). Furthermore, societies have alternated between optimistic and pessimistic views of the nature of reality and man. Four modes of imaging the future emerge from various combinations of attitudes to the basic categories of *Seinmüssen* and *Seinsollen*:

1. Essence optimism combined with influence optimism; the world is good and man can make it even better.
2. Essence optimism combined with influence pessimism; the world is good but it goes of itself and man cannot alter the course of events.
3. Essence pessimism combined with influence optimism; the world is bad but man can make it better.
4. Essence pessimism combined with influence pessimism; the world is bad and there isn't a damn thing man can do about it.

Influence optimism can be further divided into direct and indirect influence optimism, depending on whether man is perceived as running the show or acting in partnership with the supernatural.[3] Clearly, a society suffering from both essence and influence pessimism is not generating any dynamic images of the future, and the social paralysis engendered by the lack of positive images of the future will lead to the death of that society, according to Polak. The most dynamic society is one with both essence and influence optimism, and if the image has eschatological elements with a sense of the possibilities of breakthrough to a totally new order, this adds to the dynamism. These eschatological elements always present a danger to any society, however, in that there is a tendency to spiritualize the other reality and come to think of it as realizable only in heaven, or in an afterlife, and not in this world. This is what happened to Christianity. The ever-deferred parousia, conceived as imminent in Jesus' time, was finally thought to be not for this world at all.

Out of the turbulence of the Middle Ages, when conflicting modes of viewing the future were doing battle with each other both inside and outside the Church, came the great surges of influence optimism that

---

[3] Questions may be raised concerning the nature of relationships between man and the supernatural which are not dealt with in Polak's theory. This relationship is formally specified as nonhierarchical, but the specification is exceedingly fuzzy given the difference between the dimension "human" and the dimension "supernatural."

characterized the Renaissance. From that time on the utopian and eschatological streams diverged more and more, as the Church retreated in the face of increasing confidence in man's capacity to shape his own destiny with the aid of science. In the end, only the Pentecostal and Adventist sects kept intact the concept of "the peaceable kingdom" as coming on earth; the rest of the Christian church settled for a spiritualized kingdom within man or located at a comfortable remove in outer space.

Two sets of discoveries released the pent-up energy of the Middle Ages for utopian construction of possible future societies: scientific discoveries that opened up the possibilities of using nature as a tool to shape the environment, and voyagers' discoveries of exotically other cultural patterns which revealed that human society was highly malleable.[4] The sixteen, seventeen, and eighteen hundreds produced a heady array of "futures." These ranged from classical-style Platonic utopias, such as Bacon's *New Atlantis*, which drew on a prevision of future scientific and technological development to outline a kind of universal communism, through romantic, satirical, and rollicking utopias which combined a sharp critique of the times with glimpses of an upside-down right-side-up society — Rousseau, Rabelais, Defoe, Swift, Fénelon, Holberg — and on to the socialist utopias of Owen, Saint-Simon, and Fourier. This is the point at which social scientists got into the utopia-building business; Comte and Marx each constructed utopian future societies based on "natural law," though Marx vehemently attacked the concept of utopism itself.

Utopian writing about the future interacted with social experimentation and the more popular imagination to create social innovations in every sphere from the economic (the trade union movement, profit sharing, social security, scientific management) through the political (parliamentary democracy, universal suffrage) to the social (universal education, child welfare practices, women's "emancipation," New Towns, social planning. As Polak says, most features of social design in contemporary Western society were first figments of some utopian writer's imagination.

In the 1800's, however, something began happening to the "other space" and the "other time" of utopian fantasy. It began in Germany, home of the universalistic utopians Lessing and Kant, in such works as Fichte's *Geschlossene Handelsstaat* (1800) which designs a specific future for a specific country — Germany. From this time on, national-

---

[4]   There is some danger of overemphasizing the role that contact with other people's "differentnesses" has in generating a sense of transcendence. Such contact may simply extend the range of an invading culture's manipulative abilities rather than stimulate the envisioning of totally new kinds of social structures. If there were a direct correspondence between contact with other cultures and transcendence generation, the West would not now stand accused of having done so much harm to the world.

ism and an orientation toward the immediate future begin eroding the creative imaging powers of the utopist. The sense that man can breach time and create the totally other was lost.

It is Polak's contention that in any culture the capacity to image the future is a core capacity that is manifested in every aspect of the culture. Therefore, the decline in the ability to envision totally other "realities," the compressing of the mental perceptions of time and space into the here and now will be revealed not only in the literature of an era but also in its art, architecture, poetry, and music, in its science and philosophy, and in its religion. Polak documents the decline in imaging capacity in science, philosophy, and religion in the twentieth century. The predominantly Orwellian tone of twentieth-century science fiction is presented as the most damaging evidence of the diseased futurism of the present. Prometheus is rebound, tied up in knots by his own science and technology and by fear of a future he had thought to master. What went wrong?

The cultural lag in ability to generate new visions appropriate to the complex knowledge structure of a hyperindustrialized society has been examined at length in contemporary social science literature. The rate of change itself is usually seen as the culprit. Whether or not the human imagination can adapt itself to reconceptualizing reality as fast as reality changes in this century of exponential growth curves is a subject for debate. An element usually left out of the debate, however, is the disappearance of the eschatological sense of a totally other order of reality. The divorce of utopia from eschatology which characterized the Enlightenment appeared as a liberation of human thought at the time, but Polak points out that the utopian and eschatological modes are symbiotic and either without the other goes into decline. Once the eschatological otherness of utopian images of the future was weeded out, utopias themselves came to be conceived as more and more static images of a boring end-state of man. The true utopia is not static, however, but historically relative.

It carries within itself the seeds of its own elimination through progress in time. The vision which it holds up of the best conceivable future at any given time, is by definition a vision subject to change, and utopias do change both in form and content with the course of history. (Polak 1961: I, 442)

Our weakened capacity to image the future may therefore not be due to the rate of social change (which we probably adapt to more effectively than we think) but to a general cultural loss of the sense of transcendence. Whether such a culture trait, once lost, can be reconstituted again is the question. Polak takes the position that it has not been lost, only weakened, and that awareness of its weakening can lead to new insights concerning the importance of otherness and a rejuvenation of the capacity for imaginative construction of the other.

CONTEMPORARY FUTURISTICS

No general survey of contemporary images of the future will be attempted here but only a brief examination of relatively specialized developments that have taken place in futurism in recent decades.[5] Within social science, futurism has taken various forms, including specialized and general systems-type planning, the development of special techniques such as brainstorming for inventing new futures, and the development of a variety of conceptual tools for predicting the future in the manner of Kahn and Wiener, Helmer, etc. Straddling the social and engineering sciences are the evolutionary nucleators such as Mead, Platt, and Doxiadis. The ecological futurists range from Ward and Boulding, who offer a Spaceship Earth vision of the future, through social geographers and ecologists to Whole Earth romanticists and pre-Raphaelite Aquarians. Finally there are the revolutionary futurists, some political, some nonpolitical, some militant, some gentle, and all dedicated to a completely new society for humans — and there are the science fiction writers. Each of these will be briefly discussed.

Social Planners

Conceived in the womb of the socialist utopia, centralized government planning for total societies first caught the world's imagination in the 1920's when Lenin announced the first of a series of Five Year Plans which were to build the socialist New World by stages in the Soviet Union. Many socialist planning principles have now been accepted in the world at large. The accompanying problems, caused by the tendency of plans to bog down because of the large number of uncontrolled variables at work, have also had to be accepted. Competing economic and political interests loom large among the uncontrolled variables, whether the economy is socialist or capitalist. Regional and urban planning in the United States has been forced into continual *ad hoc* deviations from plans that may have had little merit in the first place, with end results that no one will take responsibility for, such as the urban renewal fiascos that leave the poor more ill-housed than before. The disillusionment with social planning is most complete

---

[5] Every reader is bound to feel that his or her favorite futurists have been left out, but a high degree of selectivity is unavoidable in a short paper. Polak's *Prognostics* (1971) deals more fully with the topic.

among those who have the greatest concern with reconstructing society, to the point where planning bureaucracies are viewed by the New Left as instruments for the deliberate exploitation of minority groups.

For liberals still committed to planning, the push has been toward total systems planning in order to gain control of more variables. Boguslaw (1965) calls these total system designers "the new utopians." They have identified the human element as the source of failure in previous planning and seek to design mechanical systems that minimize the scope for human action. He points out the paradox of this Skinnerian Walden II-type development:

It is perhaps a significant commentary on contemporary psychological and social science that its efforts often appear directed toward making men less than human through the perfecting of behavioral control techniques, while contemporary physical science seems to be moving in the direction of increasing the number of possible machine responses to environmental stimuli (Boguslaw 1965: 18).

Optimists think they see a general trend toward the humanization of planning. Toffler (1970: 400–405) for example, predicts the death of the present econocentric technocratic planning and its replacement by public and private planning which will place the highest value on human welfare. Since planning has always been clothed in the rhetoric of human welfare, one could say *"plus ça change, plus c'est la même chose."*

Even while the significance of the surrender of critical human decision making in sophisticated systems planning is being hammered home by social philosophers, the practice of elaborate systems planning goes on apace. The weapons system approach developed within the Department of Defense is the prototype and is rapidly spreading to the civilian sector, particularly in the area of urban planning (Schon 1967). A spurious sense of control is achieved by establishing a logically complete program to accomplish specified objectives and then ruling out any possible feedback from the environment which might lead to changing the parameters of the situation. Some New Town planning is done this way too.

Development economists engage in a kind of modified systems planning when they go into a nonindustrialized society and draw up a blueprint for industrialization. If people in a given society do not happen to behave in the way the economic model used in planning calls for, so much the worse for them. The golden era of development planning initiated by Tinbergen is grinding to a reluctant standstill with Myrdal's pessimistic discovery that people do not in fact behave as plans call for (Myrdal 1968).

Some systems engineering is, quite properly, trying to design people back into the systems. An example of this is the proposal to train people for "societal engineering" (Lewis and Pinkau 1968). The key concept here is long-lived societal systems which "are people-oriented, structured arrangements of processes and elements responding to a real need (or needs) of the society" (1968: 111). System design approaches, however, even when they explicitly try to provide for feedback and changing values, rule out radical long-term changes by their very need to tidy up the variables. Short of an explicitly evolutionary approach (Maruyama 1963), systems planning tends to narrow down alternatives and shorten time horizons. At its worst it threatens us with an oppressive and frozen anti-utopia. At its best, it can only move us toward a well understood and thoroughly probed alternative structure which lies well within the grasp of the contemporary mind.

Brainstorming

For those who are concerned with generating radically different possibilities for the future, the technique of brainstorming (Osborn 1963; Gordon 1961) has been developed; this is designed to jog people loose from their customary mental ruts and help them imagine wildly different "somethings." Problem-solving groups are given a series of exercises which free the mind for totally unexpected solutions. Since the technique is frequently used for such elevated purposes as coming up with a new name for a deodorant, its future-creating potential has not been very evident. Corporations do hire "blue sky" thinkers to dream up remote possibilities, but according to the report of at least one such tame visionary, the job is very bad for the imagination! Toffler, who is very concerned about warding off "future shock" by dreaming up alternative futures before they arrive, proposes the establishment in every community of " 'imaginetic centers' devoted to technically assisted brainstorming" (1970: 410). He would create a profession of "imagineers" who would work with technical specialists to make sure that all permutations and combinations of given sets of relationships are examined.

One significant limitation upon brainstorming is contained in Barnett's point that "the expectation of change always envisages limits upon its operations. Change is expected only between certain minimal and maximal boundaries" (1953: 57). Barnett cites the example of the Samoans who set a high value on innovation in design, but the range of total variation is so narrow that the untrained Western mind has difficulty in detecting differences between one design and another, whether in textiles, songs, or dances. Whether the range is wide or narrow, the cultural limits are firmly set. In short, the proverbial man from Mars might not be very impressed with the alternative futures dreamed up by the wildest of blue sky imagineers. While this kind of limitation operates on all human fantasizing, it operates much more strongly in a technique-oriented setting such as brainstorming than it does for the lone fantasist.

Professional Futurists

The difference between the professional futurist and the planner is that the former specializes in the delineation of alternative futures from which, presumably, the planner may choose. Waskow (1970) divides them into the technocrats, the humanists, and the participatory futurists. European technocratic futurists include Bertrand de Jouvenel (1967) who has directed the Ford Foundation-sponsored "Futuribles project" at the Société d'Études et de Documentation Économiques, Industrielles et Sociales in Paris since the fifties; Dennis Gabor (1964), University of London physicist; and Fritz Baade (1962), development economist of Kiel University. In the United States, think factory specialists Olaf Helmer (1966), developer of the Delphi technique for long-range forecasting, and Herman Kahn (1967), writer of scenarios of the future, are leading examples. So is Charles Osgood (1966) using the computer at the University of Illinois to develop future contingency models. A variety of efforts in this direction were coordinated by Daniel Bell in his capacity as chairman of the American Academy of Arts and Sciences Commission on the Year 2000. The Institute for the Future at Middletown, Connecticut, which Bell helped to establish, carries out research on the social technology of forecasting. The World Future Society and its journal, *The Futurist*, have provided a very useful communications network for this group of futurists, but they also extend their net more widely and report on the whole gamut of future-oriented work in the United States. The futures work of the Club of Rome (Meadows et al.) represents another more complex variant of technocratic futures.

    The technocratic futurists operate largely within the frame of reference of the present national and international distribution of power and resources and on the assumption that present trends of technological development and scientific breakthroughs will continue. It is perhaps not surprising, therefore, that the future which they project is being vigorously rejected by an increasing number of younger scholars and activists.

Hampden-Turner outlines some objections to the forecasting approach:

The projection of present trends into the future represents a vote of temporary approval for such trends. Yet the trends themselves are the consequence of thousands of individual human decisions ... the decision not to change direction [is] a decision. By concentrating upon the technical and material aspects of the trends, the impression is fostered that these things "are," like stars and planets around us, so that "realistic" men must humbly subordinate their minds to these physical "facts." ...

But these projections of existing trends are quite *unlike* the physical universe of dead objects. They are *cultural, political* and *social* choices. Men have the capacity to rebel against any trend at any time, in any place, by deciding to stop it, or alter its direction, or persuade others to do so ... the shared expectation that the trend whose direction you oppose will *not* be continued in the future may be politically essential to any success in halting or redirecting it.

The obverse is also true. The acceptance of a trend which is implicit in projecting it into the future, the gathering together of technical statistics, scholarly opinions, and humanistic concerns about what this trend will mean by the year 2000, has the *inevitable effect of strengthening that trend and making it more certain to occur*. Much of the efforts of these scholars would be wasted if by the year 1975 a major social rebellion against certain trends were to succeed (Hampden–Turner 1970: 305–306; original emphasis).

Typical of an even more serious type of criticism is Waskow's observation about the technocrats (1970: 138):

For them "planning" was clearly a way of helping those who now hold power to know what they must do in order to keep holding power thirty or fifty years hence. What must they change, where should they beat a strategic retreat, what new organizations and technologies should they invent, when can they hold the line?

To the extent that these criticisms imply intentional malevolence, they are unfair. In fact, the memorandum written by Lawrence K. Frank to Hudson Hoagland, then president of the American Academy, which led to the establishment of the Commission on the Year 2000, raises questions very similar to those contained in the above criticisms:

If we are to maintain a free social order in the face of the discontent and anxiety [we] will probably provoke, we must attempt the Promethean task of renewing our traditional culture and reorienting our social order as a deliberately planned process ... (Bell 1967).

But if Polak's theory has validity at all, it has validity in relation to the work of these futurists; they are indeed reenforcing the possibilities for one kind of future.

The second group of futurists, the ones Waskow calls the humanists, are worried about precisely this aspect of current social-technological trends. Polak himself belongs in this category and so does Robert Jungk, the Austrian-born futurist who founded the Institut für Zukunftsfragen in Vienna in 1965 and sowed the seeds in Europe and North America of the idea of internationalizing the effort to work for better futures. Mankind 2000 was created by this group, which in turn helped to form the World Future Studies Federation, which now has its headquarters in Rome. Mankind 2000's aims were:

A. To ensure that the future of mankind be person-centred and democratically determined. To this end, to encourage personal involvement and choice in defining and realizing the future course of events, on the understanding that failure to participate is, in effect, to abdicate responsibility and to choose by default, unless such responsibility is intentionally delegated.

B. To promote a comprehensive (total systems) approach to the problems and possibilities of the near future, in the context of futures research and planning, having as a time-horizon the end of the present century. To this end, to encourage inter-communication and co-operation between cultures, disciplines, and people generally.[6]

The humanists are an older generation of futurists who have observed the seamy side of central planning in Eastern Europe and fear a similar sacrifice of human values to planning in Western Europe and the United States. The disillusionment which the many failures of the much-looked-to socialist planning aroused in both the socialist countries themselves and among their admirers in the West cannot be overestimated in relation to imaging the future. The buoyant optimism of the twenties about possible new futures cannot be evoked again, particularly in the face of the difficulties which creative new variants of socialist planning in countries such as Czechoslovakia have met.

The humanist futurists seek to protect humanity's future by involving individuals in planning and in helping them generally to think creatively about longer time spans. The idea of a traveling exhibit of possible futures has been a feature of the Mankind 2000 project from the beginning. Perhaps even more important, these humanists come out of a cultural milieu in which the perfume of the empty eschatological vase (to misquote Renan) still lingers, and their forecasting is tinged with a visionary quality of otherness not to be found in their younger colleagues. William Irwin Thompson, historian founder of Lindisfarne typifies this otherness (1974).

The participatory futurists (among whom Waskow counts himself) are equally distressed by what they consider to be the authoritarianism

---

[6] From a July 1969 mimeographed report from the Secretariat of Mankind 2000 in London, England. Since 1971 the headquarters of Mankind 2000 has been located in Rome.

of the technocrats and the fuzziness of the humanists. They are committed to what Waskow calls creative disorder and act on their chosen visions of possible futures by building chunks of that future from the bottom up (without permission from the authorities). Johann Galtung (with Eleanora Masini a major moving force in the World Future Studies Federation) is the apostle of creative disorder in Europe, as Waskow is in the United States. Galtung is a rather unique "chunk of the future" in himself, in that he takes the world as his home in a way that very few twentieth-century scholars have been able to do. Also, his images of the future take account of the entirely new order of social innovations taking place in the People's Republic of China, thus giving his futurism different dimensions and broader perspectives than that of most of his contemporaries. The increasingly action-oriented younger generation of scholars who find themselves naturally at home in this group already find both Galtung and Waskow too conservative. Not all "movement" people qualify as participatory futurists, but to the extent that their community-building experiments are based on larger visions, they are indeed futurists. Neither are they professionals in the conventional sense, but they will breed professionals!

Certain fears about professional futurism shared by the humanists and participatory futurists are reflected in the Postscript to the published proceedings of the first Mankind 2000 Conference in Oslo. Pointing out that four fifths of the work done in the new speciality of futurism is financed either by governments, military establishments, or large corporations, they warn against futurist expertise becoming a monopoly of power groups within nations and of rich nations in the international community. Internationalization and democratization of future research is urgently needed.

The onesided use of "technological forecasting" . . . can lead us straight into new forms of totalitarianism. If we tamper with the time ahead of us, as we have already done with the space around us, in an egocentric, power-directed, narrow-minded spirit, if we spoil the future as we have spoiled our environment, then we are in for an epoch of despotism and desperation — a tyranny of a new modernistic type, which like all tyrannies will loudly proclaim its virtue and benevolence. This must not happen. The future belongs to all of us. . . (Jungk and Galtung 1969: 368).

Differences and mutual criticism aside, all three types of futurist have one strong trait in common: they are interested in realizable futures with a turn-of-the-century time horizon. Regardless of differences in their prognostic styles, they have all been caught up in the twentieth-century version of that chiliastic enthusiasm which swept Europe in the decades preceding the year 1000. None of these futurists would admit to millennialist thinking, but the basic cultural undercurrent is a powerful one and probably therapeutic. I detect in the writings of all these futurists a note of unscientific enthusiasm for a time when things will be better than they are now, which may act as an antidote to the time neurosis and fear of the future which Polak diagnosed twenty years ago. As we near the year 2000, the long-forgotten cultural heritage of millennialism may penetrate a three-centuries-old shell of rationalism and infuse a new quality of otherness into thinking about the future.

The Social Evolutionaries

When Margaret Mead called for purposeful attention to social evolution in 1964, she put into words what an increasing number of future-oriented thinkers were feeling:

If we can create living networks of the diversely gifted and the diversely trained whose concern it is to safeguard our present heritage and to learn from and teach those who will be the carriers of this heritage, we shall automatically focus our inventiveness on the very center of the evolutionary process (Mead 1964: 322).

Rather than being committed to any particular image of the future, these evolutionists are committed to a kind of high-level brainstorming — a mutating of new conceptions of social forms, structures, and ideologies in order that selections may be made from a far wider range of alternative possibilities than are conventionally considered.

These living evolutionary networks are bound to be as diverse as the nucleating minds which form their various centers. Many of them overlap. A list of the people who have joined architect-planner Constantine Doxiadis's famous yacht cruises into "Tomorrowland" would reveal a fairly dazzling network. The scholars who have come to the Center for Advanced Study in the Behavioral Sciences in Palo Alto in the last two decades have spun off a number of new networks as a result of the nucleating power of "the Palo Alto experience." Hutchins's Center for the Study of Democratic Institutions is intended to perform this same nucleating function. John Platt, the physicist and social philosopher, Buckminster Fuller, and John McHale of World Design Science Decade and World Resources Inventory fame are all nucleating groups of people committed to designing alternative world structures that will make life humane and enjoyable for every kind of social group. So is Marshall McLuhan although he operates in a different dimension from most futurists. Hazel Henderson of the

Princeton Center for Alternative Futures and Jean Houston of the Mind Research Center also represent futurists working in new dimensions.

Such nucleating individuals tend to think at a very fast pace and be tremendously optimistic. Most of them are not young but they are extraordinarily at home in the midst of accelerating change, as if to demonstrate that there are no inherent problems for humans in the need to adjust to exponential growth rates. Nothing smaller than a world will do for the Richard Meiers (1965) of the twentieth century to think in and about. The 700 million megalopolis on the Bay of Bengal planned for the middle of the next century is for them a perfectly "natural" conception. To optimists like John Platt the present situation represents a temporary lock-in for society, and we need only move through a period of inertia to get a significant choice point, when we can start using the systems design capability we now have. With our

... knowledge of feedback stabilization, cybernetic goal-seeking, and hierarchical decision-systems ... of the biological and psychological bases of individual and group behavior ... and our new abundance, it is possible to make new designs ... for the benefit of the whole society ... designs that will satisfy both urban and farm, suburb and central city, workers and intellectuals, managers and consumers, blacks and whites, males and females — designs that can permit and encourage pluralism and diversity of tastes and life styles, with abundance for every group (Platt n.d.:5).

He feels that utopias are definitely realizable because they "will be enormously profitable for everybody, in economic as well as human terms" and that they can be demonstrably profitable "for every individual or group involved in the (social) change." The sheer audacity of suggesting the imminent possibility of pay-as-you-go utopias in the midst of today's welter of social problems gives Platt's image of the future that prophetic touch of otherness which is characteristic of the evolutionists. Their images are not precise, but they give a sense of movement, of direction.

Ecological Futurism

Since ecology deals with metastable systems in the ecosphere, it seems a contradiction in terms to link ecology and futurism. Until Earth's time clock runs down, however, a good deal will still happen on what Ward (1966) and Boulding (1966) have both called "Spaceship Earth." Boulding's image of the future (as extracted from his *Meaning of the 20th century*, 1964) pictures an Earth with a stable closed-cycle technology. Since biological processes are much more efficient than mechanical processes, the technology of the future will probably be based on biological processes. Evolution within this closed-cycle spaceship requires the careful spending of capital to build complex social forms and, according to the laws of entropy, should result in a gradual diminution of the evolutionary potential of the system. There are, however, antientropic processes at work. One relates to man's knowledge and learning and consists of "the capacity of his images — that is, the knowledge present in his mind — to grow by a kind of internal breeder reaction: the imagination" (Boulding 1964: 141). The other, even more antientropic capacity is *agape*.[7] "It always builds up, it never tears down, and it does not merely establish small islands of order in society at the cost of disorder elsewhere" (1964: 146). For evolutionary potential *agape* clearly wins hands down. The imaged future, then, is one in which men have learned to be economical with their geological capital by relying as far as possible on biological rather than mechanical systems for energy and work. They live in a society structured in such a way that the human capacities to learn and to love are maximized, in turn creating ever higher-level institutions and relationships. New mutations may well enlarge the capacity for spiritual experience. That is about as specific as an ecological image of the future can get. It also brings back the eschatological element missing in the "man-as-the-measure-of-all-things" utopia and draws on the great Catholic biologist-mystic Teilhard de Chardin's vision (1959) of the noosphere.

Boulding is hardly a typical ecologist, but much of the writing of members of the Society for Human Ecology and of the environmentalists who are increasingly weaving their own scientific specialty into the larger social fabric evokes this sense of humans moving toward higher things.[8] The promise of release from the wheels, gears, and smells of mechanical technology seems to have a very liberating effect on the imagination. Edward Goldsmith's *Ecologist* (Britain) and Stewart Brandt's *Coevolution Quarterly* (U.S.A.) are both unique blends of science, intellectualism, and the visionary.

The ecological perspective moves along an imperceptible continuum from utopian applications of scientific ecology (the New Alchemy Institute) through a fairly robust back-to-the-land Whole Earth romanticism (*Whole Earth Catalog*, 1970) to a pre-Raphaelite fantasy-world Aquarianism (*Aquarian Oracle*, 1970). The image of the future eventually turns into a blurry fantasy about a return to a golden age in

---

[7] *Agape* can be translated as "love" in the sense in which that word is used in 1 Corinthians 13.

[8] The term "higher things," for those not accustomed to this mode of discourse, may be taken to mean "as yet unspecified potentials."

the past, much as in the romantic nineteenth-century utopias of Hudson (1922 [1906]) and Morris (1966 [1890]). The intellectual and spiritual vigor of the best ecological visions of the future, however, gives the lie to economists and chamber of commerce types who maintain that industrialization must proceed apace and that zero growth would mean stagnation and social decay.

The Revolutionary Futurists: Political, Social, and Literary

POLITICAL: VIOLENT LIBERATION MOVEMENTS. Liberation movements from all continents have in common an overriding preoccupation with tactical strategy, a vivid sense of the enemy, and a burning conviction that they are building a new world. An apocalyptic sense that oppression has reached an intensity which can only represent the death throes of an inwardly rotten world imperialist structure gives an immediacy to the revolutionary image of the future which is lacking in more sedate sectors of society. But the need of the guerrilla to act, to seize every momentary advantage in case this is *the* moment (in his millennialist frame of mind every moment could be the moment) also gives a child's picture-book quality to his images of the future. An attempt to analyze the images of the future which appear in *Tricontinental*, the monthly publication of the Organization of the Solidarity of the Peoples of Africa, Asia, and Latin America (OSPAAL) brings this out very clearly. Every guerrilla and liberation movement carried out anywhere in the world (even occasionally in North America) is reported on here, but the content does not vary very much from country to country. A recently reprinted "Appeal for Patriotic Emulation" by Ho Chi Minh in 1948 gives the flavor of most of the writing:

Each Vietnamese, old or young, boy or girl, rich or poor,
must become a fighter struggling in a front which is either
military or economic, political or cultural,
To realize the slogan:
Nation-wide Resistance.
Thus we realize:
The whole people will have enough to eat and dress.
The whole people will know how to read and write.
The whole army will have enough food and armament to kill
the invaders.
The whole nation will be entirely unified and independent.
Thus we realize:
Independence for the nation.
Freedom for the people.
Happiness for the people (Ho Chi Minh 1969: 17).

This is a poignantly modest image of the future, hardly a greedy, power-grasping one. This image of a future in which people shall have work, food, knowledge, dignity, and joy is the same image held by the militant minority movements in the United States. (red, black, brown, yellow, female), and the fact that violence seems the only road to this simple, basic vision for increasing numbers of people on all continents speaks for itself. Can our futurists tell us how to fit the evolutionary potential of *agape* into this scene?

The most striking feature of this image is its ordinariness, for all the millennialist fervor with which it is held. It involves no technological breakthroughs and asks nothing that is not easily realizable in strictly nonpolitical terms. The revolutionary lives with very narrow time horizons. The quality of otherness in his vision lies mainly in his refusal to accept existing political constraints as real. In this sense, he would indeed make a breach in time in the best utopian tradition.

POLITICAL: NONVIOLENT LIBERATION MOVEMENTS. Political thinking and *agape* are hard to marry, and most people who try to effect the union in their own lives or in the movements they work in wind up being those very well-meaning, fuzzy-minded humanitarian liberals everyone despises these days. The next significant social mutation will be the one which enables skills of political and economic organization and the capacity to love to be maximized in the same person. (Charles Hampden-Turner wrote his book, *Radical man* [1970], to help bring this about.) A century of relatively ineffective Euro-North American peace and humanitarian movements gives no evidence to date that this combination is as yet workable. (Some observers feel that such a mutation is taking place in China. Examining the evidence for this would require a separate paper.)

A. J. Muste, a life-long politically activist Christian, pacifist, and organizer in the labor and peace movements, gives a clue to the possibility of such a social mutation in the West. The combination of political insight and *agape* which he embodied was such that in the turbulent last years of his life, when violence was becoming the order of the day in hitherto nonviolent civil rights movements, he was still in the mainstream of the action. Consulted by everyone, present at everything, he was able to move through the maelstrom of violence and respond at another level. But images of the future were almost incidental to a life of action. Martin Luther King was developing an image of the future which people could respond to, but he did not have enough time, and much of the nonviolent thrust of his image of the future has been lost since his death — a sad parallel with Gandhi. David Harris, leader of the nonviolent branch of the draft resistance movement, on his last tour with his wife Joan Baez before entering jail seemed to realize the need of the movement for a positive image of the future. He is one of the few in recent times who has tried to spell out the details of alternative social structures for a nonviolent world. His main contributions in this direction still lie in the future. I have left out a whole generation in between A. J. Muste and David Harris. That is my generation — currently caught in a life-and-death struggle between images of the future based on *agape* and on the sword. In the clash between vagueness and fury, my generation does not come off well.

I note that this attempt to delineate images of the future from the peace movement has produced nothing more than a few individual biographies. This would seem to indicate that powerful images of the future of this genre have yet to be formed.

NONPOLITICAL: INTERNATIONAL ORGANIZATIONS.   The international movement for a peaceful, integrated world, reflected in the rapid proliferation of nongovernmental associations which are creating international networks based on every kind of human interest, has moved both forward and backward in the last fifty years. It has moved forward in the sense that there were 202 international organizations in 1905 and 3,000 in 1975. From one point of view, the noosphere appears to be meshing more tightly. But recently there has been an awareness that these organizations are almost entirely Euro-North American[9] in conception, ideology, and ways of working. The Third World components of international organizations are beginning angrily to let their international leaders know that they must change drastically if they are to represent the international community and not the West. This is equally true of peace organizations, church organizations, and cultural, civic, and professional organizations. While international secretariats are beginning to respond to this pressure, and more international headquarters are now to be found in Africa, Asia, and Latin America year by year, it will be a long time before any international organization can honestly call itself representative of the world community, quite apart from the issue of China's participation in such activities. This means that one cannot accurately speak of "world" images of the future emerging from these organizations. The images of the future so far generated by nongovernment organizations are Western images. Until the transition to a more reality-based internationalism has been effected, one cannot look for guiding images from this sector of world publics.

NONPOLITICAL: THE "NOW" PEOPLE AND THEIR IMAGES OF THE FUTURE.   The familist-oriented communes reported on in the monthly, *Modern Utopian*, the new Dionysians for whom Norman O. Brown speaks so eloquently in *Love's body* (1966), and the self-actualizers that Maslow

[9]   Even the concept Euro-North American is an illusion, since this culture area contains a number of indigenous nonwhite cultures such as Eskimos, Indians, Aleuts, and Lapps.

(1954, 1968) wrote of, all protest against mechanistic images of the present or the future which are based on manipulation of things instead of on openness to the unique creative qualities of the individual human being. The "Now" orientation is a reaction against "jam yesterday, jam tomorrow, but never jam today." While they are not explicitly in the "future-creating" business, to the extent that the "Now" people live in communes or interact in groups of some kind they are developing working models in the present of a desired future society. Some of them would deny the validity of thinking for others or of designing social structures, but some of them are in the communitarian tradition of trying out models of society for mankind. Toffler's suggestion (1970: 414) that intentional communities should experiment with new superindustrial forms rather than "back-to" agrarianism is in fact now being taken up in a few groups that are designing new types of instrumentation and intermediate-type technology for developing countries instead of making candles or milking cows. Transforming the toy industry has been the goal of several communes.

The present flowering of communes in the United States is an indication of the same social vigor which stimulated the numerous utopian communities of a hundred years ago, described by Charles Nordhoff (1965 [1875]). There is more than a touch of transcendence in many of these utopian communes, ranging from identifiably Christian to exotic cultic features. Even the far-left rationalist Weathermen communes have their own eschatological style following Marx. Many of these groups belong to the "participatory futurists" mentioned earlier. To the extent that they are acting out a part of a larger vision for society, they are indeed participatory futurists. To the extent that they are retreating into a private "Now," they do not belong in that category.

It is difficult to make generalizations about the "Now" people, individually or in groups, because the scene changes so rapidly. Communes form, break up, and re-form and the average life expectancy of a commune is probably a few weeks. In general, these groups can be ranged on a continuum from private escapism to model building for the future. The model builders are most certainly in the minority.

SCIENCE FICTION. No discussion of revolutionary futurists can be complete without mentioning science fiction. The great majority of science fiction writers, like professional futurists, make projections based on the present. They present us with galactic bureaucracies, fantastic physical and social technologies (including ESP), and citizens with a cowboy mentality — an all-too-convincing image of the future looked at from today's world. Whether they are written as social criticism, as just plain yarns, or as images of a naively hoped for future, the cumulative impact of the majority of science fiction is precisely toward self-justifying expectations of galactic bureaucracy.

There are gifted minds in science fiction which do play with alternative futures and imaginatively construct other worlds in the tradition of the Enlightenment at its liveliest. The sheer feat of constructing a totally other kind of society, with different basic values and totally other institutional patterns for dealing with what we think of as the economic, social, political, and cultural-religious aspects of life in groups is very liberating to the social imagination of the reader. Hence, books like Frank Herbert's *Dune* (1965) leave one with a feeling of reverence for the evolutionary and adaptive capacity of human beings in the face of grimly limited resources, even though the features of such a society are only remotely relevant for proximate human futures. A book such as Ursula LeGuin's *Left hand of darkness* (1969), imaging a society whose members are without permanent heterosexual attributes, opens up the possibility of human futures which would leave behind today's kind of sex-role patterns. Science fiction fans will know who the creative future-inventors are among science fiction writers. No attempt is made to survey them here.[10]

The science fiction tradition of picturing men as evolving into a higher, more spiritual order of beings, which Olaf Stapledon (*First and last men* 1930) contributed to so brilliantly earlier in the century, has found a more contemporary expression in Arthur Clarke's *Childhood's end* (1953). Polak mistrusts this tradition, insofar as it represents an abdication of human effort in the hope of being rescued by a higher spiritual being or by a chance mutation. It is a durable human trait, however, to hope for rescue from "outside." Since Polak has also recognized the importance of the eschatological element, we must conclude that science fiction would not be doing its job if it did not give glimpses of a totally other future state of the human race.

THE FRAMES OF REFERENCE OF FUTURISM

The social planners and systems designers, the brainstormers and the technocratic futurists all operate within a cultural frame of reference

---

[10] Hampden-Turner (1970: 340) cites research in the performance of different categories of people on Terman's Concept Mastery Test, which measures "... verbal intelligence, breadth of knowledge and interest, the capacity to deal with ideas at an abstract level, to associate meanings, think divergently via analogies, and to converge logically." Creative writers are far out ahead and engineers, military officers, and independent inventors (Edison types?) at the bottom. It is attractive to speculate as to what might ensue if we turned over government policy making to our most creative science fiction writers.

well summarized in Kahn and Wiener's list of "Thirteen Basic, Long-Term Multifold Trends" (1967: 7) which involve a worldwide extension of Western socioeconomic and political developments coupled with a nostalgic revival of the golden age of Greece in the twenty-first century. This is the "Standard World" that Kahn writes about. The projections allow for "Canonical Variations on the Standard World" in terms of the degree of political and economic success of the communist world. In general, they picture a Sorokian twenty-first-century West abandoning its achievement orientation and returning to a sensate Hellenism based on high-level technology, some reduction in the world-leadership roles of the United States, an unspecified development of China and the communist world, and a somehow minimal level of organization and industrialization with no one getting in anyone else's way. The most far-out changes they expect, apart from the usual technological projections of innovations in communications, transportation, human physiological capacity extension and general productivity, are things like the extension of life expectancy well beyond 150 years, possible modification of the human species, and interstellar travel.

They have left an escape hatch by allowing for the "psychologically upsetting impact of new techniques, ideas, philosophies and the like" (1967: 24). Three concepts missing from their projections are:

1. The possibility that a totally other path to decent physical levels of living, bypassing the Western sequence of technological developments, might develop in China or elsewhere in the Third World, and that this path might be followed by the rest of the Third World.
2. The simultaneous not-so-remote possibility that the West will choke on its industrial effluence and become China's (or country X's) pupil in a different order of technologies.
3. Spiritual breakthroughs which would develop the human capacity to love and lead to totally different cultural values and socioeconomic patterns.

Points (1) and (2) are not meant to imply an idealization of China as the *deus ex machina* but rather to suggest the likelihood that there will be a major shift in the locus of cultural innovation on the planet, following in a line of such major shifts in the past (shifts which are hardly reflected in the world history books studied by Americans or Europeans). China is the most likely candidate for new leadership because of her protective isolation from Western developments for a quarter of a century. On point (3), I do not wish to make any predictions about where love could make a breakthrough!

The professional futurists are too tied to present spatial distributions of social, economic, and political resources and too wedded to thirty-year projections based on artificial isolation of a Hellenic-European stream from the total stream of history, to be able to conceive of the breaches in time and space that history in its planet-wide dimensions should lead us to expect. Their man-computer symbiosis allows for no sense of the totally other, transcendent or otherwise. The paradoxical thought arises that it may be precisely the most professionalized of the professional futurists who will be in for the most violent "future shock."

The humanist, participatory, evolutionist, ecological, and revolutionary futurists all have some kind of intellectual and moral commitment to thinking in a wider frame of reference than the Western one. Whether they succeed is another matter. At the least, they extend the range of conceivable futures portrayed for humanity because of their commitment to exploring a radically different set of social possibilities than those indicated by present trends. That same commitment to otherness reintroduces the note of transcendence which is missing in much professional futurism. In all likelihood, this will not mean a return to earlier prevailing Christian conceptions but rather a different sense of the relationship of man and nature to other orders of reality.

Polak's critique of the future-imaging capacity of contemporary man shares with much professional futurism the tendency to think of the West as an isolatable compartment on the planet. The scope of Polak's own ideas, however, goes beyond any such compartmentalization. If we review the humanist-to-revolutionary futurists in the light of his most urgent concerns about that imaging capacity, we see some interesting developments:

1. *The time horizon.* This is both foreshortened and extended in that participatory futurists are creating "chunks of the future" now and visualizing social orders that will not come into being for a long time. Guerrilla movements have a very narrow time horizon, yet they are acting for a socially distant future. The "Now" people are similarly split. The evolutionary nucleators and the ecologists operate with very distant time horizons indeed, as they attempt to visualize very long-term planetary processes, but they also show considerable concern about how to deal with the immediate present.

2. *The spatial sense.* Increasingly, futurists are thinking in planetary (and interplanetary) terms, though their conceptualizations are often inadequate to the scale on which they are attempting to think.

3. *Otherness.* Openness to the possibility of radically different types of social structures is very widespread, but only in some militant political groups is there a doctrinaire futurism intent on a specific future pattern. Many militant groups are as open to possible futures as

the evolutionary nucleators — if only because they do not have much time to think about it.

4. *Transcendence.* The possibility of transcending presently conceived human limitations is very widely accepted among futurists. Whether achieving this transcendence with the aid of computer technology or through a new perception of the nonphysical world represents an ultimately significant distinction in terms of the power to transcend is not clear. Either form of transcendence has a significant impact on man's images of the future.

5. *Optimism.* There are signs that the creative minority which generates images of the future in the West is climbing out of the pessimism concerning the nature of reality and human capacity generated by two world wars and a prolonged cold war. The discovery that the "colossus technology" has feet of clay has encouraged creative thinking about alternatives among people who until recently felt oppressed and paralyzed by technology-based life-styles. Furthermore, the cultural heritage of millennialism leads to a widespread feeling of hope that rounding the bend of this last thousand-year cycle will usher in a new and better era for humanity. Perhaps it will.

REFERENCES

Aquarian Oracle
 1970   Article in the *Aquarian Oracle* 1 (1). Los Angeles, California.
BAADE, FRITZ
 1962   *The race to the year 2000.* Translated from the German by Ernst Pawel. Garden City, New York: Doubleday.
BARNETT, H. G.
 1953   *Innovation: the basis of cultural change.* New York: McGraw-Hill.
BELL, DANIEL
 1967   The year 2000 — the trajectory of an idea. *Daedalus* 96 (Summer): 639–651.
BOGUSLAW, ROBERT
 1965   *The new utopians: a study of system design and social change.* Englewood Cliffs, N.J.: Prentice Hall.
BOULDING, KENNETH E.
 1964   *The meaning of the 20th century: the great transition.* New York: Harper.
 1966   "Expecting the unexpected: the uncertain future of knowledge and technology," in *Designing education for the future, No. 1. Prospective changes in society by 1980 including some implications for education.* Edited by Edgar L. Morphet and Charles O. Ryan, 199–215. New York: Scholastic Books Service.
BROWN, NORMAN O.
 1966   *Love's body.* New York: Random House.
CLARKE, ARTHUR
 1953   *Childhood's end.* New York: Ballantine.

DE JOUVENEL, BERTRAND
1967   *The art of conjecture.* New York: Basic Books.
DRUCKER, PETER F.
1968   *The age of discontinuity.* New York: Harper and Row.
GABOR, DENNIS
1964   *Inventing the future.* New York: Knopf.
GORDON, WILLIAM J. J.
1961   *Synectics.* New York: Collier Books.
HAMPDEN-TURNER, CHARLES
1970   *Radical man.* Cambridge, Mass.: Schenkman.
HELMER, OLAF, BERNICE BROWN, THEODORE GORDON.
1966   *Social technology.* New York: Basic Books.
HERBERT, FRANK
1965   *Dune.* New York: Ace Paperback Books.
HO CHI MINH
1969   Appeal to the entire people to wage the resistance war. *Tricontinental* 44, 4 (November): 16–28.
HUDSON, WILLIAM HENRY
1922   *Crystal age.* New York: Dutton.
JUNGK, ROBERT, JOHANN GALTUNG, editors
1969   *Mankind 2000.* London: Allen and Unwin.
KAHN, HERMAN, ANTHONY J. WIENER
1967   *The year 2000.* New York: Macmillan.
LeGUIN, URSULA
1969   *Left hand of darkness.* New York: Ace.
LEWIS, FREDERICK J., JR., IRENE PINKAU
1968   Societal engineering: a new career for societal systems. *Engineering Education* (October): 111–114.
MANKIND 2000
1966   "Report of developments since the conference of overseas sponsors held in London in November, 1965." London: Preparatory International Secretariat.
MARUYAMA, MAGOROH
1963   The second cybernetics: deviation amplifying mutual causal processes. *American Scientist* 51: 164–179, 250–256.
MASLOW, ABRAHAM
1954   *Motivation and personality.* New York: Harper and Row.
1968   *Toward a psychology of being* (second edition). New York: Van Nostrand-Reinhold.
MEAD, MARGARET
1964   *Continuities in cultural evolution.* New Haven: Yale University Press.
MEADOWS, D., et al.
1972   *Limits to growth.* New York: Universe Books.
MEIER, RICHARD
1965   *Developmental planning.* New York: McGraw-Hill.
MORRIS, WILLIAM
1966   *News from nowhere.* New York: Monthly Review Press. (Originally published 1890.)
MYRDAL, GUNNAR
1968   *Asian drama: an inquiry into the poverty of nations.* New York: Pantheon, Random House.
NORDHOFF, CHARLES
1965   *Communistic societies of the United States.* New York: Schocken Books. (First published in 1875.)

OSBORN, ALEX
1963   *Applied imagination* (third edition). New York: Scribners.
OSGOOD, CHARLES
1966   *An alternative to war or surrender.* Urbana: University of Illinois
         Press.
PLATT, JOHN
         "How men can shape their future." Mimeographed Paper. Distri-
         buted by the World Future Society.
POLAK, FRED L.
1961   *The image of the future,* two volumes. Translated from the Dutch by
         E. Boulding. New York: Oceana Publications. (Abridged version,
         1972. New York: Elsevier.)
1971   *Prognostics.* New York: Elsevier.
SCHON, DONALD A.
1967   *Technology and change.* New York: Delta Books, Dell.
STAPLEDON, OLAF
1930   *First and last men.* London: Methuen.
TEILHARD DE CHARDIN, PIERRE
1959   *The phenomenon of man.* Translated by Bernard Wall. New York:
         Harper and Row.
THOMPSON, W. I.
1974   *Passages about Earth.* New York: Harper and Row.
TOFFLER, ALVIN
1970   *Future shock.* New York: Random House.
WARD, BARBARA
1966   *Spaceship Earth.* New York: University of Columbia Press.
WASKOW, ARTHUR I.
1970   *Running riot.* New York: Herder and Herder.
Whole Earth Catalog
1970   *Access to tools.* (summer). Menlo Park, California: Portola Institute.

Toward Human Futuristics

MAGOROH MARUYAMA

Human futuristics, as a study of future cultural alternatives, limitations, and choices, will not be another branch of "science" in the traditional sense. Its function will differ from that of science in many respects. First, future cultures are not existing "objects" to be observed, analyzed, and explained. Second, future cultures cannot be predicted by extrapolating the past pattern of change, the past rate of change, or even the past rate of acceleration of change. There are too many unprecedented innovations taking place which render extrapolation invalid. Third, culture changes do not just happen. People make them happen. Therefore, culture changes are subject to people's goals, imagination, will, and choice.

In this third sense human futuristics is more like engineering than science. But here again, the philosophy and principles of human futuristics differ from those of engineering. First, engineering is mainly a matter of designing an object for a specifically given purpose, while in human futuristics the cultural goals are not given *a priori*. New goals are generated by reciprocal morphogenetic interaction of heterogeneity among people. Engineers work from a given goal downward; human futuristics needs to work upward from the grass roots. Second, cultural goals are heterogeneous because people's needs vary from individual to individual and from group to group. Therefore, human futuristics deals with diverse-goal systems while an engineering project is a central-goal system. Consequently an engineering project is a one-goal efficiency system while human futuristics is concerned with multipurpose symbiotic versatility systems. Third, people's goals are not constant over time. The goals are the unknown variable, not only in the sense of being quantitatively unspecifiable although confined in a known range and dimension, but also in the sense of being capable of jumping into dimensions which are not yet known. The product of engineering is usually a constant-goal system. The object of human futuristics, on the other hand, is an evolving-goal system. It is even a goal-evolving system. Fourth, and most obvious, engineering deals with inanimate objects, while a culture consists of people with self-determination.

Science deals with knowledge. Engineering deals with the practical application of knowledge when a goal is given. Goals are generated by people. Human futuristics does not aim at generating goals but aids people in generating their own goals. Its function is catalytic. Therefore, human futuristics differs from utopianism as it is usually understood. Most utopians, both by profession and by inclination, tend to proceed from their own goal downward, assuming that their goal is "good for" people. Human futuristics prevents the growth of "professional" goal generators and self-appointed utopia designers.

In the past, the members of a society did not need to generate cultural goals. In most cases cultures were either stationary or changed very slowly, and cultural goals were transmitted from the older to the younger generation in the process of socialization. Sudden culture change, which did occur from time to time, was merely a matter of transition from one stationary or almost stationary pattern to another. But we are now entering an era of transition of a different nature. It is a transition from a chain of stationary or quasi-stationary patterns, which the population accepted as given, to a period of perpetually transforming patterns which depend on people's will and choice. It is a transition between types of transitions. This can be called *metatransition*, from homeostatic transitions to morphogenetic transitions.

In the past, education could aim at transmitting relatively stationary goals and relatively known means of attaining these goals. Education could be thought of as information-giving and answer-giving. This type of education will become inadequate for people preparing to enter the period of nonstationary cultures. We must *unlearn* to expect information on ready-made goals and means. Education will increasingly become a matter of developing an attitude, ability, and skills to transcend the existing cultural goals and means, and to challenge our present ways of thinking, logic, science, and epistemology.

Imagination must be accompanied by realistic elaboration. Human futuristics must prevent the individual from delivering himself to pure fantasy. It must encourage the individual to develop new methods for new types of reality testing. It must stimulate reality-directed inventiveness in the individual. In short, human futuristics aims at developing a scientific attitude, an experimental attitude, and an engineering attitude rather than at teaching scientific data *per se*. Above all, it must help people develop the attitude that technology should serve human goals. Human futuristics will not be merely a body of knowledge as many other "ologies" are primarily. It will make use of knowledge, but it will not provide us with ready-made answers about our future society. Its usefulness lies not in information-giving but in its catalytic function.

For example, suppose we desire a nonhierarchical, symbiotic, pluralistic government structure. A large nonhierarchical, symbiotic system requires complex channeling of communication as well as finding symbiotic combinations of heterogeneity. Special computers and computer programs must be invented to facilitate this process. Such goal setting and subsequent mobilization of computer technology are possible only if there are persons capable of designing the overall system as well as the component subsystems. These persons must have knowledge not only of computer science but also of government organization, the composition of ethnic and professional groups in the nation, the culture of such groups, psychological and political motivations for agreement and disagreement, etc. Human futuristics cannot stock ready-made answers for this task. But it can help people to equip themselves with a framework of mind and ways for self-training to generate a new methodology for tackling such complex problems.

Currently, scientific "training" often tends to make the student internalize as a moral principle the ready-made methodology of his field of specialization. Such an indoctrinated student feels guilt about deviating from that particular methodology and may even consider the methodologies of other fields of specialization to be morally inferior. Even many proponents of new movements are trapped in old logics (Maruyama 1977a, 1977b). Human futuristics must devise ways to help people unlearn such fixations.

Human futuristics as an evolving system will undoubtedly develop other functions as time goes on.

TYPOLOGY OF FUTURISTICS

The study of the future has a long history. But it has recently entered upon a period of rapid proliferation. Books are being published, conferences held, and seminars and lectures given at a rate much faster than anyone can hope to survey. But one can recognize certain patterns of focuses and orientation in the field. In terms of the focal topic, technological and economic studies of the future formed the first wave of the contemporary futuristics boom. However, a new wave of ecological and environmental studies is catching up with this. There have always been a number of architectural publications and urban planning publications as well as some sociological research into the future. But studies of the cultural aspects of our future society are still scarce. I would like to present here a somewhat tentative and over-simplified typology of the attitudinal orientations implicit in futuristics studies. I am offering this simply as a kickoff for further discussion.

1. *Descriptive.* This deals with trends in social change; it can be sociological or historical.

2. *Predictive.* This may be subdivided into:
   A. *Extrapolative.* Inferences regarding the future are derived from the past rate of change or past rate of acceleration of change.
   B. *Speculative.* An estimate is made of change resulting from innovations which have no historical precedent.

3. *Pragmatic.* A study is made of what can and should be done to affect the direction of social change. This can be subdivided into:
   A. *Reactive.* It can be further subdivided into:
      i. *Defensive.* This is mainly concerned with how to preserve the old patterns (for example, family structure, population size, clean air over cities).
      ii. *Instrumental.* This is mainly concerned with how to use new tools for old purposes. (For example, how to replace accountants with computers while keeping the accounting system intact; or how to replace school teachers with teaching machines while keeping the education system intact).
      iii. *Adaptive.* This is concerned with how to modify culture in order to fit it to technological changes, i.e. let culture be dictated by technology.
   B. *Goal-generating.* This first asks what the goals of mankind *can* be, then adapts and develops technology to serve these goals. It can be subdivided into:
      i. *Uniformistic or homogenistic:*
         a. *Constitutional.* A numerical majority imposes its decision uniformly upon minorities (so-called democracy).
         b. *Planned utopia.* A small number of "planners" design the society "for" the rest of the population.
      ii. *Pluralistic or heterogenistic.* There are no *a priori* goals. It builds on goals generated by people; accommodates diversities and differences; studies examples of intercultural ecology such as cultural symbiosis and cultural parasitism.

The descriptive study of social change deals with the past and the present. It sometimes seeks to derive general rules of social change from past and present data. It may claim that we can learn from past mistakes and can therefore avoid making similar mistakes in the future. But beyond this, the descriptive study of social change is of little help in our exploration of the future.

Predictive futuristics, so long as it remains merely predictive, tends to be based on the assumption that most social change occurs beyond the individual's will and that the individual has little or no choice but to live with it. There is an undertone of the inevitability of the "course of the history," which is thought to have a suprapersonal or impersonal reality. Predictive futuristics sees its function as limited to preparing the individual for inevitable social change. Within predictive futuristics, extrapolative futuristics is less imaginative and reflects a pattern of thinking based on bookkeeping. Speculative futuristics is more imaginative but tends to attribute innovations to a small number of geniuses while considering the role of the people as culture changers to be negligible.

Pragmatic futuristics assumes that man can influence social change. Reactive futuristics is the most common and popular at present. Defensive futuristics is politically and intellectually conservative. Instrumental futuristics is scientifically liberal but politically conservative. Adaptive futuristics is technocentric. Goal-generating futuristics is practiced by humanistic liberals. Uniformistic futuristics is produced by armchair idealists who live relatively comfortably and have never shared the sufferings of minority groups or dissenters. Pluralistic futuristics is associated mainly with those who have got their feet wet in grassroots life or are perceptive enough to recognize the cultural diversity of society.

A NEW EPISTEMOLOGICAL THRESHOLD

We have said that we are entering an era of metatransition, that is a transition between two types of transition: one of these types consisted of transitions between stationary or quasi-stationary cultural patterns; the other will consist of perpetually transforming cultural patterns. Our era is also characterized by an epistemological transition. By "epistemology" we mean here the framework and internal structure of the reasoning process. The basic epistemology of American culture was derived from Greco-European epistemology, which is based on deductive logic, an assumption of nonreciprocal causal flow, and hierarchical social order (Pribram 1949; Maruyama 1965). It is mixed with the peculiarly American worldview (Mead 1942, 1946) which includes a unidimensionally rankable universe, competition, conquest, technocentricism and unicultural assimilation. Under this epistemology, even "democracy" takes the form of majority rule over minorities, i.e. domination by quantity.

This epistemology is being challenged by the emergence of alternate epistemologies. Some of these have long existed among the ethnic minority groups in the United States, unrecognized by the social majority: for example the nonhierarchical mutualism of the Navajos (Dyk 1938; Kluckhohn 1949; Maruyama 1967a) and the Eskimos (Freuchen 1961); the philosophy of harmony of nature held by most Native Americans (American Indians); and the mutual complementarity (Chang 1938) brought in by Chinese and Japanese immigrants. Hippies, rebelling against traditional Americanism, borrowed these epistemologies, imported the practice of Zen from India and the kibbutz way of life from Israel, and added some contributions of their own, such as psychedelic art. The black movement stimulated the brown movement and both inspired the yellow and red movements. The Asian American Political Alliance, the first organization of the yellow movement, was formed in 1967, and in 1969 Indians moved onto Alcatraz. Ethnic consciousness sprang up in various ethnic groups, and the black-white contrast has provided an impetus for cultural heterogenization and political pluralism.

Improved birth control methods led to an increase in experiments in forms of sexual relationship, such as multifamilies and multimarriages. The nuclear family system tends to foster a hierarchical, monocephalic, and uniformistic view of the universe (Maruyama 1966). It can be expected that multifamilies and multimarriages will enable children to develop more naturally a nonhierarchical, mutualistic, and symbiotic epistemology.

Our society is thus suddenly faced with not only one but several sets of epistemological discrepancies between established ways of thinking and emergent ways of thinking. Most conspicuous of these discrepancies are: (1) competition vs. sharing; (2) technocentric transgression vs. harmony with nature; (3) material efficiency vs. cultivation of mind; (4) hierarchism vs. nonhierarchical mutualism; (5) leadership vs. interactionism; (6) majority rule vs. symbiotism; (7) homogenization vs. pluralism. The single epistemology in which most Americans sought to find psychological security is being challenged and undermined. They feel therefore as if the whole universe is collapsing. Never having been aware of the existence of other epistemologies and never having learned to find a foothold in another epistemology, these people are panic-stricken and are desperately trying to fight their own insecurity by reinforcing their conservatism.

Recently conservatism has been gaining strength. Some say that this is a matter of cycles between conservatism and liberalism. In the past there were cycles. But these cycles were oscillations within the same epistemology. This time it is likely to be a jump into another orbit of new epistemologies. The shape of the new orbit is still unknown. It may be circular. It may be elliptic. But it may be parabolic or even hyperbolic. Then there will be no return.

Elise Boulding calls this type of jump "totally other," and the capacity to imagine such a jump "eschatological" or "transcendent." The notion of paradigm shifts (Kuhn 1962) can be applied to sudden social restructuring which follows a period of increasingly pervasive incongruence between emerging patterns and the old structure. According to this model, at the beginning the occasional incipient new elements are dismissed as deviations or temporary irregularities. But gradually, the incongruent elements grow in number and are found all over the place. After a time, the obsolescence of the old system comes to be recognized as fundamental, and eventually the component parts suddenly snap into new relationships. The time needed for such restructuring is unpredictable. But when it comes, it comes like lightning, though the adjustment of details may take several years. The reason for the speed is that the change is prepared for everywhere at once. Whether it is called "transcendence" or "quantum jump," a basic epistemological restructuring is becoming inevitable in our society.

GOALLESS DISSATISFACTION, GOAL-ORIENTED DISSATIS-FACTION, AND GOAL-GENERATING DISSATISFACTION

Jean-Paul Sartre said: "As long as a person is immersed in the historical situation, it does not even occur to him to realize the defects of a specific political or economic system, not because he is 'used to' it, but because he sees it in its full presence and cannot even imagine that it could be otherwise" (Sartre 1943: 509–510). Sartre distinguished two ways of being: "in-itself" and "for-itself." The being in-itself is one without awareness of the possibility of being otherwise. The being in-itself is complete without any vacuum or fissure where a negation can enter. The being for-itself, on the other hand, is a double negation between the wanted and the actual: the wanted is a negation of the actual, and the actual is a negation of the wanted. This double negation characterizes the "authentic" human being.

Such negations involve dissatisfaction. Therefore dissatisfaction is inherent in the authentic mode of human being. Dissatisfaction is the source of change. I would define progress as change which is desired by people (Maruyama 1967b: 174). If progress is desired change, and if change is desired only when there is dissatisfaction, then dissatisfaction is a prerequisite for progress. I have distinguished two types of dissatisfaction: goalless dissatisfaction and goal-oriented dissatisfaction. Both can be either goal-generating or non-goal-generating (Maruyama 1967b).

There are times when only one side of the double negation is present: a person has a desire not to be what he is or not to be in the situation he is in, without knowing what he wants to be or what situation he wants to be in. He is not a being in-itself, yet he has no precise goal. This is the state of goalless dissatisfaction. This state has been described by various thinkers in various ways. For Søren Kierkegaard (1844), it is a state of awakening awareness of possibilities, a state in which a person emerges from his anxiety-free stage of ignorant innocence. Erik Erikson (1956) calls it a state of "psychosocial moratorium" in which the young person, in search of experiment and identity formation, shuns any step leading toward permanent commitment.

Goalless dissatisfaction may originate in different ways: (1) in discontent with the self or with society; (2) in past satisfaction which has ceased (for example, extinction of the buffalo for the Plains Indians); (3) where a goal is made impossible (for example, through discrimination based on race or sex, or by being physically disabled); (4) through the opening of unprecedented possibilities, the extent and implications of which have not yet been fully assessed.

The ways to channel goalless dissatisfaction are accordingly different: For (1), by producing goals; for (2), either by restoring the past means of satisfaction or by producing new means; for (3), either by making the goal possible or setting an alternative goal. The fourth type of goalless dissatisfaction must be dealt with somewhat differently. This type is inherent in any experience of growth, the extent of which is not yet known. It can happen to an individual when he is growing out of childhood, and it can happen to a culture when an innovation occurs which affects the basic philosophy of the culture.

When a young person grows up, physical and mental capacities change. What is crucial in this experience is not so much that the change occurs but that the ultimate extent of the change is unknown. The growing youth does not know whether he will eventually attain the height of six feet two inches or five feet nine inches, whether he will be sufficiently skillful to become a surgeon or whether he must settle for being a dentist. He cannot set a fixed goal. And in many cases he refuses to set a goal. Even if a reasonable goal is proposed, he wants to explore all other possibilities first. He must learn to avoid fixing his goal and yet at the same time he must look for a goal. He must learn to generate goals. This is why the youth is inherently dissatisfied, not only with his present situation but also with proposed plans for the future. In a sense he wants to remain goalless, at most setting up only temporary goals. Some young people even keep the future completely blank as if there were no such thing as future.

A newborn nation may experience a similar need to avoid goal-fixing. For example, Israel experimented with various forms of kibbutzim searching for its own cultural pattern. Erikson (1956) called this a "historical moratorium."

Whether temporary or permanent, when a goal is set which is different from the present situation, there arises the double negation between the present and the goal. This double negation is goal-oriented dissatisfaction.

When an individual has attained a goal, he may fall into a state of static satisfaction or he may generate a new goal. After falling into static satisfaction, he may become the victim of boredom. For example, there was a man who had set himself the goal of obtaining a Ph.D. degree. He considered this the ultimate goal in his life. Working toward his degree became his way of life and gave "meaning" to his life. After obtaining his degree, he entered the Civil Service and attained a comfortable income. He became apathetic toward life and could not understand why he was not happy.

Whether goalless or goal-oriented, a dissatisfaction can be goal-generating or non-goal-generating. Non-goal-generating dissatisfaction tends to end in stagnation, boredom, apathy, or disgust.

We should not assume, however, that everybody is dissatisfied and desires to generate goals. Our society should contain niches for individuals who are satisfied and do not want to generate goals. To some extent our society already has niches in which a minimal amount of goal-generating is required, for example factory assembly-line work, the military, or the civil service. Unfortunately, not all of the people who work in such places have chosen to be there. Some are there because they were denied other opportunities. Our society must create a more satisfactory system of matching the needs of individuals and the opportunities available to them.

NEW ADAM'S APPLE AND NEW PHILOSOPHICAL CONCERN

For some centuries humans have traveled along a course of history without needing to question it. There were wars and there were times of peace. There were political revolutions and there were religious reforms. But these were regarded as inevitable and normal events of history stemming from "human nature." "Human nature" included such basic "facts" as marriage, death by aging, parents' chronological seniority over their children, and man's "superiority" over animals.

Contraceptives, organ transplants, body freezing, and possibilities of extraterrestrial intelligence, which have all occurred within the past few years, have challenged these basic "facts" of "human nature." For example, if a parent is frozen for a later resuscitation, his child may in the interim grow older than the parent. Then what happens to the parent-child relationship which is as old as human history and has been considered part of "human nature?"

Until now, discoveries and inventions did not change our view of "human nature" which was regarded as something given and beyond humans' power to change. The invention of nuclear explosives was only an added tool for "human nature" to use in fighting a war. Anthropologists' "discovery" of many nonwhite cultures did not affect the way of life of ordinary whites. Philosophy, whose function was to speculate about "human nature," was mainly indulged in as an intellectual luxury far removed from the "banality" of daily life, and was seldom intended to have practical consequences.

But we are now entering an era in which discoveries and inventions will not only change a part of what has so far been considered "human nature" but will also give humans the power to change it. This is a new Adam's apple. This time the apple is not from the tree of knowledge about good and evil conduct. It is an apple which may transform human's body, mind, and culture. Humans may transform themselves into monsters unfit to survive or may attain a new and unknown civilization. Our choice requires some philosophy. Philosophy, for this purpose, becomes as indispensable to our action as a navigation map is to a pilot. But existing philosophy is inadequate to serve as a guideline for our future decision making and action. We must develop a new type of philosophy.

GENERATING CULTURAL GOALS AHEAD OF TECHNOLOGY

When "human nature" was considered as given and constant, cultural goals were considered to be naturally derived from "human nature." Those who regarded human nature as essentially "good" and cooperative thought that the role of cultural goals should be to facilitate the goals of individuals. Those who regarded the individual as essentially harmless to himself but egocentric thought that society should regulate the activities of individuals in order to minimize conflicts among them. Those who regarded human nature as essentially base and evil thought that individuals should strive for "higher" purposes in order to counteract their evilness. In each of these cases the cultural goals, once generated, discovered, or given by "God," were permanent and there was no need to question them. Most people did not even suspect that there could be other ways in which a culture could exist. Western civilization was in a state of in-itself.

Then came anthropology. But for most people in our society it remained an exercise in intellectual curiosity having no application to their own lives. Many people in our society still have never heard of anthropology. Among those who came in contact with it, many regarded "primitive cultures" as museum pieces outside their immediate personal reality. The more informed took the existence of different cultures more seriously, but many of them decided that each culture should mind its own business. Some people even found an intellectualized way of bypassing the philosophical question of differences in cultural goals: They looked for "universals," and after choosing their favorite universals, settled themselves in their old way of life because other cultures must only be variations on the universals which their own life exemplified. More sophisticated people argued that life-style is governed by the cultural context, and since our life-style fits our cultural context, we should not change it. Thus, the overall effect of the "discovery" of other cultures upon our own cultural goals has been virtually negligible. Even many of the proponents of "new" philosophies, such as hippies and "consciousness" advocates, have epistemologically misinterpreted the non-Western cultures which they borrowed (Maruyama 1978a).

Technological change, on the other hand, has affected our society more broadly. Automation has touched the average person, especially the less skilled worker, in the form of vocational displacement and unemployment. Average parents can no longer fulfil the role of model and adviser to their children because their job and their knowledge are becoming obsolete. This type of massive and rapid obsolescence of cultural goals is something people in our culture have had little experience with and are unprepared for. Therefore, haphazard attempts are made at modifying our economic, educational, and other systems in a retarded effort to catch up with technological change. The result is that technological change is dictating culture change. Culture is in danger of becoming a tool of technology. This, of course, is putting the cart before the horse. Obviously we need to generate cultural goals ahead of technology and orient technology toward the achievement of cultural goals.

It is people who generate cultural goals. Most utopians have made the mistake of assuming the role of goal generators. This is one of the reasons why many of the utopias failed. People's goals must be recognized as the goals of the culture. Since people are diverse, the cultural goals which they generate are also diverse, varying with the needs and tastes of individuals and groups. The future society must aim squarely for diversity and heterogeneity (Maruyama 1978b), not merely "making allowance" for "marginal" diversities. Uniform imposition of majority decisions upon minorities is obsolete.

RESONANCE

Though goals vary from individual to individual, there may be a symbiosis of different goals among combinations of individuals. I have termed such a symbiotization of goals and purposes "relevance resonance" (Maruyama 1961b, 1969). There are other types of resonance (Maruyama 1961b). For example, complementary levels and ranges of intellectual interests create intellectual resonance. Shared experiences create experiential resonance. Individuals who are in resonance can derive mutual gratification and appreciation from interaction. When there is no resonance, interaction may cease, becoming boring, artificial, exploitative, phony, or even explosive.

At present there is often a lack of relevance resonance between businessmen and ecology-minded people, between students and college administrations, between the ghetto and the middle class, and so forth. Karl Mannheim (1952) pointed out that there are many logics and epistemologies, and that the choice of a particular logic or epistemology that an individual makes is based on translogical factors (factors outside, beyond, and independent of logic). The specific social and historical conditions of each social group generate specific feelings which are shared by the members of that group; and these shared feelings, in turn, generate goals and purposes. These feelings, goals, and purposes generate the particular logic and world view of the social group. Lawrence Kubie (1956) and Lewis Feuer (1959) pointed out that even among scientists and philosophers there usually are translogical emotional needs behind the choice of a particular logical theory or model. Relevance resonance depends on these translogical factors.

Lack of resonance, when it occurs, is usually felt by all the interacting parties concerned. But sometimes, only one of them may be aware of it. This happens especially frequently in the case of relevance resonance. The relationship between the ghetto and the middle class is an example. A more extreme example is the relationship between prison inmates and academic researchers. Many middle-class people were convinced that the programs they and their government ran "for" the ghettos were relevant to the ghetto residents, while from the point of view of the ghetto residents many of these programs were irrelevant and useful only as a means for a "hustle." Such lack of relevance resonance can easily occur when plans for the future are made from the top down.

Because relevance resonance is important in understanding social friction, I shall briefly discuss the prison inmates' case, mentioned above, as this illustrates the nature of relevance resonance more clearly (Maruyama 1968, 1969) than other cases available. Prison inmates often perceive an academic researcher as coming for the purposes of testing his hypothesis, proving and perpetuating his theory, producing publications as a means of achieving recognition, enhancing his reputation and improving his chances of promotion, gaining prestige from having worked with "criminals," or simply earning his research salary. Such purposes are irrelevant from the point of view of the inmates, whose own purposes are to have the abuses and harassments by the guards reduced, the food made edible, or the educational and vocational training programs updated. Prison inmates are thoroughly familiar with the psychology of academics, and have in stock several sets of ready-made, sophisticated, phony answers which satisfy the researcher and at the same time safeguard themselves. They can also play "stupid" in order to avoid arousing anxiety in the researcher. They can even fool some of the prison psychiatrists. They manufacture "symptoms" and play them out in front of the psychiatrists; they gradually reduce the symptoms from month to month or from year to year in order to obtain a report of "improvement." The inmates are skilled at making the researcher believe that his research is relevant to them.

When lack of relevance resonance occurs between hierarchical levels, as in this example, the result is frequently that a delusion of relevance is created among those on the higher level while those on the lower level feel that they are being exploited, resent this and make an attempt at counterexploitation. The power hierarchy perpetuates the situation, and a solution is extremely difficult unless the system is dehierarchized.

When lack of relevance resonance occurs between groups in nonhierarchical relationship to one another they may cease interacting or enter into a conflict blaming each other for being "illogical," "irrational" or "immoral" (Mannheim 1952; Maruyama 1962, 1963b). This is partly because epistemological differences are mistakenly perceived as logical or ethical errors. This type of conflict is likely to occur in a heterogeneous society; it is easier to avoid if the members of each group become aware of the epistemologies of other groups.

INTERACTIONAL DYNAMICS: CHANGE AMPLIFICATION AND CHANGE COUNTERACTION

In a heterogeneous society with a wide range of differing cultural niches, an individual can seek out an existing group with which he finds resonance, or several individuals in symbiosis may form a new group. Individuals — whether heterogeneous or homogeneous and whether they belong to different groups, to the same group, or to no group — interact and influence one another's goals.

Until recently the concept of reciprocal causality was taboo in Western thinking (Maruyama 1961a, 1963a, 1965). This was because the structure of events was confused with the structure of Aristotelian logic which prohibited "circular argument." As late as 1953 Hans Reichenbach, a leading philosopher, considered that reciprocal causality was impossible (1956: 39). But reciprocal causality exists in many biological, ecological, physical, and social processes, as various branches of science have gradually begun to recognize (Prigogine 1977; Morin 1977).

A reciprocal causal network may be hooked up in such a way that it works to amplify change, counteract change, drift randomly, or form any combination of these (Maruyama 1963a). A deviation-amplifying reciprocal causal system may generate complexity, increase differentiation and structuredness, or go beyond the boundary of viability. Examples are: interspecific competition in the evolutionary process; growth of a city; and arms races. A deviation-counteracting reciprocal causal system maintains equilibrium. Examples are: the ratio between predators and their prey; a thermostat; an automatic steering mechanism.

Change-amplifying reciprocal interaction is a useful concept in our discussion of goal generation. One of the properties of the deviation-amplifying reciprocal causal system is that a small initial kick may result in a large change. This property has several consequences. One is that two identical systems with almost identical initial conditions may produce very different results depending on a small difference in the direction of the initial kick or on a minute difference in the initial condition. In such a system the old principle that similar conditions produce similar results no longer holds. Another consequence is that a relatively small "investment" in the initial kick will produce a disproportionally large "return." The third consequence is that once an amplification has started, it may be very difficult to stop or reverse the process. The fourth consequence is that when the initial kick is left to inconspicuous random fluctuations, the produced result has an appearance of unpredictability because of the invisibility of the initial kick. Much of the unpredictability of history can be attributed to deviation-amplifying reciprocal causal processes rather than to some "unknown" variables.

Goal generating, as a reciprocal interaction process between individuals, between groups, or between levels of hierarchy, possesses these characteristics which can be utilized to advantage. But they may also cause dangers. For example, an administrative policy of suppressing dissenters tends to further widen the gap between the dissenters and the administration instead of reducing it. The people who support the administrative policy reinforce one another's conservatism, aided by administrative sanction and its perception of the dissenters. This may lead to an impasse and bloodshed.

INTERCULTURAL ECOLOGY: SEPARATISM, SYMBIOSIS, PARASITISM, ANTIBIOSIS, AND MUTUAL ANTIBIOSIS

There are several ways in which the component groups in a heterogeneous society can interact. Groups may coexist with no or very little interaction between them. This is separatism. Or groups exist in mutual benefit. This is symbiosis. Or the relationship may be such that one group's gain is another group's loss. This is parasitism. Or one group may harm another. This is antibiosis. Or many groups may harm one another. This is mutual antibiosis. These relationships can be classified into zero-sum and non-zero-sum. Zero-sum relationships are those in which the total gain and total loss cancel out. Non-zero-sum relations are those in which this does not occur. Table 1 summarizes these relationships.

The ideal relationship, of course, is symbiosis. There are two ways of conceptualizing symbiosis. One is organismic (Pribram 1949) and the other is mutualistic. The organismic view assumes that there is a whole, to which the parts are subordinated. The parts cooperate with one another in order to fulfil the task of the whole. There is a hierarchical, causal, and teleological priority of the whole over the parts. The whole is the cause of the parts. The whole is more important than the parts. The mutualistic view, on the other hand, is that there are only parts, and parts create a system of interaction. There is no "whole" prior to the parts.

The strategy of planning in a heterogeneous society varies depending on whether the organismic view or the mutualistic view is taken. In organismic planning, a hierarchical planning center is set up, and the planning flows from the top down. The component groups conform to the outline issued by the center. In mutualistic planning, the ideas originate from the component groups and are pooled for symbiotic combination. Solutions are explored in various dimensions until one is

Table 1. Classification of types of group interaction in a heterogeneous society

Type	Gain	Loss	Remarks
Separatism	No group	No group	No interaction
Symbiosis	All groups	No group	Positive sum
Parasitism	Some groups	Other groups	Zero-sum
Antibiosis	No group	Some groups	Negative sum
Mutual antibiosis	No group	All groups	Negative sum

found which satisfies all the groups or at least does not produce hardship for any group. No majority vote is imposed on minorities. One of the tasks of human futuristics can be to help develop mutualistic symbiosis in a heterogeneous society.

HORIZONTAL MOBILITY, HOMOGENIZATION, AND HETEROGENIZATION

Tönnies (1887) pointed out several differences between two types of organization: *gemeinschaft* and *gesellschaft*. One difference, which concerns us here, is that a *gemeinschaft* is an entity in which the individual must stay permanently, while he can move in and out of a *gesellschaft* relatively easily. For example, a business firm or factory in North America is a *gesellschaft*, while a business firm in Japan tends to be more of a *gemeinschaft*. Since a *gemeinschaft* cannot eliminate its members easily, it must accommodate individual variations (Maruyama 1967b). It must either allow for heterogeneity, or suppress it.

Another interpretation of *gemeinschaft* is as an organismic or totalitarian society, in which the purposes of the individual are subordinated to those of the society. But for our present discussion let us define *gemeinschaft* as a nontotalitarian society with noncancellable membership. There are many tribes which are *gemeinschaften* of this type, for example the Navajo tribe before the beginning of urban migration. It accommodated individual variations to a remarkable extent (Kluckhohn 1949; Maruyama 1967a). A *gesellschaft*, on the other hand, needs no built-in device to accommodate individual variations. A dissatisfied individual can cancel his membership and move out. The *gesellschaft* itself may expel "deviant" individuals, or maneuver for "resignation" of nonconformists. Therefore a *gesellschaft* can easily become homogeneous (Maruyama 1967b).

A culture or a society may be a *gemeinschaft* or a *gesellschaft*, and may contain subgroups which are *gemeinschaft*-like or *gesellschaft*-like, or both. A predominance of *gemeinschaft*-like groups tends to produce low horizontal intergroup mobility of individuals, and a predominance of *gesellschaft*-like groups tends to produce high horizontal intergroup mobility of individuals.

In a society with high horizontal mobility, the individual can move around until he finds an organization whose members are congenial to him. In a *gesellschaft*-like organization, elimination of uncongenial individuals and new supply of congenial individuals may tend to have an inbreeding effect, and the idiosyncrasy of the organization may be gradually amplified. The organization may deviate more and more from other organizations. Therefore a society with high horizontal mobility may be characterized by a high degree of homogeneity within each organization, low tolerance of deviation within each organization, and a high degree of heterogeneity between organizations, at least in principle.

But this is a simplified model. In real life there are complications. American society, for example, has high horizontal mobility, and there are diverse organizations in it which are *gesellschaft*-like. Each organization, professional, industrial, or otherwise, has its own idiosyncratic unwritten philosophy, and has a low tolerance of deviations. All this is in accordance with the model discussed. However, the degree of heterogeneity between the organizations is much lower than the model would anticipate. In fact, the whole country is rather homogeneous in terms of ideology and philosophy and has low tolerance of ideological and philosophical deviations.

This may be accounted for in two ways. One explanation is that people in the U.S.A. are so used to thinking in a partisan way that they cannot think effectively in heterogeneistic terms beyond their own organizations. They are so *gesellschaft*-oriented that they regard the whole country as an aggregate of unrelated groups rather than as an ecology of intergroup relations. One of the principles of American democracy is that each person votes for his own interest, his faction, or his party. He does not need to think beyond these. A statistical tabulation of votes is supposed to take care of the rest. Of course this is a fallacy, and the result is domination by quantity.

The second explanation is that the whole country started as a *gesellschaft* of immigrants, not as a *gemeinschaft*. Immigrants left their home countries, freeing themselves from the concept that their countries were *gemeinschaften*. The new country they entered was a *gesellschaft* for them because they chose to enter it instead of having been born into it. Since the new country was perceived as a *gesellschaft*, it was expected to be homogeneous, at least in ideology. Anybody who disliked the country shouldn't have come in the first place and should go back. Thus started the policy of "assimilation" to make a "standard American" out of every immigrant. And the immigrants were eager to become "standard Americans."

After several generations, the U.S.A. has become more of a *gemeinschaft* than a *gesellschaft*. But a *gesellschaft*-like ideology still persists. American culture has never learned to be a nontotalitarian *gemeinschaft* which knows how to live with heterogeneity. American culture has a fear of heterogeneity. A symptom of this fear in an exaggerated form is the spreading logic that everything that is not standard-American must be communist-inspired. This logic cannot be dismissed as a phobia of a small number of fanatics. Fear of heterogeneity is found even among some of the supposedly most liberal people: the academics. It suffices to think of the departmental and organizational infights in many fields of the humanities and social sciences on many university campuses: the "orthodox" factions trying to eliminate or demote, openly or secretly, often with invented reasons or secret allegations, those whom they consider unorthodox; faculty members with a multidisciplinary background being considered as impure and relegated to the periphery; the administration vetoing the appointment of those with nontraditional past records; research-funding agencies preferring those research proposals which have a standard research design; editors of professional journals trying to make authors conform to the format of their journals (an attitude unheard of in Europe). This climate fosters unproductive politicking, suspicion, use of "confidentiality" as a vehicle of unfounded rumors, and reluctance to express opinions frankly. Fortunately the natural science and engineering fields are much freer from such practices.

We must learn not only to tolerate but also to appreciate and to make positive use of heterogeneity.

INDIVIDUAL VARIATIONS IN THE OPTIMAL PACE OF CHANGE

Many people say that rapid changes in patterns of living cause psychological disequilibrium or insecurity. But as Elise Boulding points out, some people are perfectly comfortable with a rapid pace of change. As I have pointed out before (Maruyama 1959), mental health is a matter of matching the individual's optimal pace and level of input and output with the pace and level the society imposes on him. While individuals whose optimal pace is slow suffer in a society which demands a faster pace, it must also be recognized that individuals whose optimal pace is fast must suffer in a society which permits only a slower pace. A culture cannot be mentally "healthy" or "unhealthy" for all of its members. Each culture is mentally healthy for some of its members and unhealthy for others. For example, Danish culture is healthy for individuals oriented toward nurturance or dependency but unhealthy for those inclined toward achievement (Hendin 1964), in-itiative, and highly expressive behavior (Molesworth 1694; Schiødt 1957), or direct communication of feelings and conversation on factual subjects (Maruyama 1959, 1961c). Swedish culture, on the other hand, provides gratification for individuals inclined toward high achievement (Hendin 1964; Maruyama 1961c) but frustrates those with high depen-dency needs (Hendin 1964) or with low communicational capacity (Maruyama 1959, 1961c).

Similarly, the increasing rate of change in the pattern of living in the future may be mentally unhealthy for many individuals but will be healthy for some other individuals. Toffler (1970) proposed numerous arrangements to alleviate the effects of a fast pace of change. But we must also examine ways to channel individuals, for whom a fast pace of change is optimal, toward activities which provide them with outlets for their high rate of transformation.

EDUCATION AS TRANSEPISTEMOLOGICAL PROCESS

We have discussed several characteristics of our era: metatransition into nonstationary cultures; new epistemological threshold; goal generation from the grass roots; change from *gesellschaft*-like homogenism to intercultural symbiosis in a heterogeneous society. All these require that we undertake an epistemological overhaul of our culture. The main tool for such an epistemological overhaul is education. But the type of education we need for this purpose differs in *goal, methods, form*, and *content* from the education now being offered.

The *goal* may be defined as transepistemological process: development of the individual's ability to grow out of the traditional epistemology and explore, discover, invent, and reality-test new epistemologies. The *methods* I propose are (1) exposure to various existing epistemologies such as non-Aristotelian logics, the nonhierarchical epistemology of the Navajos and Eskimos, the Mandenka logic of heterogeneity, Einstein's cosmology, the quantum versus the wave theory of light, the principle of reciprocal causality in cybernetics, measurement versus topology, etc; (2) minimizing psychological dependence upon a single epistemology in order to minimize psychological defensiveness toward other epistemologies; (3) developing the habit of questioning established theories and definitions; (4) open-minded examination of what is excluded from current science; (5) use of imagination; (6) discipline in data collection and field experiments; (7) exercise in inventing new cultural patterns and in elaborating on the implementation details of such patterns. I would like to elaborate on the second and sixth methods.

Many students ask me whether they would not get confused by learning to think in more than one epistemology. One of the students in a seminar gave a very compact answer to this question: "Being able to think in two epistemologies is like having binocular vision; you can see three-dimensionally, but you don't get confused." This fear of possible confusion, common among students, reflects a fear not of invalidation of their own epistemology but of demonopolarization. Persons who are brought up in a nuclear family system with one set of parents tend to develop a dependence on one authority, one theory, one truth, etc. This I have called "monopolarization" (Maruyama 1966). On the other hand, persons brought up in an extended family or in a communal situation seem to be relatively free from monopolarization. Monopolarized persons tend to be trapped into one way of thinking and believe that theirs is the "universal" way of thinking. In this respect Americans are handicapped in preparing themselves for transepistemological processes, and special methods may have to be developed to facilitate their demonopolarization.

Anthropology, which is supposed to be the least culture-bound of disciplines, has suffered, nevertheless, from some degree of epistemological and methodological monopolarization. Until now, most anthropologists were Europeans or Americans. Their point of departure was inevitably Western epistemology. Even though they strove not to be culture-bound in terms of the content of their observation, their framework of perception remained epistemology-bound to varying degrees. Furthermore, many anthropologists remained monopolarized with regard to what they called "objectivity," and put heavy emphasis on "objective" methods, without realizing that such emphasis is in itself a culture-bound tendency to reduce events to measurable shadows for the sake of manageability and being able to convince colleagues. Without fully appreciating the distortions inherent in such "objectivization," some anthropologists even claimed that observers from outside a culture have a more "objective" and therefore supposedly more "correct" perspective than cultural insiders. However, the subjective perceptions shared by the members of a society are as much a cultural reality as are objective measurable quantities. Moreover, the subjective perceptions of insiders are much more relevant to the understanding of the culture than objectively "correct" perceptions. Comparison of two subjective perspectives — one by insiders and one by outsiders — would produce more insights into both cultures than insistence on agreement on a single "objective" perspective.

Anthropology needs to demonopolarize itself. Subjective differentials may become more important than objectivity in future research (Maruyama 1969b). Efforts in this direction have already begun. Endogenous research — study of a culture by its participants with their own epistemology, conceptualization, hypotheses, methodology, research design, and data analysis — has been carried out by Navajo and other ethnic groups (Adair 1967; Maruyama 1968, 1969b). Plans are being made by nonwhite anthropologists to conduct studies of white cultures in order to obtain a binocular vision of them. In fact, we will obtain a polyocular vision as a variety of nonwhite cultures begins to produce researchers.

The sixth method — discipline in data collection and field

experiments — is very underdeveloped in our primary education system, although the fifth method is being increasingly encouraged. Pure fantasy without reality-testing is not only useless but may be harmful. For example, in a workshop for schoolteachers which I held recently, one teacher said that a boy in her class came up with the idea of a flying chair, and she though that this was wonderful. The teacher did not explore the feasibility of designing a flying chair with the child. This type of teaching is harmful; it encourages the child to be a wishful and capricious dreamer without the will and capacity to work hard to materialize the dream. On the other hand, if the teacher explores with the child the means of propulsion, various possible designs for the engine, and, if possible, conducts experiments to test out the designs, then the teaching becomes meaningful and useful in preparing the child for future society.

Another teacher mentioned that children in her class said they see ghosts which grown-ups do not see. She thought that this was a wonderful example of imagination. Here again, the teacher should have taught the children to set up experiments to verify what they said they saw. For example, if the children say that there is a ghost in the classroom which the teacher does not see, then the teacher can have each child write up a detailed description of the ghost independently of the others, and then make them compare the descriptions to see if they agree. If the descriptions disagree, then there is little validity to the ghost. But if the descriptions agree, then further tests for spurious factors can be developed. For example, all the children might have read the same ghost story and have come up with the same description of an imaginary ghost. One possible test to check this point is to let one group of children read one ghost story, another group a different ghost story, etc., and see how this affects their descriptions of the ghost in the class.

Scientific rigor should not be confused with rigidity. While an emphasis on rigorous reality-testing is necessary, the criteria for "reality" should not be too narrow. There is a tendency among those who have a blind faith in the established form of science to reject phenomena which cannot be explained by our present level of science. For example, emotions and feelings are considered unreal by some of those who define reality as quantity measurable with laboratory instruments. Extrasensory perception is considered nonexistent *a priori* by those who limit perception to events which are manifested in known physical forms. Unidentified flying objects are explained away as hallucinations by those who limit flying objects to birds and man-made machines. The history of science abounds with examples of discoveries which necessitated revisions of the previously established laws of science.

The scientific attitude is one of open-mindedness toward unorthodox possibilities, coupled with rigorous testing. Dogmatic denial, like dogmatic assertion, is unscientific. Each possibility must be given an opportunity to be tried out. For example, in the case of children claiming to see a ghost, it is unscientific to dogmatically tell them that they see nothing. All possibilities, including optical illusion, hallucination, extrasensory perception, unknown physical or nonphysical laws, and even the possibility that some animal, more intelligent than *Homo sapiens*, is playing a trick, must be considered and tried out. Each fantasy can be used as a starting point for rigorous (but not rigid) experiments and data collection.

For older children and adult students, fieldwork can be added, especially in the social sciences. One serious defect of the traditional education method is that students are made to read books and take books as reality. This has several harmful effects: first, it tends to isolate students from the community and people instead of helping students to interact with people in the community. The community becomes a distant object, and people in it become animals in an exotic country. Many students even develop fear of the community and the people in it. Second, students learn to fit people into theory instead of learning to develop a theory from direct experience. Theory becomes more important than people. Students start looking at people from the point of view of their utility for theory, instead of questioning whether the theory may be irrelevant to the actual situation of the people.

Third, the students' perceptions become filtered by the theory, and dimension-reduction (Maruyama 1961b, 1962) and dimension-addition occur: the students perceive whatever the theory wants them to perceive and ignore whatever is not in the theory; and they may project a theoretical dimension onto people which is actually nonexistent or almost irrelevant. This tendency is particularly reinforced by the research procedure which requires a hypothesis to be set up before the researcher goes into the field and the data collection to be limited to what pertains to this hypothesis. This procedure does not allow students to go into a community open-minded and open-eyed.

Fourth, students are prevented from developing that awareness of the limitations of research which the researcher develops in the course of his research. For a researcher, research is something which generates a need for further research, because one piece of research tells him only one part of the story and generates more questions than it answers. The researcher always feels a need to refine his research further. In this sense he has an awareness of the incompleteness of his research. This awareness is developed only by doing research. Students, who are made to learn from books, lack this awareness. They tend to take the printed research report as absolute truth and see research results as an answer rather than a process to generate questions.

Getting students' feet wet in the field can remedy many of these tendencies. Fieldwork can be carried out concurrently with book learning. But it is still more effective for students to have some field experience prior to book learning. This allows them to experience the community without theoretical bias and will provide them with a basis for interpreting books meaningfully.

There are several ways of conducting field experiments in the community. The least effective is as a tourist, a zoo visitor, or an interviewer. A somewhat less but still ineffective way is as a "community worker" with an agency role or an organizational affiliation. A more effective way is stepping into the streets directly, into a laundromat, a pool hall, a bar, a barber shop, etc. as an individual without agency role or organizational connection and meeting people on a person-to-person basis, in order to learn the point of view of the people in the community rather than selling them a point of view. The student goes into the community with the attitude of an apprentice being initiated into a new culture. This is called the "walk-in method" (Maruyama 1970). Even young white girls were successful in going singly into black ghettos and learning the ghetto point of view using this method.

Still more effective is the transspection method (Maruyama 1969) combined with the walk-in method. Transspection is an effort to put oneself into the head (not shoes) of another person. One tries to believe what the other person believes and assume what the other person assumes. For example, if someone claims that he sees a ghost and is scared, you try to visualize his ghost and see how scared you become. If you have questions about his ghost, you ask these questions not as an interviewer, but as someone who visualizes the same ghost. Transspection differs from analytical "understanding." Transspection differs also from "empathy." Empathy is a projection of feelings between two persons with one epistemology. Transspection is a transepistemological process which tries to *experience* a foreign belief, a foreign assumption, a foreign perspective, feelings in a foreign context, and consequences of such feelings in a foreign context, as if these have become one's own. In transspection a person temporarily believes and feels whatever the other person believes and feels. It is an understanding by practice.

Younger children who cannot conduct field experiments can be trained in transspection by means of autobiographies. There are many autobiographies available with "adult material" suitable for exercises in transspection (Dyk 1938; Malcolm X 1964; Mitsuko 1969; Slim 1967a, 1967b; Green 1957). But unfortunately there are very few such books for children (Clark 1951). More books as well as teaching techniques for encouraging transspection must be developed.

Education must also initiate children into nonhierarchical mutualistic patterns of life. Cooperative games (Bavelas 1950) instead of the usual competitive games should be emphasized. Nonhierarchical group activities, mutualistic interaction and latitude toward diverse individual styles should be encouraged. Leadership and *a priori* division of labor should be discouraged.

Education as transepistemological process will continue during the whole lifetime of the individual. Therefore its *form* needs to be different from the current one which concentrates on preadult education. Olof Palme (1970), Robert Butler (1970), and others suggest that "recurrent education" should be institutionalized to allow adults to take time off periodically for education, travel, or new experiences to widen their horizon.

Heterogenistic diversification of structure in education is also needed. For example, American Indians may wish to set up an education system of their own which would be appropriate for their culture. Canada, Denmark, and Sweden are much ahead of the United States in this regard. They have education systems designed for, and to some extent *by* Indians, Eskimos, and Lapps, while the American philosophy and method of education so far has been to include Indians, Eskimos, Aleuts, Polynesians, and Micronesians in the education system developed for white children.

We also need "exchange programs" between ethnic groups, age groups, etc. These programs should not be aimed at standardizing and homogenizing society but at improving intergroup respect and understanding and promoting symbiotic intergroup relations.

As for the *content* of education, a greater part of education must be devoted to developing students' capacity for exploration and their skills in self-education rather than to storing information in their heads. This part of education will become less knowledge-oriented. In some fields of study, such as pharmacology and law, much of the present knowledge-oriented education will remain. But even in these fields, knowledge will be regarded more and more as something subject to constant revision rather than as eternal truth. In knowledge-oriented fields, too, recurrent education will become a necessity. Paul Armer (1970) stipulated in his "Paul principle": "Individuals often become, over time, uneducated and therefore incompetent at a level at which they once performed quite adequately."

These are some of the differences in goal, methods, form and content between traditional education and education as trans-epistemological processes.

SUMMARY AND CONCLUSION

Human futuristics, as conceptualized here, is not a science of ready-made information but a science designed to help people develop the attitudes and capacity for self-education which will enable them to move through the present epistemological metatransition into an era of nonstationary culture and knowledge, nonhierarchical mutualism and heterogenistic symbiosis, not as followers of culture change but as changers of society in which technology must be directed by cultural goals generated from the grassroots.

REFERENCES

ADAIR, J., S. WORTH
1967 Navajo as filmmakers. *American Anthropologist* 69: 76–78.
ARMER, P.
1970 The Paul principle. *Futurist* 4: 77–78.
BAVELAS, A.
1950 Cummunication patterns in task-oriented groups. *Journal of the Acoustical Society of America* 22: 725–730.
BUTLER, R.
1970 The burnt out and the bored. *Futurist* 4: 82.
CHANG, T. S.
1938 A Chinese philosopher's theory of knowledge. *Yenching Journal of Social Studies* 1.
CLARK, A.
1951 *Little Navajo herder*. Lawrence, Kansas: Haskell Institute, Bureau of Indian affairs.
DYK, W.
1938 *Son of Old Man Hat*. New York: Harcourt.
ERIKSON, E.H.
1956 The problem of ego identity. *Journal of American Psychoanalytic Association* 4: 58–121.
FEUER, L.S.
1959 Bearing of psychoanalysis upon philosophy. *Philosophy and Phenomenological Research* 19: 323–340.
FREUCHEN, P.
1961 *Book of the Eskimos*. New York: Bramhall House.
GREEN. P.
1957 *I am Eskimo*. Juneau: Northwest Publishing Co.
HENDIN, H.
1964 *Suicide in Scandinavia*. New York: Grune and Stratton.
KIERKEGAARD, S.
1844 *Begrebet angest*. Copenhagen.
KLUCKHOHN, C.
1949 "The philosophy of Navaho Indians," in *Ideological differences and world order*. Edited by F. S. C. Northrop. New Haven: Yale University Press.

58 MAGOROH MARUYAMA

KUBIE, L. S.
1956   Some unsolved problems of the scientific career. *American Scientist*
        41: 3–32.
KUHN, T.
1962   *The structure of scientific revolutions*. Chicago: University of Chicago
        Press.
MANNHEIM, K.
1952   *Ideologie und Utopie*, Frankfurt am Main: Schulte-Bulmke.
MARUYAMA, M.
1959   A critique of some widely held assumptions on the relationship
        between culture and mental health. *Revue de Psychologie des Peuples*
        14: 273–276.
1961a   Morphogenesis and morphostasis. *Methodos* 12: 251–296.
1961b   Communicational epistemology. *British Journal for the Philosophy of
        Science* 11: 319–327; 12: 52–62; 12: 117–131.
1961c   The multilateral mutual causal relationships among the modes of
        communication, sociometric pattern and intellectual orientation in
        the Danish culture. *Phylon* 22: 41–58.
1962   Awareness and unawareness of misunderstandings. *Methodos* 13:
        255–275.
1963a   The second cybernetics: deviation-amplifying mutual causal proces-
        ses. *American Scientist* 51: 164–179; 51: 250–256.
1963b   Basic elements in misunderstandings. *Dialectica* 17: 78–92; 17:
        99–110.
1965   Metaorganization of information: information in classificational uni-
        verse, relational universe and relevantial universe. *Cybernetica* 224–
        236.
1966   Monopolarization, family and individuality. *Psychiatric Quarterly* 40:
        133–149.
1967a   The Navajo philosophy: an esthetic ethic of mutuality. *Mental
        Hygiene* 51: 242–249.
1967b   Goal-generating dissatisfaction, directive disequilibrium and prog-
        ress. *Sociologia Internationalis* 5: 169–188.
1968   Trans-social rapport through prison inmates. *Annales Internationales
        de Criminologie* 7: 19–46.
1969   Epistemology of social science research. *Dialectica* 23: 229–280.
1970   Walk-in exposure projects in the ghetto. *Mental Hygiene* 54: 261–
        270.
1977a   Heterogenistics: an epistemological restructuring of biological and
        social sciences. *Cybernetica* 20: 69–86.
1977b   New movements in old traps. *Futurics* 2: 59–63.
1978a   New theories in old epistemological traps. *Proceedings of Society for
        General Systems Research 1978 Annual Meeting*. Washington, D.C.:
        Society for General Systems Research.
1978b   Heterogenistics and morphogenetics. *Theory and society* 5: 75–96.
MEAD, M.
1942   *And keep your powder dry: an anthropologist looks at America*. New
        York: Morrow.
1946   An application of anthropological techniques to cross-national com-
        munication. *Transactions of New York Academy of Science series 2*,
        9: 133–152.
MITSUKO, I.
1969   *Honolulu madam*. Los Angeles: Holloway House.

MOLESWORTH, R.
1694   *An account of Denmark as it was in the year 1692.* London.
MORIN, E.
1977   *La méthode.* Paris: Seuil.
PALME, O.
1970   Are young people getting too much education? *Futurist* 4: 79–80.
PLATT, J.
1970   "Hierarchical restructuring." Communication 269, Mental Health Research Institute, University of Michigan.
PRIBRAM, K.
1949   *Conflicting patterns of thought.* Washington, D.C.: Public Affairs Press.
PRIGOGINE, ILYA, GREGOIRE NICOLIS
1977   *Self-organization in nonequilibrium systems.* New York: Wiley Interscience.
REICHENBACH, H.
1956   *Direction of time.* Berkeley: University of California Press.
SARTRE, JEAN-PAUL
1943   *L'être et le néant.* Paris: Gallimard.
SCHIØDT, E.
1957   Selvmord og dansk folkekarakter. *Perspektiv* 5: 39–42. Copenhagen.
SLIM, I.
1967a   *Pimp.* Los Angeles: Holloway House.
1967b   *Trick baby.* Los Angeles: Holloway House.
TOFFLER, A.
1970   *Future shock.* New York: Random House.
TÖNNIES, F.
1887   *Gemeinschaft und Gesellschaft.*
X, MALCOLM
1964   *Autobiography of Malcolm X.* New York: Grove Press.

Anthropological Insights for Social Policy: Western View

The Possible and the Desirable: Population and Environmental Problems

STEVEN POLGAR

There are a number of desirable conditions for the future that would surely meet with approval from most people. Among these are the continued existence of humans as culture-bearing animals, opportunities for individual development and inquiry, increasing the choices for action of future generations, and stringent limits on violence against other people. In the context of this symposium,[1] I would put greater emphasis on the above than on more technological goals such as protection from harsh weather conditions or good communication facilities, although many of the latter are also noncontroversial.

When we turn to "practical futuristics" (to use Maruyama's term) finding out how to reach the desirable future has usually been more difficult than agreeing on the nature of the desirable conditions. Indeed, as I shall try to illustrate, one of the most serious problems of practical futurology is the tendency to pinpoint "goals" first and to worry about "means" later (cf. Peattie 1960).

POPULATION PROPHESIES

A great deal of current writing about the population problem, which might be classified as "reactive, defensive futuristics" (again using Maruyama's terms), suffers from this "ends first, means later" syndrome. The population threat is so immediate and overwhelming according to neo-Malthusian doomsters such as Paul Ehrlich (1968), that to defend against it we must accept policies which would preclude many other desirable conditions, such as individual freedom in the

[1] This paper was originally delivered at the 1970 meeting of the American Anthropological Association in San Diego, California.

United States or health improvement abroad. Population trends are extrapolated by these people in simplistic ways. Positive measures (e.g. family planning, social security, income redistribution) are casually dismissed. And other types of ultimate danger are either ignored or subordinated to the particular brand of doom with which the doomsayer is most involved (e.g war and poverty are considered to be consequences of overpopulation).

To justify reprehensible means (such as involuntary sterilization or withholding food) by the end of stabilizing the population is to lose sight of the goal of a better quality of life for all, which for most people is the wider objective in attempting to stabilize human numbers. The long struggle to provide people with access to modern means of birth control and to do away with restrictive laws on contraception and abortion has been fought in the name of individual freedom, health, and equal rights for women. Despite this long struggle, a realistic opportunity to obtain modern birth control assistance is still available to only a small proportion of humankind. It is sadly ironic, then, that Kingsley Davis, Garrett Hardin, Paul Ehrlich and like-minded commentators are busily preparing the ground for a demographic dictatorship where the legal freedom of voluntary reproduction would once again be taken away (particularly from the less politically powerful such as welfare recipients and minority groups).

Population problems are not an unprecedented phenomenon of the post-World-War-II period; also, they include difficulties related to the uneven distribution of people, not just the growth in their numbers. The basic explanation of population problems will have to be sought in economic and political processes. Psychocultural factors are only the mediating variables. In order to understand population problems we must have a thorough knowledge of social history. Significantly, however, the writings of the neo-Malthusian prophets of doom reveal their authors' ignorance about human evolution. These writers are not merely ethnocentric Westerners, they are also "chronocentric" in looking at humankind from a late nineteenth- and twentieth-century perspective. By contrast, the central mission of the anthropologist in futuristics is to look at the future from the panoramic standpoint of humanity.

POPULATION AND HUMAN EVOLUTION

Soon after the transition from ape to human, the maintenance of demographic balance changed from a biological to a biocultural phenomenon (Birdsell 1968; Polgar 1972). Voluntary learned behavior came to be a part of the mechanism that kept reproduction well below the biological maximum. These voluntary measures, furthermore, had seldom any connection with the act of sexual intercourse. Thus, in evolutionary and cross-cultural perspective, such "coitus-connected" methods as withdrawal or the diaphragm, which were important in the decline of early twentieth-century birthrates among European populations, are highly atypical. Infanticide, abortion, prolonged breastfeeding, and delayed marriage, in contrast, are "coitus-independent" methods of great generality. Also, regulation of births was usually concerned with spacing them, not with limiting their number in a direct sense (Polgar 1969).

The greatest proportionate increase in human numbers, perhaps as much as a 100-fold jump, accompanied the transition from hunting-gathering to food production. The period of preindustrial cities and feudalism saw relatively little population growth. Then, with colonialism and industrialization there occurred another spurt of major proportions (Polgar 1972). Political centralization, under both preindustrial state regimes and colonialism, has in the long run stimulated the natality of subject populations. The increased supply of labor was required to provide more revenue for the rulers. In feudal societies, much of the resulting population increase was often rolled back in great epidemics. But the establishment of large-scale food transportation networks and the suppression of tribal warfare, among other factors, helped to lessen mortality in colonialist situations in the long run.

In the home countries of the colonialist powers, meanwhile, wider opportunities for socioeconomic advancement stimulated the emergent middle classes to reduce the size of their families, concentrating their nonagrarian capital among fewer heirs. In industrial societies where legal abortion is easily available, particularly in Japan, Scandinavia, and Eastern Europe, natality has closely approached the replacement level.

POPULATION PROGRAMS

The "scenario" for the future painted by those like Paul Ehrlich includes famines and epidemics caused by a relentlessly surging tide of reproduction, and attempts to control this tide by cajoling, persuading, or coercing people to have fewer children. My scenario, in contrast, mainly involves continued progress in lowering death rates, equality between the sexes, liberation from the colonial relationship, and greatly expanding the facilities and techniques for good quality birth control.

Lowering death rates can help to reduce the number of births considered necessary to ensure the survival of at least some children to an age when they can assist their elderly parents (May and Heer 1968). The demographic transition to low birth rates, where it has occurred, has usually been linked with rapidly falling death rates. Lowering death rates is also good in itself. It is desired by everyone and is a continuation of current trends.

Equality between the sexes is also good in itself, although its acceptance as a desirable goal is not quite as universal as is the reduction of mortality. There is a strong movement afoot, however, both in the Third World and in industrial countries, to speed women's liberation. There appears to be some relationship between high birth rates and lack of participation by women in economically significant pursuits. Or, to put it the other way, women employed outside of households generally have fewer children (Weller 1968).

The demise of administrative colonialism has certainly not meant the end of political or, more importantly, economic colonialism. I would suggest that stabilization of prices paid for primary products exported from the Third World would do more to reduce population growth than donating transistor radios (for the reception of antinatalist propaganda) to every household in Asia, Africa, and Latin America. The uncertainties of financial return from agriculture are an important factor in stimulating peasants to send some of their children to town while keeping others at home to help with farming. To "spread one's bets" in such a way between the uncertainties of urban employment and the uncertainties of agricultural income, usually requires several offspring. By the same token, the subsidized development of better fertilizers, seeds, and tools suitable for tropical and subtropical conditions should take precedence over sending manufactured consumption goods to Third World countries. Big alterations in the ecosystem, such as the Kariba dam, have usually been not only harmful to many local inhabitants but often also technological and economic failures on a wider scale. Industrial development in the Third World — with more recycling of resources than is now done in the metropolitan countries — should certainly be speeded up, but urbanization as such is clearly not the answer. The redirection of foreign aid efforts will be difficult, but certainly possible within the context of concern over the population problem and other persistent difficulties.

The last item on my list is not the least important. A great expansion of services for contraception is certainly possible within present political, technological, and administrative circumstances. New, effective and safe methods of birth control need to be developed, and more attention should be paid to cultural factors in their distribution and use (Polgar 1970). Techniques for choosing the gender of the next child would also be very useful. The adverse effect of such techniques on social organization would not be as great as claimed by critics who ignore the long precedent for unbalanced sex ratios in many cultures where female infanticide was practiced. Legal abortion services are also expanding — we will soon see them even in Latin America.

One great shortcoming of present family planning programs in many countries is the lack of emphasis on child spacing. Influenced by neo-Malthusian theories, policymakers have neglected the long and widespread cultural tradition favoring voluntary control of the timing of marriage, spacing of children, and the circumstances under which the period of childbearing is interrupted or terminated. By focusing too narrowly on the goal which they have defined for the program, those in charge have given short shrift to the advantages the people themselves see when family planning is defined as more than just limitation of the number of children born.

SOCIAL COMPLEXITY AND ENVIRONMENTAL MODIFICATION

Human evolution, in several important features, has been a combination of inorganic, organic, and social evolution (Polgar 1961). Perhaps the most important trends in human evolution have been the increase in social complexity and in environmental modification. Both of these can be seen as beneficial. Social complexity allows more individuals to get together in more different ways, permitting (but not ensuring) greater freedom of individual divergence. Social complexity has now also come to encompass the whole human species in a single interdependent system. Environmental modification allows humans to live in a wide range of climates, allowing them to "prosper" as a biological species to an almost unprecedented degree.

But social complexity and environmental modification also have a dangerous side. The further humans have gone up these slopes the further, one might say, they can fall. The social complexity of the nation-state permits not only egalitarian but also dictatorial modes of governance. While in the main, humans have come to abhor cruelty, and to include more and more categories of people in their definition of common humanity against whom cruelty is wrong, the lapses into cruelty in this century — both within and between nations — have been on an unprecedented scale. Complexity allows for individual privacy and utter neglect. Environmental modification permits sending aid quickly to disaster victims continents away, but it also threatens disaster to our air, water, and land.

There is an interesting relationship between social complexity and environmental modification; increased social complexity has often been accompanied by — or even depended upon — simplification of the ecological system. During the hunting stage of evolution humankind displaced several other species of carnivores and, through the use of fire drives, changed large areas of forest into grasslands. More dramatically, with the change to food production, techniques were developed to keep the ecological system in the early stage of ecological succession in which both the production of organic matter and the amount of energy used are very high (Odum 1969). By contrast, the mature stage of ecological succession involves great complexity and relatively slow "throughput" of energy (Odum 1969). Monocrop agriculture is an outstanding example of a simple ecosystem, with high energy use and organic production and, by the same token, extreme susceptibility to disastrous losses from sudden climatic change or invasion by "agricultural pests" of various kinds. But there is another kind of agriculture which has been held in contempt by Western technologists (Geertz 1963). This is the swidden method — more pejoratively known as "slash and burn." Under this system a large number of plants are grown on the same plot, each with slightly different susceptibilities and requirements. While not as productive as monocrop planting, swiddens are also much less exposed to natural disasters.

The growing enthusiasm for "organic" foods in the wealthy industrial countries of the West signals a disenchantment with the intensification of the chemical control in agriculture that came in the wake of destroying ecological complexity. Many of the same people who seek to eat "natural" foods — not surprisingly — are also seeking to get away from the social complexity of industrial society.

ENVIRONMENTAL IMPROVEMENT PROGRAMS

Many arguments on how to deal with problems of resource use and pollution compare the "technological" approach with the "attitude change" approach. I agree that much greater investments need to be made in improving the technologies for waste treatment, recycling of metals and other minerals, cheap and clean energy sources for small communities, etc. Attitude change is equally desirable — particularly in the metropolitan countries, where even electric pencil sharpeners now seem to have sales appeal. But neither technology nor attitude change will be of much help unless we change the economic systems which treat air, water, and soil as "externalities" not represented in calculating costs (Coale 1970; Goldman 1970).

Governments are beginning to recognize that oil slicks and radioactive clouds do not respect national or city boundaries and that humankind and its works are no longer just a minor part of the planetary ecosystem. But to move toward a solution, governments will have to dismantle the hegemony of giant industrial enterprises over the economic system. More power will have to be given to international agencies and more power returned to individuals and small groups. It is probably unnecessary to reduce overall social complexity; the tendency to expand interdependence between groups of individuals to regional, continental, and planetary scales has been a significant feature of social evolution. However, the consolidation of power in the hands of nation-states has delayed progress toward meaningful world government. Also, the haphazard development of large cities has decreased the importance of residential neighborhoods, with severe consequences.

We can regard the cancerous growth of metropolitan areas and the delay in forming supranational governments as temporary deviations in the long sweep of human history. They may indeed turn out to be fatal deviations, but from an evolutionary perspective they were neither inevitable nor are they now necessarily permanent. At the risk of being accused of being an anthropological romanticist, I would prefer to think of the two million years of human evolution before the advent of feudalism as "good" and hope that — with much effort — we may return to the healthy path of development which includes human equality and environmental integration.

REFERENCES

BIRDSELL, J. B.
1968 "Some predictions for the Pleistocene based on equilibrium systems among recent hunter-gatherers," in *Man the hunter*. Edited by R. B. Lee and I. DeVore. Chicago: Aldine.
COALE, A. J.
1970 Man and his environment. *Science* 1970: 132–136.
EHRLICH, P. R.
1968 *The population bomb*. New York: Ballantine.
GEERTZ, C.
1963 *Agricultural involution*. Berkeley: University of California Press.
GOLDMAN, M. I.
1970 The convergence of environmental disruption. *Science* 1970: 37–42.
MAY, D. A., D. M. HEER
1968 Son survivorship motivation and family size in India. *Population Studies* 22: 199–210.
ODUM, E. P.
1969 The strategy of ecosystem development. *Science* 164: 262–270.
PEATTIE, L. R.
1960 "The failure of the means-ends scheme in action anthropology," in *Documentary history of the Fox Project*. Edited by F. Gearing, R. M. Netting, and L. R. Peattie. Chicago: Department of Anthropology, University of Chicago.

POLGAR, S. P.
1961   Evolution and the thermodynamic imperative. *Human Biology* 33: 99–109.
1969   "Cultural aspects of natality regulation techniques," in *Proceedings of the VIIIth International Congress of Anthropological Sciences, 1968,* volume three, 232–234. Tokyo: Science Council of Japan.
1970   "Specifications for new birth control methods." Paper presented at the VIth World Congress of Gynaecology and Obstetrics, New York, April 13–18.
1971   Population history and population policies from an anthropological perspective. *Current Anthropology* 13: 203–277.
WELLER, R. H.
1968   The employment of wives, role incompatibility and fertility. *Milbank Memorial Fund Quarterly* 46: 507–526.

The Prehistory of Homo sapiens: Touchstone for the Future

JAMES C. GIFFORD

In order to comprehend, even in small measure, why we are the way we are today and thereby help place ourselves in a position to think and work constructively on human problems of the future, information from prehistory is of singular importance, constituting a ring of keys without which we cannot penetrate the origins of *H. sapiens* reality. Margaret Mead discusses contributions which can be made by the discipline of anthropology to a science of the future (this volume). In this paper I wish to focus more specifically on the value of gathering data from archaeological and evolutionary sources that will help to guide man's search for rational culture change in the future.

In reviewing "the Australopithecines and the problem of brain size and behavior . . . one is faced with understanding the significance of the almost 1000 cc. increase in capacity since this stage of hominid evolution, in terms of behavioral complexity" (Holloway 1968:185). Archaeological findings disclose that increased cranial capacity "was the final great change in hominid morphology, following basic reorganization of the locomotor apparatus, dentition, and skull" (Washburn 1959, 1960). But that is only part of the picture. Neural reorganization has also taken place and this "means that quantitative shifts between components or substructures of the brain, as measured in terms of area

It is difficult to properly credit persons and sources in an essay of this nature. Many discussions with colleagues have contributed to these thoughts. I also express gratitude to those students at Temple University who have participated in my course, "Introduction to Archaeology." Each semester they have contributed to my better understanding of prehistory by their own efforts to grasp the subject matter that lay between us. Appreciation is also extended to Elmer S. Miller, Chairman of the Department of Anthropology at Temple University for providing an atmosphere conducive to research activity.

or volume, have taken place under natural selection such that the outputs of the systems are different between the species. By shifting interactions between components in quantitative ways, the product of the whole is altered" (Holloway 1968: 175).

THE BIOLOGICAL BASIS OF *H. SAPIENS*

Taxonomic references to the early forms of man reflect these distinctions. "Generic separation does not indicate a degree of difference so much as a difference in the utilization of the environment. *Australopithecus africanus* with a mean brain size of 500 cc. filled such an entirely different niche from *H. sapiens* with a brain of ±1500 cc. that generic separation is abundantly justified" (Mayr 1970: 381). So various changes in the brain, as human evolution proceeds through genera and species to *H. sapiens*, not only lead to greater awareness, greater ability to think new and unique thought patterns, but to other abilities that together tend to prescribe the parameters of behavior differently as time advances toward the present. What the creatures could do, then, has never been static through time, nor is it likely to be in the future. Human evolution has not terminated and, barring generic extinction, never will as long as there is any environmental shift and biological range of variation within the human population as a whole. "Much that is puzzling about man can be understood only when man is considered as evolved and evolving" (Mayr 1970: 375). Within human evolution not only do the creatures become able to think abstractly enough to move from the manufacture of pebble tools to the building of Apollo-Luna space vehicles, but they develop thinking capacities that relate to artistic expression and then, in conjunction with both of these dimensions, develop thought mechanisms that can successfully handle greater and greater numbers of variables that can combine to become the major selector configuration in any given environmental context. The more variables successfully handled, the greater the ultimate biological success of the population consummating that handling. In human evolution, natural selection, including the everwidening cultural factor, favored those creatures who most advantageously handled the many variables surrounding them. The feedback mechanism permeates every aspect of the totality.

The process of natural selection, as now understood, is complex rather in its concrete working and its interactions than in its basis. That basis is simply differential reproduction correlated with genotypic constitution. If some individuals in a population have more surviving and breeding offspring than others, and if there is a consistent average difference, however small, in the genotypes of those who have more and those who have fewer, that is natural selection at work. The actual selection — that is, the determination of which individuals have more or fewer offspring that survive to breed in their turn — is an interaction between environment, in the broadest sense, and the population, in all its individuals throughout their complete ontogenies . . . . Behavior is subject to particularly strong selection, and it is probably farthest removed from the genes and also most elaborately polygenic as a rule (Simpson 1969: 34–36).

The ongoingness of evolution and the continuous operation of natural selection may, then, be taken as universal givens. It is further understood that human evolution is distinct from all other evolutionary trends in biology by virtue of the constant presence of the cultural dimension in some proportion. "The origin of man surely was not a sudden event but a response to continuing selection pressures . . . . What are the major factors that shifted human evolution into channels so totally different from those of the anthropoids? There are two classes of such factors: changes in behavior and changes in the environment." The search still continues for

. . . the decisive factor that led to the spectacular increase in brain size in the one million years between 1.3 and 0.3 million years ago. The late J. B. S. Haldane liked to emphasize that this dramatic increase in brain size was the most rapid evolutionary change known to him. It is even more astonishing because it does not involve a superficial structure but an organ as elaborate as the central nervous system. What then is responsible for this dramatic evolutionary event?" (Mayr 1970: 383–384).

Mayr himself feels that "all answers to this question are largely conjectural" (1970: 384). I would argue, though, that the crucial aspect is not necessarily "the decisive factor," and that we have somewhat misled ourselves by looking too assiduously for too much that would be too specific. Most decisive would seem to be rather a sequent series of lifeways, each more complex than the previous one and more elaborate from a cultural standpoint, requiring of the participants greater and greater facility in the handling of increased numbers and kinds of variables. "Natural selection operates in favor of those most capable of understanding and exploiting their environment" (Clark 1970: 96). Ability to do this through the use of their thinking capacity meant the margin of *Homo* success, a success that eventually became extraordinary by comparison with that of any other primate.

Archaeological probing has yielded stone tools and other artifactual remains as well as skeletal material. The data of prehistory have accumulated to the point where comprehensive assertions can be put forward concerning ancient lifeway patterns (Howell 1965). Each sequent lifeway follows upon the one before it with ever increasing rapidity. Some lifeways were, are, and will be in the future, better than others. A mental apparatus has been needed that could accommodate speech, think abstractly, handle a multitude of shifting variables, adapt quickly and easily to new and complex situations evermore of a cultural order, and commit large volumes of vital information to a memory resource. Any lifeway horizon in time, however, depends not only on the biological creatures or populations but on the natural environment and the cultural environment as well. The articulation of these components yields the lifeway.

That man is a product of natural laws can be a primary assertion. Secondarily, culture is produced by man. Culture is free of or apart from natural laws only to the extent that man's thinking can be apart from natural laws. Inasmuch as human thought is produced by the interaction of a number of biological or biologically derived phenomena, it seems difficult to prove that human thought does indeed, even at times, transcend the effects of natural laws. It is on this account that the cultural products of the mind do in fact resemble the biological, and artifact types and varieties do resemble species and subspecies, and cultural development does resemble biological evolution to the degree that many anthropologists refer to cultural evolution rather than to the development of culture. The primary attribute of culture or of any cultural item, however, is that it is *not* alive. Culture does not live and so does not truly evolve in exactly the same sense that living organisms do. Culture changes through time and in retrospect looks as though it had evolved only because the mind of man has in fact evolved. Concomitantly, successful mutation in any part of the human brain or its biological connectors always holds open the possibility of new and entirely unique thought processes, mental images, and thinking. In this way man does achieve the production of new ideas and under favorable circumstances transforms these ideas (the genes of culture) into new cultural constructs. There is a sequence of past lifeways because human evolution has taken place and there is the probability of new lifeways in the future because evolution continues.

Will the new lifeways or future lifeways be designed *by* man for his greater comfort or will they be designed *for* him by the interaction of natural selection and a cultural dimension that has simply come about without the benefit of conscious forethought? The former is a viable alternative because man alone makes culture and yet he is a product of natural laws. Culture is a derivative; it is solely a secondary product of natural laws. Accordingly, culture has no inherent living existence of its own and simply responds to and is a reflection of man's mental processes as manifested in his behavior.

If man were knowingly to influence his own biological evolution, he would inevitably be influencing his culture of the future; however, in this approach man himself must directly decide who among his numbers will be the reproducers and who will not. This has occurred to man and when tried, primarily for powerful cultural reasons, has acted more to his disadvantage than to his advantage. On the other hand, because the feedback mechanism is constantly present and because it permeates every aspect of the totality, if man were knowingly to set out the culture of his future, he would inevitably influence his own biological evolution. The feedback mechanism ensures that the biological nature of man is, and will be, strongly influenced by the culture that he makes. In addition, the fact that man is a product of natural laws renders the definition of a comfort index for him a feasible possibility in terms of his biological self. A lifeway or lifeways that included a high *H. sapiens* comfort index could therefore be calculated. This can be conceived of on an individual basis, on a population unit basis, or possibly on a worldwide basis for the *H. sapiens* population as a whole.

In this assessment of *H. sapiens'* future disposition, the central fixity has to be the basic nature of man as he has been and as he is. He has to recognize himself for what he has been and for what he is. From an understanding of man as he is and of how he has become what he is, we can consider the position of cultural planning with respect to potentially more advantageous and constructive directions in his future. It can be asserted that cultural planning *is* man's future because the human mind gives rise to ideas and ideas are the genes of culture (Gifford 1960). Ideas that originate in the human brain make culture move, so in the circumstances of the future where culture has largely replaced the natural environment, biological evolution and change will be greatly determined by culture change. Man's ideas in coalescence with his belief patterns, will largely make him what he will be in the future. "Like other animals, man develops, is born, grows, reproduces, and dies. He bends the qualities of nature to his own ends, but he is as fully subject to nature's laws as is any other animal and is no more capable of changing them. . . . Let us not forget those aspects of man's nature" (Simpson 1969: 97). Although he cannot at the moment change nature's laws, through the exercise of forethought, man can influence them to change him in directions that he believes will coincide with advantage, an increased comfort index, positive position, constructive output, and general success. The tool with which this can be accomplished is culture. The engine or force behind the use of this tool is the mind of man (individually and collectively), his ideas and beliefs (ideas from individual minds, beliefs motivating the minds of the many).

Futurology, or human futuristics, is cultural planning, and cultural planning is the ultimate in applied anthropology. Sound cultural planning, however, is dependent upon prehistory for the story of what man has already tried, for information about where his cultural envelope has done well by him and where it has failed him. Contemporary *H. sapiens* activity includes much that he has tried before that failed. Prehistory is the only means we have of knowing how man has articulated with his culture over the past three to five million years. In order to achieve a high comfort index for himself in future, man as a biological creature must articulate successfully with the culture he makes for himself in that future. To do this he must know and pay attention to how that articulation worked out for him in the past.

"Man is a species of animal . . . but no more tragic mistake could be made than to consider man 'merely an animal'. Man is unique; he differs from all other animals in many properties, such as speech, tradition, culture, and an enormously extended period of growth and parental care" (Mayr 1970: 375). Man uses nature to make artifacts, feed himself and so on; nature is exploited by man through his understanding of it, but the more complex his cultural dimension becomes, the more he is able to duplicate nature at his own will and by his own activities. At the simpler levels of complexity in terms of culture, man had to make do with what was provided by nature; as complexity advanced, however, man developed the ability to synthesize nature, adjust his natural surroundings or alter them profoundly.

Man has always been a product of his environment and this is irrevocable in his future, but now his environment is largely of his own making in a cumulative sense rather than being predominantly natural as it was for the australopithecines. The australopithecines' environment was essentially natural and hence similar to that of the other creatures of their biome. Although what was cultural was crucial in their particular differentiation, their lifeway envelope was perhaps cultural only to a comparatively minute degree; in an orbiting space station the opposite is true. As hominid evolution steadily advanced toward *H. sapiens* of today, the cultural dimension constantly enlarged, the complexity of that culture constantly increased, and the rate of culture change constantly accelerated. All along it is correct to say that man has been the product of his environment. But that environment is an extremely different mix now compared to what it was for the australopithecines. In addition to being of larger proportion than the natural dimension, the cultural aspect of the environment is of man's own making and he is constantly changing what still remains of the natural environment. Finally, the empirical perimeter of man's world has continuously enlarged, first to include all of the world, then to include outer space and on to the extent of considering other galactic configurations (Blakeslee 1971) — quite a contrast to the square-mile world of an australopithecine. The more elaborate and complex the cultural dimension becomes, the more man is the product of that which he himself produces.

The ingredients are the biological organism (man); the feedback mechanism; and the environment. The results have been that the human brain interacts successfully with an ever-increasing number of variables; the feedback mechanism while encouraging the brain toward larger volume and greater internal interaction capacity, moves culture in directions of greater complexity and elaboration. One literally feeds upon the other. Because the cultural component is not alive, it offers no resistance to acceleration in the rate of change. The feedback mechanism operates more rapidly, parts of the biological component evolve more rapidly, and the rate of culture change progresses more rapidly, unless nature intervenes or man himself intervenes through some conscious effort of his own. Unless overtly countermanded by man or nature, this entirety also favors those human population units which can successfully adapt most rapidly not only to new, but to expanding, lifeway totalities.

THE CULTURAL ENVELOPE

This prologue explains that the past as well as the present is speaking to us. It tells us clearly that the survival and success of any creature depends upon whether or not that creature interacts with all of his habitat in such a way as to ultimately confer upon himself a biological advantage.

If the creature in question creates a physically hazardous, psychologically tortuous, biologically harmful habitat for himself and others of his kind, both the past and the present scream out at him that he can hardly expect to prosper; on the contrary, he will doom himself. Evidence from the past, the archaeological record, shows that short-term self-interest is often man's hood of self-destruction (Bacon 1963; Cottrell 1962). This seems to have been true of small social groups as well as of entire cultures. The evidence also tells us in stark, undeniable terms that a cultural environment, a man-produced environment, has, in varying measure, taken the place of the natural environment since those fateful days when certain australopithecines first experimented successfully with the rudiments of the cultural phenomenon (Hubbert 1967). Hominids have moved from the manufacture of pebble tools to the projection of Skylabs.

"In current NASA planning, large laboratories housing 12 men, many of them non-astronauts, would be developed and launched by

1978" (Schneider 1970).[1] Implicit in such futuristic thinking is the existence of small social groups within entirely man-directed "artificial" environments traveling at incredible speeds through space. Despite our touching the realm of large-scale artificial, man-directed cultural environments, our record of the past, which is in excess of three million years, tells us that in the final analysis culture lives not by itself; that man can and does make the culture even though he himself is shaped by what he has made; and that once begun, the cultural envelope moves in the direction of greater and greater complexity unless man decides to make it otherwise.

What man really believes and comes to decide on through the thinking processes of his brain, individually and then collectively, will greatly, perhaps entirely, determine his nature and fate tomorrow. This is a realistic projection because the cultural envelope has already replaced the natural encasement to a considerable degree, and the cultural envelope is undeniably man's very own creation. Should he come to really understand this, his cultural envelope would *in fact* be his own to mold and shape just as his ancestors shaped their flints and molded their clays and thought the thoughts that enabled some of them to select certain grains for the first agricultural enterprise.

What man believes, his view of himself and of what he has made to surround himself with, could confer upon him an advantage in tomorrow's world or it could pave the way to an abysmal morass. Will tomorrow hold comfort for *Homo* or will it hold sorrow, pain, and the aggravations of intense human discomfort? The answers are at man's fingertips, but the seat of finger instruction is, as it was in the beginning, in his brain — from the very start a brain unique among all others in its capacity for conceptual thought. The challenge for anthropology seems to be how to influence man so that he will appeal consistently to his senses rather than to the supernatural, think realistically rather than mystically, and behave constructively rather than destructively in order to ensure his own comfortable survival in a world which to many a contemporary resident often appears to be one of mindless despair. The urgency centers on the use to which he puts his unique brain package to think without bias about what will confer on him and generations of the future "constructive advantages," not only biologically with reference to the genetic matrix but with regard to immediate physical and psychological needs.

Those who would be involved in culture change must be influenced to look and listen, because for the first time anthropology can on a grand scale communicate with and inform those who wish to be

---

[1]   Since 1975, large orbiting space communities, each accommodating 5,000 to 10,000 inhabitants, have been designed. See *Space settlements: a design study* (NASA Publication SP-413). — *Editor.*

involved in culture change. There are large numbers of people who are concerned and who would be willing to help effect certain kinds of culture change if they knew what to do; the cumulative evidence suggests that this has never before been the case insofar as transposition of desire to constructive action is concerned. Now there is an opportunity for many people to assess the potential consequences of changes that will result from the interlockings of human evolution and cultural development.

To reach responsible conclusions man must look intensely at what he did before today. A first step toward tomorrow's balance lies in the realm of self-awareness. Questions must come before answers. Many questions vital to man's future have not even been asked; others have been asked but not probed; still others, profound in their implications, have been answered hastily without reference to basic data and information.

Does the seeming relationship between human anxiety and ritual eventually lead to the preoccupations clearly noticeable in most high civilizations of the past? The Maya cultural configuration was quite possibly preoccupied to the point of obsession with their concept of religion (Thompson 1967; Coe 1965, 1967) as the Aztecs were with human sacrifice (Caso 1958) and the Assyrians with war (Dyson 1960). With greater knowledge from archaeological finds this listing grows until those who study societies of the past come to know ancient peoples through their preoccupations. That which is left behind by a civilization always tells of its preoccupations. The archaeological evidence reveals what people actually did do through time.

Does the seeming relationship between growing societal complexity, population densities, and pressures on the individual eventually lead to increases in societal tension to the point where urban disintegration is (as it seems to have been up to now) inevitable? Cities in the past have rarely endured indefinitely. All were founded amid value orientations that irrevocably related to the agricultural lifeways of previous as well as contemporary, surrounding populations. Again and again elaborations, wealth, and achievements of great variety occur but it seems that, to date, the population has always failed to achieve truly *new* value orientations geared to the new urban cultural envelope *Homo sapiens* fashioned for himself. In the absence of a new and workable "value orientation" suited in real ways to man's changed surroundings, tensions and societal abrasion move into the intellectual and philosophical vacuum bringing the people to despair and the cultural envelope to ruin (Riley 1969). This suggests that in the context of high civilization man has never before *in situ* been able to move himself successfully into a new value orientation commensurate with the dimensions of his altered cultural envelope (Piggott 1961). In the past he seems to have failed to maintain any given civilization, but then, having failed, he always moved from the scene of cultural disaster to try again. As long as he has lived, prehistory clearly shows that he has never stopped trying to move his cultural setting toward greater heights of elaboration and complexity.

Certain australopithecines had a desire to shape some things in their environment to suit their own purposes (Pfeiffer 1969), and they habitually indulged this inclination to the extent that it separated them from all other creatures then in existence. This inclination remains man's primary interest and it has been his basic preoccupation. But the word "some" must be changed to "all" things in his environment. The prehistoric record indicates that within man as a whole there is a consistent and determined desire to exercise control over that which he finds around him. But as populations increase the world over and one man, one population, cannot escape another, we seem to find the realization pressed upon us that no one man can control his own destiny without influencing that of others and that such progressions widen. Consequently *H. sapiens* cannot afford total individual freedom, and the occupants of the driver's seat tomorrow must possess rational thought and be committed to responsible, constructive action patterns which are shared by many, rather than by one man or by nature, as was the case when the australopithecines began their tiny piece of the cultural envelope.

Today, immediate recommendations are often called for. We must, however, first further delineate some of the philosophical truths that relate to *Homo sapiens* (Tax 1960). If we can recognize and accept these for what they are, other dimensions of appreciation and understanding will follow as will realistic projections for avenues of action, large and small. The alternative is to join those in the past who, often at frightful expense, accomplished little more than becoming prisoners of their cultural preoccupations. Out of desperation they generally parlayed or flailed these into obsessions that ransacked rational thought and so brought human misery on a wide front (Kramer 1967, Leonard 1967).

The problem often seems to be stated in the following way: "The long-range question is not so much what sort of environment we want, but what sort of man we want" (Sommer 1969: 172). But this kind of thinking ignores the contribution that prehistory can make to the problem. Prehistory shows us that in order to achieve the "sort of man we want" the environment can be our mold. Prehistory shows us that, as we move through time our environment becomes steadily more cultural in its makeup and the cultural dimension is ours to construct as we wish, should we have the desire to exercise this potentially creative prerogative. If we ask the right questions about the kind of man we want and about the kinds of environmental factors most likely to favor such a creature within future generations by virtue of the feedback mechanism, perhaps directions will be perceived that will genuinely hold comfort and constructive advantage rather than discomfort and disadvantage for man. If we ask the right questions, then, do we have the capacity to discern the right answers? I believe we do, but despite the overwhelming urgency of this task it will take much coordinated effort and some time to achieve. The most important element, however, will simply be people's desire to achieve it.

The ability to channel the desires of a population along certain lines and in certain directions remains something of a mystery to us. Setting aside this part of the problem at this juncture, let us ask another question: if we did know how to channel the desires of large numbers of ourselves, how would we define what is best for us, how would we differentiate the desirable from the undesirable and the advantageous from the disadvantageous with respect to man in the future?

We can say that unless man consciously decides to the contrary, cultural development will continue in directions of greater complexity and elaboration, and human populations will incline toward greater density patterns. That has been the irrevocable trend since the advent of pebble tools (Berreman et al. 1971). We can also say that man's biological development responds to his interaction with the cultural envelope produced by him so as to adapt, in a general sense, to the greater degrees of cultural complexity (Geertz 1964). This means that the biological nature of the species as a whole has changed and will change as the totality of the cultural envelope changes. This in turn means that any conscious changes in the cultural envelope of tomorrow will ultimately and without question also change the genetic construct of man. At the same time, however, we must fully realize that change will occur anyway because natural selection and the feedback mechanism will continue to operate within all human population units. The issue is whether or not man will enter this process consciously and decisively. He can do this if he has but the desire to do it.

Beside the complexity factor we can say that there is also a rapidity factor. As cultural complexity increases, the feedback mechanism functions with greater and greater speed, unless conscious steps are taken to inhibit it. This means that any alterations we might succeed in making to the entire cultural envelope would register an effect upon the *Homo* gene pool more quickly than ever before. The variables involved here, however, are predominantly cultural and could be consciously manipulated by men themselves if they so desired. Prehistory implores man to think about that and ponder the implications; the call is for a new kind of flexible thinking and fluid conceptualization to accommodate the unending and necessary ongoingness of change itself. Fixed human goals are only flashes in history, and tomorrow's thought about human futuristics must take this into account.

If the species were to effect overt, conscious manipulation of its own environment, what should be its control mechanism and what should be its guidance system? If the human brain, functioning within a framework of rational thought, were to be the control mechanism, a new flexible and tolerant value orientation could be visualized as a guidance system. To move the desires of man in this direction, however, the framework of rational thought itself must be acceptable to the *Homo* population of the world as a whole. The flexible and tolerant value orientation would flow from this and of necessity relate and apply differently to individual societal elements the world over. A double objective of this kind needs satisfaction because we know that we are one of the more homogeneous species the world has ever known, and yet no two individual genetic templates are exactly alike. What is comfort for one *H. sapiens* creature need not be comfort for another. Anthropology shows us again and again, in contemporary society as well as in prehistory, that *Homo* needs both change and stability, organization and disorganization, regularity and irregularity in that which surrounds him (Kluckhohn and Murray 1953). So he will need a rational framework that is encompassing and to which he can subscribe without doubt or fear; at the same time he will need lesser dimensions within that framework that he can tinker with — situations in which he can exercise immediate individual and small group choice, in which individual and small group idiosyncratic behavior can be tolerated and encouraged comfortably, and in which individual and small group innovation and creative experimentation can be accommodated.

This could mean individual freedom within a societal framework built upon responsible rational thought. The prehistoric record outlines in detail how man has devised and engaged in many culturally different behavior patterns (Cohen 1968). He has the capacity for constructive or destructive behavior, for aggressive or peaceful behavior, for enjoying a meat-oriented or a vegetable-oriented diet, for thinking patterns that we would define as hate-producing or patterns that we would define as loving, and so on (Young 1970). Man's beliefs influence the mixture as to what extent he indulges this capacity or that. Influence his beliefs and you will influence his activity patterns in directions that will emphasize one capacity and deemphasize another. At any moment man may be limited to a definable spectrum of capacities hinged to the extant range within his genetic matrix, but the choice can be his as to how and to what extent each capacity is behaviorally manifested by a population unit or by any number of population units. Define these capacities with precision and the future could rest, figuratively, in the palm of his brain. Subsequently, the job shifts from general, often abstract considerations, to the task of getting the *Homo* population to desire to undertake the emphasis of certain capacities and the deemphasis of others.

- Up to the present, man has developed a variety of cultural orientations (Thompson 1969; Lenski 1070), each of which, apart from many other considerations, operates as a protective device, as a sort of shield protecting man from himself and from the inclusiveness of his environment. These and other functions will have to be served by tomorrow's world view. We must know them well before we proceed. Societal trajectories to the future will be fallacious unless they are based on a thorough knowledge of the fundamental nature of man and one on which most could and would come to agree. This achieved, the rest would be no more difficult than a successful Skylab, and no one doubts the possibility of a Skylab if man but desires its existence. We must also honestly desire to know the functions of culture before we can hope to make it work consistently for us and to our continuous advantage.

Each individual has his own absolutely unique genetic template. Tenable cultural trajectories into the future depend on the acceptance by *H. sapiens* of such basic givens. Against this and other givens like it (discussed in Tax [1960] and Gifford [1970]), value orientations become philosophical windows to tomorrow; a new value orientation composed of new belief patterns grounded in a valid milieu of demonstrable but newly phrased fundamental *H. sapiens* truths, could be built into a firm cultural foundation that could serve man's best interests free of the harshnesses of past and present struggle.

But man's mind, his thoughts, govern his beliefs and his desires. His mind, his ability to think conceptually, and his thinking capacity are among his most valuable treasures. Ideas are the genes of culture. Ideas come from man's mind. What in the way of ideas should we begin to work with in order to make a future predictably advantageous for the *Homo* population living that future? Simpson tells us

. . . a chemical reaction, even though it proceeds in time, is completely devoid of a history; it always has and always will occur in the same way under the same conditions. It is that lack of any historical factor that makes observations in the physical sciences indefinitely repeatable, that makes exact predictions possible, and that makes prediction and explanation simply different ways of looking at the same conclusions . . . a study of living things, inevitably and always has a historical factor, and the physical principles of repeatability, predictability, and parity of prediction and explanation do not apply to the historical aspects of biology (1969: 8–10).

This is so because change is everpresent with respect to the many variables that attend any given biological condition or circumstance at any point in time.

...no two organisms, not even identical twins, are exactly alike. Each is the product of a history...and each history is different from any other,...and inherently unrepeatable.... Their diversity is not incidental, not interpretable as deviation from a norm or type. It is part of their nature as organisms, a universal and necessary phenomenon of living things at the population (or specific) level. If organisms did not vary, and had not done so for some billions of years, they would not exist at all (Simpson 1969: 8–10).

No two biological organisms, then, are ever equal. Change is a basic universal and it has made everything that lives and has lived unique "...each derived from everything that went before and conditioning every thing that will follow" (Simpson 1969: 8–10). So with respect to living things, including *H. sapiens*, exact prediction has very little value. General prediction, however, is possible because archaeology and anthropology have shown that there are demonstrably repetitive patterns in the expression of human nature through time (Kroeber 1957). A move toward the relatively general rather than the overly specific is more compatible with seriousness of purpose in human futuristics.

AN INTERNATIONAL-EXTRATERRESTRIAL CONFIGURATION

Probably in an overall sense the future of man will need an international-extraterrestrial configuration of negative imperatives. This configuration will be composed of those things that *sapiens*, in his own best interests, cannot be allowed to do. Of necessity, the overall configuration will probably include little by way of alternatives. But on the secondary level, alternatives between and within the various tolerated social situations should be encouraged. Decision making on lower levels that does not violate the primary level sanction configuration would appear, perhaps, to be very desirable. To enforce the totally new primary level international-extraterrestrial configuration of negative imperatives, the world would need an agency with the power to enforce. A new agency with new guidelines, new motives, and new means of enforcement is clearly a corollary. Degree of enforcement must be total upon the primary level. This is a most important consideration. No group or individual anywhere can be permitted to violate the new primary level international-extraterrestrial configuration of negative imperatives. On the secondary local level, however, no set means of enforcement need be prescribed with respect to day-today living. Whatever serves the local comfort index best would serve the world best.

Dator (1970) has made a critical observation to the effect that potentially man's "nature is certainly more subject to his own control ... than was previously expected, and thus man must finally assume responsibility for the modification of himself and his nature, and take this into account when designing future sociopolitical institutions and procedures."

With the technical or technological aspects of any situation open to the fullest mastery in both the realms of biology and culture, responsibility moves from the ethos, the mystical, the spiritual, the philosophically abstract, directly to the shoulders of man himself. Man can no longer shift responsibility to spirits or a pantheon of gods; it is with him to stay. The individual must now look to himself alone and to other men about him, to his mind and the minds of other men for beliefs and belief patterns that lead to responsible individual as well as collective behavior and decision making. A new philosophical morality might replace law in the ultrasophisticated dimensions of tomorrow, but responsibility as a basic value orientation would probably be deemed necessary on all levels of societal articulation. The worldwide sense of responsibility would permeate all aspects of the new primary level international-extraterrestrial configuration of negative imperatives.

To agree on primary level negative imperatives is not exactly to predict the future. Neither will it answer the many intriguing specific questions that can be brought up such as: "Should legislation be proposed to prevent further research into techniques for modifying the genetic structure of humans?" (Dator 1970). Local populations on the secondary level may wish to deal with such questions in a variety of different ways. In the long run biology interacting with the totality of culture by means of the feedback mechanism will ultimately show which answers are best. Deciding answers ahead of time to all questions for secondary level interaction patterns would cause one prescribed society the world over. Many would argue that this is less than desirable and with regard to secondary level population units seems far from being compatible with the idea of diversity in comfort indices.

As long as the primary level configuration of negative imperatives was not violated, tolerance could be championed throughout the secondary level from one population unit to another. Each in varying degrees, would have its own "simple social system design." Adherance to this basic tenet would make it possible for the world at large to note the efficacy of this or that "simple social system design" and evaluate the possible advantages of wider implementation. Each would constitute a test designed from within, beneath a framework of concomitant worldwide negative imperatives. At the present stage in the evolution and development of human society it seems important that the *H. sapiens* population as a whole provide a world environment wherein Bushman and astronaut can live out their lifeways without threat of forceful extinction or cultural annihilation. If the Bushman lifeway is positive in essential feedback content, it will flourish and expand; the same can be said of the astronaut lifeway. If not, a relatively static or declining lifeway will result.

Having thought out with utmost care a set of negative imperatives, and having obtained worldwide *H. sapiens* acceptance of it, futurologists could set about devising alternate futurologies for differing *H. sapiens* population units. Some of these population units might experiment with particular futurologies. The world *H. sapiens* population could then appreciate to what extent "success" or advantages would attend any given futurology. In this way a "good" futurology might expand by virtue of voluntary adoption on the part of other population units. A "bad" futurology might be abandoned in favor of a better one. It seems perhaps an error to think that futurologists, or any other segment of society, should want to "get" all *H. sapiens* populations to participate in a world based on science, or one based on technology, or even a world that would function as a unity beyond upholding a fundamental set of negative imperatives.

Without violating the negative imperatives, some population units may wish to undertake strict population controls, some may wish to undertake conscious programs of genetic guidance, others may not wish to limit their populations at all but rather build enormous artificial territories, others may elect to do as close to nothing as possible. Apart from the issue of population control itself (discussed by Polgar in this volume), such a schema in general principle would not seem to be disadvantageous to *H. sapiens* the world over. Quite the opposite, it would seem to take into account much that we have to accept as "true" with respect to the basic nature of *H. sapiens* as we know him today.

A fault in present futurological social thinking may have to do with its implications: it often seems implied that somehow it is necessary to devise *a* lifeway and that all *H. sapiens* everywhere must be prevailed upon to join in it. Perhaps this level of conformity is needed only with respect to negative imperatives. As to the rest, evidence relative to the nature of man and to the mechanisms and processes affecting his evolution and cultural development suggests that so much is variable, so much remains unmeasurable, that it may be disadvantageous to suggest a single lifeway for all of *H. sapiens* at this time. No human problem area brings this more forcefully to our attention than that of how to deal with *H. sapiens* population increases. There are two polarity positions: limit human populations everywhere through the adoption of birth control mechanisms, or, at the other extreme, do nothing or little in this regard and devote every technical resource to the development of new space for people to live on, in other words, expand our territories artificially.

As to the first polarity, beliefs will ultimately govern the acceptance, utilization, and effective implementation of birth control mechanisms. Technical achievement and the availability of both demonstrably good and alternative methods represent only a part of the problem. What individuals or populations think about the use of birth control mechanisms, and what they think about the "idea" of limiting the size of their families represent at least two crucial areas of belief. If a population believes that it will not be adversely affected by the self-limitation of its size, or that there are individual and collective advantages in undertaking self-limitation, then possibly it might attempt to do just that. In spelling out advantages and in dispelling fallacious notions concerning real or imaginary disadvantages of a population control method harmonious with belief patterns and other aspects of the lifeway and thought patterns, an argument which has proved to be successful in one population element may not necessarily be successful in a different population element.

On a primary level, then, a philosophy, a rationale, a belief pattern is needed with regard to the self-limitation of populations advantageous to people (*H. sapiens* creatures) the world over. Complementary to this but upon a secondary level of belief, we must be able to develop a myriad of locally applicable rationales. The first would be the "why" for us all, the second the "why" for differing population units or elements, custom tailored in each case to a particular value orientation. Number of children per family would vary from culture to culture in accordance with what each considers, by virtue of its values, to be a "nice" family. But the primary overall view could emphasize in the most meaningful ways possible that individual and collective advantages lay in the avoidance of excessive numbers of children per family, that it is up to each family unit to wait until it can comfortably not only afford to have children but afford to bring them up within a milieu that embraces a high comfort index for both the children and the adults.

Addressing ourselves to the second polarity, some might question whether, in suggesting the limitation of population size, the availability of new territories resulting from advanced technological environmental controls has been sufficiently explored. Large populations could now realistically be maintained in the intensely cold arctic and polar regions, beneath the ocean, in outer space itself, and possibly on other celestial bodies. Might we not serve all purposes better by moving forward swiftly in areas of technology that will provide large-scale artificial environments that can be set anywhere on earth? Rather than limit the population inordinately, given the desire, a world organization might be able to provide the everexpanding population with large, new, artificial living areas.

Regardless of which polarity is chosen or if some other alternative is pursued within the spectrum of possibilities, thinking is best accomplished on two dimensions (primary: overall orientation; secondary: local orientation). One of these concerns general desirability and the broadest of purposes and when defined and agreed to, aims to influence the behavior and attitudes of all *H. sapiens* creatures. The other secondary dimension is directed toward *H. sapiens* population elements, and asks how each population element will react to such an overall sentiment. Comprehending this, it asks how each population element can be induced to undertake the articulation of primary overall dimension sentiments with the idiosyncratic components of its own particular cultural manifestation. Operational effectiveness is one of the goals here and it is on this elemental secondary dimension that individual or small group choice can be stressed in order to attain that goal.

A GENERAL SYSTEM OF BELIEFS

"Living systems evolve in order to meet the challenge of the environment" (Mayr 1969). Mental evolution is the key to *H. sapiens* viability in tomorrow's world. The *H. sapiens* mind must find the ability as well as the ways and means to believe in man. This belief in man must include trust in one another and trust by one small population unit in another; it must also include a real value for life and the living. Faith would not be synonymous with trust nor would love be equated with a real value for life. Faith and love are emotions differently defined and variously manifested by the many population units the world over. To solve the numerous clusters of problems that can be raised, the minds of men must move to new belief systems. I would argue that new belief patterns must be arrived at and must be favorably met by the minds of men before the myriad of empirical problems, large and small, can be advantageously solved. In the absence of a general system of beliefs a solution to one urgent problem is likely to be advantageous to one population unit but at the same time disadvantageous to another.

H. sapiens needs to adapt not only to a new living environment, by embracing an overall set of negative imperatives, but to a new mental environment as well. Now, both can be uniquely the product of forethought. In between the mental aspects of primary and secondary level environments, a new philosophical environment on an intermediary level of abstraction would have a profound bearing on the character of solutions adopted to cope with living problems, whatever their setting or their dimensions might be. Such a new mental environment must not be fixed but must be flexible and susceptible to change.

A new intermediary level mental environment is needed as a flux to make primary and secondary level considerations interrelate because the past has been dominated by a plethora of population unit belief patterns which have often conflicted disastrously with one another for lack of any overall conceptual articulation. A philosophical unity of purpose will not be achieved easily because each existing population unit has a belief pattern of its own that ordinarily has successfully resisted breakdown. Idea and belief recombinations have, in most instances, been tested over and over again. Over numerous generations a hardness is attained that resists profound changes in its internal integration (Kluckhohn and Strodtbeck 1961). Individual population units have survived in the past in considerable measure because each has been able tenaciously to maintain the distinctiveness of its belief pattern despite the biological similarity of all of the population units. Beliefs have kept us culturally apart in the near past; tomorrow certain beliefs must weld us together the world over. Something new has to happen. A belief in people that is not superficial has to transcend the value orientations of local population units (Kluckhohn 1958). If this were to happen, primary level negative imperatives would provide meaning for secondary level lifeways, each as unique and distinctive as any population unit could wish.

In summary, I have been talking about a primary level of *H. sapiens* unity based on a configuration of negative imperatives fluxed to secondary level phenomena by a philosophical belief in people founded on reciprocal trust of one man in another and of one population unit in another. A basic subscription both to a set of negative imperatives and to a belief in people founded on trust is essential if population units are to reside permanently within artificial environments. To the present, most population units have not wished to remove themselves from an economic and subsistence base they could manage, protect, or control for themselves because no population unit has thus far had complete confidence and trust in all of its neighbors. International, intertribal, and interpersonal mistrust have been so prevalent that one sounds naive, unrealistic, almost a simple-minded wishful thinker to suggest such a philosophical orientation and to use the word "trust" as I have. And yet space flight to the moon is a first step in this direction. The men in the spaceship are completely dependent on men on the ground. The belief patterns of men in a spaceship must be totally tuned to the idea of trusting those on the ground directing their flight. Spacemen must trust their ground directors, they must have confidence in them, they must believe in them, and responsible behavior must be a common code between all parties. From the standpoint of philosophical value orientation, this lifeway is a kind of capsule view of a belief pattern that has to prevail generally in the world of tomorrow.

We are, of course, a long way from that; but how else can we expect societies that are rudimentary in complexity and degree of elaboration to throw off their economic base and embrace a new one that will increase their comfort index but which is dependent on far more elaborate cultural configurations located in removed and relatively far-off places? How else can we expect whole population units to live comfortably and permanently within completely artificial environments in the arctic regions, on the ocean floors, and possibly within intensely desert regions, or in space? The space way, as I see it, is perhaps philosophically the only way. The question is how could it be managed on a worldwide basis. It seems at times so far removed from the distrust of contemporary survival. Perhaps if *H. sapiens* came to want a comfortable, peaceful existence as much as the space participants wanted to go to the moon, and if subscription to the set of negative imperatives was an accomplished fact, there might at least be a basal podium of desire.

On such a foundation, overall principles and belief patterns could be developed to which population units would adhere. Individual population units could then be fostered, each embracing, if this seems desirable, its own secondary culture and its own secondary value orientation; some located in places familiar to us today, others in the arctic, beneath the sea, and in space. But somehow, capacities such as invasion, subversion, hatred, and animosity must be replaced or minimized by emphasizing others that lead in different directions. The integrity of the secondary cultural and belief patterns of every population unit must be guaranteed in exchange for adherence to primary level negative imperatives and the intermediary philosophical outlook. Without unbreakable and enforceable guarantees as to secondary configuration integrity there can be no commencement to these thoughts.

Enforcements, nevertheless, are one thing — necessary, yes, but hardly the absolute crux. I cannot visualize any kind of futurology without "desire." *H. sapiens* must desire the future that will be his if a relatively high comfort index is to be part of that future. The sources of human desire and how to influence them in relatively constructive and advantageous ways remain comparatively obscure and enigmatic. *H. sapiens'* behavior does not by any means always match predicted behavior. Should we conceptualize a futurological schema that did meet the many diverse demands in need of satisfaction, we would still be left with the problem of how to bring it in conjunction with *H.*

sapiens himself. I can visualize primary imperatives, a belief pattern flux, and distinctive secondary cultural configurations the world over constituting a single integrated smoothly meshed *H. sapiens* whole. But *H. sapiens* will have to desire their coming together. How do we explore this matter of desire — this vital ingredient so close to *H. sapiens* himself?

I wonder if rather than thinking of it in terms of grand primary level solutions simply because it will be a primary problem, it might not be best to examine it within the array of secondary level cultural configurations. Jacobs (this volume) reminds us of individual space needs, of noise tolerance levels, and of language problems among other things. In these there are many answers to comfort index factors — what one cultural manifestation regards as just the right proximity value, noise quotient, and vocal means of communication another population might feel to be the epitome of discomfort. So to seek a precise or the "perfect" universal in these is perhaps to entertain an illusion. Perhaps futurologists will conceptualize a valid futurological schema and then teams of anthropologists may be needed to effect a smooth mesh between that schema and population units by defining as many desire patterns as there are secondary population units. Once defined the desire pattern in a particular population unit could effectively be tuned into the schema itself thereby accomplishing a mesh.

Examples can easily be presented which demonstrate how culture change and the idea of culture change differ from one cultural configuration to the next. Secondary level population units the world over can perhaps be expected, as McKnight indicates (this volume), to appreciate that change is to some extent vital, but at the same time they are apt to discourage it. Each can also be expected to deal with change differently. Culture change seems rarely to be just a shift or accommodation; unless consciously directed to the contrary it more often appears to involve the attainment of some degree of greater cultural elaboration or complexity, even though this is ever so slight. Prehistory tends to support such a contention.

If we were to agree to the need for general adherence to a set of negative imperatives, we would also have to agree to a means whereby such adherence could be invoked. As an extension of this there would have to be means whereby population units everywhere could be assured of self-determination with regard to culture change. Population units must each be assured of a position which would allow them to govern their own rate, degree, and direction of culture change. Population units must be positioned within a futurological schema in such ways as to enable them to elect for themselves the degree to which they will or will not embrace greater elaboration or complexity. A population unit must be able to attempt to stay as it is if that is what the people within that population unit see as most appropriate (provided adherence to the overall primary level set of negative imperatives is not compromised by this).

Because the natural environment is eternally shifting, culture change as such is universal. On this account no futurological schema would be complete without allowance for change. Indeed, I feel the better futurological schema would be one that made use of change itself to ease individual population units each in its own way toward high-comfort-index adherence to the primary set of imperatives.

THE FUTURE

The idea of thinking about the potential effects and biological advantages or disadvantages of technological goals within a particular cultural envelope *prior to* the initiation of those goals would in itself be new. No population has ever really done this till now. Such an effort is now being made, however, because the SST program was in part evaluated in this way, and other developments in the Space Program are being subjected to similar scrutiny. Calculating the effects of this or that alternative course of action is exacting and expensive, but it can be done. Society can now avail itself of this capacity. To encourage its use on a wide front is essential to the discipline of futurology. In order to suggest how to choose among alternative directions for the future we must be able to evaluate consequences with as high a degree of certainty as possible. Then technology as well as the other arms of operative culture, such as values and beliefs, can be "directed toward serving generated cultural goals" as Maruyama points out ("Toward human futuristics," this volume).

With particular regard to technology, the study of the past contains a multitude of lessons for us. What man has done in the past can be a major contributor to the perspective needed for choosing among future alternatives. It can also define which activity patterns are likely to be disadvantageous to the general population or to discrete population units of the future.

Although I prefer to talk about "cultural planning" rather than "engineering," there will probably be more rather than less "futurological engineering" of the overall world value orientation because when perfected the primary value structure will more nearly resemble a "one-goal efficiency system" in its cumulative sense. It will be unlike any "one-goal efficiency system" ever previously devised, however, because one of its very basic elements will be a flow into the future, a built-in fluidity, a flexibility to accommodate what will come, a constantly present everchangingness that will directly associate with change, since change itself will be one of the principal norms of the future. On the other hand, "cultural futurology" or "human futuristics" will endeavor to work with "concurrent-multipurpose versatility systems" on the secondary level of tolerable cultural diversity. Here the futurologist "facilitates people in generating their own goals" within the framework outlined by the primary overall value orientation. Here, too, on the secondary level, the futurologist's "function is catalytic," while at the primary level he is perhaps a humanist, philosopher, social scientist, engineer, cultural planner, and more, all wrapped into one.

Prehistory demonstrates that for the most part man has responded or been pushed into what Maruyama terms "predictive futuristics" which "as long as it is merely predictive, tends to be based on the assumption that social change occurs mostly beyond the individual's will, and that the individual has little or no choice but to live with the predicted social change. There is an undertone of the inevitability of the course of history which is thought to have a suprapersonal or impersonal reality" ("Toward human futuristics," this volume). In a general sense man has been swept along for over five million years (Reinhold 1971) by the consequences of his deeds. The average Old Empire lowland Maya (Morley 1969) or Sumerian (Kramer 1963) did not have an opportunity to plan out the future of his society. He decided from moment to moment what he would do and what he would not do and in so doing he shaped his future. What he did or did not do from one minute to the next added to what those about him did or did not do and shaped the course of his civilization. The feedback mechanisms operating within the Old Empire lowland Maya and Sumerian gene pools shaped the genetic matrix and cultural milieu of each through time, shifting this way among the Maya and that way among the Sumerians until encroached upon and overwhelmed by Mexican, and Elamite and Amorite forces respectively.

The genetic construct has never been planned knowingly and knowledgeably, nor has the cultural aspect in a broadly successful ongoing sense. But now the responsibilities of planning can no longer be avoided. Prehistory can show us what happens if man does this and that over a wide spectrum of situations. Prehistory shows conclusively that although exact circumstances never repeat themselves, man attempts to do the same generalized things over and over again. It shows that he has a certain number of capacities, each of which can be defined. It shows that he is very likely to heavily indulge one capacity under certain circumstances and another capacity under others, and it shows dramatically what will come of it in each case. On the basis of this kind of evidence (and it is available in considerable amounts), we can state with some certainty that future man must emphasize certain capacities and deemphasize others if he wishes to live tomorrow in a particular way. For the first time in history many men could join in a meeting of minds to define in the broadest of terms what that particular way should be.

Prehistory cannot help us measure rates of culture change in the future nor can it assist us in any kind of exact quantification, but archaeology together with the physical anthropology of prehistory can show us with crushing clarity exactly what man has done, what has happened to his genetic self, what among all that he does repeatedly brings disadvantage to him, what kinds of activities have again and again brought advantage to him and what kinds of activities bring about swift culture change, or conversely, slow it down. Knowledge on these matters is of the greatest importance.

Thanks to the perspectives afforded by archaeology (Adams 1966; Daniel 1968) and paleoanthropology (Bishop and Clark 1967; Coles and Higgs 1969; Klein 1969), we can now define what might be disadvantageous and what carries with it advantage if we encourage culture change in certain directions. Volatile, aggressive behavior seems disadvantageous to the many in the context of complex civilization and an urbanized condition, or wherever peoples cannot, in a lifeway sense, remove themselves from one another's company. Adaptability seems to hold advantages; simply to maintain biological and cultural adaptability seems distinctly advantageous. Cultural obsession is strikingly disadvantageous; extremes in cultural behavior are disadvantageous more often than not. Blending cultural themes seems to hold advantages. All these and others in the long view, of course, extend over the tens, the hundreds, and the thousands of years, but that is the essence of responsibility in futurological planning. Biology will continue to be the final arbiter because man will either adapt biologically to the consequences of plans, make his inability to adapt known by changing or doing away with plans, or become extinct. There is no future without the living creature. That part we cannot alter no matter whether the future is partly devised or simply unfolds without intense conscious direction.

I can visualize a world construct unlike anything presently extant, in which the general and individual comfort index is quite high. This to me would carry with it correspondingly low general and individual dissatisfaction indices. Today progress is defined differently by different peoples. Tomorrow, progress could simply be defined as biological and cultural change in directions that would mean a higher and higher comfort index both in general and for the individual. I do not believe that overt negativism is necessarily inherent in the dominant human condition tomorrow any more than I believe that overtly aggressive behavior is inherent in the general lifeway of the future. Possibly the retention of a negative quotient along with an anxiety factor would be desirable to forestall undue complacency, but that the general outlook should be one of negativism and/or anxiety is not essential in my view.

My position is based on the concept of potential self-awareness both in a general sense and with respect to the individual. The means whereby self-awareness can be achieved today are primitive. Suppose, however, that one primary goal of tomorrow were the rapid attainment of individual self-awareness. Suppose sophisticated means of attainment were readily available. Suppose education were not as it is but that its basic objective were to teach self-awareness (self-awareness for man and self-awareness for the individual). Human desires might then be quite different; the individual could swiftly determine for himself and to his own satisfaction where his own highest comfort index lay and he could move rapidly toward its attainment so that a major portion of his life span could take place within it. Potentially there seems to be much *H. sapiens* satisfaction and peace of mind to be found in real self-awareness itself. A new philosophy is an obvious corollary, and a new, and perhaps for the first time, true comprehension of human nature is an obvious necessity.

Apart from self-awareness, that which is needed by *H. sapiens* everywhere could be delineated as a series of "concerns." Wherever we examine or observe *H. sapiens*, we find that he is concerned about a configuration of entities: subsistence, ceremonialism-ritual, craftsmanship-art and artistry, and so on. These concerns may focus on different entities in different areas, but everywhere a series of concerns can be observed. This is equally true of the prehistoric record. Man cannot function properly unless his basic concerns are satisfied. These concerns must be fulfilled one way or another or the population unit will disarticulate or distort. Accordingly we can move on the premise that *H. sapiens'* long-term cross-cultural concerns are necessary to his existence. Concerns that consistently recur could be abstracted by cross-cultural study so that the futurologist could build a valid model composed of an irreducible number of consistently recurring concern entities vital to *H. sapiens* existence.

Once the necessary concern inventory had been established, we would turn to the method by and the degree to which each separate concern is fulfilled, seeing that the method and the extent of fulfillment vary infinitely from population unit to population unit throughout human society. Some population units may very nearly avoid fulfillment of one or more of their basic concern entities; degree of fulfillment will vary and all will go about fulfillment differently.

How a population unit fulfills its concerns is secondary, as long as the fundamental concerns are in some measure fulfilled. This is important because if we were to subscribe to an overall international-extraterrestrial primary level configuration of negative imperatives, that subscription might block certain fulfillments in certain population units. Blocked fulfillments could not be left unfulfilled. They would have to be unblocked by thoughtfull redirection of the concern so as not to leave the population unit in a distorted condition. There is no reason to suppose that concerns which have been fundamental during the past thirty thousand years will not continue to be basic during the immediately foreseeable future. On the other hand, because of population density trends there is every reason to suppose that these concerns, however fundamental they may be, will have to be fulfilled in ways that will differ profoundly by conscious intent from past ways of fulfillment. New ways of concern fulfillment must be devised to accord with new man-directed environments that will in part be those of the newly "emerging urban systems." With an appreciation of the *H. sapiens* concern pattern inventory, we can address ourselves more cogently to the question of what will be desirable ingredients of tomorrow's social fabric. It will then be a question of how man might best handle these ingredients to achieve the highest possible comfort index the world over.

THE MODEL

In the area of immediate answers, I believe that what is needed is an operational model composed of various discrete *H. sapiens* population units. These population units would be submodels in the sense that they would be units willing to subscribe to the model and willing to embark within it on new lifeways geared to their particular nature and to that which we presently know about man as a whole — for example, his ability to believe in entirely new conceptual abstractions.

Population unit components of the model would not have to be geographically contiguous; the only common bond necessary would be desire to participate in a new world view. However, without absolute guarantees of population unit integrity on a worldwide basis within the framework of a set of negative imperatives, there is no real possibility of freedom from the breaking force of vested interests which are often rooted in beliefs that are disadvantageous for present or subsequent *H. sapiens* generations.

In an overall sense the most urgent need is to consider the problem of what should constitute the international-extraterrestial configuration of negative imperatives. In constituting this configuration of negative imperatives perhaps it will serve *H. sapiens'* best interests to encourage the human brain, our uniquely conceptual thinking apparatus, to function within a milieu of rational thought. In this way it would act as a control on deliberations, while at the same time encouraging a flexible and tolerant value orientation that can provide guidance to those deliberations.

There is no reason in my view why a single population unit might not commence the model. As other discrete *H. sapiens* population units joined, it would come increasingly to function as an international or extraterrestrial model. In this way we could avoid trying to provide one set of right answers for all of *H. sapiens* at this juncture in world history regarding intermediary and secondary level considerations. The model could be altered and adjusted as our knowledge increased and discussions and deliberations bore fruit. If the model did not emerge, or having emerged, did not enlarge, obviously failure would have attended the effort, and new designs would have to be conceptualized. The model itself, then, would represent a test. The world could watch, the world could participate, the world might profit greatly, the world would seem to stand to lose little in the effort.

Let us assume for the sake of discussion that the international-extraterrestrial configuration of negative imperatives has been arrived at and *H. sapiens* agreement and subscription to them have been achieved. An absolutely effective means of implementation has been devised and is operative. We are dissatisfied with the particular cir-cumstances of our immediate surroundings. We wish to embark on the model rationale. We wish to get outside present conditions and at-tempt "cultural planning" to build or rebuild anew. We wish to design a cultural envelope in the hope of achieving a high *H. sapiens* comfort index for the inhabitants. The parameters of our experiment are limited by the negative imperatives, but at the same time, if we desire viable patterns within the basic strictures of those negative imperatives, our patterns are guaranteed by them. The extent to which we might succeed is up to us and relates to how well we are able to think things out through the exercise of forethought. Inasmuch as we are designing the first envelope within the model, we have to think broadly, but at the same time we have to deal with a vast armada of concrete specifics as well.

We might begin with a study precisely documenting the *H. sapiens* obsessions that we should consciously attempt to discard or avoid (Jacobs, this volume). We might find it useful to explore envelope designs that would inhibit obsessions of any kind within the scope of the model, realizing that *H. sapiens* capacity to become obsessed is a disadvantageous capacity to indulge even in limited ways or along particular lines. We might undertake subsequent studies to consider other *H. sapiens* capacities: capacity to become obsessed, capacity to become spiritually involved, and so on. In each case interest would fasten on how best to handle a particular capacity within the structure of the model and within the design of a specific envelope — the large ongoing (philosophical?) dimension and the immediate particulars as reflected by concern fulfillment needs.

REFERENCES

ADAMS, ROBERT M.
1966   *The evolution of urban society: early Mesopotamia and prehispanic Mexico.* Chicago: Aldine.
BACON, EDWARD, editor
1963   *Vanished civilizations of the ancient world.* New York: McGraw-Hill.
BERREMAN, GERALD, et al.
1971   *Anthropology today.* Del Mar, California: Communications Research Machines.
BISHOP, WALTER W., J. DESMOND CLARK, editors
1967   *Background to evolution in Africa.* Chicago: University of Chicago Press.
BLAKESLEE, SANDRA
1971   "Special report: California astronomers detect two big galaxies near Milky Way." *New York Times,* January 11.
CASO, ALFONSO
1958   *The Aztecs, people of the sun.* Norman: University of Oklahoma Press.
CLARK, GRAHAME
1970   *Aspects of prehistory.* Berkeley: University of California Press.
COE, WILLIAM R.
1965   Tikal, Guatemala, and emergent Maya civilization. *Science* 147: 1401–1419.
1967   *Tikal, a handbook of the ancient Maya ruins.* Philadelphia: University Museum, University of Pennsylvania.
COHEN, YEHUDI A., editor
1968   *Man in adaptation: the biosocial background.* Chicago: Aldine.
COLES, J. M., E. S. HIGGS
1969   *The archaeology of early man.* New York: Praeger.
COTTRELL, LEONARD
1962   *Lost worlds.* New York: Doubleday.
DANIEL, GLYN
1968   *The first civilizations.* New York: Crowell.
DATOR, JAMES
1970   "State of Hawaii task force on political decision-making and the law in the year 2000," in *Symposium on cultural futuristics: pre-conference volume.* Edited by Magoroh Maruyama. Washington, D.C.: American Anthropological Association.
DYSON, ROBERT H., JR.
1960   The death of a city. *Expedition* 2: 2–11.
GEERTZ, CLIFFORD
1964   "The transition to humanity," in *Horizons in anthropology.* Edited by Sol Tax. Chicago: Aldine.
GIFFORD, JAMES C.
1960   The type-variety method of ceramic classification as an indicator of cultural phenomena. *American Antiquity* 25: 341–347.

1970   "Prehistory: perspectives from the past as trajectories to the future,"
        in *Symposium on cultural futuristics: pre-conference volume.* Edited by
        Magoroh Maruyama. Washington, D.C.: American Anthropological
        Association.

HOLLOWAY, RALPH L., JR.
1968   "Cranial capacity and the evolution of the human brain," in *Culture:
        man's adaptive dimension.* Edited by M. F. Ashley Montagu. New
        York: Oxford University Press.

HOWELL, F. CLARK
1965   *Early man.* New York: Time.

HUBBERT, M. KING
1967   *Time and stratigraphy in the evolution of man.* Publication 1469.
        Washington, D.C.: National Academy of Sciences and the National
        Research Council.

JACOBS, SUE-ELLEN
1970   "Ethnocommunication: past, present and future," in *Symposium on
        cultural futuristics: pre-conference volume.* Edited by Magoroh
        Maruyama. Washington, D.C.: American Anthropological Associa-
        tion.

KLEIN, RICHARD G.
1969   *Man and culture in the late Pleistocene, a case study.* San Francisco:
        Chandler.

KLUCKHOHN, CLYDE
1958   *The scientific study of values.* Toronto: University of Toronto Press.

KLUCKHOHN, CLYDE, HENRY A. MURRAY
1953   *Personality in nature, society, and culture.* New York: Alfred A.
        Knopf.

KLUCKHOHN, FLORENCE R., FRED L. STRODTBECK
1961   *Variations in value orientations.* Evanston: Row, Peterson.

KRAMER, SAMUEL N.
1963   *The Sumerians.* Chicago: University of Chicago Press.
1967   *Cradle of civilization.* New York: Time.

KROEBER, A. L.
1944   *Configurations of culture growth.* Berkeley: University of California
        Press.
1957   *Style and civilizations.* Ithaca: Cornell University Press.

LE GROS CLARK, WILFRED E.
1967   *Man-apes or ape-men?* New York: Holt, Rinehart and Winston.

LENSKI, GERHARD
1970   *Human societies.* New York: McGraw-Hill.

LEONARD, JONATHAN N.
1967   *Ancient America.* New York: Time.

MARUYAMA, MAGOROH
1963   The second cybernetics: deviation-amplifying mutual causal proces-
        ses. *American Scientist* 51: 164–179.

MAYR, ERNST
1969   "The evolution of living systems," in *Evolutionary anthropology.*
        Edited by Hermann K. Bleibtreu. Boston: Allyn and Bacon.
1970   *Populations, species, and evolution.* Cambridge: Harvard University
        Press.

MORLEY, SYLVANUS G.
1969   *The ancient Maya* (third edition). Revised by George W. Brainerd.
        Stanford: Stanford University Press.

PFEIFFER, JOHN E.
1969   *The emergence of man.* New York: Harper and Row.
PIGGOTT, STUART
1961   *The dawn of civilization.* New York: McGraw-Hill.
REINHOLD, ROBERT
1971   "Bone traces early man back five million years." *New York Times,* February 19.
RILEY, CARROLL L.
1969   *The origins of civilization.* Carbondale: Southern Illinois University Press.
SCHNEIDER, WILLIAM C.
1970   "Special report." *New York Times,* July 2.
SIMPSON, GEORGE G.
1969   *Biology and man.* New York: Harcourt, Brace and World.
SOMMER, ROBERT
1969   *Personal space: the behavioral basis of design.* Englewood Cliffs: Prentice-Hall.
TAX, SOL, *editor*
1960   *Evolution after Darwin,* three volumes. Chicago: University of Chicago Press.
THOMPSON, J. ERIC
1967   *The rise and fall of Maya civilization* (second edition). Norman: University of Oklahoma Press.
THOMPSON, LAURA.
1969   *The secret of culture.* New York: Random House.
WASHBURN, SHERWOOD L.
1959   Speculations on the interrelations of the history of tools and biological evolution. *Human Biology* 31: 21–31.
1960   Tools and human evolution. *Scientific American* 253: 62–75.
YOUNG, LOUISE B., *editor*
1970   *Evolution of man.* New York: Oxford University Press.

Ecosystems and Economic Systems

ANTHONY WILDEN

Western society has promised traditionally that our conquest of nature would result in social progress. The power that science and technology exercise over nature would liberate mankind from scarcity.

The successful development of capitalism since the seventeenth-century economic and scientific revolutions tells a different story. Since capitalism depends upon growth for stability, it has relied on increasing exploitation of the nonhuman environment and on the pillage of anything it chose to define as an exploitable environment, e.g. the Third World.

As in many other dichotomies in our obviously irrational and potentially self-destructive system — subject and object, organism and environment, self and other — the struggle with nature projects its own exploitative violence onto nature. Nature is "hostile" and must therefore be subjugated.

Development of new knowledge has not given humanity as a whole increased control over nature. Science and technology have remained the property of the dominant classes and nations. Increasing control over nature has in fact been matched by increasing technological and economic control over people. As C. S. Lewis once pointed out, "...what we call Man's power over Nature turns out to be a power exercised by some men over other men with Nature as its instrument" (Leiss 1972: 26).

The Christian idea of humanity as God's viceroy in nature is qualitatively different from modern domination, which is allied with both exploitation (economics, technology) and knowledge (natural

The original version of this paper was presented at the American Anthropological Association's Symposium on Cultural Futuristics, held in Toronto, in December 1972.

science). Francis Bacon (1561–1626) was the major modern propagandist for the scientific study of nature designed to make her the slave of men. Bacon invented the research grant and successfully promoted the myths of "pure knowledge" and "pure science." He distinguished himself by originating the ideal of an apolitical, objective, and totally ethical scientific elite, and then got himself fired for taking bribes while Lord Chancellor of England (Leiss 1972).

AN ECOSYSTEMIC PERSPECTIVE

Most people are acquainted with ecology and with the "environmental crisis" — some to the point of being sick and tired of it. And yet, in spite of ten years of publicity about it, in spite of daily newspaper reports about it, what is actually happening is not easy to understand. On the one hand, a number of ecologists predict our imminent extinction — which, of course, nobody can believe. On the other, people write, read, and talk of such matters as air and water pollution as if they were analogous to a rising crime rate accompanying rising population. But the crime rate, under more or less normal social conditions, always refers to a more or less fixed percentage of the population. The population of criminals is constrained to a major extent by the same factors as those constraining the population as a whole (with due allowance for special cases of social disruption, e.g. the rise in hard drug addiction stemming from the Indochina War). Unlike air and water pollution, the crime rate is not necessarily accumulative.

Accumulated air and water pollution are, however, still no more than symptoms of underlying processes, and it is these processes we need to understand. What I am seeking to show is that the current "problematic of the future" is not an "ecological" crisis in the usual sense of the term, but a crisis in the relationships between the economic organization of the global ecosystem, its social base, and the organization of nature. Since economics is concerned primarily with the fundamental relationships between people in a given economic system, rather than simply with those between people and goods — as well as with our socialized relationship to nature as an implicit social category (Lukács 1971) — the ecological crisis is a mere symptom of an unprecedented kind of social and political crisis. The "problem of the environment" reveals itself to be an unconscious ideological smokescreen. Just as the phrase "the Negro problem" projected the psychological and economic fact of white racism onto the very people it exploited and oppressed, so the phrase "the environmental crisis" projects the responsibility for that crisis away from its actual source. It implies that it is the natural environment that is the problem, rather than its exploitation by our present economic system.

This ideological process of projection occurs at every level of the social ecosystem. It is complemented by the idea that it is men and women who are responsible for the crisis (i.e. "human nature"), whereas what has in fact been involved historically are the specific conditions of exploitation, by the new form of socioeconomic organization which we label "industrial capitalism," of everything it chooses to define as its environment: nature, other classes, other races, the Third World.

The "ecological" danger to the future is expressed in an ideology extolling the benefits of economic growth. This must be seen as a covert metaphor for the systemic and objective necessities of accumulating productive capacity in order to maintain the present stability of the system. The exponential and superexponential increases in population, in pollution, and in the exhaustion of the nonrenewable matter-energy reserves of the planet, are not the result of subjective ideas or values, nor are they simply the result of Western ethics, of Genesis, or of our ways of thought. The basic structure of Western ideology and its epistemological base, like that of any other society, is ultimately derived from its socioeconomic organization, rather than the other way round.

Naturally, our ideology — based on the myth of free, equal, and autonomous individuals in open and symmetrical competition in a free marketplace of commodities and ideas — says the opposite. Nevertheless, this myth of the abstract individual should not deter us from trying to analyze what is happening to real people in the real world, especially once we realize that our survival is at stake.

Since ecosystemic processes are interlinked — increased population increases energy use which increases pollution, for instance — it is not possible to talk of these processes in the traditional linear terms of cause and effect. Whereas we have been trained and educated to think in a language of causality which says that "like causes produce like effects," the ecosystemic perspective requires us to think in terms of a different vocabulary. For example, in the biosphere (the life-support systems of the planet) seemingly insignificant causes can produce enormous and unexpected effects, because very small disturbances in the complicated system of natural relationships may undergo amplification as they are transmitted throughout that system. Changes in one part of the system may also have effects on other parts which do not at first sight seem to be very closely connected with the area in which the changes first occurred. Our failure to see the connections is part and parcel of the way we have been trained to think about cause and effect. We have inherited our doctrine of causality and metaphors of change from classical physics. But the relationships between the inorganic particles and forces studied by classical physics are of a different type of complexity from the relationships between organisms.

What is significant is that one of the basic tenets of the ecosystemic perspective: *the synergistic multiplication of causes by their effects*, applies in all biological and social systems. For example, a relatively small withdrawal of affection or a lack of sensory stimulation or both in the first year of a human child's life can become amplified into relatively large psychological and developmental changes in later life. Some of these changes, like ecological changes, may prove to be irreversible.

An ecosystemic perspective involves radical changes in our way of thinking about all kinds of relationships. But such changes in thinking are useless without equally radical changes in ways of behaving. Such changes in behavior, however, are not usually possible for the single individual. Individual behavior is linked to sets of values, on the one hand, and to socioeconomic organization, on the other; individual values are, within certain clearly defined limits, transforms of the values of our culture. Consequently, any valid ecosystemic perspective must necessarily seek to locate the real source of the problem in cultural and economic values and not in individual values. It seeks change in the socioeconomic sphere, not simply in the individual.

As Paul Sears and others have been pointing out for years (cf. Shepard and McKinley 1969), the questioning by ecology of what is inaccurately called "growth for the sake of growth" — it is really a question of growth for the sake of short-term economic and political stability — makes it a subversive science, so subversive in fact that it generates problems of almost intolerable difficulty which shake the values of our culture and of the various countercultures to their foundations. To take the simplest example: population stabilization through birth control is one thing for the relatively affluent white majority in the United States. It is quite another for members of the racial minorities in that country, many of whom see no possibility of significantly affecting the economic and social discrimination against them by the white majority except through an increase in numbers.

The solution of this sort of problem depends upon the introduction of the idea of "context." The context of white values may call for a stabilization of population growth. The context of the minorities may call for population increase. It is not possible to apply the same set of values, in the abstract, to both populations. A contextual approach — which is undoubtedly unacceptable in principle to the white majority (although presently occurring in fact) — would call for a decrease in the white population matched by an increase in the minority populations. Population stabilization would then be achieved by altering the present ethnic ratios and not by a general limitation on growth which has the effect of maintaining the differentials at their present level.

Alfred North Whitehead once said that Western civilization is still living on the intellectual capital accumulated in the seventeenth century. He also said that the culture that cannot break through the framework of its own concepts is doomed. The seventeenth century was, after all, the period of the capitalist revolution, of the fundamental reorganization of social relations resulting from a historically novel type of commodity production. The technical and technological innovation represented by capitalist social organization was accompanied by two allied events: (1) the invention of the abstract, autonomous individual and the atomization of social relations through a quantitative and one-dimensional principle of social performance (currently represented, in particular, by the IQ test); and (2) the invention of the Newtonian-Cartesian scientific method based on mechanics, closed systems, a new atomism, and linear causality. It also depended on three basic, nonecosystemic principles: (1) that no effect can be greater than its cause (the "scientific" basis of Descartes's ontological argument for the existence of God); (2) that like causes produce like effects; and (3) that action and reaction are equal and opposite (symmetry).

I cannot go into the complex historical process of these changes in detail. It is enough to say that (1) it was precisely at this period that "nature" was defined by science, by ideology, and by economic relationships as an object to be controlled, exploited, and dominated; (2) at the same time, the development of capitalism was being financed through the designation of the nonwhite world as a similar environment for the system to exploit (Western economic development depended essentially on the de-development of the civilizations that we now call "underdeveloped" — as if it were their natural or genetic condition); (3) the physicist model of atoms and closed systems, related by self-regulating internal forces, was immediately imported into biology, psychology, and the social sciences, where it still remains, based on one version or another of the Benthamesque and utilitarian "pleasure principle"; (4) the same model was imported into political theory (the United States Constitution) and became the foundation of modern left- and right-wing liberalism and conservatism (cf. Wills 1971). Liberalism-conservatism is based on the idea of free and equal social atoms in one-dimensional and symmetrical relations of competition (with or without "equality of opportunity"), each with separable and individual responsibility for their own situation. (However, given the real relations of oppression and exploitation in our society, it eventually became necessary ideologically to show that some atoms are "genetically" less equal than others); (5) the same model of symmetrical equilibria naturally turned up in the deep structure of all economic theories seeking to justify or rationalize social relations under modern capitalism.

In a word, science, ideology, and economics all became united around a conception of the individual and the organism as isolated systems, like billiard balls governed by "forces" ("instincts" in psychology and ethology), all on the same plane of being, all separate from their own environments and from the various levels of the general environment. Organism, atom, and person became ontologically and ideologically equivalent — and explained or designated by the same overt or covert mechanical metaphors. The "freedom" of the individual was (and still is) a metaphor for her or his status as a commodity in the marketplace, measured against the linear yardstick of money or a similar general equivalent of performance. The accompanying ideology sought to homogenize and digitalize the individual, just as the factory system devalued the qualitative aspect of human labor (creativity) and made it both abstract and quantitative (cf. also the IQ test), making the laborer the equivalent of an interchangeable machine part in a social system conceived as a production line.

What is significant is that none of these basic conceptions or values has changed significantly over the last two hundred years. (Note, for instance, that both relativity and indeterminacy in physics reinforce the closed-system basis, as well as the idea that not only are all atoms equal, but that all standpoints for interpretation are also equal.) The liberalism of the university and society is still based on these notions (in spite of certain inconsistencies). The academic notion of the "free marketplace of ideas" not only reflects the fact that by the nineteenth century knowledge and art had become commodities (as detailed by Balzac in the 1820's, for example, in *Lost illusions*), but it also implies that ideas themselves are atoms. Hence the general resistance of academia to explicitly systemic interpretations of social reality (the systematic nature of the liberal ideology is allowed to remain unconscious). As Gary Wills points out (1971), this ideology of the free enterprise of people and ideas is based on the "self-regulation" of the commodities market — Adam Smith's hidden hand — in spite of the fact that if unregulated free competition actually existed, our economic system would have fallen into stagnation and collapse long ago. In a word, this whole complex of ideas and realities militates against the kind of ecosystemic understanding and behavior that are undoubtedly essential if we are to have a properly human future.

The general point of view advocated here can be summarized as a set of general requirements (Wilden 1977, 1976; d'Arge et al. 1973):

(1) There is the need to understand the multiplication or amplification of causes through feedback processes.

(2) An attempt should be made to anticipate the fact that events in one part of the whole system may be transmitted into unexpected events in other parts.

(3) The nature of organic and social complexity and the inadequacy of present methods of explaining it in detail should be recognized.

(4) A properly contextual analysis of the values and behavior of any given system should be made.

(5) It should be recognized that open systems are goal seeking and involve levels of communication and control.

(6) A distinction should be made between energy-entity explanation and communicational-relational explanation.

(7) It should be assumed that all behavior is in effect communication.

(8) It should be recognized that like a Dedekind "cut" (Schnitt) in the sequence of the real numbers, the distinction between "organism" (or "system") and "environment" is not a boundary equivalent to a barrier, but a necessary and essential locus of communication and exchange.

(9) The problem of dealing with relations between relations (i.e. between systems, environments, and ecosystems) should be recognized.

(10) The distinction between long-range and short-range effects, e.g. the potential transformation of adaptivity into counteradaptivity over time, should be understood.

(11) The protective and stabilizing nature of redundancy in such systems and the instability of efficiency as such should be recognized.

(12) It should be understood that what survives in nature is not simply the fittest individual but, more significantly, the fittest ecosystem, i.e. that what must survive above all is not the "entity" in an environment, but rather the relation between system and environment.

(13) The distinction should be made between causality and constraint, i.e. between determinism and the relative semiotic freedom of a given subsystem to produce, reproduce, and exchange within a given context of constraints.

(14) It should be recognized that levels of communication and control can be distinguished by their logical typing, and that these hierarchies of systemic relations can be reversed — at least temporarily — in human ecosystems.

This is a somewhat programmatic list, and obviously it is impossible to deal with all these questions in a short paper. But it serves to indicate what is usually unrecognized in traditional epistemology and ideology, neither of which can be properly applied to the kind of human and biological reality which is our primary concern here. One final point of major importance: if open systems seek goals, this involves values which are hierarchically ordered. Consequently, the epistemology and the science of such systems should be primarily and overtly qualitative at a level higher than that at which they are necessarily quantitative.

ENVIRONMENTAL IMPACT: LINEAR CAUSALITY AND FEEDBACK

Significantly enough, the United States federal government now requires "environmental impact" statements on all major projects in the country. But the very term "impact" reveals the traditional dependence on a mechanical conception of linear causality that simply does not apply adequately to ecosystemic relationships.

In any ecosystem or at any level of the overall ecosystem, interventions (impacts) result in reciprocal feedbacks. But the kind of causality involved in organic and social ecosystems means that this feedback is in no way comparable to the cause-and-effect relationship implied in the mechanistic term "impact," for example the impact and rebound of a rubber ball. The momentum of the ball is absorbed or dissipated through impact with a soft medium and is largely reflected through impact with a hard one. In any case, the ball returns with less than its original momentum or "force," and its return follows predictable paths. The feedback from a disturbance induced in a biosocial ecosystem is quite different. It is not primarily a sort of reflected or deflected and predictable "force." Because the system is made up of goal-seeking, reproducible, and adaptive subsystems and because both matter-energy and informational relationships are involved, ecosystemic feedback may appear as totally new and unexpected disruptions — or kinds of disruption — elsewhere in the system, or at another level in that system, as the ecosystem itself seeks to adapt to the original disturbance.

This is especially so when the difference between short-term and long-term effects in ecosystems means that the major feedback is delayed. In fact, such feedback is much more likely to be delayed than immediate, because of the capacity of ecosystems to make up for their losses temporarily by, for example, increased reproduction, altered expression of gene frequencies, or longer-term mutations. Part of the reason for this is that impacts on ecosystems do not just leave "scars" behind, like scratches on rock or craters on the moon. They also affect the future behavior of the system, and restrict or enlarge the scope or the range of its future possibilities. In mechanics causes produce changes rather than adaptations, and by the "laws" of physics, for example, no cause can change the higher- or lower-level sets of constraints that restrict the functional behavior of the system and govern its possible activities. But an ecosystemic disruption may well change some level of the ecosystem's constraints on the subsystems within it, at some level of their behavior — the "phase space" of their semiotic freedom (cf. Wilden 1977; Marney and Smith 1969).

We may elaborate this notion by making a comparison with constraints governing the expression of messages by individual goal seekers employing a common code of communication or language. The deep structure of contemporary English, for example, permits functional changes in the selections and combinations permissible in the construction of messages, i.e. it permits dialects (subcodes) or relatively different organization of messages in its surface structure (e.g. a novel, a poem, a scientific report, a textbook). It does not, however, permit structural change. Even the "word salad" of the so-called schizophrenic is a functional manifestation of the deep structure, and no matter how one tries, the basic code of English cannot be manipulated to produce messages in Chinese. This is the ultimate limit on the semiotic freedom of the speaker of English.

Similarly the four-unit code of the nucleotides and its twenty-unit articulation in the code of the amino acids is the ultimate constraint on the instructions for reproduction of all organisms, a constraint subject (at another level) to the "laws" of physics. But within this set of informational constraints, the expression of many different species is possible. The genetic code may thus be compared to the universals of language (operating in all languages), and the genetic instructions of a particular species to the deep structure of a specific language.

In natural and social ecosystems, disruptions are not necessarily, or primarily, received as the impact of matter or the transformation of energy but more importantly as messages. The kinds of adaptation that come about as the system and its subsystems seek to "obey" their goals are thus directly comparable to the way errors or noise in the transmission of an order between human beings might change one instruction into another. (The basic analogy, of course, is again with the genetic instructions in the DNA molecule, which can be wrongly "punctuated" and produce mutations.) At some point, given sufficiently high, short-term disruption or continuous low, long-term disruption, the subsystems or the ecosystem will adapt by mutating or evolving into new systems. In a social ecosystem, we call such mutations "revolutions" — as when the factory system fundamentally and irreversibly changed the face of the relations between capital and labor.

In ecosystems causes do not necessarily have specific, single, visible, predictable, or isolated effects. Moreover, given that their subsystems are goal seeking and reproducible, feedback from environmental messages may not simply be displaced, transformed, or delayed. The messages may be, and very often are, amplified during the process before they reach other parts or levels of the system or their original source. Here they reappear as new causes of other effects or as new constraints on the possibilities of the system or the source. This is in part the result of the fact that such systems involve levels of communication and constraint. A small input at the right level in the system will be multiplied and accelerated by the system's information processing capabilities. This is an aspect of what most clearly distinguishes biosocial ecosystems from mechanical or purely matter-energy systems, namely the way they employ information to constrain their own behavior and organization, to trigger and measure and time energy output, and to govern the disposition and control of the matter-energy available to the system (e.g. the biological control of phosphorus).

For example, in an economy undergoing recession, a relatively small adjustment in the bank discount rate or the allowable tax depreciation rate will usually have large effects. In recession, investment in the capital goods circuit (plant, labor, and materials) constrains the behavior of the consumer goods circuit (with feedback between them of course [cf. Tustin 1952]). Government or bank action to make liquid capital easier to get or cheaper to use encourages investment in capital goods and new labor, which reduces unemployment and increases production. Increased production increases total incomes, which increases consumption, which increases production and decreases unemployment further, and so on. At least this is so until the positive feedback effects of rising real wages and the tendency of production to overshoot possible consumption, along with other factors, begin to reduce the rate of profit and make outlets for capital investment scarcer or less attractive at the very moment when industry is beginning to overproduce. In a given national system, the result is another recession—the expression of negative feedback—with too little money chasing too many consumer goods.

This is a classic case of the inapplicability of the linear causal model to ecosystems. Government action in, for example, making money cheaper at a given point in a recession cannot be properly called a "cause" at all. The government's action is not a force driving the system to change, because the system is not an entity that can be pushed or pulled around (like a billiard ball), but rather a set of relations. Rather, the government action involves changes in a set of informational constraints at a specific level. There are many goal-seeking subsystems (corporations) in the economic ecosystem which are placed in a more favorable potential profit position by the government action. Consequently, a large number will freely follow their own judgment and (yet) be "induced to invest." Some will act in order to get the jump on their competitors. Others, if they are monopolies, for example, will be provided with necessary outlets for accumulated investment capital. Each corporation will have acted not because it was caused to do so but because the degree of semiotic freedom or available flexibility for it to follow certain courses was raised, or the constraint on its possible courses of action at a specific level was lowered.

We might carelessly say that the government's action had "an impact on" the economy, but that is an ingrained habit of speech not a scientific statement. The term "impact" itself is a metaphor for the kind of linear relation of causality between self-subsistent entities (involving, for example, momentum, mass, inertia, gravity) described by the Newtonian mechanics on which physics was first founded. What happens to a causal impact — say between two billiard balls — in a mechanical system? The impact has a certain effect (e.g. cue ball strikes eight ball), but the fundamental operation is the dissipation of one kind of energy into the mechanical environment by its transformation into another kind, usually in the form of unusable heat ("bound energy," which is energy no longer capable of work).

This process is a one-way, irreversible, nonretransformable conversion of energy. The change in the discount rate is something quite different. Since it involves information, it is itself reversible and retransformable. It is multidimensional (affecting some parts of the economic system, such as banks, differently from others) and (at least) two-way: it feeds back, for example, as an effect on both government revenues and political stability apart from its effects on the accumulation of capital.

But there is a significant difference in the definition of the reversibility and transformation of the systems involved (as distinct from the definition of that which changed their disposition). Other matters being equal, time and place have no significance for the single-level billiard ball system (which has no internal source of energy and seeks no goals in its behavior). The application of the same force will always — i.e. with a very high statistical probability — produce the same result, so that its application in the opposite direction will always return the system to its original state. This is not the case with the multidimensional economic system, nor with any biosocial ecosystem. Such systems have an essential relation to both time and place, and no transformation of the system is ever truly reversible. The same input at different times will not have the same results, except in very general terms (e.g. the economy is "expanding" or "contracting"). The introduction of an identical input at different levels of communication in the system will also produce different results, as may its introduction into different subsystems within the whole. Moreover, the way in which ecosystems use information to control their organization, development, and reproduction, means that a given input may eventually come to affect itself, — a relation that is impossible in a linear, mechanical system.

In an unlimited environment these differences between the two types of system and inputs may not be more than theoretically significant. Moreover, so long as the environment is believed to be unlimited, like Newtonian space — i.e. so long as people believe that unlimited future transformations and expansions are possible — then the theoretical difference will *not in general be perceived or recognized at all.* In consequence, people will tend to model the second, highly complex ecosystemic relation on the first, the mechanical relation, which is more simple, more immediate, and more "visible." Only when the entire system begins to approach its own limits will the enormous range of practical effects implicit in this theoretical difference begin to be generally recognized — by which time, of course, it may well be too late to do anything about them.

THE IDEOLOGY OF GROWTH

Historically, belief in the automatic benefits of growth and in increasing economic efficiency through technology have each performed the same ideological function. Growth in the contemporary sense of increased production, increased capital investment, and expanding markets, has traditionally been used by apologists for our economic system to explain away economic inequality in the distribution of incomes. Any suggestion of limiting growth thus puts the entire fabric of their argument in question. The argument has traditionally run as follows: economic expansion and continued development of technology provide the only true road to economic justice. As production and sales rise, the economic divergence between the incomes of the affluent and the incomes of the poor will necessarily tend to decrease. As the rich get richer, the poor will also get richer.

The proponents of this theory have characteristically ignored the considerable evidence which shows that, under our present type of development, growth has historically created greater and greater economic disparity between the "haves" and "have nots." Their illusions about increased economic justice have always depended on an explicit or implicit isolation of part of the economic system from its total context. Thus, before the publication of Michael Harrington's *The other America* in the early 1960's, the official line of apologists for the American system was that economic expansion had made poverty negligible in the United States.

French apologists for the economics of neocolonialism in Africa use similar arguments. They have made much of the "economic miracle" of the Ivory Coast, for example. They have conveniently forgotten that recent increased per capita income in that country is unevenly distributed between the white capitalists and their local *compradores*, on the one hand, and the local (especially rural) population on the other (Vignes 1972). They have also neglected the size and effects of the repatriation of profits to the industrialized countries, to say nothing of the wholesale destruction of the forests of the Ivory Coast by European lumber companies.

This last feature of the European exploitation of the Ivory Coast is particularly significant. It is estimated that the exploitation of the forests will result in their effective disappearance within eight or ten years. Lumber exports represent about 20 percent of all exports, a figure that happens to be equivalent to almost the entire surplus of exports over imports in the trade of the Ivory Coast. Thus, Jacques Vignes can go on to argue effectively that the current economic prosperity of the country can be said to depend almost entirely on the destruction of its limited forest reserves (1972).

The "economic miracle" of the Ivory Coast, a country now busy seeking trade and contact with South Africa through French intermediaries, typifies the economic dilemma of most of the former colonies in Africa; these are characterized by economic growth through energy-intensive European exploitation of natural and human resources, without any accompanying real economic development of the country.

This example reinforces the necessity for contextual explanations of the system-environment relations involved. The only properly critical scientific judgments that can be made about the economics of the Ivory Coast must include its situation as an object of Western and Westernized industrial exploitation. French economic planners create an unscientific and invalid model of an "economic miracle" by concealing the total set of relationships involved. They treat the Ivory Coast as if it were an isolated, self-regulating system, whereas it is in fact an environment controlled by foreign industrialists from outside the country who regulate the form and character of its supposed development. In this sense, the Ivory Coast is defined by the industrial countries, on the model of "mastery over nature by mankind," as a "nature" for "mankind" to pillage in the quest for profit.

From the moment that the ideology of growth and expansion into all environments — geographical, technological, organizational, and temporal — can no longer legitimately be used, like the Christian idea of heaven, as a justification of present economic inequities by the promise of future blessedness, then all the values of Western society are put on trial.

USE VALUE AND EXCHANGE VALUE

Many people anxious about the human future — to say nothing of the present — find themselves explicitly or implicitly in an "anticapitalist" or "anti-Western" position. Unfortunately, this position is most often a purely ideological stance — sometimes even revealing an unconscious identity with the mythical ethic of free enterprise under early capitalism — and is not very often based on an adequate critical analysis of the deep structures of socioeconomic organization in our society. Ideas have an important role to play in change, but the finest set of ideas can have no effect unless the economic constraints on the system are also changing. If, for example, Keynesian economic theory had not been necessary to save capitalism from its own inherent instability — necessary in the sense that it codified and explained what people in the world of politics and business were already doing — it is unlikely that we would ever have heard of Keynes. Consequently, it is worth remarking on a few of the significant basic characteristics of state and private capitalism in order to correct the deficiencies of purely ideological approaches to futuristics and at the same time show that the economic conditions for radical change are indeed being produced by the logic of capital itself.[1]

In spite of similarities with other socioeconomic systems — especially in surface structure (cf. Sahlins [1972] on market exchange as distinct from a market economy) — the industrial capitalism that evolved from mercantile capitalism displays unique characteristics,

Briefly, any division of labor in any society results in processes of exchange within it. The division of labor may be the result of biological differences in the process of natural reproduction; it may be the result of myth, ritual, training, initiation, and kinship rules in the reproduction of ideology (tradition) and socioeconomic organization; or it may be the result of specialization in economic activities (cooking, hunting, crafts, and so on). In kinship-controlled societies, the modes of production, reproduction, and distribution are in general all constrained by the collective control of the means of production (nature, technology, technique). In a monetary economy of simple commodity production, the individual producers control their means of production and sell one commodity in order to buy another they need, e.g. one sells clothing to buy food, another sells food to buy tools, and so on.

The system of exchange in such economies is governed by the

---

[1]   In what follows I have deliberately avoided basing the argument on the labor theory of value (the self-evident idea that only human labor can expand the value of raw materials so as to produce commodities, including the machines used in manufacture) in order to avoid the possibility of the argument being sidetracked into an irrelevant discussion about "value" and "price."

necessity of circulation, as in any kind of biosocial organization including all communication systems; but here the circulation of goods and
people is constrained by naturally and socially defined real needs.
Moreover, different spheres of exchange — e.g. food, weapons,
"wealth objects," marriage and descent — remain separated from one
another. There is no general equivalent of all exchanges (like money in
our economy) which can make of any relationship a commodity
relationship. (Cf. the *kula* in Malinowski [1961] where the two kinds
of shell circulate as information, fulfilling a linking and organizational
function within and between groups and persons. In Australia, correlations have been made between the degree of informational complexity
of social structure and the environment, such that a given individual in
a harsh environment may be the marker, or bearer, of well over 100
"bits" of relational information binding him to others within the social
structure.) In such systems, exchangeable items therefore circulate
primarily in terms of their social and economic use value (or "utility")
in the ecological-economic system as a whole (cf. Rappaport 1968).
They are exchanged primarily on the basis of their qualitative differences from each other. If money is involved, one sells in order to buy.
Both the concrete social function of such exchange, as a system, and
the individual's subjective consciousness of what is involved are therefore closely connected.

Under modern capitalism, including state capitalism in the socialist
countries, a new factor appears: exchange value measured against the
yardstick of money. The dominance of use value over economic
exchange value in noncapitalist systems is inverted. With money as a
general equivalent, it is possible for all social and ecological relations
to become commoditized. Land, labor power, and capital (capital in
the dual sense of productive capacity and control over it) are shaken
from their original, ecologically defined, hierarchical relation to one
another by the historical process of commoditization. Although land
(photosynthesis) is ultimately the necessary condition of labor power,
and labor power the necessary condition of capital, commoditization
inverted the hierarchy of constraint at the same time as it symmetrized
each of these three basic conditions for society by reducing them to the
single plane of interchangeable commodities. This process reduced to a
single dimension what had been socially — and still is ultimately —
defined as an ensemble of levels (or logical types) of constraint and
control between which no ultimate "tradeoffs" are possible (no amount
of labor or capital can be "traded off" against photosynthesis, for
example).

In this way the use value of all exchangeable items, including people,
became dominated by their monetary exchange value. Originally and
primitively represented in the merchant, and later in the industrialist,

the "capitalist" does not sell in order to buy, he buys in order to sell — and he sells for profit. Simply put, the class of capitalists — a complex and nonhomogeneous set of people in whom capital is "embodied" — enter the market with money. Money is used to buy the two essential commodities necessary to production: the total "means of production" represented by (1) the labor power of the worker as a commodity (wages and costs, called "variable capital"), and (2) the required capital goods (machinery and so on, called "constant" or "fixed" capital or "manufacturing assets").

The capitalist mode of production — its means of production and associated social relations of production — organizes labor power and machinery to produce other commodities from raw materials. The expanded (exchange) value represented in these commodities is then "realized" (i.e. extracted) on the market in the form of money. This money is then available for consumption by the capitalist in various ways, but also, and more important, it is available for reinvestment in a further quantity of constant and variable capital. Until it is so invested, money remains as money (liquid capital). When it is invested in new capital goods in the basic processes of production it becomes new industrial or agricultural capital — the most important kinds of capital. Thus there is a fundamental distinction between the accumulation of money and the accumulation of capital as such, because money, like knowledge and information, may accumulate almost indefinitely without taxing its environments. In contrast, the accumulation of productive capacity eventually generates a localized or generalized overtaxing of the "resource environment" (that which constrains the input of raw materials) and the interlinked "sink environment" (that which constrains material circulation rates and the output of wastes).

Remembering the distinction between money and capital, we can see why both Aristotle and Marx labeled this type of process (whether mercantile or capitalist) as "unlimited." Money — in the sense of that which can be converted into capital through investment in plant and machinery — is the beginning and end of the process. The relationship commodity-money-commodity, based on the primacy of the exchange of use value (selling to buy), becomes converted to money-commodity-money (capital), based on the primacy of exchange value (buying to sell). And whereas there are limits on the expansion of use values, there are no such immediate limits on the expansion of exchange values.

Capital governs the circulation of commodities so that it may be expanded. The qualitative differences in the various use values represented by commodities and labor power are consequently reduced to quantitative differences ("price"). Commodities therefore serve in the main as instruments of the expansion of capital, their use value being on the whole a mere secondary or subordinated characteristic. Hence the well-known tendency of capitalism to produce more and more essentially useless goods under a system of planned obsolescence, and to rely on advertising and other means to make such goods "needed," not by responding to the requirements of the consumer but rather by adapting the consumer to the requirements of the system.

The expanded value realized in the market is never simply that which is required to replace worn-out, depreciated, or outmoded capital equipment, for the accumulation of capital is not like simple interest on money. Nor, as it turns out, is it like compound interest (exponential increase). Because of the logic of expansion, capital accumulation always tends towards superexponential increases (increases in the rate of accumulation). This is so even though capitalism is prevented by its own logic from actually realizing this kind of increase in any given industry, country, or market (i.e. in any relatively closed system).

By "capitalism," of course, we refer to the system as a whole, not to a particular person or group. And "capital" refers both to the power over organization represented by capital (the organization of organization) and to the means of exercising that power. In the wide sense, then, "capital" refers not to a thing, but to a system of relations organized by power. Since its rules of relation and rules of production are based entirely on exchange value for profit under competition, then objectively the capitalist mode of production is a system of expanding exchange value which the individual capitalist or corporation does not control. An analogy might be made between the capitalist and an individual speaker of a language (an example used by Marx).[2] Our semiotic freedom to produce, communicate, and exchange words and messages is governed by the different levels of constraint in the deep structure of the language system. This is a set of constraints of which we are unconscious, and which no particular set of individuals controls. Similarly, the individual corporation is subject to basic economic constraints beyond its own control, and ultimately beyond even the power of oligopolic relations in the economy. These constraints are systemic — embodied and imbedded in the system as a whole and not in individuals or groups as such.

Certainly the "human nature" of individual investors or managers has nothing to do with the workings of advanced capitalism. It is

---

[2] In this sense we are not concerned with the "laws of motion" of our economic system, but rather with its deep structure or grammar. The question then becomes that of considering to what extent the constraints embodied in the grammar of the economic system ultimately fall inside or outside the (higher-level) grammar or deep structure of its environment — "higher level" in the sense that the grammar of inorganic and organic nature ultimately constrains all other viable or long-term grammars possible in the universe.

perhaps not even true to say that capital is based mainly on the maximization of profit as such. More fundamental to the workings of the system is the fact, recognized by most economists, that the accumulation of capital within a given system is an overall positive feedback process with its own, lower-level, negative feedback controls. Economists will say that there is a tendency for the rate of profit to fall as capital accumulates in any particular business cycle. Consequently, in order to protect the overall process of accumulation, new outlets for investment capital must constantly be found. The system must expand if it is to remain viable in its own terms. This positive-negative feedback relation may certainly be referred to by such terms as the "need for maximization of (the rate of) profit." But what is more fundamentally involved is the need to protect profitability itself, the need to protect the continuing possibility of profit. This is the sense in which economists agree that capitalism must expand to ensure its own stability; and the positive feedback of accumulation at this level is not constrained by the logic of the system itself but only — and ultimately — by that of its environment.

As a result, there is a tendency to oscillating instability, stemming from the tendency toward underconsumption (overproduction, recession) in the business cycle. Capitalism also tends toward disproportionality between the capital goods and consumer goods circuits. The production and consumption of capital goods (the locus of accumulation) has historically tended to increase at a faster rate than the production and consumption of consumer goods. What makes the system even more unstable and dependent on expansion is the fact that not simply one kind of capital or one kind of industrial production is involved, but many. These different types of capital remain in competition with one another. If a given monopoly restricts investment in its own area, for example, then other free capital will seek out less restricted areas, in retailing or new industries, for example. Thus, at every level, the capitalist system tends to promote its own uneven development, creating new depressed areas and industries, such as railroads, within its own sphere (cf. Mandel 1962: 705–722).

It might be expected that the system would "learn" to avoid such disruptive cycles by greater foresight. Historically this has never happened because of the constant appearance and creation of new markets for capital, especially just as the system begins to recover from recession (e.g. the Second World War). New markets for capital include: (1) geographical extension (into noncapitalist areas or into less advanced areas of capitalism, such as the American invasion of both the Third World and Europe); (2) new industries resulting from technological advances and necessities, such as integrated circuits, pollution control; (3) realignments or bankruptcies of domestic and international competitors; (4) government defense spending; (5) other government programs, including antipoverty projects, freeways, and so on; and (6) population growth.

The export of capital is an especially important factor. It reduces the amount of spare capital seeking investment in the home country, which would normally put pressure on the labor market and drive up the cost of labor, tending to bring about a crisis. But workers are not generally free to move from one area of the world to another; consequently, wage rates are never equalized globally. Thus, in a systemic and general sense, the export of capital has the effect of maintaining the domestic rate of profit as well as providing high profits from low wage costs abroad. A high rate of profit at home may also assist a corporation in underselling its foreign competitors abroad, if necessary by "dumping" — with or without government assistance through subsidies. The raw materials controlled by exported capital in the Third World do not simply provide an essential source of supply, but are also an essential source of profit. With the low wages and high profits in the Third World a corporation is protected from the dangers of underconsumption (it has greater freedom to control prices, for example), and it is doubly protected from this effect of overaccumulation because of the vast possibilities for new investment in industrialization in such countries.

THE PARADOX OF ACCUMULATION

The contradictions inherent in the (continued) growth of capital for the sake of capital — or of production for the sake of production, rather than for the sake of human beings — are truly paradoxical. Logically it means that the economic system views itself as a closed system operating in an infinite environment (much like a diesel-generating plant supplied with unlimited resources of cooling water, spare parts, and fuel), whereas in fact it is an open matter-energy and informational system in a finite environment.

Paradoxes involve situations where, if you take one side of the question, you are then forced logically to take the other side, and so on, without limit. The paradox involved here is that if capitalism is to survive, it can neither obey nor disobey its own organizational imperative — growth. Whereas purely contradictory relationships in both logical and ecological systems can in principle continue indefinitely, paradoxical relations in ongoing systems sooner or later move the system to a point where it can continue to survive only by a radical transformation to a new level of organization, one where the particular paradox is no longer in effect because the original constraints controlling it no longer operate.

This notion depends on the "theory of the double bind" developed by Gregory Bateson (1972). Consider the following example: a child gets two T-shirts as a birthday present, instead of the expected fancy leather boots. The next morning, swallowing his disappointment and trying hard to please, the child appears at breakfast wearing one of the shirts. There's a heavy silence for a moment — then, just as the first mouthful of Cracky Crispies goes crunch, one of the parents looks across the table with a complicated air of "we've-been-through-all-this-before" or "how-come-you-never-do-anything-right" or "when-are-you-ever-going-to-shape-up-kid," and says: "What's the matter? You didn't like the other one?"

Here we see the use of logic as an instrument of oppression: the use of double binds against a "victim" in a context of power and pathological communication. Double binds are explicit or implicit paradoxical commands (not contradictions): commands that, within a given context of communication and at a specific level, can be neither obeyed nor disobeyed (like a freeway sign saying "Disregard this sign," or the well-known paradox in ordinary logic: "I'm a Cretan. All Cretans are liars."). The widespread potential for such commands stems in part from the fact that, as Warren McCulloch pointed out, every message in any communications system, linguistic or biological, is both a report about a situation and a command to do something about it (which may of course be nothing). So long as the victim accepts the context, which is defined for him or her at more abstract levels of communication and constraint than that at which the double bind is communicated, there is no escape. Such a situation sets up a self-perpetuating oscillation between impossible alternatives; if you take one, you are then forced to take the other, which returns you to the first.

Frantz Fanon (1967) located the fundamental double bind of white colonialism (foreign or domestic) in the implicit message of the white power structure: "turn white or disappear." Women's Liberation members have analyzed the paradoxical injunction imposed upon them by sexism, which subjects each female to an impossible, schizoid — as distinct from normoid — either/or choice between being the woman-as-mother (sexless mom) and the woman-as-whore (supersexy chick). So long as she is programmed to accept this male definition of the context of constraint, the woman will live out a culturally sanctioned schizophrenic existence, oscillating between a "self" and an "other" (as in *The three faces of Eve*), one of which is the proverbial "other woman." The way to get out of a double bind is through the door. One has to refuse the context, deny the levels of control, break the rules and metarules that define the permissible communication in the system, escape the trap of trying to respond at the same level. In a word, one must metacommunicate (cf. Wilden and Wilson 1976).

We can translate this analysis into a socioeconomic perspective by comparing the positive-negative feedbacks of the business cycles of boom and recession around the exponential growth trajectory of the accumulation of productive capacity — produced by the "challenge of profitability" or the "challenge to accumulate" — with the "challenge to perform" in alcoholism. Bateson views alcoholism as the product of a battle between "mind" — the alcoholic's self-control, his or her ability to perform according to the dictates of our system — and "body" — the bottle with which the alcoholic is in a relation of competitive symmetry. Even the implied injunction in the word "self-control" (cf. Wills 1971) depends on the schizoid dualism between mind and body in our culture (Wilden 1977). But as Alcoholics Anonymous has always insisted, this battle between mind and matter cannot be won. So long as the alcoholic sees control over drinking as a challenge, all is lost. Taking up the challenge to his power of "self-control" means going on the wagon. And once on the wagon, he is at one pole of a double bind. Having met the challenge, he has destroyed it; there is no longer an opponent against which to measure his "strength of character." The contextual structure of sobriety has been transformed by its achievement. Hence the only way of checking one's ability to conform to the linearized symmetries of the performance principle of our society (Marcuse 1962) is to recreate the challenge, to start drinking again. Thus, the alcoholic oscillates interminably between his "self" and his "other" — "the Demon Drink" — unless he can break the double bind by metacommunication, by going beyond it. That is precisely what the religious experience of AA is all about.

We can see that our economic system is in exactly the same paradoxical relation to its own future, as Marx points out (1962: vol. 1, pp. 504–506, vol. 3, pp. 242–245) when he deals with the economics and the ecology of capital. In a finite environment, the economy cannot continue to expand. If capital accumulation continues, it necessarily reduces the future flexibility of its own relationship to the natural and social environments. It trades adaptivity for counteradaptivity by reducing the scope of its own future potential for change. As a result, it may well destroy us all. On the other hand, if the capitalist system were "voluntarily" to stop expanding, it would cease to exist as "capitalist" — its deep economic structure would necessarily have been restructured (cf. Wilden and Wilson 1976).

CONCLUSION

The only long-term solution, it would seem, is the emergence of an economic system based on the circulation of socioeconomic use values rather than one primarily based on the production and circulation of economic exchange values. But this likely imperative involves more than commodities as such; it also involves people. At present, all forms of labor — skilled and unskilled, manual and intellectual, individual and collective — are effectively reduced to exchange values or commodities that are bought and sold in a marketplace structured by the challenge to perform under quantitatively measured competition. But labor potential is in essence qualitative and creative; it is not a commodity *per se*, and only becomes one in the context of the power of capital to expropriate and control it.

It is the creativity of labor potential that makes each of us, not an abstract individual — not an economic abstraction exchanging human value for monetary exchange value, not a commodity in the economic machinery worth a specific, competitively defined, quantity of dollars per hour to a part of the system over which we have no control — but a qualitatively differentiated individual, inseparable in the long run from our dependence on complex and undefinable sets of nonexploitative communications and exchanges with our fellow human beings, and ultimately with nature.

However, so long as quantified labor potential circulates as the primary commodity in the social ecosystem, and so long as nature remains commoditized — rather than simply used — it is impossible to see how any viable array of properly human solutions to our economic-ecological crisis will be available to us. We have to discover a way of circulating between each other the qualitative component of labor potential: the creative aspect of the human ability to organize and "in-form" matter and energy and relations. This is the aspect of labor potential expressed when we give form (i.e. organization) to an amorphous lump of clay on a potters's wheel, for example. The same organizing power, in a systemic sense, was at the roots of human evolution at the time when we collectively evolved from the simple levels of group organization found among gregarious animals, to complex forms of social organization based on social and ecological use values, as distinct from the commodity exchange values of the modern economy.

These are the forms of value-for-use employed and expressed in the evolution of a division of labor going beyond the procreative division of labor; in the systems of kinship that organize and control the production and reproduction of the means of life and society itself; in the production of economic surpluses going beyond biological needs, providing goods that can be exchanged as information-bearing gifts — as links — in redistributive relations between individuals and groups (cf. Malinowski [1961]; Sahlins [1972]); and in the organization of the exchange and communication of other kinds of information: words, knowledge, symbols.

In a society based on the circulation of creativity and the true recognition of human diversity and difference, the economic abstraction and reification represented by the so-called free and equal autonomous individual — the modern "self" — would disappear. In such a society, the exploitation of nature, class, race, and sex as we know them could no longer exist. For, in matters of creative capacity, as distinct from the ability to perform in a rigid economic system of caste and class, all human beings are truly equal.

Moreover, such a change in the deep structure of the socioeconomic system would reintroduce into the ecosystem of society-plus-nature many of the factors we believe to be responsible for the long-range survival of natural ecosystems: the diversity of species, the redundancy of pathways for exchange, the heterogeneity of relations, the constrained use of materials and energy, and the preponderance of constrained competition, symbiosis, and systemic cooperation and coevolution in nature.

In contrast, whether we single out energy-intensive monoculture in food production, or the spreading of the deep structure of wage labor and capital throughout the world, we see little more than an increasing reduction of diversity and stability in the world ecosystem by the effects of nonnatural competition. For, whereas competition in nature clearly contributes to long-range stability by encouraging diversification, the unprecedented kind of systemic economic competition defined by the present dominant mode of production and exchange is clearly contributing to the homogenization or "eutrophication" of the planet and its peoples.

Consequently, what ultimately faces us is clearly not the question of restoring or maintaining the "delicate balance of nature." Natural systems are not delicately balanced; rather they are ruggedly "inefficient" and "wasteful" systems of enormous redundancy. The myth of the delicate balance of nature is simply one more instance of projection. What is in fact delicately balanced and potentially unstable is not the environment — which will "save" itself no matter what we choose to do — but rather the relationship between our economic system, as such, and all its environments: nature, human beings, the future.

REFERENCES

BATESON, GREGORY
  1972   *Steps to an ecology of mind.* New York: Ballantine.
D'ARGE, RALPH, R. J. ANDERSON N, JR., S. BLACK, *et al.*
  1973   "Design of urban ecosystem indicators." National Science Foundation-Institute of Ecology, Urban Ecosystems Workshop, Austin, Texas.

FANON, FRANTZ
1967 *Black skins, white masks.* New York: Grove.
HARRINGTON, MICHAEL
1962 *The other America.* Harmondsworth: Penguin.
LEISS, WILLIAM
1972 *The domination of nature.* New York: Braziller.
LÉVI-STRAUSS, CLAUDE
1969 *The elementary structures of kinship.* Boston: Beacon.
LUKÁCS, GEORG
1971 *History and class consciousness.* London: Merlin.
MALINOWSKI, BRONISLAW
1961 *Argonauts of the western Pacific.* New York: Dutton.
MANDEL, ERNEST
1962 *Marxist economic theory.* London: Merlin.
MARCUSE, HERBERT
1962 *Eros and civilization.* New York: Vintage.
MARNEY, M. C., N. M. SMITH
1969 "The domain of adaptive systems: a rudimentary taxonomy," in *General systems yearbook* 9: 107–131.
MARX, KARL
1962 *Capital,* volumes one and three. London: Lawrence and Wishart.
MEADOWS, D. H., D. L. MEADOWS, J. RANDERS, W. W. BEHRENS
1972 *The limits to growth.* New York: Universe Books.
RAPPAPORT, ROY A.
1968 *Pigs for the ancestors.* New Haven: Yale University Press.
SAHLINS, MARSHALL
1972 *Stone Age economics.* Chicago: Aldine.
SHEPARD, PAUL, DANIEL McKINLEY, *editors*
1969 *The subversive science.* New York: Houghton Mifflin.
TUSTIN, ARNOLD
1952 Feedback. *Scientific American* 187: 48–55.
VAYDA, ANDREW P., *editor*
1969 *Environment and cultural behavior.* Garden City, New York: Natural History Press.
VIGNES, JACQUES
1972 Article in *AfricAsia,* January 10.
WILDEN, ANTHONY
1976 "Communication in context: a systems perspective." Mimeographed.
1977 *System and structure: essays in communication and exchange.* London and New York: Social Science Paperbacks.
WILDEN, ANTHONY, TIM WILSON
1976 "The double bind: logic, magic, and economics," in *The double bind.* Edited by Carlos Sluzki and D. C. Ransom. New York: Grune and Stratton.
WILLS, GARY
1971 *Nixon agonistes.* New York: Signet.

Futurism in Man: Humanism, Social Technology, and Survival

ARTHUR M. HARKINS

If I were asked to select a number of contemporary thinkers who have had considerable impact on my recent life the process would be fairly easy, and would result in the following list: Maruyama, Fuller, Clarke, Reiser, and Helmer. In one way or another all these names are associated with attempts to unscramble many confusions about human life on and off Earth, about the ecology of our planet, and about the nature of man himself. What is man? Implicit and explicit treatments of this question are in some fashion a part of the concerns of each of the thinkers I have singled out. What is man? Let R. B. Fuller answer;

Man?
    A self-balancing, 28-jointed adapter-base biped; an electrochemical reduction-plant, integral with segregated stowages of special energy extracts in storage batteries, for subsequent actuation of thousands of hydraulic and pneumatic pumps, with motors attached; 62,000 miles of capillaries; millions of warning signal, railroad and conveyor systems; crushers and cranes (of which the arms are magnificent 23-jointed affairs with self-surfacing and lubricating systems, and a universally distributed telephone system needing no service for 70 year if well managed); the whole, extraordinarily complex mechanism guided with exquisite precision from a turret in which are located telescopic and microscopic self-registering and recording range finders, a spectroscope, et cetera, the turret control being closely allied with an air conditioning intake-and-exhaust, and a main fuel intake.
    Within the few cubic inches housing the turret mechanisms, there is room, also, for two sound-wave and sound-direction-finder recording diaphragms, a filing and instant reference system, and an expertly devised analytical laboratory large enough not only to contain minute records of every last and continual event of up to 70 years' experience, or more, but to extend, by computation and abstract fabrication, this experience with relative accuracy into all corners of the observed universe. There is, also, a forecasting and tactical plotting department for the reduction of future possibilities and probabilities to generally successful specific choice.

Common to all such "human" mechanisms — and without which they are imbecile contraptions — is their guidance by a phantom captain.

This phantom captain has neither weight nor sensorial tangibility, as has often been scientifically proven by careful weighing operations at the moment of abandonment of the ship by the phantom captain, i.e., at the instant of "death." He may be likened to the variant of polarity dominance in our bipolar electric world which, when balanced vanishes as abstract unity I or 0. With the phantom captain's departure, the mechanism becomes inoperative and very quickly disintegrates into basic chemical elements (1971).

Is this man? In the past I have read these short selections from R. B. Fuller's *Nine chains to the moon* to my students and received responses largely of horror, amusement, or disbelief. In this day of incredibly rapid social and technological change I rather imagine that a serious reading of Fuller's definition of man in effect fights fire with fire; one may emerge from momentary paralysis, as I did, with a more functional and sympathetic viewpoint on the creature of our concern. In the last half of the twentieth century, we are beset with many alternative ways of regarding humanity in its homogeneous and disparate senses. Perhaps Fuller does us a favor with his mischievous but compellingly respectful dissection of the only creature on this planet allegedly possessed of "real culture."

Here in the post-industrializing West, particularly in the United States, the comparative affluence produced by industrialism has resulted in so many "successes" that old forms of human homogeneity and diversity are being pressed on all sides by new social patterns. White ethnic groups, once at the bottom of the class hierarchy in large cities, persons of blue-collar and rural ghetto circumstances alike find themselves engulfed in the waves of newly proliferating groups: youth movements, gay liberation, hippies, women's liberation, blacks, Indians and other minorities, urban gangs, and many more. There are also signs of still greater pluralism to come — systems analysts, human components in man-machine interactions, a burgeoning leisure class, corporate radicalism, the rise of the technician, and the coming of the cyborg and genetic control — heralding for some the emergence of a golden age and for others the beginning of *Level VII* or *THX 1138*. Reacting characteristically to this confusing explosion of rearranged and new human styles, Loren Eiseley has expressed his own particular anxiety about what man is and might become:

Man, at last, is face to face with himself in natural guise. "What we make natural, we destroy," said Pascal. He knew with superlative insight, man's complete necessity to transcend the worldly image that this word connotes. It is not the outward powers of man the toolmaker that threaten us. It is a growing danger which has already afflicted vast areas of the world — the danger that we have created an unbearable last idol for our worship. That idol, that uncreate and ruined visage which confronts us daily, is no less than man made natural.

Beyond this replica of ourselves, this countenance already grown so distantly inhuman that it terrifies us, still beckons the lonely figure of man's dreams. It is a nature, not of this age, but of the becoming — the light once glimpsed by a creature just over the threshold from a beast, a despairing cry from the dark shadow of a cross on Golgotha long ago.

Man is not totally compounded of the nature we profess to understand. Man is always partly of the future, and the future he possesses a power to shape. "Natural" is a magician's word — and like all such entities, it should be used sparingly lest there arise from it, as now, some unglimpsed, unintended world, some monstrous caricature called into being by the indiscreet articulation of worn syllables. Perhaps, if we are wise, we will prefer to stand like those forgotten humble creatures who poured little gifts of flints into a grave. Perhaps there may come to us then, in some such moment, a ghostly sense that an invisible doorway has been opened — a doorway which, widening out, will take man beyond the nature that he knows (Eiseley 1970: 180–181).

It is precisely Eiseley's conservatism, contrasted with the eager, flexible, and good-naturedly aggressive approach of Fuller that raises a point which is obvious to us all in some fashion: that the answer to the question "what is man?" can partially be found in terms of explicit and implicit constraints on the *flexibility* and therefore the *alternative futures* of man. Conceptual differences over the nature of man and his concomitant alternatives were brought to the level of national discussion by the emergence in 1971 of another book by the behaviorist, B. F. Skinner. In his novel, *Walden II*, Skinner indicated years ago his preference for a form of social technology (or social cybernetics) which would level out the highs and lows in human society and ensure law and order and survival. In *Beyond freedom and dignity*, Skinner pleads for an official definition of mankind which would recognize the programming effects of culture and environment and the spuriousness of notions of unlimited human alternatives. Following this he suggests that positive reinforcement be employed to generate a man-made social environment that would take into account the need to stabilize man's behavior through engineering of the programmatic context itself. The mechanism for this redirection of mankind would be social experimentation:

An experimental analysis shifts the determination of behavior from autonomous man to the environment — an environment responsible both for the evolution of the species and for the repertoire acquired by each member (1971: 214).

Skinner and Fuller are in agreement on where we should begin in our attempts to improve the human condition: don't attempt to change man; change his circumstances.

Perhaps we should look to a common source for some assistance in our search for answers to the question "what is man?" The *Unabridged*

Random House dictionary of the English language (1967) refers to man's "high position" *vis-à-vis* other animals, to his exceptional mentality, and to his singularity. This same source identifies things human as having to do with man's interests in human welfare, values, and *dignity*. Humanitarian interests are *operational* interests, we read, aimed at converting the high thoughts of humanism into practical changes in men's lives. In *Social technology*, Olaf Helmer is concerned with what he regards as epistemological errors in the social sciences. Such errors adversely affect the capability of these sciences to contribute to the employment of humanitarian goals intended to improve man's interests, values, and dignity. With characteristic economy of style, Helmer identifies a central misconception about the style and task of the social sciences:

In the first place, the comparison of the social with the physical sciences is a spurious one, based on an epistemological misconception regarding the nature and purpose of scientific activity. Second — and this is the crucial point —there is every reason to believe that, by effecting specific changes in attitudes and procedures, we can substantially narrow the gap between physical technology and sociopolitical progress (Helmer 1966: 4).

Helmer's statement of the problem follows a short discussion of what he considers to be the essentially pessimistic outlook on mankind's current condition and future possibilities of many social scientists and intellectuals. Given what is already known about self-fulfilling social prophecy, we are told, pessimistic and passive outlooks must be tempered by something else. It is to this end that Helmer devotes himself in *Social technology* and other works concerned with the development of intentional epistemologies and methodologies designed to galvanize social scientists in the interests of man's quest for a desirable future. In similar critical style, Magoroh Maruyama says that:

. . . scientific "training" often tends to make the student internalize as a *moral* principle the ready-made methodology of his field of specialization. Such an indoctrinated student would feel guilty about deviating from that particular methodology and may even consider the methodologies of other fields of specialization to be morally inferior. Human futuristics must devise ways to prevent such fixations and to help people *unlearn* them ("Toward human futuristics," this volume).

Maruyama's observations tend to support the idea of freedom and dignity for human beings to develop common and disparate relationships with one another. While he proposes no step-by-step means of achieving this mixture of human similarity and diversity, Maruyama goes a long way toward exposing some straw men that dichotomize cultural components — such as young and old, black and white, male and female, communist and capitalist, hippie and square, past and future, and so on. It is Maruyama's contention that as men we can share certain broad cultural understandings while pursuing forms of pluralism unimaginably more diverse than those common today or on the postindustrial horizon.

In 1966 Oliver Reiser published *Cosmic humanism*, an attempt to develop an *operational* "pantheistic" point of view on mankind and its problems in the twentieth century. Eschewing the "paralyzing relativism" that so many clear thinkers of our times feel themselves obliged to accept, Reiser argues for a synthesis of all things into "cosmic" or "scientific humanism." "A faith," he says, "in the intelligibility of social evolution is necessary to a stabilization of the world of the future" (1966: 9). Central to the development of clear, intelligent understanding are the social sciences. For Reiser, the goal of scientific or cosmic humanism is to "apply knowledge for the purpose of controlling social change" (1966: 11). Calling for a return to notions of orderliness and lawful behavior and to the idea of human beings engaged in the great adventure of creation, Reiser calls for nothing less than "self-evolution" leading to more numerous and abundant freedoms for all mankind. Two constituents of his viewpoint are:

A Faith and an Idea — a conviction that man's archetypal concept of man can be put to work intelligently to create the environment essential to this new humanity.
A Program of Action — unified, super-personal, super-national action, made up of the collective decisions of many individuals, gripped by a universal loyalty, motivated by common purposes, guided by a shared wisdom, directed towards polarized objectives — all of which together will then determine man's planetary future (1966: 10).

In addition, Reiser declares that the twin foundation stones of his scientific humanism are the two closely related principles which stress the value of the individual and the responsibility of the individual.

Not one of us is without power to contribute to the making of the future. Not one of us is free from responsibility for making the future (1966: 10).

Thus Reiser joins R. B. Fuller, Weston LaBarre, Marshall McLuhan, Teilhard de Chardin, Magoroh Maruyama, Elise Boulding, among the growing number of those generally interested in planetary man and planetary society as prerequisites for the enhanced general welfare freedom, and dignity of mankind.

In this paper I propose to start from the ideas of Helmer and others concerning the epistemological difficulties of the social sciences, and the need to develop viable social technologies. Specifically, I will explore three types of humanism which I believe to be necessary for the maximization of both the pluralistic and local community alternatives awaiting mankind. Using the definition of humanism as "anything and everything falling within the self- or other-protective interests of any man or human group." I will examine three types of anticipatory, operational humanism:

Type 1. Locally Defined Humanism. This is essentially identified with highly developed pluralist groups and stresses, among other alternative goals, the maximization of survival on the local level. This is the most common and operational of humanist types.

Type 2. Cosmocentric Humanism. This may also stress survival, but in the more flexible and inclusive scope of meanings provided by the universe itself and all the events, creatures, matter, intellect, and energy within it. This form of humanism is difficult to operationalize broadly because it is largely rhetorical — even verbally ritualistic.

Type 3. Knowing Humanism. This is humanism of an active, exploratory, process- and information-oriented type. It cuts across both local and cosmocentric levels, acting to link informatively many types of culture, energy, and other components into evolving information loops. The loops may be tapped voluntarily by any type of culture; no information is secret; all process skills are open to examination; no epistemological lock-in characterizes either style or content. It is distinguished from contemporary science by its flexibility, openness, full respect for different world views, and provision of two-way terminals between different cultures.

The context for this exploration will be that of long-term human travel in space involving colonization of other planets and possible encounters with other intelligent beings. If this approach is considered far-fetched, note that permanently removing a few representatives of mankind from the earth is already the expressed goal of a new institute (see Hubbard 1971); and that a removal of the setting of the argument over humanism, freedom, and dignity to points away from Earth may serve to add something to the "either-or" arguments that have surrounded the theses of Skinner and others.

A good deal has been written about the day when men will leave the Earth in space vessels to embark upon long and difficult trips to distant celestial points. Almost all the more futuristic of these speculations have touched upon the tremendous lengths of time such travels will probably consume. The distances between even the closest planets of the solar system preclude rapid transit for a very long time, if one may judge from the projected development periods for certain sophisticated interplanetary and interstellar propulsion systems. It follows that, for considerable periods of time, men will be grouped together in confined physical and psychosocial conditions as they conduct trips among the planets, their natural satellites, and artificial manned outposts orbiting them. With the first unmanned spaceship designed for travel outside the solar system now being constructed in the United States, the moment for consideration of human "living space" on manned versions of such vehicles is at hand.

Let us first concern ourselves with some of the general problems, both physical and psychosocial, which may beset early groups of humans traveling long distances within the solar system. For virtually any discussion of human groups it is useful to keep in mind the conditions of the physical environment in which they exist. For space travelers, the environment outside the ship will be fraught with a variety of dangers, including temperature extremes, radiation, varying levels of gravity, illumination and atmospheric extremes, and many factors related to vast distances.

Within the human living space of groups engaged in long-distance space flights will lurk other hazards, among them psychological interactions which cause friction, imbalances in the crew's social system, upsets in the ecological interactions between the human group and elements of the complicated life-support systems, and many psychosocial effects of the long distances involved in space flight. The entire interacting complex of problems awaiting long-distance space travelers is summarized by Peter Ritner in his book *The society of space* (1961):

In Space, where there is no water or oxygen or anything else the human physiology requires, man has only his brain with which to design substitutes or store up supplies. Instead of ignoring a routine autonomic activity like breathing, as man can do on Earth, in Space he must think about it all the time, and devise intricate apparatuses which *allow* him to breathe. [That] he *must* breathe is no longer a casual matter; it is a critical weakness in his fortifications. On Earth a man breathes air. In Space a man will breathe a gas, artificially evolved, stocked in guarded containers, its composition calculated by biophysicists down to the third or fourth decimal place.

In addition to providing man with none of the essentials of his physical being, Space seems to regard life with a supererogatory indifference that may only be classified as malice. If a pilot ventures too near a strange star he may be shriveled up by a blast of a new kind of radiation. A tiny puncture the size of a pinhole in a space suit will detonate the helpless operator inside like an exploded can of overheated whipped cream. One brush with a number of kinds of cosmic particles, one large meteor punching through the main power plant, one over-long exposure to temperatures above 100 degrees Centigrade or below −10 degrees, one rupture in the plumbing that recycles wastes or recovers water or generates electricity and oxygen, one indiscretion with a major circuit, one error or blind spot or incompetency and the spell is broken, human daring and deserts are utterly lost (1961: 3).

What makes travel in space itself so much a consideration for planners of crew composition and interaction as opposed, let us say, to the manning and control of an atomic submarine is essentially the incomparably greater inaccessibility of the spacecraft once it is launched. It is easy to envision a rescue ship caring for a disabled submarine or even evacuating it in the event of a serious misfortune, but similar aid cannot be mustered for the long-distance spacecraft once it is underway. All one can reasonably hope for is a second or third vessel traveling with the stricken ship, allowing for crew transfer after disaster has occurred. But even these measures, while they offer the opportunity to continue life, leave one with all the problems we have discussed, and perhaps a few more. If three ships are traveling a long way together and the crew of one transfers to the others, life is continued but problems will probably mount.

The reasons for this situation are many, but the fundamental problems are tied to the factor of distance. Although many bombard us with the reminder that our solar system is astronomically quite diminutive when compared in size with other systems or with the distances between them, a round trip to Mars will nevertheless require at least eighteen months for spaceships constructed within the next ten to fifteen years. The "void," as many writers label it, is just that. A trip to the moon, our nearest celestial goal, is a six-day round trip. It is a very short space journey indeed, but allows time and distance enough for disasters of many kinds to occur.

The paramount demand upon any group of humans sent into space is the performance of given tasks in the "best" possible fashion for survival — a Type 1 requirement. To properly manage the control and monitoring functions allocated to them by the designers and planners of spacecraft, operators must be aware of certain minimum standards below which their collective output may fall only at the peril of everyone on board. The concern for life must be paramount with space designers to ensure the continuing survival of the crew. It follows that crew members necessarily will be human engineered to a degree, whether more or less depending upon the sophistication of their equipment, the dangers of their mission, the flight distance, and the type of society which is sponsoring them.

What might a "made up," locally defined humanist culture of Type 1 conceivably face in reasonably long-term space travel, and what might some of their responses to stress be? Below are some very brief scenarios for implementing locally defined humanist influences when humans are brought together for trips into the solar system or for long orbits around Earth.

Control of Bereavement Situations. In the event of the injury or death of one or more crew members or passengers, certain "automatic" behavior patterns are employed to preserve the efficiency of crew operations. Emotional abreaction or expressions of grief and horror are as brief and complete as possible to prevent recurring memories of the deceased from interfering with individual performance. The use of strict, well-defined rituals, carefully set up before the voyage begins, accomplishes this. Such normally revolting acts as euthanasia, abortion, and burial in space, are anticipated and made ready for while the crew is still in training. The use of a death ritual is necessary for the swift reaffirmation of group solidarity and morale, so that survival functions may continue uninterrupted.

Maintenance of Leadership. The head of an expedition and his aides demand the complete subordination of all other locally defined human-ist philosophies adhered to by different crew members. All crew members are indoctrinated under the same Type 1 humanist auspices prior to takeoff. The captain of the vessel becomes — artificially and naturally — endowed with a powerful charisma. Humanist authority and ritual materially assist this situation, particularly in times of stress or when training responses begin to fail and strong leadership becomes a necessity. Drugs and other means provide leadership with backup support.

Sanctification of the Mission. Assuming that the voyage in question is to Mars, it will last at least six months each way and probably six months will be spent on or near the planet. That is obviously ample time for members of a scientific passenger group to begin questioning moral objectives and to conclude that it is somehow "wrong" for such a journey to take place. With the composition of such crews likely to include many brilliant young men and women trained in the natural sciences, such a possibility is not without some justification. They will not, presumably, be as occupied as the crew with the control and maintenance of the vessel while in flight. Therefore, they are involun-tarily hibernated for most of the trip and are not allowed access to "privileged" information, such as political developments on Earth.

General Use of Ritual. Ritual opposes anomie. It encourages integra-tion of purpose, emotionally (we-feeling) as well as rationally. Locally defined humanism provides a very potent and continuous force in attempts to shape behavior and to help ensure continued in-group feeling and identification with the objectives of the spaceflight mission. Appropriate observances are introduced as, for example, regular ser-mons and services conducted and participated in by the crew members and passengers alike. A "physician-chaplain" is at the head of the "congregations," or they could be led by the captain. Spontaneous humanist leadership — or leadership of any kind, for that matter — is not allowed to spring up from outside the controlling elite. The provision of an on-board "physician-chaplain" appeals to everyone; the necessity of his function as healer, and his charisma as a spiritual leader are quite imposing when combined. On-board ritual and feeling are supplemented, where possible, by selectively used broadcasts from Earth of familiar persons conducting more elaborate reintegration functions.

Further Rationale. From what has been stated above it is seen that local humanism can make definite contributions to the maintenance of a society in space. It does this by ritually channeling the attitudes of the crew into expressed values that serve to aid the mission rather than hinder it, and by helping crew members to envision the nature of their obligations to the group and to the vehicle. It provides a restraining power against unwanted tendencies and serves to underwrite with reverence and respect the inviolable local mores fundamental to the success of the voyage. To achieve greater efficacy, it is completely reasonable that some or all of those social controls peculiar to the vessel should be couched in quasi-religious terminology. Locally defined humanism, when functioning as a psychologic "prop," helps to provide for stability in situations which would otherwise be more or less chaotic.

It is not my intention to suggest that local humanist influence is the only solution to the detrimental effects of stress in space. Specific training is the best answer, along with the cohesion of the primary group. Local humanist influence, however, helps to bind together a society on the verge of collapsing below the minimum standards of performance necessary for survival. Even though "religious" overtones to required functions may be recognized as labored and superimposed — in varying degree, depending on the perceptiveness of members — the nearly universal social conditioning to react with respect toward religious sentiment and symbols augments the establishment and maintenance of basic, indispensable social controls. Without these, groups in remote space could not survive.

Now that some of the social aspects of travel within inner elements of the solar system have been briefly examined, I should like to consider the much more exacting conditions of outer-planetary travel and colonization.

The technical problems associated with such journeys are enormous. In addition to the dilemmas already discussed in the context of more modest solar flight, it has been estimated that to achieve a respectable speed for interstellar travel a mass the size of the moon would have to be emitted as rocket exhaust. Even then, because of limitations imposed by relativity, the spaceship would require over four years to travel to the nearest star. Due to the length of time envisioned for such journeys, the physical and cultural survival of passengers and crew may take on additional and fundamental meaning. The group that begins a given journey, should it survive physically, may not be the group that finishes it but a subsequent generation of the starting group. The scientist Arthur C. Clarke, estimates that speeds in the region of that of light will not be attained for centuries yet. He does envision, however, spaceships traveling at fractions of this velocity much sooner. If we assume that a manned vehicle completes a journey to the nearest star system at a hundredth the speed of light, that is at one thousand, eight hundred, and sixty miles per second, we have contemplated a trip lasting about fifty years — one way. As Clarke states the problem:

> Since several decades of traveling through space would be an ordeal even to the most enthusiastic astronauts, one cannot help wondering if medical science might come to the rescue with some form of suspended animation — another theoretical possibility still outside the range of present achievement. If this became practicable, it might extend the range of space flight almost indefinitely — assuming that travelers could be found willing to return to earth perhaps generations after their departure, when everyone that they had ever known was dead and society itself might have changed out of all recognition (1951: 178).

Continuing Clarke's line of thought is another writer, Carsbie Adams:

> The idea of generation travel is so immense in its philosophical scope as to befuddle the twentieth-century imagination: the dedication to a purpose that neither the parents nor their children or grandchildren could ever hope to realize directly would be amazingly difficult to instill. To live for one's children seems natural; to live only that one's remote descendants can land and live on an alien planet is at best difficult to imagine. After several generations had been born, had matured, and had expired, the relationship of the spaceship and its occupants to the home planet would become quite vague.
>
> Alone in the cosmos, these people could know of the earth of their grandparents only through books and by word of mouth. Elaborate sociological systems would have to be worked out, together with an extremely refined version of space psychology and perhaps even a specialized religion. We can be sure that some psychological props would be necessary. The predicament of these space travelers would be a vastly intensified version of life on earth (1958: 269).

We must assume, however, that medical aids for interstellar flight such as the one Clarke suggests will not involve most members of the crew; someone must remain active to provide maintenance and control.

Another aspect of stellar flight concerns the effects on the passage of time aboard ship as the speed of light is approached. After reaching about 96 percent of the speed of light, a space crew would supposedly note the passage of only one "ship year" since the start of, let us say, two-gravity acceleration. But, due to the effects of the special theory of relativity (already demonstrated experimentally in certain cases) an observer on earth would ascertain that the same ship had been accelerating at two gravities for five and one-half years instead of one. Even considering the effects of "time dilation," as the compressive effect is termed, the social structure of a human group moving at nearly the speed of light would have ample time for alteration — assuming the landing point were distant enough.

So there will be plenty of time for sociocultural changes to occur on the home planet, within the space crew, and upon the planets where colonies have been established. It seems prudent to consider implementing some strong Type 1 bond to help keep these distant nomads as culturally alike as possible, in order that communications and trade can be sustained. (The trade in mind here is primarily that of ideas and specific technological skill.) It could be that a Type 1 humanism, with the tenacity of Judaism, would be needed, or it could be that a kind of enlarged humanism or "cosmocentrism" (Type 2) would supplement anthroposocial creeds. But it is certain that some cohesive force which can conjure ample collective sentiment to ensure the brotherhood of widely separated peoples will have to be worked out by the time the first colonists embark. It seems apparent that if we are to deal with forms of *Homo sapiens*, altered culturally and genetically through conditions peculiar to their stellar habitats, we will need the palliatives of a cosmocentric or Type 2 humanism. But Type 2 humanism is essentially fragile because of the overriding survival imperatives of the Type 1 variety. Therefore, some other kind of humanism, nonlocal and nonuniversal, but *in* and *of* both, is required. The major service of a Type 3 humanism would be to keep many kinds of alternatives open to many kinds of ordinary and extraordinary human groups.

A wag has referred to the little old lady who felt that spacecraft were an invention of the devil, and that man should continue to travel by jetliner "as God intended." It is this sort of bias — a rather quaint example, it must be admitted — that may cause extreme difficulty in dealing with the impact of the rocket upon our own civilization. If we should reach the stars (or they should reach us) and we come into contact with other civilizations however, uncomprehending and stunned reactions may be replaced by two culturally induced reactions: fear, followed quickly by aggression. Again, Clarke states the problem aptly:

[One suspects that some people] are afraid that the crossing of space, and above all contact with intelligent but non-human races, may destroy the foundations of their religious faith. They may be right, but in any event their attitude is one which does not bear logical examination — for a faith which cannot survive collision with the truth is not worth many regrets. Whether or not man is alone in the universe is one of the supreme questions of philosophy. It is difficult to imagine that anyone could fail to be interested in knowing the answer (1951: 191).

Obviously many people are not interested, and some of them occupy the highest positions in Western civilization. But we will have to display far more of the qualities of compassion and tolerance with altered forms of humanity and with other races than is common in everyday racial interaction in this world today. The world of tomorrow may only be one of many, and the destructive forces of today are probably puny beside those to come. If and when we meet our betters or our peers in space, we should have developed (down to the lowest echelons of humanity) an innate operational respect for and tolerance of the differing ways of all others, because if not, we may fall into the patterns of agression that fear and suspicion have always caused. And, if we are wont to do battle, it is well to consider the possibility of defeat; our ships may appear as painted war canoes confronting a modern navy.

Something is needed other than a self-destructive Type 1 reaction or a limitedly operational philosophy of the Type 2 kind. To quote Ritner:

In this era, we want to say, the community of man first came to view *knowing* not as a means but as a way; not as a weapon but as a destiny; not as the province of specialists but as the central stabilizing energy of the Society of Space (1961: 81).

This seems to me a statement of implicit support for Type 3 humanism.

If we come face to face with members of another race, quite possibly an aesthetically repulsive race, what might such a contact be like? In an effort to promote Type 2 cosmocentrism, Ritner makes this intriguing appeal:

... what if the Scorpion's (this is Ritner's symbolic alien) notions of interstellar diplomacy include the closest sort of bodily contact — a kind of quasi-sexual byplay between Man-explorer and Scorpion-receptionist, not of course, with the object of procreating anything, but in order to exchange body warmth as a token of good faith and affection. At this even the crustiest spider lover in Arizona would balk. But where will humanity be then? The Scorpion is man's *brother!* And we loathe him. Man must steel himself *not* to loathe the Scorpion. That is the teaching of Space (1961: 52).

If we feel that we are not such a long way from embracing celestial bugs, let us consider the difficulties human beings now have embracing their fellows, who differ from them but little.

The best case Ritner makes for the development of cosmic humanism based on love may suggest a kinky kind of togetherness on a universal scale, but it does not seem unattractive as rhetoric:

> Let man understand at last that the Mind can do nothing without the aid of the Passionate Soul. That any entity possesses the audacity to organize and metabolize in this dungeon of the Universe should be enough for us. We can love any such entity, and this love will enlarge our own audacity, and life will conquer (1961: 53).

A Type 3 process-and-information-oriented humanism is necessary, it seems to me, for the practical working out of such lofty aims in space or on Earth.

That there are people within our society afraid to contemplate the prospect of man afoot in the cosmos is demonstrated by our slow progress in that field. Carsbie Adams notes that Western man's concept of a jealous god ruling the universe is the source of most philosophic misgivings about the genesis of space flight:

> ... here is the crux of the ultimate dilemma: Man is terrified by the prospect of a deity who is jealous of his command of the universe, but not so much because of the element of apparent omnipotence (which could also be kindly) but because he, man, will himself not rest until he attains all within his awareness. But there was never any doubt, once man ate of the forbidden tree of knowledge, that there would someday be a day of reckoning. Maybe the odds, when they are known, will prove to be hopeless. We will not know until we are finally face to face with the infinite. In the depths of our being, we must feel that we have a chance or we would not try (1958: 363–364).

The on-board social problems of space flight to inner planets of the solar system are clearly very great, but colonization of the inner planets and later stellar journeys and colonization will require investigation of powerful elements for controlling human groups in time of stress and for aiding them in maintaining their essentially human characteristics — assuming that this is always desired.

It is suggested that consideration be given to the use of very rigid, heavily ritualized humanist mystiques to aid in controlling and maintaining group cohesion during flight through space or under adverse planetary conditions. But it also seems necessary to prepare a mandatory and preferably automatic humanist reaction to other space-faring human groups and extraterrestrial races, to come into play upon initial contact. Such planning should include opportunities for "dress rehearsals" of such eventualities to aid in familiarity, timeliness, and quality of reaction. The problem here is the obvious antipolarity of the two humanist systems: ritually structured humanism in a context of fierce, almost tribal rigidity and formalism necessary for physical survival in space on the one hand; and the flexible, cosmocentric sophistication of men who are rhetorically one with the universe on the other. Against the backdrop of the stars, however, lie more than small ships; whole planets such as Earth must somehow develop the art of survival with as little recourse as possible to the primitive mechanism of aggression. It is to this end that a Type 3 humanism must work — to provide information, as well as process skills, allowing for expansion of the closed, tribal groups and for enhancement in the operational capability of (rhetorical) cosmic humanism.

Let us leave space and return to Earth. What of the continuing problem of clashes at close quarters between different varieties of humanism operating at Type 1 and Type 2 levels? If it is quite easy to understand why the challenges of space to man's future might lead to Skinnerian solutions, should Earth be excluded as a sector of the universe where behaviorist styles of Type 1 humanism might function? Is there no room among the earth-bound cultures of man for this variety of pluralism? If not, how easy is it to operationalize Type 2 humanism and make it work?

Very difficult, I would guess, for many liberal professionals and other ideologues who do not choose to label their own Type 2 proclivities "ideologic," but only "correct." Very difficult too, I would suppose, for fem lib zealots, youthful radicals, and some ethnic politicians whose very *raison d'être* and popularity are often linked to anomic gaps and lags in the overall mechanisms of social harmony. In short, lip service is currently paid to Type 2 humanism in some Earthly quarters but must bow to locally defined humanist influence. This might have been an imperfect but essentially workable situation before large-scale technological development, but how does it work in 1978 or how will it work in 1999? Is it necessary for men to travel deep into space in order to remove themselves from this dilemma? Will we leave "Spaceship Earth" because there may be no cultural room for the many varieties of highly developed technological societies? Is it inevitable that some must leave the planet to save it and themselves? While I cannot answer these questions adequately either for myself or for others, I hope that I have made it easier to consider the recent pronouncements of B. F. Skinner not so much as depredations but more as the early expression of a Type 3 approach (with definite Type 1 undertones) to alternative human futures. But perhaps this is what "Spaceship Earth" needs at this point in the 1970's: more human alternatives operationally spelled out, and greater willingness on the part of informed people to consider these alternatives with intellectual and emotional openness and honesty.

I have purposely provided some "far out" examples of humanist activities and reduced the definition of humanism to refer to local, cosmic, or information-and-process assumptions that are not handed down from supernatural sources, but are, as Kurt Vonnegut says, "just" made up. But the little word "just" contains, I believe, a great potential for mankind if we can but realize it. A mixture of reason in the arguments over proposed behavioral modification in man would help a great deal, I believe, in removing us from the level of the witch hunt to the responsible search for workable viewpoints on man. Skinner is not Hitler, and we should realize that. Cosmic humanism is at present little more than high-sounding rhetoric, and we should know by now how difficult it is to operationalize rhetoric. I believe Skinner has made a marvellous contribution to the sophistication of an argument debated too long in stereotyped emotional and allegorical styles. Let someone come forth to help us clarify the *full* range of alternatives for social control and freedom available to man in social space and the near space of the mind; in the region of the stars and on "Spaceship Earth."

I believe that formal education systems, with the help of competent analysis by many kinds of specialists, generalists, and citizens, can begin to operationalize our abilities to provide both Type 1 and Type 2 kinds of information for young people and their elders within the open information-and-process context of a Type 3 approach. Under the right conditions, we may find ways to augment that process by encouraging more, not fewer, controversial scholars like B. F. Skinner. Their contributions may never be sufficient, but they are necessary if we are to raise the level of our debate about freedom and dignity above the twin totems of scare scenarios, such as *1984* on the one hand, and the fragile, conservative, and appallingly nonoperational rhetoric of today's official humanists on the other. Type 3 humanism is precisely the open provision of information, and therefore alternatives, for all. It does not itself solve the problems of Type 1 and Type 2 humanists, but it offers continuously sophisticating alternatives generated by the constant feedback of information arranged according to many world views. Sparked by some men, augmented by computers and displays, it is the guts of the noosphere, the world village, the cosmic sensorium, or the world university. It is science expanded, the universities made competent, the media made honest. It accommodates East and West, male and female, black and white, Earthly and extraterrestrial. It is Reiser's cosmic brain but without a single cortex. It is the newest extension of our ecology, and, I submit, contra Eiseley, it is *natural*.

REFERENCES

ADAMS, CARSBIE
  1958   *Space flight*. New York: McGraw-Hill.

CLARKE, ARTHUR C.
1951   *The exploration of space.* New York: Harper and Brothers.
EISELEY, LOREN
1970   *The firmament of time.* New York: Atheneum.
FULLER, R. BUCKMINSTER
1971   "The phantom captain," in *Nine chains to the moon.* New York: Doubleday.
HELMER, OLAF
1966   *Social technology.* New York: Basic Books.
HUBBARD, BARBARA
1971   From meaninglessness to new worlds. *The Futurist* 2: 72–75.
REISER, OLIVER L.
1966   *Cosmic humanism.* Cambridge: Schenkman.
RITNER, PETER
1961   *The society of space.* New York: Macmillian.
SKINNER, B. F.
1971   *Beyond freedom and dignity.* New York: Alfred A. Knopf.

Anthropological Insights for
Social Policy: Third World Views

The Concept of Heterogeneity and Change Among the Mandenka*

SORY CAMARA

> He who is motivated by some desire for
> domination will never really understand
> how extremely diverse human beings can be
> within the range of human existence. His
> universe is confined in quantitative dimen-
> sion and reduced to the concept of the least,
> the most and degrees between them.
>
> SORY CAMARA

The purpose of this article is to discuss how the Mandenka of West Africa perceive the future of humanity, based on their concepts of beings and things. The Mandenka see the universe as having evolved according to a principle of heterogeneity. In nature, beings differ greatly, and the differences are amplified by the fact that things, beings and the elements of the universe are in constant interaction. Thus, life develops as a process of incessant change.

Humans try to introduce a certain degree of stability by organizing society according to principles which would be invariable. This ac-counts for the importance of customs and rites which were what caught the attention of ethnologists first. By discussing rites and customs, ethnologists could talk about "societies without history."

However, this effort to create stability has its limits. The inevitability of change must be taken into account if a collapse of norms is to be prevented. Norms must be such that changes are relatively easily integrated. Even the rituals, which greatly impressed observers from outside by their seeming regularity and invariability, differ from region to region, from village to village, from clan to clan, and both their form and content change over time, because those who perform them are

* Translated from the French by Magoroh Maruyama.

never the same. It is not without nostalgia that the Mandenka say:

Bɛ ni tumɔ   Everything has its moment

Bɛ ni i tele   Everything has its sun

During the course of his life, an individual goes through several phases of activity and experience. He is never the same and he acquires the ability to see things from different points of view as he goes through several phases of his life. A person at the age of six is different from what he was when he was five years old. Adolescents are assigned certain tasks to perform in society; young adults perform other tasks. In their early thirties the men assume the administrative responsibilities of the society. Their roles are often misinterpreted by Western scholars as those of "chiefs." The functions they assume, however, are not those of authority figures, but of caretakers. They must do all the worrying for other people but they have no special privileges. In their late thirties, the men retire from these heavy responsibilities and take up other functions. Old persons are respected for their wisdom because they have gone through many phases of life. These phases are seen as radically different, even opposite. Heterogeneity and change are two complementary principles and are the origin of harmony. This is because a person who has gone through different experiences can understand different situations and different types of individuals.

Westerners frequently ask if heterogeneity does not create conflicts, but the Mandenka think that conflicts are caused more by homogeneity. If people are forced to be homogeneous, they will inevitably try to find ways to be different and there is only one way open to them: they become competitive, attempt to eliminate or separate from one another. This creates conflicts. The Mandenka are skeptical of Westernization for two reasons. On the one hand, they suspect that some homogenization will result; while on the other hand, they fear that specialization brought about by Westernization will lock each person into one task and one function, preventing him from going through other types of experiences, and consequently making him incapable of seeing a situation from another person's point of view.

The basic heterogeneity, which has change as its temporal dimension, entails a certain harmony. It also involves antagonistic, conflictual relations among beings which the Mandenka are keenly aware of, and which they strive to attenuate.

The Mandenka believe that N'Maba Taala, the Great Ancestor, created all sorts of beings, each according to its own fundamental nature. Regardless of the point of view from which they are considered, beings are fundamentally different, physically, morally, and spiritually. The Mandenka say that this was the way the Great Ancestor proceeded in his great wisdom.

In the environment in which man creates, produces, and reproduces his life, even the most insignificant grass has a history, a course of development, a foundation for its individuality and a destiny unique to itself. This phenomenon is much more evident among animals. The *kūbējalo*[1], who are clown-critics and hunters, wise concerning the things and beings of forests, point this out clearly to us. Each animal, descendant of a primordial ancestor, is born in unique circumstances. Not even blood ties produce the notion of "species." Often a *kūbējalo* is able to distinguish up to seven individuals among one species of bird, each having its own name depending on the tree upon which it perches habitually, or the manner in which it alights by slowing down the movements of its wings. Man's imagination is exhausted in his admiration for such a diverse and heterogeneous universe.

Human beings are also differentiated. Even the Mandenka (people of Manden, a country situated on the border between Mali and Guinea) are grouped by different lineages[2]. Each lineage is descended from an ancestor who, in primordial and historic times, had distinct and peculiar experiences. Each lineage enjoys a monopoly on certain activities in which it is considered to excel. This does not mean, however, that each member of the lineage is endowed with a miraculous talent. It simply means that they have a higher probability of success in lineage-specific activities than in others.

The difference goes further. It seems that even people have different origins. Certain families seem to have descended from a life composed of elements different from those of other families. This is the case, for example, with the blacksmiths and the clowns. In certain myths, the clowns are said to have participated in the creation of other humans. They enjoy a special status in the social life of the Mandenka (Camara 1976). They are empowered to perform certain ritual tasks which, if performed by others, would compromise the moral and physical integrity of the performers, such as the shaving of hair, circumcisions, excisions, announcements of deaths, and washing of corpses. It is as if they were of a special nature which justifies some of their privileges. It is accepted that they may sing sweet words which will excite all sorts of passion, or they may make offensive and indecent statements in public. They have the right to criticize kings. In times of peace, they cannot be punished; in times of war, they cannot be made captives. But as the Mandenka consider it important not to mix things, the clowns are not allowed to have access to political power, which has to be left to other

---

[1] Derived from *kūbē*, a musical instrument they play while they tell stories.
[2] The Mandenka word is *si*, symbolized by the names *jamū*.

people. The clowns live on what other families give them on those occasions which mark important moments of life, such as birth, circumcision, marriage, and death and at other times when they make unplanned visits. One cannot afford to refuse to give them gifts because they could make embarrassing statements in public.

The clowns provide "feedback" or act as "checks and balances" in a society which appears to have a hierarchical structure. From the point of view of formal structure, Mandenka society is highly hierarchical in many respects. However, there are a number of built-in systems of feedback which make it nonhierarchical in practice. The role differentiation between men and women is a good example illustrating the complexity of relations which might appear hierarchical to superficial observation.

Men and women are considered to be so different that their union is highly problematic. While containment of affectivity expression is believed to characterize man, perpetual profusion of emotions is attributed to woman. Education contributes to the development of courage, control of anger, and suppression of tenderness and longing in man. Woman is required to suppress neither tenderness nor longing. Man is judged by his capacity to keep secrets (gbūdū doo), while woman is believed to be fundamentally incapable of doing so. Therefore it is understandable that men suspect women and keep away from them as much as possible. It would be debilitating for men to engage in feminine tasks. If a man touches the metal cylinder used by women and girls to gin cotton, he would suffer sudden powerlessness. Young men are advised to postpone sexual intercourse for as long as possible. Sexual precocity results in a disease called sede, a bad influence of woman on man characterized by a slowly developing and insidious weakening of the body accompanied by chills. This disease can be fatal for young males who are too precocious. Even adult males lose their moral strength and see their undertakings fail if they engage in excessive sexual activities with women. Chastity was considered the most important weapon of warriors: those who had never had sexual intercourse were considered to be invulnerable to metal weapons.

Heterogeneity is not limited to sexual differentiation but is also found within the individual. Even if the behavior of the male is distinct from that of the female, his invisible nature does not exclude the female principle. In myths and tales, a young man must travel through a thicket before or during an important undertaking. In the course of his voyage he meets an old woman. If he does not ignore her and behaves with friendliness — for example, helps her with some domestic chores such as finding firewood or carrying it for her — he will succeed in his undertaking. The woman reveals some secret to him, gives him magic power, physical prowess, or intelligence which will allow him to overcome all obstacles. Not infrequently he is given an amazing virility. Occasionally the woman advises him not to disclose the secret to women, and especially not to his wife. If the young man walks through the thicket without noticing the old lady of destiny, or discloses the secret to the village women, he always fails, and may even lose his virility.

Here we begin to glimpse the complexity of the system and the difficulty foreigners have in understanding it. Though physically weaker than the male, the female is nevertheless the foundation of his strength. Physically she is apart from him, but psychologically she proves to be a component of the profound essence of his being. While he seems to guard himself against her in his daily life, he must reconcile himself with her in his psychological life in order to accomplish his male tasks. This point calls for further elucidation. In moving from the level of observable behavior to psychological processes which the myths and tales reveal, one discovers a different man. The man who wants to stand in good relation with woman is no longer the man who suspects the woman as something dangerous and contrary to his destiny. But are we talking about the same woman? Actually we are not. The woman he suspects is the real woman in his daily life; the other is the woman-in-himself. The first is the one he marries, she is of his generation. The second cannot be a possible marriage partner for she is the old lady.[3]

We thus realize that we are dealing with two different beings. A man cannot maintain the same attitude toward both of them. When he passes from the one to the other, he cannot remain the same. He must change. In effect, the old lady, a being within himself, means that he is heterogeneous within himself. This heterogeneity gives rise to the question of harmony: how do you make these two beings work together? The conciliation does not come about by itself. One must make efforts to respect the other-in-himself.

One begins to see how the Mandenka endeavor to solve the problem inherent in a concept of life based on heterogeneity and change. If the

---

[3]   The language, in fact, gives them different names. In the language of the Mandenka in Guinea, the young woman can be called *sŭkudŭ* (from *sŭ* or *sī* meaning 'breast,' and *kudŭ* meaning 'short' or 'small'), and the old woman is denoted by the term *musokɔdɔ* (from *muso* meaning 'woman,' and *kɔdɔ* meaning 'old' or 'aged'). Usually one calls her *musokɔdɔ nɛ̃* or 'little old lady,' with a diminutive indicating an older age. As one gets old, his body withers and he walks with an arched back, giving the impression of becoming smaller and smaller. The images which these two types of women evoke are therefore completely different and incomparable. The language of the Mandenka in Eastern Senegal makes a similar distinction. The young girl is called *sŭkŭtɔ́*, where *sŭ* comes from *sŭjɔ́* or 'breast,' and *kutɔ́* conveys the quality of being short or small. One can also say *karafa* (from *kara*, 'breast'; and *fá*, 'full'). The old woman is called *mùsùkɔ́tɔ́* or *musukɔtɔrĩŋo*. Often in the tales and myths her name is *tɔ̃kɔ̃fɛ̃dá* which implies her great knowledge and mysterious powers.

woman is different from me, it is possible that our movements become contradictory, and we create conflicts. But it is inconceivable that I do not moderate my hostility, because there is within myself an element which works in the reverse direction, leading me to understand the other outside-me in its difference.

If the heterogeneity is not free from conflicts, it must allow for conciliation. It even requires it. If homogeneity is the only principle in operation, we would see conflicts arise which, without conciliation, lead to incapacitation and even elimination of one of the parties.

Family structure plays an important role in the social, economic, and political systems of Mandenka society. At first glance, it may appear that the principle of identity (and therefore of homogeneity) dominates the system. All the members of the same lineage and of the same clan have the same name. They are considered to have descended from a common ancestor. They share the same resources. But "we are all the same" has never been the establishing principle for any society. All groups make some degree of separation or distinction among their members, if by nothing more than status and function. Once identity has been established, the only possibility for differentiation lies in the establishment of a hierarchy and the distribution of authority. The males take and exercise all authority, while the females are given none of it, and remain subjects of the males. Among men, age and primogeniture seem to determine the hierarchy. The father exercises authority over his children, and older brothers exercise authority over their younger brothers. This authority cannot be challenged, regardless of circumstances. In case of a conflict between a younger brother and his older brother, the blame is always laid, in public, on the younger brother. It cannot be otherwise, because the younger must be silent and obey. It is only in private that the older can be reprimanded in the absence of the younger — in order to save the hierarchy. It is this conspicuous aspect of inexorable authority which impressed observers from outside. It appeared to them that the differentiation was between the most and the least. But if this differentiation by hierarchy — which, by the way, is an illusion — were the only principle at work, social life would be unviable, and there would be layers of authority which would crush those at the bottom.

But in practice the Mandenka exercise a principle which counteracts the hierarchical order. That is the system of criticism known as the "joking relationships" or "joking relatives." Joking relationships exist within a family, and a similar concept is extended to the relationships between social groups, as will be explained.

Within a family, the joking relationships are between: (1) the grandfather and his grandchildren, (2) the maternal uncle and his nephews, (3) the younger brother and the wives of his older brothers, and (4) the younger sister and the wives of her older brothers. By means of joking relationships the hierarchically inferior can channel complaints and criticisms to a person who has direct authority over the one under whom he or she stands.

One may begin his criticism by making fun of physical or moral defects of the person to be criticized. Joking relatives benefit from their right to criticize publicly or privately, and they do not fail to take advantage of these rights. In order to ensure that the purpose of this system is achieved, the joking relatives are not allowed to attack one another. They must not get angry at one another. On the contrary, they are obligated to mutual assistance and protection. All authoritative behavior is prohibited between joking relatives.

If we superimpose this principle of joking relations on the authority structure, we obtain a system with feedback loops as illustrated in the following figures.

Let us first consider Figure 1. We see that the grandson is not subjected to the authority of all the preceding generations. Though his father has authority over him, his grandfather has none; he is considered to be a friend and an equal of the grandson in all respects. Two consecutive generations are in a vertical authority relationship, while two generations separated by a third generation interact by joking, in

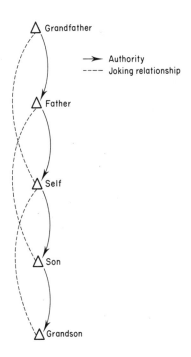

Figure 1.

friendship and mutual support. In this system of feedback, the hierarchically inferior can control his superior. If there is a conflict between a man (Ego) and his father, he can appeal to his grandfather. The grandfather will exercise his authority to protect his grandson, and the father has no alternative but to obey the grandfather.

Figure 2 shows the relationship between Ego and his parents and uncles. He is under the authority of his father and his father's brothers. His mother, too, exercises authority over him, but hers is an attenuated, tender authority. Her brothers, however, have a joking relationship with him. An equilibrium is established between the authoritarian side (the paternal side) and the friendly side (the maternal side). He is protected by his maternal uncles. If Ego's father or one of his father's brothers punishes him too severely for some misconduct, he can appeal to his maternal uncles. The younger brother of his mother is in joking relationship with his father as well as with his father's brothers; he is in a strategic position to intervene on behalf of Ego. Furthermore, Ego's mother's older brother is in the position of a creditor with regard to Ego's father and his father's family because he has given his sister to them; his intervention is totally effective.

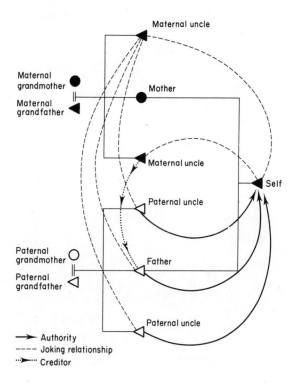

Figure 2.

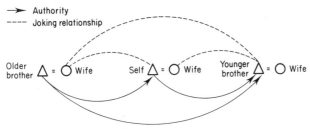

Figure 3.

Figure 3 shows the third channel of control. The younger brother, Ego, is under the authority of his older brothers, even though he, as the youngest, may receive the uncontained affection from his parents. On the other hand, Ego has a joking relationship with the wives of his older brothers. He is also in the position to mediate between his older brothers and their wives in case of marital problems. This gives him an important leverage. For example, if one of Ego's older brothers has a marital quarrel and his wife runs away to her parents, Ego can talk with her as well as with her brothers in order to solve the conflict and bring her back to her husband. The possibility of such an event makes his older brothers refrain from abusing their authority over him. If, in spite of everything, an older brother wants to tyrannize Ego, Ego can use his brother's wife as a mediator.

It should be noted that there is *no* joking relationship between an older brother and his younger brother's wife. This is because only the subordinates need protection.

Women are also protected in this system. If Ego behaves unjustly toward his wife, her younger brothers can ridicule him because of their joking relationship with him. Thus the wife is protected against her husband through her younger brothers. She must obey her own older brothers, but here again she is protected against them through their wives, who in turn are protected against their husbands through their younger brothers.

Joking relationships serve another purpose. If Ego is criticized by a joking relative, he must not get angry but must accept the criticism. The result is that Ego considers himself from another's point of view and questions his own viewpoint. Ego succeeds in doing so to the extent that there is within him a role, a different person so to speak, which corresponds to the situation in which he is involved. For example, he is a brother-in-law to his sister-in-law in addition to being himself. Thus the joking relationship teaches and enables him to change his roles instantaneously, and makes him heterogeneous in himself.

There is a distinction between "authentic" and "inauthentic" differentiation. Authentic differentiation has as its purpose conciliation and composition, while inauthentic differentiation aims at separation and hierarchization. Joking relationships reconcile and symbiotize; therefore the role differentiation is authentic.

The principle of joking relationships can be generalized outside the family structure to the social system as a whole. Clowns are formally considered members of an inferior caste whom the members of other castes cannot marry. However, as we have seen, these clowns have the inviolable right to criticize everyone including the chiefs. The formal caste differentiation which separates the clowns from the other castes is inauthentic — because one can prohibit, in principle, endogamy but not exogamy. Exogamy aims at uniting the different. Endogamy is either a formal error, an error by passion, or a result of the desire to preserve superiority. In the latter case, it separates and hierarchizes, and is therefore inauthentic. On the other hand, the role of the clowns as critics of those who govern, aims at conciliation and composition, and is therefore authentic.

The concept of joking relationships applies also to the relations between clans. When groups which are considered different come in contact, they either intermarry or joke about one another. Each Mandenka clan intermarries with a certain number of other clans. With those clans which it does not intermarry, it maintains the relationship of teasing and criticizing (these clans are called sanākū). In both cases we are dealing with heterogeneity. In intermarriage, one exchanges only what is different. In the joking relationship, one makes fun only of what he himself is not.

One might wonder if the teasing and insulting does not cause overt conflicts. As is the case with the joking relationship within a family, clans which are in a joking relationship cannot attack each other. Not only is anger prohibited between these clans, but they are obligated to mutual assistance in all circumstances. The old customs required that they could not kill each other in war, and they had to release each other's members if they were captured.

Does this not show a frank willingness to recognize and accept differences? One does not hide or ignore them; one expresses them as they are. One names them with antagonistic terms; one readily makes explicit the latent conflict which underlies any heterogeneity, in order to control it more adequately. One accepts the differences, and "plays" the war which they imply in order to prevent the war from becoming real. This is the procedure the Mandenka follow whenever they live near another tribe. They unfailingly establish joking relations with it: such is the case, for example, between the Peul and the Mandenka who live in close proximity in several regions.

Whites who have lived close to the Mandenka in positions of exchange rather than positions of authority, particularly traders, have always been integrated in this type of relationship.

To accept differences without overt conflict is to accept change and the necessity for it. All tribes and ethnic groups with which Ego comes in contact make him conceptualize, understand, accept, and integrate new elements. With each contact, he becomes different. A Mandenka proverb says: "Human beings do not cease to change as long as they live." At each contact with another person, something from the being of this other person enters Ego's being. Therefore in each person there is something which comes from his father, something from his mother, something from his ancestors, something from his wife, something from the neighbors, something from the plants he eats, something from the trees he fells, something from the animals he hunts. This something (*nãma, nãmɔ* or *nãmãdin* [diminutive]) changes his being. It can also harm his spiritual force or his efficiency. In extreme cases it can destroy his very being if he cannot come to terms with it. Fortunately it is possible to arrive at a composition with these forces in spite of, or perhaps even thanks to, these differences.

Mandenka philosophy takes this possibility into account. The universe is seen as a set of infinitely composed things. Nothing is simple, elementary, or homogeneous. In this regard there is always a possibility of openness of beings and things toward one another. The human is not only a human. He is also a certain animal called *tana*, and a certain phenomenon called *yɛlɛmã*, of which he can take an appearance. By real or symbolic actions he can modify the course of the phenomena which are called "natural phenomena" by Westerners. Only a logic of heterogeneity and of composition makes it possible to conceptualize such a system.

Westerners who could not go beyond the logic of homogeneity and exclusion have misinterpreted the logic of so-called "primitive" people. Some Westerners have called this logic "animistic," believing that "primitive" peoples confused two categories of things which are mutually exclusive: the principle of human action relevant to the mind; and the laws of natural phenomena. According to them, the primitives had an anthropomorphic interpretation of the universe, considering all things moved by anthropomorphic agents fashioned after the human mind. This is the theory of Tylor (1876). Others like Levy-Bruhl (1949) have seen in the primitive man an indication of absence of logic due to the underdevelopment of the mind: the primitives were at the "prelogical" stage of evolution. Such an idea obviously assumes that there is only one logic, and that anything different must fit into the earlier history of its development. We must recognize nevertheless that Levy-Bruhl considerably modified his ideas on this point toward the end of his life. In his notes published in the *Carnets* (1949), he conceded that the primitives were not incapable of logic, but that they were merely indifferent to the notion of contradiction.

But it is necessary to go beyond this and raise the more radical question of the possibility of an alternative logic, which is not to be confused with the illusion of affective participation. This would open the way for a new direction of inquiry in which authentic change is thinkable. But it is very difficult for European philosophers to take this step. Plato, for example, conceived of the being as one and identical with itself. Perceptible differences resulted from a sort of temporal degradation. Perceived things strove to imitate, but never attained, the perfect identity of the proto-being. They attempted this through a closed cycle of change. This excludes the possibility of the real and authentic change of which the Mandenka philosophy permits formulation: our actions change the universe and ourselves. Thus all things become more and more different, because different elements continually enter them. We honor people in their old age because of their authentic wealth of diversity and because of the wisdom they have mastered in order to keep it all together and not let it destroy them through the effect of latent conflicts. The Mandenka have a profound respect for this type of change.

They also recognize the danger of error that change may induce in a society. If the members of a society in contact with another society change to the extent of believing that they have become identical with those they are in contact with, and of identifying themselves with these others, they are negating their authenticity. We say that they have erred (fili). Those who have erred dispute with their parents and become incapable of understanding the values which govern the latter's behavior without even becoming identical with the others.

Others cannot contribute anything to Ego's being, and he cannot enrich himself from contact with them unless he is and remains different from them. Otherwise he will lose himself in the illusion of identity. If he says: "I am like him," he alienates his being. If Ego says: "He is like me," Ego negates the other, and remains alone in his poverty.

A few months ago I had the idea of putting a question about intercultural contact to some old Mandenka of Eastern Senegal. Some of them said that intercultural contact would increase the probability of wars and conflicts. Others thought that intercultural contact would contribute to an increase of differences in customs, cultures, and patterns of thinking. But they were almost unanimous in affirming that any conflict that might arise would be caused by a lack of wisdom in recognizing differences and by a lack of respect for others.

In contrast, Western societies are oriented toward homogenization which seems to be based on considerations of technical efficiency in the management and manipulation of things and human beings for maximum gain. In this context, differences which exceed certain limits immediately become bothersome for the system. Breeds of animals, fruits, and plants must conform to standardized norms of size, shape, and color for manufacturing specifications. Human beings are more difficult to standardize. However, the system permits expression of individual differences only within certain limits, and tasks are defined in such a way that the individuals who accomplish them are easily interchangeable.

In this framework, introduction of authentic differentiation seems difficult. Therefore one resorts to erecting hierarchies: hierarchies based on status, values, and positions. Here reigns the tyranny of quantitative measurement. Things and persons are classified according to how much they show certain characteristics.

It is in the field of human sciences that this tendency has surprised us most. All researches are reduced to more or less the same question: how much? Even when dealing with subject matter as complex as attitudes and feelings, this tendency cannot be escaped. For example, in a psychological test one is asked to rank a number of things, often very heterogeneous, in a one-dimensional order of preference. This would be regarded as absurd in many other cultures. One of my European friends asked a polygamous Mandenka the other day: "Which of your wives do you like best?" The Mandenka answered: "All of them, because none of them alone has satisfied me all by herself." When pressured to choose, he thought for a while and answered with a smile: "When I am hungry, it is the one that can cook fast." But he cannot be reduced to his hunger only, and the wife cannot be reduced to her speed of cooking only. The very notion of preference becomes unthinkable in such a complexity. It is completely impossible for me to say: "Here is the being which I love most in the whole world," a statement common in European literature and European daily life. Such a way of thinking reflects an affective alienation by reduction under the tyrannical influence of hierarchization.

This principle of homogeneity generates conflicts which are difficult to solve. With this principle, one endeavors by all available means to surpass and dominate others in order to find a way of differentiating himself from others within the homogeneous system. When he fails to dominate others, he is left with one possibility: to set obstacles to the enterprises of others whom he considers to be competitors or adversaries, to limit them or to eliminate them physically. Competition is the other side of the coin of homogeneity.

A Mandenka sage expressed this in a paradoxical tale. He once passed by the court of a great king. It was teeming with healthy and beautiful youngsters who were children of the king. The sage exclaimed: "What disastrous ruins we see there?" His disciples were puzzled. The sage explained to them: "This stupid king has kept his grown children around him. They all live in the hope of taking over the same inheritance. When the king dies, the internal conflicts among his children will ruin the kingdom." For a Mandenka, wisdom consists in orienting his children in different directions before his death, because common interests, far from uniting men, often divide them.

The testament of Mahan Soundiata, the founder of the medieval empire of Manden reads:

The day death reached Mahã Sõjata
He called his sons.
Come! he said to them.
Each of you tell me what he wants.
Each tell me the place he has in mind to establish himself.
That I may bless him.
If I die leaving you at each other's throats,
My efforts will have been wasted.
When a man dies leaving his many children at each other's throats,
It is as if he has left ruins behind him.

The oldest son whose name was Ba,
He came to his father,
He brought the hoe and the grain.
Father, he said, bless me by the handle of the hoe,
I have in mind the land behind the river,
The place is called Figida.
He wanted, he said, to go and settle at Figida.
He blessed him.
He went to settle at Figida.

The next son,
Fodakaba Keta,
He brought the book,
With the ink pot,
With the reed,
With paper.
He asked that his father bless him by the Koran.
Said that he had a vast land in mind beyond the river
Here at Mãdē.
He said that the place was called Kiñɛdɔba.
He said that it was at Kiñɛdɔba that he wanted to settle.
He blessed him with knowledge.
He departed to settle at Kiñɛdɔba.
In the whole of Mãdē
It was at Kiñɛdɔba that the first flames of knowledge were lit.

The son who was born after him
Was Kulũfãba.
He also brought the hoe and the grain.
Asked that his father bless him by the hoe.
Said the land he had in mind was along the chain of mountains, and that the place was called Kiñera
He wanted to settle at Kiñera
There, all the people around the mountains come to buy grain.
Till today, these people have not known hunger.

Next son,
Nɛtɛwulĕba,
He brought the gun,
With the powder.
He said: It is here at Kaaba that I will settle, in your place.
Bless me.
He blessed him by the gun and by the powder.
He became war chief.

The youngest son,
He came to ask that his father pray for him to have a long life,
And health,
And tranquility.
He said that he had a land in mind not far from here.
The place was called Dɛgɛla.
It was at Dɛgɛla that he wanted to settle.
Mahã Sõjata blessed him with long life,
With health,
And with tranquility.
Even today, if you go to Dɛgɛla
You will find people with red hair[4] (Camara 1973).

From all of the foregoing discussion we would like to single out one idea: the heterogeneity of beings and things seems to be the basis of the Mandenka philosophy, and this enables them to conceptualize change and to prepare themselves for it.

Differences in modes of life are the basis of peaceful coexistence and a harmonious community. Exemplifications of this principle may be found in the life of animals. For example, dogs fight more often with other dogs than with cats, because all dogs like the same food — bones — which cats do not like. Hunters say that a vulture and a lion make good friends because the vulture is satisfied with what the lion despises: carrion. It seems, therefore, that homogeneity generates conflicts whereas heterogeneity does not. One would think that anthropologists would be in a better position to understand this principle than other students of the human sciences.

Paradoxically, however, anthropology appears to have been dominated by an entirely different conceptualization for a long time. Evolutionism which contributed to the founding of anthropology as a "science" with its use of the comparative method took the unity and psychic identity of human nature as its basic postulate. Establishing this seems to have been its main preoccupation. What is the basis of the argument of those who say, "We are all alike" other than the knowledge they have of themselves and their personal experiences?

---

[4] Among the Mandenka, it is not white or grey hair which is the sign of old age. The hair of extremely old people turns red after having been grey.

These are their primary data. By affirming, "We are all alike," they say nothing more than, "You are like me." This is typical of the cultural alienation of Europeans which we, who were considered "primitives," found so shocking. But that is not all — there is much more to it. The travelers and conquerors of the nineteenth century drew the attention of theorists to differences in customs between the populations they encountered and European societies. Their descriptions reflect the culture of the authors more than anything else. Imperialist theory quickly reduced these differences to simple variations of secondary importance. After having eliminated the content from non-European religious and kinship systems, by means of skilfully manipulated comparisons the differences were reduced to variations found in the past history of Europe. It suffices to read Tylor (1876) and Morgan (1971) to realize this. Though it was no longer possible for European scholars to say: "They are like us," they had the satisfaction of being able to assert: "They are what we used to be." Other theorists following the philosophy of Auguste Comte (1830–42; 1884) have identified the minds of primitives with the minds of children: "They are like our own children." They assumed that there was only one way the human mind could develop. By so doing, they sacrificed the non-Europeans to the glory of their intellectual imperialism and to conscious or unconscious justification of their colonial ambitions.

How else could this phenomenon be explained? Why take so much trouble only to say "They are all like us," or in other words that there is nothing new under the sun? Such an effort was hardly worth undertaking. But a "scientific" justification was needed for something else: if non-Europeans are primitives or infantile beings who have not reached the normal level of evolution, those who have attained this level can take upon themselves the duty of educating and elevating the non-Europeans to their level — the level of "civilization." To this end, armies, missionaries, and salesmen of all sorts worked, each in his own way.

The theoretical anthropologist, having classified cultures according to a hierarchical scheme in which his culture represented the apex, could gloriously assert: "There is not a plurality of civilizations; there are only inferior cultures." By denying cultural differences, the ethnology of the nineteenth century could establish a hierarchy among peoples, completing and justifying the work of the military powers. In this way it became an intellectual weapon in the tragic process which is far from being ended even today.

Contemporary anthropologists have not yet been able to get rid of this mentality. European anthropologists and many of their disciples from other parts of the world have retained some of the imperialistic attitude discussed above. This attitude is expressed in their belief that they, as "scholars," are in a position to reveal to a population the truth about the latter. This is a paternalistic attitude, to say the least. They feel uncomfortable about facing the concept which other cultures have of themselves and of the universe. That would entail becoming a humble disciple of the other and assuming the role of a simple interpreter. The "scholar" would lose prestige by doing so, but anthropology would gain a great deal.

In a preliminary discussion at a recent congress, I said to one of the members of the discussion group that the purpose of my paper was to present psychology formulated by Mandenka themselves. He asked me with a smile of amusement and surprise: "Are you sure that they do psychological research?" Obviously, if psychology is defined solely as a discipline practiced in a specific place by a certain group of persons, and as something which provides a way of making a living for those who study it, then I am not at all sure whether the Mandenka practice psychology. But I am not sure either whether that is the only way of conceptualizing psychology or of dispensing psychological knowledge. This apparently unimportant incident has wider implications. One cannot practice the human sciences in the same manner as the natural or physical sciences. Each cultural group has its unique point of view on all types of questions. Sociologists and psychologists develop theories and systems of explanation which are preconditioned by their own culture. Therefore their point of view is neither "scientific" nor "objective." It precedes all scientific preoccupation and perhaps constitutes the foundation of their systems of explanation. What the psychologists consider to be facts is a product of conscious or unconscious elaborations oriented by their point of view — which in the final analysis is the expression of historical, material, social, political, and cultural conditions of the society in which they live. The knowledge of an observer from outside is not superior to that of an insider immersed in the norms of the life of his people. This is a reality seen from a different angle and according to a different purpose. Therefore, in addition to the scholarly theories of anthropologists and psychologists, the point of view of the people being studied must be taken into consideration. If there is no perspective which is more objective than another in the human sciences, there ought to be a fundamental rule: "Endeavor to arrive at the other's point of view!" This would mean that one must stop talking only about himself, and listen to the other with the attentive ear of a disciple. This is quite difficult, but is the only way to hear new voices.

The world today seems irremediably engaged in a process of change which puts everything into question. We cannot help but ask ourselves what the future will be and how we will be able to direct it. Nobody has the answer to these questions. However, we believe that in this context homogenistic logic will be a mediocre solution. Even worse, homogenistic logic will only amplify any conflicts which might arise because one will never be able to exclude the other without destroying him. In a changing world in which we have no stable references nor sure knowledge, one thing still remains possible: to learn to change in order to direct the future. In this respect heterogenistic logic would seem to be an invaluable tool.

REFERENCES

CAMARA, S.
  1973   L'histoire pour les Mandenka. Bordeaux: Université de Bordeaux.
  1976   Gens de la parole: essai sur la condition et le rôle des griots dans la société Malinké. Paris: Mouton.
COMTE, A.
  1830–1842   Cours de philosophie positive. Paris.
  1884   Discours sur l'esprit positif. Paris.
LEVY-BRUHL, L.
  1949   Les carnets de Lucien Levy-Bruhl. Paris: Presses Universitaires de France.
MORGAN, L. H.
  1971   La société archaïque. Paris: Anthropos.
TYLOR, E, B,
  1876   La civilisation primitive. Paris: Reinwald et Cie.

Resistance to Early Western Education in Eastern Nigeria

CHUDI C. NWA-CHIL

"The public apathy and suspicion that greeted the first efforts to introduce modern education in Africa have given way to an almost mystical faith in education as the indispensable key to personal and national progress" (Kitchen 1962: 3). Our aim is to account for the factors which were responsible for the early reactions (public apathy) of the people of Eastern Nigeria[1] toward Western education at the time of its introduction in the region. It has very often been argued that the main obstacle to the acceptance of Western education in the region was the innovative characteristics of this form of education. My contention is that while the innovative characteristics of Western education contributed to its nonacceptance, the main factors are to be found in the cultural and institutional setup of the indigenous society and in the social relations between the Europeans and the Africans prior to the coming of the first missionaries, the pioneers of Western education.[2]

This paper is from a series of articles on education in Nigeria. A later article in the series attempts to explain why and how the initial resistance to Western education in the region "has given way to an almost mystical faith in education," particularly among the Ibos. This paper is therefore part of a study in social change.

[1] Following the Nigeria-Biafra crisis, Eastern Nigeria was divided into three states. This paper deals with the former Eastern Region.

[2] I have chosen Eastern Nigeria because of the Ibos who are today often cited as educationally most progressive and the most rapidly and thoroughly Westernized group in black Africa. Of course, what I have to say also applies, sometimes in large measure, to other societies in Africa. But I believe that it is especially interesting to follow the historical development of these people with respect to European-style development, in view of what has been happening in Nigeria.

THE EARLY CONTACTS OF THE PEOPLE OF EASTERN NIGERIA WITH THE MISSIONARIES

The first contacts between Nigerians and European missionaries began with the first missionary expedition of 1841 — some three hundred years after the start of the slave trade between the whites and the blacks. This mission, usually referred to as the First Niger Mission and sponsored by the Society for the Extinction of the Slave Trade and for the Civilization of Africa, was sent out to promote trade in the hinterland, to try to establish model farms (through treaties with the local rulers), and, not least, to spread the gospel and evangelize the Africans. The slave trade had been going on for more than three centuries and was later abolished by law, but slavery continued in one way or another; law enforcement was simply not effective.[3] It was believed therefore, that "the only way to save Africa from the evils of the slave trade would be not by law or force, but by calling out its natural resources" (Crowder 1962: 124).

This mission was a fiasco, as many Europeans in the expedition died because of climatic and health conditions. But it was significant for at least one reason: it marked the beginning of missionary activity in Nigeria.

The first European missionaries to enter Eastern Nigeria were from the Church of Scotland Mission, which arrived in Calabar in 1846. These were followed by the Church Missionary Society, which began its first activities in Onitsha, on the Niger, in 1857, and then by the Catholics, with their first mission also at Onitsha, in 1885. The Qua Iboe (Protestant) Mission was the last to arrive, and it settled along the Qua Iboe River area in Uyo.

Although these missionaries had other tasks, such as helping to abolish the slave trade and promoting legitimate trade between the natives and the Europeans, their main objective was to preach the gospel and spread their new religion. They therefore preoccupied themselves with establishing schools and churches through which they could carry out this work of evangelization.

RESISTANCE TO WESTERN EDUCATION

The activities of the early missionaries, however, did not seem to be welcomed by the people of Eastern Nigeria, who not only did not want to go to their schools and were either indifferent or opposed to their establishment and the consequent introduction of the Western[4] system

---

[3]   Britain had also tried to use force to stop the trade.
[4]   Including the American system.

of education, but sometimes even resented the presence of the missionaries in their areas. Thus, the missionaries could not penetrate inland, but remained only along the coasts and in areas of the Niger Delta. For a long time Western education did not make much headway, because the traditional social structure gave the natives a basic reason for rejecting it.

The Religious System

Before the coming of the Europeans, the native peoples of Eastern Nigeria had a way of viewing their world. At the center of their view of the world and the place of man in it was their belief in spirits — that the universe was peopled by spirits, some great, some small, some virtuous, and some deadly malignant. All were capable of swift and vindictive action as well as of rewarding good conduct. These gods either inhabited or were guardians of the land, air, and sea, and everything in them.

Among the Ibos, the supreme deity was Chukwu (or Chineken), who was responsible for creation, fertility, and the rain, and was "the source from which men derive their 'chi' or soul." (Forde and Jones 1967: 25). Chukwu was also the father of the lesser great spirits: the sun, the sky, lightning, the earth deities, the spirits of water and farms, the spirits of yams and other crops, and the ancestral spirits.

The sun represented good fortune, wealth, and new enterprises. The earth deity, Ani (or Ali), was the most prominent of the great spirits and was regarded as the queen of the underworld and the owner of men, whether dead or alive. A shrine for Ani rituals was found in each village, and there was a senior shrine in the original village of the village group or other wider community.

In Ibo cosmology, every human being had a genius or spiritual double known as his *chi* which, from the moment of conception, was associated with him, with his abilities, faults, and good or bad fortune, and into whose care was entrusted the fulfillment of the destiny which Chukwu had prescribed for him (see Forde and Jones 1967: 26).

In very close association with the deities was the belief in ancestral spirits and reincarnation. This belief manifested itself in various ritual practices connected with the ancestral shrines. Through his death the individual made a transition from the material, tangible, or bodily life to the intangible world of the ancestors. In this process of transition social status and other personal characteristics were usually carried over to the other world. The closeness of the ancestral spirits helps to explain the Ibos' strong kinship attachments. The cult of ancestors was closely associated with the earth goddess Ani.

But the Ibo world was not just a spirit world. It was a dual world in which the spirit world and the world of man were one. The world of man was peopled by all created beings and things, both animate and inanimate. The spirit world was the abode of the creator, the deities, the disembodied and malignant spirits, and the ancestral spirits. It was the future abode of the living after death (Uchendu 1965: 11). In the Ibo conception of the dead, the dead were alive and still members of the lineage joined to the real world in a mystic way. There was constant interaction between the world of man and the spirit world. This interaction manifested itself in the behavior and thought processes of the natives, for instance, in their reactions to imps and their belief in reincarnation.

Among the Ibibios and some east Cross River peoples, Abassi (Obassi) was the supreme deity. Like Chukwu of the Ibos, Abassi was the sky god and the creator of men. The Ibibios also had numerous other spirits — those associated with animals, sacred places, and objects, and all represented by varying symbols. "Worship of ancestors (Ekpo) is far more prominent. Sacrifices are offered at the ancestral shrine, which is kept in the house of the eldest member of the lineage and consists of wooden stakes two to four feet high driven into the ground. The Oron have carved figures representing ancestors" (Forde and Jones 1967: 78). The Ekpo society was a cult group whose members impersonated the dead in public ceremonies.

The other tribes of the region, too, acknowledged a supreme deity and a swarm of spirits of different denominations and varying functions. Their other religious beliefs and practices also resembled those of the Ibos and Ibibios.

To summarize, the world as conceived by the people of Eastern Nigeria was a world full of spirits and supernatural powers, a world of the visible, a world of the living, the dead, and the yet unborn, a world in which the dead formed an integral part of the social life of the living. To understand these cosmological views of the people is to understand the people themselves: the moorage of their culture; what affected their behavior and thought systems; the framework into which one must fit the beliefs in witchcraft, charms, and magic so prevalent in this society; the reasons for the respect paid to elders and traditional rulers who form the visible links between the living and the dead. To understand all these is indeed to make sense of the entire way of life of the indigenous people of Eastern Nigeria.

Then came the European missionaries who introduced their (Western) education. Central to this, at least in its early phases, were these Europeans' religious beliefs: the idea of Christianity, the Divine Trinity, the death and resurrection of Christ, atonement and salvation, the angels, the devils, and heaven and hell. "Almost from the start they condemned the indigenous religions in all their aspects" (Crowder 1962: 132). They demanded that the Africans change to their, the white man's, religion. This demand was unacceptable to the people.

But, it may be asked, what had Western education[5] in its early phase to offer the natives of Eastern Nigeria that would have motivated them to abandon their own system of thought for that of the Europeans? Was it the Christian doctrine of atonement and salvation? The practice of atonement was not, of course, unknown in the traditional culture. Among the Ibos, for instance, if someone committed murder or manslaughter, revenge could be taken by the relatives of the murdered man on any member of the murderer's family, and the property of the murderer's nearest relatives could be pillaged. But if the culprit committed suicide immediately, the whole family was saved from attack and its property from spoliation (Meek 1937: 224; 1966: 126).

Were the deliverance of the natives from evil spirits, the doctrine of heaven and hell, and the hierarchy of angels new concepts? As will be demonstrated, these were not unfamiliar in the religious doctrines of the Ibos or of any other tribes in the region.

As for human sacrifices which the Christians were said to have frowned upon, it may be asked whether the idea of sacrifice (human sacrifice) was not known to these Christians? The Christian doctrine taught that "God so loved the world that he gave his only begotten Son to be sacrificed for the sins of men." It also taught (amidst messages of love for God and for one another and the abolition of human sacrifice among the natives) that one Abraham, in demonstration of his love for God, was about to sacrifice his only son, Isaac, on the altar but for the kind intervention of a voice in the bush and a ram nearby. So the Christians were indirectly teaching that if you loved God, you would be prepared to sacrifice even your own son to Him. There were then, Christian parallels to the native practice of sacrifice. The killing of twins or the sacrificing of humans was to propitiate the particular god or gods who had been offended, and here it should be reiterated that the birth of twins in those days was regarded as "an abomination which the gods of the tribe or clan frowned upon" (Nduka 1965: 91), just as much as the God of the Catholics would frown upon any Catholic who ate meat on Good Friday or who failed to do his Easter duty — sins usually remedied through prayer and sacrifice to God.

It has often been said that the people of Eastern Nigeria were animists. By this is meant that they worshiped wood and stone and

---

[5] I consider Western education and the doctrines of the Christian missions (or Western religion) to be synonymous, the former being only an instrument with which the European missionaries hoped to effect their proselytization. For example, reading was taught essentially to enable the people to read the Bible.

material artifacts. This description is not quite accurate. They never really worshiped material objects. These objects were merely symbols of the supreme being, Chukwu or Abassi. Admittedly, there were no shrines or cult symbols for this supreme deity, except for the Long Juju Oracle of the Ibos at Arochukwu, and no priesthood or place of worship for him. And it is also true that neither Chukwu nor Abassi, nor indeed any other supreme deity of these people, received any direct sacrifices. But the people knew that they were worshiping the supreme deity, and that this rather than the material and visible objects was the ultimate recipient of their offerings and sacrifices. The lesser gods to whom these sacrifices were explicitly made served only as intermediaries. The following dialogue between a European missionary and a village chief, who apparently understood the basic tenets of the Christian doctrine in those early days, will clearly illustrate this.

Village chief: "You said you had one supreme God who lived on high. We also believe in Him and call Him Chukwu. He is the Creator of everything, including the other gods."
Missionary: "But there are no other gods. Chukwu is the one and only God. These other gods you mentioned are not gods at all. They are simply pieces of wood and stones, false gods. And you worship them as if they are the true God."
Village chief: "No, we do not. It is true that they are pieces of wood and stones. But we use them only as intermediaries. It is like your angels and saints. As you said, you do not really worship these, but you beg your Chukwu through them. This wood and these stones are made by Chukwu for us to approach Him through them."
Missionary: "And the sacrifices?"
Village chief: "Yes, indeed, the sacrifices. We made them first to the little gods. And it is right to do so. They are the messengers of Chukwu. But Chukwu is the Master. These little gods are only his servants who know His will. . ."
The dialogue continued.[6]

Even if we accept that the natives were, in fact, animists, just how much more animistic was their religion than the religion which the Christians had brought to replace it? In Catholic teaching, for example, there were the angels (or spirits) of God. These angels were the guardians and messengers of God. Everyone on earth had one of them to guide and direct him against evil deeds. If he behaved well, the angel was happy and proud; if he behaved badly, the angel was ashamed and angry.

Then there were the saints surrounding God in all His pomp and glory, in a descending order of hierarchy, the most holy of them being nearest to Him, but with Mary, the mother of Jesus, sitting closest.

---

[6]   A narration from my great-grandfather, who was an "animist."

These saints in heaven above were those dead men and women who while on earth had behaved exemplarily. Ask them, through prayers, for whatever you want, and they will help you to ask God for it. Again, according to the Christian doctrine, beneath the world was hell, a kind of depository for the souls of those who died in mortal sin without repentance and forgiveness. Their souls were perpetually punished (by burning) in an unquenchable fire. The chief of this territory was Satan or the Devil (or Lucifer) — a former chief servant of God and leader of the angels, who lost his heavenly position through disobedience to God and was cast into hell.

One wonders, in fact, what significant differences there were between these Christian teachings and the religion of the natives — for instance, between the angels of the Catholics and the *chi* of the Ibos, between the saints in heaven and the ancestral spirits, and between the cross and holy pictures in the Catholic churches and the wood and stone carvings in the homes of the natives. Were not the saints and Satan, for example, just other names for the benevolent and malevolent spirits of the Africans, such as Olisa and Ajo Mmo [Evil Spirit] or the sun and Amadiora. And when an Ibo said, "*Chim do!*" or an Ibibio man, "*Abassi do!*" [God, please!], was he not "raising his mind and heart to God," as the Christians would say?

Thus, if the natives were in any way animists, the European Christian missionaries were no less so. And yet, the latter invited the former to abandon their animism for a belief in the "true" God, in the saints and angels, in the Holy Ghost, in the mysteries concerning the Divine Trinity, in the Virgin Mary's immaculate conception, and in a better life after death. Whatever the missionaries might have meant, there is no doubt that these culture synonyms with a homonymous outlook[7] brought confusion and contributed to the rejection of Western education in the region.

The Total Culture

It was not just the introduction of another religion that led to the people's initial skepticism toward Western education. The crux of the matter was that, in trying to change the religion of the natives, the missionaries also advocated a complete change in the whole of the indigenous culture. There was nothing good in it, they said; virtually everything was bad. "Native names and costumes, native songs and dances, folklore, art, systems of marriage, were all to be consigned to

---

[7]   By this I mean that the two religions were quite similar; they only *seemed* to differ. It was this seemingness, essentially, and the missionary's approach to the situation, which caused the confusion and the people's reactions.

the scrap-heap" (Nduka 1965: 12). It was altogether a revolutionary demand.

According to Crowder, this is, of course, understandable. "The missionaries made a correct appreciation of the fact that West African religions were much more closely integrated with West African cultures than Victorian Christianity with the rest of Victorian culture. To destroy the one effectively it was essential to destroy the other" (1962: 52).

These demands naturally undermined the structure of the existing community. To accept them would mean the acceptance of a complete alienation from the entire culture. It would mean the acceptance of the individualism implicit in the Christian faith in contradistinction to the corporate concept of African life. It would make things fall apart. "A cultural group feeling itself threatened by another tends to close itself against the invasion of the other" (Ponsioen 1965: 51).

Apart from these direct demands, there were also the indirect ones, arising, for example, from the school textbooks meant for use by the missionaries in their new schools. To all intents and purposes, these books, and other accompanying materials, were designed not for the people of the region but for the schools in Britain and other countries of Europe and America. Even when meant for the region, they were prepared with little concern for the environment in which the native child lived. They had no bearing whatever on the life of the individual as lived in his traditional enclave.

The earliest European schools in the region were essentially modeled along the lines of the charity schools in England, with curricula overweighted with religious knowledge — recitation of the catechism, reading passages from the Bible, and singing hymns. When the songs were not religious, they had to be in praise of Britain and her scenery or of events in British history — Rule Britannia, Bonnie Charlie, etc. (Anowi 1965: 43). Even in such a fundamental subject as language, not much was made of the vernaculars; "it was proficiency in English that was the goal" (Nduka 1965: 37). Indeed, in most schools, not only was English taught as a subject in its own right, but it was made compulsory as the medium of instruction.[8] In such other subjects as the three "R's," the contents were imported unadulterated from Britain or from America, and no attempts were made to use local material in their preparation and teaching. In history and geography, children, mostly the sons of returned ex-slaves, who were understandably the earliest clientele of these missionary schools,[9] were compelled to learn

---

[8]   For example, in all Catholic schools in Nigeria beginning in 1882.
[9]   The other early clients of the missionary schools were the children of African traders who were involved in the exchange economy of the coastal region. Anyway, some of the early patrons of the missionary schools were said to have been "literally press-ganged into schools" (Wilson 1966: 24).

the history of Europe — out of European history books — instead of African history. They were taught more about the Alps, the Thames, the winter and summer seasons, the "land of the midnight sun," etc., than they ever were taught about their own rivers, mountains, the dry and wet seasons, the Sahara, and the equatorial climate.

No doubt these early missionaries tried to give the best of what they really knew anything of — education as it was given in their own countries. The significance of this, nevertheless, is that the education intended for the people simply was not realistic, at least from the people's point of view. It was completely foreign and far removed from their life, or as Nduka (1965: 39) put it, "the school and the environment tended to pull in opposite directions." As such, these schools did not arouse the interest and enthusiasm of the native peoples.

Conflict with Traditional Education

Also significant in the resistance to Western education was the conflict arising from the traditional forms of education. Before the advent of the Christian missions or, indeed, of Europeans in general, the indigenous people of Eastern Nigeria had their own system of educating their young ones. As in all traditional societies, school and life were one, and education consisted solely in the transmission of the culture from the older members of the society to the younger ones. There were no schools in the formal sense of the word, nor any system of organized teaching either for boys or for girls, except in scattered instances of apprenticeships for boys as blacksmiths, medicine men, and fishermen.

Broadly, education in the traditional social system was "a matter of assimilation rather than formal teaching" (Green 1947: 78), and the child learned through contact, observation, and *active participation in daily life.* This involved him in meaningful relationships with the entire community. Through his daily activities, he gradually acquired the material and spiritual fundamentals of social life: the values, customs, and traditions of his society, attitudes, beliefs, a world view, and a grasp of the meaning of life in general.

Mothers played an important part in the education of girls. They taught them everything relating to the role of the woman — how to fetch wood from the bush, how to draw water from the stream, how to tend certain crops, how to look after their younger brothers or sisters, and how to prepare family meals. Certain crafts, such as weaving and pottery, were strictly in the sphere of women. The distribution of and trade in production were also entirely in the hands of women, and girls usually learned the trade from the older women. All these skills were usually learned without the aid of literacy.

The father assumed most of the responsibility for the education of the boy. He taught him how to be a man.

Thus, a small boy might accompany his father to the farm carrying a wicker container with some fowls in it. He was taught to disintegrate a neighbouring ant hill, and on this the fowls fed. In due course he would take a small hoe in his hand and learn from his father how to clear and till the land and to cultivate the crops. This process of instruction did not end with acquiring the habit and skills of merely the labour involved. Weather signs would be taught, often in the form of runes, rhymes, and sayings. Crop pests, destructive and dangerous animals and reptiles, cross-fertilizing creatures and those advantageous to the soil were identified and their peculiarities taught (Wilson 1966: 15).

The task of educating the young was not, of course, exclusively that of the parents. The child was also a member of the community from the educational point of view. Consequently, his education was everybody's affair, and practically everybody took part in it in various ways. For instance, any adult could intervene in the education of any child and in the variously constituted groups for community education. Nonetheless, the parents alone shared the blame for the moral failures of their children.

Available evidence shows conclusively that in the traditional social system of Eastern Nigeria the child was educated and educated himself through his various contacts with adult life and in the bosom of the family. It is wrong therefore to believe that Africa had no schools prior to contact with Western culture. This was exactly what the Europeans, particularly the missionaries, claimed.

When the missionaries arrived in the region, it hardly occurred to them that the natives had cultures of their own; little or no examination or analysis of what already existed was ever made. There was, indeed, a naïve belief that the people had no education at all. The facts that education is part of the social organization of any society and that all societies, traditional or modern, have educational systems whether or not they are recognized as schools, never really caught the imagination of the European missionaries. No sooner did they arrive in the region than they "stooped to conquer." And so unfortunate misunderstandings arose.

The misunderstandings were reinforced by two other factors: the occupational socialization of the child and the parents' philosophy of education. In those days children engaged in various forms of productive activities almost as soon as they could walk. The girls, for instance, participated in various forms of household activities. They carried water from the stream, collected firewood from the bush, scrubbed floors, helped to prepare the family meals, and took care of the babies while their mothers went to the farms or the market. The boys, too, though freer than their sisters, also participated right from childhood. In the season they accompanied their parents to the farms. At home they were called upon to help either in building operations or in getting food, usually grass from the bush, for the domestic animals, or they simply watched over these animals while they were feeding in the bushes. These daily duties helped to prevent the children from attending the missionary schools and contributed to the resistance to missionary education.

There is one significant aspect that must be mentioned here. Those writers who apply the modern capitalist economic yardstick to traditional African societies have often said much to the effect that, because the African child was engaged in productive activities quite early in life, he or she was no more than "an economic utility." This is not quite true, even if the word "labor" is sometimes used to describe the traditional activities of African children; one important sociological fact has often been missed by these writers. In the traditional social system of African societies, school and life were one. Children learned mostly through imitation and participation. In taking their sons or daughters to the farms or to the market, or in giving them a few odd jobs at home, parents were doing no more than educating their children, as they believed they should be educated. No doubt, children did contribute to their family's economy through these activities, but this was not the central objective of parents. Education (or, if you like, socialization) was the main concern of the parents at this stage of their children's growth. In such a simple economy, with its minimal division of labor and specialization, the child had to follow its father (or mother) in life in general, and in occupational socialization in particular. The economic relationship between parent and child was no more than that between a teacher and his pupil. It was never an employer/employee relationship, in which the child was an instrument which could be manipulated to perform various tasks merely to satisfy the (economic) needs of the employer. It was the duty of the father or the mother to guide the child when he made his first contacts with his environment, not only in social intercourse with other people but also in work, and to help him benefit by participating, according to his capabilities, in the workings of the community.

It becomes obvious, too, from another point of view, that the occupational socialization of the native child contributed to resistance to early Western education. Parents thought it their primary duty to educate their children, but sending them to a mission school was not part of that duty, nor was it, at least as the parents saw it then, a necessary part of the children's education. Rather, as we have already noted, going to a mission school appeared to conflict radically with the child's growing up (or education), not only because it robbed the child and his parents of the time the child needed to learn at home, but also because the content of missionary education conflicted with the ideologies of traditional ways of life.

STRUCTURAL STRAIN

To understand more fully the reactions of the people to early Western education in the region, one must also look at the nature of the early contacts between the natives and the Europeans in general and at the pattern of relations which existed between these two peoples before and at the time that Western education was introduced.

The first large-scale contact of the people of Nigeria with Europeans began in about 1495, with the colonization of the two islands of St. Thomas (São Tomé) and Fernando Po by some deported Portuguese Jews, exiles, and converts. These islands were said to have a rich volcanic soil and, with the heavy rainfall of the tropics, were found extremely suitable for the growing of certain tropical crops and sugar. Sugar, in particular, was a readily marketable commodity in Europe. But neither São Tomé nor Fernando Po had any indigenous population, and as a result these two islands lacked the necessary labor force to work the plantations. Benin, in Western Nigeria, could supply the needed manpower, and, by 1510 trade with Benin was almost exclusively in human beings, later slaves.

At Mina, on the Gold Coast, the Portuguese had already established a fort and were trading in gold from this region. Men were needed to work the gold mines, and the gold merchants were said to be prepared to pay for them at twice their original cost. This meant huge profits for the human traders and soon Benin was exporting slaves to Mina, too.

Trade in other goods dwindled after the start of the slave trade, and, in fact, before the turn of the century, men and gold were the main market commodities in West Africa. The slave population on the two islands of Fernando Po and São Tomé was also becoming so large that it was imperative for the slave dealers to look for markets elsewhere. By this time, fortunately for the traders (and unfortunately for Africa and the world), the Portuguese had begun to settle along the coastal plains of tropical Brazil, which was soon to become another huge plantation center. This was a prospective market for slaves and led most of the original sugar planters on the islands of São Tomé and Fernando Po to transfer their activities (now as slavers) across the Atlantic to South America, where they found a ready market for their goods — a Negro labor force of West African origin.

The silver mines of Mexico and Peru were discovered by the Spaniards about the middle of the sixteenth century. Here, too, as in

São Tomé and Fernando Po and the gold mines of Mina in their early phases, there was a labor shortage. The population of America was small. The natives of Mexico and Peru were thought to be unable to work in the mines; and the indigenous inhabitants of the West Indian islands had been almost completely exterminated. Of the Europeans themselves, not many were willing to leave home and work in the mines. The solution to the problem of labor supply, therefore, was to import laborers from the outside. The Spaniards naturally turned to West Africa where there was an abundance of people who were known to be well fitted for hard work of this nature, who could adapt easily to the climate, and could be transferred from the mines to the plantations if need be. By the latter part of the sixteenth century the Atlantic slave trade was in full swing. Slaves from Benin joined those from the Congo and Mina — at the island of São Tomé, the center of the seventeenth-century slave trade — in large caravans, for sale in the Americas.

About 22,000 slaves were shipped annually from ports in Nigeria: 4,000 from Benin and the Colony of Lagos, and 18,000 from Bonny, the New Calabar (the Present Kalabari), the Old Calabar, and the Cameroons (Crowder 1962: 63). Such was the first phase of contact between Nigerians and Europeans, and for many years this human traffic continued.

What were the implications of this early contact and how did this relationship pattern affect the acceptance of Western education in Eastern Nigeria? First, the slave trade made the natives suspicious of any white man, be he trader or missionary. As part of the slave trade, one hears of the nasty slave raids, inter- and intratribal wars, and the resultant death toll. One hears also of those killed during actual slave raids, of those wounded and incapacitated by the wars, of those who died of hardship on the march to the slave coasts, and finally of the millions of souls subsequently shipped across the Atlantic to the Americas to work in the mines and plantations there. More than 40,000,000 people, the majority of whom were able-bodied, were said to have been lost to West Africa alone in this period (Crowder 1962: 63).

As a result of this huge traffic in slaves and the human destruction that went with it, the African developed an attitude of suspicion and apathy toward the European — if not suspicion, then a feeling of insecurity, of uncertainty, and of fear. And since he made no distinction between European trader and European missionary, this affected his response to the missionary calls. True, there had been slavery in Africa before the arrival of the first Europeans on that continent. But this was mainly for the performance of servile or domestic duties and existed on a relatively minute scale. Besides, slavery in those days was neither so humiliating nor so frightful as it turned out to be during the

Atlantic slave trade. In the traditional African social system, slaves were usually acquired as domestic laborers and personal servants of their master. They often became integrated into his family and were subsequently acculturated and became integrated into the entire community with the full rights and duties of free citizenship. In some societies it was even possible for slaves to rise to positions of prominence. One remembers the biography of one Pepple, a slave of Ibo descent, who later became the King of Bonny in the Rivers Province.

The second implication of the early contact between Nigerians and Europeans may be summarized as follows: the difficulties of the early missionaries were largely the result of their close association with trading interests. The missions were dependent on traders from the interior for transport and supplies, and inevitably in the minds of the local people the missionaries became identified with the hated traders (Crowder 1962: 147).

Following the legal abolition of the slave trade (first by Britain and later by America and other European countries), Britain sought to increase her other trade with Nigeria, buying raw materials from the country, such as palm produce, timber, and beeswax, and selling her finished products from British industry. But, more importantly, Britain also sought to deal directly with the inland people and the markets of the interior rather than restrict herself to the coastal regions. She sponsored a number of explorations along the Niger in search of inland highways for this purpose. Before then:

The marketing of goods, including slaves, was handled entirely by the African middle-men of the coastal kingdoms who secured their monopoly on the basis of their exclusive knowledge of conditions in the interior and of the fact that the climate was too unhealthy for Europeans to penetrate beyond the coastal fringe (Crowder 1962: 118).

It was said that Europeans did not want to trade directly with the interior. The supply of Ibo slaves to the delta ports, for instance, was under the control of the Aros of Arochukwu who were believed to be representatives of the Long Juju Oracle or the supreme deity of the Ibos, Chukwu. Incidentally, this oracle was recognized as the final court of appeal by virtually all the inhabitants of the hinterland and the delta regions so that the Aros acted as mediators between the oracle and the different tribes of the hinterland. Because the Aros commanded great respect among the Ibo and delta states, they were "the only people who could safely travel from village to village unharmed" (Crowder 1962: 72). They were, therefore, the most convenient intermediaries between the hinterland and the delta regions.

In genuine fear that they would lose the huge profits that hitherto accrued to them as a result of their intermediary position in trade, the

Aros middlemen did not welcome the idea of the Europeans trading directly with the markets of the interior. This led to friction and resulted in outbreaks of hostilities against the "new" traders, as these Europeans were now called. For instance, in early 1860's, throughout the lands of the Niger Valley, factories set up by the Europeans were attacked and destroyed (Crowder 1962: 146).

The point then is this: It was the very group of European traders, bitterly hated as they were (because of their intrusion into the hinterland), who provided transport, supplies, communication, and sometimes protection for the European missionaries. "As the missionary bodies were not rich enough to own their own ships, these trading firms helped them by transporting them from place to place as the former's ships plied up and down the main rivers and creeks" (Nduka 1965: 23). No wonder then that the missionaries became identified with the traders the natives so bitterly hated. No wonder also that the "attacks on the trading posts at Onitsha in 1859 and 1860 brought to a standstill the work of the CMS (Niger) Mission at Onitsha"[10] (Crowder 1962: 147).

In conclusion, it can be said that the difficulties of the early missionary attempts to establish schools in Eastern Nigeria were partly due to the clash of cultures and the resultant culture conflicts between the Europeans and the natives; partly due to the fact that many natives, after more than three hundred years of subjugation into slavery, were not in those early contact days disposed to associate with any Europeans, be they European traders or European missionaries — as they could not distinguish one from the other; and partly due to the fear and insecurity of the native middlemen as their position in trade was threatened to the point of collapse. As Nduka (1965: 10) tells us, the missionary "did not want the wealth from the Nigerian soil, nor the fruits of her forests, nor any portion of her soil, but her soul," but this was not enough to induce the natives to go to school.

REFERENCES

ANOWI, J. O.
1965   "The role and function of voluntary agencies in Nigerian education," in *Education in Nigeria.* Edited by O. Ikejiani, 40–53. New York: Frederick A. Praeger.
CROWDER, M.
1962   *The story of Nigeria.* London: Faber and Faber.
FORDE, D., G. I. JONES
1967   *The Ibo and Ibibio-speaking peoples of South-Eastern Nigeria* (reprinted edition). London: International African Institute.

[10]   This Niger Mission, it should be remembered, had begun activities only two years previously, in 1857.

GREEN, M. M.
   1947   *Igbo village affairs.* London: Frank Cass.
KITCHEN, H.
   1962   *The educated African.* New York: Frederick A. Praeger.
MEEK, C. K.
   1937   *Law and authority in a Nigerian tribe.* London: Oxford University Press.
   1966   "Ibo law," in *Readings in anthropology* (second edition). Edited by J. D. Jennings and E. A. Hoebel, 221–231. New York: McGraw-Hill.
NDUKA, O.
   1965   *Western education and the Nigerian cultural background.* Ibadan: Oxford University Press.
PONSIOEN, J. A.
   1965   *The analysis of social change reconsidered.* The Hague: Mouton.
UCHENDU, V. C.
   1965   *The Igbo of South-east Nigeria.* New York: Holt, Rinehart and Winston.
WILSON, J.
   1966   *Education and changing West African culture.* London: Oxford University Press.

The Relevance of African Traditional Medicine in Modern Medical Training and Practice

KIVUTO NDETI

It would seem inconceivable that any group of people, irrespective of their level of cultural development, should not have some empirically tested knowledge of medical science. The mere fact that they have lived in their environment for a prolonged period suggests that they have acquired enough homeopathic adaptation to enable them to survive. The factors of time and space are crucial variables in man's struggle to overcome the selective pressures exerted by the pathology of his environment. This point cannot be overemphasized when one realizes that human knowledge is on the whole aquired by trial and error. In other words, so long as individuals living in a particular territory are singled out by "mystical forces" (variously known as demons, diseases, spirts, germs, parasites, and viruses) it would seem most nonhuman not to discover some remedies to ward off these challenges to existence and the perpetuation of the species. Experience of any nature is man's best teacher; hence time and space provide a laboratory in which man can experiment with reality in order to perpetuate his kind in the dynamic struggle for existence.

Here we shall attempt to show the evolution of the types of men who, while believing mortality to be the natural end of all living organisms, still challenge its causes and attempt to give rational explanations for its occurrence. The methods used in explaining the existence of these men draw upon the physical, social, and humanistic sciences. Such people are known by various designations in African societies (see Table 1).

From Table 1 several contrasts based on some features of the surface structure of the languages can be made (the terms "deep" and "surface" structures are used to characterize two very important components of a language). Deep structure in this sense means the

Table 1.   Sample of African languages contrasting wisdom, sorcerer, and witch doctor

Informant	Language	Wisdom (W¹)	Sorcerer (S)	Witch doctor (W²)
Maloba	Kiluhia	Obu-kesi (β)	Omu-losi (θ)	Omu-lesi (γ)
Muga	Dhaluo	Ri-eko (β)	Ja-jouk (θ)	Aju-oga (γ)
Bujra	Kiswahili	Bu-sara	M-chawi	M-ganga
Joroge	Kikuyu	U-ugi (β)	Mu-rogi	Mundu-mugo (γ)
Elsie	Luganda	Ma-gezi	Mu-logo	Muganga
Ndeti	Kikamba	-ue (β)	Mu-oi	Mundu-mue (γ)
Elaso	Kumamu	Ry-eko	Aj-wok	Emu-ron
Gutosi	Lumasaba	Kama-khula	Umu-wosi	Umu-sawu
Onyonka	Ekegusi	Ehi-semi	Mu-rogi	Omonya-mosira
Cecilia	Kisagara	—	Mh-awi	Mla-guzi
Yasufu	Arusha	—	—	Olo-ibon
Msaki	Chagga	Mh-re	Ms-awi	Mw-anga
Mblambuka	Matumbi	L-unda (β)	Mw-abi	F-undi (γ)
Masongo	Nyamwezi	Ma-sara	Ml-ogi	Mf-umu
Kingoria	Meru	U-ume	Mu-rogi	Mu-gaa
Keriasek	Maasai	Eng-eno (β)	—	Olo-iboni (γ)
Musikari	Bukusu	Bu-kesi (β)	Omu-losi	Omu-ng'osi (γ)
Msawi	Kirombo	—	Ms-avi	Mw-anga
Makama	Lusoga	Ama-gezi (β)	Omu-sezi (θ)	Omulu-guzi (γ)
Ejiogu	Ibo	N-zu	Omu-su	Di-bia
Vanda	Kikinga	Ama-aka (β)	Mh-awi	Ug-anga (γ)
Akiiki	Rutoro	Om-gezi	Omu-rogo	Omu-fumu

semantic aspect of language while the surface structure applies to the phonological aspect. The two components are the most basic characters of a natural language (Lenneberg 1968: 397). For the sake of analysis W¹, S, and W² are used where W¹ = Wisdom, S = Sorcerer, and W² = Witch doctor. Also β, θ, and γ are used corresponding to the W¹, S, and W² to indicate the categories of overlapping. The contrasts are as follows:

1.   W¹ versus W² = 40.9 percent overlap of the basic components marked by β and γ respectively
2.   W¹ versus S   = 13.6 percent overlap of the basic components marked by β and θ respectively
3.   W² versus S   = 13.6 percent overlap of the basic components marked by γ and θ respectively

Column S, on the basis of the surface features, seems to fall into three broad categories. The morphemes of category $[\text{-o-i}_{(o)}]$ consist of 45.5 percent of the total column entries. The second morphemic category of $[\text{a}_{(e)}\text{-il}]$ consists of 31.8 percent of the total. The rest falls in the third category which for convenience will be indicated by [-n], meaning a different language family or a prolonged separation which lacks obvious contrast. The morphemes in this category consist of 22.7 percent of the total. Although the writer depended entirely on the orthography of the informant in writing down these morphemes, the fact that such nice morphemic categories are not obvious in W^1 or W^2 suggests the uniqueness of S in the cultures represented in the sample. The factor of the language family in the sample does not seem to play a significant role in establishing the overlap correlations of W^1, S, and W^2.

However, the table was used to establish the fact that there is a basic correlation between the terms "wisdom" and "witch doctor" in many traditional African languages. Although this sample includes mainly East African Bantu languages and only a few Sudanic languages, it shows conclusively that there is a 45.5 percent overlap between W^1 and W^2 on surface structures and to a certain extent on deep structures. Thus the name of a witch doctor in the majority of African languages coincides with wisdom. He was always a man with wisdom based on practical knowledge. Unlike his counterpart, the sorcerer (a sinister character or night runner), he practiced his work in public. In the majority of cases, there was little mystery surrounding his art. It was an open secret that anyone could scrutinize.

On the other hand, lower percentages of overlap between S and either W^1 or W^2 may be attributed to chance or uncritical orthography of the informant. This means that, while most African medical practices have been identified with S, there is little or no empirical evidence to support the identification. Whatever functions S may perform in a given African society, there is little or no correlation with either wisdom or the art of healing. At least this is true for the above sample. However, no one should be under the impression that this sinister character has no function in African society. He has his place, mysterious as it may be.

Let us now take another aspect of the art of the traditional doctor. He is often accused of being "jack of all trades but master of none" by his professional colleagues in modern medicine. Like a philosopher, he knows everything about all diseases but nothing about any particular one. His diagnoses are marred by the aura of mystery surrounding them and so are some of his therapies. Furthermore, he has no formal scientific training in modern medical science. Most of his work is guess work. He does not understand the magnitude of things like germ theory, or the cause and effect dynamics of disease. His surgical practices are to say the least, very primitive and backward. Although he may give a herbal prescription, in the majority of cases this is nonscientific. He is a clever rascal and, to a certain extent, an extortionist. He is a barrier to the progress of modern medical practice in the rural areas of the developing countries and a threat to progress as a whole. He relies too much on the spirits of ancestors when diagnosing obvious cases such as diarrhea, malaria, gonorrhea, syphilis, goiter, schistosomiasis, trypanosomiasis, pains, or the common cold. Most diseases can be effectively cured if scientific methods are properly applied.

Many of these accusations do apply to some traditional doctors. Not all witch doctors are good doctors or are motivated by a desire to alleviate human suffering. Some of them (like some modern doctors) can be racketeers and exploiters who overcharge their patients in exchange for very mediocre medical services. This is an accusation which can be leveled against professionals in other areas as well. There are those who enter a profession with specific motives of material gain. These characters are interested in their profession as a means to an end rather than as an end in itself. There is no doubt that in the practice of traditional medicine, which carried so much honor and prestige in African societies, such "unprofessional" native doctors existed. Even now, some are still around, human nature being what it is.

The allegations against them however apply largely to some part-time witch doctors, and no intelligent person would condone the barriers they put in the way of progress in medical science and public health programs in the developing countries. In some cases they are so notorious that the government is called upon to curb their activities. In this way the government protects its citizens against fanatic ideas of practitioners who are emotionally disturbed, and the exploitation of certain traditional medical arts as a convenient means of personal aggrandizement.

On the other hand, there are individuals who enter the profession in response to a vocational call. They take their vocation with seriousness and purpose. They take the training in the same way. Such vocational dedication seems to come from the individual's serious consideration of the meaning of the human condition and its relation to general schemes of human destiny. It is even possible that some individuals might be motivated by selfishness but still work for noble ends insofar as they consider the welfare of humanity. Others might be motivated by sheer honesty and tenacity of purpose. In such cases vocation is conceived of as a realization of man's spiritual fulfillment.

In traditional "medicine-man-ship" there were many individuals with such a noble view of their vocation. This can be seen from the various terms describing the qualities of the witch doctor in Table 1. In Kisagara he is called *mlaguzi* [diviner or person who possesses the ability to divine]. In Kirombo he is known as *mwanga* [light]. In other words, he is a leading star of his community. In Luganda he is described as *muganga* [curer, healer, remedy]. In Ekegusi he is known as *omanyamosira* [he who posesses power to treat any organism]. In Kikuyu he is known as *mundu-mugo* [wise man, seer, diviner]. In Kikamba he is called *mundu-mue* [diviner, seer, rainmaker, wise man].

In Bukusu he is called *omung'osi* [cultural hero, big powerful man]. In Maasai he is called *oloiboni* [he who performs good acts and has no counterpart anywhere else].

All these designations point clearly to the fact that a native doctor in traditional African societies was a man of critical mind endowed with many abilities and that he was dedicated to his vocation. He was well informed about the problems of his environment and possessed practical knowledge of botany (herbistry), pathology, psychology (divination), surgery, animal and plant curative agents, climatology, cosmology, sociology, and psychiatry. He was a man renowned for his critical abilities. Thus criticisms leveled at him by his modern professional colleagues do not apply in all cases. It is true that questions can be raised concerning his medical education. But no one should forget that the native doctor worked within the means and provisions of his culture. Lack of effective media of communication such as writing and the proper keeping of professional records limited the transmission of professional ideas from generation to generation.

This, however, does not mean that the traditional doctor was not professionally competent. Oral history, folktales, stories, and folklore kept alive many important ideas for generations. Such means of keeping ideas and records of the significant events in the history of a community may not seem effective and accurate because of our own biases. It is known, however, that events recorded orally can be as authentic as historical documents (Vansina 1968). Limited though the media of transmission may have been, important ideas still managed to survive. Also in many cases the witch doctor had an apprentice or heir apparent who guarded and carried the medicine man's herbs, divining apparatus, and other items involved in the art of healing. Upon the death of the witch doctor, his apprentice or close follower always inherited his healing arts.

Let us now turn to another matter raised in criticisms of the native doctor which brings up a very fundamental problem in medical science. The medicine man was thought of as one who employs all types of techniques and therapies to treat his patients. The handling of patients in this manner, however, takes into consideration pathology and the nature of the human body, and the witch doctor's therapeutic techniques stemmed from these considerations. Disease will be discussed both from the witch doctor's and the patient's point of view. The following cases, observed some time ago, represent various efforts to understand the concept of disease dynamics. The cases were observed in villages in Tanzania and Kenya.

The first incident took place in 1953. The case involved a little girl who had recurrent illnesses including abscesses, malaria, measles, and eye infections. The uncle in charge of this little girl was undoubtedly familiar with these diseases. But what he could not account for was the fact that the illnesses followed one after another; and even after the cycle was completed some of them reappeared. In the second cycle the eye infection progressed to a bleeding stage. At this point the uncle decided to break away from modern medical practice which had proved ineffective. He was convinced by then that there was a spiritual force behind the patient's illnesses which had not been taken care of by the drugs. He decided therefore to offer a special prayer to the ancestral spirts, asking them for an explanation of the misfortune and also for a remedy. While the prayer was being said, flour and water were sprinkled on the patient as if to cleanse her from the wrath of the ancestors. The chanting of the prayer was as follows:

Mvose mwe akena Nhelua na mwe kena Anatoli mkagone. Nagwee Nhelua mwenyego haukanilongela nimsole ayumwana. Sambi ni choni mala ino ni maipu, mala ingi ni mtwe mtwe mala ingi ni meso negano meso gasambi ninhali kugaona na damu yangulawa umo! Mkagone mwvose, akina Mwambalile, mlekeni mwana asome.

The uncle was talking to her dead father and mother requesting them to leave the child alone. He reminded them of their decision, when they were in this world, to give him (the uncle) charge of the girl. He urged them to rest in peace. To his great satisfaction and in accordance with his belief, this alternative therapy worked. Eventually the girl got well.

Another case took place in 1966 and involved a sixteen-year-old girl who was attending a girls' boarding school. The headmistress reported to her parents that she was ill. When the parents arrived at the school they found her somewhat deranged. She was taken to a hospital where a physician diagnosed a case of cerebral malaria. She was treated for a while and finally recovered. However, she developed other complications later. Her eyes began to bleed, a condition which continued for almost two years. During this time she was taken to several eye specialists including some at Kenyatta Hospital. The doctors examining her eyes could not diagnose any defect whatsoever. The girl was sent home. Her parents, who were modern in their ways and education, decided to try traditional medicine. They called a traditional medicine man and secretly asked him to treat the girl.

One of the first things the medicine man did on diagnosing the case was to consider at great length the girl's genealogical history. To everyone's surprise it was found that some of the dead ancestors on her mother's side had had cases of eye disease. The native doctor told the patient's parents that it was the ancestors of the girl who wanted some blood. He ordered that they kill a goat and have the girl wash her face and eyes with warm blood. The witch doctor went into the bush and fetched some herbs which he then mashed. He added some soup from the goat meat and asked the girl to drink it. The following day he brought in another herbal medicine in the form of powder and applied it to the patient's eyes. He advised the parents to make arrangements for a traditional dance in which the girl would be invited to participate. The native doctor's orders was carried out and to the amazement of the parents the girl was cured and since then she has gone back to school.

The third case took place in 1967 in a small village in Kenya. The incident involved a man of about thirty-five years. He had been complaining for a long time of pains in the chest, headaches, and aching knees. A native doctor was called and he diagnosed the case as being caused by witchcraft. Someone in the village had introduced some little organisms which caused the pains that he was experiencing. The pains and aches resulted from the fact that the little organisms moved like grazing cows from the head through the chest to the knees. The native doctor told the patient that he was going to arrest the organisms while they were migrating into different areas. He made incisions in the aching parts of the head and covered the bleeding parts with a cow's horn, called *chuku/mbibi*. By drawing out air from the horn chamber he caused blood to flow from the head through the incisions. He repeated the same process with other aching parts. In all cases coagulated blood came out. He then applied a thick liquid-like herbal concoction on all the incised parts. He took some of the coagulated blood from different areas and asked for a live chicken. He forced the chicken to swallow the blood. He took both the chicken and the patient with him to a place where several paths converged. He released the chicken at the spot ordering it to take the patient's illness to the person who had caused it. He came back with his patient and a few days later the man was cured. The patient had a child of about six years of age who had a swollen leg. The witch doctor examined it and said it was a case of a boil situated near the bone, adding that he would prescribe a specific medicine that would draw the boil from the bone area to a particular spot on the surface of the leg. He went out to collect the medicine and came back with roots and leaves of various plants. He crushed them in a mortar with a pestle until they formed a paste. He then located a place on the leg where he wanted the boil to come through. He applied the paste, and a few days later the boil appeared on that spot. He pierced the boil and a lot of pus flowed out. Then he washed the wound with a herbal solution and in a few days the child was cured.

These incidents, observed in different parts of East Africa, raise a fundamental problem in medical science as conceived by African traditional practitioners. From the citations and the general understanding of the operations of the native doctor, several theories or ideas of disease emerge. There is no doubt in the mind of a native doctor that disease is an external force which enters a human body in a specific way and interferes with the normal bodily functions. For the sake of analysis these external forces may be divided into two classes.

In African medicine, the concept of disease first takes into account the role of the spirits of dead ancestors. This concept is found in almost all African societies. Because of the organic and psychological relations that exist between the living and the dead, the spirits of dead ancestors seem to take a keen interest in the affairs of the living. They regulate the general conduct of individuals in African societies in mysterious ways. Those who deviate from the normal activities of the culture, by refusing to offer sacrifice to ancestors, disobeying cultural norms, injuring others, refusing to cooperate with others for the general good, or shirking responsibilities, for example, must pay the price individually. The spirits do not discriminate in their attacks. Their victims include both adults and children, though they tend to concentrate on adults. Children are hardly ever possessed as adults are. The attack on children seems to be a consequence of adult negligence in maintaining peaceful coexistence with ancestral codes. Animals and plants also follow suit because of this general ignorance.

This concept of disease as originating with mischievous and dangerous spirits takes into consideration the cultural reality of human life. The fact is that the memory of dead ancestors haunts human reality. Culture helps us to rationalize the reality of death as an inevitable ending of human life. Although man is a mortal being, as the maxim states, fundamentally man is afraid of death. The fact that death is the greatest shock is deeply rooted in human consciousness. In African culture this psychological shock constantly reminds man that the only conceivable relationship that exists, after the disintegration of the dead body, is in an intangible form. The encounter between the living and the dead must therefore be through spirits. Also the fact that after death only spirit remains raises the question of the power of spirit. If spirit cannot die then it must be above the power of death and consequently it must control death. This is a logical construct, but when one considers the whole phenomenon, including the theology of death, one cannot help feeling that the native doctor's involvement of spirits in his therapies is not as foolish as it appears from superficial analyses by modern doctors. Perhaps the concept of disease could be further clarified by taking another line of approach. That is, the psychological myths of African experience which bind the living to the dead through the spirits. The living are a culmination of a long historical chain tracing back to the beginnings of things. This is what every culture in fact teaches its followers. Why, then, should a modern doctor find it so difficult to understand the native doctor's method of incorporating the psychological and cultural realities of African experience in therapy? It would seem, human nature being what it is, that all diseases, real or imaginary, are to a large extent psychosomatic. Physiological malfunctions in a human body will undoubtedly have an effect on the psychological orientation of the individual and vice versa.

Let us move to the second concept of disease. Unlike the first, this concept reduces the cause of the disease to the organic level. This is quite evident in all citations. The fact that a special effort is made to treat the human body with herbs or by some other means of an organic nature indicates existence of an assumption that sickness in a human body has an organic basis. The organic antagonists interfering with normal bodily functions can be interpreted as antigen-antibody reactions as they are in modern medicine, or as *Nyamu/Nhamu* as they are in the native doctor's terminology. In medical science today antigen-antibody reactions are seen as being due to the fact that when foreign bodies enter a "normal" human body the natural resistance of the body mounts an attack to counteract the foreign organisms. The native doctor recognizes these foreign objects, too, and he names them *Nyamu* or *Nahmu* which, in some Bantu languages, literally means "vicious little organisms" which cause death and can be passed from one person to another. These organisms, as understood in the witch doctor's language, seem to adhere beneath the human nails and when swallowed with food or drink cause illness and sometimes death. Among the Akamba there is an old saying: *vai utinda na mukundu ndakunduke* [he who stays around a person suffering from skin rash is also likely to get it]. It can be seen, therefore, that it is untrue to claim that witch doctors do not understand the concepts of germ theory or infectious disease, and disease dynamics. It is very likely that they do not understand the biology of organisms, nor do they categorize them into viruses, bacteria, and parasites. Nonetheless, their healing techniques and use of drugs leave no doubt about their knowledge that organisms cause some diseases. On the whole one can argue strongly that the native doctor had a clear understanding of the psychological and organic bases of diseases.

The standard technique of modern medicine is to use physicochemical means for controlling pathology. Remarkable strides have been made in this approach to human disease. Indeed, the area has grown so fast since the beginning of this century that it has been almost impossible for any physician to keep up to date with literature on the production of drugs. Because there are many full-time scientist-physicians engaged in pure research in such areas as nuclear medicine, space medicine, and the technology of medicine, we may expect more startling medical discoveries in the future. The trend now is to have specialists who keep up with these advances in medicine and who can advise the general physician on the use of new drugs and techniques. The specialist's advice, however, is not always immune from human error. When the advice is uncritical, it can have serious consequences, as in the case of thalidomide. This drug was widely used in many Western countries as a means for relieving tension and pain in pregnant women. But the drug proved to be mutagenic; women who had been taking it for some time gave birth to deformed children. Because of professional cults and private financial interests, it took some time to convince medical practitioners and entrepreneurs that the drug was responsible for the deformations in children. Consequently, there is now a whole thalidomide generation. Similar mistakes have been made in other areas of scientific activity as well. Nonetheless, this is the price that man must pay for his scientific activity if precautions are not taken.

The discovery of antibiotics was another landmark in the progress of medicine. They are used to boost the energy of resistance factors to many pathological agents in the body. Surgery is another area which recently has caused mixed reactions because of heart transplants. Although still disputed by some physicians because of its inability to produce effective drug therapies, psychiatry is another active area of modern medicine. The impact of psychiatry is felt in the area of mental health. Mental illness is a serious problem in the technologically advanced countries; according to some experts there is a correlation between its incidence and the fast rate of technological change in these countries.

In many of the developed countries, social institutions have not kept up with the rapid and vast changes brought about by innovations in science and technology. Because of the urgent need for industrial development in the underdeveloped countries if they are to survive, the incidence of mental illness is likely to increase in them. Hence, facilities for psychiatric treatment become a necessary corollary. For instance, in eductional institutions such as universities or colleges, in addition to having a physician to take care of specific diseases, there is also a psychiatrist who takes care of the mental health of students. In the law courts, prior to a trial for murder or any other serious crime, a psychiatrist is usually consulted to ascertain whether the criminal was in a responsible mental state when the crime was committed. Thus whether or not this aspect of modern medicine is scientific, its importance cannot be denied. If he fails to recognize it, a physician's work is incomplete.

The native doctor is not as sophisticated as his modern counterpart, nor is his training as formal as that of a modern doctor. However, he follows closely what seems to be the ideal practice of a physician. He recognizes the important role that culture plays in human diseases. He refuses to accept the simpleminded philosophy that a diseased human body is a collection of pathological states. Or rather, he accepts that philosophy but goes beyond factual information. The physico-chemical approach to disease involving the use of liquified or powdered herbs is a clear indication of factual cognition of the basis of human disease. It is in this physico-chemical approach to the treatment of disease that most triumphs in modern medicine have been achieved, and nobody doubts that greater triumphs are yet to come. Advances in molecular medicine for the treatment of human diseases are currently a popular idea among many modern practitioners. Indeed, this is one of the reasons put forward for more emphasis on biochemistry, physics, and molecular biology in the curricula of many medical schools. This emphasis helps to upgrade medical education from its present status as a "service science," based on ideas discovered in other branches of science.

The witch doctor shares this belief to the extent that he is a herbalist. But he transcends the limits of the molecular approach. He takes into account the powerful interplay of an individual with his family, his culture, and his environment. All these affect his bodily states. He also recognizes the fact that human beings are constituted of psychic and physical realities which are distinct but not separate. They interact and influence each other in all conscious and subconscious acts. For example, the unhealthy body threatens the existence of the soul which forms the principle of life. On the other hand, psychic derangement is easily translated into physical acts. In view of these two realities constituting the phenomenon of man, no treatment or therapy would be complete if it considered only one of the two. The native doctor is extremely aware of the two distinct aspects of man, and they form his philosophy of medical practice:

The shaman, like the physician tried to cure his patient by correcting the causes of his illness. In line with his culture's concept of disease, this cure may involve not only the administration of the therapeutic agents, but provision of the means for confession, atonement, restoration into the good graces of the family and tribe and intercession with the world of the spirit. The shaman's role may thus involve aspects of the roles of physician, magician, priest, moral arbiter, representative of group's world view and agent of social control (Kiev 1964: vii).

The above statement about the work of the shaman would be quite appropriate in defining the functions of a good modern doctor. There is a lot of psychology involved in the doctor-patient relationship. While a doctor must use objective methods in evaluating the patient's health problem, he should also pay serious attention to other factors such as the patient's verbal self-diagnosis. In order to understand and interpret his illness it seems absolutely essential for a good doctor to know his patient's background. This issue raises a very important point in the training of doctors. In older countries medical education strongly emphasizes curative medicine. In fact, great advances in medicine are found in this area. Although the cliché that "prevention is better than cure" is still kicked around among medical men, not much allocation of money or staff is given to preventive medicine, particularly in the developing countries:

Mr. Chairman, one thing you said which I find difficult to accept, is that there is an over-emphasis in Africa between preventive services and curative services, and that the emphasis is in favour of preventive services. I will agree with you that in the last 10 years there have been unfortunate repetitious statements about the need to emphasize preventive medicine, but the emphasis has not been reflected in actual services. . . . If there is an over-emphasis, let it be reflected in the allocation of staff or funds (Sai 1968: 34).

This area of medicine is also difficult because so much of its success depends on understanding cultures and the behavior of the people on whose behalf health programs are being implemented. Thus, the training of doctors must take into account, all factors relevant to human behavior. The inclusion of social and behavioral sciences in a medical curriculum is not just an additional unnecessary burden for medical students but a means of providing them with extremely useful knowledge which will prove most effective in their professional practice. The call for a rethinking of medical education, especially in the underdeveloped countries, is heard in many medical encounters. The old, orthodox approach to medical training has come under severe attack from critics, as reflected in the following statement:

The "biological principles" bandied about by an earlier or older generation of physicians are, most of them, nonsense — among them the deep-seated and all but ineradicable belief that natural dispositions and adaptations are well-nigh perfect, and that sickness and other disabilities are part of a long-drawn-out expiation for leaving nature and leading unnatural lives. A case can be made for thinking out medical education anew and building it upon a foundation of human biology. . . . As matters stand, human genetics makes its appearance, if at all, as a supernumerary course fitted somewhere into the clinical years; demography is mixed up with sanitation, and human ecology is treated as something which, though it may help us to understand the medical predicaments of foreigners, is barely relevant to our own cosy domestic medical scene (Medawar 1964: vi).

The British Medical Association recently announced the inclusion of behavioral sciences in medical training curricula, possibly in response to calls similar to the one cited above by Medawar.

Needless to retort that the native doctor knew all along that human diseases of whatever nature were psychosomatic. By psychosomatic is meant that health problems of whatever magnitude are likely to affect the "normal functions" of an individual on both physical and psychological levels. Because of this realization the native doctor made sure that the diseased body got its share of herbs, and psychological imbalances were restored. The psychotherapies took the forms of divination, confession, restoration of faith in dead ancestors, offerings, and "bibliotherapy." The native doctor prescribed dances in accordance with traditional culture. The dances were meant to entertain the spirits so that they would ward off all the afflictions which cause human suffering. Voodoo and *Zambi*, found in many African cultures, are in this category of dances. In addition, the dances formed an excellent basis for group therapy. They provided an appropriate climate for catharsis.

In sum, a witch doctor treated effectively the three broad categories of disease recognized in modern or scientific medicine:

1. SPECIFIC DISEASES: The diseases in this class were fairly well known to the witch doctor. He knew specific herbs that he could administer to get the expected result. In modern medicine diseases in this category are not many.

2. SYMPTOMATIC DISEASES: The diseases in this group involved both herbal treatment and a psychological result. In other words the witch doctor gave a herb which reduced the symptoms of disease in the patient without necessarily changing his pathological state.

3. PSYCHOLOGICAL DISEASES: The witch doctor gave psychological therapies in addition to bibliotherapy. In this way he was able to improve the feeling of the patient without necessarily changing his pathological condition. A good doctor in the modern sense has to be more or less like the traditional native doctor; he is not just a specialist who treats only specific diseases but one who treats nonspecific diseases, that is, symptomatic and psychological ones which make up as much as 90 percent of all known diseases.

Finally, the art of healing, whether modern or traditional, cannot escape the paraphernalia which surround the mystery of curing agents. There is a great deal of emphasis on science in modern medicine, and this is well and good in all fairness to science. However, in view of the quackery and mystery of healing agents, and human nature being what it is, scientific medicine would do better and would advance its professional goals if it recognized the legitimacy of the so-called nonscientific approach to human healing. This nonscientific approach seems as if it will always be there in one form or another. To date, beliefs such as Christian Science, divination, palmistry, superstition, occultism, fortune-telling, magic, soothsaying, miracle healing, exorcism, possession, witchcraft, will of God, fatalism, shamanism, juju, and voodoo, are still in existence. These beliefs are as old as man. They figure greatly in the inner reality of human life. So far they have been a hindrance to the progress of so-called scientific medicine in many parts of the world. Modern medicine would do better if it stopped adhering to the cult of science and professionalism. Even the most ambitious program geared to eradicating a specific disease is doomed to failure if the planner fails to recognize the complexity and relevance of cultural institutions in the matter. An example of such failure was the effort made by the World Health Organization to eliminate schistosomiasis in the countries of the Nile Valley where this disease is endemic. One of the barriers to complete eradication of schistosomiasis is Islamic tradition. The religious rite of washing the genitalia after excretion acts as a medium of transmission of the disease. In order to institute an effective control of the parasite, modern medical men would have to ban the rite. Yet it does not seem likely that devoted Muslims would give up an age-old holy rite in response to medical advice. It would be a wise move for scientific medicine to meet tradition halfway in such matters.

This also applies to the relation between the witch doctor and his modern counterpart. In view of its activities, powers, limitations and the very nature of the subject, modern medicine must accept and recognize the reality of the native doctor. He is a very important part of the medical scene and possesses legitimate knowledge essential for medical science. The professional jealousies, cults, and god-complexes surrounding modern medicine should be shunned, and all the attendant hypocrisy. The witch doctor's therapies and treatments should be examined critically and the relevant elements adopted into modern medical practice. These therapies and treatments touch many vital areas which are beyond the imagination of current medical education and they are wholesome in approach. This is a virtue which modern medical science cannot afford to condemn.

REFERENCES

HARRISON, G. A., J. S. WEINER, J. M. TANNER, N. A. BARNICOT, editors
  1964   Human biology: an introduction to human evolution, variation and growth. New York: Oxford University Press.
INTERNATIONAL PLANNED PARENTHOOD FEDERATION
  1968   The role of family planning in African development. Hertford: Stephen Austin and Sons.
KIEV, A., editor
  1964   Magic, faith and healing: studies in primitive psychiatry today. London: Collier-Macmillan.
LENNEBERG, E. H.
  1967   Biological foundations of language. New York: John Wiley and Sons.

MAHLER, H.
1975 "A crisis of purpose: dilemmas and opportunities," in *The 17th International Congress of Midwives report.* Lausanne.
MEDAWAR, P. B.
1964 "Foreword," in *Human biology: an introduction to human evolution, variation, and growth.* Edited by G. A. Harrison et al., v–vi. New York: Oxford University Press.
NDETI, K.
1972a *Elements of Akamba life.* Nairobi: East African Publishing House.
1972b Socio-cultural aspects of tuberculosis defaultation: a case study. *Journal of Social Science and Medicine* 6: 397–412.
1973 "Social change and mental disorders: a Kenyan case," in *The use and abuse of drugs and chemicals in tropical Africa.* Edited by A. F. Bagshawe. Nairobi: EALB.
1977 "Future of human family: cross-cultural perspective," in 6th ECUS, ICF. New York.
NDETI, K., C. NDETI
1977 *Cultural values and population policy in Kenya.* Nairobi: D. L. Patel Press.
SAI, F. T.
1968 "Useful entry points for preventive medical services," in *The role of family planning in African development.* Edited by International Planned Parenthood Federation, 34–36. Hertford: Stephen Austin and Sons.
VANSINA, J.
1968 "The use of ethnographic data as sources for history," in *Emerging themes of African history.* Nairobi: East African Publishing House.

Managing the Ecosystem of World Nations

SAMIR I. GHABBOUR

THE PAST HISTORY OF THE HUMAN SPECIES

In discussing the future of the human species, it is essential to interpret its past history in the light of the present if we are to recognize the trends which are likely to prevail in the future.

It is often said that man is a social animal. But where are the signs of his sociality? Man is the descendant of the armed hunting bands of the Palaeolithic, and this loose level of social organization was man's first experience of sociality. The human species is still a new species which cannot be said to have fully developed its potential for sociality. The other species belonging to the family *Hominidae* were extinguished before any form of social organization beyond coteries could be developed.

Other primates have stabilized social systems which may be similar to those of the Cro-magnon stock of *Homo sapiens*; we might have retained these systems were it not for the extraordinary ability of our species to radiate into a multitude of different environments and for our endowment with a bigger brain which gave us the power of speech and fostered curiosity and inventiveness.

Homo sapiens is still in the process of acquiring an appropriate social system through a painful process of trial and error. Every historic period is different from all others because innovations take place and there are always changes in the physical and cultural environments. It is illuminating to compare the brief span of human history with the

This contribution draws from such a large number of texts in ecology, history, anthropology, and economic geography that I am unable to cite them all, but I am indebted to their authors for helping me to view the world nations as an ecosystem that may be managed.

millions of years which were available to the primates related to man or the scores of millions of years which were available to the social insects. In their beginnings as clear-cut species the primates and insects must have passed through agonizing processes of socialization much like the one we have been passing through since the Palaeolithic. Now, at the end of the trail, we can admire the perfected social systems of the termites, the ants, and the bees. We also understand a great deal about the social organization of several primates. Their social systems must have been established through trial and error, or, to use evolutionary terminology, by mutation and natural selection. There is very little human social organization that is solidly established for the whole species in a way that is comparable to that of the social insects or the primates.

The social norms of social insects and primates appear to us to be well adapted to the environmental requirements of the respective species. When man first appeared with his unique properties of speech, versatility of hand, large brain size, lack of fear of fire — in short, with his innovative capacity — he had to evolve social norms which would ensure his survival. Since he was able to spread from his original home, which may have been an African savanna, into a multitude of different environments, he could not rely on the social norms inherited from his ancestors or on a single set of norms. He had to modify and adapt his norms to the rigors of every new environment into which he ventured. Because of this, the human species was unable to establish a definite and durable set of social norms.

The appearance of the human species coincided with the great climatic vicissitudes of the Pleistocene. The Palaeolithic was a long period marked by a series of abortive efforts to establish a permanent adaptive set of social norms. When man emerged safely at the end of the Würm Glaciation, about 20,000 years ago, he had a very limited heritage of useful and adaptive elements of social organization on which to draw. Perhaps only the human populations in the intertropics, which had been relatively less affected by the glaciations, were able to evolve useful general principles of social organization upon which to build their present social structures. The Neolithic populations of the Middle East, India, and China, which may have been in close contact with the former populations, were able to build more elaborate social systems than their intertropical fellows.

The small units of social organization which were suitable for the gathering economy of the intertropics — the family, the clan, and the tribe — were developed by the riverine populations of the Middle East, India, and China into the village, the nome, and the kingdom, when they adopted agriculture. When they became pastoralists, the nomadic populations between the rivers developed the tribal system into a much more coherent system than it had been in the intertropics. All these developments took place over a period of only 5,000 to 10,000 years. The new systems were so well adapted to the local environments that they continue to the present.

Nevertheless, despite the successful social experiments of the Holocene, human social norms are not as firmly established as are those in societies of baboons, monkeys, or the higher primates. Even the biologically fundamental male-female relationship is not well fixed. There is a lot of uneasiness about this relationship everywhere in the "civilized" world, and the period of experimentation with it is not yet over. Some youth groups in the United States and Scandinavia are carrying out new experiments or repeating old ones that were discarded a long time ago. These experiments emanate from a rejection of present-day norms and show that these norms may no longer be functional due to innovations generated by the societies in which the experimenters live.

Devising strategies of social organization which would be most appropriate for the environment was much easier for nonhuman primates, even for those which evolved in the Pleistocene with man, because they were not handicapped by man's innovative capacity. It is this capacity which emancipated man from the animal world and from nature. It caused constant instability in social organization, so that we speak of *forms* of human social organization, while there is only one form of organization for each species of social insect or primate. Man, though a social animal descended from social animals, is not yet as social as his relatives. True, there are a number of highly elaborate and sophisticated human social systems, but these are highly local and confined to small communities. They are in a perfect and delicate balance with the environment and are inappropriate if transferred elsewhere. Hundreds of these communities coexisted and interacted slowly in the world for millennia, but they were readily crushed when exposed to foreign influences from societies with more labile forms of social organization. Subsequently, these balanced communities, which have erroneously come to be termed "primitive," have tended to replace their stabilized and functional social achievements with foreign labile forms.[1]

---

[1]   A stable society is one which is in a harmonious balance with its environment. It is one which does not exhaust or deplete its natural resources. Labile is a more appropriate ecological term for "advanced" (unstable) societies. Labile societies exhaust their own or others' natural resources. It is to the credit of stable societies that they are able to remain stable, i.e. in harmony with the environment. This explains why a number of human societies remain at the gathering, subsistence agriculture, or subsistence pastoralism stages. It is because they are in perfect balance with the environment.

THE ORIGIN OF THE ECOSYSTEM OF WORLD NATIONS

The unstable systems had no chance of reaching a state of balance with the environment because neither the physical nor the cultural environment was ever allowed to become stabilized. The story of instability started in the great river basins of the Middle East, India, and China where man began to change his physical environment purposefully by a series of engineering inventions. The instability of the environment, compared to that in the intertropics, was a challenge to the innovative genius of the human populations which settled on the banks of these rivers. The seasonal flood, which pumped life into the valleys and allowed luxuriant plant and animal life to flourish, was followed by markedly contrasting dry and parched conditions for the rest of the year. In these unstable conditions the local populations were forced to find a way of surviving the dry season. The proximity of a permanent water supply was a deterrent to migration, and there was nowhere to go but the nearby inhospitable desert or other equally unpleasant environments.

In the savanna, the local populations were obliged to migrate seasonally even where rivers were present; in fact, they had to migrate away from the rivers in flood time. Disease, insects, and flooding were repellent factors. These populations came back to the river when it was low. This still happens today in southern Sudan. In arid regions, where there is a river it is the sole life-giver; in the savanna, rain makes the river of secondary importance. It was vital for the riverine populations in arid regions to remain near the river even though they might starve in the low season. Food had to be stored for this period. Food production had to be improved by agricultural methods which involved making the best possible use of the available flood waters. Basin irrigation was the outcome of the innovative power of the early Egyptians. This system of irrigation required the construction of levees between basins, the digging of canals, the calculation of areas, the establishment of land ownership, etc. It also required a centralized government to administer these and other activities. Perhaps it was in Egypt that the institution of centralized government originated, and it is possible that the Egyptian model influenced the later rulers in Europe more than any other model in the Middle East. The Egyptian governmental institution was the most ancient, elaborate, efficient, and stabilized in the Middle East when Alexander the Great led his armies to conquer these lands. Julius Caesar was suspected of contemplating the establishment of an "Oriental" monarchy.

With the introduction of Middle Eastern innovations in Europe during the Graeco-Roman period, the state became much cherished and fought over. While this institution was penetrating into temperate latitudes, the savanna populations were developing elaborate forms of the tribal institution. In both regions, the institution adopted was the one best fitted to the environmental needs — in the former case, the need for agriculture and in the latter for transhumance. The wandering tribes of Europe took a long time and sacrificed much before finally accepting the institution of centralized government. It was developed in the first place to fit basin irrigation in a dry country and then tailored to fit the conditions of each country that accepted it. It was only in the nineteenth century that centralized government spread throughout Europe — Germany and Italy being the last European countries to adopt it.

It was also toward the end of the nineteenth century that the European powers became determined to conquer the whole inhabited land area of the globe. They either conquered tribes or deeply influenced their cultures. Thus a new flow of innovations from centrally governed states to tribal societies was established. This resulted in the tribal societies adopting European ideas about social organization. The oppressed tribes longed to free themselves from the colonial powers in order to build a state like the one which ruled them. The former colonies all adopted the institution of the centrally governed state once they obtained independence. It was impossible to return to the tribal system which had been successful before the Europeans came. Now the whole land surface of the globe is divided into centrally governed states. Gone are the days of the tribe as an independent political unit. The state, in the form in which it began in Egypt, has now been adopted by countries which did not develop it as an answer to their own local environmental requirements. In fact, this form of organization may be antagonistic to such requirements (for example, the frequent lack of coincidence between tribal and state boundaries in Africa). Today, the centrally governed state is universal.

All of the people living on earth now have a nationality (except in a few colonies, mostly in Africa). They are subjects of a particular nation. They live within boundaries they did not choose, which were drawn in many cases as straight lines on a map to satisfy the dominant powers and may be meaningless to the inhabitants whose interests are sometimes jeopardized by these lines. People are not allowed to move from one country to another without permission from the two countries concerned. Nor are citizens allowed to move goods from one country to another without permission.

All international relationships and exchanges are firmly controlled all over the world by centrally governed states, notwithstanding some smuggling. The human species is thus totally distributed over a number of states which control its future. The interrelationships of these states now covering the globe constitute an ecosystem which has been growing over the millennia through the spreading of innovations and the reaction of tribes to them. The tribe which was the appropriate form of social organization for the human species at the subsistence stage and also at the pastoral stage in the intertropics, is now obliged to merge with other tribes within the boundaries of the state. The once independent tribe is now being pressured by the emergent centrally governed state to abandon subsistence for cash-crop production in order to boost exports.

It is important to note not only that the human species is divided into nations and that these nations have filled all the space into which they can expand, but also that these nations now have to learn to coexist. They will have to develop a pattern of interrelationships that will help to maintain the global environment in a healthy condition. Pollution, for example, is the responsibility of all nations, each contributing in its own measure and proportion. Pollution is not an inevitable curse. In many of its aspects it is the result of faulty recycling of matter. Since the movement of matter is now controlled by nations, it is their collective responsibility to politicize its cycling according to the same rules which guarantee its cycling in healthy and mature biological ecosystems.

THE STRUCTURE AND FUNCTION OF THE ECOSYSTEM OF WORLD NATIONS

The division of the world into independent states is a new situation that has come about only in the last couple of decades with the freeing of former colonies from foreign rule. The new states fitted themselves into the formerly smaller and simpler ecosystem as new members with new endowments and characteristics different from all other previous members. Every new state not only enlarged the size of the ecosystem but also introduced new relationships between itself and other members and modified the relationships that existed among the former members before its entry. Every former member had to adjust its relationships with other members to accommodate the new relationship established with the new member. These relationships are mostly manifest in trade but also include variables such as emigration, immigration, grants and loans, exchange of services, armaments, repayments of loans, and foreign investments. The pattern of these variables had to undergo modification with the establishment of a new network of such activities with every new member joining the ecosystem.

An ecosystem is not just an assemblage of components. It is, in addition, a pattern of interrelationships which render the system homeostatic. The degree of homeostasis increases as the ecosystem matures. If the newly established ecosystem of world nations is allowed time to mature, it should reach a degree of homeostasis comparable to that of mature biological ecosystems. The ecosystem of world nations can be helped to reach maturity and homeostasis by deliberate steering or management to shorten the time required for the completion of the maturation process. In this ecosystem, nations are analogous to species in a biological ecosystem. The mature biological ecosystem has a characteristic structure and function, and all its species interact in harmony and may survive as active components indefinitely.

The ecosystem of world nations is at present undergoing continuous adjustment because it is very recent, but these adjustments may eventually allow all the components to fit into a functional pattern that will be beneficial to the parts. The ecosystem may then continue in a state of dynamic equilibrium with a considerable degree of homeostasis.

Structure. By the middle of 1970, before the creation of Bangladesh, there were 152 nations in the world (see Tables 1 and 2). The distribution of these nations in terms of area or of population on a logarithmic scale shows a characteristic pattern, with a preponderance of medium-sized nations and fewer very small or very large nations.

Table 1. Classification of world nations by area.

Area in square kilometres	Number of nations
Less than 10	2
10^1–10^2	2
10^2–10^3	13
10^3–10^4	7
10^4–10^5	32
10^5–10^6	69
10^6–10^7	26
More than 10^7	1

Table 2. Classification of world nations by population size

Number of individuals	Number of nations
Less than 10^3	1
10^3–10^4	1
10^4–10^5	11
10^5–10^6	22
10^6–10^7	69
10^7–10^8	41
10^8–10^9	7

About 46 percent are within the 10^5–10^6 km^2 area group and within the 10^6–10^7 individuals population-size group. About 83 percent are within the 10^4–10^7 km^2 area group and about 86 percent within the 10^4–10^8 individuals population-size group. The majority of world nations fall within these limits of area and population size. There is a higher proportion of smaller nations, however, than of larger ones. It is noteworthy that exactly the same number (69 nations) is present in both the majority area and majority population classes. There are also more larger nations on the population scale than on the area scale. This is understandable because nations can swell their population but cannot add to their area now that all lands belong to one nation or another.

If the nations of the world are the biotic components of the ecosystem, their natural resources, including living resources, correspond to the abiotic components. Whether the natural resources of a nation are living or nonliving does not affect the nation's function (or niche) in the ecosystem. The distinction between renewable and nonrenewable resources is much more important. Nations with renewable resources (if well managed) are in a much better position to continue functioning than nations with nonrenewable resources, even if the former are poorer. The latter group, no matter how rich they may be, will lose their place in the ecosystem when their resources are depleted. They will either disappear as nations, or, if wise enough, will change their niche by wise investment of their income.

A nation's natural resources are those which, when properly utilized, enable it to satisfy the needs of its population and to trade with other nations. It is the second aspect which is essential to the structure and functioning of the ecosystem.

Function.   The amount and kind of natural resources is what determines the niche which a nation occupies in the ecosystem. The form in which natural resources are traded determines the level of productivity of the nation. If a nation exports its resources in crude form, or as raw materials, it is said to be a primary producer. A primary producing nation may be important in one resource and not in others. If a natural resource, such as cotton or petroleum, is processed in a country other than the one which produced it in crude form, this second nation is said to be a secondary producer, or primary consumer, and its importance depends on the amounts of such resources that it handles. A third level of production and at the same time a second level of consumption is where a nation imports manufactured goods from secondary producers and consumes them or processes them further.

When the world was divided into several smaller, simpler ecosystems of two levels only, composed of colonial powers and their colonies, there was little exchange between neighboring ecosystems, but there was heavy traffic between each colonial power and its colonies. The colonial powers imported raw materials from their colonies and exported a high proportion of their manufactured products to them. Cycling of matter was ensured, and the colonies were able to absorb the secondary production of the colonial powers. Secondary production consisted mainly of manufactured goods, such as textiles, which the colonies could use. What made a society become a secondary producer was that it learned to innovate because of physical and cultural environmental instability. This, in turn, created a demand for raw materials and produced a surplus of manufactured goods. Both conditions could be satisfied only by trade. Maps of trade routes show that they are established only by secondary producers. The same pattern is found on maps of the ancient world and maps of A.D. 1960; the only differences are that the number of secondary producers in A.D. 1960 is larger and the routes span the globe. The trading areas have expanded to include all the inhabited continents, but the pattern of relationships — between primary and secondary consumers — has not changed.

A similar pattern dominates international trade today, but it has undergone a number of modifications. Foremost among the modifications are: (1) the increase in trade among secondary producers, which are now 10–15 in number according to how they are defined; (2) the introduction of a new type of production which is at a higher level than the processing of primary products. This is tertiary production, represented by complex machinery such as sophisticated electronics, rockets, satellites, and atomic devices. Two countries are involved in tertiary production ahead of all others, for which reason they are termed "superpowers"; (3) the diversion of the bulk of secondary production to the tertiary producers which thus become large-scale secondary consumers; (4) the establishment of some trade among the primary producers.

The colonial powers and their colonies which constituted separate small ecosystems in the nineteenth and first half of the twentieth century, have now coalesced into a single large, complex ecosystem. The appearance of a third level of production (simultaneously a second level of consumption) which gave the new ecosystem its new complexity of structure and function would not have been possible without the coalescence of the former small ecosystems.

Biological ecosystems are distinguished into trophic levels which are stratified into a pyramid of numbers. The number of species on any level is usually ten times the number of species on the level above. In the ecosystem of world nations, the 10:1 ratio in the pyramid of numbers holds. The superpowers are two (not exactly equal). The rich nations, which are the secondary producers, are about 10 in the Western world and about 4 in the Eastern Bloc, depending on definition. This leaves us with 130–140 primary producers (the less-developed countries). If we take the production size of the Soviet Union as 0.4 of that of the United States, the ratio becomes 1.4 : 14 : 136 (137 with Bangladesh). This ratio depends, of course, on definitions and is open to modification, but the overall 10 : 1 ratio remains. The question of definitions is not settled yet, but a nation's level of productivity is a suitable guide.

Within each level, every nation has a predestined role which no other nation can play in the same manner. Every nation has its own definite geographic position that cannot be shared with any other nation; this determines its assets in terms of natural resources. Thus no two nations enjoy the same complement of natural resources. This leads to a natural division of labor among nations which is not so much imposed by external political and economic pressures as by each nation's original endowments of natural resources (climate, topography, waters, soils, plants, animals, fossil fuels, marine resources, etc.). Immediately after they obtained independence, the primary producers endeavored to increase the quantity and to improve the quality of their primary products (cotton, cocoa, coffee, jute, rubber, timber, livestock, wool, petroleum, coal, tin, copper, etc.). Although they now have the choice of changing old colonial production patterns it is difficult for them to do so. Even if a primary producer can develop some sort of secondary production, it is either difficult to market it or it must be sold to nations at a higher level in the pyramid which are able to maintain their advantage as secondary producers because of their higher innovative efficiency. Thus the gap is maintained and even widened. Primary producers should not feel embarrassed by their position in the pyramid as long as feedback is maintained in the ecosystem. It is this vital feedback which is lacking or faulty at present. This is what creates crises.

A biological ecosystem does not consist only of producers and consumers; it has its parasites and decomposers. The ecosystem of world nations also has these two categories. In today's world, there are two or three "hot spots" where militaristic groups suck enormous amounts of material from upper level consumers and impose a constant threat of destruction on the regions around them, thus putting the countries of the region on the defensive and obliging them to slow down their development and allocate the proceeds from their resources for protection. An ecosystem made up of human beings should remove this ugly and destructive form of feedback and replace it by direct constructive input for peace loving primary producers.

MANAGEMENT

The ecosystem of world nations may not be an exact replica of a biological ecosystem — we may not wish it to be — but the salient features are present. The flow of energy and the cycling of matter must be distinguished in great detail. The bottlenecks which hinder these movements must be identified and treated. Humane feedback must be encouraged and sustained.

In order to realize these objectives, mathematical models which include all forms of exchange among nations must be constructed to give an exact picture of the situation. Such models will help in predicting the results brought about by emergence of a new nation, an increase or decrease in the trade in a commodity, the outbreak of a war, or other changes. A state of dynamic equilibrium of some sort exists now and will continue to develop automatically if left without intervention. It will develop along the lines of the law of the jungle. The law of the jungle is the result of the automatic development of biological ecosystems. In a human ecosystem, development into a mature stage must be oriented, diverted, or corrected as required, by rational management. With our awareness of the functioning of our ecosystem, we know that management by external intervention is necessary to help the ecosystem mature in the shortest possible time while avoiding inflicting suffering through wars and revolutions — both forms of destructive blind rectification. Management should aim at helping the ecosystem to produce, consume, and recycle matter by giving every nation the chance to exchange with others goods that will satisfy its needs.

Management can be carried out by the United Nations and its agencies or by specialized international authorities governing each of the natural resources separately, e.g. for oil, whales, fishing, and cocoa.

Instead of having associations of producers on the one side confronting associations of consumers on the other, there should be something that might be called "The International Authority for Managing... Resources" which would bring producers and consumers together for their common benefit and in order to prevent the use of force and the generation of hostility. The managing authority should work with the full consent of the producers and consumers. Its decisions should be fully implemented by those concerned. Wars and revolutions are the result of lack of any proper ecosystem management of natural resources. If such management were established, perhaps the human species would be able in the future to discard forever the militaristic tendency which performed the feedback function in the past.

Social Determinism and Social Change: An Analysis of Alternatives for the Future Development of Papua New Guinea

T. K. MOULIK

The major stimulus for far-reaching social changes in a predevelopmental society comes from its exposure to external influences in ideas, communications, institutions, and technology. In other words, the principal source of social change in underdeveloped countries is exogenous in the sense that the change in the traditional culture starts as a process of intersocietal culture diffusion brought about through contact. This is not to suggest that the traditional society is stagnant; there is ample evidence that social change is an ongoing process. But there is little doubt that exposure to new ideas as a result of intersocietal contact is the major stimulus for large-scale and intense social change. In stressing the role of tradition in modernization, a misleading impression is often given that the sources of change are to be found in tradition itself (see various studies in Singer [1959]). Tradition comes in at the stage of responding to new stimuli, not as their source.

Almost by their nature, the processes of social change produce strains or intensify strains which are already present in the society. These strains cause the most tortuous problems in the recipient "undeveloped" societies where there is always a race with time. The challenge of social change is more taxing for a primitive society like Papua New Guinea than for many other developing countries, first, because of its unique sociocultural heritage which in most respects is in complete contrast with the cultural heritage of the Western societies from which the major stimuli of change come; second, the short span and depth of the nationalist movement in Papua New Guinea make it an unsuitable vehicle and training ground for social and economic reform; and third, the sudden and rapid nature of the modernization sequence necessitates simultaneous changes in many sectors of the society, thus making it difficult to develop any coherent scheme of priorities.

Working from this assumption — that the principal stimuli for social change in a traditional society are exogenous, originating in the physical or social environments of modern societies and that the role of tradition is to respond to these stimuli — the fundamental question concerns the way in which the traditional society adapts to the exogenous stimuli.

In the colonial situation, which is a cross-cultural product of superimposed interethnic contacts, the traditional society's adaptation to the introduced "modern" stimulus invariably takes place through imitation rather than innovation. Although imitation would not seem to require the exceptional personal qualities associated with the Schumpeterian model of entrepreneurship or innovation, in underdeveloped countries it is, nevertheless, a pioneering step, as daring in its way as innovation in the developed countries. Moreover, the imitative action is not just a passive adjustment to the introduced change, but a process by which certain action patterns associated with the induced change are acquired. In this process the imitator is motivated to attempt to reproduce the model's pattern of action in his own pattern or project of action (see Hurh [1968] for a scholarly discussion on the process of imitation). Over a period of time, through selective adoption, elimination, and reshaping of the borrowed elements, the imitative action becomes essentially innovative. In other words, the traditional society, in responding to external stimuli, introduces action patterns which are already available in the developed countries and in this way orients its innovational efforts to meeting specific internal problems or needs.

But the problem of imitative action is that it is always segmental or partial, in terms of similarity to the original model (that is, the introduced stimuli). A perfect identity between the model (or the exogenous change-producing stimuli) and its reenactment is inconceivable. Time is the most important factor in explaining this. Yet, the success of the imitative action is generally evaluated in terms of its similarity to the original. The apparent incongruity is due to the intervention of *determinism*. Broadly speaking, there are three types of determinism involved in the ultimate outcome of the imitative action:

1. Determinism inherent in the nature of the model's action or of modern technologies. Examples are as numerous as the number of modern technologies in fields such as politics, biology, chemistry, the physical sciences, economics, sociology, and psychology. In the economic field, the deterministic role of production factors, land, labor, capital, and technical know-how is well known. Directly relevant to the present paper is the market determinism combined with the institution of a money economy which provides a generalized facility

for acquiring desired goods and services, although certainly not an unlimited range. The deterministic role of the supply-and-demand relationship between monetary rewards and efforts is also relevant.[1]

2. Determinism arising out of the unique sociocultural heritage of the imitating society.

3. Determinism caused by the sociocultural heritage of the model or developed society which is the source of the stimulus for change.

The last two categories of determinism include the whole gamut of attitudes, abilities, personality characteristics, social structure, and socialization processes. Obviously there is a whole range of degrees of similarity between the imitated action and the action of the model, depending on the nature of the similarities and differences among these three kinds of determinism.

Against this background of the nature and requirements of a theory of social change I shall examine the rural communities of Papua New Guinea. My aim is to provide a characterization of traditional communities which have been exposed to an advanced economy, with a view to showing what aspects of the advanced economy are likely to be adopted in a continuing process of adaptation and with what types of modification.

Various aspects or elements of an advanced economy were introduced into the primitive society of Papua New Guinea by the incoming colonial powers, but my main concern here is with the introduction of monetary exchange. My choice of this aspect stems from the fact that I have recently done fieldwork in rural communities in Papua New Guinea, investigating the responses of the indigenous inhabitants to the cash economy. I have also chosen this aspect because the introduction of "general purpose" money into a purely subsistence economy is the most influential of the exogenous change-producing stimuli; it causes a ripple effect in other facets of socioeconomic life and leads to a thorough reevaluation of traditional values and social structures. In fact, the social, political, psychological, and economic changes going on in present-day Papua New Guinea can be viewed as direct and indirect effects of the indigenous reaction or response to the monetary exchange economy.

[1] The deterministic nature of the market economy is emphasized by Talcott Parsons: "Since there is no important contemporary economy which closely approaches the ideal type of *laissez-faire* and pure competition of the nineteenth century, it has become fashionable to hold at least among certain intellectuals who are not professional economists, that markets and more broadly economic considerations no longer count. This is clearly an illusion which, if taken seriously, may have disastrous consequences. The market, though both 'oligopolistic' in its most important sectors in free-enterprise societies, and publicly controlled, remains a critically important aspect of modern societies, and though given much less scope in the socialistic societies, the fiction of market evaluation becomes indispensable to economic policy" (1970: 620).

PRECONTACT SOCIAL AND ECONOMIC STRUCTURES

Before discussing the social changes associated with the introduction of a money economy, the major characteristics of the traditional social structure of Papua New Guinea should be outlined. It is not my intention to give a detailed account of the social structure of precolonial Papua New Guinea and in some ways it is a gross violation to attempt to characterize such a complex socioeconomic structure in just a few broad strokes. My hope is, however, that this broad characterization will help to bring to mind the type of society that we are dealing with and the nature of its inherent forms of cultural determinism. My intention is to focus on specific aspects of the primitive social structure of Papua New Guinea especially those which affect that society's participation in the monetary exchange economy.

In broad terms, precontact Papua New Guinea can be regarded as a typical primitive or subsistence economy in isolation; all consumption depended on subsistence production; there was no specialization, no trade, no division of labor outside the group; and no "general purpose" money was used as a medium of exchange. Market exchange transactions were entirely absent or limited to a relatively narrow range of goods and services. They were therefore of only minor importance to livelihood.

Traditionally the indigenous people of Papua New Guinea had few political institutions beyond the tribal group inhabiting a known territory. The tribal groups were divided into clans, with subclans of 50 to 100 people occupying a hamlet area and claiming a common ancestor. Each clan or hamlet group belonged to a village. The clan was the largest effective unit in the village. The functional social unit within the village was the lineage group (matrilineal or patrilineal) which recognized a common ancestor and consisted of an expanded family with known relationships. Its members engaged in mutually beneficial activities, and this system of traditional obligations ensured that the lineage remained a functioning unit.

The basic economic activity of the villages was producing food for subsistence using the typical Melanesian techniques of the bush-fallow system. The skills required were simple. Even a child of ten or eleven could be trained in them and would be able to handle the most common agricultural tools efficiently. Subsistence production was undertaken collectively by the lineage group, in accordance with the traditionally accepted principle of food production and distribution. Traditional economic activity was geared to employing the labor and natural resources close at hand in order to obtain a sufficient and not long-deferred net return. The collective cultivation system was a highly effective means of attaining this primary objective. When need arose, fellow subclansmen, kinsmen, and affines could be called upon by the individual family household to help in fencing, housebuilding, and garden preparation, to contribute to marriage or death payments, or to participate in other ceremonial feasts. Relationships of mutual aid in terms of work and financial support within or outside the clan were mainly between affines and were always carried out on a reciprocal basis buttressed by moral and social obligations. Intergroup and interpersonal relations were sustained by obligatory exchanges based on ceremonies marking marriages, deaths, births, initiations, or peacekeeping. Traditionally, pigs, plums, subsistence foods, ornamental shells and other decorative items were the only valuable items of exchange. In short, the two important economic functions of a society — production and distribution — were expressions of underlying kinship obligations, tribal affiliation, and social and moral duty. Labor, land, services, and goods were allocated, exchanged, or appropriated by means of transactional modes of reciprocity and redistribution rather than through the familiar commercial mode of market exchange (see Polanyi, 1947). Perhaps, such an economy may rightly be described as small-scale "utopian communism," in contrast to the kind of socialism we associate with modern communist countries.

Contrary to what might have been expected, the village community on the whole lived well above a bare subsistence level; it did not just eke out a living from what could be found in woods or water. Every household in the village had the right to use some land (usufruct) mainly acquired by inheritance according to traditional clan laws. Except in very rare circumstances, the two main factors of production — land and labor — were available to the indigenous people in relative abundance and they lived in a state of primitive affluence. This means that they were able to produce, from their own resources, as much of their normal staple foods as they could consume together with a reasonable surplus for entertainment, display, and emergency. They were able to provide a standard of housing, clothing, and entertainment that was considered acceptable, by employing a relatively small part of the total potential resources of labor and land available to them. This means that the productivity of their labor was very high and it is still quite common in these regions to find substantial groups able to sustain this level of consumption from their own resources at the cost of an average labor input of about three hours per man-day.[2]

Finally, I should like to make a few comments on the traditional system of social stratification and touch on the question of status

[2] Unless otherwise interfered with by uncontrollable factors, such as natural calamities or internal social upheavals. The term "primitive affluence" was first used by Fisk (1962).

mobility. The traditional society of Papua New Guinea was to a high degree egalitarian, and there was a strong conviction that social equality demanded equal distribution of wealth to all members of society. Social stratification or economic differentiation were therefore opposed. In this social system personal achievement brought considerable prestige so long as it was shared with others, "almost *pari passu* with his own" (Belshaw 1955). There seemed to be a socially tolerated limit to the amount of wealth an individual could accumulate for personal use; anyone who indulged in conspicuous consumption without sharing was considered selfish and antisocial. He could "arouse jealousy with the possibility of envious sorcery being directed against him" (Belshaw 1955). Failure to observe established social norms governing the distribution of wealth was frowned on as it was felt that it would undermine the entire society. As a result, there was very little differentiation in living standards.

In this traditional, egalitarian society, the leaders of the village were the leading personalities of the lineage groups. They gained influence by traditional means: through wealth and garden produce; through ceremonial wealth and other decorative objects; by means of oratorial skill; knowledge of traditional customs and skills in war and magic; because of mature age; and last but most important, through generosity in distributing the wealth they had acquired. A leader's prominence in village affairs was dependent on his skill in fending off rivals and on continuing ggenerosity. Since leadership was not hereditary nor based on the political or judicial powers associated with an established position, no leader had absolute influence or authority. The normal pattern of decision making in the villages depended on consensus among clan members rather than on the exercise of formal authority. All men had some influence and all who exhibited the desired qualities could take on leadership roles. A community remained without a leader until someone emerged with the necessary qualities. In general, these people did not like to be forced or pushed in decision making. An impatient, pushing type of leader was most likely to evoke opposition from the villagers and would eventually lose the leadership, even when this might be to the general detriment of the village community.

The broad generalizations about the precontact society of Papua New Guinea made here are not meant to obscure the existence of differences within and between groups. There were real and important differences between communities and these differences became more pronounced after exposure to the modern economy. However, the differences between communities seem to have been differences in degrees of emphasis rather than in direction. For example, social sanctions against behavior which endangered the norm of egalitarian mutual dependence were much more severe in some communities than in others; in communities where the leadership structure was organized more along the lines of a "big man" system there was greater economic differentiation than in others. These are differences in degree of emphasis only; the traditional social philosophy and structure were basically the same throughout the society. The significance of inter-community differences will be discussed later in relation to social change.

THE INTRODUCTION OF A MONEY ECONOMY: A CAPITALIST MODEL

The three colonial rulers of Papua New Guinea — the Germans, the British, and the Australians — were interested, though to varying degrees, in developing the economic infrastructure for purposes of colonial exploitation. Like much of the rest of the colonial world, the pattern of development in Papua New Guinea was the familiar one of improvements in transport and communications, discoveries of new mineral resources, introduction of cash crops for the export market, and import of large-scale foreign enterprise (plantations, trading companies, etc.), whose chief economic need, at least initially, was for cheap, unskilled labor. The major stimulus for introducing money into colonial situations is so that the incoming colonial power can act as a middleman between the indigenous cash-crop growers and the world market, and to stimulate the indigenous demand for imported goods. To commit the indigenous subsistence growers to the cash economy, the colonial "package deal" also includes forced labor, compulsory cultivation of export crops, head taxes, school and church fees, and many other coercive and noncoercive monetary obligations.

The type of cash economy introduced into Papua New Guinea by the colonial powers was basically the Christian-capitalist one. This is the most important point to remember in discussing social change in Papua New Guinea. What Papua New Guineans were given to imitate or emulate was the "spirit of capitalism" which is radically different from their own traditional value system. At the risk of being tautological,[3] a few of the characteristics of the spirit of Christian capitalism should be mentioned here in order to indicate the degree to which it differs from the traditional system of values of Papua New Guinea.

1. The rise of capitalism was based on the exploitation of subservient labor and the concentration of control of manufacture in the hands of a few individuals who reaped all the profits (see Marx [1887]).

[3] Much has been written by economic historians on the rise of capitalism, and the theories propounded often have a large element of tautology in them, making it difficult to test them empirically.

2. Economic freedom — *laissez faire* — is typical of capitalism. Freed from the control of manorial customs and traditions, enterprise was able to make quick use of new improvements, of investment opportunities etc. (see Sombart [1927]).

3. Capitalism has its own "spirit." It is an unshackled, accumulating, profit-seeking spirit, careless of social consequences and communal relationships (see Sombart [1927]).

4. The "profit-maximizing activities of capitalism are justified by the religious values of thrift, diligence, sobriety, and frugality. Thus the Reformation gave to the capitalists a clear conscience to pursue profits to the best of their ability. According to these Christian values, profits and interest are not necessarily evil gains; the cardinal sin is idleness. On the other hand, the spirit of capitalism has justified a marked class distinction and socioeconomic differentiation and forbade open dissatisfaction on the part of oppressed labor" (see Weber [1958]).

5. Last, but not least important, and the feature which has found its way most frequently into theories of economic growth, is the emphasis on individual entrepreneurship as the vital force in the spirit of capitalism. According to Schumpeter, a wholehearted admirer of the capitalist system, the entrepreneur is, among other things, a social deviant, egocentric, untraditional, and ambitious. His "characteristic task — theoretically as well as historically — consists precisely in breaking up old, and creating new tradition. Although this applied primarily to his economic action, it also extends to the moral, cultural, and social consequences of it. It is, of course, no mere coincidence that the period of the rise of the entrepreneur type also gave birth to Utilitarianism..." (1934: 91–93). An essential aspect of Schumpeter's idea of vigorous capitalist development is rapid circulation of this type of entrepreneurial elite, whose success under unbridled capitalism, is highly rewarded by society and leads to the top of the social ladder if not for the individual himself, then at least for his son or grandson.

It is apparent that the spirit of the Christian capitalist money economy is radically different from the indigenous social and economic institutions and values of Papua New Guinea. However, it is often argued that there has been some degree of capitalism in all civilizations and that all societies for thousands of years have been acquisitive; therefore the spirit of the capitalist exchange economy is not so radically different from that of the primitive economy. For example, superficial resemblances between shell money and traditional exchange transactions in Papua New Guinea, on the one hand, and modern all-purpose monetary exchanges, on the other, have been noted, as has the apparent similarity between the "big man" system in Papua New Guinea and the Western capitalist entrepreneur. But it is often not understood that in primitive economies these practices and institutions are differently organized and perform different functions from their counterparts in the capitalist exchange economy.[4] The essential point is that in analyzing the social changes in Papua New Guinea caused by the introduction of a money economy, attention should be focused not on the monetary exchange system as such but on its embeddedness in the philosophy and practices of Christian capitalism. In other words, the exogenous stimulus for social change in Papua New Guinea was the capitalist ideology of monetary exchange activities, and the imitative process of social change began as an attempt to emulate this model of capitalism.

SOCIAL CHANGE: TOWARD INDIGENOUS CAPITALISM

With the introduction of a money economy into Papua New Guinea, there were changes in the style of the economic function. First, the production of a few exportable commodities, such as copra, coffee, and rubber was expanded; this had repercussions on the rest of the economy and eventually linked the indigenous subsistence producers with international trade and markets. Second, a single means of exchange, that is, notes or coinage, was channeled into all economic spheres and applied to the full range of exchangeable goods, including those which had been traditionally ceremonial. Third, part of the labor resources of the traditional economy were drawn into wage-earning employment. Fourth, the internal market demand for subsistence produce and traditional valuables was expanded. These four changes in the economic function had both immediate and more long-term effects on the incomes and consumption levels of the subsistence producers.

Let us first examine the effects on income. It is a reasonable guess that at least 90 percent (if not 100 percent) of the population of Papua New Guinea have access to some money income for spending on

---

[4] Shell money or traditional valuables certainly do not serve as a general medium of exchange; they are at best "special purpose money" as distinguished from modern "general purpose money" (Polanyi 1957: 264–266).

In the case of the "big man" system, the socially approved social and economic differentiation between the "big man" and the commoners is matched by obligations on the part of the "big man" to provide emergency subsistence for the unfortunate, to reward the services of followers, provide community feasts, defence, and a generous sharing of wealth. The commoners do not begrudge the material payments and services to the "big man" because he is generous in sharing his wealth; his affluence is therefore identified with community affluence. Certainly, a "big man" has some characteristics akin to a modern entrepreneur, but the ultimate purpose and function of his entrepreneurial activities are distributive rather than accumulative. If the "big man" uses his traditional power to acquire European goods and cash earnings for himself, his followers feel unjustly exploited and various kinds of social sanctions and social ostracism follow.

nonessentials.[5] The economy of Papua New Guinea has become less and less a pure subsistence economy in isolation. For most of the indigenes, subsistence has been supplemented with cash production. There are four main sources of cash income for subsistence producers: (1) sale of cash crops; (2) sale of subsistence produce and traditional valuables in local markets; (3) wage remittances and gifts; and (4) other business transactions such as storekeeping, trucking, and handicrafts. However, among the rural majority (more than 90 percent of the total population live in rural areas) the major component of the cash income is derived from cash crops. For example, in a recent survey[6] it was found that the average monthly cash income of a rural household was $A12.00, about 57 percent of which came from cash crops, 26 percent from the sale of subsistence produce (and traditional valuables), 9 percent from wages and remittances, and the rest (8 percent) from other businesses (mainly trading stores) and occasional gifts.

What happened to consumption levels? Obviously, with the advent of a monetary economy and the "demonstration effects" of imported European goods and European standards of living, there was the usual enlargement of consumption patterns and wants. This is clear from the cash expenditure patterns of indigenous households. In a survey of the day-to-day cash expenditure of 67 rural households whose monthly cash income was about $A21.00, the average monthly cash expenditure was found to be about $A16.00. This cash expenditure was intended to meet two distinct patterns of demand: (1) exogenous demands or the demands made by external agencies, such as council taxes, school fees, and contributions to church funds; and (2) endogenous or internal demands, such as day-to-day consumption items, marriage payments, traditional obligatory exchanges and ceremonies.

Exogenous cash needs are periodic, but the payments have to be made at a specified time, and often the amount of cash required (as in the case of fees for children at boarding school) is relatively large. Because of these two factors, exogenous demands for cash are generally followed or preceded by periods of intensive cash-earning activity. On the other hand, endogenous or internal cash needs comprise both occasional and regular day-to-day demands. Occasional internal cash demands are those where cash is used in the traditional sphere of life, such as for marriage feasts and bride price, other ceremonial feasts and exchanges, or for settling past obligations and disputes.

---

[5] See Fisk (1966: 25). In 1966 Fisk estimated that 80 percent had access to some money income. Since then the figure must have increased considerably.
[6] The survey was carried out by the present author in 1970 and 1971 among 366 rural households in the three district regions. For details, see Moulik (1973). It is to be noted that most of the factual observations and empirical data cited henceforth in this paper pertain to that study, unless otherwise indicated.

In the traditional sphere of life, cash (either in the form of hard cash or trade store goods) is less important than subsistence or nonmonetary items. Nevertheless, cash demands are often conspicuously high (as in the case of bride price which may range from $A100.00 to $A600.00 in hard cash depending upon the status of the parties). In the rural households surveyed, an average 20 percent of net disposable cash income was spent on feasting and ceremonies. Many of these expenditures, irregular as they are, are often shared by a community or immediate clan group on the basis of reciprocal obligations in the future. As in the case of occasional exogenous demands, these internal periodic cash demands are followed or preceded by greater than normal intensity in cash-earning activities.

Within the second category of cash needs, that is, regular day-to-day consumption, trading store purchases (mainly European foods, such as tinned fish, tinned meat, sugar, rice, and stimulants such as cigarettes, cigars, tobacco, beer, and other varieties of alcohol) are the most important. In fact, by far the greater part of cash is spent on such store-bought foods which would seem to be superfluous considering the "affluent subsistence" level of the village economy. (In view of the nature of the subsistence diet, however, tinned meat and fish are perhaps useful in providing protein). In the rural households surveyed, more than 60 percent of monthly cash expenditure (of $A16.00) was on these foods. It must be noted that some of this store-bought food (about 15 percent) was used or given away in the traditional obligatory exchanges. It is also interesting to note that, if the monetary value of subsistence produce and other traditional valuables used in traditional exchanges were considered in the calculation of a household's cash expenditure, it often far exceeded the total cash income of the household. This shows the primary importance of the subsistence sector of the economy in the traditional sphere of life. In other words, money has not replaced the subsistence sector, it merely adds prestige in ceremonial exchanges by supplementing the subsistence produce and traditional valuables which remain of prime importance.

It is conventionally accepted that there should be some direct relationship between income and expenditure, at least, at a certain stage of the demand curve. There is some empirical evidence to suggest a gradual increase in the consumption expenditure of indigenous households with the increase in cash incomes up to a certain maximum level. After this expenditure tends to reach a plateau (see Blyth 1969). The problem is that the point at which the consumption expenditure of indigenous households flattens out is fairly low, indicating a demand ceiling at a relatively low consumption saturation level. In the rural households surveyed, for instance, an average monthly consumption expenditure of $A4.00 per consumption unit was found to be the saturation level. Blyth has shown that in the subsistence economies of the South Pacific, as household income rises, income elasticities for most classes of goods and services, except for a limited number of relatively unimportant luxury items, contract, and that this occurs at a relatively low level of expenditure. This is so not only for actual consumption expenditure but also for anticipated cash income aspirations as well. For example, in the rural households surveyed the maximum level of nominal income, after which the plateau in income aspirations occurred, was $A18.00, and the income aspiration limits at which stabilization tended to occur was around $A28.00. This is a clear indication of a psychological demand ceiling characterized by narrow consumption and investment vistas.

However, the patterns of cash use show that cash demands have become established in day-to-day life. Cash is being used to meet ends ranging from external demand such as taxes and school fees to traditional exchanges. But the proportion of cash used or needed by an indigenous household is as yet relatively small. It may be argued that the indigenous people are not acquainted with the existence and availability of various consumer goods and that this stultifies the demonstration effect. But this argument is difficult to defend. The level of linkages with the advanced economy and the availability of merchandise in the local stores mean that a large majority of the village households can find plenty of things on which to spend their entire cash income and still leave many desirable things which they cannot buy because of shortage of cash. The absence of items such as torches, scissors, hammers, bicycles, watches, and radios in a large majority of rural households was certainly not because they were unavailable or difficult to find or because of lack of familiarity with their use. Once the immediate necessities are satisfied, discretionary purchasing power or consumption expenditure is limited at a low saturation level.

Why is there such a low demand ceiling for consumption expenditure? What is perhaps most important in analyzing this phenomenon is to consider the kinds of motivations and incentives that the money economy offers to the indigenous people to stimulate the process of adopting the capitalist model. In this context two very important interrelated factors need to be considered. First, the psychology of the indigenous people which is a psychology of affluence — not affluence of the type found in developed economies such as North America, but the kind of affluence which Fisk has aptly termed "primitive" or "subsistence affluence" (1962). In this form of affluence not only basic needs such as food, clothing, and shelter are catered for but also derived needs such as prestige, status, and security are adequately satisfied with relatively little effort and exploitation of production factors. Subsistence affluence with its relative freedom from the irritant of socioeconomic necessity (both physical and psychological) has allowed the indigenous people to view the choices open to them dispassionately and to feel very little compulsion to choose between them. Being deprived of war and head hunting by the colonial powers' pacification program, the indigenous people lost one of the important challenges of life, and it has not been replaced by any equally motivating new challenge. The introduction of a capitalist exchange economy soon led to conflict between the two economic systems — subsistence and monetary — resulting in a *sui generis* connection in which the subsistence sector seems to ensure the monetary sector. Thus, it is possible for the villagers to grow subsistence crops mainly for home consumption so that they have sufficient food for the family unit and obligatory exchange purposes symbolizing the continuity and existence of the kinship group, whereas cash crops are directed toward the "outside world" with its different expectations and value orientation patterns. The two production systems tend to coexist as a form of "inner dualism" with the subsistence activities remaining dominant and the cash-earning activities substantially and quantitatively peripheral if not deviant. The net result is a mere supplementing of the subsistence economy by the monetary one and a consequent limitation of monetary needs or lack of dependence on the cash economy.

All conscious and unconscious monetary wants are instantly gratified. For the average villager the money income needed does not require much exertion and he is able to make purchases beyond his daily needs. For example, our survey showed that in one time period an adult male villager would spend a maximum of four hours labor in various productive activities, out of which less than an hour would be spent in cash-earning activities. This was enough to satisfy his existing cash expenditure demands. At another time the same villager might work eight to ten hours a day, often most of it in cash-earning activities. A closer look at the reason for such heightened activities would reveal that the incentive was either direct or indirect compulsion in the form of taxes, school fees, bride price, "pay back," or some sort of traditional festival. It is equally interesting to observe that once these wants were satisfied, the old patterns of maximization of leisure would reassert themselves. This incongruity causes everything about the indigenous mind to exist in dual focus and results in a backward sloping supply curve of efforts in cash-earning activities. If it is possible for the villager to earn the same extra cash income with less labor, he prefers this to earning a higher income at the cost of a little extra effort. This not to suggest that the backward sloping supply curve of labor effort is unique to Papua New Guinea. It is not. It happens even in advanced commercial societies. But, because the villagers of Papua New Guinea have a limited fixed set of wants which is more readily satisfied, or in other words, because of the limited and inelastic demand for cash income the backward slope starts at a relatively early stage. This is one of the reasons why the labor market (particularly in the monetary sector) in Papua New Guinea is in a state of continual flux with what often looks like a totally uncommitted, irresponsible and extremely choosy labor force which will not respond to the bait of money regardless of the type of work involved.

The element of target production and target effort is noticeable in all kinds of indigenous economic activities especially in the monetary sector. Once the villagers' modest target oriented money requirements are satisfied, they prefer to buy leisure. Because of the periodic nature of the target demand for cash income and the "elective affinity" for leisure, the labor efforts of the villagers of Papua New Guinea manifest a certain irregular periodicity rather than a sustained work effort. This can be seen clearly in the way cash crops are harvested and marketed and in the pattern of response of migrant plantation laborers to the incentive of extra cash income for working overtime. In my survey of rural areas, for instance, as much as 30 to 60 percent of cash crops (coconuts and coffee) remained unharvested and the plantation workers rejected the offer of overtime with the characteristic remark: "Why should I have to work more when I am happy with what I am getting?"

Traditionally the indigenous people were accustomed to irregular bursts of diligence, rather than to the steady unremitting toil characteristic of the capitalist commercial economy. The absence in the traditional culture of a positive compulsion to work hard in a sustained way greatly inhibits the transformation of Papua New Guinea into a society which will give its whole attention to the production process and to increasing the productivity of labor, rather than to enjoying life to the full through leisure. A capitalist commercial society which sees labor as man's vocation on earth and repose as merely a preparation for fresh exertions is quite alien. Apart from the built-in disincentive to sustained effort there is an odium, attached to labor as a marketable commodity which does not necessarily attach to work performed in the traditional sphere of life. Indeed, the degree of odium attached to work in cash-earning enterprises can be gauged from the fact that such work ceases during events associated with life crises — mourning for the dead and a host of other traditional rituals and ceremonies — while it is perfectly within the social norms to work on subsistence gardens at these times.

The capitalist cash economy provides neither cultural nor monetary incentives to spur most of the villagers to greater efforts. Most participate in it for reasons of practical expediency; it enables them to supplement their subsistence living with some monetary fringe benefits or to comply with the coercive requirements (taxes, school fees, etc.) imposed from without rather than generated from within. Their deepest interests and most basic psychological drives are not involved at all; indeed they cannot be involved since work in the monetary sector is neither an extension nor a vindication of the traditional concept of living. One supposes that in itself there is no particular harm in this sort of masquerade. But in social and psychological terms it obviously implies rejection of the capitalist monetary exchange economy and surrender to the traditional way of life.

The second major factor influencing the low demand ceiling is the societal evaluation of the capitalist monetary exchange economy. Indigenous participation in the monetary sector involves the possibility of greater social and economic differentiation between individuals, and rising levels of expectation or expansion of wants for goods because of the demonstration effect of the advanced economy. But exposure to goods alone is not sufficient to arouse an effective want — effective in the sense of creating a willingness to put in the extra effort necessary to obtain the goods. The arousal of an effective want requires that there should be reinforcement by some kind of reward or punishment. It is cultural conditioning or the norms and sanctions of the culture that regulate the particular ways in which a given need is accepted and satisfied. As noted before, in Papua New Guinea there is great opposition to social and economic differentiation or stratification, and the social norm favoring egalitarian distribution of wealth determines the range and kind of expansion of wants. The prevalent egalitarianism supports the view that monetary wealth should not be used to create more money or to make the individual independent of family and kinship ties. This does not mean that monetary wealth is not valued. In fact money income and monetary wealth are one of the means of achieving social prestige which is the prime goal in life. But prestige accrues to the man who shows his affluence by reckless spending or generous sharing. So long as it is understood and can be demonstrated that wealth will be shared "almost *pari passu* with his own" (Belshaw 1955: 60), personal achievement in the monetary sector is applauded and can be a source of prestige. In reply to a question about the qualities which confer high prestige on an individual in the eyes of the villagers, monetary wealth was given lower priority by the rural respondents than traditional wealth, age, land ownership, family size, knowledge of clan history, and speaking ability. It should be noted, however, that all respondents added the rider that both traditional and monetary forms of wealth could confer prestige only when they were used for the common benefit of the villagers and distributed through ceremonial feasting, contributions, and exchanges.

In addition to the low priority given to monetary wealth, social sanctions, particularly sorcery, contribute to the limitation of want expansion. They act as strong negative reinforcements or social punishments. The difficulty is that it is almost impossible for the individual to demonstrate his willingness to share his wealth before actually doing so. There is always suspicion about anyone who hoards money and does not share it to the desired degree. Conspicuous accumulation and consumption are equally repudiated, and social pressure is exerted to dampen any extra effort in cash-earning enterprises. The severity of social sanctions and the amount of social pressure applied to ensure conformity with the social norms depend upon how strongly the community has held to these norms despite the demonstration effect of the capitalist economy. In the relatively isolated coastal villages of Milne Bay District, for instance, a deviant who indulges in conspicuous manifestations of monetary wealth without sharing to the desired extent could expect to be killed by sorcery (reported by 78.5 percent of the respondents). On the other hand, in the relatively less isolated villages of the Eastern Highlands District, more than 50 percent of the respondents thought that such a man could possibly become a leader in the village and that other villagers would seek advice from him.

The social norm of egalitarianism integrates the individual into a tightly woven complex of social obligations, which naturally causes him to think in terms of the social duties that he is expected to perform (see Lloyd 1967). There seems to be little sense of absolute ownership of monetary wealth. Rather, in keeping with the society's primary emphasis on social relationships, various kinds of property are symbolic of particular types of social obligations; this makes it possible to acquire a particular good simply by admiring it openly.

Apart from the internal controls, there is another factor limiting expansion of wants among the indigenous people. In Papua New Guinea the demonstration effect comes mainly from the very high standard of living and wealth of the expatriates. The gap between the indigenous and expatriate standards of living is so enormous that it produces invidious comparison rather than inducing efforts at emulation. It soon becomes apparent to any indigene who has risked incurring severe social sanctions by working extremely hard in an attempt to emulate the standard of living of the expatriates, that the goal is extremely remote and probably unattainable. Such a distorted demonstration effect leads to frustration and often to the type of fantasy known in Melanesia as "cargo cults." The indigenes seem to expect that the expatriate wealth will be distributed as it is in their own society. This projection of their own social norms is natural and logical. Unfortunately, it was reinforced by the corrupting paternalism of the colonial powers and Christian missionaries to such an extent that the indigenes became extremely dependent on the generosity of the administration and the missions. This has led to problems because the impersonal capitalist money economy could not continue to fulfill such expectations. A further aspect of the demonstration effect is that the indigenous people's desire for monetary wealth may be no more than wishful thinking, a spontaneous desire which does not produce pain if it is unsatisfied. The individual may prize the thing desired if he gets it by good luck or through another's generosity, but he will not bestir himself to get it.

It is not being suggested that these are the only consequences of the demonstration effect, nor that the social norm enforcing egalitarianism means that the society is composed of homogeneously structured personalities. There are individual differences and there is competition between individuals; there are deviations from the social norms; there are instances of experimental spending on new and untried goods and services; there are striking examples of entrepreneurship, innovativeness, and willingness to participate in new cash-earning enterprises. These have even involved initial over-response to the opportunities offered by new cash crops such as oil palms or tobacco, cattle projects, development bank loans, storekeeping, cooperatives, and trucking. It is also true that many traditional notions and customs are not wholly accepted any more or, at least, not with the same intensity. For example, gift giving in present-day New Guinea is not always carried on as willingly as in the past. This is not only the case among educated indigenous people; uneducated villagers, too, often express, though sometimes covertly, their reluctance for gift giving which brings no immediate material return. But the central point is that the cultural heritage undoubtedly continues to have a strong influence on the form and content of the decisions made by individuals.

To illustrate the persistence of the traditional cultural heritage, the investment motivations of indigenous entrepreneurs may be looked at. Investment of resources in business activities[7] is highly esteemed in Papua New Guinea. Investment is mainly in cash crops such as coconuts and coffee, in trading stores, trucks, cattle, and in the marketing of subsistence foods and traditional valuables. Because manufacturing industry is fairly new in Papua New Guinea and because of the pronounced shortage of such essential elements as information, skill, capital, and experience among the indigenous people, the indigenous entrepreneurs are mostly microtraders, not industrialists or the "creative entrepreneurs" of Western capitalism. At this point it is customary to point to the Schumpeterian model of the capitalist entrepreneur, which is a man engaged in purposeful activity undertaken to initiate, maintain, or aggrandize a profit-oriented business unit for the production and distribution of economic goods and services and whose ever present desire for profit and the dream to found a

[7] Papua New Guinean's perception of business enterprise is much broader than the conventional Western concept. For detailed discussion on this, see M. Strathern (1972).

private kingdom can only be satisfied by ever increasing investment opportunities and by attaining industrial and commercial successes (Cole 1959: 12). In terms of this definition the microtraders of Papua New Guinea are certainly not entrepreneurs. But the dividing line is by no means clear. Insofar as the microtrader ploughs back the limited resources in circulation into his business of purchasing commodities for resale at a profit or lending money or trading store goods, and insofar as he uses ceremonial exchanges and traditional clan obligations to raise money for new commercial enterprises (such as trucking and trading stores), he is a capitalist entrepreneur. The entrepreneurial touch in the indigenous microtrader's investment decisions comes from the fact that it is he who first sees the opportunities in raising, organizing, and channeling resources into some potential profit making enterprises. Because he is willing to take the social and economic risks involved in departing from the usual pattern of behavior, he is both an innovator and a deviant.

But the similarity between the bourgeois capitalist entrepreneur and the indigenous microtrader entrepreneur does not go beyond the characteristics mentioned above; in terms of the aims and motivations of investment decisions, they are far removed from each other. A. Strathern (1972) brings out clearly the differences between the motivations of New Guinea's entrepreneurs and those of full-blown capitalist entrepreneurs. He shows that the entrepreneurs of New Guinea are from the start anchored in their own communities and partly set in the mold of the big man whose primary aim is to climb the ladder of social prestige even to the detriment of profit rather than to achieve profit maximization if this involves doing without prestige. In terms of the "big man model," prestige is enhanced by generous distribution or sharing of wealth, whereas individualistic profit maximization incurs considerable social costs and social sanctions. As a result, profit making becomes the secondary aim in investment decisions. In fact, given the prevalent social norm favoring egalitarian distribution of wealth and the social sanctions that go to enforce it, the economic aim of profit maximization has to be secondary to the primary aim of gaining social prestige in order even to get an enterprise off the ground. But the extent to which profit making has to be sacrificed depends upon: (1) how far the goal of profit deviates from the norm governing acceptable economic differentiation; (2) the degree of severity of expected sanctions; (3) the level of available opportunities to form an alternative reference group for whom the economic goal is acceptable; and (4) the social position and personality traits of the entrepreneur. Based upon these four factors, the indigenous village entrepreneur has three patterns of behavior open to him:

First, he could completely give up the goal of investment and conform with the existing social norms. Obviously, such behavior will occur in places such as the Milne Bay villages which are relatively isolated and interact less with the advanced economy. There is greater face-to-face interaction in these communities in which the closely knit kinship group is the only available reference group. Because of their cohesiveness and because of the limited choices open to the deviant entrepreneur, the social sanctions, such as sorcery, are enforced more quickly and effectively in such communities. The degree of deviance which is tolerated is extremely low. An illustration of this pattern of behavior is provided by the case of an entrepreneur in a Milne Bay village who abandoned a nicely built European-style house for fear of sorcery. In another case, an entrepreneur gave up his efforts to start a trucking business after a few months of hard work on cash crops to raise the money. When his aim became known to the members of the community he was threatened with sorcery.

Second, the entrepreneur could arrive at a mutually acceptable compromise between his economic goal of profit making and the existing social norms governing wealth; he could lower the level of his profit aspirations so that the degree of deviance from the social norm would not be large enough to attract social sanctions. The behavior of most entrepreneurs in the villages of Papua New Guinea belongs in this category. The entrepreneur skillfully maneuvers his social relationships (this is comparatively easy for the established, traditional "big man") by participating in and even encouraging the traditional obligations and ceremonial exchanges which involve parting with a considerable share of his wealth. Giving his kinsfolk goods on credit without any chance of payment or giving them free rides to the town in his truck, are the kinds of concessions aimed at gaining acceptance of and support for his deviant behavior. Similarly, the entrepreneur may make considerable expenditures on ceremonial exchanges, and conspicuous entertainment of his supporters. This second kind of behavior is most common where the entrepreneur has accepted help (both financial and in terms of labor) from his supporters in starting the enterprise. Such behavior enhances the entrepreneur's social prestige and at the same time levels out economic differentation. On the other hand, it often brings about the ultimate collapse of the wealth generating enterprise. The poor financial state of indigenously owned trading stores (out of 17 surveyed, only three were breaking even and the rest were running at a loss) and trucking businesses illustrates this. This kind of compromise is relatively easily made in areas like the Eastern Highlands which have greater linkage with the advanced economy and where the social sanctions are not so fearsome as in the isolated Milne Bay villages. The high degree of development of the "big man" system also permits relatively greater socioeconomic differentiation.

Third, the entrepreneur could maintain his original economic goal of profit maximization for personal use and satisfaction in spite of social sanctions and community disapproval. In this case he has to rely on external agencies such as administration officials and development bank loans, for support and become a typical, egocentric, ambitious, capitalist, entrepreneur. In the villages of Papua New Guinea it appears to be very difficult to maintain this kind of behavior for long periods of time in the face of existing social norms and community disapproval; it requires a tremendous amount of psychological strength. Persistence in such an extreme form of deviance leads to frustrations in relationships with other people in the community and ultimately to social ostracism. Consequently, this type of entrepreneur is rarely found, at least not among the relatively uneducated small-scale village microtraders. Of course, in the "urban" areas or in their immediate vicinity, some elite entrepreneurs are beginning to engage in this extreme form of deviant behavior and they have influential links with government agencies. But, as yet, they are very few.

The essential motive of the indigenous village intrepreneur is to increase his social prestige by accomodating his economic aim of profit making to the existing social norm of egalitarian distribution of wealth. Every time the entrepreneur tries to make a compromise by sharing wealth he hopes to gain social prestige and social approval. In the process his enterprise may fail and this is often the case. But he is not a complete failure because he has achieved part of his primary aim of gaining social prestige. The fact that the entrepreneur is able to start a trading store or buy a truck, is enough to gain initial social prestige among his group. In the process of running it he adds to his prestige because he shares his profit. Unlike the Schumpeterian model, the indigenous entrepreneur has to be concerned with social success even if this is the cause of economic failure. The net result of this mixture of aims and values is that much wealth flows from the entrepreneur directly to his own community thereby creating relatively less sharp economic differentiations and class divisions in the society.

Having discussed some aspects of the changes in Papua New Guinea's primitive economy under the influence of the Christian capitalist monetary economy, a final question remains: What will or should be the future direction of social change? Should the goal be to arrive at the Western model of Christian capitalism? The question is too broad for me to answer in this paper. But on the basis of the present trends some reasonable suggestions can be made. One thing is certain, whatever Papua New Guinea's ultimate course turns out to be, its gaze is no longer fixed exclusively on a subsistence-based economy with its traditional social values and outlook. The growth of the monetary exchange economy is inevitable. But this does not mean that the money economy will replace the traditional economy completely or that all the traditional values and structures will disappear with the development of Christian capitalism. Much will depend upon the ability of cultural and social traditions to provide cohesion in the face of the modernist onslaught. Up till now, the clash between the opposing determinisms of traditional egalitarianism and exploitative Christian capitalism has resulted in a "mix" between the antecedent and enacted models; and it will remain a mix for a long time to come or perhaps for all time to come. The key parameter is the nature of the mix that will survive in the future. Ultimately, national aims and aspirations about the future shape of the society, especially as envisaged by the leaders who are involved in development decisions, are the most important determining factors. For example, an accelerated rural development approach with emphasis on developing and diversifying subsistence agriculture and creating labor intensive, agriculture supporting, and import displacing industries will have the advantage of mass participation, self-reliance, and maintaining many of the desirable traditional values. However, such a policy may have to be geared to a relatively lower level economic goal, and the pace of development may have to be reduced; the level of aspirations may have to be adjusted accordingly. On the other hand, if the development policy is capital intensive, urban-oriented and capitalist, emphasizing industrial technologies, the confusion, tensions, and destructive discontents may increase to the extent that the purpose will be defeated; this may not only create severe social dislocation, it may also cause a vigorous revivalist movement with renewed emphasis on traditional or modified traditional ways of life.[8]

REFERENCES

BELSHAW, C. S.
   1955   *In search of wealth.* American Anthropological Association, Memoir No. 80.
BLYTH, C. A.
   1969   Primitive South Pacific economies: their consumption pattern and propensity to save out of cash income. *Economic Record* 45: 354–371.
COLE, ARTHUR M.
   1959   *Business enterprise in its social setting.* Cambridge: Harvard University Press.

[8] Such revivalist tendencies can often be observed in Papua New Guinea, even among the Western educated elites. In part, they are symptoms of aggressive nationalism; they are also a defense mechanism to compensate for the frustration caused by a rapid rate of imposed change.

FISK, E. K.
1962   Planning in a primitive economy, special problems of Papua New Guinea. *Economic Record* 38: 462–478.
1966   "The economic structure," in *New Guinea on the threshold*. Edited by E. K. Fisk. Canberra: Australian National University Press.

HURH, W. M.
1968   Imitation: its limits in the process of inter-societal culture diffusion. *International Social Science Journal* 20 (3): 448–463.

LLOYD, P. C.
1967   *Africa in social change: changing traditional societies in the modern world*. Baltimore: Penguin.

MARX, KARL
1887   *Capital: a critical analysis of capital production*. Edited by Friedrich Engels. London.

MOULIK, T. K.
1973   Money, motivation and cash cropping in Papua New Guinea. *New Guinea Research Bulletin*. Canberra: Australian National University Press.

PARSONS, TALCOTT
1970   The impact of technology on culture and emerging new modes of behaviour. *International Social Science Journal* 22 (4).

POLANYI, KARL
1947   Our obsolete market mentality. *Commentary*, February: 109–117.
1957   "The economy as instituted process," in *Trade and market in the early empire*. Edited by Karl Polanyi, Conrad M. Arensberg, and Harry W. Pearson. Glencoe: The Free Press.

SCHUMPETER, J. A.
1934   *Theory of economic development*. Translated by R. Opie. Cambridge: Harvard University Press.

SINGER, MILTON, *editor*
1959   *Traditional India: structure and change*. Austin: University of Texas Press.

SOMBART, WERNER
1927   *Der moderne Kapitalismus*. Leipzig.

STRATHERN, A.
1972   Entrepreneurial model of social change: from Norway to New Guinea. *Ethnology* 11 (4): 368–379.

STRATHERN, M.
1972   Absentee businessmen: the reaction at home to Hageners migrating to Port Moresby. *Oceania* 43 (1): 19–39.

WEBER, MAX
1958   *The Protestant ethic and the spirit of capitalism*. New York: Charles Scribner's Sons.

Discussions: Chicago

Chairperson: MAGOROH MARUYAMA

Participants: AJATO AMOS, SORY CAMARA, SAMIR GHOSH,
BEATRICE MEDICINE, CHUDI NWA-CHIL, ALVIN TOFFLER

MARUYAMA: Recently there has been increasing concern about the future of human civilization and of our planet. But so far most of the thinking, writing, and planning about the future has been done by economists and technologists in rich countries or by people who have little understanding of the cultural diversity of the world. As a step toward remedying this situation, we held a cultural futuristics symposium at the American Anthropological Association annual meeting for the first time three years ago and this has since become an annual event. So far most of the participants in these symposia have been Americans or European-born Americans, and we have felt the need for input from the Third World. We decided that the International Congress of Anthropological and Ethnological Sciences was the right occasion to obtain this input, and this particular session was planned with that in mind. We made a great deal of effort to recruit a number of participants from developing countries and we succeeded in doing so. At least they have written papers and sent them to us. However, with the exception of Chudi Nwa-Chil, they could not get the money to come. But fortunately we were able to find, among those who have come to other sessions, four participants who are interested in our topic. They joined our panel today.

First, I would like to mention the papers that were written for this session. Samir Ghabbour from Egypt wrote a paper on the nations of the world as an interacting ecosystem. Lalitha Gunawardena of Ceylon wrote about two social classes in that country and about their differing aspirations for the future. T. K. Moulik wrote about the failure of the cash economy system introduced by outsiders into New Guinea. Chudi

These discussions took place at the IXth ICAES, Chicago, Illinois

Nwa-chil, who is with us today, wrote a paper on the resistance to early Western education in Eastern Nigeria. On our panel, in addition to Chudi Nwa-chil, we have Sory Camara from Guinea, Beatrice Medicine who is a Native American (American Indian), Alvin Toffler, Samir Ghosh and Ajato Amos.

Now, let me briefly formulate what we mean by cultural futuristics. The initial impetus was not so much to predict the future as to study cultural alternatives and cultural possibilities in the future. What kinds of cultures can we imagine? What kinds of cultures do we wish to choose? These were the basic questions. So today you are not going to hear our predictions about the future, but rather discussions of what cultural possibilities and alternatives there are in the future and which we would like to choose.

It has been our experience in the past that every time we started talking about the future, we ended up talking about the present or the past. We would like to avoid this today. That is why I have prepared a list of questions to focus our attention on the future. One question is: Can cultural goals be generated ahead of technology? Most people think that culture change occurs because of technological change. But that is putting the cart before the horse. Can we generate cultural goals in such a way that technology can be utilized to further cultural goals instead of the culture being shaped by technology? A second question is how to channel goals generated from the grass roots rather than some professional planners' goals. Another question is: Will the post-industrial paradigm be heterogenization and symbiotization? Most technologists and industrialists are talking about homogenizing the whole world. The counterculture people are thinking in terms of making our society heterogeneous. And a related question: Can developing countries bypass the homogenization paradigm and go directly to the heterogenization paradigm while they are industrializing? Another crucial question is: Does current social and cultural change involve not only change in terms of more cars, more people, more pollution or less pollution, but also a change in logic, philosophy and paradigm? If that is the case, then are we capable of such an epistemological change? If culture change involves a paradigmatic or logical change, then perhaps one way to prepare ourselves for the future would be to develop an ability to change logic and to invent new logics. Do we have that capacity? Do we have institutional ways of doing it? Do we have educational systems to do it? These are some of the questions we are asking.

In other sessions held during the week of this Congress, you may have noticed that some people were insistent on sticking to their basic premises or basic paradigms and tried to reduce everything to them. You also have found that some other people were more flexible in moving between paradigms. Alvin Toffler has been talking about future shock and more recently he has said that the social change we are experiencing right now is basically anthropological. He means that it is cultural change, and not just economic or technological. I have requested Professor Toffler to be our discussant and respond from the Western point of view to the presentations by the panelists from the Third World. We are going to hear each panelist present very briefly some of his or her ideas. This will be followed by questions and discussion. The first speaker is Professor Camara.

CAMARA: I feel a little constrained by Professor Maruyama's suggestion that we should only discuss the future in this session and not digress into considerations of the present or the past. But I would be less than honest if I promised to talk only about the future of the human species. I will confine my discussion to the conceptualization which the populations I study, the Mandenka of West Africa and particularly of Eastern Senegal, have of some of the questions which we are dealing with in this session.

Actually I feel guilty, as an ethnologist and as a Mandenka myself, to realize after several years of research, that I used to think it was sufficient to observe people, analyze my observations and draw theoretical conclusions which seemed appropriate to me. I did this without ever asking myself whether the subjects I was studying might have theories of their own concerning what they do and what they say. Perhaps they would be in a better position than any observer from outside to provide us with a real vision of their society, founded on experience. When I realized this, I began asking them the questions that I had previously been asking myself.

In order to stay within the topic of this session, I shall mention only their thoughts about their society, the way it functioned, its relationship with other societies, and its future. Following my friend Maruyama's suggestion, I will not go into details but summarize briefly.

The Mandenka perceive the elements of society as heterogeneous, as are the elements which constitute the individual. This heterogeneity seems to be the basis of the principle of change. During his lifetime an individual goes through several phases of development. These phases are conceived as being radically different from, and even opposed to, one another. Heterogeneity and change are two complementary principles and form the basis of a certain harmony. It is because the individual has very different experiences during his lifetime that he becomes capable of understanding different situations and different persons.

The Mandenka view of the future is this: they say that increased contacts between peoples will cause their elements to become increasingly different from what they used to be, but that this does not mean that they will become identical. The evolution of society and of the world does not lead to homogeneity but to increasing heterogeneity because, to use their terms: "When a log stays in water for a long time, the water changes the log considerably. But this does not mean that the log will turn into a crocodile."

Then I asked them the question which a Westerner would have asked: "But will this heterogeneity not create conflicts?" Their answer was that conflicts originate more from similarities than from differences. If you increase homogenization, people are forced in one way or another to become similar, even identical. They will look for some way to be different. There is only one solution open to them: to try to subordinate one another, to avoid one another, or to destroy one another. This creates conflicts. It is not a viable solution. On the other hand, when goals, functions, and attitudes are no longer identical, conflicts disappear and it becomes possible to find grounds for harmony. This insight is not a trivial one. It indicates a considerable degree of wisdom.

The fears expressed by the Mandenka regarding the future evolve around the influences of Westerners. The Mandenka feel, for example, that Western influence will lead to an increase in certain types of homogenization, on the one hand, and to ossifying specialization on the other, the latter to such an extent that each individual's jobs and functions will be defined for his lifetime and it will be impossible for him to get out of them. This will lead to a lessening in the variety of individual experiences and render individuals incapable of understanding each others' points of view.

Many of the old Mandenka are of the opinion that those who have responsible positions in society ought to change roles regularly. For example the planners, who theorize about the products on which the peasants' livelihood depends, ought to work the land with a hoe themselves and become apprentices to the peasants from time to time in order to obtain a concrete understanding of the problems the peasants face (see Camara i.p.).

I will stop here in order not to encroach on the time reserved for discussions.

MARUYAMA: Thank you very much. I think this raises a very interesting question of different logics. If you think of the relationship between animals and plants, you see that animals consume oxygen and convert it into carbon dioxide while plants do the opposite. But this does not create conflict. On the contrary, it creates symbiosis. Plants and animals help each other by being different. And if you observe the ecology of tropical forests or the coral reefs around tropical islands, what is striking is the heterogeneity of the species living there. It is because of their heterogeneity that so many species can live together. If all individuals were of the same species, they would be fighting for the same food. So the idea that homogeneity creates conflict and heterogeneity creates symbiosis is excellent, as contrasted to the more usual type of argument which calls for unity through similarity. Thank you very much. Are there any questions at this moment? Professor Toffler, do you have any comments on this?

TOFFLER: I would rather wait.

MARUYAMA: Next speaker is Professor Nwa-chil.

NWA-CHIL: I think the future of any society depends on its past, and it is very difficult to talk about the future without thinking about the past. The future of most developing countries depends on the past, on the fact that they were colonial countries dominated by the big powers. I would like first to deal with the question of whether culture determines technology or technology culture. I think it is a question of interaction between the two. What is happening in Tanzania, where I come from, provides a good example. We try to blend the past with the future. In our traditional society we lived as groups of families, and we believe that we can build our future society on the basis of this group cohesiveness. Our goal is to build socialism based on family solidarity. Tanzanian socialism does not mean that you cannot own individual property. It simply means that the means of production are held in common. Instead of adopting so-called scientific socialism, we find it preferable to go back and tell the people that the sort of thing we are trying to create is not something different from what we were before. A group of villagers who consider themselves descendants of one ancestor move as a group from their existing area to a virgin land and create another village. This is a natural transition from the traditional to the modern. What I would call "the rational path" is to develop agriculture rather than industry. We cannot neglect industry completely, but we know that we can develop ourselves by developing the resources we have. Again, this relates the past to the future. We have land; we have people; we are poor. We do not have the capital to establish industries. Besides, we cannot compete with the industrialized societies. When I arrived in Chicago, the first thing I saw on the table in my room at the hotel was a list of the Conrad Hilton Hotels throughout the world. We cannot compete with enterprise on such a gigantic scale.

We are at a disadvantage by virtue of the fact that primary products in the world market depreciate every day. We are also at a disadvantage because we do not have equal bargaining power with the industrialized societies. Because of their economic power, the industrialized societies can decide how much they will pay for our coffee or tea. It is easier for us to change our people by introducing modern means of agriculture. An important consideration with implications for the future is that we do not need a radical change in our people's attitudes and orientation. They are used to agriculture; all we need to do is introduce gradually modern methods of agriculture. In this way, the transition from the traditional to the modern can be natural. It is possible for culture and technology to go hand in hand.

MARUYAMA: Thank you. Any questions at this point? Then we would like to hear next from Professor Medicine.

MEDICINE: *Mita piepi chanta washteyana apichiespi.* This I know none of the translators can translate. It is Native American[1], and every woman and man who speaks before a group must say this. It means simply: "My kinsmen, I greet you with a good heart and a warm hand." Much of my speech was written in my native language and my son was to interpret it for you. However, he has gone to the blessing ceremony of a Native American grammar school. This is a part of the new self-determination efforts on the part of Native Americans to decide their future. I think this is a very, very significant kind of movement and I feel that this is where the future of the Native Americans will go. So what I will say is an English translation of my speech in Lak'hota. Anthropology, whatever that term means, and all that implies and what strength or directions that takes, depends upon the total efforts and combined commitments of mankind and womankind to the preservation of the natural world. We Native Americans consider the natural world sacred, and we are becoming very, very concerned about what is happening to it. We have had many prophecies about the destruction of the world and, indeed, we who live in this part of the world are seeing it occur. The sacred world encompasses both the two-leggeds and the four-leggeds. This is very much part of our philosophy and world view. Because of the sacredness of the world we are concerned with the thoughts and aspirations of the Third World peoples throughout the world and *worlds.* We, the darker-pigmented people of the world, must be considered in the development of new perspectives in both theories and methodologies in anthropology. An infusion of non-Western perspectives into anthropology is needed, and by this I mean that anthropology must be willing to accept and pursue new insights and alternative ways of exploring, communicating, and activating itself if we are to implement the theme of this Congress "One species, many cultures." English is not my native language and I am glad that you try to understand what I am saying. Thank you.

---

[1] "Native American" refers to the original inhabitants of the American continents before the arrival of the white man and their language. They were called "American Indians" by white people.

MARUYAMA: This is very easy to say but very difficult to communicate to those who do not know what we mean. In this Congress we non-Westerners have had many discussions with Westerners. Somehow their minds are structured in such a way that what we say does not get through. They just reconvert everything we say into their Western way of thinking and say: "Aha! We understand you very well!" Actually quite often they do not. Professor Medicine's talk was very brief but very profound if you can see what is in it the way we see it. But most of you cannot really see, even though you think you can. Let us move on to Professor Ghosh from India.

GHOSH: Indeed we are very much concerned about the future, if only for the reason that we are going to live in it. We are all included in it, nobody is excluded. It is somewhat mistaken to think that the Western way of thinking, the Western model, and Western logic are all wrong. By the same token not all non-Western logics can be elevated. We have to see what we can learn from the Western model. But certainly we would not advocate that Western logic should be used throughout the non-Western world. By the way, I do not like the term "Third World" because it covers more people than there are in the "First" and "Second" worlds. Moreover, it is a misnomer, in that it implies homogeneity, whereas it includes all kinds of people. The world we live in is composed of different cultures, different colors, different kinds of food habits, different languages.

Perhaps in another hundred years all the men will wear the same kind of clothing and all the women will have similar possessions. But we cannot change skin color. We cannot change languages. We cannot even change food habits and ways of thinking. So the world will still be heterogeneous. What is wrong with Western logic and the Western way of thinking is that they more or less assume that the world is based on competition and not on cooperation. The future as we envisage it will be more or less based on cooperation. There will be some kind of coexistence, not in the political sense but in the cultural sense. What we need is good communication instead of a lot of technological products.

As to whether culture will determine technology or technology determine culture, technology should be controlled and geared to the needs of particular communities and nations. Unless we have methods to control technology, there will be human crises. There already is a crisis in some of the Western cultures.

MARUYAMA: Thank you. According to Western logic, people communicate through similarity, but according to a different logic, it is heterogeneity that creates communication. Symbiosis is possible only when there are differences. Professor Camara would like to make some comments now.

CAMARA: In order to encourage the audience to ask us some questions, I will ask a question to myself. We are talking about the future, about changes in the future, about whether technology is determined by culture or culture by technology, and so forth. I think the basic problem is whether or not we *can change* the future, whether or not we can influence the direction of the future. My colleagues in France believe that the process of nature is governed by God and cannot be changed by man. They accuse me of being an animist, because in the philosophy of my culture, man can intervene in the natural process and change it to some extent. One of the criticisms which my French colleagues have often directed at me is: "You (people born in the Third World) are involved in a process of change determined by industrialization, and you cannot change this direction no matter what you do." I often answer: "But what does it mean to be engaged in the process of industrialization if not that I am going to be able to operate a car, a tractor, or, perhaps, a radio or television station?" Does a television station which I operate have to have the same meaning for me as for my French or English colleagues? When colonization was established in Africa and in my country, the missionaries tried to teach us the precepts of their God. We changed because many of us adopted Christianity. But does this prove that you cannot change the future because you have become a Christian? The Christianity which resulted is entirely different from the Christianity which is found in Europe. The missionaries who came to change us have themselves been changed. Can we change the future, or can we not? In our culture there is a saying: "Regardless of whether you want to or not, you influence the condition of your life and your future. Whether you act or do nothing, you change something because your behavior is integrated in the movement of the universe in a harmonious way." I shall stop now to allow for questions on this problem.

MARUYAMA: In a very interesting previous discussion which I had with Dr. Camara, he mentioned that in his culture each person changes from year to year. Change is a basic paradigm, so to speak. Perhaps such a culture is more geared to change and is more flexible and adaptable. According to Japanese philosophy, everything changes. So if something changes, you are not surprised, whereas Americans suffer from future shock. Professor Amos would like to make his presentation now.

AMOS: Previous speakers have already dealt with the wider questions. I am going to concentrate on just one geographic area and a process that has been changing that area; this is an example of industrialization in the Third World. I am going to talk about Lagos, one of the twelve Nigerian states and the one which contains the federal capital. It has had a long association with the Western World, changing its role from that of a slave port to an exporting center for raw materials. Today it is a point of interchange between those things which Nigeria gets from the outside world and those things which Nigeria sends to the outside world. Processes that have operated here have been mainly pushing Lagos toward full industrialization. Until 1954 when Nigeria was still under colonial influence, Lagos served mainly as a port for bringing in goods for the Europeans in Nigeria and things that could not be manufactured in Nigeria. By the time Nigeria became independent, people were beginning to think in terms of import substitution, which meant producing certain things to save the money previously spent on importing them. This brought many foreign firms to Nigeria; they set up subsidiary firms to manufacture these things more cheaply, or to assemble vehicles. But this did not do Nigeria much good in terms of keeping the profits within the country. Our government decided that the firms must be established in Nigeria. This has led to the new indigenization decree which has had the effect of stopping the participation of foreign firms in Nigerian industries. Certain firms cannot be operated by foreigners. By next year Nigeria will have to make many of the foreigners who are operating there now leave.

Raw materials processing formed another dimension of industry in Lagos. Previously the industries there had been basically engaged either in assembling goods which had been manufactured elsewhere or in finishing them off. But now there has been a shift to intermediate processing.

The current question is whether or not to bring in heavy industries. These cost a lot of money and a certain threshold level is required before they can be brought in. There should also be industrial linkages so that there are enough industries of other types to use the output from the heavy industries. Would it not pay Nigeria to remain a raw material producer, or engage in final-stage processing, or intermediate processing, leaving the heavy industries to the outside world? Here national politics come into consideration. No country wants another country to have the right to decide when it can have basic products like steel, weapons, or petrochemicals. So the decision as to whether or not to have heavy industries has to be made sooner or later. The decision in Nigeria will be taken by the federal government. There is also, the problem of where to locate the heavy industries. We have a labor pool now assembled in Lagos, but it is not the type of labor force that these industries need. It is a predominantly rural labor force that has not been transformed into an industrial labor force. So there is a problem of bridging the gap between training an industrial labor force and limiting the number of people who migrate into Lagos. At the same time, the national goal is to force industries to disperse into other areas. Each of Nigeria's twelve states demands that industries be located in its area. Industry is supplementary to agriculture in providing employment; agriculture is basic to our country. The agricultural sector has to be developed at the same time as the industrial sector. This is the problem Nigeria is faced with. It is a typical Third World country.

MARUYAMA: Thank you. Since there has not been any reaction from the Western point of view, perhaps Professor Toffler would like to speak.

TOFFLER: I think I should begin by disabusing anybody who is under the illusion that I "represent" the Western World. As I listen to this conversation, I hear an objection to the use of the term "Third World" on grounds that it implies a uniformity or homogeneity in the non-Western World. I would like to take that idea and apply it, in turn, to what is commonly known as the Western World. Just as we tend to look upon the Third World as one big undifferentiated mass, it may be that many people outside the Western World and indeed even inside it are taking too simplistic a view of what the Western World consists of.

There is, I believe, no single Western culture, although it may well be said that there is a single industrial culture. Industrialism, it seems to me, has certain more or less fixed imperatives and characteristics, and these crop up wherever it is implanted. However, what is happening now, I believe, is that the industrial world is going through a fundamental transition, a breakdown of the industrial system.

In each of the highly industrialized or high-technology nations, a new society or a new system is struggling to come to birth. This system has characteristics that are diametrically or sometimes dialectically different from those of the industrial system that precedes it. To be unaware of this new phenomenon and to look at the Western World in terms of the classical model of industrialism is to make a serious error. Under the traditional industrial system there are certain fundamental principles, for example standardization — standardization of product, standardization of time units, standardization of people, standardization of the value system — as well as centralization of control, maximization of scale, and so forth. All of these are characteristics of the traditional industrial society. The new system that is beginning to emerge in the United States and in some of the other high-technology nations has characteristics quite different from these. They are moving away from standardized end products toward a mix of standardized components and creation of mosaic products and services. I use the term "configurational" for the kind of society that is beginning to emerge in the high-technology countries, and I believe it should never be confused with the traditional image of industrial society.

When "the West," including Japan, is undergoing such a radical transformation away from the traditional industrial system, it seems to me a mistake in strategy for countries that are not yet industrial to attempt to adopt the traditional industrial model based on Manchester 1870. I do not know what the answers to the questions of world development are. I am certainly not an expert on that. But I have been impressed by some discussions and some developments that I have come across in India where a friend of mine working in a laboratory is developing microtechnologies or intermediate technologies that require very little capital investment, make possible large-scale employment, and do not require Ph.Ds to operate them. This system of using local materials, local labor, and low capital, however, collides with the idea of modernization or industrialization based on petrochemical plants, nuclear power reactors, and high technology. It seems to me that it may well require from us an imaginative planning strategy which sets aside certain zones (not geographical zones but technological zones) where we will use low-scale technology and not permit competition from high-scale technology, while in another zone we may move toward the most advanced technologies possible. I do not know whether that strategy is even plausible, but it seems to me that it needs to be thought about. There are a few people beginning to think about it.

As for the question of whether culture follows technology or technology follows culture, I think it has always been a feedback relationship, a loop relationship. But even though that was true, it is possible within a feedback system for one part to carry more weight than the other, and until now technology has been a very dominant shaping force. I think that now in the high-technology countries this force is beginning to be moderated and cultural factors are taking on a little bit more weight. For one thing, we have developed a large technology for creating and diffusing culture change, whether we are talking about the media or news system among researchers. We have found ways to accelerate the innovation of ideas and the diffusion of the ideas we have.

On the other hand, we have not found much technology to help us innovate institutionally. So we have a tremendous gap between our institutional structure and cultural ideas. One of the critical ways in which the emerging technology differs from the traditional industrial technology is that instead of producing uniformity, it encourages, produces, and perhaps even demands diversity or heterogeneity in the high-technology countries themselves. To me the breakdown of the old melting pot ideal in the United States and the shift from assimilationism to a new kind of ethnic policy in which Italians and Ukranians are joining with blacks and other people in saying, "My culture has a right to live also," are very significant. It has to do, I believe, not just with ideology or with accidents of political leadership but with underlying technological and deep cultural trends in the society. This cultural change is not unrelated to technological and organizational change in the society.

Finally, if we do move toward greater heterogeneity, I am not so confident on the question of conflict. For those of us who would like to see more heterogeneity, it is easy to adopt the view that this can happen without conflict. On the other hand, if there is maximum diversity or heterogeneity in a system, there is no guarantee that this heterogeneity will be symbiotic. There is at least some likelihood that it will be antisymbiotic and that there will be plenty of conflict. It seems to me that the greatest danger we face in this sudden, and, I think, good, development of diversity in our societies is the absolute obsolescence of our political institutions for dealing with it. Certainly the institutions in the United States and in other industrial nations were set up and have been engineered to deal with uniformity and standardization in societies dominated by large blocks of people who are all the same. They were not set up to deal with the kind of increasing variety that we are now creating. Unless we in the United States and other high-technology countries begin to develop radically new political institutions, I can see an enormous amount of highly destructive conflict arising out of this process.

MARUYAMA: Thank you very much for this very thought-provoking presentation. The "configurational" concept is a very important one. There are two ways to heterogenize. One way is through localization, such as Chinatowns, black communities, and so forth. In this the differences become localized, but within each community there is homogeneity. Another way is to interweave heterogeneity within each locality. In this format, two cities may look alike but within each city there are all sorts of variations. In an interweaving system, a white person may choose to live like a black or a Chicano[2], and a Chicano may choose to live like a white. A Westerner may choose to live like a Zen Buddhist. This might well be the pattern of the postindustrial society.

Every time I talk about diversity or a nonhierarchical system, people jump on me and say: "Well, you must be an anarchist." In Western logic you have either hierarchy or anarchy. There are other possibilities in other dimensions, not just these two poles within the same Western dimension. For example, there are models of nonhierarchical interaction networks that are neither hierarchical nor anarchistic, nor are they between the two. They exist in a different dimension. Government institutions may be set up for this type of arrangement, but this

[2] "Chicano" means an American of Mexican descent. Chicanos comprise the second largest racial minority group in the USA.

would require a new logic or a new paradigm. Our so-called "democracy" is based on the old logic. It is based on majority rule which amounts to homogenizing domination by quantity. It is no longer adequate for a heterogeneous society; new systems must be developed. I think this is where anthropology can contribute. Professor Nwa-chil would like to make a comment.

NWA-CHIL: Dr. Amos mentioned that Nigeria is trying to go agricultural, like my country Tanzania. The following question occurs to me: Is industrialization the best alternative for the developing countries? In Nigeria, there is economic growth but no economic development. I am distinguishing the two. To me, economic growth means increase in per capita income with an uneven distribution. Some people are disproportionately advantaged or privileged while others are not. The fact that the industrialized societies have a high income does not necessarily mean that countries in the Third World can develop by becoming industrialized.

REFERENCES

CAMARA, SORY
  i.p.   *Saison sèche, ou entretiens avec les vieux de la brousse.*

Discussions: Frascati

Chairperson: MARGOROH MARUYAMA,
Cochairperson: ARTHUR HARKINS

Participants: SAMIR GHABBOUR, LALITHA GUNAWARDENA,
T. K. MOULIK, KIVUTO NDETI

MARUYAMA: This session should have been held in Chicago. But you were unable to obtain travel funds to come to Chicago. Fortunately, we are able to get together here today. Let us begin with a short summary by each person of his or her work.

GHABBOUR: When I received the invitation to participate, I felt it was an opportunity to put down on paper some ideas that I had been nurturing, based on an article by F. F. Darling and R. F. Dasmann entitled "The ecosystem view of human society" (1969). Darling and Dasmann apply the idea of ecosystem to human communities in towns and cities and say that every group of professions has a niche in society just as any species of animals or plants has a niche in an ecosystem. I thought that this could be applied on a larger scale to the community of nations. There are several types of nations. First, there are nations which act as producers. They produce vegetable products, animal products, or fossil fuels. Most of their production is for export and very little is used inside the producer nations. Second, there are the countries which import these raw materials and transform them into manufactured products. The relationship that was prevalent between each colonial power and its satellite colonies was typical of the relationship between these two categories of nations. But since the Second World War and especially since 1960, most of the former colonies have become independent except for a few pockets in Africa. The ascendance of the U.S.A. and the Soviet Union to the status of superpowers and the coalescence of the former small ecosystems of each colonial power and its colonies into one single community have produced three

The panelists who were unable to come to Chicago due to lack of travel funds had an opportunity to get together later in Frascati, Italy. The Frascati discussions complement the discussions which took place at the Chicago session.

levels of structure in the world ecosystem: the producers; the primary consumers which we used to call the rich nations; and the secondary consumers which are the two superpowers. The U.S.A. deals with the rich nations of Western Europe and with Japan, and these nations deal with countries which are mostly former colonies. Similarly, the Soviet Union deals with a small group of comparatively rich nations in Eastern Europe, which in turn deal with a number of producers which are centrally controlled.

An ecosystem has certain principles which must be obeyed if it is to function and be viable. One of them is the principle of recycling. What is happening is that all materials rise from the producers to the primary consumers, and then to the secondary, superconsumers and accumulate at the top. I have extended my Chicago paper (this volume) and elaborated it into another paper to be presented in Frascati with data showing, for example, that the amount of iron discarded in American city dumps is equal to ten times the production of iron in Egypt.

GUNAWARDENA: My paper (written for the Chicago session) was partly prompted by the present economic crisis and political situation and by the emergence of a new political party, outside the parliamentary system, in Ceylon. This party consists mainly of students in secondary and higher education and of the educated unemployed. My study focuses on the political aspirations of the major social classes in Ceylon as a function of their social practice, that is, as an abstraction, correlation and projection of their social activity as a group. It defines a social class in terms of mode of production and appropriation of surplus produced by the society. My paper focuses attention on the manner in which one class takes away the surplus produced by another and examines as a separate category the group of individuals produced by the universal free education system introduced in 1945. These individuals are the unemployed, the part-time employed, and the students, none of whom produce a surplus. The school system is treated as a method of training individuals as wage laborers, on the one hand, and as managers and controllers of capital, on the other. The political aspirations of various groups are analyzed as a function of their post-school experience of the society into which they are thrown. The organization of students and the unemployed under discussion decided to confront the power of the state at the 1971 election; the attack failed, and since then the organization has been completely suppressed. My paper analyzes some of the political beliefs and background of the members of this group.

NDETI: My paper (this volume) developed mainly from my teaching experience in the medical school of the University of Nairobi. When I returned from the United States in 1967, we started our medical school and I was entrusted with teaching the medical students behavioral sciences and some aspects of human biology. But I found that I was more interested in the treatment by traditional African doctors. There are linguistic bases to the names of various categories of healers and diviners. One of the things I deduced from the overlap of meanings and sounds was that in traditional medicine the concept of a doctor or healer is really that of a wise man and not of a sorcerer or witch as Westerners have interpreted it. After clarifying the semantic meaning of these men in their cultural context, I went on to study the actual therapies. I took three cultures as examples.

I found that the basic idea is first of all that of the healer, the diviner and that the concept of healer and diviner is associated with the concept of herbalist. The healer is thought of as a spiritual person. The initial treatment which these people employ is to try to restore the patient in his own culture. In other words, they try not so much to go into the mechanics of the disease itself, but first of all to establish some kind of harmony between the patient and his culture. I consider this type of harmony to be sociopsychological. After that has been done, the doctor goes to the herbalist or consults someone who knows local herbs, and the patient is treated with the herbs.

I felt that in the training of medical students in Nairobi this traditional method should be introduced at least in dealing with rural patients. We established a training program for field doctors. We have an area about 40 miles from Nairobi where the students go during the first and the fifth years of their training to gain an understanding of the social context of the diseases which they have to treat and an insight into the customs of the people. It is quite clear that disease, medicine, philosophy, and language are really not separate, but complement one another. Disease is not a technical problem, for which you have a technical solution. Disease is related to other cultural factors in a complex way. I think that this approach made a great contribution to our social medicine and public health. The idea was really to try to bring traditional ways of treatment into modern medicine, so that the doctor would not be just a technocrat but a diviner in the real sense and not a witch doctor as he is now — the modern doctor is a witch doctor.

MOULIK: I am glad to hear Dr. Ndeti's presentation, because my research produced a similar point of view. I was at one time very closely connected with the diffusion research organized by Michigan State University. I felt at that time that a sort of deterministic, or ethnocentric, interpretation was being made of the Indian situation. They said that peasants in India were apathetic, not motivated, and that they did not have the characteristics which allow innovations. I think they produced some fifteen books on this theme. My assessment of those fifteen books was highly critical, and I became very disliked.

Luckily the Green Revolution came, and all their theories were proved wrong and mine proved right.

It was at that point that I left India to work in a completely different country, one which had a subsistence economy, was based on kinship, and was purely egalitarian. I had been assigned to the Australian National University to study social change in Papua New Guinea in the context of the cash economy. Ironically, while I was there, I gave a seminar paper on why the cash economy did not fit with the subsistence economy as it existed at that time in Papua New Guinea. I was labeled by one of the professors there as "American determinist." It then occurred to me that the development programs and technical experts coming into a developing country create a problem because of their basically deterministic nature. That is how this paper was born.

Traditionally, Papua New Guinea had a purely subsistence economy. Then came the colonial powers: Germany, England, and Australia, in that order. They brought in a highly developed capitalist cash economy, an exchange economy, and a market economy. They introduced cash crops as a sort of lever. They thought that once the Papuans began to have some cash, they would automatically switch over to the cash economy. But this did not happen. Even today, in some areas, sixty percent of the cash crops are not harvested. The Papuans do not need cash, they are perfectly happy without it. But they expect to share the Europeans' wealth. This is what some anthropologists call a "cargo cult." But I can see some rationality in it. The "cargo cult" expectations are consistent with traditional Papuan thinking. In their traditional culture, all wealth is equally distributed. No one is supposed to keep or accumulate wealth. The Papuans therefore expect that the wealth of the Europeans will be distributed to them. The problem, as I saw it there, was the agricultural contact point. Changes take place basically as a process of imitation. This process is determined by three forces: the incoming culture; the existing culture, and technology itself. I showed in my paper (this volume) why Papua New Guineans could not fully accept the capitalist exchange economy. But they would accept part of it. So the result would always be a mix. This creates problems and frustrations for the planners, the experts, and the colonial powers. They ask: "Why are these lazy people not doing things?" By forcing them into this economy, they are ruining what the developed countries are striving for, such as an egalitarian society, a sense of community and a happy society. The Papua New Guineans are given only one model of development. As an alternative, I suggest the mixed model. It has to be mixed. It can never be a purely capitalist exchange economy.

(This completed the panelists' summaries of their work. Maruyama then gave a short summary of the session that had taken place in Chicago, to which the panelists responded as follows:)

NDETI: I would like to comment on Professor Camara's remarks. I was very happy to hear that the way of thinking he describes is found in other parts of Africa. I mean the recognition that the world is not explained by just one principle. It is possible to have a world which can be explained in more than one way. In terms of my research, if we look at Western medicine we see that it takes a very monistic approach. Only the pathological states of the human body are considered. But the social, psychological, and cultural dimensions should be considered as well as the physical nature of the disease. These dimensions do not oppose but complement each other. What we need to do now is to recognize that those people who are incorporating traditional methods of treatment are making a positive contribution to our health services. It seems to me that the complementary, as opposed to monistic, view of the world is one thing we should develop in this conference. There can be more than one system of logic. According to the Western way, things fall from God, and everything is deduced from higher principles. Things are not that way, they complement one another. There may be differences, but these differences have a useful function. This brings in the idea of symbiosis. From my examination of the structures of many African societies, I can say that most of them are very egalitarian. Nobody at any time within the society is made to feel useless, whether he is old or young. Each age group performs a particular role, and all the groups together fulfill a symbiotic function.

GUNAWARDENA: You said "egalitarian." What do you mean by that? A democratic system? Ownership of land? Or a collective?

NDETI: Well, in the traditional sense, egalitarian in every respect. A chief is regarded as the custodian of people's interests. He is responsible for ensuring redistribution.

MOULIK: That is all, he is the guardian.

NDETI: Precisely.

GUNAWARDENA: How does he become a chief? Because everybody agrees that he should be appointed or . . . ?

NDETI: If I can take some East African examples, a chief is not a lasting force as such; he happens to be one of the gifted people around. An exception in East Africa is Uganda, where there is a fairly structured system. In Uganda, a kingdom started around 1800, but before that even Uganda was really egalitarian on the clan level. The head of each clan was really a custodian. But because of the missionaries, the Kabaka became the chief; originally he was just one of the clan heads.

GHABBOUR: This ties in perfectly with what I have just written.

When the missionaries came, they mistook tribal advisors for chiefs.

GUNAWARDENA: Wasn't there something in your paper about certain communal things they do? Is it a collective thing?

MARUYAMA: That is a completely different structure. You are trying to classify it into either capitalism or communal land ownership. But it is neither. For example, the Navajo system is neither capitalist nor communist. There, as long as you use a certain portion of land it is yours. But as soon as you stop using it, somebody else can use it.

GUNAWARDENA: But I thought there must be some communal idea which makes the Navajo system work.

MARUYAMA: It is individualistic too, because as long as you use a portion of land, it belongs to you. But it does not belong to you permanently.

GUNAWARDENA: Oh, you cannot inherit it, you cannot pass it on to your children?

MARUYAMA: It is not ownership in the capitalist sense.

MOULIK: Use right, is it?

MARUYAMA: Just use right. As for production and distribution, you grow anything that you want to grow. You might grow corn or you might grow pumpkins or something else. You might herd sheep. But eventually everybody can eat everything. One of the methods of distribution goes like this. If somebody in my family gets sick, I call for a "sing." I call a medicine man to sing for my patient for three nights. A lot of people come to hear the sing.

NDETI: Do they treat the symptoms?

MARUYAMA: Yes, very much so, psychologically as well.

GUNAWARDENA: Yes, we have this too...

MARUYAMA: People bring food. Some people bring corn, others bring sheep. Some people bring a lot and others bring almost nothing. Then all the food is cooked together, and everybody can eat as much as he wants. So the people whose crops are not very successful can still eat. The sing happens very often. When I was on the Reservation for a month or two, there were two or three sings every week within a five-mile radius. So if you are really hungry, you keep going to sings. Nobody starves. Nobody can get rich either.

GUNAWARDENA: At harvest time, do people help one another? Is that common?

MARUYAMA: Yes. Traditionally the arrangement was this. If you have a big field and you need many people for harvesting, people come to help. Next day you go to somebody else's place to help. It was not planned, communal activity, with somebody issuing orders. It was an individualistic system which functioned in a communal manner; so it was neither communist nor capitalist.

GHABBOUR: In such a system, there may be some individuals who do not want to work, and, as you say, move from one sing to another. If many people did this, the system would collapse. Are there any checks?

MARUYAMA: Nobody behaves like that because the basic idea is that of the harmony between individuals. If you destroy the harmony, you become sick.

GHABBOUR: There must be social sanctions.

MARUYAMA: Once in a while you find mentally ill people. That is possible too.

NDETI: This demonstrates the value of harmony. Harmony becomes a very powerful force. It teaches you to be responsible, and at the same time . . .

MOULIK: In Papua New Guinea there is a similar system. It provides a powerful social sanction. You hear that a rich man is a "sick" man.

GUNAWARDENA: In Ceylon, families helped neighboring families to harvest and were paid by them. But more recently with the free education system, young people's aspirations turned away from agriculture toward the towns and getting jobs. The system is breaking down because more people are getting educated, not working in the fields or helping their families but migrating out to get a university degree or to the towns to look for work. Village communities no longer have this cooperative or communal sharing. We now have to employ labor and pay for it. So the system is breaking down. This is mainly due to free education and to the aspirations that it has inspired.

MARUYAMA: There is some Westernization taking place on the Navajo Reservation. People get jobs and start getting money. There is now a housing project in which you have to buy both the house and the land. These changes are breaking down the Navajo system.

NDETI: That process is also causing a lot of disorganization in our country. It is producing a landless class, or a class without means.

GHABBOUR: The problem is not just that of having a landless class, but a landless class together with a land-owning class.

NDETI: I am writing something for the Kenya government on cultural policy, and these are some of the things I am going to recommend. We need to rethink certain relationships which we can learn from our traditional cultures. These systems probably were not perfect and may need some modification. But the basic logic was, I think, quite sound. Under Western influence, the majority of people are being completely excluded; therefore, I think we need to do some very serious rethinking. I hope that in our futuristics research, we can come up with a positive contribution.

GHABBOUR: I would like to return to the subject of social sanctions among the Navajos who are both individualistic and communalistic. In Navajo society no man can live without working, just depending on being fed. Perhaps you have heard of something called the "tragedy of the common." This is a model of an island with many shepherds each of whom has one sheep. Each of them thinks that if he could acquire just one more sheep, nobody would actually be harmed but he would double his income. If every one thought that way, the island system would be ruined. This example shows what happens to natural resources if everybody pursues his own goal without thinking of the others. Can we apply social sanctions in a modern society to prevent this "tragedy of the common?"

MARUYAMA: That is a good question. How can people who have grown up in the other system be converted to...

GHABBOUR: How did the Navajo system originate?

NDETI: In a wider context, we can infuse complementary logic into the technological Western model...

GUNAWARDENA: In Ceylon, since it was the education system which drove people away from the communal tradition, many people are suggesting that we should not have a free education system which imparts these values, and that we should go back to a grass-roots system of education in which people can work on the land while getting educated part-time in schools.

MOULIK: Has this idea been implemented?

GUNAWARDENA: No. It has been discussed but it is very difficult to propose it to the government. There is a lot of it in the Chinese system.

NDETI: Professor Maruyama, you raised the question of industrialization and Westernization. Could you elaborate on this as it is very important?

MARUYAMA: By Westernization I mean things like becoming a Christian, wearing a tie, eating three meals a day...

NDETI: Fork and knife...

MARUYAMA: All that goes with the Western way of living, but which may have nothing to do with industrialization per se. It quite often includes a Western system of government, the majority rule system in which the biggest number wins. Also the idea of competition...

GHABBOUR: Competition is not typical of all Western societies, because Soviet society has not yet...

NDETI: No, that is a Western society.

GHABBOUR: You are right. It has no competition. So competition is not typical of all Western societies, only of capitalist Western societies.

MARUYAMA: That is correct. The idea that as long as I only think of my own interest, I can benefit and it does not matter what happens to other people: that is what I mean by Westernization. The African way of building a house is much more suited to the African climate. If you build a European house in Africa, you have all kinds of health problems. African dress is appropriate in that climate too. If you start wearing Western clothes, you get skin diseases.

MOULIK: Let me talk about futures research, and what you said. The basic problem seems to be that we have become dreamers. In every second paper that I saw here (at the conference in Frascati), the word utopia appears. That means that the futurists themselves seem to be doubtful about the future. If you have to think in terms of utopia, you are looking for something unattainable. That means that you are defeated at the outset. Such an approach will not influence the decision makers at all. We must present real solutions for practical problems. As Professor Ndeti says, it would be very practical to integrate the methods of traditional medicine in the modern medical system. On the recommendation of some economists and anthropologists, this has been done in Papua New Guinea. But many people say that the communal system is the reason why Papua New Guinea is not going to develop. As late as 1970 and 1971 it was said that capital could not be formed because of the communal system. But as I have pointed out, a cash economy can never work in Papua New Guinea. Nor can we just say: "We do not want technology," or "we do not want Westernization." The world is so small now. You cannot keep people unexposed to these things. The futurists' research would be to explore the kind of mix that will work.

NDETI: The Japanese have industrialized to a certain extent, and I do not think they have broken with all their traditional institutions. One of the things we can explore is how to symbiotize Western technology with non-Western tradition. I think we have the potential for developing a completely different society. We are going to have problems if we allow foreign economists and advisors to come and plan everything. That is what is happening in Kenya.

MOULIK: I am suggesting what you are suggesting. I want experts of a different kind, experts who have much more patience, who are interdisciplinary, and who can see the situation in the proper perspective. Before 1960 it was a puzzle how Japan could industrialize so quickly, how feudal loyalty could work for the capitalist system. Japan worked it out. But Western experts did not learn. They made the same old mistake in India and other developing countries, ruining the traditional system and imposing a foreign system from above.

MARUYAMA: Unfortunately, Japan is becoming Westernized to a greater extent. Take houses, for example. It has become very popular to build Western-style houses in Japan. This is silly for many reasons. First of all, they do not suit the climate. Second, it is not economical and it is not even rational. In a Japanese house you do not have furniture. You have folding tables and folding bedding which is stored away when not in use. One room can serve many purposes, and the whole space is free from furniture, available for human movement. Walls are removable, and there is continuity between the outdoor and indoor environments, which is very important from the point of view of

Japanese philosophy. There are no rooms for individuals, and the whole family feels that it is living together. The Western-style house destroys all this. There is an acute housing shortage in Japan because of the conversion to Western-style houses. A Western house needs many rooms, and much of the space is taken up by furniture. In cities, there is not enough space for big houses. I hope the Japanese people will realize their mistake.

NDETI: We had a conference in February, in Nairobi, organized by the East African Medical Research Council, and we invited the Chinese for the first time. They came and talked a great deal about acupuncture and other traditional methods. They also showed some films. The general theme seemed to be that there is nothing wrong with traditional ways, and there is nothing wrong with technology as such. They exemplified this by comparing surgical operations using acupuncture with operations using anesthesia. You see how much can be achieved by combining the two. They say, of course, that there are some operations which require more of one than of the other.

GHABBOUR: The value of acupuncture is not that it helps anesthesia or reduces the need for anesthetics, but that it performs the mix that you are speaking about, and something else. It shows that there is something wrong in Western medicine, because the places where you put the needles have nothing to do with the organ, and this destroys the theory of Western medicine.

NDETI: Yes. Well, actually, during that conference, the Americans and the British came up and said: "Look, I think it is about time to become diviners. We have been witch doctors for too long." They recognized the need to look at the disease not just as a technical problem, but as something which must be treated with more than technical methods. The very fact that people in Africa have existed for so long in their environment means that they must have attained some kind of adaptation, they must have developed some technique to be able to live in it. We should think twice before we replace this with something from outside.

GUNAWARDENA: There is something else which the Chinese have done for medicine. They have decided that there are certain medical tasks at the village level which a student, after two years of medical studies, can perform. They have different grades of training.

MARUYAMA: I heard a very interesting paper (Kehl, 1972) presented last year in an anthropology meeting. The paper was on the Chinese concept of waste as compared to the American concept of waste. According to American philosophy, a thing is a substance. It is permanent. It has its identity. So when this thing breaks a little, it is no more the same. If your pencil breaks, it is no longer a pencil. Therefore it is no good any more. You have to do one of two things;

either repair it to exactly the same shape, or throw it away. But according to the Chinese way of thinking, nothing ever remains the same anyway. Everything changes all the time. It is normal for a pencil to break or something else to change its form. And it is not considered as waste. All you have to do is to find a new use for this changed thing. So you keep using it for different purposes. It is different from recycling because recycling is to make the same thing again, whereas the Chinese idea is not to make the same thing.

GHABBOUR: There are certain factories in Cairo which collect discarded things and make something useful out of them. And this is the technology of the Third World.

GUNAWARDENA: I have seen cigarette cans all stretched out and a suitcase made of them.

NDETI: Actually, I can recall quite a few examples from my own country. People there have developed a secondary industry and it is a big industry. Discarded things are converted into something else. And now I can see the difference between recycling and using something in another stage of its change.

MARUYAMA: Some of the films on China showed that the conversion is done in small houses. Certain houses specialize in collecting old objects of a particular kind and convert them while other houses collect and convert something else.

NDETI: I think that is very creative. Our faculty of architecture is involved in small-scale, locally based industries. Uses for discarded materials which can be converted into something else is one of the things they are working on. Industry of this type is developing in the so-called ghetto areas of the town. That is where the creative thinking is taking place. It is called "village polytechnic" and can be found all over the slum areas.

GHABBOUR: May I comment on Professor Maruyama's paper on heterogeneity? I agree that heterogeneity by itself is not enough, there must be interrelationships between the heterogeneous parts. Heterogeneity has two functions. First, it serves to maintain the viability of a system, whether it be a nation or a biological system. Secondly, it guarantees the continued growth of this system. As Maruyama (1978) has shown, it is the cause of evolution and embryonic development. But I wish to add something new to this. That is the creation of the first molecules of living matter.

NDETI: Primordial soup.

GHABBOUR: Yes, because all theories so far have succeeded in explaining how protein came about. But protein alone is not enough, because nucleic acids are absent from this model and they are essential for life. Protein without nucleic acids is not living matter. So I think this is something worth doing further research on, using the idea of deviation-amplifying reciprocal causal processes which generate heterogeneity.

MARUYAMA: Some of the counterculture people are making one mistake. They are not familiar with the reciprocal causal model. Therefore, when they reject hierarchy, they fall into the atomistic pattern. "Do your own thing. I do my own thing. We do not worry about anything else. We just mind our group." There are little encounter groups which are very popular. But in these encounter groups they do not think about anything outside the group. I met an encounter group institute director who hates black people, but loves her little encounter groups. The mistake the counterculture people are making is to become isolationist. Heterogeneity might fall into that pattern if the groups are not interrelated. It is not just heterogeneity but interrelationships which make for a viable system and symbiosis.

GHABBOUR: And then comes division of labor. The division of labor is also essential because it is the essence of heterogeneity.

NDETI: Precisely. Not hierarchical stratification, but division of labor.

GHABBOUR: And every old man, every person has a function, and his loss will be a loss to the whole society. But in a society of homogeneous people, every individual is like every other individual and his loss means nothing.

NDETI: Extinction. That was the problem with the dinosaurs. They just specialized on one particular form of vegetation.

GHABBOUR: And they grew without differentiation.

MARUYAMA: Well, there are several ways to heterogenize. One way is to have localized heterogeneity. For example, in San Francisco we have a China Town, a Japanese section, a Russian section. So the city looks heterogeneous. But if you go into each locality, it is very homogeneous. The other way to heterogenize is by interweaving. For example, in some other American cities the Japanese people live scattered all over the place but eat Japanese food, and the Chinese people live scattered and eat Chinese food. Furthermore, you do not have to be Chinese to eat Chinese food. White Americans can eat Chinese food in their homes.

NDETI: I think I see the danger. Homogeneity can lead to extinction if people localize too much and overspecialize.

MARUYAMA: I can think of the individual heterogenizing himself. Today I eat Chinese food and tomorrow I eat African food, and so on. A white person might become a Buddhist for a few years and a Chinese might become a Muslim. I can also have several different jobs and heterogenize myself that way.

NDETI: There is an old saying that variety is the spice of life. It is a very fundamental principle.

MOULIK: Are you suggesting that all individuals should heterogenize?

MARUYAMA: Not necessarily. Some can specialize or remain homogeneous.

MOULIK: You see the prospect of heterogenization in the future?

MARUYAMA: I think it is becoming more and more possible. I can go to a store and buy all kinds of food because of canning and freezing processes. Now people are talking about shorter working hours, perhaps three days a week. In that case they could have two jobs. The more free time you have, the more different things you can do. I think a lot of people are interested in doing that, even though some people might want to specialize.

GHABBOUR: Well, I am finding myself heterogenizing in this meeting.

NDETI: That is the only way to survive. In a fundamental sense, it is not the survival of the fittest as Westerners interpret that.

GHABBOUR: It is not the survival of the strongest, but...

NDETI: No. Survival of the one that can heterogenize.

GHABBOUR: Yes, the survival of the most symbiotic.

NDETI: In the Western sense, the survival of the fittest is very much the survival of the strongest.

GHABBOUR: But the fittest could be the strongest in one sense and the most symbiotic in another sense. Who is the fittest?

NDETI: In the capitalist system of thinking, the one who is the most competitive, the one who is at the top, the one who is imbued with the Protestant ethic, the one who is assured of heaven because he has managed to kill everybody else around. That kind of fittest...

GHABBOUR: It goes with the homogeneity of society.

NDETI: But what you are saying is survival of the most symbiotic, survival of that which has heterogenized...

GHABBOUR: Survival of the one which has established as much interrelationship with the surrounding world as possible.

MARUYAMA: That is a new formulation. We have several formulations now. Let us write them down.

1. Survival of the most symbiotic.
2. Survival of the most diversified (not too specialized):
   A. diversification within each individual; and/or
   B. diversification between individuals.
3. Survival of those who are most interrelated:
   A. among themselves; and/or
   B. with the surrounding world.

It has been a fruitful discussion. I think what has come out of this session is not necessarily a recommendation for some kind of utopia, but principles for survival. Would anyone like to make a concluding statement

NDETI: Perhaps heterogeneity is the sort of principle that we should encourage in futures research. In order to diffuse the work load of those doing futures research in Western societies, some research can be carried out in non-Western societies to articulate the idea of heterogeneity and perhaps the Western societies might be brought to accept it.

REFERENCES

DARLING, F. F., R. F. DASMANN
  1969   The ecosystem view of human society. *The Impact of Science on Society* 19(2): 109–121. UNESCO.
KEHL, F.
  1972   "Chinese cities under capitalism and socialism." Paper presented at the American Anthropological Association meeting, November, 1972.
MARUYAMA, MAGOROH
  1978   "Psychotopology and its application to cross-disciplinary, cross-professional and cross-cultural communication," in *Perspectives on ethnicity*. Edited by R. Holloman and S. Arutiunova, World Anthropology. The Hague: Mouton.

Conceptualization of the Future in Various Cultures

Past and Future Culture Change: A Quest for Variant Explanations

ROBERT K. McKNIGHT

Not knowing about culture change, how can one presume to know about the future and the cultural changes it may bring, much less espouse a discipline termed "futuristics?" In this paper I contend that social scientists in Europe and America have been derelict in their efforts to comprehend how culture change is regarded and managed in non-Western societies. Western scholars have, on the whole, asked the wrong questions, or only questions that would enable them to propose cultural alternatives for the future based on their own past cultural experiences. That this provincialism is inadequate to the task of attempting to understand or project man's future on this planet should be evident without elaboration. It appears, however, from early reviews of this paper, that the importance of an effective cross-cultural perspective in the study of culture change is not clearly understood. Perhaps the confusion can be corrected by looking retrospectively at the experience of Western scholarship in the study of religious ideology and behavior.

Before Edward Tylor's reduction of basic, pancultural religious ideology to "animism" (*Primitive Culture*) and Emile Durkheim's subsequent reduction of pancultural religious functionalism to "social cohesion" (1954), European students of non-Christian societies maintained that many of these societies were devoid of religion. Prior to Tylor and Durkheim, for the most part, religious ideologies and institutions were only recognized to be such insofar as the observer

This paper is based on research conducted at California State College, Hayward, by the author with L. Hazell and T. Allen, both advanced students in Anthropology. The original research from which this paper is abstracted is detailed in a paper titled: "A charter for innovation: toward a cross-cultural understanding of culture change" (unpublished manuscript).

could detect parallels with European religious practice. European and American social scientists only began to take a scholarly approach to the study of religion on a planetary scale after this provincial perspective had been effectively abrogated.

A scholarly approach to the study of culture change, particularly when that study purports to comprehend the future of the whole human species, necessarily involves a similar abrogation of provincialism. In this paper I will demonstrate a methodological strategy that can provide a more fully cross-cultural approach to the study of culture change, and tentatively I will suggest some of the possible implications of a nonprovincial perspective on cultural futurology.

"WESTERN" AND "TRADITIONAL" SOCIETIES

All social systems change. Some societies are, perhaps, more conscious and articulate about change than others, but the question of how change is described or expressed as an experience in nonliterate, non-Western societies has rarely been put in reasonable terms.

An objective scanning of behavior in Western society will indicate that culture change, when defined as socially significant by accepted observers, is generally described in a manner that is basically Orwellian: that which is sensed as new is made relevant and assigned a positive or negative value in relationship to established and persistent social trends. The frame or validation field is our own experience with past historical conditions and changes. For Western observers the validation field for culture change has been in the process of being defined by European observers since the thirteenth century, and by the end of the nineteenth century it was deeply embedded in the popular rubrics of evolution and progress. Culture changes or descriptions of culture change that are incongruent with Euro-American conceptions of cultural evolution and progress are, in the main, dismissed as irrelevant or inconsequential. This tends to be the case whether the changes being described take place in Western or non-Western societies. The neoevolutionism of contemporary anthropology, supposedly a product of refined observation and sensitivity to cultural relativity, remains about as unilinear as its nineteenth-century antecedents. It is suggested that the locus of evolutionary progress may shift from the West to Africa or elsewhere, but the epistemology involved does not deviate from the basic Spencerian assumptions about progress. The features of culture change are deeply shrouded by the macroevolutionary trends defined by Western social science. On a more detailed level, case studies of societies undergoing change are distorted by the emphasis given to reactions to Western influence.

Observers of such societies, who are generally Western social scientists concerned with or about Westernization, focus chiefly on the specifics of responses to the introduction of Western technology and institutions.

Of deepest concern to many social scientists is the fact that in our application of the social sciences in political, economic, or broadly social development programs there is abundant evidence of ethnocentricity and little evidence of freedom from the biases of nineteenth-century evolutionary lineality. Technologically underdeveloped societies undergoing programs of directed culture change are guided away from their own institutions toward Euro-American society with only a few minor deviations depending on the political calling of the director. In religion, this is explicit in foreign mission work. The missionary knows that he is weaning his congregation away from one set of religious practices toward another that he holds to be fundamentally superior. The missionaries of political and economic development, however, are generally less candidly aware of their actions. The administrative directors of political and economic programs frequently assume that they are "filling a vacuum" by introducing institutions where none existed before. In anthropology we recognize that this is seldom the case: the presence or absence of an institution is determined by its function, which may be political or economic, whether or not it happens to conform to a familiar structure.

From the anthropology literature it is abundantly clear that the same recognition does not pertain to culture change. Terms and concepts such as "neolithic New Guinea," "Stone Age Australian," "primitive isolate," and "limited good" convey far more than operationally functional objectivity, and easily document the epistemology of the anthropological assumption that only technologically advanced societies are provided with techniques for managing culture change. When the ideologies and technologies associated with culture change in our society are not detected in another society in their familiar forms, we tend to lump that society along with numerous other non-Western societies in a category termed "traditional." Hence, when Western influence is present in a "traditional" society, there is a tendency to assume that a vacuum is being filled (whether we like it or not) and an ideology of change introduced.

This paper is based on the recognition that all social systems change, and we assume, therefore, that all have experienced changes. We hypothesize from this that all societies have described such experiences and that these descriptions incorporate elements that are functionally analogous to the Western notions of evolution and progress, however dissimilar and unfamiliar in form.

METHODOLOGICAL CONSIDERATIONS

How does one go about determining how others have defined the experience of culture change? A people's experience with change, if the change is recent, is likely to be a more or less crude effort to depict some chronologically ordered segment of reality or sensed action — simplified, warped by perceptual failure and sometimes crassly personalized. Akutagawa in his novel *Rashamon* caught the essence of recall for the recent past. But as age overcomes an action sequence, if it is recalled at all, the description of it begins to drift toward harmony with culturally defined reality. No doubt this process of harmonization occurs more rapidly in societies which lack the fossilizing technology of the written record and rely instead on oral historians, but it occurs nonetheless to a greater or lesser extent in all societies. With the passage of time, descriptions of change begin to lose the crudeness and crassness of oversimplification and personalization and gather about them a particular and, I would add, functional cultural perspective. The recall of change becomes the perspective of a people conscious of their past and prone to put it to use in a purposeful fashion. The titles of several books on prehistory, variants on the theme "uses of the past," suggest the motivations involved. The tendency is by no means limited to Western students of ancient history and archaeology.

We hope to show that a people's recall of the past includes the reshaping of past changes in a manner that helps to explain the society as it now exists. Hence, to the extent that contemporary societies differ from one another, we should expect to find different frames or validation fields by which to view humanity's experience with culture change. We may anticipate that each such validation field is shaped by the particular contours of the society of the narrator, and that it portrays in more or less coded form the society's motivations and aspirations for the present and future. Rather than a single perspective on the future, then, we should be able to detect as many perspectives as there are significant differences between societies. Among the variant perspectives, we should be able to locate particular types that include various technologically developed societies, including our own. This suggests that each society, through its histories, myths, commercials, legends and novels, presents for its members ideals or models of behavior relevant to culture change — the stimuli that shape the enculturation of the innovator or agent of change. In this paper a brief analysis, along these lines, of three nonliterate, non-Western societies is attempted.

Ultimately the ramifications of this research strategy suggest that we shall need to reinvestigate with less astigmatic lens the legends and myths that shape our own innovators and those in other technologically developed nations. In this short paper, however, I will restrict myself to speculating on the applicability of some of the more general features of culture change as illustrated by three non-Western societies in an effort to frame some questions relative to innovation in America and Japan.

FIELD DATA FOR THE CROSS-CULTURAL STUDY OF CHANGE

In research conducted along the lines suggested above, the oral literature of three societies — Andaman, Trobriand, and Ulithian — was examined. The first two societies (Andaman and Trobriand) were selected to provide an alternative view to that of their ethnographers, Radcliffe-Brown and Malinowski respectively. In both instances the ethnographic description is chronologically "flat," and both ethnographers argue that this perspective is appropriate for the societies involved — both societies are described as lacking an ideology of culture change. We hoped to demonstrate that this was not the case. Ulithi was chosen because of the availability of Lessa's *Tales from Ulithi Atoll.*[1] The general research strategy can be applied to any society for which there is a resonable collection of oral literature.

In each case, of course, attention was focused on narratives depicting past changes, such as how the islands were formed, how the people learned to make a fish trap, or how a particular variety of food came to exist. We scanned such narratives for consistent themes and preconditions associated with innovation and change in the society. In the original monograph reporting this study considerable space was given to illustrative material. Here I shall concentrate on abstracted consistent elements and themes.

THE ANDAMAN IDEOLOGY

Andaman myths and legends as presented by Radcliffe-Brown proved to be a rich source of native descriptions of innovation and culture change. Two features in particular stand out from these descriptions: First, the Andaman folk historian telescoped changes back to what was referred to as the "wonderful time" of the ancestors when the Islands took shape, when all knowledge was acquired, and when rules for social conduct were established. Events involving innovation and change were located in the past. While this ideological gymnastic served to reinforce Radcliffe-Brown's determination to treat the soci-

---

[1] The publications used in this study are the classics by Radcliffe-Brown (1964), and Malinowski (1929, 1961, 1965). For Ulithi see Lessa (1961).

ety as static, it may as readily be described as a way of managing or adapting to change and innovation. Second, change and innovation are typically accompanied by or are sometimes the result of anger. Radcliffe-Brown himself observes that the Andaman equates anger, heat, and fire and that the latter, a prized cultural possession, could be observed to have great power to change things. In the Andaman view, anger appears to have creative and adaptive qualities. It is tempting to expand the Andaman conception into a basic statement about systems and energy.

The Andaman Islands are situated in a region frequently disturbed by typhoons and subject to seasonal monsoon. When the Andaman harvested his main crops, which ripen during the monsoon season, he believed that his gods were angered. Despite this belief, harvesting continued, and in time it was perceived that the gods had been appeased through their display of anger, and harmony returned to the universe. The fisherman was often aware of the anger of the gods, but the storms would pass, and persistence in the face of anger was seen to be adaptive. Hence it would appear that in the Andaman ideology positive adaptation including cultural gain through innovation was achieved by patient persistence in the face of resistance and anger. The latter were essential for appeasement to occur and harmony return to a universe that was essentially cooperative and reciprocative. What is perhaps most striking is the neat fit of this ideological system with the Andaman environment: the same formula that applied to ongoing ecological adaptation was made applicable to culture change with the additional feature that, in time, the folk historians antedated change making it congruent with the past and providing a sense of stability and continuity.

THE TROBRIAND IDEOLOGY

In the Trobriands, two major themes stand out in the materials presented by Malinowski: First, changes described by the Trobrianders had their origin outside the temporal and geographic boundaries of their culture. In general terms, in narratives concerned with past changes, a native Trobriander was described as having left the Trobriands to return with a new variety of banana, a new song, etc. Innovations came from the outside. Second, the role of the agent of change is described as difficult and hazardous, demanding unusual personal characteristics such as strength, endurance, skills in magic, and virility. Since, as Malinowski observes, the Trobrianders regarded canoe travel on the open sea as dangerous, the second feature is not incongruent with the first.

It would appear that the Trobriand legends concerned with past cultural changes had woven into them many of the features of the *kula*, the trade system that linked the Trobrianders with distant neighbors. The role characteristics and experiences of the legendary innovators were very similar to those of the *kula* trader. From a variety of perspectives, excepting perhaps Malinowski's own, we can posit that the *kula* may best be viewed as the institution through which the Trobriander anticipated novelty, innovation, and change. Curiously, Trobriand innovators often encountered stressful sexual experiences before returning to their homes with their innovations. Is this an encoded form of the Andaman concern for heat or energy which, in the Andaman materials, was expressed as anger? Is it too farfetched to suggest that the association between innovation, sex, and advertising connotes a similar code in the United States?

THE ULITHI IDEOLOGY

In the Ulithi materials by far the most dominant theme is reciprocity — unless the would-be innovator engaged in generous exchange relations with the source of innovation, no innovation would take place. In one legend involving undersea swimming, the woman possessing the secret received shoddy treatment from her community during a period of food scarcity. In the end, when the villagers discovered that she knew the secret of undersea swimming and came to her with gifts, she destroyed herself in flames rather than teach them the secret.

Other themes, some of them familiar, occur in the Ulithi materials. The source of innovation (often a sea spirit) resided outside the local community. The innovator was one who was not intimidated when facing dangers or the unknown. The Ulithi legends stress the importance of perseverance, learning skill, and stealth or cunning in creative innovation. We suspect that these are the characteristics generally ascribed to the Ulithian canoe navigator who, like the *kula* trader in the Trobriands, is the most likely agent of change.

The dominant theme of reciprocity in Ulithi is, of course, of wider significance than might be implied by associating it specifically with innovation. Indeed, a reverse sort of relationship is suggested. In the Ulithi legends culture change, rather than being epiphenominal, is allied with a dominant institutional base the importance of which in an atoll environment has frequently been recognized in the anthropological literature. Sahlins expressed this as follows:

When surpluses are relatively small and deficiencies liable to arise in different localities, a premium is put on direct or reciprocal types of distribution, not types that travel up and down hierarchies (1958: 236).

Thus we find that themes connected with culture change are closely allied with dominant concerns and institutions of the existing community and with ecological conditions that are relevant to it — innovation and monsoon harvest in the Andamans, innovation and the *kula* in the Trobriands, innovation and reciprocity in Ulithi.

THE IDEOLOGY OF CULTURE CHANGE AS AN ASPECT OF ETHOS

We found it fairly easy to depict the specific differences between the three societies that emerge from their narratives concerning past innovations, and we were able to note some common features. How these differences may be classified in terms of categories or typologies, however, and how widely the commonalities may extend beyond these three examples remain for future study.

No theme that occurs commonly in one society is completely absent in the others. For example, the interesting complex of ideas formed by the association of anger, heat, energy, and adaptive change which seems central to the ideology of culture change in the Andaman materials reappears in the Trobriand materials in the need to overcome fear in sea travel and in the Ulithian, in confronting a sea spirit. Nowhere in the Trobriand or Ulithian materials, however, did we find such a fundamental acknowledgment of the importance of energy (ultimately "heat" but manifest as wind, storm, anger) as in the Andaman formula for system change. The stipulation that the source of innovation should be external to the immediate human community is found in each society, and it occurs in practically every narrative. Andaman innovations antedate the society of the immediate present. In Ulithi the source of innovation is typically a sea spirit. The notion that innovation comes from outside seems most strongly emphasized in the Trobriands, where a native resident may be sent away to return, after trials and suffering, with some new song or other novel item. The idea of mutual benefit through giving, the offering of a portion to the spirits, and the exchange of gifts or sexual favors occur in each of the three societies in the context of innovative gain. However, the theme of reciprocity seems to dominate the legends dealing with innovation in Ulithi.

Rather than being a disease which the static metabolism of the social system strives to reject, change in the perspective illustrated here is juxtaposed with a dominant ethos which is associated with the adaptive vitality of the society. In none of the legends of these three societies, however, is the role of the agent of change made congruent with that of the commonplace person, and, as we have emphasized, the locus of innovation is described as being outside the immediate local, human, or temporal context. We are led to suggest that culture change is a theme that occupies a central place, and that it is given importance by association with dominant institutions or social conditions, while the idea that anyone can easily be an innovator is strongly discouraged.

Scanning beyond these three societies we wonder if this kind of ambivalence — change is vital but discouraged — may not be universally associated with ideologies of change? One who contributes to the well-being of his community through innovation may well be granted fame, but this does not mean that any society, including Euro-American, encourages its neophytes to define themselves willy-nilly as free agents of innovation. The theoretical consequence would be chaos. Societies would seem to provide guidelines suggesting the course to take to gain the license to innovate. However, the particular features of that course are carefully constricted, and, in consequence, few persons may define themselves casually as innovators. None may do so overtly (and successfully) without first showing ability and determination to accept the core principles upon which their particular society is built — this is especially evident in the Ulithi materials.

The ideology of change in Western society seems congruent with the preceding if we accept the centrality of the idea of specialization. Perhaps in no other social context is the would-be innovator subjected to so severe a struggle or to so many initiation ceremonies, tests, graduations, and conformity rituals as is the Western student in his endeavor to emerge as a licensed specialist — a shaman of innovation. The formula is one that would seem to ensure compliance with the core principles upon which Western society is based. But at the same time the student is groomed to be an outsider; he must leave his society and return as a specialist with a new appropriate label or identity associated with a craft or science in order to contribute in a manner recognized to be creative; indeed it is expected that he is now going to innovate, like the *kula* trader returning home. However, as the students struggle to complete their ritualized journey toward specialization, their capacity for significant innovation becomes severely limited, bounded by the very walls that their own efforts have erected to secure their conformity and to separate them from their society. Perhaps nowhere is this removal or separation more evident than in the rigidly maintained boundaries of academia, itself a potential source of innovation and the most marked of separated domains.

SPECULATION: IDEOLOGIES OF CHANGE AND THE ASPIRATIONS OF NATION-STATES

Ruminating on the materials developed thus far, I found myself trying to gain a new or slightly tangential perspective on the special case

represented by Japan. I dealt mostly with two features — conformity
and specialization — that have been emphasized thus far, noting that
specialization is a particular variety of "outsideness."

When the Japanese leadership decided on a course of rapid modernization, around the mid-1800's, the country had just emerged from a
hundred year period of carefully controlled social conformism, the
Tokugawa era, during which Japan had maintained relative isolation
from other nations, and centralized government had developed detailed procedures for enforcing social conformity and detecting deviation. Techniques ranged from systematic control over dress to the
development of a system of taking political hostages. Conformity was
never perfect, but Japan was probably the most highly controlled
society of its size that the planet has seen. Concurrently, Japan had
developed considerable diversity and specialization in art, craft, and
commerce. Before the "opening" Japan had developed a formula for
controlled innovation that subsequently gained worldwide recognition
in art, architecture, landscaping, and commodity marketing. With the
"opening" the same general formula was put to work for modernization with the added ingredient of the overseas scholar as "outsider-
specialist." The epitomy of the process by which Japan achieved
alarmingly rapid modernization was the government-sponsored overseas scholarship student.[2] These students were carefully selected after
years of conformity rituals in schools that combined memorization and
tests with moral education. They came from family backgrounds that
tended to ensure kin pressure for conformity, and they were sent from
Japan to Europe and America to gain highly specific training in areas
considered relevant for modernization by the Japanese leadership. The
scholars returned and innovated rapidly and efficiently, making a
particular and specialized rather than general impact on the course of
Japanese destiny.

In time, with the development of the appropriate technology, Japan
began to implement the legends of the past. The fabric of the legends,
including repeated rewriting of the nation's present successes to conform with the directionality suggested by the legends, was (by and
large) accepted by the public. Japanese leaders were able to make use
of the mobilizing energy of the national legends as well as the increasing cadre of highly sophisticated technological specialists. Among the
latter were many professionals who professed no belief and a few who
protested, but they were easily controlled. The vast majority of the
educated elite assumed the peculiar role of the outsider-specialist,
gaining rewards from society for their particular skills and otherwise

---

[2] A number of studies of Japanese modernization have made this point, including
Bennett, Passin, and McKnight (1958).

not interfering with or questioning the society that was rewarding them.

Leading up to and during World War II the driving purpose for the Japanese public was the realization of Japan's destiny — a religious and national obligation to the world. In retrospect it seems difficult to understand why the very process of developing a highly sophisticated education system did not in and of itself produce an effective counter-ideology, a debunking of the national legends. The myths of Japan's origin and destiny are at least as grotesque as those of other cultural entities. Yet education, whether sponsored by government or religious institutions, cannot or does not maintain effective detachment from the national myths and legends — these are part and parcel of enculturation — and in adapting to the paradox of supporting both legend and knowledge, education continues to produce the outsider-specialist who, although he may be given a license to innovate, is shaped, rewarded, and seduced by his society so that he conforms generally and innovates particularly.

Innovation in technologically advanced societies seems to be char-tered and legitimized through formulae that, in some general features, resemble those that were evident in the Andamans, the Trobriands, and Ulithi. The pioneers at the frontiers of science, the nuclear physicists, the computer specialists, and the hundred-and-one other specialists are the Andaman ancestor, the Trobriand *kula* trader, and the Ulithian navigator, with better technological tools and, perhaps, an even more effective form of outsideness — detached but dependent on the success of their nation.[3]

If we look about us today it is evident that there is no established destiny for the nation-state beyond the realization of its own legends, and, given the technology to do so, it seems logical that each nation will strive to realize its legends through formulae generally resembling those described here. The future of society on this planet, if this is the case, may simply be based on a ramification of this quandary: the predicament of a hundred different nation-states each striving to achieve lineal evolution!

A STRATEGY FOR CULTURAL FUTURISTICS

On the basis of the above analysis it seems clear that there is a sizable research area in anthropology that has thus far been shrouded by stereotypes such as "traditional" and the notion that many non-

---

[3] Slater (1971) traces a legacy for outsideness in American culture. While his discussion is tangential, it would appear that specialization qualifies for this legacy.

Western societies "lack ideologies of change." The naiveté involved in such stereotypes has been fostered by: (1) the anthropological suggestion that contemporary societies lacking the technological development of Western societies are analogous to societies of the ancient past and the inference that such societies have remained unchanged; (2) the overwhelming attention that anthropologists have bestowed on the impact of Western societies in their political and economic expansion on the planet and the inference that this impact has brought with it the first experience with culture change for most non-Western societies. Both inferences are spurious by-products of anthropological methods and focus. A cross-cultural understanding of man's experience with culture change has not been achieved as yet for the profession and must be a necessary component of a discipline concerned with man's future changes on the planet. A methodological strategy has been suggested in this paper for determining the content of ideologies of culture change in cross-cultural studies. The results obtained using this method seem to indicate that such ideologies are closely associated with the enculturation of neophytes in the mainstream of their culture, creating agents of change who are well indoctrinated in the legends and aspirations of their society.

If this is the case, it would appear that among the important tasks of an anthropology action-oriented toward the future would be the re-orienting of education toward the creation of licensed innovators whose boundaries of sensitivity and conformity are those of humanity and whose skills and contributions in innovation are geared to motivations more widely based than those of any particular society or nation-state. What may be needed is a legend for mankind, and a philosophy for man, broadened beyond the particular myths and goals of a hundred separate nations.

REFERENCES

BENNETT, J. W., H. PASSIN, R. K. McKNIGHT
    1958   *In search of identity.* Minneapolis: University of Minnesota Press.
DURKHEIM, EMILE
    1954   *Elementary forms of the religious life.* New York: Free Press.
LESSA, W. A.
    1961   *Tales from Ulithi Atoll: a comparative study of Oceanic folklore.* Folklore Studies 13. Berkeley and Los Angeles: University of California Press.
MALINOWSKI, B.
    1929   *The sexual life of savages.* New York: Harcourt, Brace and World, Harvest Book Edition.
    1961   *Argonauts of the Western Pacific.* New York: E. P. Dutton.
    1965   *Coral gardens and their magic,* volume 1. Bloomington: Indiana University Press.

RADCLIFFE-BROWN, A. R.

1964   *The Andaman Islanders.* Glencoe, Illinois: Free Press.

SAHLINS, M. D.

1958   *Social stratification in Polynesia.* Seattle: University of Washington Press.

SLATER, P. E.

1971   *The pursuit of loneliness — American culture at the breaking point.* Boston: Beacon Press.

TYLER, SIR EDWARD BURNETT

1958   *Primitive culture,* part two: *Religion in primitive culture.* New York: Harper and Brothers.

Ideas Concerning Maya Concepts of the Future

JAMES C. GIFFORD

The unique kind of high civilization embraced by the Old Empire Maya, to which we can unquestionably relate the Zinacantecos of present-day Mexico, was indicative of a cultural configuration that had become elaborated to an unusual degree, especially in directions of ecclesiastical and ritual development. As one dimension of this elaboration, so spectacular in its religious aspect, we can think of the southern lowland Maya Old Empire as being not only socially stratified but as relying on the existence of two different worlds — the village homeland and the major ceremonial center. As this high civilization unfolded through time, these two patterns of living became more and more remote from one another, and full-time specialization became increasingly accentuated as well as characteristic of the ceremonial center lifeway. As they gradually became differentiated from one another, two lifeway patterns arose which, though recognizably distinct, combined with one another to form, in their cumulative articulation, the high civilization. The Old Empire Maya participated in their kind of high civilization with full knowledge of these two very different worlds. A crucial societal difference between these two worlds, evidently not at all so obvious to every participant in this ancient configuration, lay in the fact that the major ceremonial center was dependent on the village homeland, while the homeland was self-sufficient. Despite its unparalleled theological opulence, its ritualistic splendor, and its hierarchic superposition over homeland population units, the world of the major ceremonial center could not exist without its articulation in the setting of the village. When that articulation

In developing my interpretation of the Maya cultural continuum, I have relied heavily on the written works of Evon Z. Vogt, Gordon R. Willey, Eric S. Thompson, and Sylvanus G. Morley.

ceased, the world of the ceremonial centers vanished and so did this kind of high civilization.

Within the Zinacanteco setting, the village homeland world survives in much of its absolute reality; but the highly specialized ceremonial center world, so much the outward symbol of the Old Empire, survives only as a glimmer and a shadow appearing sporadically at various places in the overt behavioral manifestations of the Zinacanteco people. Evidence of the ancient empire pattern, diffused and altered, appears most clearly in the components of Zinacanteco belief and thought patterns. The Zinacantecos hold on to the essence of what was once a second world in their ancient high civilization by means of intangible images and symbols which now reside deep beneath more tangible expressions of their ritualistic and philosophic rationale. Many seem at first to be so obscure and unrelated that their derivational interpretation might easily have remained unrecognized but for our knowledge of Maya prehistory. But these dimensions of the second world of the major ceremonial center, today dimmed among the Zinacantecos and other population remnants, were all-pervasive for over 800 years after Christ in the natural biome of the Petén lowlands, with its infinitely more productive agricultural system, far greater societal wealth, and the resources of many tribal units held together by the empire.

As a consequence of the empire's cultural mechanisms, there existed throughout the lowland jungles a vast expanse of contiguous tribal homelands, constantly interacting with one another and with numerous ceremonial centers of varying sizes. In this extensive cultural milieu, which increased in complexity through time, each tribal unit provided different cultural essentials for the others. Today as well, the Zinacantecos rely on their Chamula neighbors for *metates*, sandals, and other items. They turn to various sources for special essentials and use Ladino musicians on certain occasions rather than providing this service for themselves. Many more examples could be given. In the ancient village setting and homeland world, population units relied on one another for goods and services and for the fulfillment of certain roles. This was an internal reliance within the empire. The population units provided the empire with its food base — maize. Their system of maize production was efficient and, among other things, resulted in a labor surplus which could be a potential source of power under the direction of full-time specialists of comparatively exalted rank.

Within the ancient empire's structure, the other world — the world of the full-time specialist and the major ceremonial center, the second world which perished with the disarticulation and disintegration of the empire — vigorously tapped this surplus labor through the ancient version of the Zinacanteco "cargo" system. The cargo of a villager was in significant measure the *labor* he owed to the empire's second world. With that labor, the "Great Ones" of the empire, supported by the religious, ritualistic, administrative, and other full-time specialists surrounding them in a hierarchical system dedicated to the most intense ecclesiastical devotions, built their ceremonial centers into a physical setting for a cultural environment of massive proportions in which the empire's second world existed. Although the ancient cargo system may have strongly resembled what we see among the Zinacantecos today, the participant provided his society with something above and beyond what was required of him for the satisfaction of strictly homeland commitments. In the ancient system, men went to their ceremonial center on a part-time basis to help build the monumental structures considered to be essential to the perpetuation of their civilization. The future of the ceremonial centers came to depend on labor contributed as a ceremonial aspect of the cargo system; this no longer exists because ceremonial centers of the ancient type no longer exist. A comparable concept of the future is not, however, necessary in the homeland setting. A world view holding men's minds to a central theme was necessary only for the maintenance of the *empire* and so was vital only to the permanent denizens of its second world, the world of ceremonial centers and the elaborate religious dimension. The Zinacantecos today need no preoccupation with the future on this level of abstraction and do not seem to have one. On an operative level, their cargo system has now reverted strictly to the village setting where it is used by them to maintain local ritual and ceremonial essentials. In the beginning of the Maya Classic interval, however, the rituals and ceremonialism were necessary to the life of a high civilization and as such eventually came to justify the *empire*. They remain necessary but now they simply justify *life;* and since that justification is complete and total to the Zinacanteco, they take their cultural future for granted. No overt concern for the future in the sense of world view is needed if from a practical standpoint the world view rests entirely with the ancestors.

One's view of the future more or less relates to the fulfillment of a good life and does not go far beyond day-to-day goals. For a Zinacanteco, a major concern with the future relates to *his* specific cargos. According to Vogt (1970: 73–74):

Following his wedding, a young Zinacanteco ordinarily has to work diligently for a few years not only to provide for his new family, but to pay off the debts incurred by his marriage. He and his wife also look forward to having a house of their own, and this stage is usually achieved by the time he is about twenty-five. Between about twenty-five and thirty he can begin to think about serving in the cargo system. . . . When a Zinacanteco calculates that he will be ready for his first cargo some years in the future, he takes a bottle of liquor to present to the *moletik* ("elders") on August 8th. On this date each year the *moletik* sit outside the wall of the church of San Lorenzo and receive requests for cargos. The "waiting lists" are kept by the Scribes in hardcover notebooks which have a page or two devoted to each year in the future for which there is a cargo requested.... A man might ... request in 1966 the cargo of Senior Mayordome Rey for 1980, only to be told that 1980 is already taken and that he may have the position in 1986.... Once his name is recorded in the sacred book, he must reappear each August 8th, present another bottle of liquor, and reaffirm his intention to serve.

This was not so under the empire. The lifeway of those who occupied the ceremonial centers was dependent on the perpetuation of their world view. Without this kind of orientation toward the future, there would have been no reality to the second ceremonial center world of the empire even though the functional role of the ceremonial center may well have included complex and important trade and other dimensions. Consequently, as an empirically believable concept of the future became increasingly difficult to maintain and as philosophical and conceptual involvement became more abstract and removed from the homeland settings, difficulties mounted with respect to the balanced effectiveness of the empire.

The empire itself had been built up based upon an internal reliance on homeland belief in the validity of an overall view of the future propounded by the occupants of the ceremonial center. Toward the end of the empire there is evidence that the societal lifeline between homelands and ceremonial centers may have been pulled very taut by the demands of the world of major ceremonial centers (Willey, et al. 1965). These connectors may also have become badly frayed by a deepening sense of incredulity concerning the effectiveness of ceremonial center activities and the view of the future held by the occupants of ceremonial centers. These and other factors, heightened by a wide variety of circumstances (Willey and Shimkin 1971), including a threat of invasion (Sabloff and Willey 1967), may have caused the homeland world to sever irreversibly its ties with the now-remote ceremonial center world.

To the Zinacantecos the inner self, their system of beliefs — its maintenance, proper functioning, and credibility — is life itself. If those beliefs could no longer be held supraordinate with regard to the empire's second world, the empire itself would vanish with astonishing rapidity — its inner soul fragmented, its parts disarticulated, it would quickly die. The remnants of this inner soul have survived in the Chamula, the Zinacantecos, and other population units who for the most part embrace only the village-life aspect of what was once the empire.

The great ceremonial centers are gone, the stupendous architecture is gone, the real Great Ones are gone, but it is all ritually remembered

and Zinacanteco ancestors live today within pyramid-shaped mountains, where they preside over Zinacanteco societal life, care for inner
souls, and know and control the future. As long as close touch is
maintained with the ancestors, there is no need for concern with the
future — the ancestors are the future. The role of the cargo system is
still the same — it links the people with their rulers. Yesterday the
rulers lived in the ceremonial centers and the cargo system helped to
build and maintain their special lifeway within an empire. Today the
people live in villages and the cargo system maintains their lifeway by
providing a means of communication with the ancestors. The cargo
system does not accomplish this among the Zinacantecos by itself; the
shamans, too, are always needed. These shamans are the closest
remaining approximation of the full-time specialist residents of the
imperial ceremonial center. The empire needed both of its worlds; the
Zinacantecos need *real persons* to fulfil both categories of functions.
The three-year renewal ceremonies among the Zinacantecos provide
an insight into this matter. According to Vogt (1970: 99): "The ceremony has deep structural significance for Zinacantán since it links
together the two peaks of sacred terrestrial power — the top-ranking
cargoholders and the top-ranking shamans — and relates them both to
the all-important Ancestral Gods in the supernatural world."

The village homeland setting still retains three basic essentials: the
production of food, a dependence on other population units for certain
special goods and services, and a reliance on a system to provide the
society with special role actors and special role fulfillments. Among the
Zinacantecos, all of these, but particularly the last, are achieved on a
part-time basis. Structurally, it was profoundly different within the
empire, where tribal population units were the maize producers who
were part-time builders of the empire's second ceremonial center
world, furnishing full-time specialists who became residents of the
large ceremonial centers.

The point that requires emphasis here is that the homeland settings
contributed some individuals on a permanent basis for the performance of full-time roles in the ceremonial centers themselves. Thus as
a societal unit the Zinacantecos had a role to which they contributed
some of their people from generation to generation. And these people
acted out a particular Zinacanteco role in the second ceremonial center
world on a continuing (perhaps lifelong) basis as full-time specialists.
This, then, was a third and vital contribution to the empire and its
existence, made by each of its population units. Although each population unit made this contribution in its own way, it was largely determined along lines which paralleled homeland tribal interdependence
for the exchange of goods and services on local levels, and perhaps also
by factors more internal to the population unit itself. For example,

among the Zinacantecos, "a younger brother spends his life in a struggle for status in a system that has led his older brother to resent him" (Vogt 1970: 68). This setting favors the older brother within the homeland context. If an alternative lifeway were available, however, the same kind of system might encourage a younger brother to travel from the homeland setting to the second world of the ceremonial center. In staying there on a full-time basis in a capacity or position that was traditionally occupied by Zinacanteco tribesmen, he could move unimpeded toward a level of achievement and prestige comparable to or exceeding that accorded an older brother remaining in his homeland.

Within the ancient configuration, special roles no longer extant were primarily concerned with the future of the empire. Old Empire Maya astronomy, mathematics, numerology, hieroglyphic writing — these and many other arts concerned with prediction — were necessary because the Great Ones relied on the experts in these extremely specialized fields in order to comprehend the Maya future and rule their empire. Conversely, without the Empire structure, tribal units need only to govern themselves as separate units; there is consequently no need for a long-range view of the future as long as total confidence in the ancestors is maintained and communication with them is uninterrupted.

Accordingly, one has the impression that the Zinacantecos of today are preoccupied with what the ancestors accomplished in the past, with pleasing the ancestors who now reside in the spirit world (mostly inside mountains), and with day-to-day Zinacanteco activities which will not change in the future because they have been determined and set by the ancestors. Since the Zinacanteco world was fixed in all its dimensions by the ancestors, and since the present Zinacanteco system of beliefs is absolute with respect to the inviolability of what has been determined by the ancestors, there is no need for concern with the future because the future will always be as the present. While the myth of Quetzalcoatl related to the return of a Great One and ancestors, in the present state of our knowledge there is no great myth among the Maya paralleling this view. Therefore there is not even an abstract philosophical expression of future "deliverance" from that which now prevails. The future will be as it is now for Zinacantecos because the ancestors control the future and fixed it the way things are now. If change does come, it will be because the ancestors have so determined it. If communication with the ancestors has been kept in good order, Zinacantecos will know what to do.

Homeland settings of the Old Empire may well have held a similar absolute view, and the absoluteness of this view, so complete and so obvious to this day, may have been a major factor in the building and perpetuation of the empire. The most far-reaching difference is that the ancestors of the Zinacantecos are fixed abstractions; their counterparts in the empire were alive as the Great Ones and their advisors. These Maya peoples, the Great Ones and their advisors, evidently concerned themselves very much with ideas of the future. This is apparent even though our evidence comes entirely from the prehistoric record. What is known about the lifeway of the Old Empire second ceremonial center world has been inferred from data amassed by archaeologists rather than ethnologists.

These data strongly suggest that this second ceremonial center world was committed to a world view which was deeply concerned with the future. There are indications of a philosophical dimension to certain activities and certain highly specialized roles. In the archaeological record, some of these are more obvious than others. There is considerable evidence, for instance, that some individuals were totally involved with astronomy and the making of permanent records relating to astronomical observations which were not only incredibly accurate but which required extremely long periods of uninterrupted observation. These records were accumulated in book form and transcribed by means of a hieroglyphic writing peculiar to the Maya Old Empire. "Actually, as the Maya priests reckoned hundreds of millions of years into the past, it is probable that they grasped the concept of time, and therefore perhaps a world, without beginning" (Thompson 1966: 261).

In discussing the first public showing of a newly discovered, eleven-page fragment of a manuscript executed on bark cloth coated with stucco and folded like a screen, M. D. Coe perceptively touched on the extent to which certain activity patterns must have been emphasized in the ancient configuration.

The eleven-page fragment . . . is part of a larger book that originally must have been twenty pages in length. It deals exclusively with cycles of the planet Venus as seen from the earth (M. D. Coe, unpublished data).

Each cycle was measured by Maya priests as 584 days. . . . Modern astronomers have calculated this cycle to average 583.92 days. So you see, the figure is extraordinarily accurate. The complete codex would have given 65 Venus cycles, so that the whole table would cover slightly less than 104 solar years . . . the Maya were the greatest thinkers of the entire New World! (Gent 1971).

No other people in history has taken such an absorbing interest in time as did the Maya, and no other culture has ever developed a philosophy embracing such an unusual subject. . . . For the Maya time was an all-consuming interest. . . . The Maya wished to know which gods would be marching together on any given day because with that information they could gauge the combined influence of all the marchers, offsetting the bad ones with the good in an involved computation of the fates and astrological factors. On a successful solution depended the fate of mankind. . . . Each lunar month in the series and each division of each revolution of the planet Venus had its divine patron, and the influences of all those gods had to be taken into consideration. The Maya priest-astronomer was anxious to find the lowest common multiple of two or more of these cycles, or, to state it in the Maya pattern of thought, how long would be the journey on the road of time before two or more of the divine carriers reached the same resting place together. . . . So far as we know, no other people in Middle America used tables comparable in accuracy to those the Maya developed to predict possible solar eclipses and to compute the synodical revolutions of Venus, nor, so far as we know, did any other people in Middle America measure the length of the tropical year with the skill the Maya attained (Thompson 1966: 162–183).

It is clear from an abundance of archaeological data that a deep feeling for the future and correlative prediction in inself became a vested interest of the Great Ones and for associated specialists, and that this vested interest was vital to the world of the second ceremonial center for the maintenance of its highly specialized lifeway.

GENERAL CONSIDERATIONS

An inordinate interest in the future and in ways and means of influencing it may have become an obsession with the leaders in Maya prehistoric society. In the name of this obsession they may have made demands on their society which exceeded the society's capacity to meet them. The consequences may have included severe societal dislocation which, combined with other difficulties (such as threats of invasion), resulted in the sudden disintegration of the belief system of the empire. Without the binding mechanism of this system of beliefs, the physical disarticulation of population units and the abandonment of the cere-monial centers may have occurred swiftly, causing the disappearance of the second ceremonial center lifeway.

One wonders if it could be said that vested interests when trans-formed into rulership obsessions, have lethal potentialities for their societal hosts. Certainly it is possible to think that the Maya and Sumerian kinds of high civilization were actually victims of this pro-cess. Perhaps the same could also be said of the Aztec and Assyrian high civilizations. The obsession and its specifics, of course, differ from one civilization to another. Also interesting and potentially suggestive is the dynamics of change in a culture's view of the future. It is possible to observe the debilitating nature of a population-wide over-concern with the future which can lead to obsession. In the past, however, leadership obsession has been a more common behavioral pattern because education and communication have been limited. Despite the universal presence of cultural change, systems are developed for introducing and maintaining societal order and efficiency within a cultural configuration. This is often profitable to those in power, so the systems are maintained, strengthened, and elaborated in order to inhibit or prevent additional change and perpetuate the status quo, thereby protecting vested interests.

As a line of evolution, our chances for survival and success were enhanced by a certain mobility factor. This kept our population units in contact with each other, thus encouraging the exchange of genetic information on a wide front and favoring the perpetuation of a broad genetic base rather than one or a series of separate narrow ones. The former situation is genetically advantageous in the face of change, especially rapid change. This process not only continues today but has accelerated dramatically. As the genetic base for *H. sapiens* becomes even more homogeneous the world over, it will be necessary to foster cultural diversity, especially with reference to beliefs or ideological outlook, beneath a configuration of negative imperatives (Gifford, this volume). This will be needed to prevent a single mental outlook from prescribing the boundaries of the future biological development of the worldwide *H. sapiens* population. The genetic resource of the Maya was certainly bounded by the confines of their ideological outlook, total value orientation, and system of beliefs; this was the case, too, with the Sumerians and the ancient Egyptian high civilization. The priesthood of ancient Egypt managed a "comeback" time and again, thereby fixing the Egyptian high civilization in its image and perpetuating perhaps the most lengthy among the various high civilization continua (Riley 1969).

In the future *H. sapiens* genetic pool of the world, and with respect to its development, we cannot afford a narrow base caused by adherence to a single ideological outlook. Diversity in mental propensity may hold distinct advantages for the *H. sapiens* genetic base of the future, especially in a societal context where imaginative or creative forethought may be a paramount asset to a constructive cultural continuity.

A further advantage may rest with a capacity, in this *H. sapiens* "mental pool," to react favorably to sharp changes in outlook. The potential to react successfully to a rapid rate of ideological change could confer a decided advantage. This would be true even though one will recognize that there may not be a limit to complexities but a limit to the number of variables and a limit to the rate of culture change, with which the human mind can cope in such ways as to achieve psychic comfort.

In a more immediate circumstance than that of the ancient Maya, involving a potential contemporary obsession, it may not be that technology *per se* is the villain — rather, technology may simply be the most obvious, tangible indicator of too rapid cultural change which is causing psychic distress to associated population units. These observations may have suggested more questions than they answer. It is my firm view as an anthropologist that, in order to gain insight into contemporary human nature and that which will evolve in the future, one must achieve a basic comprehension of the prehistoric derivation of the *H. sapiens* populations that exist today.

REFERENCES

GENT, GEORGE
  1971   "Manuscript part may alter theories on Maya religion." *New York Times*, April 21.
RILEY, CARROLL L.
  1969   *The origins of civilization.* Carbondale: Southern Illinois University Press.
SABLOFF, J. A., G. R. WILLEY
  1967   The collapse of Maya civilization in the southern lowlands: a consideration of history and process. *Southwestern Journal of Anthropology* 23: 311–336.
THOMPSON, J. ERIC
  1966   *The rise and fall of Maya civilization* (second edition). Norman: University of Oklahoma Press.
VOGT, EVON Z.
  1970   *The Zinacantecos of Mexico.* New York: Holt, Rinehart and Winston.
WILLEY, G. R., W. R. BULLART, JR., J. B. GLASS, J. C. GIFFORD
  1965   *Prehistoric Maya settlements in the Belize Valley.* Papers of the Peabody Museum, 54. Cambridge, Mass.: Harvard University.
WILLEY, G. R., D. B. SHIMKIN
  1971   The collapse of Classic Maya civilization in the southern lowlands: a symposium summary statement. *Southwestern Journal of Anthropology* 27: 1–18.

Traditional Greek Conceptions of the Future

ROGER W. WESCOTT

Of all those civilizations which have, throughout most of their histories, been distinct from the Western European world (in the narrow sense of this phrase), there is none about which we have more extensive documentary data over a longer period of time than the Greek. In this regard, Greece's closest competitor is undoubtedly China. But, from a linguistic point of view, what makes Greece easier for us to comprehend — aside from its Mediterranean locale and its philological kinship with English — is the fact that spoken Greek never underwent the process of extreme dialectal fragmentation which led Mandarin and Cantonese, like French and Spanish, to become mutually unintelligible. Ever since Greek was first written (in the Mycenean Linear B syllabary) in the fifteenth century B.C., all Greek speakers have been able, so far as we know, to engage freely in verbal communication with one another.

We have yet, however, to determine how much of Greek history may plausibly be covered by the term "traditional." If "traditional" means substantially unaffected by the intellectual and technological transformations that swept Western Europe between the Renaissance and the Industrial Revolution, then Greece remained a traditional culture at least until its achievement of political independence from Turkey in 1830. But insofar as traditional means non-Western, and non-Western is a negative rather than a positive cultural category, it may be desirable to subcategorize Greek cultural history in terms of a sequence of phases or stages. Those most generally recognized by

I wish to acknowledge the generous bibliographic assistance I received, in the preparation of this paper, from my colleagues James Macris, Professor of Linguistics at Clark University, Anna Motto, Professor of Classics at Drew University, and Charles Sleeth, Associate Professor of English at Brooklyn College.

historians are as follows:

1. The Mycenean Period, ca. 1400–1100 B.C.
2. The Dorian Interregnum, ca. 1100–800 B.C.
3. The Era of Mediterranean Colonization, ca. 800–500 B.C.
4. The Athenian Golden Age, ca 500–300 B.C.
5. The Macedonian or Hellenistic Era, ca. 300–100 B.C.
6. The Roman Imperial Age, ca. 100 B.C.-A.D. 300.
7. The Byzantine Christian Era, ca. A.D. 300–1500
8. The Ottoman Turkish Period, ca. A.D. 1500–1800

Of these eight cultural phases, only two or three are recognized by most historiologists, or students of the comparative study of civilizations (of whom Spengler and Toynbee are perhaps the best known), as constituting important components of major civilizations of quasi-continental scope. These three are: the Mycenean, often accorded autonomous status; the Athenian, generally regarded as the peak of a larger Hellenic civilization to which the Dorian, Mediterranean, Macedonian, and Roman cultures also belong; and the Turkish, usually considered part of a larger Levantine civilization. In terms of these groupings, only the Byzantine phase remains ambiguous in status, Spengler attaching it to Levantine civilization, Toynbee treating it as autonomous, and most other historiologists appending it to Hellenic civilization.

According to the doctrine that is conventionally termed "the Sapir-Whorf hypothesis," which was first enunciated by the German linguist Karl Wilhelm von Humboldt in the early nineteenth century, the systematic thought of any people cannot be understood apart from the structure of the language which they speak. If forms expressing a concept are not found in either the grammar or the vocabulary of a given language, then, according to Humboldt, it is doubtful at best that any awareness of the concept exists among the speakers of that language.

In the case of early Greek ideas about the future, we can say without hesitation that a Humboldtian affirmative should be rendered. For future forms occur in both the grammar and the vocabulary of Greek from an early period. Before citing specific forms, however, we would do well to make these citations meaningful in terms of a sequence of linguistic stages similar (though unfortunately not wholly equivalent) to the sequence of cultural stages presented above:

1. Mycenean Greek, ca. 1400–1100 B.C.
2. Homeric Greek, ca. 110–600 B.C.
3. Classical Greek, ca. 600–300 B.C.

4. Hellenistic Greek, ca. 300 B.C.–A.D. 600
5. Byzantine Greek, ca. A.D. 600–1500
6. Modern Greek, ca. A.D. 1500–

In seeking to determine the degree of embeddedness of future concepts in the structure of a language, linguists generally put grammar before vocabulary, since lexical borrowings are everywhere more frequent than grammatical borrowings. Within the sphere of grammar, they likewise tend to put morphology before syntax, since the reordering of words is more susceptible to external influence than is the process of affixation. With these understandings, the linguist, particularly if trained in Indo-European comparative philology, will look first of all for a sigmatic future-tense suffix in the Greek verb. He will, moreover, find it in the earliest known stage of Greek — Mycenean itself, where we encounter the trisyllabic form *do-so-si* (phonemically interpreted as dōsontsi) [they will give], cognate in its base with Classical Latin *dōnum* [gift], and, in its suffix, with Old Latin *faxont* [they will make].

This sigmatic future persisted in Homeric and Classical Greek and proliferated in Hellenistic Greek, yielding two forms in place of one, the first exhibiting a durative aspect (I will be doing it) and the second a punctive aspect (I will do it). As if this increment were not enough, Hellenistic Greek supplemented these one-word forms with a variety of periphrastic future constructions consisting of auxiliary verbs followed by infinitives (as in English "I will go"), by participles (as in English "I am going"), or by subjunctives (as in English "would that I went").

Byzantine Greek eliminated all of these periphrastic futures except the two auxiliary verbs *thélo* [I wish], and *ékho* [I have], followed by the participle *nà* [that] (from Classical Greek *hína*) plus the subjunctive of the main verb — a type of construction that was, and still is, widespread among Balkan languages.

Modern Greek has only one future tense. But that tense has three different aspects, having added a perfective to the two already found in Medieval Greek. The result is three different future forms for each person and voice of the verb in question. The durative future (I will be doing it) consists of *thà*, the shortened form of *thélo nà*, plus the present subjunctive of the verb. The punctive future (I will do it) consists of *thà* plus the aorist subjunctive of the verb. And the perfective future (I will have done it) consists of *thà ékho* plus the infinitive of the verb, though it should be noted that this three-word future is little used in ordinary speech.

Among verbs, *méllō* [to be about to], is found in both Homeric and Classical Greek. Among nouns, the phrase *ho méllōn* [the future tense], occurs in Hellenistic Greek. And the phrase *tò méllon* [the future] (referring to time rather than to tense) occurs in Classical Greek. Among modifiers, the participle *essómenos* [(coming) to be], occurs in Homeric Greek. The participle *epiṓn* [coming after (the present)], occurs in Classical Greek. And the adjective *epíloipos* [remaining after (the present)], also occurs in Classical Greek. In Modern Greek, the equivalent modifier is the adjective *mellontikós* [future]. Among adverbs, the indeclinable forms *opísō* and *ópisthen* [in future] both occur in Homeric Greek.

In sum, it appears that the linguistic inventory of both morphemes and lexemes referring to the future has been abundant throughout the thirty-four centuries for which Greek has existed as an identifiable language. (The fact that only one form designating the future is found in Mycenean Greek is probably indicative not so much of the poverty of its lexicon as of the fragmentary nature of the tablets surviving from pre-Homeric Greece. Indeed, the fact that the so-called sigmatic future in the verb-tense system is more deeply embedded in the lexicon than any syntactic construction would seem to indicate that a lively sense of futurity has always been part of Greek speech. In this regard Greek contrasts strikingly with English, which has never had future inflection in its verbs and in which even a periphrastic future involving the auxiliary verbs *shall* and *will* was not firmly established until the fourteenth century.)

There seems, then, to be little doubt that the Greeks always conceived of the future as an experiential reality, even if some metaphysicians, such as Parmenides of Elea, argued that time was ontologically illusory. But there is considerable difference of opinion as to the value which the Greeks placed on the future — more precisely, as to whether they saw the passage of time leading predominantly to improvement or to degeneration in man and his world. Outside of a doctrinal religious context, this question was not seriously posed in the Western European world until the early Renaissance in fourteenth-century Italy. From then through the Enlightenment in eighteenth-century France, virtually all classicists and historians seemed agreed that the dominant, if not the exclusive, attitude of the early Greeks had been positive with regard to the passage of time and its tendency to bring about a continuous betterment in both human nature and the human condition. The only question in their minds was whether it was the ancient Greeks or the modern Europeans who were more progressive in their viewpoints and their accomplishments — a question whose polemic aspects were satirically summarized in Jonathan Swift's famous *Battle of the books*, written in the late seventeenth century.

It was not until the early nineteenth century that the French sociologist Auguste Comte put forward the unprecedented view that the Greeks had, compared at least with the heirs of the Industrial Revolution, been archaistic in their outlook and basically pessimistic about the long-range future. Because of Comte's doctrinaire positivism, however, and his consequent insistence that any scientific orientation is intrinsically more progressive than any philosophic orientation, his reversal of the conventional assessment of Greek historical ideology was not at first taken seriously. Perhaps partly because the trauma of World War I led Western Europeans to question their Victorian-style optimism, the intellectuals of the interbellum era were inclined to accept Comte's skeptical pronouncements about pagan Greek futurism. This skepticism found its most authoritative expression in *The idea of progress: an inquiry into its origin and growth* by the British historian John Bury in 1928.

In recent decades, classical historians have veered back somewhat toward pre-Comtean views of Greek thought about time and the future. There seems, however, to be no real consensus on the matter. This, it seems to me, is as it should be, since the Greeks themselves were never unanimous in their conceptualizations of the future. Individual thinkers differed sharply on the issue in every period of Greek history for which we have adequate evidence. The only generalizations that can reasonably be made, I think, have to do with the preponderance of views in selected periods. Mycenean inscriptions are too fragmentary in nature and too confined in subject matter to yield any quotable pronouncements on the future. Yet it seems reasonable to infer that, just as the wandering Teutons of Western Europe's Dark Ages lived in the shadow of Roman grandeur and so tended to be revivalist rather than progressivist in outlook — a fact which we may deduce from their resuscitation of a more northerly and more "holy" Roman Empire — so the Myceneans must have lived with the memory of Minoan glory and in the hope of recreating the Cretan thalassocracy rather than of originating anything distinctively Greek.

The Dorian Interregnum was probably even more backward-looking than the Mycenean Period, since the Minoan syllabary had been lost and the Phoenician alphabet not yet acquired. Overall, this was doubtless the era of greatest social instability in Greek history, when internal migration was at its height and even the Hellenic equivalent of a Charlemagne was lacking. Homer, who, it is believed, lived toward the end of this period, implicitly bears out this assessment. The two great epics that he composed ignore the three centuries or more of Dorian tribal incursions which preceded his lifetime and instead focus exclusively on the martial and nautical exploits of the late Mycenean aristocracy.

The major spokesman of the Era of Mediterranean Colonization was the Boeotian poet Hesiod; his *Theogony* became a source of religious authority and his *Works and days* a manual of moral instruction. There is no question about Hesiod's view of human history; it was for him a melancholy record of steady degeneration, beginning with an Age of Gold, and declining, through successive Ages of Silver, Brass, and Heroic Metal, to the nadir of a contemporary Age of Iron. Nonetheless, there are reasons for inferring that other Greeks were beginning to enjoy a more hopeful view of the future. Chief among these is the evidence of a vast outpouring of Greek colonists from the Aegean area into those of the Mediterranean and Black Seas and the rapid foundation, especially during the seventh century, of new Greek city-states from Spain to the Caucasus.

At the opening of the Classical or Athenian Period about 500 B.C., progressivism as an explicit ideology made its first appearance. Foremost among early Greek futurists was the Ionian philosopher Xenophanes, who openly derided Homer and Hesiod for having revered boorish and barbarous deities and praised the Lydians for having invented coinage and the Milesians for having instituted scientific speculation. Xenophanes, who later founded the Eleatic school of philosophy in Italy, was the first Greek to describe ethnocentrism (noting that Nordics worshiped blond gods and Negroes black gods) and to articulate an evolutionary biogony. He inferred from marine fossils found on mountains that all life had emerged from water and thought that men had achieved rationality only by passing slowly and painfully through a series of prerational stages.

Xenophanic views quickly supplanted Hesiodic pessimism among fifth-century thinkers. The philosophers Anaxagoras, Protagoras, and Democritus all believed that prehistory, though undocumented, was a record of human progress. The Sophist Hippias of Elis coined the term "archaeology" to denote the study of antiquities, which he recommended to anyone in doubt about the remarkable advances in the quality both of life and of thought that had transpired within his memory. The dramatist Sophocles exulted, in his tragedy *Antigone,* that "never planless does man meet the future." And the retired admiral Thucydides, who did not hesitate to declare his *History of the Peloponnesian War* "a perpetual treasure," asserted at its outset that, epic tradition notwithstanding, "no truly major events had occurred" in Greek annals prior to the catastrophic conflict between Athens and Sparta.

Despite the political eclipse of Athens in the fourth century, most Athenian and other Greek literati continued to embrace a progressivist ideology, albeit in the more moderate form advocated by Aristotle. Reactionary views, such as those of the comic dramatist Aristophanes, who ridiculed Socrates, Euripides, and all other intellectual innovators, were regarded more as satirical jests than as fundamental insights.

Between the Macedonian and Roman conquests, however, optimism was more sharply qualified. In matters relating to science and technology, such Alexandrian scholars as Archimedes, Eratosthenes, and Hipparchus persisted both in expecting and in exemplifying continuous improvement. But in social and personal affairs, as the labels Stoic and Cynic suggest, the thinking of the Greek intelligentsia was taking on a more somber tone.

Between the Roman conquest and the advent of Islam, Greek faith in the future waned but was never extinguished. Prior to the Christianization of the Roman world, the Athenians continued, as the Apostle Paul observed, to equate novelty with value. And as late as the sixth-century reign of Justinian, the Byzantine Greeks still hoped not merely to reunite but to extend the Mediterranean Christian ecumene.

By the seventh century, however, Greek Orthodox civilization was on the defensive — first against Sassanid Zoroastrians, then Western Christians, and finally Turkish Moslems, under whose political yoke it remained for nearly four centuries. During all this time, as the term "Byzantinism" implies, the overwhelming tendency of Greek thinkers and writers was to look nostalgically to the past for consolation and inspiration.

It might be assumed that Greek attitudes toward the future underwent a dramatic change between 1769, when Czarist Russia first fomented Greek revolt against Turkish rule, and 1843, when Greece became an independent constitutional monarchy. While there is no doubt that Greek morale improved greatly during this period, it appears that most modern Greeks still look to the past rather than to the future for historical self-fulfillment. Even Nikos Kazantzakis, the most ebullient and powerful of contemporary Greek authors, evinces no clearly positive attitude toward the future — at least insofar as one can judge of this from his major work, the verse tome *The Odyssey: a modern sequel* (1958). Kazantzakis's Odysseus lives in a timeless realm in which elements of the legendary, the ancient, and the contemporary are psychedelically commingled. His domain is that of mythology, not history; his vision, that of Dante and Goethe superimposed on that of Homer and Hesiod.

The reason for the apparent lack of strong Greek feeling for the future today is not far to seek: since the early nineteenth century, Greece has been, culturally speaking, a satellite of Western European civilization. Moreover, despite the fact that Greece is now nominally independent, while under the Turks she was formally in bondage, she is a far more minor component of Western civilization than she was, before "de-Turkification," of Levantine civilization.

To recapitulate our discussion of Greek attitudes toward the future: beginning with her face turned resolutely toward the past in the fifteenth century B.C., Greece slowly turned in the eighth century till, in the fifth century, her gaze was more ecstatically fixed on the future (that is, the secular future rather than some unworldly eternity) than that of any other urban culture prior to the Italian Renaissance. Then, in the second century B.C., Greece turned again, till, by the seventh century A.D., she was as pietistically spellbound by the past as in her infancy. The attitudinal wheel had come full circle.

To be sure, the dipolarity which we have set up between archaistic and futuristic outlooks is oversimplified. As Charles Van Doren points out (1967) in his revisitation of John Bury's theme, there are significant differences between those futurists who view progress as continuous and those who view it as intermittent; between those who view progress as necessary and those who view it as contingent; between those who view it as eternal and those who view it as finite; and between those who view it as human and those who view it as cosmic. Furthermore, it is questionable whether such terms as futurist, progressivist, Xenophanic, Athenianate, and Promethean can be accurately used as interchangeable synonyms to describe that explicitly positive or optimistic view of the future which the classical Greeks seem to have originated and modern Europeans and Americans to have revived and enlarged. Yet to do justice to such semantic nuances would require far more space than this paper affords. Within the scope of such a sketch, it seems to me, the descriptive silhouette offered here is a fair outline of the phraseological and attitudinal evolution of historically attested Greek concepts of the future.

One further disclaimer may be in order: the reader will observe that no attempt has been made here to include an examination of either pagan or Christian Greek concepts of the individual afterlife. Aside from considerations of space, the chief reason for this deliberate omission is that the destiny of discarnate souls — like the career of Kazantzakis' Odysseus — belongs outside the temporal realm and is therefore beyond the scope of a time-bound excursus such as this.

REFERENCES

ADRADOS, FRANCISCO RODRIGUEZ
  1963   *Evolución y estructura del verbo indoeuropeo.* Madrid: Instituto Antonio de Nebrija.
ATKINSON, B. F. C.
  1933   *The Greek language.* Second revised edition. London: Faber and Faber.
BLAKENEY, E. H.
  1937   *Smith's smaller classical dictionary,* revised edition. London: Dent and Sons, Everyman's Library.

BROWNING, ROBERT
1969 *Medieval and modern Greek.* London: Hutchinson University Library.
BRUGMANN, KARL
1888 "Morphology," in *Elements of the comparative grammer of the Indo-European languages.* Translated by Joseph Wright. New York: Westermann and Company.
BUCK, CARL DARLING
1933 *A comparative grammar of Greek and Latin.* Chicago: University of Chicago Press.
BURY, JOHN BAGNELL
1928 *The idea of progress: an inquiry into its origin and growth.* London: Macmillan.
DURANT, WILL
1939 *The life of Greece.* New York: Simon and Schuster.
EDELSTEIN, LUDWIG
1967 *The idea of progress in classical antiquity.* Baltimore: Johns Hopkins University Press.
GRAY, LOUIS H.
1939 *Foundations of language.* New York: Macmillan.
HAHN, E. ADELAIDE
1971 "The Greek language," in *The Encyclopedia Americana,* volume 13, 434–439.
KAZANTZAKIS, NIKOS
1958 *The Odyssey: a modern sequel.* Translated by Kimon Friar. New York: Simon and Schuster.
KROEBER, ALFRED LOUIS
1944 *Configurations of culture growth.* Berkeley: University of California Press.
KURYLOWICZ, JERZY
1964 *Inflectional categories of Indo-European.* Heidelberg: Carl Winter Universitätsverlag.
LIDDELL, HENRY GEORGE, ROBERT SCOTT
1940 *A Greek-English lexicon.* Revised by H. S. Jones. Oxford: Oxford University Press.
PAPPAGEOTES, GEORGE C., JAMES MACRIS
1964 *The language question in modern Greece.* Special Publication 5, Papers in Memory of George C. Pappageotes. London: William Clowes and Sons.
REINHOLD, MEYER
1946 *Essentials of Greek and Roman classics.* Brooklyn: Barron's Educational Series.
VAN DOREN, CHARLES
1967 *The idea of progress.* New York: Praeger.
VILBORG, EBBE
1960 *A tentative grammar of Mycenean Greek.* Göteborg: Göteborg University Press.
WESCOTT, ROGER W.
1970 The enumeration of civilizations. *History and Theory* 9(1). Middletown: Wesleyan University Press.
WHIBLEY, LEONARD
1931 *A companion to Greek studies* (fourth edition, revised). Cambridge: Cambridge University Press.

The Future in the Past: Toward a Utopian Syntax

EVAN VLACHOS

Man has always had a yearning for paradise and for a society better than his own. He could look back with nostalgia and attempt to revive "the good old days" or build the myths of a coming golden age, Garden of Eden, Arcadia, or Valhalla — heavenly and earthly para- dises of a hope to be fulfilled. Incipient utopianism is to be found in almost every culture: in prophecies, apocalyptic visions, millennial dreams, myths, ideologies, and finally, in more definite accounts of utopias or semiutopias. Despite the range of forms — biographies, travel literature, romances, philosophical dialogues and treatises — all utopias have incorporated, from time immemorial, the hope of a better future or the longing for a good society which has been kept alive in the historical memory of a living culture. This yearning has always been particularly acute at times of cultural despair or historical up- heaval when people longed for the perfect or just society and a stable form of social organization which would permit both individual and collective happiness. Revelations, apocalypses, and mythologies of things to come have often been the vehicles for symbolic and imagina- tive treatment of the future and the precursors of later more concrete models of the "good society." In the utopian vision the hope and effort and the imaginative quest for a better society would be fulfilled when the moral order became internalized and part of a definite intelluctual scheme. As succinctly stated by Negley and Patrick (1952: 2), "What indeed could be of more significance in the history of civilization than that man, since he first began to read and write, has continued to dream of a better world and to speculate as to its possible nature."

There already are well-documented histories of utopian thought and the remarks that follow do not attempt to paint in full detail the colorful picture of visionary icons throughout human history. Rather, they are intended to provide a backdrop for understanding the utopian syntax, the continuity of themes and preoccupations as well as some important conceptual distinctions. Finally, they are intended to underline the need to include the ability to dream in our present thinking, along with a purposeful image of the future.

In trying to describe the utopian and millennial mentality, we need to realize that visions and dreams have been the constant companions of man. Thinking about the future has to do with the basic problem of coping with present anxiety. Reliving the past and hoping about the future have always been powerful weapons in man's struggle to endure the difficulties of the present or escape the repression of contemporary despots. As they surveyed the ruins of their time, different generations have sought either to recapture the better society of a past golden age or to develop the patience and fortitude to wait for better days in a future Arcadia. Arnold Toynbee took comfort in what he called the "etherealization" of mankind, i.e. the tendency in many societies to move from a material existence to one that is more spiritual, from the sterility of secularism to the mythic avenues of the future.

In another paper by the present author (Vlachos 1972), four periods of utopianism and imagery of the future are discussed in detail and described as coinciding with various phases in the evolution of culture. The four periods illustrate a transition from early optimism and faith in a better society, to the more recent abysmal pessimism about the future. While classical utopianism and the early images of the future exhibited individualism, humanism, and pervasive optimism, the romantic utopianism of the last half of the nineteenth century was marked by institutionalism and economism. The growth of highly centralized structures and the preoccupation with rule making indicate a third stage of utopian thought, that of "technological utopianism." As the industrial revolution advanced, the image of the future became permeated by the hope that the efficiency of machines would compensate for wasteful human habits. However, even those optimistic images were finally extinguished as extreme institutionalization and a vengeful technology became tools for destroying life instead of enhancing it. Thus, the dreams of humanity slowly changed into nightmares and the hope of better things to come produced a new stage, a flight from negative utopia to the mythology of a paradise lost. Indeed, the quest for utopia now rests on how to avoid its actual realization rather than on hopeful expectations about the future. Thus, the image of the future has lost not only its positive character, it has become a rational, nonimaginative instrument for projecting the pernicious trends of the present.

The future is part of a continuum incorporating two other elements of temporal perspective: the past and the present. As we stand in the present we use the past to enable us to look with more positive expectations toward the future. The past provides an historical memory which enables us to interpret the present and gives us a perspective on, if not a projection of, things that may happen. The image of the future, on the other hand, provides hope of a "better" society. Thus, by remembering the past and anticipating the future, we come to an understanding of our present predicament and are able to create positive images of the future.

In the literature dealing with images of the future there are three key concepts which are frequently used interchangeably — ideology, myth, and utopia — and its is necessary to distinguish between them in order to analyze the visionary aspirations of a society.

Ideology is a relatively recent concept which has been defined as "all systems of thought that aim at justification and preservation of the status quo" (Mannheim 1946). The key elements that characterize an ideology are historical consciousness and emphasis on the *present*. Since they emphasize the present, ideologists do not have to invent futures or rely on the past. Although ideology and its historical consciousness incorporates a sense of tradition and a commitment to the future, there is a concreteness of emphasis which separates it from the messianic flavor of myth and the visionary character of utopia.

Myth and the millennial vision, on the other hand, are characterized by what may be called traditional consciousness. Here the emphasis is on the *past* and on the sacred and timeless understanding of the cosmos (e.g. see the selections in Murray 1968). Myths attempt to sanctify a society's existence, explain its origin and its importance, and underline the continuity of universal human experience, not with what happens but with the typical or recurring elements in action. Since myths emphasize eternity, symbolism, and the recurrent aspects of human action (Mullins 1972: 505), they lack the uniqueness that tends to characterize ideology.

Utopia in its classical sense, is similar to myth in that it often conceptualizes time as recurrent and not historical. However, utopia also includes a vision of things hoped for, the substance of things not seen. Utopias are mostly characterized by visionary consciousness, and a timeless "ought," with the major emphasis on the *future*. There is another important element in utopias. Because of their emphasis on a reconstructed world without sin or human frailty and their preoccupation with a perfect social structure, they do not recognize or accommodate the dynamic aspects of the historical process. This was the major criticism made by Dahrendorf (1958: 117) when he observed that because of the absence of historical change, "all processes going on in a utopian society follow recurrent patterns and occur within, and as part of, the design of the whole." But the distinction between utopia and ideology, one as a historical and the other as a more or less visionary (unhistorical) presence, breaks down in the later stages of the evolution of utopian thought. After the French Revolution, for example, utopias began to differ greatly from the early classical models. There was greater future-directed activism so that utopias began to enter the stream of history as possible future societies (Mullins 1972: 506). However, with the introduction of the distinction between ideology and utopia, a serious attack was made on the utility of utopian thought. This was particularly the case with Marx who postulated that to be utopian means to be out of step with modern economic development and to ignore the class struggle and the role of the proletariat in it. But as Hunt observed (1957: 181), when Marx went on to describe the communist state of the future, his language became more utopian than that of the French socialists from whose influence he never freed himself.

It is simplistic, indeed, to attempt to draw sharp distinctions between ideology as present-oriented "historical consciousness," myths as past-oriented "traditional consciousness," and utopia as future-oriented "visionary consciousness." The terms have been used interchangeably throughout history and there is often a thin line separating actual political ideologies, visionary societies, and timeless millennia. Millenarism, in particular, has been a difficult concept because it incorporates political, religious, and mythological as well as utopian elements. The most important characteristic of the millennial dream is the preparation for imminent salvation, and it is exactly this central idea which separates the millenarians from the utopians (Thrupp 1962). Fantasies of a miraculous realm, messianic hopes of things to come, and various forms of militant apocalypses have provided the backdrop not only for utopian expectations, but also food for specific political movements and for the emergence of sociopolitical trends which borrowed their durability and rhetoric from the religious impulse (Tuveson 1949; Cohn 1957).

The term "utopia" has had a variegated definitional career. A first definition conceives it as a specific literary genre and its essential nature is sought in certain formal literary qualities. The definition preferred by Marx and Engels, is of utopianism as a naive, prescientific mode of thought. Finally, a third definition of utopia incorporates a more critical view of the alternative society. Whatever its definition and form, however, there are some major characteristics which are typical of a utopian mentality, such as its openness, its imaginative and visionary character, its nonelitist approach to the alternative society, its cautiousness about cultural upheaval, and its preoccupation with static and unchangeable societies. Underlying the definitions or basic premises of utopia is a preoccupation with "order" as opposed to "regularities," and an emphasis on *telos* or what "should" or "ought" to be in the future society.

This last point needs additional explanation before we proceed to examine some examples of the image of the future and of the utopian vision throughout history. "Regularities" imply an emphasis on empirical observation, on interpretation of reality without forms, models, or plans that can be used as a guide for action. The objective world is a diffuse substance — a view first expressed by Protagoras. "Order," on the other hand, implies a cosmos, a purposeful world characterized by moral order and *telos*. Utopias, therefore, incorporate an emphasis on teleology and in this respect differ from the mainstream emphasis in the social sciences on etiology. In the following summary form we may see the distinction between "regularities" and "order" which lead respectively to ideologies and utopias.

"Regularities"		"Order"
ETIOLOGY		TELEOLOGY
were	are	should-ought
Past	Present	Future
Experience	Reality	Vision

We now need to reintroduce an idea presented earlier. The future, or the image of the future, is pushed and pulled in two directions simultaneously. Starting from the present there is a pull as far back as possible, expressing nostalgia for and a desire to recapture a paradise lost and a golden age that have long passed. At the same time, the future is pushed forward toward some unspecified time and this is associated with the eternal quest for a paradise that has not as yet been attained. Looking backward or forward also involves a number of parables which can perhaps best be illustrated by referring to Figure 1.

As this figure indicates the search for the ideal state or for a better society starts because of discontent generated by what may be described as "bad times." We always find utopian visions at times of societal stress and tension, often reinforced by messianic hopes of delivery. The utopian icon is thus formed with reference to one of two time directions — either backward or forward. Its realization rests on what may be called "Heaven Above," or an extrahuman, supermundane, theocratic salvation; or, on "Heaven Below," a rational philosophical, socialistic, if not revolutionary achievement of Eden on earth. Thus, there are two dimensions in our first map of utopia: space and time. Historically, the early utopias were always situated in space, mostly on islands. However, the publication in 1887 of Bellamy's

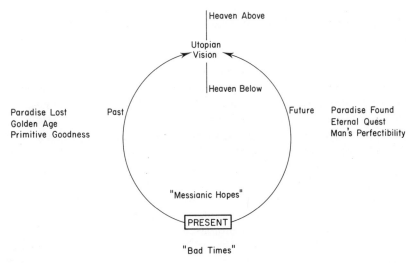

Figure 1.

Looking backward marks a break. Here utopia is situated not in space but in time. Since there are few unexplored places left on earth, and the known planetary system does not seem to be particularly hospitable, the distant future has become the mechanism for imagining the future society.

The historical search for utopia has taken a number of forms based on the distinction just mentioned, namely movement in time and movement in space. We have tried to incorporate the distinctions involved in the quest for utopia in another simplifying figure (Figure 2). This will permit us to delineate more clearly our proposed typology of utopian visions.

A major part of the search for a better society has to do with what one might call the *upward* utopia or the theme previously described as "Heaven Above" (A). This extramundane conception of utopia underlies the whole Judeo-Christian tradition. It is also part of many other religious systems in which utopia awaits man in a life after death freeing him forever from present suffering so that his soul rests in eternal peace.

A second form of the utopian search may be called the *outward* utopia (a term borrowed from Rhodes 1967) (B_1). This notion of utopia rests upon the belief that utopia exists now, somewhere, but not here. The outward utopia is the one found in the works of More, Campanella, Andrae and the other classical utopists who tried to find the perfect society on islands or in hidden valleys. The outward utopia expresses the quest for new frontiers or the search for an ideal community in some remote corner of the earth which has not yet been

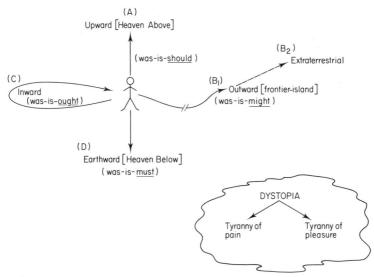

Figure 2.

touched by the evils of modern civilization (if such a place still exists). Stories, such as James Hilton's *Lost horizon* with its Shangri-La perhaps afford a modern example of the outward utopia. A modern variation of this search would be the space flight and the *extraterrestrial* quest for other hospitable planets (B_2).

A third form of the visionary utopian impulse may be described as the *inward* utopia (C). Here the emphasis is on what ought to be and how man can arrive at perfection by means of a personal quest for excellence. Inward utopias incorporate the search for true self and perfection; they contain a mystic element. A classic statement is to be found in Plato's *Republic*, in the discovery of the just man.

A fourth form of utopian quest may be designated the *earthward* utopia (or perhaps *downward* utopia to differentiate it from the first category of upward utopias) (D). Here, once again, we have the quest for a heaven on earth, mostly exemplified in the socialist tradition of attempting to create communitarian societies and aspiring to achieve the better society on earth and in the not very distant future.

As can be seen in Figure 2, certain verbs are associated with each of these four categories, indicating the degree of moral commitment to the achievement of the utopian end.

Lurking at the back of all these utopian maps is, of course, the dystopian nightmare promised by a threatening technology and rising political tyrannies. Rather than "Heaven Above" or "Heaven Below," here or in other places, in the future or inside one's self, the dystopian hell promises a tyranny, a nightmare. And this hell may become possible either through the tyranny of pain, as exemplified in Orwell's

1984, or through the tyranny of pleasure and mindless hedonism as in Huxley's *Brave new world*.

Concern for the better society and the vitality of visions of the future rest on the continuity of ideas which have been shared by all social theoreticians regardless of when they lived. Three key questions seem to be repeated throughout time:

1. What is society? What are social forces and processes; what is the origin of society; how is it organized?

2. What is the form of social control which assures the existence of society? How can the individual be controlled most effectively for the good of the collectivity?

3. What factors determine and shape social change? Can man control it or is it out of his hands?

In trying to answer such questions we encounter the central element of utopian thought, namely the attempt to create a "just" society. Early civilizations such as the Babylonian, Egyptian, Chinese, or the Hebraic placed stronger emphasis on affective elements rather than on concrete principles of social organization. The key theme of these early civilizations was emphasis on the supernatural and on the continuous idealization of society.

We should, however, concentrate briefly on the Hebrew prophets who seemed to have caught a glimpse of a larger social and religious purpose in life and a protoutopian vision of the ideal society. The problem of the prophets was the same as that of all other later utopian and social reconstructionists, namely the breakdown of an old moral order and the disintegration of the socioeconomic system of their time. This disintegration and destruction resulted in innumerable evils that had to be identified and contained. At the same time, optimism had to be introduced to make it possible to endure the present hard times and to provide motivation for eventual ethical, social, political, and cultural rehabilitation. Thus, the prophets were preparing their people for an ideal future state conceived in ethical and social terms. This ideal state as well as the whole tone of their prophecy was centered on a feature that has always been a central heroic axis in any utopian vision: the hope for the Messiah, or the coming of the Deliverer, through whom the glories of the future age were to be realized (Hertzler 1923: 49).

As Hertzler put it succinctly, in his book on the history of utopian thought, the important thing about the utopianism of the prophets is that it demanded not only proper human relations but also an extrahuman, theocratic relationship (1923: 49). The early Hebrew prophecies, and the continuous historical destruction of the promised kingdom of

Israel led inevitably to the development of the so-called apocalyptic writings, in which the major emphasis was on deliverance through miracles. These apocalyptic writings (not confined entirely to Jewish and Christian writers) are essentially of a predictive and miraculous nature and treat of a future which is highly artificial.

The prophets and later apocalyptics are also part of the beginning of the visionary orientation which combined with the secular thinking of the early Greek philosophers to provide a more tangible scheme for expressing utopian thought and hope for the future. It is very interesting to notice that all the great philosophies of the world flourished at about the same time, that is around the sixth century B.C. The Hebrew prophets appeared at approximately this time, as did Thales, the earliest Greek secular thinker, Zoroaster, Buddha, Lao-Tse, and Confucius. The Druidism of the barbarian people beyond the Rhine also coincided with this period of crisis. In many cultures, "bad times" seem to coincide with the appearance of new social philosophies and visionary dreams of better societies to come. There are, indeed, striking parallels between the renaissance after the sixth century B.C. and the renaissance of the Middle Ages. The major parallels have to do with exploration and the increasing knowledge of the surrounding physical world. They have to do, too, with invasions and population shifts, which led to a rearrangement of social values, the growth of cities, the domination of the rural economy, and the challenging of outworn customs. Cities not only produce emancipated minds but they challenge the continuity of a living culture based on tradition.

The earliest Greek philosophers of the sixth century B.C. were interested almost exclusively in rational explanation of the physical world. Here we have the first major breakthrough from the exclusively supermundane preoccupation and heavy theocratic orientation in the thinking of earlier societies. The earliest Greek philosophers, initiators of a tradition which was to become much stronger in later years, saw in the universe a "cosmos" (order) which could be grasped. This intangible order of the physical universe brought forward early the idea of a "law" governing the universe and its changes. Thus, around the sixth century B.C. we can trace the origins of social utopian thought as a result of two major developments. On the one hand, the old world and the traditional order were collapsing because of political events, wars, and intrigue. This provided the impetus for seeking answers to questions of social justice. On the other hand, the traditional basis of established institutions was under strong attack from three major philosophical movements: from natural philosophy which maintained that the gods could not possibly exist in the form in which the city had inherited them from Homer; from the Sophist movement which maintained that the laws of the city had no divine sanction; and from mysticism and the strong tradition of Orphism which introduced the subversive doctrine of individual sin, the idea of brotherhood, pantheism, and individual responsibility. The Orphic movement is of considerable significance in philosophy because of the communal organization associated with it and the conviction which it inspired that philosophy is a way of life rather than a simple satisfaction of curiosity as advocated earlier by the Ionians.

With the Orphic movement and the growth of the ideal of communal organization, philosophy began enquiring into modes of life. Utopia and communal organization became expressions of the quest for the virtuous life in which the relationships among men would be ordered on the basis of some design or purpose. With Solon, justice began to acquire intellectual attributes and an attempt was made to internalize the moral order and make it an intellectual pursuit. From this point, it was not difficult to make the jump to Socrates and Plato. What was needed was a theory of ideas which would bring these concerns together. The philosophical and social backgrounds existed; the hard times were there; what was needed was someone to bring this cosmos and organization together.

Plato, a devout disciple of Socrates, inherited the Socratic notion of order or cosmos with its emphasis on the idea that goodness is an arrangement of the parts into a whole. Moreover, goodness is not something with which we are born; it is something acquired by training. Plato came along at the right time to elaborate, with admirable dialectical method, not only the philosophical ideas but also the more detailed political outlines of the ideal state. In his *Republic* and *Laws* Plato began the great debate about the best kind of social system which runs right through to Marx and has been taken up by thinkers from More to Orwell (Clarke 1972: 75). All of them, in their own ways and with their own philosophical underpinnings, deal with the same problems and questions about society and man: the problem of political order, the quest for social stability, the search for universal justice and ultimately for the happiness of all citizens. In addition, all these thinkers exemplify the dramatic dilemma inherent in all utopian thinking: that of individual happiness and individualistic pursuits, on the one hand, and the benefits to be derived from a stable, highly organized society on the other.

Plato was a product of the bad times described above. During the first twenty-four years of his life he witnessed the results of continuous warfare, constant slaughter, and finally the collapse of Athens in the subsequent terror of the Thirty Tyrants. His book was intended as an indictment of the contemporary political system. Observing the politicians of his time, much as Marx later on observed the harsh effects of industrialization, he saw that no miraculous plan could really save the city-state. Its salvation would depend on the followers of true philosophers and searchers after the ideal form.

The theme of Plato's *Republic* is too sweeping and detailed to be dealt with fully in a brief analysis of the utopian background of contemporary futuristic thinking. For our purposes, it is sufficient to say that Plato discusses the nature of justice and the forms of social relationships that would make it possible to achieve the perfect state. If nothing else, Plato has provided us with a yardstick against which to measure later utopias and a method for writing utopias. As Clarke observed (1972: 80) the pattern of utopian narrative has changed little since the days when Plato taught at the Academy. Later utopians gave the model a greater degree of realism and added the convention of the voyage to the unknown land or, more recently, the trip through time.

We need to compare Plato with his predecessors, especially the Hebrew prophets who were as close as one can come to utopian thinkers. The prophets had a common characteristic in that they suggested no concrete methods of bringing about anticipated states. In essence, the prophets were presenting abstract ideals for a transfigured humanity. Plato, on the other hand, perceived society not as an aimless mass of aggregate individuals but as a self-conscious entity and order capable of directing its own form and processed by its own deliberate action. He saw philosophy and the utopian vision as instruments for remolding and not just interpreting society (Hertzler 1923: 118).

It is worth noting here that while many people delve into Plato's *Republic* for the utopian model of the perfect state which it portrays, little attention is paid to the latter theory of social order expressed in the *Laws*. The latter is truly a statesman's handbook and contains a generalized history of the evolution of mankind. While the *Republic* reflects the ebullient and hopeful utopian vision of Plato as a young man, the *Laws* is in a sense the dystopian dream of an elderly, more conservative philospher. In the *Laws*, Plato begins his account with a flood, from which only a few shepherds are saved. Conditions for the survivors are primitive, and change is incremental (*Laws*, Book III). The narrative in the *Laws* is more reminiscent of the quest for a paradise lost than of the bold expectation of the ideal state delineated in the *Republic*. There is no strife or war among the survivors since all are kindly disposed to one another. They are the same "simpleminded" primitive people who appear in many present-day dystopian scenarios revolving around the return to a primitive civilization. What we need to keep in mind here is not so much the rather inappropriate parallel between a philosophical treatise on the one hand, and contemporary speculative fiction on the other, but the continuity of ideas that is involved. "Bad times" may provide the impetus either for envisaging sweeping changes and a new society, or, after the disaster (be it a flood, a drought, a nuclear war, or any other apocalypse) for anticipating a return to primitivism and the beginning of a new cycle of civilization.

Plato is important because he was the first to express the conviction which has been so influential in Western civilization, that social change could be consciously directed toward the realization of previously formulated goals. Although other Greek philosophers attempted to describe the ideal utopian state and had interesting conceptions of the future (see Wescott, this volume), Plato's was the distinct breakthrough from oriental fatalism and the theocratic and millennial visions of earlier civilizations.

The utopian writing of Plato did not have any immediate follow-up. As a matter of fact a huge gap of seventeen centuries stands between Plato and the first modern utopian writer, Thomas More. There are many historical and philosophical reasons for the eclipse of utopian writing. The Greeks' successors, the Romans, produced many competent and realistic men who understood how to create a powerful state and a major civilization, but very few dreamers. The Romans were preoccupied with practical and technological matters rather than with theories or abstract ideas which might have promoted utopian thought. As a matter of fact, the Romans have been accused of a "failure in inspiration" because of their intellectual leaders' preference for Stoic and Epicurean philosophies. Commenting on the Roman aversion to utopian thinking, Nell Eurich observes that the deeply held belief or faith in the grand destiny of the Roman race made any fanciful vision of better worlds to come pointless (1967: 74). Eurich speculates further that when people know the direction in which their society is moving and feel sure it is best, they have little reason to create dream worlds or search for new knowledge unless it solves practical problems encountered en route to the accomplishment of their grand design. This is an interesting indirect comment on the influence of "bad times" on the emergence of utopian thought. Once again one is tempted to make the comparison between the ancient and "the new Romans" found in so many respectable accounts of American civilization today. A directionless, futureless, American society has become fertile ground for the emergence of utopian and visionary alternatives to the present cultural predicament.

Christianity provided very little scope for the emergence of earthward utopias. It is characterized by a completely structured universe, divine in purpose, in which man follows set rules of behavior which leave very little leeway for individual choice. Supernatural mysticism, monastic life, fixed institutions, blind faith in and acceptance of authority, and the idea that happiness exists in the remote regions of Heaven do not provide a fertile environment for wishful speculation or for dreams of a better society on this earth. Yet, even in the midst of an environment infertile for such thinking, expressions of utopianism were to be found during the Middle Ages in peasant revolts, in various accounts of trips to the moon, in the idealistic accounts associated with feudalism and chivalry, and in legends of saints (Hertzler, *passim*).

A comment is needed on the influence of Christianity on utopian thought. Like other visionaries, Jesus was a product of "bad times." At that time, people were living in a changing moral order under the iron, but slowly disintegrating, rule of Rome. The great theme in the message of Jesus was the brotherhood of man and the divine fatherhood of God. However, expressions such as "Kingdom of Heaven" or "Kingdom of God" are devoid of political significance. Thus, the "Kingdom of Heaven" is always understood in terms of a moral relationship rather than a quest for an ideal political state. As a matter of fact Jesus always refused to offer any specific utopia but emphasized rather the righteousness of the social order that he proclaimed, and not its form. The Kingdom promised by Jesus was not to come about by force, or through an apocalyptic dream of a better future, but by what we indicated above as the progressive sanctification of individual human beings (inward utopia). It would become the true Kingdom of God, a new external social order, once it was realized internally in the individual. In contrast to Plato (although Plato ultimately depended on internal acceptance of utopian goals) the Kingdom of God is seen as a gradual process of social and spiritual progress. It begins and perhaps ends in the hearts of men. Thus, the utopianism expressed in the concept of the Kingdom of God, although its ultimate goal was social, was mostly individual and subjective (Hertzler 1923: 67–74).

The Christian inward utopia had, however, a built-in problem in the doctrine of predestination. Liberation from this deterministic doctrine only occurred in the wake of the conflict with Pelagius, a British monk who propounded a heretical degree of free will. The issue of free will is one that Christianity has frequently had to grapple with. It is expressive of one of the oldest dilemmas confronting man's thinking, namely that of individual freedom of choice against some form of determinism. There can be no earthward utopia unless human beings have free will and can make free choices.

Thomas More rediscovered both Plato and utopia in the sixteenth century. This, too, was a period of "crises" and "bad times." Plato wrote the *Republic* in the midst of defeat after the continuous wars with Sparta. Attica had been devastated. Political ethics and public morality were at a low ebb, and Plato felt that only a newly designed and built ship of state could survive the stormy waves of history. The equivalent motivation for More can perhaps be traced to the historical rearrangements and new philosophical directions which were making the old ship of traditional community and Christian conventions unable to withstand the battering of a new moral order. During the Middle Ages two independent images of the future had finally crystallized. Each had another world as its ultimate goal. However as Polak has noted (1961: vol. 2, p. 165), in the one the line moves from this world toward the Other; through the image, the world is remade and raised to Heaven. In the other, the line moves towards this world from the Other; by means of the image, Heaven is stretched out like a curtain and spread like a tent to dwell in. One represents an increasing spiritualization, the other an increasing materialization.

The events that led to the Renaissance and a new universe are many and complicated and yet they all center upon "crises" of that time, not only historical upheavals, but also the rise of humanism and naturalism while the medieval ideal of a static, divinely sanctioned, international order declined. The drowsiness of the Dark Ages and the stupendous organization of the hierarchical Church were slowly eroded by events that shook the world. The Crusades, with their spirit of recklessness, adventure, and discovery; the travels of Marco Polo; the frightful consequences of the Black Death; the fall of Constantinople which caused scholars to flee to the West; the invention of printing; and the expeditions of Spanish, English, and Portuguese explorers were all earth-shaking events which aroused people's consciences in the fourteenth and fifteenth centuries. The Kingdom of Heaven ceased to hold men's allegiance as a utopian escape as soon as other channels, other worlds, and other opportunities unfolded.

Sir Thomas More's *Utopia*, which was first published in 1516, deserves to be recognized as the first real utopia since Plato and a first expression of the dawning of a new age. More important, it began the tradition of humanistic outward utopias. It reflected vividly the new forces of rapid social differentiation. The rise of cities, their loss of independence and prosperity, the appearance of classes and increased social mobility, forced thinkers once again to look outward to other lands and later on to other times for a better society in which the difficulties of the present might decrease. Works such as More's *Utopia*, Campanella's *City of sun*, Bacon's *New Atlantis*, and Harrington's *Oceana* were not simply vehicles for safely criticizing the current political order; they were also bridges spanning the gap between the old order of the Middle Ages and developing Renaissance interest in institutions.

In his *Utopia* Thomas More invented a new term and a new form of social analysis and criticism which provided a link with the earlier tradition in social thinking. Utopias became an expression of idealism and a stimulus to belief in better things to come. They not only provided blueprints for a better society but displayed increased tolerance toward new forms of social organization and new human values. The utopians were willing to suggest the use of untried forces. They were venturesome men who devised new criteria for collective life and rejected the subjective individualistic preoccupations of the Middle Ages. Although pessimistic about contemporary conditions they were highly optimistic about the possibilities for future society. They anticipated worlds in which civilization would be rational and definitely intended. They continuously underlined the idea that given a proper environment even relatively mediocre individuals could be made socially desirable (Hertzler 1923). Thus, the utopians were true social theoreticians in that they saw society as a necessary object of study and showed increased comprehension of social phenomena. They looked toward future perfection in an attempt to have the evils of the present eradicated.

In the rationally motivated seventeenth and eighteenth centuries the idea of change, usually in the sense of improvement and progress, was introduced. The ideal of progress marks another interesting phase in the evolution of utopian and futuristic thinking. While in the past the search for an ideal society had been defined spatially, the idea of progress now permitted a temporal definition conditioned by faith in and expectation of humanity's deliverance from its present "bad times."

The vision of a millennium in this world became important leading to an upsurge of utopian socialism. The socialists were as utopian as their predecessors, although not as romantic and poetic. Most of their schemes for an ideal society were based on a dogma of "primitive goodness" which as we have seen, is usually identified with nostalgia for a "golden age" or "the good old days." The utopian socialists' search was for the natural state in which man would be happy and benevolent and for the social environment best suited to keep him so. But like other utopian thinkers before them they were faced with the spectacle of disorder and misery. For them "bad times" could be alleviated only through contemplation of an ideal commonwealth that would unify mankind and elevate it to the highest degree of power, beauty, and splendor. The utopian socialists were the first to boldly suggest, and directly attempt to implement a solution to their current problems. Despite the fact that these attempts came to nothing and despite Marx's sharp indictment of their lack of historical perspective, they provided a basis for later reforms and for renewed visions of the ideal state.

In tracing some common threads in the development of utopian speculation we have seen that each utopian vision seems to be identified with a particular dimension of the utopian map introduced in Figure 2, as well as with particular circumstances of social, intellectual, and political development. Toward the end of the nineteenth century the communitarian ideal of the sixteenth, seventeenth, and eighteenth centuries was foredoomed by rapid industrialization and urbanization. Because of the discovery of new lands, the idea of a self-sufficient community, with an uncomplicated economic structure, happy in the enjoyment of simple values of artisanship became impossible and either a vehicle of nostalgia or of satire. Centralized structures become the key element of the new utopia, foreshadowing the dystopias that appeared with Huxley and Orwell. Utopias and tales of the future increasingly moved away from what one may call the *"terra incognita"* theme to the theme of future epochs. This new theme freed authors from the difficulty of finding any more untouched islands. The coalescence of two ideas, namely technological progress and Darwin's evolutionary theory, from the 1870's on, provided the base for new forecasts about the future of humanity. The most important exponent of both ideas is H. G. Wells with whom scientific romance really began. Utopia now became filled with stories of demon scientists, space voyages, future wars, and future scientific marvels. It is only a short step from H. G. Wells to the gloominess of contemporary speculative fiction and what might be called the remnants of utopian thought. Ominous forecasts of future destruction and bitter satires are replacing the old optimism so that all the types indicated in Figure 2 (inward, outward, earthward, or upward utopias) are slowly being displaced by dystopian hells. To a limited degree, the only remaining optimists are the futurists who tend to incorporate in their scenarios the promise of better things to come.

What is happening then to the utopian vision? What remains of the noble dream? The utopian description has been superceded by studies of the future of every imaginable kind. As Henry Winthrop has indicated (1971: 85), the utopian vision was bound to disappear, first as a result of the complexity of modern social systems and subsystems; and second, as a result of the knowledge explosion which has led to a fragmented vision of the world around us.

It seems, then, that we are living in a postutopian age. But we have a desperate need to recapture the utopian vision. We are also confronted with the larger question of finding a philosophy adequate for an age of science and technology, which can at the same time counteract emerging nihilistic trends. We need a combination of futuristic etiology and scientific humanism — a utopian teleology. Perhaps the way to combine etiology and teleology is to be found in the emerging field of *mellontology*, which explores how things are occurring and some of the possible consequences of present trends, as well as reexamining the reasons for commitment to values and goals.

The search for *mellontology* which would incorporate both a rational quest for etiology and teleology has become an important theme in current writings about the future. It is true that the old static utopias have disappeared or are under widespread attack because of the rigid and unimaginative (if not boring) character of the social life they promise. We need to find images which will combat both the future-lessness and sense of impending doom that seem to characterize many present-day scenarios of the future. As Polak has observed, the degeneration or denaturalization of positive images of the future not only demonstrates the existence of a crisis, but announces what is to come (Polak 1961: vol. 2, p. 341). If we are to combat what Erich Fromm has called a necrophilic tendency in contemporary civilization we need to reexamine urgently the major assumptions on which futuristic thinking is based.

Once again, we are faced with a cultural crisis, "bad times" which impel us to think about alternative futures rather than drift toward the nightmarish visions of either Orwell or Huxley. Our brief look at images of the past and future and various utopian themes underlines the unextinguished desire to dream and plan our future. Our present concern with the future has two sources: one is preoccupation with problems besetting our society today. This predisposes us to think either in terms of the past or the future and to seek predominantly earthward solutions to the problem of coping with the genies unleashed by rapidly expanding technologies. The other source is our theoretical commitment to understanding and predicting social change. Both these concerns — anxiety about our present and theoretical commitment to understanding and predicting change — make it imperative to rediscover and reemphasize our long tradition of technological thinking and utopian vision. Although we may not be so bold or imaginative or perhaps naive as the early utopian visionaries, we need to come to grips once more with the broader questions which tend to be neglected in the narrow and limited scenarios of many futurists today. (How utopianism can contribute to modernization, for example — as in the case of Japan — is one of the major themes in Plath's volume [1971].) Winthrop has exemplified this trend very succinctly in his tableau of issues to be included in a social philosophy for an age of science and technology. The questions which he discusses, although more detailed and relevant as befits the changing times, echo many of the concerns that have been expressed throughout history. The quests for justice and universal happiness, although nebulous and overgeneral, remain as relevant and unanswerable as they were when

Plato raised them in his *Republic*. The shadows of impending apocalypse are lengthening; the alternative scenarios are becoming more complex and much more forbidding; the capacity to dream has diminished. But we have gained something since Plato's first vision of a planned future: the freedom to know that we can easily reject any of these visions if we want to. Yet, in doing so we are left with the same question: "What are we here for?"

REFERENCES

BERNERI, MARY LOUISE
1950   *Journey through utopia*. London: Routledge and Kegan Paul.
BUBER, MARTIN
1950   *Paths in utopia*. New York: Macmillan.
CLARKE, I. F.
1972   The primacy of Plato. *Futures* 4: 75–80.
COHN, NORMAN
1957   *The pursuit of the millennium*. New York: Essential Books.
DAHRENDORF, RALF
1958   Out of utopia: towards a reorientation of sociological analysis. *The American Journal of Sociology* 64.
EURICH, NELL
1967   *Science in utopia: a mighty design*. Cambridge: Harvard University Press.
FERGUSON, JOHN
1975   *Utopias of the classical world*. Ithaca, New York: Cornell University Press.
GILISON, JEROME M.
1975   *The Soviet image of utopia*. Baltimore: The Johns Hopkins University Press.
HERTZLER, JOYCE O.
1923   *The history of utopian thought*. New York: Macmillan.
HUNT, R., N. CAREW
1957   *The theory and practice of communism*. New York: Macmillan.
HYANS, EDWARD
1973   *The millennium postponed: socialism from Sir Thomas More to Mao Tse-tung*. New York: Taplinger Publishing Company.
KATEB, GEORGE
1963   *Utopia and its enemies*. New York: Free Press.
MANNHEIM, KARL
1946   *Ideology and utopia; an introduction to the sociology of knowledge*. London: Kegan Paul, Trench, Trubner and Company.
MANUEL, FRANK EDWARD, *editor*
1966   *Utopias and utopian thought*. Boston: Houghton Mifflin.
MOLNAR, THOMAS
1972   *Utopia: the perennial heresy*. London: Tom Stacey.
MORGAN, ARTHUR ERNEST
1946   *Nowhere was somewhere, how history makes utopias and utopias make history*. Chapel Hill: University of North Carolina Press.

MULLINS, WILLARD A.
1972 On the concept of ideology in political science. *The American Political Science Review* 66: 498–509.

MUMFORD, LOUIS
1922 *The story of utopias.* New York: Boni and Liveright.

MURRAY, HENRY, editor
1968 *Myth and mythmaking.* Boston: Beacon.

NEGLEY, GLENN, J. M. PATRICK, editors
1952 *The quest for utopia.* New York: Henry Schuman.

PLATH, DAVID W., editor
1971 *Aware of utopia.* Urbana: University of Illinois Press.

PLATTEL, MARTIN G.
1972 *Utopian and critical thinking.* New York: Humanities Press.

POLAK, FREDERIK LODEWIJK
1961 *The image of the future; enlightening the past, orientating the present, forecasting the future.* Leiden: A. W. Sijthoff.

RHODES, HAROLD V.
1967 *Utopia in American political thought.* Tucson: University of Arizona Press.

RUYER, RAYMOND
1950 *L'utopie et les utopies.* Paris: Presses Universitaires de France.

THRUPP, SYLVIA L.
1962 *Millennial dreams in action.* Comparative Studies in Society and History. The Hague: Mouton.

TUVESON, ERNEST LEE
1949 *Millennium and utopia; a study in the background of the idea of progress.* Berkeley: University of California Press.

VLACHOS, EVAN
1972 "Images of the future and scenarios of the apocalypse." Paper published in *Pre-conference volume on futurism* of the American Sociological Conference.

WALSH, CHAD
1962 *From utopia to nightmare.* New York: Harper and Row.

WINTHROP, HENRY
1971 "Utopia construction and future forecasting: problems, limitations, and relevance," in *The sociology of the future.* Edited by Wendell Bell and James A. Mau, 78–105. New York: Russell Sage.

Anthropological Perspectives of Social Movements and Cultural Trends

Fumbling Freely into the Future

LUTHER P. GERLACH

Twenty years can be a long time. In the twenty years following Martin Luther's defiant stand before the Diet at Worms, Western Europe was remade. There was religious upheaval, peasant revolt, political and economic reorganization, transformation in man's view of himself and his place in society and the environment. It was, indeed, multirevolution. One analyst, Preserved Smith, refers to this as the sudden coming of spring after ages of winter (1966).

Look what has happened to the United States and its people since the end of World War II or the end of the Korean War. There we were, in the fifties and early sixties, commanding the stage of high mass consumption, proud of our past, sure of our destiny, exercising our great power to bring to the world the *pax Americana*. In our abounding generosity, we reached down a helping hand to those nations, all less fortunate, who confessed their need.

We were interested in change, but mostly in how to change the rest of the world, developing the underdeveloped lands in accordance with our image of good health, progress, and prosperity. Our main worry was that these lands would follow "false prophets" and take Russian, Red Chinese, or Cuban models as their design for change. True, some Americans feared communist subversion at home, but guerrilla warfare and insurgency — well, that was something that happened elsewhere, usually because we "permitted" agents and agitators to exploit poverty, inequity, and European colonialism. Racism was something practiced by Germans on Jews or by the British, French, or Dutch on Africans or Asians. Women's rights were something to be struggled for in Pakistan or Egypt. Smoke billowing from factory stacks was a symbol of industrial resurgence; DDT was almost a synonym for man's ability to conquer his environment; the word "pollution" conjured up images of overcrowded slums in Calcutta, open sewers in Teheran, or night soil on the rice paddies of Japan. Ecology was some type of esoterica studied by specialists in their ivory towers or was the name of the game in Walt Disney's nature films.

Among the most relevant enterprises in American universities during this era were those which brought scholars and sometimes students together to examine problems of economic development, nation building, and health in other lands. The main problem seemed to be how to arouse the concern of otherwise self-satisfied organization men or would-be organization men and inspire them to do something to help the rest of the world. In short, for most deserving all-Americans, the American Dream seemed to have become reality, and it needed only to be packaged for export.

There were a few bad scenes and sputniks in the Dream, but it was felt that these could be expunged, given time, money, and concern. We could spread more civil rights in the United States and *permit* Negroes to begin to share the Dream. We could pray that under the shield of our missiles, the atom would be as peaceful as pie, and we could train many more aerospace engineers and physicists and surely beat the Russians to the moon. We could send young, idealistic Americans to carry the gospel of the American Way to other lands. We could conduct the proper technological, economic, and counterinsurgency rituals, and in time we could exorcise evil and free peoples from the chains of tradition. In short, we could help everyone find the good life. Then, boom, the sweet dream bubble burst, and by the end of the sixties and the onset of the seventies, people were saying or thinking that the dream had become a nightmare, or a succession of nightmares.

You know what happened: the United States was swept by waves of social-political-religious movements, bursting out in crisis intensity at such places as Selma, Watts, Berkeley, Groppi's Milwaukee, Detroit's inner city; in student movements at Columbia and Madison, convention Chicago, King's Memphis, Newark, Kent State, Washington, and on and on. Sit-ins, teach-ins, write-ins, protests, demonstrations, riots were happening, bombs were exploding here and there and were threatened everywhere. There was calamitous insurgency in Vietnam and unbelievable insurgency at home. It was easy enough to interpret all of this as a sign of national illness. Some blamed it on the failure of the entire sociocultural system of America; many others admitted that, while the system was basically O.K., it had wronged all too many people, and yet others feared that the United States had fallen prey to powerful agents of subversion and perhaps lost the will to defend itself.

Diverse movements grew rapidly, proliferating across the land, and bursting with life. They demanded change and focused attention on flaws in seemingly every aspect of the national life. Black Power, the

American Indian movement, the Chicano movement, the New Left, Women's Lib, antiwar and student movements, the counterculture: all these zeroed in on the American social structure and political order. In the wake of their onslaught it appeared that it was the United States itself which needed vast help in building its own nation.

The ecology movement brought Americans to the sharp realization that their environment was being ruined by the very technology and economy which the country once flaunted as a sign of its power and command of the future. GNP was pictured by cartoonists as a gross national monster gobbling up resources and spewing out junk as it clink-clank-clunked across plasticland Amerika.

The charismatic movement, the underground church, the Jesus revolution, the mushrooming of astrology, Eastern religions, upheaval in the established church: all these seemed to imply either that there were many disturbed Americans around, or that established religion was losing control.

This was indeed the time of counterculture, and people from many walks of life contributed to the genesis and spread of acts and ideas "subversive" to conventional wisdom. Minority Americans, establishment Americans, young Americans, old Americans — all played their roles. Some were as active in mocking the myths of the traditional American system, as were our overseas agents of change in attacking traditional societies in the Third World.

From many directions, Americans heard that the best the established order could hope to do was die gracefully. They found their popular reading headed by survival manuals, descriptions of eco-catastrophe and doomsday books. They learned that apocalypse is just around the corner and that in their last days they should confess the sins of their racism, militarism, and pollutionism. But seldom were they given hope that, through this, they could gain forgiveness and seek renaissance. Instead they heard over and over that, since everything is hitched to everything else, most anything they did to solve these problems would have some harmful consequence.

With respect to Vietnam, the only options it was said were that either the United States should admit defeat or hang on and achieve some sort of victory in the field, even if only vicariously through the success of the South Vietnamese. In a search for scapegoats some blamed communists and their naive dupes, long-haired radicals, or the military-industrial complex.

Indeed, the bad news seemed never-ending. Americans were told repeatedly that their cities were dying or dead, their school systems collapsing in spite of an insatiable demand for tax money. Only crime and inflation seemed on a continual upswing, while law, order, justice, and employment spiraled ever downward, and drug abuse attacked the national vitality. It was, in sum, a time of troubles. What could people do? Drop out, play ostrich, slip into nostalgia and seek to revive a golden age version of the fifties, bull ahead, hoping it would all work out in time, or live it up now, with the "after-us-the-deluge" philosophy? Or could people take command, change course, and steam into a better world and a better future?

It appeared that the whole progress ethic, so characteristic of American culture, was threatened. Americans have liked to see their history and future as a steady march "onward and upward." The unilineal economic growth and evolutionary model of Rostow (1971) is but a logical extension of this. Suddenly scholars, such as Andrew Hacker (1970), were speaking, not about the rise of the American era, but its impending fall. Would America go the way of ancient Rome, or modern Britain? Probably few Americans seriously think that this will happen, but they might be tempted to believe that we are merely on a slightly downward curve of a recurrent cycle of change. On a similar note, the classical Chinese perceived the course of change as a wave-like cycle, with families and empires rising to prosperity and power over a period of some three generations, only to slide to the bottom, and then slowly and steadily to rise again, repeating the cycle every three generations or so. (Apparently the communist Chinese, reflecting new ideologies, have now a progress-oriented view of their future and see it as one constant climb up the communist ladder of progress.) Is it quite likely that increasing numbers of Americans will come to regard the present time of troubles as but a short, bad cut of the pendulum's arc and expect that we shall soon swing back to "normal"?

We do see some manifestations of this "swing-of-the-pendulum" view in the interpretations of renewed calm on the American college campus. Some observers say that the 1970's have brought us right back to the good old 1950's, when Americans were more noted for social apathy than activism. This view, however, probably seems somehow unsatisfactory to Americans. Thus, when Art Seidenbaum, a feature writer for the Los Angeles Times, described this return to campus calm in a spring 1971 article, he implied a kind of unfulfilled urge for change. He said that he was sorry, in a sense, that the old fire seemed gone from the campus — although he hastened to add that he was relieved that the confrontations and violence were also gone. Others suggest that the calm was misleading, that it masked a time bomb waiting to explode, and that people had stopped demonstrating, not because they were apathetic but because they were terribly frustrated. They were withdrawing into themselves, and some of them were gathering energy for a new thrust for change.

Stewart Alsop (1970) was one of the first newsmen to proclaim that radical activism was dead or dying in the United States. He described his awareness of this as an impression gained through travels across the country, meeting and interviewing people everywhere. Yet he did not say that this meant that the United States would swing back to the good old days. Instead, he said that, now that radical extremism and noisy demonstrations had declined, the country could get down to the real business of necessary social change. Of course, we remember that a favorite statement of many Americans during the 1965–1971 period was that, while they agreed with the objectives of those demanding change, they did not agree with the means employed. Are we to write this off as a gambit of people who really want to maintain the status quo, or does it reflect a continuing and probably growing desire for new ways? We know that the Gallup and Harris polls in spring and summer 1971 indicated a rather widespread public belief that something clearly was not right with the United States, and that change was necessary. Our "You and Ecology" questionnaire (Gerlach and Hine 1970a) and analyses (Gerlach and Hine 1970b, 1970c) revealed similar sentiments among upper middle-class Americans.

We hear spokesmen for various government, educational, and business organizations everywhere hailing the return to reason which now seems to be pervading ecology, campus, and racial issues. They are fond of saying that, now that emotionalism and militancy have subsided, people can face up to the real problems of fighting pollution, and racism, and improving the quality of education. Is this only a smokescreen to cover a policy of status quo maintenance, or are these institutions really changing? We strongly disagree that radicalism and militancy were only noise and did not contribute to change, and we feel that most Americans do not want a return to the seemingly more stable system of twenty years ago. Like it or not, the American system is still rigged for "progress" and is bounding forward to a new future. Furthermore, it is not entirely clear that radical agitation has really vanished. Instead, it has shifted from one scene to another. Prisons are the latest to experience turmoil, resultant public attention, and explorations in change. Perhaps the now "cooler" ecology scene will burn with new conflict as expectations of environmental action are not met.

The real question is not have we changed or will we change, but how much will we change? Will the United States undergo chiefly patch-and-repair development so that the next twenty years will be but an updated version of the last twenty, or will the United States undergo revolutionary transformation in structure and culture?

Many Americans have been asking such questions, and futurologists in the 1970's are obligingly on the scene to conjure up answers. Of course, some futurologists have been around for years, either to entertain people or to help the established order plan and control the route to tomorrow. These are the more traditional, "realistic," establishment futurologists whose vision of the future is a lineal, exponential, progression from the America of the 1950's. Pontificating from their think tanks, they describe how everything will be bigger and faster — unless we have a war, which will also be bigger and faster. (For example, see Kahn and Weiner's *The year 2000* [1967].) Megalopolis is projected from the present spiraling growth rate of cities. Megaconsumption of energy is projected from the present rate of use. Ostensibly these futurologists deal in units and behaviors which can be measured and projected years ahead. They advise planners and influence corporation and government decision makers to fulfill their projections.

Science fiction writers, more popular than ever, are still busy at their trade. Some are still locked into the Flash Gordon, space invasion, or superelectronic mind-control sort of thing; or they describe a twenty-first century landscape atom-bombed back to the stone age, peopled by everything from brainy apes to superhumans who wield iron swords, wear the latest in all-weather hotpants, and ride about on rocket ships. A few science fiction writers, such as Asimov, Herbert, and Bradbury, really conjure up visions of probable or challenging new worlds, and in science fiction form preach their social, religious, and ecological sermons. They may profoundly influence those who seek to establish realistic models for the future. The editors of *The Foundation Journal*, an underground press compendium of knowledge deemed necessary to save the human race and enable it to found a new and better era, are disciples of Isaac Asimov. In a 1970 edition they say: "It was the insights of Buckminster Fuller that initiated *The Whole Earth Catalogue;* It was the insight of Isaac Asimov that initiated the *Foundation Journal.*" Asimov urges that technologists and scientists should mastermind this salvation, for after all, since "they accept credit for lowering the death rate and industrializing the world," they should seek to correct the "undesirable side effects that have accompanied these victories" (1970). Ray Bradbury, another influential science fiction writer, has been speaking to college students about tomorrow's world. In a seminar in Los Angeles in October 1971 he discussed the New American Revolution with Jean-François Revel, author of *Without Marx or Jesus* (1971).

But a new dimension in future forecasting has been added in the wake of the movements sweeping across the land. People are speaking about seeking significant alternatives to the conventional American life-style. The future will not simply be an exponential extension of the present, but something quite different. We learn that megalopolis and superconsumption may not necessarily be our fate.

A major and most obvious source of alternatives has been that network of movements once called the counterculture. In typical

American fashion, participants in these movements did not long like the label. Like all good Americans, they wanted to be for something, for new and better ways, not just against tradition. Probably sensing the potential linking of their various movements into one network, they often referred to themselves as "the movement." They described their various social, political, economic, religious, and ecological innovations as *the* alternative society. We think this diagnosis is at best premature, although much closer to the truth than the popular view that these innovations are foolish fads, expressions of mental illness, or retreats from reality. The various movements are not yet one, and the various "alternatives" are not yet any kind of complete sociocultural system, integrated and potentially independent. East Africans, who rejected tradition, for example, could copy a full-fledged and complete Western system, or for that matter, a complete Islamic system. Those who reject traditional American culture cannot yet find a complete, self-contained, and independent movement *system* to join.

Movement people are not the only ones who perceive the actual or potential presence of an alternative system. In its spring 1971 issue *Tuparts Monthly Review of the Underground Press*, explained that this system is in the making. Their subscribers seem to be business executives, university and school administrators, government officials, and others who are persuaded that through a review of the underground press they will better understand what the New Left has in store. The *Tuparts* reviewers seem to be former or moonlighting government or military intelligence analysts who have formed their own free enterprise operation. The *Tuparts* editors, with perhaps functional prerequisites of a sociocultural system in mind, list underground alternatives to nearly every conventional aspect of established life. What is more, they imply that their list is as yet incomplete, and that the underground is developing more alternatives. In sum, these will provide a complete system of alternatives. They list alternatives for established marriage and family, established police and social control structures, established religion, and, of course, established communications and media. They seem particularly fascinated by the ways the underground or counterculture helps runaways and drop-outs obtain subsistence, shelter, and legal and medical aid. One could imagine that they were speaking about ways in which the Viet Cong or NLF subsisted in government controlled areas. In any event, they are speaking about *the* movement and a system of alternatives existing as a kind of organic whole, in competition with the established order.

Writing for *Playboy* magazine, Morton Hunt and Paul Anderson (1971) both present glimpses into the future as they see it. They naturally reflect the so called *Playboy* philosophy. According to *Playboy*, sexual variety is the spice of life, and playboys and playmates should be able to live their sex lives as they see fit, even if this conflicts sharply with old-fashioned convention. Anderson and Hunt suggest that considerable diversity in life-styles is to be the condition of our sociocultural system well into its future. They project that many different styles of marriage, cohabitation, and family life, many different techno-economic life-styles, and many different residence patterns will exist in the same system. Some of these would seem to be mutually incompatible according to more conventional sociological and anthropological concepts about what elements can coexist.

Back in the fifties and early sixties, when America was changing the world, remember how anthropologists, sociologists, and psychologists described the way in which various developing peoples were becoming confused by the presence of many different and presumably conflicting lifeways? Culture was supposed to be a coherent and integrated whole, in which one set of lifeways did not conflict with another, values did not conflict with behavior, there was regularity in law and a close fit between legal postulates and legal action. Cultures were supposed to be a result of a limited selection from the great arc of possibilities. People just would not permit too much variation — or, what is more important, people *could not* tolerate much diversity in their culture. How pathetic were the tales of poor, lonely Africans and Asians caught straddling two cultural worlds. How traditional in social science were the essays which described ways in which cultures reduced internal inconsistency by modifying and reinterpreting alien patterns so that they blended into the seamless fabric of a healthy social system. We are therefore prompted to ask: is the proliferation of variation in our society a sign that we are disorganized? Will diversity give way in time to a new synthesis, blending the new alternatives with convention, or are the new alternatives of so little consequence that we can write them off as the meanderings of purposeless deviants? Perhaps the traditional models of cultural integration are defective, and the theory needs careful reexamination. In any event, the variation in the cultural system of the United States is basically a product of *internal* innovation, not an import or an imposition by some powerful alien power.

Some, like Toffler (1971), see the future as so completely different from the present that entering it will be like entering an unbelievably foreign culture. Supposedly, people newly come to live in a foreign culture, especially one quite different from their own, experience such a sense of discontinuity that they are shocked, disoriented. We do not know if this is any more accurate than the proposition that people experiencing marked diversity within their own culture will be disorganized. But it sounds good, and in any event, it helped justify countless Peace Corps training programs. Now we hear that our own future will burst upon us and be so dramatically different from the present that it will shock us. We will be complete strangers in our own land.

Or will it be our land? Maybe it depends upon our age. Charles A. Reich (1970) tells us that tomorrow belongs to the "kids" of today, and the kids are supposedly so different from their parents that the millennium will come as the parents age, retire, or die and the kids mature and take over: culture change by generational replacement. This should sound familiar enough to readers of economist E. E. Hagen (1962) who back in the glorious fifties and early sixties realized that money and technology alone were not enough to bring the gift of economic development to lands which were dominated by a traditional conservative elite which did not know what was good for them. What was necessary? Of course, replace the old obstructionist elite with a new, young, entrepreneurial, and modernizing elite. Simply stated, the kids reject the old ways and take over from their parents. Entrepreneurial Burmese kids should now be leading Burma to revolutionary growth.

Some scholars (e.g. the Minnesota Experimental City Project contributors) advocate building new experimental cities from the ground up as perhaps the only way for the United States to break away from an increasingly maladaptive urban condition and leap into the future. Like Elman R. Service (1971) and various fellow evolutionists, the advocates of the experimental city, such as Neil J. Hurley (1969), have observed that a system which is highly specialized in one form of adaptation becomes so locked into this form that it is unlikely that it will free itself to create revolutionary new modes. The adapted system is most likely to cope with stress and strain by fixing things up, by patching and repairing and updating. It becomes increasingly specialized in this way of doing things and increasingly loses its ability to set off in bold new directions. In other words, a society which is modern in the 1950's and 1960's and seeks to adapt to new pressures chiefly by repairing and reforming within conventional themes, structures, and technologies, may well find that simply to survive it will have to fight a rearguard action in the 1970's, and even then will find itself relegated to underdeveloped status in the 1980's by a society which has taken a revolutionary overleap. Hurley and some of his colleagues seem to warn Americans that this fate could be theirs if they do not do something heroic to break away from the liabilities imposed by their past development. Hurley notes that European cities and industries were so completely destroyed during World War II that Europeans were free to build anew in the most advanced design. McLuhan (1960) argues that America has the largest backlog of obsolete technology in the world, particularly in communications; and that, because of this, backward countries have an enormous advantage over us. They can exploit all the tremendous potential of the electronic revolution which we started, but are unable to realize. Elman Service (1971) speaks of the greater evolutionary potential of the less developed countries.

We can see the issue in front of us squarely as we consider the question raised by the ecology movement. For example, the United States is already highly specialized to the automobile which generates major problems. If the United States seeks to resolve some of these by building more freeways, by demanding new engines to reduce pollution, and by planting new kinds of trees more resistant to this pollution, the result is simply an increased specialization in auto transport. It will have so much capital invested in the automobile that it will find it increasingly difficult to leap to new levels of transportation, even if faced with a major energy crisis. It will be another society not yet locked in to the automobile which is more likely to take this leap.

Similarly, the United States has had to face the environmental costs of generating electricity, and power companies have had to face public opposition to the construction of new plants. One answer has been to impose improved pollution controls on such power plants. Another has been to invite representatives of environmental groups to sit in on power company decision making and help to determine where new plants will be located. This will perpetuate conventional patterns of energy consumption and continued growth. Compare this to the revolutionary proposition that we must achieve a steady state society and significantly reduce energy consumption.

The same dichotomy prevails across the spectrum of our socioeconomic system. If we seek to solve our education problems by putting up more buildings, and improving conventional textbooks and teaching methods, we will keep the educational system running but make it increasingly unlikely that we will forge ahead to new types of education so revolutionary that we cannot now see more than their multimedia outlines. If we keep our cities alive by conventional methods of building malls and high-rise buildings in the downtown areas and broadening the traffic arteries which feed these cities, we will become less likely to forge ahead into the truly innovative urban life of the future.

My colleague Virginia Hine and I have found it convenient to call such patch-and-repair change "developmental" (Gerlach and Hine 1973). Service (1971) and Geertz (1963), among others, have called it "involution." No matter what it is called, it can be distinguished from revolutionary change which implies the generation of new courses of thought and action and new modes of validation and legitimization. Kuhn's description (1962) of such revolutionary change as "paradigm change" is most helpful. In seeming contrast to Service, we regard revolutionary change as the key to evolution, not as an alternative to it. It is through revolutionary step-change that new species evolve, and once evolved, they work things out developmentally for as long as possible.

Given their desire to break free from the retarding effects of America's lead and its developmental adaptation, we can understand why Hurley and his colleagues wish to construct an experimental city from the ground up. The experimental cityists are visionaries and futurists. They began their ponderings and designings in the mid-sixties, and since then, the processes we have been discussing have seriously undermined public confidence in the prevailing cultural model. It is no longer so obvious to Americans that they enjoy a lead which needs to be maintained only by patching and repairing. If Europe eventually benefited from having its cities destroyed by war, enabling them to be rebuilt anew (itself a questionable proposition), what will be the effect of the current American view that our cities are dead or dying? Americans may never have thought too highly of city life, but it would appear that, partly as a consequence of black power, ecology movements, and other processes of change, they are now ready to regard their cities as places of ruin requiring revolutionary transformation. Bombs and artillery destroyed Europe's cities; social and technical change have debilitated America's cities, discredited their energy-intensive, pollution-generating way of life, and opened the path for rebirth. In a sense, a great number of America's large urban areas have become "experimental cities." New ideas and actions proliferate across the whole range of movement groups, interface elements, and established order responses. If it is now hard to keep many bad ideas and actions from surfacing, it is just as hard to suppress many good ideas and actions. In this context, the Minnesota Experimental City is but one of many experiments, and it will affect, and be affected by, the multitude of explorations. The future of American cities, and thus of America as a whole, is going to be "discovered" by these intersecting trial-and-error efforts.

Winding up this glimpse of influential future speculators, we should mention MIT systems engineer Jay Forrester, who advocates world social system research and planning (1971a, 1971b) to achieve equilibrium; psychologist B. F. Skinner (1971) who blends visions of utopia with fears that, given free rein, mankind would charge into disaster; philosopher Jean-François Revel (1971); and stockbrokers Merrill Lynch, Pierce, Fenner, and Smith who are "bullish" about America.

Amassing great gulps of data, Forrester and his computers proclaim impending eco-disaster if the United States and the industrial and developing nations of the world continue their exponential growth. He is thus a rising hero in the ecology movement pantheon.[1] As a skilled systems analyst, he updates conservationist Muir's and anthropologist Malinowski's concept that in this world absolutely everything *is* hitched to everything else. Calling social systems "multi-loop nonlinear feedback systems," Forrester shows that, in the complex interactive system of national and world society, you cannot simply change one subsystem without its affecting and being affected by others. The planner or change agent cannot rely upon intuition to guide him in meeting his goals; he must understand and presumably control all major interdependent elements which affect his problem — otherwise, the very things he does to improve conditions will often create even greater problems. Indeed, Forrester sounds like an anthropologist in Africa or Asia explaining to an economic development officer the need to examine economic activity in context and realize that development projects will have unanticipated and undesired consequences. For example, Forrester shows how a program to improve urban conditions by simply building low cost housing will only result in attracting more people to the city than there will be jobs available for. With incomes too low to maintain the housing, the inner city will deteriorate still further. The urban planners should change and control enough conditions across the entire country to generate a nationwide equilibrium in total attractiveness of living area, thereby preventing localized overcrowding. Similarly, Forrester says that programs which reduce pollution but do not reduce or control population and curtail industrial growth and resource consumption will only produce a short-term improvement in the quality of life which will be followed by ecological catastrophe. All elements affecting the quality of life in the nation — and the world — must be simultaneously controlled. Forrester is not optimistic about the future condition of humankind. The quality of life will decline, not rise, he says. Man will be facing problems from all sides: supression of modern industrial society by natural resource shortages and collapse of world population consequent upon pollution, food shortage, overcrowding, war. But in good old evangelical style he implies one possible hope for some salvation. He suggests that humans may have an increased ability to cope with such dilemmas if they apply the developing tools of systems analysis, using computer models as he does, not the "mental models" of systems which, he says, are inadequate and intuitive. He says that the next challenge to human endeavor is to pioneer a better understanding of the nature of our social systems — by the "orderly and organized" process that is modern scientific discovery.

[1] Since this paper was written, Forrester's student, Dennis Meadows, and Forrester's systems program have achieved fame through the *Limits to growth* study (1972).

So there we have it. Given the complexity of social systems, the belief that unplanned and uncontrolled change will have awful consequences, and the fear of eco-catastrophe unless national and world systems are properly studied and managed, we have established a reasoned and positivistic argument for faster control by systems experts. Although Forrester himself may not carry his argument to this final conclusion, there will be many who will; indeed, we find it in those who suggest that we follow the model presented in Asimov's *The foundation* (1970) or turn the management of the country over to the scientists. This idea has been around for a long time, but under the threat of ecological ruin and the growing realization of system complexity, it may well receive considerable support.

Dramatically curtailing growth and establishing a condition of equilibrium in the United States means revolutionary change. If a group of planners and managers seek to accomplish such change from the top down, they will have to change many elements almost simultaneously or in rapid sequence to prevent a downward spiral. It seems that something similar confronted the Chinese Communists when they took China on the Great Leap Forward. Unlike the patchwork reformers of the Kuo-Min-Tang before them, they seem to have realized that, if China was to break out of its downward spiral, it needed to break fundamentally with tradition and change major subsystems in one great interdependent wave. To persuade people to make sacrifices in the present for possible future gain, the Chinese leaders had to use considerable force along with thought-control education. Tight organization and powerful ideology were the keys to this Chinese attempt to leap forward.

Perhaps the work of B. F. Skinner could suggest to would-be master-controllers the means to persuade Americans to change so fundamentally. The Skinnerians, bless them, may have a better and less painful way of ensuring that people do what is best for them. Skinner appears haunted by the complexities and stresses of life and the capacity of the self-seeking human animal to upset delicate balances. His answer also is to have experts design a more rational system and then shape man's behavior to that which specialists consider more desirable and more adaptive. In short, the Skinnerians match up nicely with the Forresterians and, given enough time and support, they may yet design the great world tranquility and stability box.

In contrast to all this, Revel (1971) sounds like a positive anarchist. While he says that we live in too complicated a time for revolution simply through a sudden takeover by a gathering of idealistic and often misled "kids," he also says that to succeed necessary revolutionary change must rise from the masses. It will not, he says, come down by direction from a political elite, for politicians follow, they do not lead.

Revel also claims that adaptive revolutionary change will not come from the actions of the Marxist-oriented radicals or the religious dreaming of hippies and "Jesus Freaks." Unfortunately, he does not really describe the process of revolutionary change by which the public generates its own transformation. According to Revel, revolution will happen in the United States because it is beginning to happen.

As for stockbrokers, Merrill Lynch, Pierce, Fenner, and Smith, they may not be rooting for revolution but they feel the need to "spread a little sunshine," perhaps hoping for the magic of self-fulfilling prophecy to work its miracles. Most Americans have seen their ads in which a herd of cattle charge across the TV screen to the theme "Merrill Lynch is bullish on America." According to an article in the *Los Angeles Times* (1971), consultants testing this advertising found that people understood the imagery (of bullishness) whether they understood the word or not. An impression of optimism and progressiveness was clearly made, although not necessarily in keeping with the stock market sense of anticipating a rising market.

So who is right among all these soothsayers and prognosticators, doomsayers and sunshine-spreaders, cautious controllers and enthusiastic "let-it-all-happeners"? Where are we going, and who is really going to get us there? If we have experienced so much surprising change in the past twenty years, can we possibly imagine what the day after tomorrow will bring, regardless of how elegant our models may be? Is it to be doom or boom, supermanagement, multiple alternatives forever, or grass-roots transformation, lift-off, swing back, or collapse?

My hypothesis is that for the United States this is a time of revolutionary system change, of fundamental social and personal transformation at the grass roots, and of a magnitude at least equal to the transformations which are remaking the Third World. One difference is that the Third World was pushed to change chiefly by the invasion of the West, while the United States is changing essentially because of pressure from its own people. This is not to say that in Africa, Asia, and the Middle East peoples would not have changed, and perhaps fundamentally, had the West not played its role — but, as it is, the West had a terrific impact. And internal change in the United States is not really self-contained. It has certainly been stimulated by the rise of African independence, collisions with China, the disaster in Vietnam, and world flows of energy, food, and resources. However, conspiracy thinkers to the contrary, the movements which slashed through convention were home-grown, as have been the responses and interactions which have generated new designs for our future. A few revolutionaries sought to find new designs by urging us to copy the Russians, or the People's Republic of China, or Cuba, but they found few followers. Americans have realized that these examples will not really provide them with pertinent models for their tomorrow. Essentially, they are designed to achieve twentieth-century industrialization and growth through central command, organization, and ideology — not to stimulate people to lift off toward an uncharted postindustrial era.

Other Americans have sought to go back to their presumed golden ages to find designs for the future, but, while there will certainly be some of the past and myths of the past in the future, we cannot expect much real direction from simple retrospection; nor can we trust planning and management by experts. Skinner is not alone in believing that we can achieve a desirable future only by big planning, behavioral engineering, and the like. Look around and listen, and you will meet many people of good will who believe that in the present state of ecological, political, and social crisis we must turn to experts. Are there really "experts" around who can create the kind of brave new world in which we would wish to, or even be able to, live? Indeed, given the very real system complexity which Skinner and others see, can we really expect that a group of specialists can somehow "solve" our problems? Surely, what we must learn from the ecological, political, and social crises which so alarm us is that we customarily solve problems by creating new ones. If the experts have us all leap forward by numbers, it is possible that for a time they may pick some right directions; and the gains from this might almost justify the loss of liberty. But the risk of expert error is so great that it is even more likely that they will have us all leap into disaster and that their final solutions will spawn new horrors. Did we not have experts advising our leaders on Vietnam? Did we not have experts who endorsed the use of pesticides and herbicides as an unmixed blessing and some who thought the Aswan Dam was just great? We should regard expert solutions as nothing more than temporary strategies to achieve limited goals, which should be continuously reassessed for revision. It is best to regard our future as an uncharted, unexplored land. To find our way, we need to increase diversity of exploration, decentralize the process of discovery and innovation, and reduce the impact of failure and success so that we can find out what works through trial-and-error, which is small-scale, but nonetheless system-transforming.

A SYSTEM OF CHANGE

The system of revolutionary social change is very complex. It is an organic whole in which many different elements interact in conflict and concord, each playing a part in the drama of change. Identifying each participating element or group in this drama in even one city is an almost impossible task, but it is possible to describe a model or scenario of what happens — although clearly a mental model rather than Forrester's computer model. It is possible to identify some major types or categories of involved elements or groups and to give some case examples. Such categories include movements, established order response — both positive and negative — interface elements, conventional voluntary associations, and self-help groups. It is possible to describe some of the ways in which the elements interact in a mutually causal process of deviation-amplification or system change. The model which I will now describe, clearly does not do justice to the enormous diversity and dynamism in life but it may serve as a useful "first cut" at the issue. In describing this, we shall deal with three aspects: cause, structure, and interaction and function. The first problem is to perceive movements as initial generators of fundamental change, instead of merely consequences of failure.

Much of the literature on social movements has focused on their presumed cause. This bias tells us as much about the scholars of the established order as it does about the movements. Movements have been generally regarded as *consequences* of pathological conditions in the participants or the society that spawned them. The participants are alleged to be reacting to deprivation or disorganization. They are suffering from mental stress or personality defects, or they are simply spoiled or bored; in any case the system of social order and control has supposedly broken down. True-believer Eric Hoffer (1963) is well known as a popularizer of such views. Linton (1943) and Wallace (1956) have pioneered anthropological studies of this type to show how movements help people restore social order and mental balance. Lanternari (1963) follows a well-trodden path in religious studies when he shows how religious movements arise as a reaction to and compensation for oppression, while Beals (1953) sees religious movements as a reaction to radical change. Ted Gurr (1967) and Chalmers Johnson (1966) are far more sophisticated in their analyses, attempting to construct elaborate multivariate socioenvironmental models of the causes and early growth of movements, although a key element is relative deprivation. While Gurr is bold enough to say that he can predict insurgency from this (declining to do so because governments would abuse the information), Johnson (1966) claims that it is impossible to construct a statistical measure which will predict the occurrence of a phenomenon as multiplex as a movement of revolutionary change. Instead Johnson aims to discover measures of the "disequilibriated social system," an approach which he feels will provide a description of the potentially revolutionary situation. Harry Eckstein (1964) contributes ideas about the influence of precipitating factors which can act as catalysts to turn potential into actual revolution. Mass media reports, popular discussion, and government commission studies also reflect this preoccupation with cause.

In the United States black power was regarded primarily as a sign that black Americans were deprived and secondarily that social control had broken down. Neo-Pentecostalism and the Jesus-charisma movement among middle-class and upper-middle-class white North Americans were considered primarily a result of mental or other personal defects of the participants and secondarily a result of the fact that the established church was slipping in its ability to control and meet their emotional needs. Student protest was considered a consequence of permissive childhood training, boredom and alienation, and lax university management. The ecology movement has been regarded by some as a sign that Americans are overly emotional faddists, and by others as indicative that the United States is indeed deficient at the very roots of its Judeo-Christian, growth-oriented, profit making, super-technological society.

Commissions have been established in various national institutions to determine causes in detail and suggest counteractive and preventive measures. These commissions are as numerous and varied as the problems they study:

1. Episcopalian, Lutheran, Presbyterian, Methodist, and Catholic denominations established commissions and research and study groups to investigate the Pentecostal uprising and suggest means by which the established churches could regain control of some of their straying sheep. They also investigated areas where reforms might rekindle moderate enthusiasm. Some churches financed research to determine the extent to which such overly emotional displays as speaking in tongues could be attributed to mental abnormality.

2. The Kerner Commission Report, as well as many local government and urban coalition task force studies explained how the country could and should eliminate black power protests by combating racism and providing economic, social, and political opportunities for black Americans so that they could enter the American mainstream.

3. The Scranton Commission and other government and university commissions investigated student unrest and how it could be combated so that students and faculty could get back to the real business of learning and teaching.

4. A number of industrial and business firms are conducting studies on the ecology movement and public concern for the environment. Some studies attempt to determine how the public is learning about environmental problems, to estimate how much the public really is willing to fight for and pay for a better environment, and to determine how to communicate their "story" to the public to counter maladaptive emotionalism. In other words, they wish to restore order to a disor-

derly field. Some firms, on the other hand, see the ecology issue as one which provides them with new areas for enterprise and growth; they can capitalize on the concern for environment by making and marketing pollution control devices, and providing ecology study courses, and the like.

In cases where pertinent established orders in the United States defined the cause of movements and accompanying conflicts as economic, political, or other deprivation, the remedy seemed obvious — counter insurgency by countering deprivation. In effect, the established order said: "Now that you have made us realize that we have not given you what you expect, we will make amends. Sit tight and let us do it. Just don't make unreasonable demands." When the protests and the conflicts continued in spite of these first steps at reform, the social control exponents in established orders could be heard proclaiming that order could really only be restored by better police, better technology for the police, punitive sanctions for the transgressors, and identification and arrest of the key outside agitators.

In short, established orders proposed both the carrot and the stick as means of restoring equilibrium. (Indeed, our Vietnam policy was much like this.) If we can't win friends and influence people by helping them economically and technologically, then make our enemies and those they have misled repent by hurting them with our power. It may well be presumed that the United States will repeat this set of approaches with respect to prison riots. Commissions will focus on the causes of the riots and then seek ways to reduce these causes and restore equilibrium to the prisons.

All of this is a prescription for reactive developmental change. Of course, some of those who propose such patch-and-repair operations will say that it is only a temporary measure, to cool things down while fundamental change is planned and programmed. All of this is also based on the conventional, but probably quite incorrect assumption that experts can really find — and then eliminate — the cause or causes or something as nonlinear, multilooped, and based upon feedbacks as a movement of change. Certainly this approach is a reflection of the basic control-oriented model for finding the cause and eliminating the undesirable effect, and is characteristic of the way Americans treat all phenomena which they regard as undesirable, pathological, or dangerous.

We suggest an alternative approach. We regard socioenvironmental conditions of deprivation, disorganization, and disequilibrium as movement-facilitating rather than sufficient or necessary conditions for movement genesis and growth. Attempts to counter deprivation and induce reform often stimulate revolution. We note that once a movement is under way, it helps generate the very conditions which foster its continued growth. For example, a movement can produce an ideology which exacerbates perceptions of deprivation. A movement can increase social disorganization and grow in its ability to impose sanctions, even as it reduces the control capability of the established order. (The rise of Islam in the seventh century A.D. is an illustration of this process.) Furthermore, we suggest that attention be paid to the process by which movements help generate change.

Given this perspective, people could ask different and more appropriate questions about movements. Established churches, for example, could ask how the charismatic and social change movements in the church can propel that church to new levels of thought and action, of community involvement, and spiritual growth, instead of focusing on how to control these movements. Government and urban coalition commissions on black power could look chiefly at how this movement is working to generate pride among black Americans; sparking new and exciting experiments in community organization, in police-community relationships, in art, music, economic organization, and education; and how it has ignited movements of change in other fields among other peoples; how it is helping futurize the United States so that it can cope more effectively with the rising nations of the Third World. Government and university commissions on the student movement could look chiefly to the potential of this movement for generating fundamental and exciting experiments in education, for involving young Americans in the quest for a better and more humane future, for channeling the great energy of youth and vitalizing educational endeavor. Industry and business could regard the ecology movement as creating a great opportunity for us to extricate ourselves from the retarding effects of our fading industrial lead and discover new ways of providing necessary goods and services, measuring gross national product, perceiving progress, and living within energy limits. People generally could apply themselves to facilitating such processes of change and reducing concomitant pain. People could learn to appreciate that everyone can play an important role in this process of fundamental change instead of turning it all over to supposedly expert government management or radical movement leadership. People could indeed consider this a time of vast and far-reaching fundamental social exploration.

Putting aside the conventional idea of the cause of movements, we investigate what they are made of; how they work; and how they interact with established orders and a range of other interface groups, such as conventional voluntary associations and self-help organizations. We examine the social organization of movements, their recruitment and commitment processes, their ideology and perception of opposition. Then we examine the social organization of interaction among the various groups involved in generating change. In sum, we suggest that the total process of revolutionary change is analogous, if not isomorphic to the process of biological evolution. In this process of change, the range of possible behavior, thought, and action is greatly extended through social mutation and cross-fertilization of ideas and actions. In time, the future is discovered and settled through processes of selective adaptation.

MOVEMENTS

We regard movements, irrespective of their causes, as generating the initial means by which a society can break out of its locked-in modes, overcome the retarding effects of its past lead in one form of adaptation, and lift off into a revolutionary new system. Movements have this capacity because: (1) they destroy or counter the retarding effects of convention, and force people to think new thoughts and try new actions; (2) they generate sociocultural variation and possible ideas and actions. It is from this expanding range that the design for the future is worked out through the dynamics of selective adaptation. Movements are facilitated in their ability to accomplish this by their typical characteristics of segmentation and decentralization. (But once movements initiate such a process, they interact with a range of other elements which contribute to change.) Once the process of sociocultural change has been kicked off by the thrust of one movement, many other elements in the whole system contribute to such change as they interact in a complex mutual causal deviation-amplification process. For our purposes in this essay, we can identify the following additional elements: (1) other movements of personal transformation and/or sociocultural change; (2) responses, positive and negative, of the established orders; (3) groups standing at the interface of movement and response; (4) energized conventional voluntary associations with local and limited focus; (5) self-help groups.

Let us now turn to a brief examination of the structure of a typical movement. In such an analysis, we concentrate on five factors: social organization, recruitment, commitment, ideology, perception of opposition.

Organization

When Americans, both movement participants and their opponents, think of organization they often think of a pyramid structure with central authority, leadership, and a clear channel of command. If the activity does not have such a structure, Americans usually believe that it is disorganized. Our research indicates that, while movements are not thus bureaucratically structured, they have a special type of organization highly effective for generating change. We call this organization segmentary or many-celled; polycentric, with many local leaders; and networked.

1. Movements are segmentary. A typical movement is composed of many different semiautonomous cells or segments. Such segments are formed by splitting of ongoing groups, the genesis of entirely new groups, or by a combination of these. Cells frequently overlap and intertwine in complex fashion so that participants are often simultaneously involved in several groups. It is not unusual for a man to be a leader in one group and a follower in another. Yet another characteristic of this segmentary structure is that there is considerable variation in both the specific goals pursued and the means used by each group. An individual group is encouraged to "do its own thing," performing according to the special capabilities of its members.

2. A second characteristic of movement organization is that it is polycentric, and has many actual or potential leaders. Movements do not have a paramount leader who rules through a coordinated bureaucracy. Each group may have its own temporary head, but such a man is no more than a *primus inter pares*. He can retain the leadership only by continually proving his worth. If a leader falters or fails or appears to sell out to the establishment, he will quickly be replaced since so many participants feel a need to contribute to the group and its mission.

3. A third characteristic of movement organization is that it is reticulate or networked. Even though it is composed of many different, often competing groups and does not have one leader, a movement is not a disorganized, formless mass. The individual groups of a movement interweave in a flexible network based on the personal interaction of "cell" leaders, through overlapping membership, and by having a common ideology, common cause, and common opposition. Traveling spokesmen or "evangelists" move across this network, contributing to its cohesion and ideological unity. This network also provides a effective grapevine communication system and logistical financial support system. The network of any one movement can rapidly expand to interweave with the network of other movements, temporarily tying all together in a giant coalition.

Let us consider the functions of such organization. Both observers and members generally regard such a loose structure as defective, and seek to centralize it, tighten its command structure, end "unnecessary duplication," and otherwise "rationalize" its organization and operation. Our research leads us to propose that such an organization is highly adapted for exponential growth and for generating and promoting revolutionary change. It is adaptive because: (1) it promotes effectiveness in new environments. The injunction that each cell should contribute in its own way, doing "its own thing," maximizes cellular variation, innovation, entrepreneurship, and trial-and-error experiment and problem solving. The failure of one group does not cause the whole to fail, but the successes help the whole movement; (2) it permits a movement to penetrate and recruit from a broad social range. An individual, attracted by what he sees as the general purposes of the movement, can find within the many cells a group of peers whose goals, tactics, personal life-styles, and backgrounds appeal to him; (3) it prevents effective suppression or absorption of the whole movement through redundancy, multiplicity of leadership, and the self-sufficiency of local groups; (4) it generates an escalation of effort and forward motion through rivalry and competition among its various segments and leaders.

Recruitment

Essentially recruitment is to a local group or cell, rather than to the movement as a whole. New individuals are recruited to such cells primarily through face-to-face contact with members. That is, recruitment follows lines of significant preexisting social relationships. Members recruit from family, friends, neighbors, associates, and colleagues. Recruiters use the capabilities, emotions, rights, and duties already existing in these relationships. The movement as a whole grows exponentially as each recruit becomes a recruiter of others. Such growth would not be possible if members recruited from loners or drifters. Pentecostals take personal pride in recruiting capable, effective associates.

Although it should be obvious that recruitment proceeds along these significant links, casual observers assume that people are drawn to membership through exposure to mass media, advertising, large demonstrations, and the like, or through contact with a single charismatic leader. Members' attitudes are changed in like fashion through interaction with fellow members in small group activities, not through large-scale "propaganda" or public information. In any event, such personal recruiting of effective people contrasts sharply with models which portray movements as giant magnets, or vacuum cleaners sucking up loosely articulated social particles.

Ideology

Movement ideology has a number of dimensions. At one level it provides a vision and master concept for the future, often in symbolic, easily communicated terms. At another it affords to individual members a sense of personal participation in shaping the future. At yet another level it affords to individuals a feeling of personal worth and power; it contributes to reshaping the individual's self-image. Such ideology encourages individual and group persistence, risk taking, and sacrifice for the cause and the local cell. When striving in this way participants do not easily acknowledge failure. Rather they interpret even that which, objectively, is failure as either a sign of future success or a temporary test of devotion and courage. Since the established order uses a different set of criteria to keep score (theoretically more rational, objective, and realistic), it misjudges the ability of the movement to persist in the face of setbacks.

Opposition

The participants in a movement characteristically perceive that they are facing opposition — *unjust* opposition. Opposition, either real or imagined, is necessary to promote the movement, offer it a basis for its commitment, and a force against which to unite. Opposition is optimum for movement growth when it is sufficient to be seen as a threat and challenge, but is not so strong that it cannot be overcome.

Commitment Process

People can be committed to change their ways of living fundamentally and strive to change others by emotional experiences and one or more "bridge-burning" acts, through which they identify themselves with the movement against the established order. We term this combination of identity-changing experience and action the "commitment process."

Effective participation in a movement such as Pentecostalism, black power, or ecology involves just such a process. It sets the participant apart from the established order of things, it cuts him off from past behavior patterns and past associations. It involves him with other movement participants and provides high motivation for changed behavior and striving to accomplish group and movement objectives. In the commitment process individuals must frequently stand on the firing line to demonstrate their new identity and validate their faith. By taking risks, they show which side they are on. The term "radicalization" is now commonly used to describe the effects of commitment, with particular reference to the ways individuals were changed during involvement in antiwar and black power demonstrations.

Interrelationship and Feedback

It is, of course, only for analysis purposes that we isolate these factors. In the actual stream of events, they intersect complexly. It is in their combination and interaction that these factors produce the energy and action that enables the movement to help generate major change.

In this discussion of the process of futurization, the analysis of the social organization of the movement is most important. Segmentation, so deplored by most observers, provides the first major impulse for variation and revolutionary change in the established sociocultural system. As new movement groups spring up they contribute not only to countering the established order and conventional wisdom, but to the growth of ideas and actions which are trial-and-error experiments and alternatives to the conventional. As movement groups deviate in concept and action from the established system, they constitute social mutations. Under the operation of selective pressures some mutations work, others don't. Those which are successful reproduce or spread their message in a variety of ways. In some cases they split into two or more groups, usually because of internal strains or differences about means and ends. In many other cases the example, or even the leadership style of one successful group creates a spin-off effect so that many new groups follow the successful model. Given time these create new permutations and variations around the central theme, and sometimes take off in bold new directions. In some instances, just the idea of a type of action or approach is spread, stimulating the birth and growth of new groups; in others the new group copies an almost complete package of ideology, purpose, and tactics. In various cases a new group may use a basic philosophy and tactic copied from an ongoing movement group, but then apply these to a somewhat different set of problems, or to a different target. In some cases, the offshoot may retain and perfect the model it copies from a parent movement even as the parent movement sets forth on new approaches. The new group may be created consciously and deliberately by a parent group, or it may come into being because the new group admires some movement action, idea, or *modus operandi*. Of course, this attempt to identify some of the modes of movement, group or cell reproduction and proliferation greatly oversimplifies a highly complex and dynamic process. For example, new groups can be created and assume characteristics of action and concept through a combination of several of these modes. It is important to realize that some participants in some of the various movements refer to fission and spin-off as the formation of "daughter" or "sister" groups.

The movements which proliferated in the United States during the sixties and early seventies may seem new phenomena and certainly in size, range, and power they were. The germ from which each grew, however, has been present for years in the sociocultural system of the United States. We can identify each of them in the years before 1965 as a kind of tolerated, constantly recurring mutation. An "open" social system, functioning effectively, can tolerate a few such mutations. It can tolerate, often with barely disguised amusement, a few conservationists, social or racial activists, religious "nuts," butterfly-chasing women's or minority rights protesters, and attempts at utopia-seeking communes. Small associations of such "deviants" keep alive the spark of counterculture, of alternative models of protest and design for change. The established order can control or suppress any marked proliferation of such elements by using sanctions ranging from ridicule to physical force. As long as the mutations do not multiply rapidly or proliferate and become noticeable forces for change, their presence can help the established order to maintain its desired image of freedom. If nothing else, they may seem to provide little safety valves for those who do not quite fit in, and certainly they give the sociologist, anthropologist, and psychologist something small, unprotected, and unusual enough to study.

Under certain complex, interacting conditions, the idea, alternative mode, or latent design for action of the tolerated mutation becomes energized and an explosive process of deviation-amplification begins. The tolerated, cautious, barely perceptible carrier of the germ is suddenly upstaged and even swept aside by new proponents of increasingly radical versions of idea, action, and alternative. It is as if the rate of sociocultural mutation itself is suddenly, dramatically increased. Side by side with this explosive growth of new mutations with ever more radical design characteristics, there is a correspondingly explosive growth of "sister" and "daughter" cells as the various mutations are reproduced many times over, in every city in the country. There is great reduplication, redundancy, and overlap of movement cells, even as there is a continuing progression of diversification and variation.

For example, the United States has long experienced some form of black protest, struggle for change, attempts to carve a niche in the mainstream and even to provide alternatives to the mainstream. Such mutations and adaptations were suppressed by the white majority or at best tolerated. Some were perpetuated or wrapped in religious movements, a few of which, notably the Black Muslims, carried within them a strong element of antiwhite sentiment and black pride. Some took the form of sociopolitical associations, aimed at ultimately securing integration within the rules laid down by the white majority.

Then, quickly, in the mid-sixties the civil rights, followed by the black power movement, grew exponentially. From the narrow base of usually cautious Negro advance, increasingly action-oriented civil rights groups proliferated and risked life and limb in sit-ins and marches, chiefly in the South. The Black Muslims and Malcolm X grew to command national attention and spark the birth of considerable Muslim-like spin-off groups, chiefly in the North. Suddenly, following

Stokely Carmichael's cry of "black power," a multitude of new groups came to life and action in Northern cities and, in various forms, echoed the black power and black pride themes. The expanding range of black power groups can usefully be described as a continuum or spectrum of groups from conservative to radical or from traditional and bureaucratic to charismatic and militant. In many cases, the newer the group, the more radical its position. Growth was typically greater at the radical end of the continuum. In time this competition and example sparked the more traditional and conservative to become more militant and aggressive in statement and action.

We have elsewhere (Gerlach 1970b) described many of the typical groups which constituted the black power continuum in a Midwestern city in 1967–1968 and again in 1970. The Urban League and NAACP stood at the conservative pole of the spectrum and constituted the constantly recurring and socially tolerated mutation. Black Panther-type groups, subscribing to the propositions of Fanon (1966), were at the radical pole. Between these poles ranged myriad black economic and educational projects, black pride efforts, community centers, parapolice and community control organizations. Black churches were vitalized by all this and moved from their characteristically cautious approach to a frequently aggressive demand for change, for funding from "guilty" whites, and for experiments in new community action programs.

Similar growth patterns can be seen in the other movements which we have studied. Environmental conservationists have been around in the United States for ages in the form of such established organizations as the Audubon Society, Conservation Foundation, Isaac Walton League, and the Sierra Club. But by 1967, the Sierra Club was becoming too activist for some of its officers, and in an ensuing power struggle the club split. Dave Brower left to start a new and more activist group, Friends of the Earth, which has divided since then. As this was happening, new conservation-environmental, ad hoc, grass-roots groups were springing up in communities across the land in response to specific cases of environmental degradation. The Environmental Defense League came into national prominence as it sued "the bastards" who were polluting the land. Richard Means called this the time of "the new conservation." (1969). By 1968 we referred to it as the embryonic movement of "participatory ecology" (Gerlach 1970a). The concept of ecology began to be voiced by laymen in struggles to stop jetport and power plant construction, arrest highway and development projects, and fight the use of pesticides and herbicides. The more traditional conservation organizations were stimulated to more activist positions by this growth of new and increasingly militant groups. Undoubtedly, this explosion of ecology movements was also sparked by the example and ideology of black power, antiwar, and student protest. Among other things, it offered whites, rejected by blacks what seemed a less dangerous focus for their desire to do something. And it offered representatives of the counterculture and the New Left a beautiful target for their general assault on the establishment. By Earth Week in the spring of 1970, the ecology movement was in full swing, displaying a broad and growing range of groups from traditional conservationists to new, radical elements referring to themselves as "ecology freaks." It seemed that in every community normally cautious middle-class and upper-middle-class Americans were forming angry little groups with such names as: "Get the Oil Out," "Stamp Out Smog," and "Women Against Pollution." An ideology of ecology was developing, which was in fact or potentially subversive to conventional wisdom and the established industrial order. Concepts such as "no-growth economy," "limited good," and "spaceship earth" were enunciated by all manner of seemingly straight Americans. We have indicated elsewhere that these concepts and the ecology movement itself were potentially revolutionary and certainly represented more than a mere artful dodge engineered by the government to sidetrack the antiwar express (Gerlach and Hine 1973: 38).

Consumerism, always present but muted and controlled by the established order, also expanded exponentially during this period from the mid-sixties to the seventies. The example of Naderism alone illustrates this. Many efforts are the direct progeny of Nader and his cadre, and he apparently monitors all of them. But Nader-like groups and actions are also springing up everywhere, some of which seek to come under the Nader umbrella, while others retain full independence.

Pentecostalism has also long been on the American scene; tolerated within the framework of religious freedom; regarded as an escape valve for the deprived, the over-emotional, and under-educated; and laughed at as "Holy-Rollerism." Its focus on deep, and personal religious experience and small group brotherhood, its manifestation of glossolalia or "speaking in tongues" as a symbol of baptism in the spirit, its quest for other gifts of the spirit such as prophecy and interpretation, were well out of the mainstream of American religion. Pentecostalism was concentrated in a few increasingly routinizing churches such as The Assemblies of God, and in various scattered revivalist sects. Then in the late 1950's Pentecostalism burst out of this confine and in the form of the charismatic revival, sometimes called "the tongues movement," it proliferated throughout middle- and upper-middle-class adult America. It popped up in home meeting groups and small underground-like cells hidden within the major Protestant churches. By 1967, the neo-Pentecostal movement had spread into the Catholic Church involving nuns, priests, and laymen in a quest for the "Gifts of the Spirit." Often Protestant Pentecostals helped Catholics to try to receive these gifts. The movement also caught on among Catholic university students at major centers of education. By 1970, the cutting edge of neo-Pentecostalism was in the many and varied groups of young people referred to loosely as the Jesus movement or Jesus revolution.

In short, this decade has seen the rapid and exponential growth of large multicelled movements exploding from germs long dormant, latent, or constrained. Each cell of each movement is like a mutation with a potential for proliferation and, under selective adaptation pressures for reproduction and growth to dominance.

We have elsewhere described a movement of change as an organic whole, a system of interrelated parts, in which each group plays a role in the growth and function of the movement (Gerlach and Hine 1973: 188). We give here a few examples of this interactive process. In one city where we did our research, black activists and some white supporters sought funds and assistance to establish a new type of militant black and minority community center in which to teach black pride and mobilize young people for change. They had many difficulties until very militant Black Panther-type groups appeared and threatened to attract a large youthful following. Against this threat and the more general danger of rioting by young blacks who were not being reached by ongoing programs, the established order did fund the new-type community center. It was relatively less radical than the Panther-type groups, and it "gives the kids something constructive to join" and "keeps them off the streets." In time it appeared that, while the community center did compete with the Panther-type groups, it also helped them by providing a meeting place, informal message center, and even a tap for financial help. The almost constant controversy surrounding the center made it a focal point for clashes between conservative Negro and militant black, for conflict between black and white, and for confrontation with the police. This provided a useful battleground for the Panther-type groups. Thus the presence of each black group helped the other and the escalation of the black power movement.

Similarly, the threat of rioting by militant blacks, following the death of Martin Luther King, moved the urban coalition and the mayor's office to permit and pay for a black community parapolice patrol with two-way radio communication. Had it not been for this threat, the patrol would not have been authorized. Blacks wanted the patrol as a device to foster black pride, keep the white police out, and generate local community control of the police. Others thought that it could be a buffer between establishment police and the black community and reduce the likelihood of an explosive clash.

Once the community center and parapolice patrol were going concerns, their design was reproduced by fission and copying, as we
outlined above. A number of similar militant-type community centers
sprang up in other parts of the city and in a neighboring city. One was
started by leaders of the initial center, others were just copies of it
stimulated by its example. Funds were obtained for this from various
establishment sources, including a local foundation. Presumably they
were motivated to give their support because of the success and
originality of the first center — and because they feared that without it
more militant groups would attract restless young people.

In time, the activist community center idea diffused to the neighboring urban Indian community, and the white supporters of moderate
Indian activists. They established a variant of this type of community
center which seemed most appropriate for helping Indians to cope with
city life.

Several other black groups and one black and white integrated group
established other community parapolice patrols in this city, each somewhat different from the original. One was more militant, armed itself,
and saw itself as a kind of vigilante group to protect the community
from the presumed threat of white citizen backlash. Another concentrated on serving as a kind of rumor control, conflict-countering effort.
The integrated team patrolled on foot, seeking mainly to mediate
disputes and act as a buffer in the event of conflict. Research by other
scholars has indicated widespread national experimenting with black
community parapolice patrols during the late 1960's (Cohen 1973;
Braun and Lee 1971; Knopf 1969).

As the American Indian movement suddenly came to life and
expanded in 1970, the more militant members within it established a
parapolice patrol for the urban Indian community. It was to function
also as a focus for Indian pride and reduce harassment of the Indian
community by the establishment police. The patrol prevented Indians
from getting drunk, fighting in public or doing other things which
would cause the white police to interfere. The patrol was modeled on
the black patrol, although the Indians themselves apparently dislike
admitting this. After the formation of this Indian patrol, a
counterculture-alternative-culture community near the urban university sought to establish a parapolice patrol. Their motive was to keep
the establishment police out of the community and achieve community
social control themselves, in accordance with the values and structures
of their alternative life-style. Above all, they wanted to prevent the
police from arresting drug users, and felt they could do so by concealing evidence of drug abuse.

The community parapolice patrol concept continues in this urban
center. It has been established in a low-cost minority housing project,

in this case to counter theft and assault. The establishment police and the urban coalition cooperate with this effort by equipping the patrol with two-way radio. The patrol wanted arms, but this the police and mayor's office refused them. However, more or less in response, the city has established a small volunteer force of unarmed police within the conventional department. This force cooperates with the housing project parapolice. Both serve as buffers between the residents of the housing project and the conventional police.

In the ecology movement we find many examples of the movement generating effect of group interdependence. The radical, emotional, nonnegotiable demands of some militant new ecology groups help make the "requests" of more conventional environmentalists seem positively reasonable to harrassed industrialists. And, of course, the radical action of eco-activists can stir moderate environmentalists and old-line conservationists to more radical action. For example, after the president of one Isaac Walton Association was labeled an "Uncle Tom of ecology" by a student ecology group, he decided to show them that his association could and would play a leading role in saving a wilderness area from developers and a river from pollution by power generation. He could tell his friends and business peers that, if they did not act dramatically to save the environment, then disillusioned young people would become even more radical.

Not only do the various cells or groups within a movement interact with each other in an organic system, but movements of change can also interact with each other in a system of movements. As they interact, in both conflict and concord, they generate new configurations through cross-fertilization and they considerably extend the range of alternatives and experiments. For example, most black power groups have regarded the ecology movement as a white middle-class cop-out from the real issue of racism. Certainly, they saw that whites had a new bag to work in and were no longer so concerned with contributing to black causes. Some black power groups said that programs of population control associated with the ecology crusade were really attempts to limit the black population — some even labeled these programs genocidal. Some participants in the Zero Population Growth variant of the population control wing of the ecology movement wanted black support for population control and, in any event, did not want to be accused of racism. In a newsletter circulated in many cities, ZPG spokesmen asked readers to contribute to the Black Panther legal defense fund for the Chicago trials in 1970–1971. They also advised their adherents to regard the fight against racism as just as important as the fight to save the environment. Indeed, they implied that each fight was part of a single effort to remake the total system. Some other ecology activist groups urged environmentalists to realize that racism and pollution are all part of the same problem — a defective society which needs fundamental change.

There is, of course, considerable reticulation between activist ecology movement participants and those in the New Left — alternate or counterculture. We see examples of this in some types of commune living, where communards seek to live "ecologically," escaping or combating the growth-consumption-competition treadmill. Characteristically, such communes have also sought to escape the tyranny of advanced technology and, in some cases, have gone back to earlier, less complex technology. Some new communes are being formed by groups which seek to use the most advanced technology, overleaping the locked-in modes of industrial society. They hope to show by this that revolutionary technology can become the tool of man in his fight to live humanely in ecological balance. For example, one such commune is being planned by some engineers on two hundred acres of Ozark farm and woodland. These prospective communards consider using solar energy to power their commune. They wish to pioneer ways of achieving a steady-state system.

New food-buying cooperatives are formed to combine alternative cultural life-style objectives with ecological, energy-conserving objectives. Natural foods, organic foods are sold in bulk pretty much on a basis of trust between buyer and market managers. Bringing their own containers to conserve packaging material, participants themselves select, weigh, determine the cost of, and check out the items. In this atmosphere shopping is fun and provides a chance to meet and talk with friends and strangers. This contributes to the achievement of sociability and the counter-alienation objectives of various life-style groups.

Some neo-Pentecostal groups, have formed urban and rural cooperatives to pursue religious objectives and achieve close brotherhood. It is true that most aspects of neo-Pentecostalism seem so concerned with personal religious transformation that social and ecological issues are ignored, but we have observed a few instances of overlap with antiwar and environment efforts. The potential for overlap is considerable. Other religious change movements, such as those often termed "Eastern religions," should also overlap with ecology, antiwar and, perhaps, racial issues.

Some radical Catholics, aiming at changing the structure of Catholic Church ritual and practice, have formed alliances with Catholics focusing on social action and antiwar activities. Associates of the Berrigans used Pentecostal-type terminology to describe their opposition to the draft. Members of the Association of Catholics for Church Renewal in one city contributed to the cost and activity of the militant community center described above.

ESTABLISHED ORDER RESPONSE

By definition, movements of change interact with the established order, or rather with various established orders. In a sense, each movement has its own established order against which it operates, and often each movement group has its own specific established order, opposition, or target. We call the established order a response to a movement and we distinguish between positive and negative response. Simply stated, negative response seems designed to stop the movement, while positive response seems designed to meet some of the movement's objectives. Most responses, whether positive or negative, are initially designed to eliminate the presumed cause of the movement so that things can go back to "normal." But in attempting to counter a movement, established orders themselves change as they interact with that movement.

Maruyama (1965) gives us an excellent illustration of how mutual causal interaction between two species can, under certain conditions, lead to the considerable amplification of deviation in each. He notes that:

... a species of moth has predators. Because of the predators, the mutants of the moth species which have a more suitable cryptic coloration (camouflage) and cryptic behavior than the average survive better. On the other hand, those mutants of the predators which have a greater ability than the average in discovering the moth will survive better. Hence, the cryptic coloration and the cryptic behavior of the moth species improve generation after generation, and the ability of the predators to discover the moth also increases generation after generation (Maruyama 1965).

The movement groups which do better than their competitors in interaction with their respective established orders will survive better. They will reproduce by fission and copying. Rapid communication along the movement network will facilitate this. On the other hand, those established orders which show a greater than average ability to cope with movement groups will survive better, and such success will be communicated across the established order network stimulating other established orders to copy their methods. Additionally, both movement groups and established order will continually experiment with new means to cope with the increasing ability of their respective opposition and challenge. The end result is that each changes considerably because of pressure from and response to the other.

Negative Response

One thing which became painfully clear was that attempts to suppress movement action by force often led to greater action by that movement and involved radicalizing fence sitters, and some neutrals, and often polarized public opinion. We have elsewhere described how opposition created the situation of risk which committed participants to movement goals and actions (Gerlach and Hine 1970d: 183). It often helped to bind participants together in tighter networks. Mass arrests of demonstrators brought strangers together and helped them forge communication links. If established orders wished to use force to crush the movements, they realized that it would need to be so massive and severe that the United States would be changed fundamentally in the attempt to avoid change.

In some cases the established order took the bit between its teeth and seemed to be leading the change. For example, university officials set in motion experimental education programs in response to student demand. Industrial and other firms contributed to some programs. Even where student interest seemed to fade, the established order pushed the programs forward. As a further example of established order response, we note that some policemen have become so "turned on" to *change* that they run for office to get more leverage.

Established orders came to realize that force and suppression were not sound responses to movements. Force did not work well and it violated the self-image of many participants in the established order. For these and other reasons, participants in the established order sought alternative modes of response. Some of these were no more than carrots to complement the big stick, but some were very new, quite innovative, and certainly change-generating.

Experiments in Established Order Response

On the individual city level, we see a profusion of experiments in established order response to movements of change. For example, there are new modes in police-community relationships including civilian observer ride-alongs, foot patrols, patrols by unarmed police, establishment of local neighborhood police offices, ongoing college education for policemen. Even where the police seek technical aid from engineers and specialists to provide them with better technology, they may get more than they bargained for and change in the process. For example, a notable engineering and systems management institution agreed to help the police of one large California city modernize its technology. But this institution is taking every opportunity to tell the police that they must not rely upon force and technology, but instead change their approach to presumed law breakers. The institution plans to monitor use of the system to see if the police are abusing their new capabilities. One may be cynical and say that nothing will control the police, or that the technologists and systems types are really just playing word games. One might even suggest that the technologists cannot measure abuse of the new system. But what is important is that a major attempt is being made by this institution to improve conditions. In the past, such technology and systems institutions would simply build to specification and ignore possible abuses of the capability. The credentials of this institution are such that the police are likely to listen to it, and this will be another confirmation of a message the police are getting from many quarters.

Stimulated by so much experience and continuing education, individual police forces are experimenting with new ways of interacting with their communities. And in turn, communities are experimenting with their approach to the police. Experiments range from outright local community control and demands that the police curtail the use of force on the one hand, to integrating diverse neighboring community police forces in one communication network or demanding that police use vastly more force on the other. At some point such experimenting will taper off and we shall have some new nationally copied models. It will be trial-and-error experiments and communication of results which will produce these new models.

The ecology movement generated considerable ambivalence in established order response. Key executives and public relations departments in business, industry, and government realized that their firm or institution would lose public goodwill if it took an overt anti-environment-protection stance. Yet the PR boys could also foresee all manner of trouble for them and their principals after an outright admission of eco-guilt and submission to ecology movement demands. The only answer was to play it cool; play a cautious eco-game for a time; achieve some compromise solutions, while waiting for the air to clear. Perhaps the eco-fad would fade away, perhaps it would continue and demand more change. In the meantime they would compromise and perhaps even find a way to capitalize on the movement.

We all know the result. Firms can be ranged along a continuum of positive to negative response to the movement. Some firms have attacked ecologists as irrational butterfly chasers who will ruin the local economy and put people out of work by blocking progress. Others have jumped onto the eco-bandwagon by advertising their products as more environmentally sound than that of their competitors. Some, of course, have made money by building pollution control devices, or have modified their plant or enterprise, making them advanced examples of pollution fighting firms.

Companies which produce electric energy have seemed to take all possible positions along this response continuum. At the negative end, we still have powerful power generating utilities which encourage their customers to use ever more energy and warn that unless more power plants are built, the public will suffer by not having enough power for industrial and domestic use. At the positive pole we have a handful of power companies which draw representatives of the public and of ecology movement groups into company decision making about power plant siting, and even into company policies affecting consumer demand. We can refer to such attempts as an "open-planning policy,"[2] which is somewhat similar to the open-planning and open-hearing approaches of the urban coalition. The urban coalition developed in response to the black power uprising and its objective was the achievement of problem-solving interaction between representatives of the protesting public, the established elite, and some elected officials. The power company's open planning was developed in response to the ecology movement uprising which blocked power plant construction and made power company officials and their plans and policies look bad. It is probably not accidental that the chairman of the board of the power company which led the way in this open-hearing approach had been one of the founders and sparkplugs of the urban coalition in the same city. There is an overlap here between these two established order response efforts.

A characteristic of open planning is that it represents in itself an experiment in decision making and social structural change and lends itself to the generation of other experiments in social action and concept formulation. Thus, through open hearing the power company has at least overtly changed its advertising policy to reflect a new awareness of the environmental cost of power generation and the concept that resources are finite and should be conserved.

Another feature of this structure is that it appears to be different from simple mediation or arbitration, in which both parties seek compromise through traditional trade-offs. It also differs from adversary procedure in which both sides seek to win. The complexity of the issues and the diversity of group interests involved reduce the likelihood of solutions being achieved within established frameworks. Thus, what we see emerging is a new form of open-ended, flexible community decision making, through which people cooperate in seeking adaptive strategies for coping with situations instead of calling upon experts to find permanent solutions. Similar structures (such as

---

[2] I completed research for this essay and wrote its first draft in 1971. By 1973 in Minnesota, the innovation of open planning for energy facility siting had evolved into a formal state-level system incorporating lengthy hearing processes and citizen participation before a board of state officials representing the governor's office and the main state agencies, and selected citizen representatives. By 1974, Minnesota farmers resisting powerline construction over their land were already beginning to force revisions in this system. This social evolutionary process continues as established orders respond to continuing citizen resistance. With a team of researchers, I am continuing to study this and have described and analyzed it (Gerlach, 1978).

the urban coalition) were developed to cope with racial strife and campus upheaval.

In any event, we can expect to find this community-oriented open-hearing forum emerging in the context of other complex environmental issues. It also came into being during controversy over jetport sitings in southern Florida and Minnesota and it seems to be emerging in the context of numerous small-scale issues involving housing or industrial development which affect community resources.

The Midwest power company which tried open planning was further motivated to contribute to new and quite experimental education projects at the local university. These experiments are themselves the product of change within the university and reflect broad currents of change throughout the city and the country. One of the power company's contributions was to help finance an intern program which would enable certain university students to spend half a year observing the operations of various institutions and businesses and, hopefully, monitoring them for corporate responsibility and concern for the public interest.

This particular power company is also interacting with what we have termed "ecology interface groups" at the university and local colleges. These groups are involved in environmental study programs and interdisciplinary environmental study seminars. The power company contributes lectures for these seminars and programs — in an effort to be sure, to spread the message of its environmental concern and keep abreast of what the environmentalists are doing. Irrespective of its motives, it is contributing to a process of cross-fertilization of ideas, and this is bound to have some effect on its approach as well as on the total process of change. Interestingly, one interdisciplinary environmental study project which it has funded is to investigate the feasibility of a steady state earth — the achievement of equilibrium. This model conflicts with the usual growth model of most power companies. The virtues as well as the problems inherent in equilibrium were presented in a series of lectures to engineering students by scholars from various fields. In the series, there was more which was subversive of convention than supportive.

The Midwest power company's efforts in open planning in this one city were communicated to another environmental study interface group in a prestigious technology-oriented university on the west coast when representatives of the environmental research project met power company representatives at a government-sponsored energy and power conference in Washington, D.C. Members of the environmental research project are now telling other power companies and local government and environmental groups about the capabilities and limitations of this kind of open-planning approach. Partly through such communication, it is likely that similar experiments will be attempted elsewhere in the country. It is also likely that the open-planning or at least an open-hearing format will be attempted in the context of other complex environmental issues.

One can be quite cynical about these open-planning and interface assistance efforts and say that the established industrial order is simply trying to defuse public opposition and co-opt leading protestors and troublesome students. But, even if this is their sole purpose, they will find that, in the process of trying to change the protestors, they themselves will be changed. Is it too much to say that the established order itself is being co-opted? Perhaps the motives of many members of the established order and of movements are not the purest, but does it matter in so far as the generation of change is concerned? Does it really matter why various German princes supported Martin Luther in the sixteenth century? They did support him, and a torrent of change was released.

SELF-HELP AND INTERFACE GROUPS AND CONVENTIONAL VOLUNTARY ASSOCIATIONS

By interface groups we mean groups or organizations which stand at the interface of movement challenge and established order response. They are not part of, or tied to, either side. Characteristically they seek to provide for problem resolution on a more or less compromise or trade-off basis. They are a combination or variant of honest broker, unbiased data source, analyst, technical expert, and focus for open-minded information gathering and study. Unlike an arbitrator or mediator, they are not chiefly interested in reducing conflict among community factions, their main objective being more to encourage adaptive change than to establish social equilibrium. Having observed all these characteristics in distinct organizations, we now tentatively propose that the term "interface group" be applied to them.

Environmental study groups, quality labs, and resource research councils (such as the Universities' Council on Water Resource Research) provide good examples of such interfacing. To some degree, the urban coalition in some cities also acted as a type of interface group, although it always had to fight to achieve this role rather than play the simple role of preventing conflict and defusing violence. The open-planning group, created during the dispute over electric power generation and power plant siting, is perhaps a kind of interface — especially as it interacts with sources of information about the impact of power generation and the real need for electric energy.

We have also observed various types of interface group emerging through the efforts of high school environmental study projects and the environmental study groups of various churches and religious denominations. Neo-Pentecostalism, particularly in the Catholic Church, stimulated interface activity. One Catholic university in particular became noted as a center for unbiased and change-oriented studies and interpretations of this religious movement.

Conventional voluntary associations also play a role in the process of change. Such associations as the American Association of University Women, the League of Women Voters, the Citizens' League, and various women's clubs have established task forces on racism, and on environmental control. These appear to be more routinized and bureaucratized than movement groups, and participants seem to have less commitment than most of those in the movements. Such conventional associations interact in both conflict and concord with pertinent movement groups on many issues. Members often bring the subject of change into neighborhood and family discussions.

Self-help and community assistance groups contribute much to change. These are groups which, we feel, lack the all-encompassing ideology and networking of movement groups but are less bureaucratized and more committed than voluntary associations. They seek to improve the quality of their lives and of their neighborhood or to help others accomplish this. Examples are inner-city neighborhood groups which fight everything from rat infestation of homes to dog infestation of parks, urban blight, and freeways; and which seek to provide free or low cost medical clinics, paramedical, legal and welfare rights assistance, and so forth.

Participants in some of these groups are also participants in or supporters of black power, Chicano, American Indian and other minority movements, Women's Lib, welfare rights and the like. Hence, such self-help and community assistance groups may articulate with these movements and we may find it more effective to simply regard them as cells in the body of pertinent movements. But for the present we consider them as a separate category.

We repeat our proposition that change in the United States is being generated by many different individuals, institutions, and groups. We have established the categories of movements, established order response, self-help, interface, and voluntary association groups simply to freeze the action of change while we identify and dissect some of its significant elements, and lineally describe aspects of interaction. Group boundaries are certainly not so neat and tidy, and the dynamic of change is not so orderly or lineal. We might equally seek to portray the process of change by constructing a continuum of all the groups or functions we have mentioned, or indeed of yet other groups and functions. Such a continuum might spread from devoted movement activists at one pole to staunch anti-change types at the other, with the various other elements ranged between these extremes.

Regardless of which method may be best for identifying the main actors in the drama of change, our objective now is to consider how they act and interact to generate change. We conceptualize each group at any point along the continuum of change as an actual or potential contributor to the design of new and adaptive structures and ways of life. Alone or through interaction, groups may generate ideas and actions which serve as models for others. The groups we are focusing on are in effect exploratory probes or sociocultural mutations. Like genetic mutations, they introduce variability and diversity into the established and conventional "pool" of working ideas and actions. Under normal conditions a few novel mutations are perhaps tolerated but will be controlled if they proliferate. However, as conventional solutions become, or appear to become increasingly ineffective or maladaptive, the established system can find an experimental design for far-reaching adaptation through such mutations. Under certain conditions of stress and searching, these mutations do reproduce and proliferate rapidly. They interact with other system elements and other movements in cross-fertilization, and a broad range of new forms emerges.

In conclusion we shall list some of the experiments in sociocultural and ecological adaptation which have emerged through the process of mutation and cross-fertilization.

SOME EXAMPLES OF ALTERNATIVES, EXPERIMENTS, AND SOCIAL MUTATIONS

We have already shown how movements, response, and interfacing have generated experiments in community social control, in police-community relations, in open planning of resource use, in food cooperatives, and in the formation of ecologically adaptive communes, including those which use advanced technology. We have also suggested that change-oriented groups within industrial firms may be experimenting in ways to humanize technology and ensure that their products are used in the public interest.

We can now list some other experiments within major aspects of our sociocultural system. This is merely a survey and summary of general examples from the broad range of experiments which we observed in 1971, chiefly in one Midwest city. We have prepared a detailed study of specific examples (Gerlach and Hine 1973: 261–293), but even this does little more than hint at the rich array of experiments which now exist. Any list of specific examples or even of different types of exploration will quickly be made obsolete by new growth and early demise.

There are experiments in intergenerational living, communal and group living, interracial understanding, varying forms of marriage and divorce, family and community organization, and sexual behavior. People are learning about the benefits and problems of living in tight corporate communities and in structures approximating to the extended family. Others are experiencing the advantages and difficulties of trial marriage and temporary liaison. Some fairly straight Middle Americans are capitalizing on the sexual revolution to have swinging fun and games while otherwise opting to maintain the established order. Young people and those of middle age are contemplating the misery which we inflict on our "senior citizens" and, perhaps realizing that such misery is not in their own future interests, a few are trying to break through into new ways of intergenerational interaction.

In political organization, social control and law, there are experiments in community control, public or open hearings and planning on a wide range of crucial subjects, and police-community interaction. There are experiments in legal clinics, free legal services, "people's lawyers," and the like. There are attempts to help people find their way through the bureaucratic tangle of the system to secure their rights. This often overlaps with medical service experiments, for some groups concentrate on helping individuals secure medical service within the conventional medical system. There are attempts to change the way prisoners are treated and to help reintegrate convicts in the community. There are also experiments in establishing community "moots" to handle disputes by discussion among peers instead of by turning the problem over to the established system.

In the provision of medical services we observe new free clinics, community cooperative clinics and the like, manned by interns, medical students, ex-military paramedics, midwives, and a few doctors. These are mainly attempts to rehumanize medicine and improve the structure of medical services. A particular purpose is to give service to poorer people who do not live within Middle America. From this designs can emerge which could help all Americans. A few of these new clinics or "people's medicals" are helping women during childbirth and then not recording the birth. Hence the child will grow up outside the records and the cognizance of the bureaucratic system. This presumably appeals chiefly to life-style radicals and to those seeking a fundamental alternative to living within the system.

Some change-motivated medics and doctors dispense the simplest medicine which can accomplish a cure rather than trying the newest and most powerful drugs. Some stress the use of herbs and "natural" or folk remedies. At least one is experimenting with acupuncture.[3] In short, a few medical practitioners are not only seeking to make conventional Western medicine work better for the public but are operating outside the conceptual framework of Western medicine. While many conventional practitioners may dismiss this as "going back," others may be motivated to observe results and also experiment.

In the economic sphere considerable innovative discussion is under way about such revolutionary concepts as equilibrium and the no-growth economy, sharing limited world resources, the anticipated demise of the work ethic, etc. The whole system of the profit-maximizing, market economy is being questioned as perhaps never before. Side by side with such assaults on conventional wisdom, there are experiments in new economic organization. We find people, especially younger ones, working for limited periods only to accomplish specific purposes — that is, target labor. We see proliferating production and sale of handicrafts, often on a target labor basis. Craft guilds are helping to guide this production and establish "fair prices." We have noted experiments in cooperative food buying and selling. "People's plumbers and carpenters" will come to help communards repair their dwellings or, better still, teach them how to do the repairs themselves. At the other extreme, new types of entrepreneurship are providing service to Middle America. Industry is being brought to open more of its planning and management to public review and participation and to consider its responsibilities to the public and the environment. New structures of consumer advocacy are spinning off from the Nader model.

There are many experiments which seek to revitalize religion, reduce church bureaucracy, and enhance experience. Some seek to make religious services more meaningful and emotional, and to involve participants in deep religious experience. Others seek new ways of providing religious services to communities of students, life-style radicals, drop-outs, or drug users. Perhaps more ministers than ever are now going into the streets, living in the non-Middle-American communities they wish to serve. There are also attempts to involve religion in fighting for social justice and a living environment. And there are continuing experiments in the establishment of religion-based communes. Some religious exploration is well apart from the conventional Judeo-Christian order.

A myriad of experiments in education proliferate across the country. We have mentioned the development of new community intern programs and environmental study projects in our research city which lead

---

[3] In 1971 this was considered quite a radical departure; its wide acceptance now shows how quickly an idea can be assimilated and spread.

to close examination of corporate responsibility and to models for growth or equilibrium. These involve students, many of them radicals, as well as members of interface groups and representatives of business and industry. Universities, colleges, and now high schools are experimenting in "living-learning" projects. Some involve faculty, students, and administration in new community education and assistance projects. Controversy and conflict relating to busing, pairing, and radical new education have aroused whole communities to take a deeper interest in the structure and purpose of schools, which has led to yet other experiments in education. Movements have generated free schools, free universities, often focusing on the student's right to study what interests him instead of what an educational bureaucracy has decided is proper. The established educational order has responded by generating its own versions of open and innovative education geared to the student's objectives. We can expect that expanding new multimedia technology will contribute to further experiments in education, including learning at home using "talk-back" cable TV and video cassettes. There is considerable fermentation in adult and community education. Intergenerational, integrated education is an idea being translated into experiment.

Characteristically we have expected that technology would be the chief locus of innovation and revolutionary change. But technology is now subject to more doubts than ever. People are exploring new ways to "humanize" it, and make it the servant, not the master of society. Some experiments in interdisciplinary environmental quality laboratories may reflect this. On the other hand, people are demanding quick technological solutions to complex problems so that they will not have to change their life-styles. Perhaps the use of new audiovisual technology will have great impact on experiments in community management, education, etc. We have already noted that members of some communes speak of using the most advanced technology to save the environment of their communes. Undergrounds within the engineering and technology professions are attempting to make these more responsive to the public, more concerned with the environmental consequences of their actions, and more humane. This generates exploration into the meaning of concepts such as "humane," and "public responsibility" and "environmental quality."

Undergrounds within the architecture and city planning professions are seeking to develop new, ecologically sound, and socially appropriate patterns of land use, residence, and rural and urban structure. Some have already generated innovative plans for experiment. We have mentioned the Experimental City Project which is an attempt by community leaders, scholars, businessmen, and government representatives to build a city of the future from the ground up. This project has attracted the support and help of some life-style radicals.

There are experiments galore in communication. In the mid-sixties it appeared that soon there would be only a few newspapers and magazines in the United States, and that many of these would be controlled by the monopolies which controlled TV and radio. But by 1970, the big news everywhere was the explosive growth of the underground press and the proliferation of underground papers, pamphlets, and magazines. Black power intellectuals were among the first in the United States to declare that those desiring change must gain access to the multimedia by which public beliefs are molded. Where they could not infiltrate the established media, they published their own papers. Subsequently, movement whites also proclaimed the need for new avenues of information as alternatives or counters to the system. They started to write and publish. Several underground papers, representing diverse movement interests, were published in the city of our research, and, of course, similar papers from other parts of the country were distributed. Side by side came the publication of innovative guidebooks or handbooks for change, such as the nationally distributed *Journal of Vocations for (Social) Change, The Whole Earth Catalogue, The Mother Earth News,* and *The Foundation Journal.* A few change-oriented middle-class and upper-middle-class adult Americans have published speciality newsletters to discuss public issues and provide people with a more neutral forum for expressing their ideas and grievances.

Underground movies and now underground or alternative videotaping and radio provide audiovisual sources which begin to challenge what Gene Youngblood (1970) has called "the perceptual imperialism" of the established order. Such growing multimedia capabilities contribute substantially to communication about the presence of various sociocultural experiments or alternatives now permeating our system. Rate of communication should positively affect the rate of reproduction and selective adaptation. What is questionable is the degree of accuracy about what works and what does not in these communications. Various perceptual filters probably influence evaluations. For one thing, participants in movements of change feel that they are more successful than would be agreed by observers or opponents of such movements. This has the tendency to generate more action and give a feeling of greater confidence in the outcome.

New methods were developed to distribute books and pamphlets across movement networks. People were also encouraged to ignore copyright and reproduce useful papers, essays, and the like, and then to distribute them locally. Gary Snyder distributed his "Four Changes" essay (1969) in this way. Movements capitalized on the expanding photocopy technology.

Man-environment explorations have sparked many innovations. We see experiments in pollution fighting and environment enhancement.

Carpooling, recycling, open planning in power plant and jetport siting, life-style change advocacy, are all examples.

Ecology issues are usually so complex, involving so many diverse interests and groups in conflict and so many interacting system factors, that the problems cannot really be resolved by simple trade-offs, compromises, or a clean victory in a law court. We suspect that, while such difficulties may cause some people to lose heart and cease trying, in the long run they may produce the most interesting and significant experiments in strategies for human survival.

The reader will have his own opinions about these experiments: their feasibility, potential impact, and the like. He can estimate the extent to which any, or all of them, will proliferate and become a significant or dominant form in our future. We anticipate a varied fate for them. Many will burst into prominence, stimulate intense effort by participants for a time, then fade away, to be supplanted sometimes by a similar activity. Some will indeed be copied over and over, or will divide into many "sister" cells. A few will have major impact.

Unlike *Tuparts Monthly Review*, we do not believe that these experiments constitute any kind of conspiracy to overthrow the established order. Indeed, as we have indicated, the established order interacts with movements to produce many of the experiments. Movement participants themselves would probably find many of the examples which we have listed counterrevolutionary, or simply patch-and-repair efforts to keep the established system going. And we certainly do not feel that these experiments at present combine to form a single alternative lifeway system. Instead, they constitute many mini-alternatives, experiments which greatly increase our cultural and social diversity.

Perhaps they will remain mere additions, often less important than established patterns. They will give Americans more options for action, involvement, and conceptualization, and perhaps in this way they will enable the mainstream to roll along basically unchanged. Perhaps the real revolution is that we shall have a sociocultural system composed of many diverse options and elements, some of which seem mutually incompatible in conventional logic. On the other hand, the real revolution may be yet to come, and these mutations and experiments provide the genes from which a new species will emerge under the pressure of selective adaptation. Energy-growth-scarcity issues seem likely to provide the stress under which adaptation will occur.[4]

---

[4] Events since 1971 and 1974, when I first made and then revised this prognosis, have affirmed its accuracy. Since 1972 my assistants and I have been conducting research on social action relating to energy and resource problems. The outcome indicates that the processes of change that are described in this essay for the civil rights, antiwar, religious and ecology movements, continue as citizens mobilize to protest against and/or seek control over the impacts of energy and water development or the shortages and rising costs of these resources. It also shows that such resource

Research is required to determine the extent to which people can live continually with marked diversity, some of them moving from one world to another and back again: "poly-people" in a multifaceted system, protean people (Lifton, 1967) continually choosing among a profusion of alternatives, a variety of life-styles, and granting others a similar right. Our hunch is that while people can live with considerable diversity, we will find that the various alternatives and experiments we have mentioned synthesize in time into a less diverse entity. In any event, we feel that the United States can now be termed an exploring society, exploring into its future, generating the design for that future through trial and error. What appears to be its time of troubles may only be its time of discovery and transformation. Exploration and trial-and-error experiments by many people in many different ways provide us with a better, more innovative, and certainly safer way of finding our future than would following a few leaders.

REFERENCES

ALSOP, STEWART
1970   "Radical chic is dead." *Newsweek* 76(24): 120.
ASIMOV, ISAAC
1970   *The foundation.* New York: Avon.
BEALS, ALAN R.
1966   *Divisiveness and social conflict: an anthropological approach.* Stanford, California: Stanford University Press.
BOULDING, KENNETH
1964   *The meaning of the twentieth century.* New York: Harper and Row.
BRAUN, MICHAEL A., DAVID J. LEE
1971   Private police forces: legal powers and limitations. *University of Chicago Law Review* 38: 555–582.
COHEN, FAY G.
1973   "The Indian patrol in Minneapolis: social control and social change in an urban context." Unpublished Ph.D dissertation, University of Minnesota, Minneapolis.
ECKSTEIN, HARRY, editor
1964   *Internal war, problems and approaches.* Glencoe, New York: Free Press.
FANON, FRANTZ
1966   *The wretched of the earth.* New York: Grove Press.
FORRESTER, JAY. W.
1971a The counter-intuitive behavior of social systems. *Technology Review Journal.*

development and citizen mobilization generate new systems of socioeconomic interdependence which in turn create a new level and a new kind of social political organization transcending established and local political boundaries and central governments. We have described movement organization as segmentary, polycentric and integrated through networks, or SPIN, and it seems that such SPIN organization is superceding centralized government as resource developers, citizen resistors, and established political institutions adapt to these energy problems (Gerlach and Palmer, 1978).

1971b *World dynamics.* Cambridge: Wright-Allen Press.
FULLER, R. BUCKMINSTER
1970 *Operating manual for Spaceship Earth.* New York: Pocket Books.
GEERTZ, CLIFFORD
1963 *Agricultural involution: the processes of ecological change in Indonesia.* Berkeley: Published for the Association of Asian Studies by University of California Press.
GERLACH, LUTHER P.
1970a "Participatory ecology: an embryonic social movement to improve the quality of man's environment." Mimeographed paper prepared for the Research 1980 Planning Conference, University of Minnesota, February 1970.
1970b "The social organization of a movement of revolutionary change: case study black power," in *Afro-American anthropology: contemporary perspectives.* Edited by N. Whitten, Jr. and J. Szed. New York: Free Press.
1978 The great energy stand-off. *Natural History.* January.
GERLACH, LUTHER P., VIRGINIA H. HINE
1970a You and ecology. *Natural History.* June.
1970b Wit, wisdom and woe. *Natural History.* October.
1970c Many concerned, few committed. *Natural History.* December.
1970d *People, power, change.* Indianapolis: Bobbs Merrill.
1973 *Lifeway leap: the dynamics of change in America.* Minneapolis: University of Minnesota Press.
GERLACH, LUTHER P., GARY B. PALMER
1978 "Global adaptation through evolving interdependence," in *Handbook of organizational design.* Edited by William Starbuck. New York: Elsevier/North Holland.
GURR, TED
1967 *The conditions of civil violence.* Princeton: Center of International Studies
HACKER, ANDREW
1970 *The end of the American era.* New York: Atheneum.
HAGEN, E. E.
1962 *On the theory of social change: how economic growth begins.* Homewood, Illinois: The Dorsey Press.
HOFFER, ERIC
1963 *The ordeal of change* New York: Harper and Row.
1965 *The true believer.* New York: Harper and Row.
HUNT, MORTON, PAUL ANDERSON
1971 The future of marriage. *Playboy* 18(8): 116–18, 168–75.
HURLEY, NEIL
1969 "The open society city." Unpublished papers prepared for the Minnesota Experimental City Project, Minneapolis, Minnesota.
JOHNSON, CHALMERS
1966 *Revolutionary change.* Boston: Little, Brown and Company.
KAHN, HERMAN, ANTHONY WEINER
1967 *The year 2000: a framework for speculation on the next 33 years.* Introduction by Daniel Bell, with contributions from staff members of the Hudson Institute. New York: Macmillan.
KNOPF, TERRY ANN
1969 *Youth patrols: an experiment in community participation.* Waltham, Mass. Brandeis University.

KUHN, THOMAS
1962 *Structure of scientific revolutions.* Chicago: University of Chicago Press.
LANTERNARI, VITTORIO
1963 *The religions of the oppressed.* Translated by Lisa Sergio. New York: Knopf.
LIFTON, ROBERT J.
1967 *Boundaries: psychological man in revolution.* New York: Random House.
LINTON, RALPH
1943 Nativistic movements. *American Anthropologist* 45: 230–40.
Los Angeles Times
1971 Article in *Los Angeles Times*, 25 October.
McLUHAN, MARSHALL
1960 "Introduction," in *Exploration and communication.* Edited by Edward Carpenter and Marshall McLuhan. Boston: Beacon Press.
MARUYAMA, MAGOROH
1965 The second cybernetics: deviation-amplifying mutual causal processes. *American Scientist* 51(2): 164–179.
MASLOW, ABRAHAM
1964 *Religion, values and peak experiences.* Columbus: Ohio State University Press.
1966 *The psychology of science.* New York: Harper and Row.
1968 A theory of metamotivation: the biological rooting of the value of life. *Psychology Today* 2: 38–39, 59–61.
MEADOWS, DONELLA H., *et al.*
1972 *The limits to growth.* New York: The New American Library.
MEANS, RICHARD L.
1969 New conservation. *Natural History* 78(4): 16ff, August.
New Yorker
1971 Commune information: the people's information center, Brooklyn, volume 47: 32. October 16.
REICH, CHARLES
1970 *The greening of America.* New York: Bantam.
REVEL, JEAN-FRANCOIS
1971 *Without Marx or Jesus.* New York: Doubleday.
ROSTOW, W. W.
1971 *The stages of economic growth.* New York: Cambridge University Press.
SERVICE, ELMAN R.
1971 *Cultural evolutionism: theory in practice.* New York: Holt, Rinehart and Winston.
SKINNER, B. F.
1960 *Walden two.* New York: Macmillan.
1971 *Beyond freedom and dignity.* New York: Alfred A. Knopf.
SMITH, PRESERVED
1966 *The age of reformation,* volume one. New York: Collier.
SNYDER, GARY
1969 "Four changes." Mimeographed paper.
TOFFLER, ALVIN
1971 *Future shock.* New York: Bantam.
U.S. NATIONAL ADVISORY COMMISSION ON CIVIL DISORDERS
1968 *Kerner Commission report.* Introduction by Tom Wicker. New York: Dutton.

VON NEUMANN, JOHN
  1956   "Probabilistic logics and the synthesis of reliable organisms from
         unreliable components," in *Automata studies*. Edited by C. E. Shan-
         non and J. McCarthy. Princeton: Princeton University Press.
WALLACE, ANTHONY F. C.
  1956   Revitalization movements. *American Anthropologist* 58: 264–281.
YOUNGBLOOD, GENE
  1970   *Expanded cinema*. New York: E. P. Dutton.

Familism and the Creation of Futures

ELISE BOULDING

SPECIAL CHARACTERISTICS OF THE FAMILY AS AN AGENT OF SOCIAL CHANGE

The family is normally thought of as an instrument for the maintenance of social stability, as primarily a conserving social institution. It is perfectly possible, however, to look at it as an agent of potentially revolutionary social change. This paper will examine those transcultural properties of the family that lead to changes in other social institutions, and also the trends in the patterning of the family itself as a social group.

The family group has a unique relation to the future for two reasons. First, owing to the age span of its members, it is a cluster of representatives of different population cohorts who have been exposed to historically different social stimuli at comparable ages. Thus, each cohort representative will have a different sense of what is "possible" in social happenings. Second, the family as a unit is continually in transition from one stage of its life cycle to the next, so no one role constellation works for very long. The family can therefore *never* be in equilibrium. It is useful to think of family life as consisting of a swiftly moving series of identity crises as members of various ages with cohort-specific life experiences engage, more or less effectively, in anticipatory socialization for new roles. The sum of these individual crises is greater than the constituent parts, since the image of the family as a whole in the minds of its members is also subject to this set of identity crises. The preschooler who faces the crisis of becoming a kindergartner has parents who face the crisis of narrowing horizons that hits adults in their late twenties when the future no longer seems wide open, and grandparents who are facing the crisis of retirement.

The teen-ager who faces the crisis of taking a role inside one of the many subsets of cultures and countercultures available to him in his late teens has parents who face both the "empty nest" crisis and the crisis of unrealized aspirations as the zenith of career activities is passed. At the same time, his grandparents face the crisis of no longer being healthy enough to be able to live independently. Needless to say, the image of the family as a whole will be different for each of these persons.

Pick any member of a family and focus on the particular identity crisis that he or she is moving into or out of, and you can trace a whole constellation of different yet concurrent identity crises for every other member of the family. The sum of these provides the family setting for the coping behavior in which each engages. In addition to the internally generated crises that stem from bio-social aging and individual bio-social pathologies, there are the externally triggered crises that may result in unemployment, separation, injury, and death of family members. One of the strangest mythologies in contemporary family sociology is that of the family as a psychological and physical haven from the pressures of social change in the outside world. The rate of change of role behaviors within the family, and the continual uncertainty about what responses to expect from other family members because of life-cycle-triggered role changes, makes the family a confusing setting for its members from start to finish.

Fortunately, the identity crises which people go through do not make them unrecognizable to one another, so there are constants as well as variables, and the group culture created by every family unit that exists for some time provides a pattern for the variations and some security and stability for individual members. But, by focusing on the continual shifts in required role performance and the accompanying identity crises, we can see the family as a workshop in social change instead of as a guarantor of social order.

Since people are undergoing similar role changes in the non-family settings in which they perform daily, the fact of individual growth and change is not in itself a unique property of the family. What is unique, however, is that only in the family are people intimately confronting role changes in others widely removed from their own age grade. Thus, the family setting continually prods individuals to locate themselves in space and time in relation to other family members. Thus, parents gain a special awareness of their past as their offspring enact childhood in the historical present, and a special awareness of their future as their parents move into old-age roles. Since the enacted childhood of their children is quite different from their recollected childhood because of the impact of changing technology and culture, children can teach their parents about the nature of ongoing social change through the attitudes and role behaviors they adopt. At the same time, the "traditional" parental role of socializing children into acceptable behavior in the adult world goes on. But this traditional socialization, more easily recognized in societies with slower rates of change, is only a small part of the learning that goes on in the family. In reality, every family member is participating in the resocialization of every other — from the youngest sibling to the oldest grandparent or great-grandparent — as different interpretation of social reality confront one another the family setting. The dynamics of this mutual resocialization may be masked by an authoritarian structure in which older members of a family refuse to give overt recognition to the differing perceptions of younger members, but even then a covert resocialization is going on.

The wide age span of members and the shifting medley of role behaviors are characteristics of all types of family groupings in all societies, regardless of culture-specific definitions of kin structures. Exposure to the very old and to the very young may not take place under the same roof, but within some type of visiting-kin network. Extended family networks may be more visible in some societies than in others, but they are present even in societies where people are as acutely obsessed with the nuclear family phenomenon as in the United States.

These structure-specific characteristics of households give a special quality to other basic human behaviors when they take place in the family setting. The capacity for social bonding fostered by the nurturing responsibilities of adults for each other and for children can expand into a rich repertoire of empathic and caring behavior when a high value is set on nurturing. By the same token, this repertoire may be severely restricted in societies that do not set a high value on nurturing. The multi-age group, however, provides the optimal setting for learning to give and receive love, since many styles of response, partly dependent on physical and emotional maturation, are interacting and mutually freeing each other.

Similarly, the play instinct finds its first expression in the family setting. The family is the first "play community." If play is indeed about the ultimately serious work of culture creation, as Huizinga describes in *Homo Ludens* (1950), then culture creation begins in the family group. If describing the family as a play community rings hollow in an era of suburban household misery and high divorce rates, it must be remembered that we are looking at transcultural features of the family which are more or less evident in all cultures and eras.

The skills, social bonding, and creative play developed through intimate interaction with others of different chronological ages and social experience, in a situation of patterned instability created by the constant identity crises of family members, can become, in the right historical circumstances, a powerful capacity for envisioning alternative futures and for creating them. What then are "the right historical circumstances?"

THE FAMILY IN SPECIFIC HISTORICAL CONTEXTS

There have been historical eras when the future has seemed wide open, when the human capacity to envision "the other," the totally different society, has flowered in a profusion of images of divine-human utopias. Sometimes God appears as the main designer, sometimes man, and sometimes the two are seen as partners in creation. I have discussed elsewhere in this volume Fred Polak's work on the image of the future (Polak 1961) which traces the interaction between the image of the future and the dynamics of the ongoing social process in the present. Polak analyzes the different qualities that images of the future have in different eras, depending on the balance of utopian and eschatological elements in the prevailing thought of each era.

Polak gives less attention to the process by which images of the future are generated than to the effects of the images once created. I am suggesting here that the family is potentially a powerful contributor to the generation of alternative images of the future because of the unique combination of experiences it offers the individuals growing up within its boundaries. In the "quiet" periods of history, the times of relative stability when few demands are made on the adaptive capacities of individuals or groups, or in periods of severe repression, the futures-creating capacities of the family may remain undeveloped. In periods of rapid social change, when each age group represented in the household has experienced critically different stimuli and pressures from the larger society at comparable ages, the futures-creating capacities of the family may become highly developed if the social bond is strong. We are accustomed to thinking of periods of rapid social change as periods of weak family bonds with high rates of dissolution. Historically, however, there have always been identifiable subcultures in such eras of flux in which family-like groups have exhibited extraordinary intrafamily stability and acted as change agents on the society around them.

In a recent international discussion on education for a peaceful alternative society,[1] a participant said that for a hundred years preceding the French Revolution, household groupings in France were continual seminars on social change, as parents, grandparents, and chil-

---

[1] International Peace Research Association Biennial Congress, Bled, Yugoslavia, October 1971.

dren of the more educated classes discussed and argued with servants, craftsmen, and peasants, in both rural and urban settings, about possible features of a new equalitarian society. It was this passionate intellectual interaction in household settings, reenforced by other social bonds, which made the ferment of new ideas about society such a powerful one. Specific subcultures such as the Huguenots in France, pietistic sects such as the Family of Love and the Brethren of the Common Life in Germany, and later the Methodists and Quakers in England, were all organized around a strongly bonded family life with solid traditions of transgenerational communication.

Clarkson's *Portraiture of Quakerism* (1800) gives a delightful contemporary picture of seventeenth-century Quakers, whose chief recreation, according to the author was "domestic bliss." That domestic bliss, however, produced children who, at a very early age, were able to carry on the social revolution while their parents were in jail — as they frequently were. The first generation of Quakers in the late 1600's included a number of twelve- to fourteen-year-olds such as the gifted James Darnell among their public preachers (Homan 1931). Although many of the subcultures mentioned happen to be religious, the spheres of activity for which members of these groups are historically noted are economic and political, and closely linked to the Industrial Revolution as well as to the political restructuring that led to a more equalitarian society in England and on the Continent (see Raistrick [1968] for an account of the role of Quakers in the Industrial Revolution).

Although Nonconformists were disfranchised until the 1830's, Nonconformist sects throughout England worked in various ways from the 1660's on for the abolition of poverty and the removal of social inequalities (Jorns 1931). After political enfranchisement, figures like the Quaker, John Bright, brought a nonstatist essentially anarchist approach to both national and international affairs into the House of Commons as he worked for the removal of the coercive privileges of the Crown and aristocracy.

Similarly the Cultural Revolution in the People's Republic of China must be traced back to the student generation of which Mao Tse Tung was a part. This group, when they became parents, taught their children to be revolutionaries; their parents had in turn brought them up in a tradition of peasant and intellectual radicalism that goes back a long way in Chinese history.

Today, in the United States young radical parents, black and white, are systematically teaching their children to be the constructors of the new society from a very early age (*Village Voice* 1971). The children's liberation movement which is sweeping some elementary schools in our larger cities under pre-teen-age leadership, cannot be understood apart from the family settings in which these children have been nurtured.[2]

The illustrations given here provide at least a hint that, if we look at any period of rapid social change, we will probably find certain subcultures that nurture strong family-like groupings which, in turn, produce powerful change agents operating out of the double context of the family bond and a special community solidarity. It is no accident that parental training for revolutionary change occurs chiefly in special subculture settings, since a powerful reenforcement is needed to enable parents to engage systematically in new types of behavior themselves, and present new patterns to their children. Parents who were trying to raise their children as pacifists in Europe and the United States in the forties know how important a community of reference was in giving courage to them and to their children in the face of the hostility of the larger society.

TYPES OF FAMILY-LIKE GROUPINGS

By using terms like "household" and "family-like grouping" in the previous sections I have skirted the issue of defining the family in terms of specific membership patterns. The whole debate about whether the nuclear family is the basic unit in all societies seems to me largely irrelevant in the face of the great variety of household patterns we find in different societies and within any one society at a given time. This variety is found at all levels of social complexity, and at various levels of industrialization. Rather than positing one optimal size and configuration for the universal family, as Levy (1965) does, or an evolutionary sequence from extended to nuclear family as Parsons (Parsons and Bales 1955), and others do, I suggest that each society has an optimal household size, including some variant of an extended-kin network suited to its particular type of socioeconomic and political organization, given conditions of relative stability. In times of rapid change or catastrophe, this size will shrink (or expand) to maximize its adaptive potential. With the return of relative stability, the family will either return to the old optimum or establish a new one.

For purposes of this paper, I will have to bypass the knotty problem of providing an operational definition of "optimal size" in any given situation. I suggest, however, that the optimal size includes, in addition to the nuclear family, some type of functioning extended-kin network. If we accept Litwak's definition of the family (1964) as the social institution best able to cope with idiosyncratic events, particularly in a

---

[2]   For further references see Boulding (1975).

complex, highly bureaucratized society, it is clear that society as such is too much either for the single individual *or* the isolated nuclear family to cope with.

The complex network of help-giving institutions in modern society, designed to assist the family to function, is in itself so complicated and demanding, that individuals and families need the cushioning effect of extended-kin ties, either biological or fictional, to protect them from excessive outside pressures.

The family, as a household group responsible for (at the least) the physical nurture of its members, can be thought of as a continuum from the single isolated householder to a multigeneration cluster of household groupings that may consist of biologically related individuals culturally defined as an extended family, or of a voluntary association of individuals living as an extended family. To emphasize the common factor between the culturally defined, extended family and the household as a voluntary association, I will use the term "expanded family" to cover both.[3] Ron Roberts's book *The new communes* (1971), quotes from the brochure of a New York City organization, calling itself the "Expanded Family," for a defininition of this term. The expanded family

> ... can be simply a close friendship of trust and respect; it may be a convenient symbiotic arrangement involving shared outings, some mutual baby-sitting and perhaps a shared vacation .... It can involve friends who rent apartments in the same building, friends who set up home together, or it can be a fully-fledged commune or a group marriage (Roberts 1971).

This same range of potential, shared functions can be found in the biologically based extended family, including the features of group marriage in those (admittedly rare) extended families that practice incest. Ranged along our continuum, then, are the following general types: (1) the one-person household; (2) informal couple arangements of varying degrees of permanency, with or without children; (3) the nuclear family with a more or less active kin network; and (4) the expanded family.

Note that Roberts's definition of the expanded family includes a variety of combinations of adults and children in one or more houses, with many or few domestic functions. No hard-and-fast line can be drawn between the expanded family and the intentional community, in which individuals and families share a common tract of land and have a

---

[3] The distinction between the biologically based extended family and the fictional extended family is not really a tenable one, of course. As Lloyd Fallers (1965) points out, many societies create fictionalized kin structures. He mentions the Jie of Africa, who maintain permanent lineage systems of equal size over time simply by fictionally regrouping individuals to correspond with their ideal lineage system.

well-defined mutual purpose beyond that of shared maintenance functions.

My hypothesis about the cyclical expansion and contraction of familistic groupings according to the exigencies of the times, within some overall parameters of optimal size for a given society, implies that any given society will have experienced various household patterns at different historical stages. It further implies that there is nothing historically unique about either the isolate householder or the expanded family experiments of the twentieth century.

A quick look at European history shows first the small-family groupings of nomadic tribes such as those of Gaul and then the small freeman landholder and his family. Each of these was superseded by the large-family system of early feudal society from the ninth to the eleventh century. The large-family system, embedded in the family-like superstructure of feudalism, developed because the individual freeman could not protect his family from continual attacks by maurauding bands such as the seafaring Norsemen.

The large-family system was gradually whittled away as a result of the population explosion that followed increased agricultural production during the relative social peace from the eleventh century on. People driven off the land provided an urban labor pool that led to economic boom for the merchants and unemployment for the masses. The result was the alternation of economic and social advances with the wildly disruptive mass movements that characterized medieval Europe. Henri Pirenne (1956) has given a vivid description of the crowds of footloose vagabonds who drifted through Europe, available for adventure in war, trade, or politics, in the era which ushered in the Crusades. These isolates were not only cut off from the traditional rural family household, but even from the possibility of independent nuclear family life in the city. We are indebted to Philippe Aries (1965) for descriptions of family life in medieval France. He points out that by the fifteenth century, married workers in urban centers, if they were lucky, were housed dormitory-style in the homes of their employers. Privacy was nonexistent, for rich or poor. In the "big houses" of the rich, beds were put up at night, taken down by day, in rooms overflowing with people twenty-four hours a day. For those not so quartered, there were tiny, often windowless rooms for married couples and the youngest of their children. No traditional nurturance functions took place in these rooms — even meals were taken at taverns. Visiting took place in the village square. Infants were sent to wet nurses when possible, and children put out to apprenticeships at the age of seven.

The impossibility of drawing social boundaries around a familistic grouping, even the nuclear family, for the urban masses in this period of European history staggers the modern imagination. With increasing (relative) prosperity, as Europe moved toward the Industrial Revolution, the reaction against the enforced loss of privacy of the early Middle Ages took some interesting forms. Not only was the private, extended family reinvented by the more affluent middle and upper classes, but many urban communal ventures were undertaken, sometimes under church auspices. Marc Bloch describes communal households of up to 200 persons organized on a voluntary basis in his *Feudal society* (1961). Many women's communes such as the beguinages were established for single working women who wished to live free of harassment in an urban setting (perhaps the forerunners of today's women's lib communes).

A proliferation of religious and secular utopian communes and communities characterized Europe in the sixteenth and seventeenth centuries. Eighteenth-century affluence led to an emphasis on biological expanded families, and to an accompanying decline in these communes, but the nineteenth and twentieth centuries have each seen a new wave of expanded family ventures. Each new wave of expanded family experiments has, on the one hand, been related to periods of social and economic upheaval, particularly economic depressions (this point is emphasized in Nordhoff 1965), and has in turn had a creative impact on the larger society.[4] This impact has taken the form of agricultural or technological innovation in some cases, of models for subsequent social welfare legislation or educational practice in others. A systematic study of the contributions of expanded family experiments to economic and social innovation has yet to be undertaken, but the flavor of the type of contribution made can be got from reading Frank Manuel's *Utopias and utopian thought* (1965).

THE CHANGE POTENTIAL IN CONTEMPORARY FAMILY-LIKE GROUPINGS

Drawing a parallel with the experience of Europe from the Middle Ages through the Industrial Revolution, we can see that (in a highly compressed sequence) the United States has moved through a period of early industrial urbanism, characterized by a substantial immigrant influx of single householders and nuclear families living isolated, yet deprivatized lives. Thomas and Znaniecki's *Polish peasant* (1927) provides the classic documentation of this. The retreat to the privacy of the modified extended family has taken pathological forms in American suburbia not (yet) observed in Europe, probably because of

---

[4] The communes studied by Nordhoff in some detail are the Shakers, Rappists, and Zoarites.

unique affluence levels in the United States. This retreat has been
paralleled, however, by two waves of communal ventures. The first
began in the early nineteenth century and was largely religiously
motivated.[5] The second, largely secular wave began in the twenties,
took a new start in the late forties after World War II, as young men
released from conscientious objector camps and their families decided
to create alternatives to a society they had rejected, and has a new
impetus today in the communes started out of the civil rights movement in the sixties.

The family-like experiments of the twenties and forties got very little
attention, partly because they were undertaken by a very tiny and not
very visible minority.[6] Today's experiments possibly get more attention
than they warrant, but in terms of social impact their significance is not
small.

How do these experimental expanded families fit into the total
picture of the family in the United States today, and what do they offer
for the future? No one knows the exact proportion of Americans living
in communal ventures of various kinds, but the figure is probably well
below one-half of one percent. It has been estimated that approximately a million and a half people move in and out of the "straight"
world. One thing social scientists have established through trend
analysis is that, in general, social change at the level of the macrosys-
tem is glacially slow. Changes in the age at marriage, number of
children born, divorce rates, remarriage rates, and frequency of ex-
tramarital sex may in the short run be subject to apparently abrupt
fluctuations, but in the long run they smooth out into steady trends.
System breaks and trend reversals occur, but not often (see, for
example, the trend charts in Boulding and Trainer 1971).

It has frequently been remarked that contemporary Americans are
the most marriage prone people in the world. Parsons pointed out in
1956 that the United States had the largest number of persons of
marriageable age, who had never been widowed, living with their
spouses and children ever recorded in the history of the country
(Parsons 1971). If the divorce rate is rising, so is the remarriage rate.
While it is true that the age of marriage is no longer dropping, but has
started rising again, the fondness for marriage will not disappear
quickly from the American scene. The best prediction about the

[5] This first wave of communal experiments does not fit the reaction-to-urbanism
model, since many European immigrants went straight into these communities without
intermediate urban experience in the United States. To the extent that Euro-North
America needs to be treated as a geo-historical unit, however, the phenomenon fits the
model.
[6] Some idea of the family base of the ventures in the twenties can be gained from
Charles Chatfield (1971). Staughton Lynd (1966) also gives some clues to these developments.

families of tomorrow is that they will be like the families of today. That, however, is not a very interesting prediction. Moreover, in the light of my own hypothesis about expanding and contracting household groupings, it is not likely to be true. We have been in a stage of contracted nuclear households and we are probably moving toward an expansion, if not of household size, at least of shared services and facilities.

Who will be the initiators of such change? In general, Middle America is very aware of the existence of the hip community, and sees in the lice-infested crash pads of urban centers and the higgledy-piggledy structures and equipment of the farm communes, a nightmare of a deteriorating society in which communal sex and drug orgies replace the orderly family routine of suburbia. Those who are experimenting with nonconformist approaches to family-like living can be divided into two groups.

One is the *reactive.* The reactors are the hippie dropouts and street people who leave school, jobs, and parental homes and wander from crash pad to crash pad, commune to commune. The reactors are middle-class young people protesting against what they feel are false social relationships at every level from the family to the public/civic sphere. It has been estimated that about half of these dropouts return to the straight world after intense communal and drug experiences. They cut their hair, marry, and live in arty middle-class houses. They usually have positive feelings about their dropout years and feel the experiences made them more appreciative of the middle-class world. Many who do not return to the straight world are probably permanently downwardly mobile and will drift into the cracks of society.

The other group of experimenters can be called the *creatively alienated.* Their response to the shortcomings of an affluent and insensitive society is to make a long-range commitment to building an alternative one. These creators may be found side by side in the same communes with the reactors, but they will be part of an identifiably creative core, never at the margins. If one looks at the life histories of the creatively alienated who founded the communities of the forties, one sees that in the middle years of life these men and women are still creating new social forms and new movements in educational systems or in economic and political structures.[7]

Looking ahead to the family forms of the future, then, we must not expect substantial changes to come from the reactor-dropouts. These young people will either be back in the mainstream or will form part of the permanently drifting subculture that every society supports to some

---

[7] A follow-up study on the communards of the forties really is needed. An outstanding representative of these communards is David Dellinger, the only member of that generation to stand trial with the famous Chicago Seven in 1969.

degree. The creatively alienated are a likelier source of long-term alternative family forms.

Which of today's subcultures are producing tomorrow's social forms? Eight may be briefly mentioned. There is the white liberal subculture that produced a cohort of creatively dissenting young people who moved from the civil rights movement of the early sixties through various protest movements into a variety of experiments in new politics, alternative schools, communal living, and community building. Then there are the ethnic subcultures, including black, Chicano, Amerindian, and Amerasian. Each of these subcultures is producing some young people with distinctive family life-styles that are self-consciously different from the middle-class Anglo style, and with a commitment to social change consonant with this distinctive style.

The red power, brown power, yellow power, and black power movements, while each contains enormous internal diversity, have a common identifiable thrust toward the development of viable family patterns for the future that draw on their respective strengths from the past. In each case this involves some concept of the expanded family. The concept of community for each of these groups is somewhat different from the middle-class Anglo concept of community, often involving a tighter integration of the family in the life of the subculture community.

The women's movement in the United States dating from the early 1800's has produced a weak but identifiable subculture that is now taking on new life through the women's liberation movement. The contribution of this movement to the restructuring of the family is in the direction of removing traditional concepts of the division of labor and visualizing the family as a flexible working cooperative of people of various ages. Another weak but identifiable subculture is the gay movement. This movement is helping society to loosen up its ideas about the composition of viable households for the maintenance and nurture of human beings. The children's liberation movement, largely a product of the same middle-class Anglo subculture that produced the dissenting youth culture of the sixties, adds a new dimension to the conception of the family as a working cooperative as it strives to remove archaic notions of age-graded status in family, school, and society.

Other subcultures could be mentioned, but these are enough to give an idea of the diversity of sources for new patterns of family-like living. Within each of these subcultures there is a creatively alienated minority who are actively experimenting, in their own lives, with new patterns. The thought experiments that find their way into the literature are important, but the living experiments are even more important, because they provide reality feedback on the viability of new patterns.

It would take another paper to outline the features of the new family emerging from these experiments, and I have been concerned here to focus rather on the social dynamics of changing family forms in the continuing historical process. This seemed important because of the tendency to regard today's experiments as examples of the disintegration of the family. A few things can be said about the common features of the creative family experiments in the eight subcultures referred to above, however. Each of them involves a strong rejection of certain privatistic family values of Middle America and seeks a new conception of the relationship of the family living group to neighborhood and community. Approaches to that new relationship vary considerably, however, from subculture to subculture. Each is concerned about a more equitable distribution of economic resources and the exploration of ways to enlarge the stock of public goods and services to be available equally to all. This does not usually imply a devaluing of private family space, but a reevaluation of it, and an exploration of alternative patterning of that space.

Each is also concerned with a more equitable distribution of role responsibilities and opportunities for personal growth among family members. This means liberating the entire world of nondomestic occupations for women, and opening the entire world of domestic responsibilities to men.

We can identify a trend to broaden the definition of the family itself as people come together with a commitment to maintaining a common household in groups not necessarily based on one conjugal pair, and rearing children not necessarily born to the household. Since these households have in recent times had a notoriously high rate of dissolution, a pattern of impermanence and irresponsibility has been ascribed to them. This is an inevitable by-product of the anomic times, and often reflects a lack of serious commitment to family-like living on the part of the participants. Rosabeth Kanter pointed out several years ago (Roberts 1971) how important commitment to common values and group discipline has been in the success of communities in the past. Expanded-family experimenters are becoming increasingly conscious of this, and the number of expanded families with a common religious orientation (the factor most closely associated in the past with community success) may well be increasing. Ron Roberts emphasizes the equality of commitment in his study *The new communes* (1971) and offers a more favorable prognosis than most other students of communes.

The phenomenon of temporary households, whether couples simply "shacking up," or group marriages that continually dissolve and reform, is a very old one — at least in the urban West — and should not be confused with serious experiments in family living. While the possibilities of birth control and abortion on request make temporary arrangements somewhat easier, the testimony of the hippie dropouts who return to the straight community to marry and live in suburbia is that transient human relationships are not satisfying.

The new expanded households all testify to the need for an enormous emotional investment in family and community living, and the fact that people make these investments over long periods is an indication of the depth of their dissatisfaction with existing society and its conventional nuclear-family living. I would like to quote from the letter of a fifty-year-old colleague who belongs to the conscientious-objector cohort of the forties, and who was personally involved in intentional living experiments after the war. He and his wife have recently embarked on a new venture, out of a lifetime of commitment to ventures that have changed form and membership over the years, but have always been carried out in the context of a dedication to the Christian peace movement. They have raised five children who are also creative community builders:

Amazingly enough we are under way — about 50 of us in several locations — Daybreak, The Gathering, Spring Garden House, Fat Man's Jug Band, Pine Street Collective, and Thorncroft, out in Chester County — small groups working out their problems of day to day living and sharing with other groups — an expression of mutual aid which can and is growing steadily. And there are various collectives through which we work — the Movement Building Collective, Training Collective, Trainers' Collective, Community Associates (a partnership open to all for economic purposes of sharing our resources, skills, and dividing them amongst us); and other things spin on and on.

Of course there are problems; living in community is not easy even when we are well prepared for it. But we have a good spirit and are hopeful we can survive and thrive in community — the name of one of our workshops! . . .

The first year of the effort is hard, and exciting; the following years may be even harder because they may not be so exciting. The long pull is what will count, and probably prove most exhausting. But we are trying to guard against all of this — to be focusing on the now with an ear to the past and an eye to the future (George Willoughby, personal communication, 1971).

The kind of expanded family these collectives represent is one grounded in a profound intention to work for a new society. The children reared in these collectives will all have been reared in the context of these intentions, and if the testimony of the nonconformist subcultures of seventeenth- and eighteenth-century continental Europe and England is any guide, the children so reared will themselves also be change agents. This is a far cry from the "hands off, let them do their thing" attitude towards children in the communes where parents who have dropped out watch their children rejecting their own back-to-the-land movement and drifting to crash pads in the city. These communes lack the structure of social intention.

Family living in the twenty-first century will probably provide more options than are open to today's individuals seeking family-like groups. It will still be possible to live as the majority of today's families live, but neighborhood institutions that provide for sharing family responsibilities, including care of the very young and very old, will be much more generally available to modify the burdens of privacy. Pressure of dwindling environmental resources will probably also help the trend toward an increase in all kinds of community-shared maintenance facilities for family units. The pioneering for this kind of sharing is coming now from the expanded-family experiments we have been mentioning.

The future of intentional expanded families is wide open. As experience accumulates, these expanded families may acquire the kind of stability expanded families have had in preindustrial eras. They will probably never be widespread, since they make special demands on human commitment and capacity for self-discipline. The climate which they create, however, will make more humanized family living possible for the average family in more humanized neighborhood communities. More important, they will provide a steady reservoir of ideas for the continual reconstruction of society.

REFERENCES

ARIES, PHILIPPE
1965   *Centuries of childhood.* Translated from the French by Robert Baldick. New York: Vintage Books.
BLOCH, MARC
1961   *Feudal society.* Chicago: University of Chicago Press.
BOULDING, ELISE, PATRICIA BOLTON TRAINER
1971   "Quality of life, U.S.A.: costs and benefits of urbanization and industrialization, 1900–1970," in the *Proceedings of the Special Session of Environmental Awareness of the 17th Annual Meeting of the Institute of Environmental Sciences, April 26–30,* 1–13. Los Angeles: Institute of Environmental Sciences.
1975   "Adolescent culture: reflections of divergence," in *Social Forces and Schooling.* Edited by Nobua Shimakara and Adam Scrupski. New York: David McKay Company.
CHATFIELD, CHARLES
1971   *For peace and justice: pacifism in America 1914–1941.* Knoxville: University of Tennessee Press.
CLARKSON
1800   *Portraiture of Quakerism.* New York: S. Stansbury.
FALLERS, LLOYD A.
1965   "The range of variation in actual family size," in *Aspects of the analysis of family structure.* Edited by Ansley J. Coale et al. Princeton: Princeton University Press.

HOMAN, WALTER JOSEPH
1931   *Children and Quakerism.* Berkeley: Gillick Press.
HUIZINGA, JOHAN
1950   *Homo ludens: a study of the play elements in culture.* Boston: Beacon Press.
JORNS, AUGUSTE
1931   *The Quakers as pioneers in social work.* New York: Macmillan.
LEVY, MARION J.
1965   "Aspects of the analysis of family structure," in *Aspects of the analysis of family structure.* Edited by Ansley J. Coale et al. Princeton: Princeton University Press.
LITWAK, EUGENE
1964   "Extended kin relations in industrial democratic society," in *Social structure and the family.* Englewood Cliffs, New Jersey: Prentice-Hall.
LYND, STAUGHTON
1966   *Nonviolence in America: a documentary history.* New York: Bobbs-Merrill.
MANUEL, FRANK E., *editor*
1965   *Utopias and utopian thought.* Boston: Beacon Press, Daedalus Library.
NORDHOFF, CHARLES
1965   *The communistic societies of the United States.* Originally published in 1875. New York: Shocken Paperback.
PARSONS, TALCOTT
1971   "The normal American family," in *Family in transition.* Edited by Arlene S. Skolnick and Jerome H. Skolnick. Boston: Little, Brown.
PARSONS, TALCOTT, ROBERT BALES
1955   *Family socialization and interaction process.* New York: Free Press.
PIRENNE, HENRI
1956   *Medieval cities.* Originally published in 1925. New York: Doubleday.
POLAK, FRED L.
1961   *The image of the future,* two volumes. Translated from the Dutch by E. Boulding. New York: Oceana Publications.
RAISTRICK, ARTHUR
1968   *Quakers in science and industry.* New York: Kelly.
ROBERTS, RON
1971   *The new communes.* Englewood Cliffs, New Jersey: Prentice-Hall.
THOMAS, W. I., FLORIAN ZNANIECKI
1927   *The Polish peasant in Europe and America.* New York: Knopf.
Village Voice
1971   "Saying hello in Panther language." Article in the *Village Voice.*
WINCH, ROBERT
1963   *The modern family.* New York: Holt, Rinehart and Winston.

Cultural Heterogeneity in Social Systems: Its Policy Implications

JACK N. SHUMAN

OVERVIEW

Analysis, evaluation planning, and decision making (in sum, the acts of policy) pose a number of semantic difficulties. These terms are not amenable to both succinct and meaningful definition. Moreover, a taxonomy of policy is equally pointless unless, of course, one happens to be Yehezkel Dror. It is clear that the disciplines and methodologies comprising policy cannot ever constitute a science, if for no other reason than the grounding of policy in values. Policy is an art and, at best, it can be made a more effectively practiced art. Policy, at least for human resource needs, can be viewed as depending on three essential qualities. It must be nonpositivist, existential, and impressionist.

The positivism of the nineteenth and twentieth century is a continuation of the eighteenth-century philosophy of the Enlightenment. All justification is based on reason and science — that is, on tested, verified, and systematized experience rather than intuition, judgment, or speculation. Nonpositivism, or in actuality genuine positivism, is based on both experience and metaphysics. The aim of a true positivist outlook should be to understand the methods and the general spirit for applying the results of the totality of human knowledge to practical life but with the realization that questions will inevitably arise which are not answerable by experimental methods.

The assertion that policy is existential does not mean that it is totally reducible to this doctrine, only that it embodies many of its features. Existentialism, and the changing perception of policy, are reactions to absolutism, which, in practice, has been translated into totalitarianism. Intelligent thinking on policy issues must be predicated on the fact that freedom is the deepest drive in man, transcending objective knowledge. Negatively, man is condemned to be free. Positively, man lives in freedom as if in a daring quest. In both instances, however, existence and freedom require the making of choices. They are perpetual either-or situations. The continuing dilemma of mankind is to make decisions in the uncharted realm of moral being.

Impressionism, like modern policy analysis, is the product of an increasingly hurried environment and momentary experiences. Social problems, like objects in impressionist paintings, are perceived and translated as fragmented and impermanent impressions. Not only does the object or issue, represented so impermanently, lose solidity it never stands still long enough to take shape in our minds. Most important, this impermanence and instability cause accompanying shifts in values as well.

Policy is a combination of form and substance, method and content, and last but certainly not least of all, perspective. Creative individuals in policy planning can give new vigor to the ideals of clarity and precise thinking. What must be avoided is an overemphasis on form and method which can have a repressive effect on the conduct of policy. Unintentionally, and even contrarily to its own purposes, modern policy analysis has contributed to the myths of form and methodology; that is, it does not matter much what we do so long as we do it right.

As far as the need for perspective is concerned, much has already been said. Because the policy-planning process is inextricably linked with the political process, it is not possible to have objective scientific planning. Yet both the analyst and the decision maker must have the ability to appreciate and understand every side of any issue. Sheila Johnson (1972) reminds us of Robert Benchley's famous solution to a Harvard international law examination. Having been asked to discuss the Newfoundland fisheries dispute between the United States and Great Britain, and knowing nothing about it, he decided to answer the question from the point of view of the fish.

In a recent planning study, prepared for the Department of Health, Education, and Welfare, Mysior (1977) rightly cautions us that nothing is certain, but that without reliance on some sort of order in the universe, intelligent life would be impossible. In terms of this paper, there is an important semantic distinction between "planning *the* future" and "planning *for* the future." Planning the future, generally produces that part of the future that is inexorable. Planning for the future produces that part of the future that is adaptive. Both are necessary.

INTRODUCTION

When an investigator initiates research on the subject of heterogeneity *vs.* homogeneity, he usually feels constrained to discuss the conditions necessary for social systems to be either heterogeneous or homogeneous. He would probably examine the components of a society such as its laws, language, religion, mores, and traditions within these two separate contexts. Furthermore, using the techniques developed in quantitative and systematic historical analysis, a social scientist can construct models which reflect an inexorable and natural transition of social systems from homogeneous to ever-increasing heterogeneous states. This mode of analysis does not imply that any individual who advocates this position is automatically a philosophical determinist. Certainly, one can make a convincing case that, if it has done nothing else, the gradual sophistication of technology has made social systems increasingly complex.[1]

From the standpoint of concrete, real-world, public policy problems, the thesis that social systems have been evolving from heterogeneity to homogeneity has little if any validity unless, as Mysior does, one goes back to the beginnings of humanity when small bands lived in relative isolation from other bands. Rather, as Von Bertalanffy (1968) argues, the history of civilization and concomitantly the evolution of policy problems shows a transition toward ever-higher orders of complexity, heterogeneity, and organization. The advocacy of social homogeneity from a historical or policy standpoint has as much meaning or usefulness as Hobbes's or Rousseau's concepts of the state-of-nature. Clearly, as Mysior asserts, this classical form of analysis is often as sterile an exercise as teaching music to the deaf, in the sense that the true "meaning" of music lies in the subjective experience of hearing it. Similarly, the pursuit of social understanding in an abstract sense is vacuous if it is not grounded in reality.

The assertion that public policy problems are becoming much more complex and difficult because of increasing heterogeneity does not imply that we have developed our capabilities to cope with these problems at even a roughly equal pace. On the contrary, as this paper will demonstrate, in most instances of domestic social policy, the instruments of public policy have largely remained homogeneous. In fact, to borrow Moynihan's phrase (1969), the domestic policy estab-

---

[1] Technology, for the requirements of this paper, can simply be defined as the development and organization of knowledge for a purpose, whether that purpose be delivering a service, solving a problem, or achieving a goal. The hardware so commonly associated with technology is only an artifact of this process. The fact that these artifacts have become so sophisticated is a reflection of rapid sophistication of the process itself — relatedly, the term "science" also assumes a different meaning. Thus, science may be more readily understood from the German *Wissenschaft*, or the Russian *nauk*. Disconnected from a utilitarian framework, science becomes a form of culture along with architecture, art, ballet, literature, and music. Admittedly, this definition of science may be correct from an anthropological standpoint. However, it is certainly to be expected that it would meet with angry cries of denunciation from the scientific communities, who would most assuredly resent being placed in a position of having to compete for resources with the dance.

lishment consists of "great simplifiers, rather than complexifiers." Since New Deal days a large measure of national thinking has been far more concerned with the expenditure of funds, euphemistically known as the science of resource allocations, than it has with ascertaining what these funds are expected to achieve or with measuring their effect or impact, if any.

Concrete demonstration of this generalization may be found in evaluations of the Title I Program of the Elementary and Secondary Education Act of 1965. Title I funds are described in the Act as special services for "meeting the special educational needs of educationally deprived children." Mark Arnold (1972) in a study funded by the Ford Foundation has analyzed the distribution and effectiveness of the Title I program in the District of Columbia public schools.

Overall, this study found that while the D.C. school system was able to identify the needs of disadvantaged children, the Title I projects frequently failed to address "the needs so indicated." As far as expenditures were concerned, the largest percentage of these funds went on salaries, particularly for paraprofessionals, and for the purchase of educational hardware. This study concluded that there was no evidence that these expenditures contributed to meeting the needs of Title I children. While certain phases of Title I programs have been successful (for example dental care, clothing, and emergency food supplies), in terms of cultural enrichment of ghetto children, the program is a total failure — at least for those children who retain any enthusiasm for learning.

Arnold's assessment clearly indicates two of the critical weaknesses in current policy analysis: first, the inability to relate expenditures directly to program or goal achievement, and second, a tendency to oversimplify the highly complex functions of organizations. By trying to make the schools into all-purpose social service delivery agencies, a role which they could not assume in relation to the Title I goals, the Title I program failed in its central purpose — that of raising academic achievement.

In spite of the foregoing evaluation, we must not assume that the entire governmental bureaucracy is incapable of functioning properly. This is most certainly not the case. For example, the National Oceanic and Atmospheric Administration (NOAA) in the Department of Commerce has for well over a century been able to deliver meteorological, oceanographic, and seismological services quite effectively and efficiently in terms of reasonable costs. NOAA does have serious problems which seem to be unique to agglomerate organizations. These include (1) difficulties of NOAA management in developing a coherent, functional, logical, and rational organization structure; (2) slowness in establishing a systematic and viable methodology for linking research and development to service delivery; and (3) a tendency to view long-range environmental program planning and evaluation as physical science rather than social science problems. In other words, this last tendency is to overemphasize the physical environment instead of perceiving interrelationships between the physical, economic, and social environments.

It is undoubtedly quite easy to dismiss the problem at this stage by accusing the bureaucracy of being corrupt or incompetent, or to blame it for being unresponsive. However, even while some of these assertions may be true, these disparagements serve no useful purpose. Instead, an infinitely more desirable, albeit more difficult exercise, is to gain insight into and understanding of the reasons for the existence of a hiatus between commitment and achievement.

Policy is a form of culture in the sense that it is one of the characteristic features of a particular stage or state of development of civilization. In another sense, policy is a form of culture because it is one aspect of the total pattern of human behavior. However, unlike the other forms of culture which constitute the sum of man's knowledge, policy does not reflect social heterogeneity. Unlike architecture, which perhaps provides the most useful comparison, public policy has generally not been responsive to social variation.

At the risk of overgeneralization, at least a partial explanation for homogeneity in policy may lie in the heuristics of policy. Heuristics may be defined as the identification or selection of components of systems. More specifically, heuristics consists of defining all significant subsystems and breaking them down into conceptually manageable parts. Policy heuristics have largely been hierarchical including, most significantly, the information systems on which policy is based. Policy heuristics are in fact one manifestation of Maslow's postulation (1959) of a hierarchy of values, attitudes, and needs based on single, directed, nonrandom upward progression.

Unfortunately, as both Von Bertalanffy (1968) and Mysior (1977) demonstrate with remarkable clarity, the knowledge base in social systems is totally inadequate. While we know that social systems function as interrelated networks, we do not really know *how* these networks function. They may function in a hierarchical manner, although it is more likely that these multilevel networks are nonlinear and self-organizing. There is presently no firm evidence to support the hierarchical heuristics of policy.[2] (A road map is an excellent example of a nonhierarchical heuristic.)

As Mysior (1977) points out, Festinger's cognitive dissonance theory

---

[2] Some subsystems do exist in hierarchical form. The United States Congress could not function as a legislative body unless it were organized into a hierarchical structure of committees. Thus, the organization of Congress allows it to pursue ends of its own. It is questionable, however, whether that organizational form is adequate to regulate a system as large, complex, and open-ended as the United States.

deals with the problem in a psychological setting. In the human being, according to Festinger, there is a drive to maintain a general sense of consonance among opinions, attitudes, ideals, beliefs, and behavior. Whenever some aspect of a person's experience becomes dissonant with another aspect, there is a drive (motivation) to reduce the gap. A commitment to hierarchical, linear, and highly structural heuristics on the part of a policy maker suggests that man is definitely a dissonance-reducing organism, attempting to keep dissonance within determined limits. In sum, Festinger merely demonstrates that social systems cannot always be controlled for desired values (goals). And, because the environment of a social system cannot have a modifying effect on these values, the system is allowed to continue despite its frequent drifts into undesirable ranges. The errors are simply ignored and the system muddles through with only marginal tinkering.

Muddling and marginal tinkering, however, do not have pejorative connotations. If we can muddle through and not make our situation any worse than it already is for at least the near future, this is in itself no minor accomplishment. In fact, since we cannot specify the parameters of our major problems all we can really do is muddle.

Actually, as Lindblom (1970) argues, effective muddling is quite a sophisticated art. In this respect, an intelligent planner ought to know the limits of systematic planning. It is one thing to have health manpower planning, since there are some reasonably standard definitions for health manpower. However, health planning is another matter entirely, since no one has yet has been able to achieve a universal definition of health. Even the notion of planning, used inappropriately, introduces a large element of unwanted simplicity. As Lindblom might well say, "if you are going to muddle, don't model."

There is of course a danger that a social scientist, by remaining purely descriptive, may in fact become normative. In other words, what is, is also what ought to be, which is not always the case. By intelligently using alternative future scenarios, we can, at times at least, give some direction to marginal tinkering.

As a brief overview, this paper is written in modular form. That is, it is composed of several separate sections which discuss one or more aspects of social complexity. Each section is a complete and independent unit, with its own introduction and conclusion enabling a reader to picture in his own mind the course of thinking in this paper. At the same time, he can also recombine the modules or substructures of this paper into new units to accord with his personal views of complexity.

HETEROGENEITY: THE META-PROBLEM

These attitudes toward policy problems are not new. Policy problems have always been complex and heterogeneous, while our approaches to them have been largely homogeneous. However, what we are experiencing today is not a different set of problems. Rather, as the Club of Rome proposal argues (1970), the present historical epoch is characterized by a fundamental mismatch between the situation we still insist on describing as a set of problems and our mental and emotional attitudes which we continue to feel might give rise to solutions. Instead, in both the present and the future, we must make the assumption that our notion of a problem is wholly insufficient for us to face whatever it is that our situation proposes — both to our intellects and to our consciences.

Orthodox problem solving postulates the fragmentation of reality into closed and well-defined problems. This fragmentation, as the Club of, Rome observes, itself creates a new problem whose solution is clearly beyond the scope of the concepts we customarily employ — the meta-problem (or meta-system of problems).

The meta-problem is derived from a threefold hypothesis:

1. The predicament of mankind is growing in complexity and variety at an ever-accelerating pace, is systematic in character, and the boundaries of the system encompass the entire planet.

2. The meta-problem transcends discrete categories of events — e.g. overpopulation, malnutrition, poverty, pollution, etc. and arises from confused patterns generated by our standard clustering of these events.

3. Any desirable or even acceptable resolution of the meta-problem will in all probability entail, at least as far as outcomes or options are seriously considered, fundamental changes in our current social and institutional structure for the simple reason that these structures were not established to operate in the dynamic and heterogeneous situation in which the world now finds itself.

From the work of enlightened systems analysts such as Von Bertalanffy and Mysior, it is obvious beyond any shadow of doubt that the vastly increased complexity of social life has created a qualitative difference, for which traditional approaches are inadequate, in the types of problem that need to be solved. These outworn methods compound the difficulties they attempt to remove. Patchwork solutions, whether a slum-clearance project or beautification program, simply shift the problem from one place to another, giving some local relief while allowing the larger setting to deteriorate further. The real problem is not that mankind is faced with greater problems now than in the past. Rather, problems of a higher order are caving in upon society, to such an extent, that society itself has become the problem. As Mysior notes, the Heisenberg principle, as far as social development is concerned, has grown in exponential progression.

In the past, it might have been, and in some cases it was possible to isolate a problem, attack it, and solve it in such a way as to cause only minor disturbances which would soon dissipate. It is analogous to throwing a pebble into a body of water; the splash causes a ripple of waves in widening circles, diminishing rapidly in intensity until the water again presents a smooth surface. For the meta-problem, however, we should imagine that this functional relationship has reversed itself. A pebble is thrown into the sea, and the amplitude of the progressive disturbance increases until the ripple has grown into a tidal wave.

Even though reality is fragmented because of our conceptual and linguistic conditioning, it is still necessary to talk about the meta-problem in generalized terms and to communicate ideas concerning it. Because no new language exists for this task, one can only approach the notion of the meta-problem in familiar terms. It is possible to break down and list the meta-problem according to its major components, both for purposes of even tenuous identification and to create a referential base. The Club of Rome's listing of continuous critical problems (1970) represents a general classificatory labeling of the meta-problem. As caveats, these disaggregations of the meta-problem are not grouped in any particular order, nor is the list to be regarded as complete. Furthermore, neither their rate of occurrence, nor their intensity is uniform throughout the world. In fact, the true list is many times larger than the following listing and actually impossible to ascertain fully even on direct empirical evidence:

Table 1.   Continuous critical problems: an illustrative list (Club of Rome 1970)

1. Population growth with consequent escalation of social, economic, and other problems.
2. Widespread poverty throughout the world.
3. Increase in the production, destructive capacity, and accessibility of all weapons of war.
4. Uncontrolled urban spread.
5. Generalized and growing malnutrition.
6. Persistence of widespread illiteracy.
7. Expanding mechanization and bureaucratization of almost all human activity.
8. Growing inequalities in the distribution of wealth throughout the world.
9. Insufficient and irrationally organized medical care.
10. Hardening discrimination against minorities.
11. Hardening prejudices against differing cultures.
12. Affluence and its unknown consequences.
13. Anachronistic and irrelevant education.
14. Generalized environmental deterioration.
15. Generalized lack of agreed alternatives to present trends.
16. Widespread failure to stimulate man's creative capacity to confront the future.
17. Continuing deterioration of inner cities or slums.

18. Growing irrelevance of traditional values and continuing failure to evolve new value systems.
19. Inadequate shelter and transportation.
20. Obsolete and discriminatory income distribution system(s).
21. Accelerating wastage and exhaustion of natural resources.
22. Growing environmental pollution.
23. Generalized alienation of youth.
24. Major disturbances of the world's physical ecology.
25. Generally inadequate and obsolete institutional arrangements.
26. Limited understanding of what is feasible in the way of corrective measures.
27. Unbalanced population distribution.
28. Ideological fragmentation and semantic barriers to communication between individuals, groups, and nations.
29. Increasing asocial and antisocial behavior and consequent rise in criminality.
30. Inadequate and obsolete law enforcement and correctional practices.
31. Widespread unemployment and generalized underemployment.
32. Spreading discontent throughout most classes of society.
33. Polarization of military power and psychological impacts of the policy of deterrence.
34. Fast obsolescing political structures and processes.
35. Irrational agricultural practices.
36. Irresponsible use of pesticides, chemical additives, insufficiently tested drugs, fertilizers, etc.
37. Growing use of distorted information to influence and manipulate people.
38. Fragmented international monetary system.
39. Growing technological gaps and lags between developed and developing areas.
40. New modes of localized warfare.
41. Inadequate participation of people at large in public decisions.
42. Unimaginative conceptions of world order and of the rule of law.
43. Irrational distribution of industry supported by policies that will strengthen the current patterns.
44. Growing tendency to be satisfied with technological solutions for every kind of problem.
45. Obsolete system of world trade.
46. Ill-conceived use of international agencies for national or sectoral ends.
47. Insufficient authority of international agencies.
48. Irrational practices in resource investment.
49. Insufficient understanding of continuous critical problems, their nature, their interactions, and the future consequences both they and current solutions to them are generating.

The meta-problem is our recent past, present, and immediate future. Four causes may be ascribed to the meta-problem.

1. The emergence of genuinely new technologies. These are almost certain to create new industries and business organizations and simultaneously render large numbers of existing concerns obsolete. These high-growth industries are likely to emerge from the scientific discoveries that have occurred largely since the turn of the century: quantum physics, the understanding of atomic and molecular structure, biochemistry and biophysics, psychology, and symbolic logic.

2. Revolutionary changes in the world's economy. Economic policy analysts and decision makers still act as if there exists an international economy in which separate nations are the units, dealing with one another primarily through international trade and fundamentally as different from one another as they are different in language, or laws, or cultural traditions. But, however imperceptibly, there has emerged a world economy, which is undoubtedly enormously complex. This economy, which shares a common information base, generates the same economic aspirations, desires, and demands everywhere, regardless of national boundaries and languages and regardless of political ideologies as well. The world has truly become in Drucker's phrase "one market, one global shopping center" (1969).

3. Rapidly accelerating changes in the political matrix of economic and social life. Today's society and polity are pluralistic. At the same time and up to the present, all social tasks of importance have been entrusted to organized power concentrations. It appears that we are also approaching a turning point in this trend in view of the rapid disenchantment with government; both with the institution itself and with its ability to perform. Other organizations are experiencing the phenomenon of rejection, e.g. the Roman Catholic Church and the large universities.

4. This final element of change, knowledge, is the most important. As Machlup observed (1962), knowledge has become the central capital, the cost center, and the crucial resource in economic and social development. This centrality of knowledge in national life has changed both the composition of the labor force and the nature of work, teaching, and learning, and the epistemology of knowledge and its politics. Above all, however, in the knowledge-intensive society we are faced with the problem of the power and responsibilities of the new power elite — the men of knowledge.

HETEROGENEITY AS A SYSTEMS PROBLEM

The subject of heterogeneity in a systems context has nothing in common with the classical systems approach which has rapidly become part of the established university curriculum. Systems, systems theory, and system science are predominantly a development in engineering science necessitated by the complexity of modern technology: man-machine relations programming and other similar considerations. The systems approach in this sense is preeminently a mathematical field offering partly novel and highly sophisticated techniques closely associated with computer science and cybernetics.

These developments, important as they are to policy analysis, obscure the fact that systems theory is a broad view which far transcends purely technological problems. The previous section on the meta-problem offered ample argument that the world is confronted with a class of exceedingly complex human problems which Alexander Christakis (1971) calls "no-technical-solution problems." However, as Christakis also points out, nontechnical solutions to any problem should not be interpreted to mean nonsystematic, nonquantitative, or nonmathematical. In broad terms, the systems approach provides the proper combination of ethical, technological, axiological, quantitative, and qualitative concepts for the solution of increasingly complex and heterogeneous human action problems. The systems approach is not so much a discipline in the conventional meaning of the word as a state of mind seeking comprehensiveness, synergism, coordination, relevancy and organization.

It is worthwhile at this stage to restate the premise that social systems are continually evolving toward ever-greater magnitudes of heterogeneity and complexity. However, unlike purely physical systems which are closed and irreversible, social systems are entirely reversible, possessing an exchange relationship with the environment. According to Von Boltzmann's second law of thermodynamics, the general trend of events in physical systems is toward the production of entropy or maximum states of disorder, probability, or randomness accompanied by a leveling of differences with the so-called "heat death of the universe" as the final outlook. Social systems, being living systems, can maintain themselves in a steady state, avoiding increases in entropy. Furthermore, they can develop toward states of increased order and organization. In other words, constant input from the environment prevents the system from running down to a state of maximum entropy.

Another major cause of complexity is found in the nature of the feedback mechanisms in social systems. In highly complex social systems, feedback exists not in the form of a servomechanism, but rather as a loop. In fact, as Forrester (1971) demonstrates so effectively, social systems belong to a class possessing multiloop nonlinear feedback systems. It is quite easy for even the most capable analyst or decision maker to be misled by this, since his intuition and judgment have been formed to expect far different behavior from particular social systems.

Largely because of this nonrational loop, social systems have structural time delays and are nonlinear. The effects of actions and policies become evident in time frames we cannot accurately predict, and in ways we would not have anticipated, depending on the course of information flow through the feedback loop. The nonlinearity of causal influences in social systems, based on Forrester's concept of the feedback loop, has a major policy ramification, namely the extreme difficulty of developing any type of criteria or indicators for measuring program adequacy and effectiveness — now or in the future. Finally, the feedback loop in social systems, unlike physical systems, possesses a degree of autonomy. It does not only affect the behavior of the system, but can alter its components as well.

There are two forms of feedback information: positive or error-amplifying, and negative or error-ameliorating. An example of positive feedback would be imbalances between prices, investments, and profits, resulting in spiraling cycles in the economy. Each time balance is sought among wages, production costs, and prices, to correct a deficit in one of these elements, error is amplified and runs throughout the system.

In social systems, however, the feedback loops that are designed are usually negative ones. As Mysior (1977) points out, the term negative loops is somewhat misleading because it implies the opposite of positive feedback. If inflation is taken as an example of positive feedback, deflation is not necessarily an example of negative feedback. Deflation is actually associated with positive feedback, while a return to a position of stability is the most important result of negative feedback. This means that negative feedback is a control device that reduces error.

In policy terms, it is theoretically possible to design complex systems that move toward prescribed goals with almost infinite flexibility by measuring the system's position with respect to the goal and feeding this information back to a control center in the system. According to this type of reasoning, any measure showing deviations from the prescribed path would automatically induce the control center to change the system's direction from perceived errors.

This paradigm of negative feedback is rather oversimplified. Social systems are composed of the most elaborate form of organization networks. The characteristic feature of these networks is that the components making up any system are linked to several communication chains simultaneously processing information. As Maruyama ("Toward human futuristics," this volume) demonstrates, the goal orientation of these networks is heterogeneous, because desires and needs vary from individual to individual and from group to group. In this respect, policy, whether it be decision making, program formulation, implementation, management, or evaluation, must deal with diverse goal and value systems which function in a nonlinear fashion, or, in Maruyama's phrase, "concurrent multipurpose versatility systems."

As both Christakis (1971, 1972) and Maruyama ("Toward human futuristics," this volume) observe, goals and values are not constant over time. They cannot be quantified with any degree of specificity. Concomitantly, while goal and value systems are continually evolving, the changes, as Maruyama's research demonstrates, cannot be predicted by extrapolating past patterns of change, the past rate of change, or even the past rate of acceleration of change.

As an alternative to understanding complexity and heterogeneity in the sense that changes are subject to individual goals, values, imagination, will, and choice, one can apply the general systems theory concept of the human action system. In general systems theory any human action system is defined as a goal seeking, value based system possessing a multiplicity of interacting subsystems in complex, nonlinear arrangement. Thus, any policy must be conceived and modeled on the basis of multilevel-multigoal-multivalue (n-level, n-goals, n-values) structure.

Social systems are clearly not single-level single-goal event hierarchical systems. Any policy based on this precept is bound to fail. Most importantly, as Russell Ackhoff (1970) explains with magnificent clarity, a policy decision process based on this simplistic mode of analysis can neither identify symptoms nor treat the causes of social turbulence. As Ackhoff notes further, in Western society of the 1970's this turbulence is expressed intranationally in social conflict and dilemmas of increasing severity. Examples are racial conflict, student unrest, changes in sexual mores, attacks on the institutions of family and marriage, drug abuse, industrial strife, the existence of poverty in otherwise affluent societies, and so forth. The major characteristic of this panoply of problems is that they pose dilemmas for all facets of society simultaneously. Social problems (like modern wars) are no longer confined to known regions of expertise but invade the lives of individuals and institutions alike. The challenge confronting any individual concerned with understanding the sheer enormity of these problems is to ascertain, not only the manner in which the variables may or may not interact, but equally, to see that only some of these variables will dominate the behavior of a social system at any one time.

TECHNOLOGY, SIMULATION, AND KEYNESIANISM: THREE KEY NONCOMPLEX INSTRUMENTS OF PUBLIC POLICY

Having dwelt at length on the growing complexity of public policy problems, it is no less necessary to elaborate in some detail on some of the methodologies available to decision makers for problem analysis and resolution. Technology, simulation, and Keynesianism are particularly amenable to this sort of discussion. Taken together, they form a composite, standardized methodology for problem solving. They offer the distinct benefit of facilitating certain short-term treatment of problems; in current parlance, the quick fix. However, technology, simulation, and Keynesianism by themselves are not useful in long-range planning since they cannot deal with what Jurgen Schmandt, in the 1968 study of American science policy by the Organization for Economic Cooperation and Development (OECD), terms "global problems." They do not provide a sufficient perspective for discerning or shaping the future. All this should be obvious to policy analysts and decision makers. But, as the philospher, Whitehead, once remarked, it requires a very unusual mind to undertake an analysis of the obvious.

Technology

For the purposes of this section, technology is defined more narrowly in terms of the standard term "technical," based on applied science and engineering.

One of the key factors in the improper use of science and technology has been the inability of many of its proponents to grasp the fact that science and technology are inseparable from their cultural, economic, political, and social wellsprings. Far too often a misconception exists among many engineers and scientists that research and development, while not totally dictating our selection of national goals or our identification of national concerns, are at least the paramount factor in this process. In Ida Hoos's phrase, these "communities are competing enthusiastically to bring the powerful tools of technology to bear on matters concerning the commonwealth."

The argument is familiar. "A nation that can send men to the moon should be capable of accomplishments closer to home." "All we need to do is apply our scientific know-how to the analysis and resolution of social problems with the same creativity we have applied to space problems." This type of argument, as Ida Hoos (1969, 1972) observes, is persuasive on two counts: first, because of the prestigious origin and logical aura of science and technology; and second, because of the growing recognition of the need for better planning, organization, and management of social affairs.

In certain cases, most notably aerospace and defense, science and technology play a significant role in achieving program goals. Fields such as medicine and transportation also depend heavily on an expanding scientific and technological science base. Yet in resolving most of our pressing problems such as racial discrimination, poverty, public service access, and decaying cities, we cannot rely on strictly scientific or technological solutions to problems that are inherently nontechnical. The notion that science and technology are worthwhile ends in themselves is nihilistic. Rather, we must determine what types of new knowledge we need to develop in order to achieve a particular goal, whether that goal be in urban planning, population control, natural resource utilization, or pollution abatement.

The main limitation of a scientific or technological approach to public policy problems arises from its fundamental inability to take into account the role of the political and ethical relationships which dominate the behavior of social systems. As Christakis notes, the successful results of laboratory control of experimental variables and the discovery of the laws of classical mechanics have given rise to the belief that physical science methods can help discover "the basic laws" of social systems. In the physical sciences, the criterion of system validity is that it works, which means that the laboratory system is an accurate representation of a natural system. In other words, the system possesses the capability of describing and predicting behavior, or of validation in some other sense. The complex interrelationships of politics, history, psychology, and sociology have nothing like the empirical justification of the phenomenology of the classical atoms and molecules of physics. In sum, science and technology by themselves are not sufficient for characterizing problems.[3]

The preceding paragraphs are not abstract discourse. An overemphasis on technology is certainly present in many programs. Two such programs that can be cited are Operation Breakthrough in the Department of Housing and Urban Development, and Research Applied to National Needs (RANN) in the National Science Foundation.

The primary objective of Operation Breakthrough, declared at the program's inception in May 1969, was to modernize the housing industry by emphasizing volume production, new technology, and advanced methods of management. Certain aspects of this program are potentially quite beneficial and important. For instance, Operation Breakthrough has made significant progress in standardizing building

---

[3] The discussion has attempted to avoid any reference to notions such as objectivity or scientific determinism. Their elaboration must be restricted to the realm of the philosophy of science. In any event, a social system is no more or less determinate than is a purely physical system. Rather, the concepts of reliability and validity, with relevance to statistical probability, are more meaningful for either type of system.

codes which acted as constraints in housing development. Also, the technology developed from Operation Breakthrough, particularly the use of modules, may also succeed in stabilizing the cost of middle-income housing. However, it is difficult to imagine Operation Break-through being of any use in resolving what is probably the most pressing single problem in HUD; namely its emergence as the nation's number one slum landlord because of the Department's failure to grasp the full ramifications of the Housing Act of 1968. This situation is reinforced by the present national pattern of welfare policy adminis-tration and the pressures of that segment of the social service industry involved in the public welfare establishment. Similarly there is nothing Operation Breakthrough can do to assist local and state governments to understand metropolitan social dynamics or inner-city instability.[4]

These criticisms should not be construed as an argument against Operation Breakthrough. It is one means of improving our national housing situation. However, by itself Operation Breakthrough is of minimal use in understanding housing problems. Its danger lies in its magnification of a limited area of research, thus restricting both perception and solution. In brief, Operation Breakthrough is a tech-nological fix for a social problem, and at best only a temporary palliative.

The objectives of RANN (National Science Foundation 1972) are somewhat similar to those of Operation Breakthrough, although RANN's mission is somewhat broader. In essence, RANN seeks to increase understanding of social and environmental problems and their underlying causes and to identify opportunities and means for applying advanced technology for the benefit of society through interdisciplin-ary research. Some of RANN's programs clearly fall within the pur-view of traditional technology. These include weather modification, earthquake engineering, environmental quality, instrumentation tech-nology, energy research, disaster and natural hazard research, etc. What is disturbing in RANN's major involvement in social problems is that it takes place largely from a traditional engineering standpoint. In fact, RANN may be regarded as a real world embodiment of Olaf Helmer's work in social technology (1965) or even of the nineteenth-century social physicists.

One of the main thrusts of RANN in social problems is in the area of developing urban technology for improving the physical attributes of new and existing communities. This is a laudable goal, except that the key aspects of most urban problems do not center on their physical

---

[4] Operation Breakthrough itself was never intended to be a social action program. It was, however, placed in this role through internal pressures and the requirements of HUD to have some sort of demonstrable achievements.

attributes. Another of RANN's concerns is in social data and community structure. Research here is aimed at developing and analyzing baseline data on the socioeconomic characteristics and the dynamic structure of significant population groups and subgroups. This phase of RANN is open to serious question from two standpoints. First, from a purely administrative or management perspective, this activity duplicates without sufficient justification a broad range of ongoing efforts in the field of social data systems operated or supported by the federal government. Second, RANN seeks to place these systems in an engineering perspective which will clearly not enhance policy-relevant research.

One of RANN's most noteworthy endeavors is its attempt to establish science policy groups at the regional, state, county, and municipal levels modeled on the Office of Science and Technology in the executive office of the President. Each of these groups would be headed by an individual whose duties and responsibilities would be analogous to those of the Science Adviser to the President who also acts as the Director of the Office of Science and Technology. Furthermore, in this activity RANN is seeking to encourage state and local government to conduct or support relevant research and development. Finally, as one of its goals, RANN urges the involvement of state and local government in national science policy formulation and implementation — i.e. the President's Science Advisory Council (PSAC) and the technical advisory groups in the federal agencies.

These objectives must be questioned separately. As far as the science policy mechanisms are concerned, RANN officials are obviously reasoning by analogy. Analogies are useful in providing a perspective in problems. However, they are not useful and can be dangerous in the design of intervention strategies for resolving complex social problems. In the case in point, the problems and concerns of federal science policy have little in common with the real needs or problems of state and local government. Additionally, the responsibilities of the Science Advisor to the President are very different in fact and in law from those of an individual functioning in this capacity at state or local level.

While federal resources are limited, state and local resources are even more limited. Thus, these entities engaging in scientific research would divert attention from more pressing and perplexing problems. Finally, in arguing for state and local participation in federal science policy decisions, RANN does not sufficiently analyze the functions of the President's Science Advisory Committee to determine what effectiveness, if any, representation by state and local government would have in the deliberations of that body. At the same time, RANN can

and should advocate increased involvement by state and local government in the technical advisory committees of those federal agencies
concerned with domestic problems.[5]

As with Operation Breakthrough, this analysis does not in itself
question the need for a program such as RANN. RANN can be useful
in stimulating innovative approaches to limited aspects of national
problems. However, while it is quite logical to place Operation Breakthrough in the Department of Housing and Urban Development, the
location of RANN in the National Science Foundation is another
matter entirely. The NSF was established over a quarter of a century
ago solely to support basic scientific research (including the social
sciences) primarily in institutions of higher education. This responsibility is sufficiently complex by itself without introducing an extraneous
program entailing even more complex responsibilities.

Many of the senior officials involved in Operation Breakthrough and
RANN have been drawn from the National Aeronautics and Space
Administration. Their migration pattern suggests that when a goal-
satisfied technology can no longer be identified with pertinent problems, it will endeavor instead to seek out either alternative relevant
solutions or even nonproblems. These sorts of actions are not, however, confined to the public sector alone. They are found in the private
sector as well. One has only to consider the predicament in which the
March of Dimes found itself in 1955 upon the successful field tests of
the Salk vaccine. Its discovery of birth defects which are too many and
varied ever to be "cured" is sufficient insurance against a repetition of
this ghastly situation.

Such judgments may not be fully applicable to Breakthrough, since
it is, in theory at least, only of temporary duration. However, it is
certainly possible to predict a blissful future for RANN, since many of
its programs are in areas that are by definition unsolvable. This
discussion does not imply that all of RANN's activities are useless.
Obviously, some benefit will be derived from RANN's activities if only
as a function of the fact that some talented people will be brought into
the project and some intelligent research will be supported.

The pressures for programs such as Breakthrough and RANN rarely
come from engineers and scientists engaged in research and development. Such individuals are fully aware of the limits of their expertise.
Rather, these programs come into being far more often through the
efforts of misguided social scientists who feel that they are not sufficiently respectable because they are not quantitative (except for the

---

[5] These criticisms concerning the involvement of state and local government in extensive scientific and technical activities do not include RANN's efforts in promoting
technology transfer at state and local levels. Taken in a limited perspective these efforts
might prove rewarding.

econometricians) and because they lack a formalized methodology. The argument that the existence of such a methodology might actually retard analysis seems to carry little if any weight with this school of thought.

These social scientists are in turn supported by engineers and physical scientists who have become administrators. Furthermore, they are convinced of the universal validity of their expertise and the infallibility of their managerial competence. In nonparlor terms, they are referred to as hacks.

The proliferation of technology (and equally, of simulation, as the next section shows) often entails a large expansion in the number of technical experts on planning staffs. Part of this number is involved in the search for intelligent applications of systems technology to social problems. The remaining (and probably larger) part devote their energies to evaluating the wares preferred by the simulation and technology mongers.

These criticisms do not imply that engineers and physical scientists should never be brought into the policy planning process. On the contrary, many more are needed, provided they recognize the limitations of their specific disciplines. Engineers and physical scientists are far more able to think critically about difficult problems than are many social scientists. Moreover, they are far more adept at innovative and novel uses of mathematical and numerical techniques.

Simulation

A corollary of the technological approach to the study of social problems has been the vast infusion, derived largely from aerospace research, of mathematical modeling and simulation into policy analysis. For example, the state of California has involved the aerospace industry located there in examining various problem areas. One of the more interesting products of this venture has been the development of a mathematical model of the state's welfare system. The only difficulty with this model is that, as one former California welfare official remarked, "it bears no resemblance whatsoever to either the state's welfare system or the problems associated with that system."

There exist certain fundamental issues of choice and responsibility which even the most sophisticated mathematical models cannot resolve. A model cannot choose between heroin and methadone maintenance. Nor can simulation effect trade-offs between economic development and environmental enhancement. Such decisions must reflect the assumptions of the decision makers. However, as James Schlesinger suggests (1967), mathematical simulations can shed some light on the total range of costs and benefits of accepting one objective at the expense of others.

Carl Hovland (1963), one of the great innovators in the use of mathematical simulation in mass communication, mentions two major difficulties in using simulation methods. The first is the complexity of the process to be simulated. At present, we consider ourselves fortunate if we can simulate by computer the typical performance of a single individual in solving a particular problem. But, as Hovland notes, for simulation to be maximally effective, we would need to be able to predict machine solutions which simulate, not only a single individual under some specified conditions, but also the effects for different individuals under different environmental conditions and after various amounts of experience.

The second difficulty of machine simulation derives from the nature of certain processes. Simulation methods have been most successfully employed where it is possible to define the performance of a task as the outcome of a succession of single steps. Where the mental process involves steps in a sequence, one can synthesize it by having a computer work first on stage one, then two, and so forth. Much more difficult are these processes where a number of stages are going on simultaneously in parallel fashion, which seems to be the way that much of our perceptual process operates. Under these conditions, Hovland concludes, it is far more difficult to untangle the processes at work prior to simulation.

Ida Hoos captures the central fallacy in the widening use of classical mathematical simulation. "By concentrating on miniscule portions or isolated variables simply because they are quantifiable, the technique may actually lead to results which are irrelevant and inappropriate. Assignment of social costs and social benefits is an arbitrary matter and even the dollar cost/benefit comparison is a matter of interpretation" (1969).

The very characteristics which distinguish the social from other systems render them resistant to treatment that tries to force them into analytically tractable shape.

1. They defy definition as to objectives, philosophy, and scope. For example, what kind of a welfare system can be regarded as valid — one which compensates for the shortcomings of other systems such as education or health, or one which focuses on individual inadequacy? As Hoos argues, a definition depends on an individual's point of view and ideological posture.

2. A "solution" of social problems is never achieved. One does not solve the problems of health or transportation. Consequently, where we start or stop is purely arbitrary and usually a reflection of resource availability and commitment.

3. Despite the semblance of precision, there are no right or wrong, true or false solutions. It is presumptuous to label anything "wrong" that is being done now and looks good on paper.

Any computer-based simulation model is of only limited utility since it can only describe what one does know about a problem. Hence, it cannot deal with uncertainty which is the major characteristic of social systems, except perhaps for fast testing of assumptions.

Fundamentally, computerized mathematical models only reveal the structures of systems as they are understood by the designers themselves. A model designer may choose to omit certain phenomena that may be far more crucial to society than his model because they resist quantitative treatment or because of his own bias. It is improbable that computerized models, being oversimplifications of reality, can alone lead to the discovery of effective policy recommendations. Clearly, there is a tendency in mathematical simulation to oversimplify the inherent complexity of social problems. Psychosocial aspects of problems, which are exceedingly difficult to conceptualize, much less measure, are often neglected. As a result, these models are inadequate as total characterizations of problems.

Mathematical simulation, as Christakis's work (1972), shows has enormously extended our means of evaluating first-order, system-wide consequences of actual or hypothetical causes of action. This is particularly so for the purposes of single value choices of nonpublic problems or fairly simple public problems. For the multigoal and multivalue choices confronting policy makers in the context of dynamic social systems, model building is fraught with danger.

The Zero Population Growth (ZPG) movement is an excellent illustration in point. Extrapolating or projecting current and historical birth rate statistics, the National Center for Educational Statistics can fairly accurately predict the school-age population over the next ten years by race, geographic region, income level, etc. These predictions in turn can form the basis for limited long-range educational planning. Yet, little attention has been devoted to ascertaining the effects of a substantially lowered birthrate on the social security system which is based on a large and expanding population of young contributors.

If this equilibrium were to shift markedly in the next decade or two, which is not unlikely, some quite difficult choices will have to be made for the social security system. Options would include much higher rates of payroll deductions, expanding the maximum baseline of deductions far beyond the present $9,000; lowered, or even no, annual increase in payments to recipients; and at least partial financing of the system from general revenue. This last option would mean either higher taxes or major reallocation of budgetary priorities which will probably also be impossible to make because of political pressure from constituent groups. The system could also be operated through deficit spending, although this option might have severe repercussions on the national balance of payments.

Finally, there is no way of knowing through simulation what would be the general public's attitude and behavior if the American people were to become convinced that the social security system was no longer viable. If nothing else, Forrester (1971) and Meadows (1972) have shown quite graphically that there is an unmistakable relationship among economic, political, and social stability. Given access to increasingly cheap technology, available through worldwide communication systems, the havoc that a frightened public could wreak is incalculable — at least it is in a standard computer-based simulation.

Keynesianism

The impact of the Keynesian revolution should not be minimized. Keynesianism has produced a more realistic theory for explaining short-term fluctuations in employment, incomes, and prices. Even if much theoretical work still remains to be done, governments have nevertheless been provided with the means for coping with the problems of maintaining full employment and economic stability.

Keynesian theory is the culmination of a long development in market economics. However, OECD economists, in attempting to assess the impact of education, science and technology, on economic growth, concluded that the Keynesian theory was inapplicable. The main factor causing this inapplicability was that the theory is static in the sense that the technological and social framework in which fluctuations in quantities, prices, and incomes take place is taken for granted. Changes to the framework are regarded as exogenous, and their influence eliminated from theoretical models by the traditional assumption, "other things being equal."

Even though changes in "other things" were sometimes assumed to have taken place, they were mostly left unexplained and unrelated to the variables of economic models, except as exogenous or residual factors. However, these changes explain a large if not the major part of economic growth. Penetrating the facade of "other things being equal," OECD economists determined that education, training, innovation, research, and development were, even by themselves, only a part of an infinitely diversified and complicated process. To arrive at even a partial explanation or interpretation of economic growth, they were forced to combine the standard methods of economic research with those of psychology, decision and organization theory, and political science.

This paper has shown that science and technology are not in themselves effective in understanding a society based on a multiplicity of nonrational individual and group needs, values, and goals. Similarly, simulation and Keynesianism do not provide sufficient insights into institutional, cultural, political, economic, or social processes. And finally, within Forrester's loop, cause and effect are largely inseparable.

These factors present any policy maker or program manager with two alternatives in planning. The first is the organic, "hang-loose" approach, advocated by both the extreme left and right, which is essentially the total absence of planning. Obviously, it would not be realistic to exercise this option. The second is to plan in the face of continual uncertainty. This option clearly presents a paradox. As Christakis argues (1972), one way in which this paradox can be effectively overcome is by using education in a cybernetic mode as the entry point to systematic planning. The cybernetically based educational system would have as input the decisions of both government and people about types of education and investment therein.

Hopefully, in the not-too-distant future, this would yield results in the form of educated individuals able to view and deal with multifaceted problems by a creative synthesis, achieved through their genuinely transdisciplinary education. This approach would maximize problem solving through a process of continual feedback between the individual and his environment. However, even the cyberneticists have neglected a major ingredient in this process. They remark on the necessity for intelligence, reason, and rationality in achieving understanding but seem to exclude a powerful and profound skepticism.

GENERALIZATIONS: THE BASES OF POLICY

We have become accustomed to a continuing reiteration of the following syllogism: consensus in American society is breaking down; policy is based on consensus; therefore, policy as a manifestation of this consensus, must inevitably be part of this breakdown.

When we begin to reflect on these statements, it becomes clear that they are unrelated. From the findings of Cantril and Roll (1971), a case can be made that there has been no serious breakdown in consensus. On the positive side, most people advocate and want better housing, health, and living standards, with widened economic opportunity. Additionally, Cantril and Roll concluded that having children and a happy family life rank fairly high as aspirations with most Americans. Even on the negative side, there was general concern about alleviating domestic and international unrest, if no general agreement on the factors responsible for discord.

Polarization should not be regarded as belonging to the same order as consensus. Polarization is a form of psychological reaction by people who feel that the *status quo* is somehow being threatened as a result of the actions of groups or individuals, whom they can neither cope with nor relate to.

Policy, however, has little to do directly with consensus, except that policies are formulated in response to what policy makers may regard as needs or opportunities based on what they consider to be consensus or political realism. The policy planning process is based rather on assumptions and generalizations. It is these generalizations and assumptions which are breaking down, rendering the process incapable of functioning properly. To state this proposition somewhat more accurately: policies, as generalizations and assumptions, function chiefly at the level of the aggregate; they break down when they are found to be not true in the disaggregate. Policies, as theoretical constructs, unfortunately, often harden into controlling myths before their premises have been carefully analyzed.

The catchphrase "the new populism" is an illustration of the substitution of semantics for thinking in policy. Moreover, it illustrates a certain symbiotic and self-reinforcing relationship between policy makers and segments of the communications media. The *New York Times* pointed out in its lead editorial on April 30, 1972, on extremely slender and ambiguous evidence that many analysts have put forward the theory that a wave of populist discontent is surging across the nation. There are, as the editorial noted, many kinds of discontent seeking some form of political expression. In a large and heterogeneous society, crosscurrents of dissatisfaction are the normal social condition. As a matter of fact, it is periods of tranquility which are abnormal and unusual.

Discontent is evident among blacks, Spanish-speaking Americans, and national and religious ethnic groups, as well as among women, who are pushing for new opportunities and new power. There are millions of submerged poor in rural and urban slums who are demanding that greater resources be devoted to lifting them out of their wretchedness. Among industrial workers and at every level of the middle class, there is a deep sense of grievance that prices and taxes are too high and not matched by corresponding increases in wages. Finally, the business community is faced with a squeeze from higher labor costs and taxes.

The striking characteristic of this catalogue of discontent, the editorial concluded, is its political and intellectual incoherence. A social theorist, who ignored human antagonisms and frailties, could conceivably put together a program which would solve or diminish almost every one of these problems. But, as a practical matter, no responsible political leader could ever attempt to bring together a workable coalition of small farmers, price-conscious housewives, militant blacks, whites angry about school busing, highly skilled workers, profit-pinched small businessmen, the poor, the elderly, and finally the middle class. The "new populism" may be a fashionable semantic umbrella to describe these diverse discontents, but it is not a major elixir to remedy them. In a policy context, the "new populism" is like the "silent majority" a theoretical model, not a political reality.

The traditional view of policy leans toward consensus, continuity, and homogeneity. What is needed, of course, is a new view which stresses diversity, discontinuity, and heterogeneity. New and substantive thinking in policy planning must begin with systematic historical analysis. With the passage of time future plans become immediate plans, and immediate plans become past history. What should be sought through this type of exercise is not the discovery of sources for assumptions and generalizations, but rather the examination of their accuracy when not aggregated. This approach is of course limited, since some facets of history cannot be confirmed, validated, or proven. Value judgments, interpretations of motivation, and analyses of character most certainly cannot.

The historical approach that comes to mind most easily may be found in the work of certain of the younger revisionist and radical American historians, most notably, those who have contributed essays to Barton Bernstein's *Toward a new American past* (1967). Their views represent a complete break with older consensus history. Their dissenting essays, while representing the new departures of recent years, do not constitute a new historical synthesis, but rather a series of novel approaches and interpretations. Certainly analysts or researchers do not have to accept the ideological predilections of these historians in order to find meaning in their work. Undoubtedly, their obvious Marxist bias renders them open to serious challenge.

The most important attribute of these historians as far as policy analysis is concerned is their total commitment to incisive, provocative, unorthodox, rigorous, and tough-minded thinking. By subjecting historical generalizations to highly critical analysis, these historians provide invaluable insights into a number of public problems that have continued to beset this nation. At the risk of incurring their wrath, this new breed of historian might be best compared with Herman Kahn. They share one common attribute with him — an enthusiasm for thinking the unthinkable, which should be the essence of proper policy analysis.

Bernstein's engrossing essay on the New Deal is clearly the most useful in providing a perspective on the supposed failure of the programs of social reform initiated over the past ten years. Peter

Drucker in *The age of discontinuity* (1969) provides a list of these programs. This type of listing usually includes the Model Cities Program, Headstart, the War on Poverty, the Elementary and Secondary Education Act of 1965, the Manpower Training Act, etc. The failure of these programs was their inability to reach their intended recipients.

The New Deal instituted a number of fairly far-reaching reforms such as the minimum wage, unemployment benefit, public housing, farm assistance, the Tennessee Valley Authority, social security, and the Wagner Act. However, as Bernstein notes, the magnitude and effect of these reforms has been exaggerated. The New Deal reforms were entirely conservative in character. There was no significant redistribution of power in American society, only limited recognition of certain organized groups, never of unorganized people.

The New Deal rarely extended government benefits beyond the white middle class. It was never intended to reach the traditional poor American in either desert or urban ghettos, or in Appalachia. The sole purpose of the New Deal, except for WPA, was to assist individuals who had been temporarily disadvantaged as a result of the depression and were capable of taking advantage of the programs and services it offered. They were considered to be the "deserving poor" in the nineteenth-century meaning of the phrase. These reforms largely succeeded. In this respect, World War II can be interpreted as a rather gigantic economy of scale.

Most important, the New Deal left intact the race relations of America. For example, public housing and welfare assistance meant the consolidation of ghettos and the robbing of individuals of their dignity. Slum clearance came to mean Negro clearance and removal of the other poor. Some of these problems can be traced to the structure of bureaucracy, and particularly to social workers who had little sympathy for the poor. But, the New Deal conceptions were also flawed because there was no willingness to consult the poor or to encourage their participation.

The reforms of the last ten years were undoubtedly directed toward eliminating the remaining vestiges of poverty in America in that they were designed to create upward mobility among the disadvantaged. However, being grounded largely in the philosophy of the New Deal, the proponents of these efforts failed to perceive the existence of a culture of poverty, implying that being poor meant far more than the lack of money. These programs have worked, but not in the manner of their original intent. They have often resulted in an enlarged and more integrated middle class. In itself, this achievement is definitely worthwhile except that it has come about at the expense of the poor, who have not significantly benefited from the existence of these programs.[6]

The reformers of the 1930's and 1960's alike endeavored to create an environment which they thought would restructure character and personality. Unfortunately, they sought to restructure America in their own image, middle-class white. One can only surmise that, if the traditional poor did not exist for these purposes, they would have had to be invented.

Being disadvantaged or poor is, to say the least, a highly complex affair. At the level of jargon, poverty is an enormosuly difficult systems problem. For the poor, the deprived, and the disadvantaged, Lee Rainwater (1970) observes in his brilliant essay, the central, existential fact of life is their near-total exclusion from the collectivity that makes up the "real" society of "real people." They are not considered and often do not consider themselves to be, as Rainwater observes, quite part of regular society. The "disreputable poor," to use David Matza's term (Rainwater 1970), may not be allowed or may not be able to participate in those activities or with those people who are defined as integral to regular society. For this reason, such groups can quite legitimately be considered disinherited in the sense that no place is made for them and their children in society, which is valued and can be taken for granted. They are on the outside looking in. Yet, at the same time, their activities are subject to surveillance and control by society in such a way that they are not truly autonomous, not free to make a life of their own.

The disreputable poor must also face a labeling process by society which constitutes a surrogate for analysis and understanding. This generalizing process is an attempt to cope with the presence of individuals who are not a regular part of society. Regrettably, as Rainwater says, the social scientist and policy analyst often bring these demeaning labels into their own work.

Matza neatly summarizes a wide range of conceptualizations of the disreputable poor, which social thinkers have brought to bear historically in their recurrent discovery of the poor. These labels include "hard to reach," "problem family," "multiproblem family," "lower-

---

[6] These summary judgments refer chiefly to blacks. They are less applicable to Chicanos, Puerto Ricans, Indians, urban white ethnics, or whites in Appalachia. However, as these groups become increasingly vocal in demanding (and receiving) affirmative action on their behalf, these judgments will become far more universal. From a policy standpoint, there are two issues involved. First, determination of reasonable limits to the demands for equalization; second, the establishment of guidelines that would hold any attendant social dislocation to a minimum. There is a further issue: the origins of affirmative action or equalization policies. In some cases these policies emanate from the Congress or the President, and in most instances from the bureaucracy itself. This factor is particularly critical, since most of the leadership of these movements seems to be thoroughly unaware of the nature of the decision-making process.

lower class," "*Lumpenproletariat,*" "spurious leisure class," and "paupers." These labels can and do exercise tremendous influences, Rainwater found, on an intellectual's grasp of poverty and, by extension, also influence the kind of policies that are imagined whenever a state of war on poverty is declared to exist.[7]

The statements that have been made in this section should not be interpreted to mean that policy planning at the national level must inevitably shift from the highly general to the highly specific. The status quo of national policy, as a series of coordinated but fairly general guidelines, should be maintained. Experiments in highly centralized national planning and decision making in other countries have not been very effective. Coordination and decentralization reflect social complexity, diversity, heterogeneity, and variations far better than even the most sophisticated, centralized and, in effect, dictated five-year plans.

What, however, is possible and desirable, within the context of this discussion is the preliminary disaggregation of general, national policy guidelines. As far as the present research has been able to determine, this type of disaggregation has seldom, if at all, been employed. It is also another way of visualizing the process of policy implementation. To be successful, this procedure would have to be based on systems analysis techniques, especially mathematical modeling. Because each disaggregate would then represent a fairly discrete subsystem, it is possible, at least theoretically, to specify the key variables with some accuracy.

This approach, if found practicable, offers the following advantages: (1) more realistic and, concomitantly, efficient allocation and utilization of resources giving Alvin Weinberg's concept of choice (Organization for Economic Cooperation and Development 1968) real meaning; (2) greater facility and accuracy in the development of adequacy and effectiveness measures, since each disaggregate would also function as an information system; (3) if the consequences or ramificattions of a proposed policy could be partially determined in advance, policy analysts would have an easier task in establishing evaluation systems which are in fact, the feedback mechanisms for planning; (4) by knowing how a general aggregate might function in the disaggregate, policy makers would have, in effect, "real-time" knowledge of how realistic their ideas were. Herein also lies the greatest source of opposition to this approach. Many policy makers, particularly those

---

[7]   There have recently been some changes in this situation. For example, the Office of Research and Statistics in the Social Security Administration has initiated a research project on the legacy and ecology of low income. Using Bureau of Census data, this project will attempt to document the extent of economic disadvantage that being born into a large family in the poor sections of the country confers.

who fear change deeply and resent innovation, could hardly be expected to embark on an exercise, which could well result in failure to "put Humpty Dumpty together again"; and (5) this procedure would demonstrate the depth of the commitment of national policy makers to Maruyama's concept of human futuristics ("Toward human futuristics," this volume).

Preliminary disaggregation, even as an experimental strategy, could provide a start toward helping people develop attitudes and ability for self-education and management, not as consumers or followers of change dictated from above, but, as Maruyama argues, as changers of society with goals generated from the grass roots. A useful prototype could well be the Indian education programs in the Office of Education. On a national basis, the Office of Education can only be concerned with the general goal of improving and upgrading the quality of Indian education as a way of raising the quality of life for the American Indian. Yet, obviously, there is no such phenomenon as a homogeneous American Indian. Not only are there a large number of Indian tribes in the United States, but, equally, many subgroups exist within each of the major tribes. These subgroups in turn possess differing goals, aspirations, traditions, ethics, and values.

Clearly, there must be a federal involvement in Indian education on a national scale, Equally, as Maruyama maintains, heterogeneity in styles and delivery of education services is also needed. Indians and other groups must be allowed to have some voice in the design of education systems appropriate to their cultures. It will require an exceptional systems analyst to achieve a state of creative biculturalism, even on an experimental or theoretical basis. Programs should not be directed to standardizing and homogenizing society; nor should they result in the isolation of individuals or groups. Rather, again as Maruyama suggests, creative biculturalism to be successful, must improve intergroup respect and understanding, and promote symbiosis of intergroup relations.

The rare type of analyst who is truly innovative is, as Wildavsky (1964) observes, a *chochem*, a Yiddish word meaning "wise man" with overtones of "wise guy," connoting an ability to grasp in humorous fashion the inconsistent and perverse sides of human nature. His forte is creativity. Although he sometimes relates means to ends, and fits ends to match means, he ordinarily eschews pat processes, preferring instead to relate elements imaginatively into new systems that create their own means and ends. Finally, he plays new objectives continuously against external and internal cost elements until a creative synthesis has been achieved. Regrettably, since no one knows how to teach anyone to be a *chochem*, combining intelligence, creativity, daring, and nerve, it is not surprising that it is so extremely difficult to define what innovative policy analysis is and how it should be practiced.

THE PHILLIPS CURVE: AN EXAMPLE OF THE FUNCTIONING OF POLICY IN THE AGGREGATE AND DISAGGREGATE

Normally, the standard procedure would be to include the ensuing brief discussion in the previous section. However, because the Phillips curve is a manifestation of both macroeconomic and microeconomic thought it is sufficiently complex in itself to warrant separate treatment. It should be noted at the outset that the following paragraphs do not constitute an examination of the accuracy of the economic justification for the Phillips curve. Rather, this section is a study of the conceptual basis of the Phillips curve as its use relates to oversimplifications in national economic policy.

The work of A. W. Phillips first appeared in 1958 and showed a significant historical relationship between the rate of money wage change and the level of unemployment in Great Britain. As a recent study by the Brookings Institution concluded (Perry 1970), the Phillips curve has become a standard part of the professional and policy making vocabulary. Essentially, the Phillips curve describes the different rates of wage increase that would accompany different unemployment rates. And with slight alterations it describes the trade-off between inflation and unemployment that confronts policy makers when choosing where to aim stabilization policies. The line of reasoning behind the Phillips curve is that as unemployment falls, the level of money wage rates in the economy will rise more rapidly due to the tightening of the labor market. Conversely, as the unemployment rate in the economy rises, it will be easier for employers to hire labor, and money wage rates will rise more slowly or may even fall.

For some time after Phillips published his results, further research on the inflation question stayed fairly close to his analytic framework. Other variables were used along with unemployment to explain wage changes in what came to be called extended Phillips-curve models. In particular, the effect of past changes in living costs and the current rate of wage increases were tested extensively. However, as George Perry (1970) suggests, the theorizing behind these models remained basically macroeconomic, in the sense that links to the traditional profit and utility-maximizing behavior of firms and individuals were at best sketched in, if they were considered at all. This state of research is not unnatural. It is part of the fundamental structure of economic theory, namely the gap between economic models that fit the facts at an aggregate level and the behavioral models of microeconomic theory.

In recent years, a number of economists, notably Perry, Eckstein, Kuh, Holt, Friedman, and Phelps have deviated from the path of straightforward Phillips analysis by incorporating a number of additional variables into the relationship. These economists have also begun to cast doubt on the validity of the trade-off between inflation and unemployment. For example, Friedman and Phelps assert that the relation results from erroneous expectations about inflation. Increasing prices, they argue, will raise employment and output in the short run, so long as labor is surprised by the inflation. When labor reacts to the loss of purchasing power it has suffered because of unexpected inflation, the whole process is reversed. Wages rise, and employment and output fall. Therefore, in the long run there is no trade-off between inflation and employment; output and employment are independent of the level of prices.

The existence or nonexistence of the Phillips curve must be outside the scope of this paper. There are undoubtedly relationships between prices, wages, and employment at least as far as demand-pull inflation is concerned. As Galloway (1971) observes, there are serious definitional questions inherent in the Phillips curve as well as the problem of the availability of data. In large measure, the Phillips curve is a specification problem in the econometric sense of the word. That is, the act of defining the variables to be considered in the Phillips curve has implications for how the equation in question is to be specified in terms of the appropriate set of weights to be assigned to each variable.

The Phillips curve, if used by itself in policy planning, can lead to serious complications, since it tends to give a simplified view of inflation and unemployment. In human and political terms higher rates of unemployment never constitute an acceptable trade-off. While the Phillips curve offers an explanation for demand-pull inflation, it does not provide an explanation for cost-push inflation. Hence, the Phillips curve cannot account for the present situation of high inflation and high unemployment. Most important, the Phillips curve does not take into account the changing nature of the labor force, which is a matter of disaggregate analysis. A Phillips analysis would treat this sort of factor only as a shift in a curve.

As an alternative approach, it would be preferable to marry the Phillips relationships with a broad and expanded manpower development policy, which would reach the entire work force, instead of concentrating, as at present, on workers with low incomes and special problems. The economic and social returns from such a coordinated effort are likely, as Holt maintains, to far outweigh its costs. Inflation could be reduced and the growth in output from several sources would be sizeable: particularly reduction in unemployment, increased labor-market participation, and upgrading of the work force to achieve its full productive potential. In addition, a really tight labor market is likely to stimulate labor-saving technological innovation and reduce resistance to its introduction.

In the long run, Morley's strategy (1971) offers a more comprehensive view of how to cope with unemployment. According to this strategy, the surest way to reduce the "natural" rate of unemployment is to eliminate the reasons for it, which are primarily the workers' uncertainty about alternative job opportunities and their inability to retrain for new jobs.

There is no cheap, noncomplex, or simple way of increasing any country's production or employment. The inflation side of the Phillips curve seems to offer an answer, but it is illusory. At best, the extra output is temporary. It is much more likely to be offset by less than normal output and unemployment sometime in the future.

THE ROLE OF INFORMATION SYSTEMS IN POLICY PLANNING

No amount of analysis can tell us whether the nation benefits more from sending a slum child to preschool, providing medical care for an old man, or enabling a disabled housewife to resume her normal occupation. The grand decisions — how much help, how much education, how much welfare, and which population groups shall benefit — are matters of value judgment. The idea of a reasonable trade-off between missiles and slums bears no resemblance to reality because of the meaning that trade-off has in a systems context. Rather, it is an expression of the personal commitment and perception of priorities of an individual policy maker. These are fundamental issues of choice, with which no analysis, however complete or sophisticated, can ever really cope.

The policy analyst cannot contribute much to the resolution of problems in this framework. What can be done, according to one former senior official in the Department of Health, Education, and Welfare, is to analyze narrowly defined areas of policy. The grand decisions, those concerning alternative programs with the same or similar objectives, within the health department for example, can be substantially illuminated by good analysis.

The analytical process serves only to clarify relevant choices (and their implications), and alternative courses of action open to planners and decision makers in certain problem areas. Yet, to be successful, this process must be supported by reasonably efficient information systems. As a RAND Corporation study pointed out (Schlesinger 1967), there are several senses in which information systems are important, the primary ones being: (1) progress reporting and control, to give an indication of how well (or poorly) major program decisions are being carried out; and (2) providing data and information to serve as a basis for the critical phases in the analytic process, especially in facilitating the development of estimating relationships.

As distinct from purely methodological bias, the more general forms of bias, which will reflect negatively on the functioning of information systems, are the pressures of large and variegated organizational structures. Specific causes of bias are asymmetry in sources of information, disproportionate attention by the analyst to preferred information sources, and the analyst's prior intellectual commitment. From these sources, according to James Schlesinger, Chairman of the Atomic Energy Commission, a great deal of bias, reinforced by careless and mechanical work, inevitably slips in even on those occasions when it is not deliberately introduced. In the highly complex process of policy planning in a heterogeneous society, the deliberate introduction of misinformation and distortion is no insignificant problem in itself. In fact, it has become a rather sophisticated art. The point here, Schlesinger (1967) argues, is that the biggest proportion of bias springs from honest and deeply held convictions rather than from a deliberate attempt to deceive.

Planning, Programming, and Budgeting

This section focuses on two systems that have been designed to meet the information needs of policy makers. The first is the Planning, Programming, and Budgeting system, perhaps more familiarly known as PPB. The second is the social indicator which, unlike PPB, is not an operational system. The social indicator at present exists primarily at the level of theoretical and nonsensical discussion.

PPB was created because of the desirability of and necessity for some sort of quantitative measure of publicly supported programs. Over the past ten to fifteen years, there has been a conscious and deliberate effort to develop and use what has come to be known as the cost-benefit approach. This technique is based on the premise that there are quantitative relationships between program goals and cost outlays.

The concept of cost-benefit analyses is not new. They have been used in the budgetary process for more than three decades. However, the formal, sophisticated cost-benefit information system has existed only since 1960–1961. Formalized cost-benefit models were first applied to the aerospace and defense programs. Here, they constituted the integral feature of the so-called "McNamara systems approach." In these areas it was feasible, at least in theory, to establish discrete and hierarchical program objectives and goals through sequential analysis. Cost data were then assigned to various subprogram areas as well as to schedules for project completion.

It was assumed in this approach that information systems could be developed to identify key variables and provide access to both qualitative and quantitative data. It can certainly be argued that useful systems, in terms of both costs and time were produced by this method. At any rate, where only hardware was involved, it was just possible to reason that PPB models were an effective management technique to attain some degree of certainty and orderliness. Beginning in 1965–1966, PPB as a formal management system was extended to all executive agencies as well as to the Executive Office of the President. Two Bureau of the Budget circulars, issued in 1965 and 1967 respectively, required all executive agencies to use PPB in their budget preparation processes. The following procedures were required in these circulars: (1) clear statements of what decisions were made and why; (2) identification of program objectives and alternative methods for meeting these objectives through systematic comparison; and (3) organization of data on the basis of major programs reflecting future as well as current implications of decisions. As in the case of budgeting in general, PPB was applied not only to current programs, but to proposals for new legislation. Normally, each agency was considered to have between five and ten major program categories, with one or more subcategories and program elements.

In theory, PPB was a near-perfect system. With reasonably articulated goals and objectives, the executive agencies should have been able to shift from one set of means and ends to another in the elusive pursuit of policy recommendations. What ensued, however, might be termed the Gresham's law of systems analysis, i.e. quantitative analyses tended to drive out qualitative analyses, when, in fact, both are supporting pillars of intelligent policy analysis.

Christopher Lasch (in Bernstein 1967: 338) observes the dominant ethos. With the growth in complexity of society, immediate experience with its events plays a diminishing role as a source of information and basis for judgment in contrast to symbolically mediated information about these events, particularly numerical indices.

Judging from the assessment of the U.S. Congress Joint Economic Committee (1969), those who introduced the PPB system into the federal government in one fell swoop did not study how to introduce the system into an organization as complex and heterogeneous as the executive branch. The proponents of PPB neglected to ascertain the actual dollar costs of introducing the system into established organizations. More important, they were insensitive to the social cost of PPB in terms of upsetting traditional relationships between the agencies and the Congress, and between the agencies and their various clientele groups, all of which have vested interests in the policies of the past.

The sort of problems for which PPB was most useful, as Wildavsky, its most persistent critic, concludes (1964), turned out to be problems that could be dealt with largely at the apex of the organization. In the Department of Defense, for example, choice among weapons systems was found to be amenable to central control. The program budget group that former Secretary McNamara established, was capable of fighting generals in Washington, but not master sergeants in supply.

The difficulties in applying PPB are further compounded when the system is extended to domestic programs. The process then automatically involves not only the federal government, but also, regional, state, and local governments. The question then becomes one of whose goals and whose objectives? They might well be those of the decision makers or the analysts at any of these levels, Congress or state and local legislative bodies. They might be those of specific constituent groups, or the varied and often divergent goals, objectives, and values of some 210 million Americans.

In effect, public organizations in a heterogeneous and pluralistic society cannot exert real control over their goals and objectives. Moreover, this capability, is becoming even more chimerical as society evolves toward ever greater states of complexity. Because such organizations cannot determine their goals and objectives, they cannot exert any great degree of control over expenditure.

Weidenbaum's work (1969) has shown that there are controllable and noncontrollable expenditures. While this statement is true, it also goes far beyond Weidenbaum's thinking. We have not only noncontrollable expenditure in terms of law, legally mandated spending, but noncontrollable expenditure in fact — moral commitments. Thus, in one way or another almost all public expenditure is noncontrollable. The existence of this phenomenon is recognized by social scientists. However, there is a tendency in the social science community, particularly among some political science professors, to throw up their hands in total despair and declare that there can never be effective control of expenditure. This need not be the case. A properly functioning policy information system can provide an analytical framework for determining where at least some degree of control can be exercised in resource allocation.

There are many weaknesses in the formal PPB system. This does not mean that PPB itself is not effective. Like any other management system there is both good and bad PPB. Additionally, one can and should understand the potential for mischief inherent in PPB and avoid accusing and blaming individuals who err in using the system. The greatest weakness in PPB is its fixation with program categories and structures. In terms of information systems, this overemphasis on structure can affect judgment by causing an analyst or decision maker to fail to recognize that policy-relevant data and information flow in what Erich Jantsch (1967) found to be two dimensions: vertical and horizontal. This concept also explains, in somewhat oversimplified terms, the dynamics of information flow within Forrester's feedback drop (1971).

The vertical dimension usually concerns planners most. In this dimension, they choose to see an upward progress toward either a general goal or a particular objective. Admittedly, this may actually be occurring. However, it is being continually affected by the course of horizontal or peripheral information. By putting too much stress on a categorical approach, it is possible, or even probable, that planners will neglect to calculate the impact of the information flow in one goal category upon another. As an illustration, the Department of Health, Education, and Welfare has as a general goal, the improvement of the nation's health. One specific objective within this general framework is the reduction of tobacco consumption, which can be measured by the standard PPB system. At the same time, the Department of Agriculture's Agricultural Research Service operates a program designed to improve tobacco production, which undoubtedly affects at least indirectly whatever progress there has been in reducing tobacco consumption.

Another aspect of the excessive attention of PPB to structure is what Wildavsky (1964) describes as the need for a program structure that provides a complete list of organizational objectives and which supplies information on the attainment of each. In the absence of analytic studies of all, or even a large part of an agency's operations, the structure turns out to be a sham that piles up data under vague categories. It hides rather than clarifies. It suggests comparisons between categories for which there is no factual or analytical basis. Examination of a department's program structure convinces everyone acquainted with it that policy analysis is just another bad way of masquerading behind old confusions. The mere observation of some fairly recent program categories of the Department of Agriculture — "Communities of Tomorrow," "Science in the Service of Man," "Expanding Dimensions for Living" — makes the case better than any comment could.

Social Indicators

As political men in a representative democracy, policy makers are dealers in preferences above all else. Because they are makers, shapers, molders, and bargainers of preferences, they need information about what people want. Related to this, as an aid in calculation, is information about where preferences differ and why, because this alerts policy makers to conflicts of preference in which they may wish to intervene.

Much of the research on policy information systems has been carried out as a corollary to the development of scientific and technical information systems, as if social science information were only a variation of engineering or physical science information. However, the needs of a decision maker transcend the rather limited needs of an engineer or scientist. The physical sciences and engineering require abstract and sophisticated information and, thus, equally sophisticated systems for providing this information. In most instances, information needed for policy is far less abstract and sophisticated. Yet, in another sense, the particular information needed for making policy demands greater sophistication and creative energy by the systems designer.

Policy-relevant information resembles strategic intelligence information. Any methods of acquiring this information should therefore resemble the concept of the strategic intelligence network. Policy makers require information about the condition of society: about how much children have learned, not about the time and money used for schooling; about health, not about the number of licensed doctors; etc.

The type of information which focuses on the condition of society rather than on the activities of government is the social indicator. This term is not yet clearly defined, but it refers to some measure of overall well-being or quality of life. It represents an attempt, in Christakis's words, "to describe with some precision and detail, the condition of society in terms of particular activities and social groups" (1971). The most generally accepted definition of the social indicator is the one used in *Toward a social report* (U.S. Dept. of Health, Education, and Welfare 1969); "A social indicator ... may be defined to be a statistic of direct normative interest which facilitates concise, comprehensive, and balanced judgments about the conditions of major aspects of a society. It is in all cases a direct measure of welfare and is subject to the interpretation that, if it changes in the 'right' direction, while other things remain equal, things have gotten better and people are 'better off.'"

Social indicators are, as Mancus Olson says (1969), measures of development in which we have a normative and moral interest evident from the purposes of public policy, but they are not measures of government activities designed to influence these developments. The national income statistics are a prototypical social indicator because they provide a measure of our level of material well-being. A large part of the existing category of social statistics is thus immediately excluded from the category of social indicators. These statistics are records of public expenditure on social programs or of the quantity of inputs of one kind or another used for socioeconomic purposes. It is not possible to say whether or not things have improved when government expenditure on a social program, or the quantity of some particular input increases.

Many of the proponents of social indicators maintain the view that these indicators are incompatible with PPB. Olson argues that this view is based on a misunderstanding of PPB. Social indicators and social reporting he says are a logical extension of PPB. PPB itself can usefully analyze certain programs as discrete categories, but cannot, as presently constituted, take sufficient account of the interdependence of different levels of government or different sectors of society. PPB is not sufficient, in principle or theory, to obtain a balanced assessment of national policy which must take into account not only the federal government, but the whole of society. This is the task of social indicators and social reporting.

Social indicators must meet, as Kamrany and Christakis argue (1970), the necessary and sufficient criteria for a theoretical as well as a working basis — including completeness, geographical delineation, effective level of disaggregation and relevance to some cohesive national process of policy making. The area of greatest interest in terms of this paper is of course the matter of effective disaggregation, hence variation and heterogeneity.

The aggregation of social accounts obscures specific problems or problem areas. Christakis points out that there is no doubt that basic statistical and information bottlenecks do exist in establishing indicators at meaningful levels of aggregation. Even economic indicators suffer from these weaknesses. For example, in spite of a rapid rate of growth in the GNP, it is generally true that the distribution of income in the United States has remained practically unchanged over the last twenty years. Likewise, while the nation as a whole has experienced unprecedented economic affluence and prosperity, it is equally true that certain depressed regions have remained economically depressed over the last two decades. In the social sphere, many findings reveal that a significant improvement in the education of children has been observed since the 1950's. Nevertheless, the learning and education of the poor and disadvantaged have not increased proportionately.

Parallel with the problem of disaggregation is the impossibility of directly quantifying certain social phenomena. As Bauer (1966) observes in his classic study of social indicators, we cannot make direct measurements of certain intangibles. As a result, we are forced to derive surrogate quantitative measures. These are indirect and serve as quantitative substitutes for or representatives of the phenomena we want to measure. For example, the price that someone pays for something is a surrogate for human satisfaction. Accepting price as a measure of satisfaction involves an assumption that there is a linear relationship between the amount of money spent and the magnitude of the need satisfied. As yet, in Bauer's words, there is "no better practiced assumption." Surrogates are useful but can be misused when they are taken too seriously. Any effort designed to increase meaning and precision in social reporting creates the need for considerable imagination in elucidating new surrogates and considerable self-restraint in not being misled by them.

At present, we are only at the beginning of effective work on social indicators. We have yet to attain Kamrany's and Christakis's (1970) last element of necessary and sufficient criteria for a proper conceptual framework for social indicators. The crucial role of social indicators in the overall process of national planning needs clarification and understanding. The relationship of social indicators to national and societal objectives, goals, and priorities needs establishing. What is required is the development of a national social theory, for which social indicators would provide the necessary social information, and from which national social policy measures would be derived. As Christakis says, the main reason for the success of economic indicators is the existence of a national income theory including economic tools (fiscal, monetary, market, and international) and some means of implementation. No such theory, tool, or system of information exists in the social sphere.

If a balanced, organized, and concise set of measures on the condition of society were available, we should have the information needed to identify emerging problems and make knowledgeable decisions about national priorities. The next step in any logical process of policy formulation is to choose the most efficient program for dealing with the conditions that have been exposed. Then, there must be a decision about how much to spend on the program to deal with the difficulty. If these two decisions are to be made intelligently, our society needs information on the benefits and costs of alternative programs at alternative levels of funding.

The fact that rational policy necessitates linking social indicators to program inputs means that social indicators alone cannot provide all the quantitative information needed in effective decision making. Ultimately, we must integrate social indicators into policy accounts. This would allow us to estimate the changes in a social indicator that would be expected to result from alternative levels of expenditure in relevant public programs. As a note of caution, it should be said that even though it is feasible to develop a comprehensive set of social indicators at relatively modest cost in the near future, a comprehensive set of social accounts is a utopian goal.

The problem which PPB and social indicators attempt to meet is an old one. How do we optimize public policy decisions by basing them on accurate and adequate information? The problem of information is central to effective decision making . Information, as Henriot suggests (1970), does not make the policy planning process work, but without it there is considerable waste of effort, misdirected motion, and eventual breakdown. Efforts are being made to correct the situation which has been described as one in which policy makers are misled by inadequate interpretation of bad information, based on obsolete concepts and inadequate research collected by "underfed and overlobbied statistical agencies."

This long discourse on information systems in policy planning is also a focus for understanding the distinction between the role of the policy analyst and that of the decision maker. The analyst functions essentially to array information. In this he obviously develops a large part of the universe of the decision maker. However, the analyst must always remain subordinate, for he can never constitute the entire universe for the decision maker. The analyst must not become, or allow himself to become, involved in the fundamental process of choice, for he is never in the position of having to accept responsibility for the consequences of choices. There is a danger that the policy analyst, by design or even unconsciously, will disguise fundamental choice problems as efficient solution problems.

This caveat is not an abstract one. The decision makers within the present administration are relatively conservative, while the policy analysts in the domestic agencies are generally quite liberal. The analysts often tend to furnish the decision maker with information distorted by their own values, and which of course does not fit his ideological preconceptions. As a result, the analyst does not prepare useful analyses, and the decisions reached are all the less effective for lack of proper information support. This situation need not arise. A capable policy analyst can array information in ways which reflect the political orientation of the decision maker, while at the same time clarifying the possible ramifications of a policy decision. This need not be at the expense of the analyst having to sacrifice his own convictions or self-respect.

This paper is concerned with the question of alternative futures of which a key element is proper role identification. If there is an identity crisis in policy planning, it is to be found far more among the analysts than among the decision makers.

THE MODULAR BASIS OF PLANNING

Within the Western world there are two established social planning frameworks: the French and the American. As Jantsch (1967) points out, both approaches are strongly function-oriented. However, France and the United States differ widely in other respects. The French approach has been mainly to centralize and concentrate their efforts within the framework of a rigid five-year plan. The United States, on the other hand, has endeavored to create a structure which allows for vitally needed flexibility in the continuous performance of decentralized planning. Judging from recent evidence, it appears that the French too are moving toward greater decentralization, perhaps in recognition of the uselessness of their inflexible planning methods.

As Lindblom (1970) suggests, decentralized and continuous planning entails starting each time from fundamentals, building on the past only as experience is embodied in a theory, and being prepared always to start anew from the ground up. Advanced quantitative procedures, such as operations research, remain mainly appropriate for relatively small-scale problem solving where the number of variables to be considered is small and the value problem is restricted.

For the foreseeable future, systematic social planning will remain suboptimal. That is, systematic social planning can be used only in solving lower-level problems. The difficulties of analysis increase and the unique competence of the specialist diminishes by an order of magnitude with each higher level of decision making. The sort of simple explicit model in the use of which operations researchers, model builders, or systems analysts are so proficient, can certainly impart most of the significant factors influencing traffic control at the George Washington Bridge. But the contribution of any such model or models to the analysis and planning of any major domestic or foreign policy decision appears to be almost trivial.

In social policy terms, suboptimization means, for example, that whatever is learned in creating a better environment in New York City might be fully or partly applicable to the Amish areas of Pennsylvania. On the other hand, these experiences might have to be discarded in their entirety. Suboptimization does imply the use of systematic means of integrating policy elements so as to build more coherent and comprehensive long-range plans. These means come under the general classification of "modularism."

Modularism, as Toffler (1970) defines the term, is an attempt to lend greater flexibility and stability to whole structures by making their substructures less permanent. In other words, a module is an independent unit that forms part of an overall structure. Modularism, as a concept, had its inception in electronics through the development of integrated circuitry. Modularism is a reflection of the reduction in the duration of man-artifact relationships brought about by the proliferation of temporary and, more importantly, disposable structures. Modularism implies a distinction between disposability and mobility. Even when modules are not discarded, but merely rearranged, there is a new configuration, a new entity, a new synthesis. It is as if one structure had in reality been discarded and a new one created, even though some or all of the components may be the same.

Some of the most significant expressions of modularism are to be found in architecture. Many buildings are constructed today so that internal walls and partitions may be shifted at will to form new internal enclosure patterns. Proponents of what has come to be known as "plug-in" and "clip-on" architecture have designed entire cities based on modular principles. They propose the construction of different types of models which could be assigned different life expectancies. In terms of social systems this view of modularism offers a novel approach in conceptualizing trade-offs.

Modularism in architecture is a reflection of both social impermanence and of heterogeneity. As Maruyama argues ("Toward human futuristics," this volume) metropolitan areas are heterogeneous in population. There are various age-groups with new life-styles and new philosophies of life, in addition to numerous cultural and ethnic groups. Moreover, Maruyama is undoubtedly right in asserting that social heterogeneity will increase rather than decrease as freedom from material restraints increases. People are becoming better able to afford diversity.

Architecture and policy planning have a common problem because we are moving from a standardized to a post-standardized society. Both must aim at complexity and heterogeneity. Glazer and Moynihan (1963) have exposed the fallacy of the melting-pot theory. Clearly, architecture and planning cannot be successful if they are blind to the cultural pluralism of the population. The overall approach to planning as a way of building the future fosters a significant relationship with design, as the visual expression of society and its development.

During the past decade, Italy has come into a position of influence and preeminence in achieving innovative and novel syntheses of architectural design and social planning based on modular precepts. For many Italian designers and planners, the aesthetic quality of individual forms has become irrelevant in the face of the common problems encountered in all industrialized countries. Consequently, they have shifted their attention to the total physical and social environment, seeing their functions as creating newer settings for more adaptable and transient life-styles. In effecting positive social change through design, the concern of this school of thought has been to make people, objects, and forms appear in all their complexity and variety. The result obviously represents unstable and changeable fragments of artifacts, events, and experiences — i.e. modules.

These apostles of counterdesign and counterplanning share one extremely important attribute with the radical historians — a willingness to give not different, but completely heretical and unorthodox meanings to key terms, namely "architecture," "the city," and "planning." Architecture becomes not a matter of design or form, but rather a means of expressing man's condition instead of his place. Similarly, the city is no longer understood as an economic, political, geographic, or even cultural unit. Rather, it is a series of variable structures for use; a heterogeneous ensemble of events, physical structures, and services based on continually shifting patterns of behavior and values among the inhabitants, allowing them maximum freedom to arrange their own system of images. What is sacrificed in this definition is the principle of harmony or to use a social term, homogeneity. Finally, planning, instead of being a formalized discipline or methodology, is a montage which permits a continuing recombination of different parts of the whole urban social structure.

The end product of all this is not a better city. It is a challenge rather to the ideology of the city. Taken as a synthesis, these ideas establish planning as a succession of contrasting logics whose basic reality is contradiction.

The shift to environmental concern has brought about serious rethinking on the function of planning and design. Design and planning, founded not solely on the concrete object, but on its sociopolitical context, entail a redefinition of the individual as an enactor. Hence, the concept of environment presupposes for man the role of active protagonist rather than of mere passive spectator, encompassing all those processes that give meaning and order to his surroundings and the daily patterns of life.

Clearly, Italian national planning is not proceeding according to the thinking of this avant-garde school of designers. Moreover, given the facts of Italy's bureaucratic stultification and social stratification, it is highly unlikely that these innovative and admittedly highly controversial ideas will exert a revolutionary impact, resulting in an abrupt change of direction, even in the foreseeable future. Rather, it would be more reasonable to expect that this avant-garde school will exert a long-term but highly subtle influence on Italy's planning.

Many of the ideas advanced by the Italian school of architectural design have been incorporated in the urban planning approach of Doxiadis (Doxiadis Urban Systems 1967, 1971). Doxiadis himself is not so much an originator of ideas, in the strict sense of the term, as a force for moving the ideas of others into creative action. Doxiadis translates the meta-problem of Drucker's global shopping center into an achievable planning framework. While Doxiadis's work has received worldwide attention, he is probably best known in the United States for his exhaustive planning study of the Detroit metropolitan area, although the Doxiadis Systems Group has prepared similar studies for other regions in this country, such as that for southwest Georgia. There are four key terms which characterize the Doxiadis planning methodology. These are: (1) ecumenopolis, (2) ekistics, (3) the ekistics logarithmic scale, and (4) the ekistic unit.

1. Ecumenopolis is the city of the future which will, together with the corresponding open land indispensable to man, cover the entire earth as a continuous network of urbanized areas forming a universal settlement.

2. Ekistics is the science of human settlements according to which every human settlement is conceived as a living organism. It develops an interdisciplinary approach to its problems. The principal concerns of ekistics are: creation of the most satisfactory environment for human activities, and selection of the most efficient means for creating this environment in a given local, national, or international setting.

3. The ekistic logarithmic scale is a classification of settlements according to their size, presented on the basis of a logarithmic scale and running from an individual man as the smallest unit of measurement, to the whole world. This scale can be used as a basis for the measurement and classification of many dimensions in human settlements.

4. Finally, the ekistic unit is based on the classification of parts beginning with man and ending with ecumenopolis.

The main thrust of Doxiadis's argument is the universality of the urban crisis, whether one is dealing with large or small cities, or with advanced or developing nations. However, Doxiadis cautions that the urban crisis, as one manifestation of a heterogeneous world, appears in varied forms. The urban crisis may appear as a traffic problem, a waster of natural resources, or as social, economic, or environmental problems. Doxiadis offers two explanations of the urban crisis. These also form part of his planning methodology. First, the city, a system of people living together and developing a community with a common economy, is getting out of balance in certain areas. Doxiadis pictures this phenomenon as an imbalance in rates of population growth, economy, and energy. Second, the city, like any other growing system, develops an increasing degree of complexity which should always be served by corresponding physical and individual clusters. However, the cities of today have not yet reached the stage where they have a structure serving their increasing complexity in the way the structure of a century ago served the complexity of those days. In sum, the real cause of the problem, in Doxiadis's view, is the gap between the size and speed of growth of cities, and our ability to cope with this.

Doxiadis is essentially a futurist. Yet, unlike many futurists, his actions in planning are not defined merely by extrapolating existing trends. Instead, he is an advocate of the use of the alternative future — the ability of man, at least in part, to shape his destiny. As Doxiadis further observes, there are a huge number of alternative futures for any large urban area. These many alternative futures result from the fact that cities consist of many elements or modules which, for the purposes of this paper, are nature-man, society, and shells (buildings and networks). Furthermore, these modules are interconnected on the basis of economics, history, sociology, technology, culture, and aesthetics.

Doxiadis has developed a methodology for searching out the best among all possible alternatives, including those based on new conceptions and on existing trends, through the aggregation of their common and desirable characteristics. There are, however, two major weaknesses inherent in this methodology. First, there is the requirement of commonly accepted goals for cities. Common goals are difficult if not almost impossible to articulate — much less to achieve in a complex institutional or organizational structure. A more profitable approach might be to use social indicators to measure concerns, expectations, preferences and, above all, values rather than the elusive goals. Second, Doxiadis arranges his alternative futures in hierarchies. This approach is useful if limited to ranking alternatives according to their importance. However, it becomes counterproductive if these hierarchies become the basis of planning, in place of the nonlinear and self-organizing socioeconomic network.

The movement of planning toward modularism also portends a change in the self-image of both decision makers and policy analysts. They can no longer be grounded in a single discipline. Their concerns are even more than interdisciplinary. They have become, to use Jantsch's word, "transdiciplinary" (1967). As such, any individual involved in the policy process will have to view himself, not as a narrow specialist, but as an architect, builder, and designer of the future in order to be effective.

SOME REASONABLE ALTERNATIVE FUTURES

What does all this mean to the shape of the next ten to thirty years? How do these issues and problems relate? There is no single answer, but we can articulate several plausible, if not always palatable, alternative futures. These are:

1. Continued high rate of economic and social growth, a great deal of emphasis on science and technology with a return to achievement orientation as the more traditional social institutions, business, and industry turn to a solution of social problems. Poverty and dissidence are substantially overcome. In particular, various integration policies

are successful, and tolerance of violence decreases. Some artificial propping of traditional institutions and values occurs, with concomitant emphasis on law and order. Partial resolution of physical environmental problems occurs through large-scale systems engineering.

2. Slow growth, a degree of stagnation, but alleviation of many social problems, particularly those which are susceptible to money and systems analysis. Despite some advances, many other social problems remain unresolved, and there is a decline in the charisma of science, engineering, and business. While most Americans participate fully in society, more small groups drop out or oppose the establishment. Problems of the environment persist.

3. Greater economic stagnation, bureaucratic stultification, and a deliberate diminishing of technological progress. There is decreasing satisfaction and pride in participating in national life. The prestige of science, engineering, and business erodes rapidly, and individual isolation increases. Environmental problems deepen.

4. Growth toward a new society becoming evident with new values and significantly changed institutions. Economic growth continues at a relatively high rate; major social problems are or clearly will be resolved. Government, business, and industry are cooperating in their solution. We learn to control or manipulate our physical environment.

Clearly some of the elements in these alternative futures are transferable from one scenario to another, while others are not. For example, it is quite possible that, even with a high rate of economic and social growth, there may be more individuals or groups who drop out from social participation. This may occur if the rate of change is so rapid that it becomes unbearable for many people. Furthermore, bureaucratization can also occur in a highly innovative society. Conversely, it is difficult to imagine science, technology, or the advancement of knowledge in general being accorded any priority in a stagnant society. Finally, the degree to which environmental or ecological problems can be resolved or not in any of these states depends solely on conscious and deliberate policy decisions and actions.

Running through these various alternative futures is what the Japanese social psychologist Yonosuke Nagai (1971) defines as the "crisis of fragmentation." The perspective shared by many social scientists is that highly energized centripetal or inward-pulling forces are consolidating huge aggregates of power. However, as Nagai persuasively argues, the crisis is the work of centrifugal forces that are pulling American institutions apart, throwing the pieces outward from the center. In other words, America is in a fairly long-term crisis because it has lost its stable majority, its ruling class, and its authority. Much of this crisis is derived from the adverse effects of what have previously been regarded as key advantages: space and freedom of movement;

abundant capital and information; tremendous systems technology; and rapid handling and control by business, with emphasis always on efficiency. But because of the multiplying effects of these factors, the United States has, as Nagai suggests, fallen into a circle of frustration and distrust.

Clearly, substantial structural problems have so shaken both society and politics that American institutions have lost much of their ability to restore themselves. Technological innovation and automation will continue to disrupt the system structures of population, capital, and information in American society. Moreover, this huge social change has come about without planning. By fanatically pushing the efficiency and rationality of each subsystem of society to the utmost limit confusion and disorder in the total system have been created.

It is by no means clear that this crisis can be overcome in the foreseeable future. However, we can at least mitigate its effects somewhat by recognizing its existence and coping with it intelligently. It seems clear that America is losing some of its national consciousness, from the standpoint of domestic issues. National goals are becoming a largely fruitless exercise, although as the more creative studies in social indicators demonstrate, more attention can be profitably paid to understanding the concerns of the American people.

There is an emerging regionalism and sectionalism in America with an accompanying heightened emphasis on particularism. America, as Nagai observes, is becoming a divided nation. Obviously, in a divided nation there cannot be a unified general will. Yet, in a heterogeneous and pluralist society, characterized by constantly shifting alignments of power, one must question whether a unified national sense of purpose is attainable, desirable, or necessary for the future, or, if in fact it ever existed at all. American history is a long record of group antagonisms and hostilities, with accumulated complaints and dissatisfactions. There is not now, nor is it likely that there ever will be anything resembling universal brotherhood in America. But with farsighted and innovative planning, blacks, Orientals, Southerners, students, women, policemen, national and religious ethnic groups, and even WASPS can continue, if only reluctantly, to coexist.

There is of course an opposing view to these preceding judgments. From economic and political standpoints, there is abundant evidence of growing concentrations of power within large organizations in the private and public sectors. Even increased social mobility will exert a certain countervailing pressure on sectionalism.[8] However, from a

---

[8] The term sectionalism, as used in this paper, should not be equated with the dynamism, force, or impact of pre-Civil War sectionalism. Rather, the current form of sectionalism is a reflection of the state of mind of an individual in understanding social complexity.

policy planning point of view the sheer enormity of these organizations, as well as the issues they must resolve, are themselves a force for a kind of sectionalism — decentralization. Policies simply cannot be administered or implemented centrally with any degree of effectiveness by either the agglomerate corporation or the executive department.

THE MISSING PROFESSIONALS

For the near future, professionals trained in policy analysis and management might be best described as poly-socio-econo-politico-technico-managers. These individuals will receive their training by adding one degree to another as, for example, a business administration degree to an engineering degree. An essential ingredient in this makeshift way of meeting the formal educational requirements of policy specialists is of course pragmatic day-to-day synthesizing of the arts and disciplines with training, motivation, and human ingenuity.

Beyond the next decade, as Simon Ramo (1971) argues, we must endeavor to create a new "profession" whose members can attack problems as a team and provide the required development for our society. These professionals will be people who have deliberately set out to become broadly expert in applying the full spectrum of information and knowledge to society, although the team will also include specialists. Certainly they will not be professionals except in the sense that their profession is to understand society, government, and business and purvey the kinds of knowledge available for application to society. It will not be enough to have liberal arts or engineering majors, who have simply taken courses outside their major area. This kind of breadth does not make up for the lack of a new kind of major. We need the interdisciplinary man, who has been specifically brought up with the idea that, when he leaves university, he will be engaged in solving the interconnected, interfacial, and intersensitive problems which are the most urgent ones of the day. If we are going to attack these problems, we must recognize them and endeavor to make an intellectual occupation out of going after them.

A third of a century ago, the momentous rise in the need for greater application of science and technology gave us the so-called military-industrial complex, a teaming up of science and engineering to meet national security needs. In the last third of this century, the rise of a social-industrial complex can be predicted. It will team up intellectual action in all the social pursuits of man, as well as his science and technology, with government, the educational establishment, the non-profit foundations, business, and industry to give the nation what it is increasingly coming to realize that it must have.

Undoubtedly we are a long way yet from having a real social-industrial complex, from building up a teaming process that yields a combination of economic payoff and social progress. At present we are only at the planning stage, but the factors that will bring it about are clear: great and increasing demand, availability of improved approaches, and the potential for private capital to generate profit under innovative public-sector leadership.[9]

CONCLUSION

This paper has attempted to provide some insight into the complex facets of policy planning within the public sector. The style employed has been to some extent diffuse for the purpose of demonstrating the diffuse nature of the policy planning process itself. Furthermore, no attempt has been made to give a succinct definition of policy. Even labeling this complex process serves only to simplify it without providing any accompanying clarification. However, to satisfy those purists who read this paper, Erich Jantsch (1967) provides a definition of policy which is as useful as any: "Policies are the first expressions and guiding images of normative thinking and action... they are the spiritual agencies of change... in the ways and means by which bureaucracies and technocracies operate." It is clear that this definition does not adequately describe those activities within government that come under the general description of policy.

Much of the difficulty encountered in public policy planning is that agencies are constituted along lines of specialization. An assumption underlying government organization is that society can be divided into a number of aspects, each of which can be dealt with separately by a controlling agency. Each agency is presumed to have the best knowledge concerning the aspect to which it was assigned and therefore is in the best position to promulgate policy and plan for the future. The trouble is that none of the aspects of society with which a government is concerned can be usefully considered in isolation except for very limited purposes — purposes which do not include policy making or planning for the future. With the increase in social complexity, there is a corresponding (probably nonlinear) proliferation of the effects of change from one aspect of society to the others.

[9] As Ramo (1971) notes, the military-industrial complex, with all its imperatives and its dangers, involves not even ten percent of our GNP. By contrast, half of our GNP is tied to problems with which the social-industrial complex will grapple. Thus, its influence for good as well as bad will be proportionately greater. The emergence of the social-industrial complex also supports Richard Nelson's judgments (1967) concerning the generally diminishing importance of the sector. There are no longer any clear-cut distinctions or delineations in social policy issues.

Beyond the next two decades we must think about establishing what Mysior describes as a special agency between the legislative and executive branches. This special agency would be designed as a cybernetic machine, a kind of supercomputer with human elements. Its function would be to coordinate the plans and control the activities of all other agencies and to feed new information back to the separate agencies as parametrics for their activities.

Many factors militate against a social control system. Few people really understand the nature of the problem and most people are not easily induced to learn new concepts. Another problem is that many promising theoretical concepts, which might contribute to the solution of social problems, call into question some of the traditional values of our society.[10] How do we properly integrate planning into our value-assumption base?

Lindblom (1970) and Mysior (1977) are undoubtedly correct in assuming that for at least the next ten to fifteen years our main strategy is going to be muddling through. A muddling-through technique is called for when no solution to a problem is known. We are faced with two alternatives in this strategy. First, the passage of time may dissipate the problem. Second, it might become clear that a problem will not disappear but will worsen with the passage of time. In this case muddling through for a while might buy sufficient time to find a solution. Undoubtedly, this last alternative describes our current situation.

REFERENCES

ACKHOFF, RUSSELL
1970   "On the ambiguity of the researcher and the researched," in *The place of research in social choice*, 21–32. London: Tavistock Institute of Human Relations.
AMBASZ, EMILIO, *editor*
1972   *Italy: the new domestic landscape.* New York: The Museum of Modern Art.
ARNOLD, MARK R.
1972   "Title I: politics, pressure, and sometimes children." *The Washington Post.* B-5, July 11.
BAUER, RAYMOND A.
1966   *Social indicators.* Cambridge, Massachusetts: M.I.T. Press.
BELL, DANIEL
1969   The idea of a social report. *The Public Interest* 15: 72–84.

[10]   It might be useful to give a definition of *values*, since this concept most assuredly affects the conduct of policy. As Mysior uses the term (1977), values are "a system of emotional conditioning," essentially meaning the "subjective experience of preferences."

BERNSTEIN, BARTON J.
1967   *Toward a new past: dissenting essays in American history.* New York: Vintage Books.
CANTRIL, ALBERT H., CHARLES W. ROLL
1971   *Hopes and fears of the American people.* New York: Universe Books.
CHRISTAKIS, ALEXANDER
1971   "The limits of systems analysis in economic and social development planning." Paper presented at the Conference on Information Technology, Jerusalem.
1972   The Club of Rome project methodology. *Ekistics* 34(210.
CLUB OF ROME
1970   "The predicament of mankind." Unpublished manuscript.
DOXIADIS URBAN SYSTEMS
1967   *Emergence and growth of an urban region: the developing Detroit area,* volumes two and three. Detroit: Detroit Edison.
1971   *Integrated program planning project: phase I design.* Prepared for the Southwest Georgia Planning Commission. Washington, D.C: Doxiadis.
DRUCKER, PETER
1969   *The age of discontinuity: guidelines to our changing society.* New York: Harper and Row.
DUNCKEL, EARL B., *et al.*
1970   *The business environment of the seventies: a trend analysis for business planning.* New York: McGraw-Hill.
EXECUTIVE OFFICE OF THE PRESIDENT, BUREAU OF THE BUDGET
1967   *Planning, programming, budgeting.* Bulletin No. 68-2. Washington, D.C: Government Printing Office.
FISHER, C. H.
1966   *The world of program budgeting.* Rand Corporation Paper 3361.
FORRESTER, JAY W.
1971   *World dynamics.* Cambridge, Massachusetts: Wright-Allen.
FREEMAN, CHRISTOPHER, *et al.*
1963   *Science, economic growth, and government policy.* Paris: Organization for Economic Cooperation and Development.
GALLOWAY, LOWELL E.
1971   *Manpower economics.* Homewood, Illinois: Richard D. Irwin.
GLAZER, NATHAN, DANIEL PATRICK MOYNIHAN
1963   *Beyond the melting pot.* Cambridge, Massachusetts: M.I.T. Press.
HELMER, OLAF
1965   *Social technology.* U.S. Department of Commerce. CFSTI, AD 460520.
HENRIOT, PETER
1970   Political questions about social indicators. *The Western Political Science Quarterly* 23: 235–255.
HOOS, IDA R.
1969   A realistic look at the systems approach to social problems. *Datamation* (February): 22–24.
1972   "Techniques for managing society: a critique." Paper presented at the 11th International Meeting of the Institute for Management Sciences, Houston, Texas.
HOVLAND, CARL
1963   "Computer simulation in the behavioral sciences," in *The behavioral sciences today,* 77–88. New York: Harper and Row.

JANTSCH, ERICH
1967   *Technological forecasting in perspective.* Paris: Organization for Economic Cooperation and Development.

JOHNSON, SHEILA
1972   Article appearing in *The New York Times Magazine* (July).

KAMRANY, NAKE, ALEXANDER N. CHRISTAKIS
1970   Social indicators in perspective. *Social and Economic Planning Science Journal* 4: 288.

LINDBLOM, CHARLES E.
1970   "The science of muddling through," in *Strategies of community organization,* 291–301. Itasca, Illinois: F. E. Peacock.

MACHLUP, FRITZ
1962   *The production and distribution of knowledge in the United States.* Princeton: Princeton University Press.

MASLOW, ABRAHAM H.
1959   *New knowledge for human values.* New York: Harper.

MEADOWS, DONELLA H., *et al.*
1972   *The limits to growth.* New York: Universe Books.

MORLEY, SAMUEL A.
1971   *The economics of inflation.* Hinsdale, California: Dryden Press.

MOYNIHAN, DANIEL P.
1969   *Maximum feasible misunderstanding: community action in the war on poverty.* New York: Free Press.

MYSIOR, ARNOLD
1977   "Society: a very large system: a systems approach to the study of society."

NAGAI, YONOSUKE
1971   A view from Mt. Fuji: the United States is disintegrating. *Psychology Today* (May): 25–27, 93–95.

NATIONAL SCIENCE FOUNDATION
1971   *Research applications III (RANN).* Washington, D.C: National Science Foundation.
1972   *Research applied to national needs: fiscal years 1971–1973.* Washington, D.C: National Science Foundation.

NELSON, RICHARD, *et al.*
1967   *Technology, economic growth and public policy.* Washington, D.C: The Brookings Institution.

New York Times
1972   "A populist wave." *New York Times; the week in review.* April 30.

OLSON, MANCUS
1969   The plan and purpose of a social report. *Public Interest* 15: 85–97.

ORGANIZATION FOR ECONOMIC COOPERATION AND DEVELOPMENT
1968   *Review of national science policy: United States.* Paris: Organization for Economic Cooperation and Development.
1971   *Science growth and society: a new perspective.* Paris: Organization for Economic Cooperation and Development.

PALMER, JOHN L.
1971   "Inflation, unemployment and poverty." Unpublished doctoral dissertation, Stanford University, Stanford, California.

PERRY, GEORGE L.
1970   *Inflation and unemployment.* Washington, D.C: The Brookings Institution.

PHELPS, EDMUND S., *et al.*
  1970 *Micro-economic foundations of employment and inflation theory.* New York: Norton.
RAINWATER, LEE
  1970 "The disinherited: some psychological aspects of understanding the poor," in *Psychological factors in poverty.* Chicago: Markham.
RAMO, SIMON
  1971 The coming social-industrial complex. *Third annual Farfel lecture.* Houston: University of Houston.
SCHLESINGER, JAMES R.
  1967 *Systems analysis and the political process.* Rand Corporation, Paper 3469.
TOFFLER, ALVIN
  1970 *Future shock.* New York: Random House.
U.S. CONGRESS, JOINT ECONOMIC COMMITTEE
  1969 *The analysis and evaluation of public expenditures: the PPBS system,* volume three. Washington, D.C: Government Printing Office.
U.S. DEPARTMENT OF HEALTH, EDUCATION, AND WELFARE
  1969 *Toward a social report.* Washington, D.C: Government Printing Office.
  1971 "HEW and the future." Unpublished report. Washington, D.C.
U.S. DEPARTMENT OF HOUSING AND URBAN DEVELOPMENT
  1972 Breakthrough. *The challenge.* 3(6), June. Washington, D.C: Government Printing Office.
VON BERTALANFFY, LUDWIG
  1968 *General system theory: foundations, development, applications.* New York: George Braziller.
WEIDENBAUM, MURRAY L.
  1969 *The modern public sector: new ways of doing the government's business.* New York: Basic Books.
WILDAVSKY, AARON
  1964 *The politics of the budgetary process.* Boston: Little, Brown.

Perception, Action, Research Paradigm, and Policy Design

Toward Polyocular Anthropology

SUE-ELLEN JACOBS

I have heard Chicanos say to anthropologists: "You will not be allowed into my *barrio* to do fieldwork. You will not be allowed to use my people to advance yourself monetarily or professionally." Native Americans have said they will not allow non-Indian anthropologists to enter their reservations to conduct fieldwork. Women in various liberation organizations are refusing to allow men to attend their meetings, or they are relegating them to nonspeaking or nominal speaking positions "in the back of the room" (e.g. Sacramento Women's Liberation). At the same time that these restrictions are being stated and implemented, Chicanos, Native and Asian Americans, blacks, and women are entering anthropology and other fields, expecting to use the techniques of the field to work with and for their own people. Some Third World People, i.e. non-"white Anglo-Saxon Protestant middle-class individuals" now doing graduate work are analyzing white middle-class America. Studying others in order to reorient the studies of own-group is recognized as providing the opportunity to return to own-group as an action-oriented anthropologist — or at least as an anthropologist less concerned with defining esoteric elements of alien cultures, than with defining specific values and norms of own-culture.

Yet, anthropologists' training involves reading, as well as field experience, debate, and discussion. Readings in ethnography should provide information that is fairly representative of the real world of people. However, certain topics are suspiciously and narrowly treated,

This paper which was originally written in 1970 was published in *Human Futuristics*, edited by Magoroh Maruyama and James Dator. It is reprinted in modestly revised form here at the suggestion of Dr. Maruyama on whose conceptual development of a "polyocular anthropology" (see Maruyama 1978) the title is based.

I am grateful to Lynn E. Kauffman for suggestions and criticisms, and for contributing some of the sections on proxemics and interior design.

almost formated into archetypical jargon — i.e. stereotyped. As an
example, in attempting to locate adequate sources for a course entitled
Women Cross-culturally, I was distressed to find that ethnographic
coverage of women's roles, women's activities, and women's talk had
been conducted largely by men. And these men usually received their
information from secondhand sources: the males in the communities
where the fieldwork was conducted. Scattered throughout the literature are statement which read "it is said that women..." or similar
hearsay statements. I have also found statements which contend that
women do thus-and-so "of course." This is just as fallacious, and has
much the same effect, as the words of a syndicated newspaper columnist
who wrote: "Approximately one in every three Negroes has double-
jointed thumbs, I'm told" (Boyd 1970). Such stories are passed on
without empirical validation. At this point, we cannot say for certain
that women in groups act as men in groups say that they do, nor do
women necessarily see themselves and their worlds in the way that
men report these things. Beverly Chiñas (1970) has demonstated some
of the discrepancies obtained when male anthropologists inquire into
women's positions, roles, communication activities, etc. More women
must be encouraged to undertake these studies. We can safely suspect
that a woman anthropologist from outside the studied culture, although an out-culture person, will, because of her sex, not cause
women to alter the normative behavioral patterns which obtain when
men are not around. This type of own-group (though out-culture)
study will enlarge the data we have on *Homo sapiens*, and provide a
more nearly total picture of the social behavior of people in various
cultures.[1]

In attempting to further develop anthropology into a discipline
which will be a source for true understanding of human conditions, it is
relatively unimportant whether a particular individual works in own-
group or other-group. What is important is that we encourage the
study of all components of social systems from all ethnic, sociocultural
and sexual perspectives. Westerman and Curtiss (1970), in the song
"Here come the anthros," say "there's nothing left to study and there's
nothing left to see." I do not believe this, but I do believe that we
should listen to the views of Akoni and others who suggest that
recruitment of Third World people into the discipline is a must if

---

[1] Since this paper was written numerous sources about and by women have been
published as well as my bibliography (Jacobs 1974). These include works on women in
societies studied formerly by men (e.g. Weiner 1976; Goodale 1970), collections of
studies of women in various cultures (e.g. Rosaldo and Lamphere 1974; Reiter 1975;
Ardener 1975), important thematically controlled, cross-cultural comparative studies
(e.g. Schlegel 1972), examinations of human developmental and evolutionary changes
(Martin and Voorhies 1975; Boulding 1976), and in-depth studies of women in revolutionary change (Cassell 1977).

anthropology is to survive. By this is meant that if anthropology is to become more than the study and documentation of *sapiens'* life-styles based on Western epistemology, and become a truly multiconcept and multimethod field, we need to encourage a greater diversity of approaches to the study of humankind. Also, it is true that the tools and methods of anthropological inquiry are as valuable for daily living as in the preparation of professional anthropologists. Again, I agree with Abdulhamid Akoni (1970 personal communication) who believes that trained anthropologists have certain advantages in coping with current crises and stress situations. But could we not enhance these survival advantages further with information gleaned from polyocular views? Can we not develop this potential by studying cultures as bodies of ethnocommunication?

In the early part of 1970 at the suggestion of Jack McCullough, (personal communication), I introduced the term *ethnocommunication* and defined it as the anthropological investigation of communication. Since then I have been working with various models of communication based on communication and information theories, linguistics, and social anthropology (Jacobs 1970a, 1970b, 1970c), and have redefined the term. Ethnocommunication is defined here as everything that people in a specific ethnically or otherwise defined group use to transfer information. It is precisely conceptualized as actions of information transfer based on cultural (or subcultural or experiential) learning. Ethnocommunications are also precisely conceptualized as particles in a range of normative behaviors based on defined cognitive orientations which subsequently affect perception of "reality." With this basis for guiding the analysis of ethnocommunications, we can easily be led to ask how we can get inside the heads of other people to really see how they view their culture (world), and is this what the study of culture is about? It is, in part, what the study of ethnocommunication is about.

As a minimum, studies in ethnocommunication must include the items listed by Hymes (1964) which constitute an ethnography of communication: participants, channels, codes, settings, forms of messages, themes or topics of messages, and a typology of communication events. Further, the networks of human interaction, formed through initial communications and maintained by other communications generated from primary events, must be examined in order to produce a factual tabloid of ethnocommunication repertoires in specific cultures and subcultures.

At this point, I should make clear what I do not consider to be contextually related to studies of ethnocommunication. The stimulus for this negative is Lévi-Strauss's article (1952) wherein he suggests that people communicate in three ways: through the transfer of women, through the transfer of goods and services, and through formal messages. These communications, he concluded, take place intraculturally and interculturally. From his analysis he determined that it was largely due to the circular distribution of women that certain societies maintain social order. Some writers think that Lévi-Strauss was thinking of rules governing the exchange of genetic material when he was discussing the "exchange of women." However, he states ". . . social organization (limited for the purposes of this paper to kinship systems, descent groups, and marriage rules) refers to a level of communication where the objects to be communicated are women, while men — or rather consanguine groups consisting of male kin — are engaged in the process of exchanging these objects among themselves" (1952: 1). I think Lévi-Strauss was concerned here with demonstrating the utility of the models to be found in the "new field of communication" (1952: 1). The ensuing arguments about his theories and those of Dumont led to conflict between descent theorists and alliance theorists (Buchler and Selby 1968). These arguments were largely devoted to showing the direction in which women actually move, in passage from one male communicator to the next. This point of view — the movement of women as a form of communication — may be based on empirical fact discerned by male anthropologists; however, in this tautological argument the primary source of data is not firsthand observation of marriage practices, but rather interpretations of some firsthand sources (but not the women in the cultures), and extrapolations therefrom.

Certainly there is much to be said for theory built on interpretation and extrapolation; nevertheless, it is somewhat disconcerting to note the tendency of these male authorities to consider women as commodities in exchange. The absurdity lies in the interpretation that Lévi-Strauss was attempting to discuss structures as empirical realities, when he admits that he was not. Yet there are alliance theorists who continue to use his words almost as clichés in defining the position of women in marriage.

Ethnocommunication studies should be, and are, studies of empirical realities, not interpretative theoretical games. There are plenty of the latter, but they do not contribute to an understanding of human interaction or reduce problems. Without using labels which designate people (individuals) as commodities for manipulation, we can simply consider that interactions constitute exchanges of information — tangible and intangible items of information flowing between people in dyadic or larger-scale interaction situations. In the past, studies that might be considered ethnocommunicational were focused primarily on ethnolinguistic or sociolinguistic factors (Hymes 1967). There was little, if any, focus on intercultural communication; intracultural communication was analyzed linguistically or through the mechanisms of transportation that might or might not allow intercultural contact.

However, various writers have undertaken studies of intercultural communication difficulties (Hall and Foote-Whyte 1960; Watson 1969; Mead and Modley 1967). There are also studies of interethnic communication (e.g. Daniel 1970; Hall 1959). The most notable weakness in these writings is the limitations imposed on information transfer. The ways people communicate are seen as the result of enculturation (Meerlo 1967: 12). That is, individuals in a given cultural milieu acquire specific verbal and nonverbal modes of expression which reflect the philosophical, ideological, and cognitive orientations predominant in that milieu. Also, some problems of interethnic communication are considered to be the result of incomplete acculturation. When interethnic communication is incomplete (i.e. recognizable units of information are not exchanged), it is postulated that the individuals involved have not brought into use the alternative communication modes to which they have been exposed and which could facilitate information transfer between them. An example would be in a task-oriented situation where two ethnically different individuals are trying to solve a problem but cannot cooperate because they perceive each other as "speaking a different language." To look at such problems without considering how they are resolved is a negative approach.

In order to provide data on similarities and differences in interethnic interactions, it would seem more positive to consider the potential vocabularies, syntaxes, nonverbal modes and media of expression, and perceptive sets which result from transcultural and/or transethnic interchanges and experience. By doing this, we are more likely to have the opportunity to note successful intergroup exchanges. Since there are few isolated homogeneous and independent groups remaining, viewing means of ethnocommunication must look more daringly at the synergism created when individuals from differing subcultures, cultures, or ethnic groups are in frequent contact. We need to know: what minimal sets of linguistic constructs are necessary to enable individuals from two different subcultures to exchange relevant (informing) information? What minimal sets of body language? What physical or structural arrangements? What time arrangements? Where do the compromises occur, so that amalgamations of differing subcultural and ethnic codes and channels result in syncretic forms which are superior for interethnic, intercultural, heterogeneous information exchange? We do not have to go outside our own American society to find the answers to questions such as these. The bio-social-cultural heterogeneity of our own geographic area provides a suitable milieu for fieldwork. But how do we get the positive answers — those that tell us what should be done, rather than what should not be done? Who are the experts who can give clues and techniques for asking and answering the right questions?

There are many bicultural individuals living in our society. They have learned to operate in two worlds: the Anglo or Caucasian working- and middle-class world, and their own. They have, through the years, developed the special expertise which enables them to get on with business outside their home communities. They shop, work, and generally mingle in the activities "out there" and they have a basic knowledge of adequate propriety for the areas where they are treated as marginals. Yet there is strong evidence that these individuals are now less concerned with placating the whims of those outside their communities, or outside their groups. Neither are we so willing to allow outsiders into our communities or groups for the purposes of study as we have done previously.

In order to discern the ethnocommunication variables operating among different groups of people, we need to consider seriously the advantage for cross-cultural understanding which the in-cultural analyst can provide. We have sufficient evidence that in-culture analysts can and do practice "disciplined subjectivity" (Mead's term 1970: 59). The primary subjective advantage is the ability of the in-culture analyst to utilize the ethnocommunications of her or his own group. The trained informant has often been cited as being an important control for objective studies. However, I do not consider that disciplined subjectivity is the only method which can be used here. Disciplined objectivity is equally useful, but I do not believe that either methodological approach alone can provide the opportunity for discovering and adequately presenting normative behavioral codes and patterns. It is possible for the native ethnographer or anthropologically trained in-culture analyst to practice both in conducting studies of own-group.

The traditional anthropologist, established in teaching and research, can focus attention on the study of ethnocommunications more efficaciously by employing some of the philosophical insights and tenets of Maruyama, especially the attitudinal approach of *transpection*. Joint endeavors undertaken by in-culture and out-culture analysts are especially useful in working toward answers to questions on intercultural and interethnic communication, as well as intragroup ethnocommunications. A balanced polymorphism of anthropological data on ethnocommunication is more likely to be obtained by a combination of in-culture and out-culture analysis. Binocular and polyocular vision with a deep field of perception can be obtained as a result of these joint endeavors. In stating this view, I do not mean to imply that one person, or even a team of trained in-culture and out-culture analysts, can give us a complete inventory of ethnocommunications in all settings, in all contextual situations. But I do believe that it is possible for one individual or team to develop and teach these techniques of analysis so that ethnocommunicationally diverse situations can be documented.

In order to obtain a gestalt of information transfer within our own groups, and in others', all of the investigator's faculties must be brought into use. In face-to-face message transfer, we must have an awareness of thermal conditions, spatial proximities, facial and other body cues and expressions. And we should know something about the outlook and perceptions of individuals in dyadic and larger situational contexts. In order to comprehend the diversity in semanticity of verbal and nonverbal communications we must listen completely, i.e. allow input of all signals and symbols which are transmitted to inform us. Too often, we are in the position of being encumbered by thoughts which do not relate to the situation in which information is being sent to us. We then employ what Kaschube (1970 personal communication) calls rapid listening, a phenomenon similar to rapid reading and with similar results: getting what appear to be the major or high points of the messages, but in actual fact, missing the cues and signals that make the message more clear, more relevant, more comprehensible. Furthermore, in the communication network, we are too often a source talking to or a destination being talked at (or to) rather than being a correspondent of information exchange. We have become quite used to one-way communication, and as is often the case, we have elected to discriminate against certain modalities of message transfer. Consequently, we have selected against receipt of certain message forms. For example, we often ignore or blank out unconsciously (and sometimes consciously) proxemic variables introduced in dyadic interactions with "different" individuals, such as when we do not understand the mechanisms intended to close, open, or maintain distance that are used by some ethnic groups.

In studying ethnocommunication, we need to examine the use of spacing mechanisms and how these contribute to information flow. In my hospital research, I have been able to measure distance between individuals standing in conversation in near absolute terms, by counting the number of tile squares between them, noting touching behavior which closed the distance between them, and by noting other nonverbal markers of space. In conferences, boundary markers used included select placement of ashtrays when several individuals were smoking (and there were only a few ash and cigarette receptacles). Placement of chairs around the conference table could inhibit information transfer, if it was determined informally that the chairs should not be moved. Use of charts and tables also limited information flow when these were held in such a fashion that only a select few could see them. It was also interesting to compare the influence that structural features had on proximity of interaction between staff members, between staff and patients, and on expressed feelings of comfort.

In the first of four contrasting hospital environments studied, the nursing care units were located in round towers. The nurses' stations were centrally located within each circular unit. The nurses could easily see each patient's room, and all rooms were equidistant from the station. In the second case, the nurses' station was located centrally between two wings of a single unit, and patients' rooms were at varying distances from it. In the third and fourth examples, the nurses' stations were located at a central corner of a cruciform unit, the difference being that the third was considerably smaller than the fourth, while the staff and equipment located in each were the same in number and quality. In the first example, some staff members who were interviewed stated that they did not like the circular structure because they were too exposed to the patients. But on the whole, most felt that it enabled them to distribute their time more equitably and accomplish their basic nursing tasks more efficiently. Patients, on the other hand, often complained that there was so much noise around the nurses' station (clanging of charts, and nurses talking) that it was hard to rest. On the other hand, most of them agreed that it was worth getting accustomed to the noise in order to have the convenience of quick response to their call signals.

In examples two, three, and four, the patients farthest from the nurses' station had the privilege of having extraneous noise reduced, but the handicap of having to wait slightly longer to have their call bells answered. Those closer got a quicker response to the call signal, but either had to develop a higher noise tolerance or ask to be moved to another room. Nurses, being generally accustomed to this basic rectangular type of structure, had no comments to make about the arrangement. However, it was noted on many occasions that if a patient who was located at some distance from the station needed more frequent attention than the average patient, that patient would be brought closer. Interesting mechanisms were used for space mainte-nance in examples three and four. In three, although individuals had to work in very cramped, close quarters, there was little physical contact, and it was apparent that they avoided touching one another. On the other hand, in the larger unit (example four), staff tended to work side by side, leaving large sections of the area unused at various times, and were in fairly frequent touch contact, either accidentally or deliber-ately.

When the effects of structural designs on communication are being considered in the future, these circumstances will be taken into ac-count, I hope, with the intention of improving working conditions and increasing the general comfort of staff and patients. Sommer has stated that:

The clearest realization of the connection between environmental form and human behavior is taking place in the institutional field. People trained in hospital administration, education, and business management are aware of the important contributions research and development have made in most aspects of their work (1969: 9).

But the examples given here are situationally specific and do not reflect any analysis of variance in ethnic norms. In many institutions and service centers, the structures are designed more for the benefit of employees than for users of the services. This might be rationalized by employees and administrators who believe that better service can be rendered if employees are comfortable. But I am not in complete agreement with this attitude. In another hospital studied, outpatients were expected to queue up at a central desk where they were issued with a number, and then told to sit in a waiting room. The waiting rooms were like small auditoriums, with chairs arranged in rows facing in one direction. A patient's number was called loudly, when it was his or her turn to go through a series of rooms where various parts of examination and treatment were carried out. The result of this system was twofold: the staff had a very rapid, functional method of operation; the patient was left feeling like an anonymous entity, a number or a condition, e.g. a shoulder rather than a person.

The patients' perceptions of the hospital environment, in each example, may be scaled along a continuum of variance. We can say that there is a wide range of reality awareness which each attempts to fit into some cognitive category that renders the hospital experience tolerable. The staff members are in a like position as they relate to patients — a group of people under their care. Patients are told that they are expected to conform to certain standards of behavior, and for the most part, they comply. Nurses and other staff members, alternatively, are expected to contribute to the recovery process and comfort of each patient. The conception of reality of these two different sets of people may be contradictory, yet within the closed system of the hospital, from the nursing staffs' point of view, the system functions adequately because people, on the whole, are cared for sufficiently to be discharged to their homes. The main concern of staff members is to maintain or improve their efficiency in fulfilling this goal.

The structural features of the hospital function largely as a means for promoting harmonious interaction between contradictory perceptions of an extended communicational situation. Behavioral instructions may be a means of "matching information to the capacity of the receivers" (Maruyama 1962), when verbal and paralinguistic messages are transmitted to patients. The staff members are expected to transmit messages in a form which patients can understand — using lay language. In Maruyama's scheme of cross-epistemological communication, this might be seen as an attempt to establish *modal resonance.* "Modal resonance occurs between people using the same mode of communication — denotative, connotative, situational-contextual, verbal, kinesic, somatic, etc." (1961: 124). However, very often the "differences in meta-intellectual level limit interpersonal communication" (Maruyama 1961: 28) between staff and patients so that dissonance, rather than resonance, occurs. Patients may have special difficulty in understanding the tactile and proxemic messages used by the nursing staff. Metaintellectual resonance occurs when individuals operate at essentially the same level of abstract thinking, and in the hospital, it is found primarily among professional nurses, as they conceptualize their duties in carrying out competent patient care. The nursing staff as a whole, on the other hand, because of the orientation of individuals at various levels of expertise, operates with resonance based on the relevancy of the contextual situation to individual expectations in the hospital. How successful an individual staff member is in establishing modal resonance with patients (or simply establishing rapport) may be determined by his or her own experience as a patient. Resonance at any level may be inhibited as a result of discriminatory communicational activities. It must be remembered that the population of a hospital is a heterogeneous microcosm of the larger community in which it is located.

If a hospital staff is primarily Anglo or Caucasian English-speaking (monolingual), the heterogeneity of the patient population may stimulate differential treatment of individuals. Differential treatment may be the result of stereotypes, or prejudices, or fears, or even of a desire to show special consideration to own-group. Certainly, the attitude of the staff members toward patients may effectively counteract any discomfort caused by the structural environment, so the question might be raised at this point, why be concerned with structures if their influence can be overcome by verbal and other dyadic personal communications? Primarily, because the concern is to develop a greater understanding of the functional requirements of institutional, as well as private residential environments and of their effects on other aspects of communication events.

Sommer (1969) has suggested that design professionals need to adopt a functional approach based on actual behavior (thus providing for transitional stages). This suggestion is neither novel nor untried in design planning, but functions have frequently been interpreted ethnically and treated in ethnocentric terms. That is to say, an individual looks at the functions as a complete outsider and judges from his monocular stance which functions are appropriate for consideration. In the hospital examples, functionalism was implemented without regard for the personal needs of those whom the institution allegedly serves. Those individuals who paid for service were treated as part of an anonymous collective, rather than as individuals. In other examples, such as urban housing planned for redevelopment areas and for urban expansion, structure and function are viewed synonomously, and ethnic variability in spatial requirements is largely ignored. Traditional modes of residential spatiality are generally shrugged off as backward or not forward-looking. The absence of front door stoops in urban rehousing is a specific example. A familiar center for gossip and information, this design feature is conspicuously absent. Open walkways fail to define boundaries between residential units, nor do they provide space in which leisurely communication may occur. The stoop acted as an extension of a defined bounded structure, one which permitted greater flow of messages between adjoining units and in-flow of information from community activity within its audiovisual range. Urban design generally discourages such communication, imposing values of residential privacy by forcing individuals to remain within the structural boundaries of the developer's blueprint. This can be changed.

Elise Boulding has stated:

I don't know how we resolve the dilemma of designing environments to maximize existing cultural strengths, in urban housing, for example, as opposed to trying to liberate people's imagination to create new environments. It should not be difficult to distinguish between *manipulation* of people by altering environments, and *liberation* of people by altering environments. But in fact it is hard because no one — rather, very few — have the interest and concern necessary to involve people in designing their own environment. ("Futuristics and the imaging capacity of the West," 1970; original emphasis).

There are some examples of urban renewal planning wherein the people of the community were consulted about their desires and needs in housing and landscape structures (one such unit has been built in Sacramento). But, admittedly, these are few. In addition, desired uses of other design concepts, such as partitioning, lighting, color, texture, pattern, scale, furniture placement, activity centers or groupings, can be determined in terms of culture-specific proxemic effect in futuristic studies. Consultant in-culture and out-culture anthropologists could readily build up a repertoire of case studies dealing with details of activities and spatial needs of specific uses of structural facilities, both institutional and residential. Robert Betchel's studies (1970) of room space and traffic patterns using the hodometer (an electrical system for recording the number and area of individual footsteps) could be useful here. Alexander Kira's monograph (1966) on American bathroom design could also be used. As Gifford notes (1970: 9–26), "once [design patterns are] defined, a particular population unit desire pattern could effectively be tuned into the [valid futurological] schema itself thereby accomplishing a mesh [between population units and that schema]." By using community consultants (in-culture specialists), design patterns for a particular population unit might be defined, offering an opportunity to maximize cultural strengths and at the same time provide liberating environments.

If the anthropological record is to become a source for understanding the environmental needs of different people, then we should attempt to provide polyocular analyses of various expectations and desires in structural designs. Perhaps we are not yet ready to consider these features of the communication interface. Even if liberating environments can be designed (and I think they can), how will people use them if they, as individuals, are not liberated from the stresses induced by stereotyped images used in intergroup interactions? There is much more to be discovered before we can teach people how to open their minds to receive relevant information in transethnic (and intragroup) dyadic-to-large group interactions. We might begin by paying closer attention to transactions in small groups, including those occurring in institutions, small business-conference groups, as well as classroom activities and "on the street scenes." In examining these situations we have an opportunity to note understandings, misunderstandings, and pseudounderstandings in message transfer.

During the two semesters I spent directing a course on culture and poverty, conducted as a small group conference, there were numerous confrontations between students who did not recognize breaches of transethnic etiquette, until these were called to their attention by the offended. There were also cases of misunderstanding. The level of resonance achieved in some cases was based largely on the ability of the student to open his or her mind to information relevant to the message which the sender was transmitting. Some examples are worth noting.

A Mexican-American graduate student was invited to the class to stimulate discussion and advise students on their approach to understanding poverty in the Chicano community. As the conversations increased in intensity, a point was reached where an Anglo student said, "I don't understand why those people on welfare won't eat the commodities they are given." The commodities in question were dry milk, flour, Karo syrup, and an assortment of unlabeled cans of vegetables. The graduate student countered with an explanation of food consumption among her people: "First of all, it is insulting to be given food, rather than money for assistance in purchasing food. Second, since food is to be given away, why not give foods that people are used to eating?" The Anglo student pointed out the nutritional value of the commodities and said that any welfare recipient could be taught how to prepare these foods so that they would be palatable. The graduate student again tried to explain that traditional foods, prepared in traditional manner, were better for the welfare client. Finally in exasperation (as she herself put it) she stated forcefully, "when you take my food away from me, you take part of me away!" Communication broke down: neither student could understand the "language" of the other. The message to the non-Chicano student was simply "you're telling me that your food, your life-style, is better than mine when you make me take your food," but she could not understand this. Other topics were raised, and this student repeatedly reentered the stream of communication. At the close of the class period, she stated that she finally understood some of the problems the graduate student had been talking about. The graduate student stated that she doubted that the student could ever understand; from her perspective, the Anglo student had pseudounderstanding of her people because she could not open her mind enough to "listen." But there were other instances where all the students listened.

During a debate on housing discrimination, a woman who was a member of the black student union, pointed out that discrimination was something that could not be ascertained by photography, questionnaire, or other innovative field techniques "...by a WASP. The subtleties of discrimination are something you learn as you grow up in a nonwhite community, surrounded and largely dependent on a white dominant society." A male student who was working out a research proposal for fieldwork on this problem challenged her statements and said he felt that *he* could tell whether or not apartment managers were being discriminatory by asking whether any blacks or Chicanos lived in the dwellings, whether he (or she) would let to blacks or other minorities if they tried to rent an apartment there, and other such questions. He also intended to hand a copy of the Fair Housing Act to the manager to determine whether or not this legislation would make any difference to his no-let policy. The woman became incensed and yelled at the student: "I am sick of blond-haired, blue-eyed people telling me what they can do, what they will do, or what they won't do!" The male student paled, blushed, then answered with "hey, wait a minute." He made no further attempt to defend his position then. The other students recognized the "charge of color," and even though it was easier to take because it had not been made directly at them, they felt the effects of prejudice based on color. Some understood the lessons in ethnocommunication as the woman talked out the problems she had in accepting evaluations of her situation by an outsider. Others did not understand. The male student later stated to me "that is the first time in my life anyone has ever told me that I'm no good because I'm white." As the semester progressed, his research proposal developed into a fine plan. He set out and was able to locate people to help him with fieldwork: he organized a multiethnic team.

A final example comes from a student whose son was put down because of ethnic cueing. He wore a pair of new shoes to school. In an attempt to call attention to his shoes, he "jived" into the classroom. The Anglo teacher told him to sit down and stop his foolish behavior. Later, when talking to the parent about the "problem her son had created," the teacher said she could not understand why he had behaved so badly that day. The parent could not explain the message complex to the teacher and ceased communication on the issue — promising to talk with her son. Later, she decided to "tell the teacher some facts of life" and explained that she felt other children might benefit from the teacher knowing about certain forms of communication used in her community.

It is not difficult to imagine a continuation of conflict interchanges with barriers to communication resulting from misunderstanding of cues and codes. On the other hand, when individuals are serious in their attempts to communicate with other people, conflict situations can become learning situations. In the above cases, relevant (positively informing) information was ultimately exchanged. However, the problems of working out programs for change in the design of cities, as well as in social and personal life are unlikely to be realized until ethnocommunications are understood. The anticipation that future generations will be more educated does not carry an automatic guarantee that they will be less prejudiced and more able to operate in diverse or multiethnic situations. But they may become less prejudiced if we are able to teach variant views of transactional and other expressive norms.

One of the elements that seems valuable to the self-determining, goal-seeking, quasi-mandates of the "revolution" in anthropology is an increased body of data on ethnocommunications from multifocal viewpoints. I believe students and nonstudents (through the use of mass media in the latter case) can be taught how to approach an understanding of communication, in all forms. For example, we might futuristically envisage the teaching of formal proxemic "language" systems, both to increase positive communication between individuals and groups and to provide cultural alternatives for new societies. To do this, an attempt must be made to isolate proxemes and build semantic and syntactic networks of all spatial variables if we are to make general statements about culturally specific groups. The suggestion that we isolate proxemes presents some serious methodological problems, but it is not an impossible task and would seem an imperative one in light of its urgency in the field of environmental planning and futuristic cultural goal development. Watson (1969), Kauffman (1970, 1971) and others are now exploring methodological techniques for in-depth spatial research.

Some other areas which I include in teaching about ethnocommunication and in attempts to aid understanding of human interaction are the study of kinesics (Birdwhistell 1970), ethnoaesthetics, small group hierarchical and nonhierarchical communication patterning, cognitive studies of kinship systems, sociolinguistics and psycholinguistics. We are beginning to have many interesting reports of particulate analysis in some of these areas. For example, Sommerville (1970) among others has demonstrated that, although physically all humans are capable of a wide range of expressive movements, each culture selects its own repertoire which limits the "vocabulary" of expression in dance. She also suggests that anthropologists have too often interpreted various sets of body motions merely as ritualistic behavior, when in fact the minutiae of finger, hand, head, etc. movements often constitute phonemic-like segments of larger constructions or total messages. Following through then, anthropologists should begin to search for choreographic isolates, in much the same way as we search for the elusive proxemes or kinemes, and the relationship these have to the totality of message-transfer mechanisms in ethnic and subcultural groups. Furthermore, there is some evidence to suggest that formal choreographic cues are modified (or amplified) to enhance dyadic, triadic, and larger group communications. It may be that choreographic expressions are derived from these latter, however. If so, we might want to further consider choreometrics as a clue to nonartistic or nonritualistic body communication. Both approaches are useful for expanding our conceptions of variant epistemologies.

Unless we encourage a variety of approaches to these studies, including introspective and transpective research, we are still going to possess and present pseudounderstanding of other cultures. We hear and issue, statements on Chicano power, black power, yellow power, red power, gay power, grey power, and women power with slogans that communicate demands for human power of specific types. These statements are from individuals no longer willing to be subjugated and denied opportunities for self-expression by male white power. In many cases, they are mandates for now that will be heard and acted upon or there will be less organized diversity in the future.

Perhaps Lévi-Strauss (1970) is right in suggesting that the increase in communication has caused an increase in the sense of nationalism, ethnicity, and other group-centrisms. If a unity of diversity is to be accomplished without further waste of human resources and energy, then the rush to that end being suggested by some planners of the future must entertain the questions of priority when designing features for verbal and nonverbal communication channel availability, for housing, and designs for urban boundaries. The various demands for group power and individual power may be the signal that individuals are aware that homogenization on a global scale is imminent, and they may form part of a general demand to forestall loss of ethnic and group identities which create and maintain heterogeneity or cultural pluralism.

If homogenization tendencies increase, we can expect to see a syncretized global cultural patterning wherein ethnic identity is lost to world identity. In such a milieu ethnocommunication may possibly be stylized so that, through the use of such things as an international sign language, communication will occur readily among all people. With the introduction of satellites, the use of global communication systems has increased. Will the continued increase in efficiency in using these facilities require a formal international language, or will we rely on computer translations of current language differences? Even if *H. sapiens* should become essentially monolingual, there would still be regional variations of basic ethnocommunication norms, creating dialectical differences. But, on the whole, we could expect mutual intelligibility of communication expression. In anticipation of reaching global-village state, some science-fiction writers who deal with the distant future refer to earth culture as a single entity, without reference to regional variations.

Concern with the near future (the next hundred years or so) causes me to anticipate more seriously the possibility that the tendency toward homogenization may be sufficiently forestalled for synergism to allow group cultures to take on communication modes and channels of intercultural interaction that will not deter the maintenance of ethnic and group identities. To understand ethnocommunication in the total context of human futuristics, I believe that many of the items of cultural activity which we have taken somewhat for granted must be scrutinized and taught. Then perhaps we can increase the potential for resonance, and by reducing dissonance perhaps there will be fewer violent confrontations when differing individuals attempt to communicate their needs and desires. To this end, we might work with the writings of Birdwhistell (1970), Kauffman (1970, 1971), Watson (1968), Hall (1959, 1964, 1966), McLuhan and Parker (1969), and Watson and Graves (1966), as well as look at the studies of queueing up, crowding effects, and other nonverbal communication complexities. These might be compiled into a general handbook on culture-specific ethnocommunications.

We can use sources such as Williams's *Language and poverty* (1970) wherein situational-contextual analyses of verbal skills demonstrate that there are no verbally deprived groups, just people who do not comprehend other-group communications. Teaching public awareness of various group norms through the mass media, may facilitate trans-ethnic communications. We can contribute to a breakdown of cross-ethnic communication barriers by encouraging Third World people, women, and other in-culture people to work with the theory and methods of anthropology, to build new theories and methods for anthropology from their perspectives, leading to self-actualization programs. McKnight has stated:

If there is, indeed, a strongly felt need in the profession to develop anthropology cross-culturally ... let us develop plans, educational programs, scholarships, and research bases for this purpose. Let's train our own students for the somewhat less romantic but far more important role they will take in the program. In the process, however, let us develop ways of protecting and enhancing the emergence of perspectives (anthropological theory-world-views) that are ethnically germane rather than simply orthodox to the profession.

In his writings on "in-culture research" Mike Maruyama has suggested an in-service training approach in which the anthropologist would serve more or less as a Rogerian enabler to a team of in-cultural researchers who specify problem, methodological approach, emergent concepts and (if relevant) solutions without particular obedience to orthodox professional methods or concepts. If Maruyama's approach were widely adopted, during an interim period, perhaps a fairly long one, the level of static in the system (profession) would increase considerably. I doubt, however, that anthropology can ever be more than a fairly sophisticated way of amplifying (either by direct analysis or mirror reflection) the Euro-American world view unless the profession programs itself specifically for receptivity to effective cross-cultural input (1970).

These statements summarize this paper fairly well. We have an opportunity to learn by listening completely to the total complex of messages sent ethnocommunicationally. We can build and teach polyocular anthropology. The question is "will we?"

REFERENCES

ARDENER, SHIRLEY, *editor*
1975 *Perceiving women.* New York: Wiley.
BAVELAS, ALEX
1950 Communication patterns in task-oriented groups. *The Journal of the Acoustical Society of Ameria* 22: 725–730.
BETCHEL, ROBERT B.
1970 "Human movement and architecture," in *Environmental psychology: man and his physical setting.* Edited by H. M. Proshansky et al. New York: Holt, Rinehart, and Winston.
BIRDWHISTELL, RAY L.
1968 "Communication without words," in *L'aventure humaine.* Edited by P. Alexandre. Paris.

1970   *Kinesics and context: essays on body motion communication.*
       Philadelphia: University of Pennsylvania Press.
BOULDING, ELISE
1976   *The underside of history: a view of women through time.* Boulder,
       Colorado: Westview Press.
BOYD, L. M.
1970   "Checking up." Syndicated column published in the *Sacramento Bee*,
       October 9.
BUCHLER, IRA R., HENRY A. SELBY
1968   *Kinship and social organization.* New York: Macmillan.
CASSELL, JOAN
1977   *A group called women: sisterhood and symbolism in the feminist
       movement.* New York: David McKay Company.
CHIÑAS, BEVERLY LITZLER
1970   "Women as ethnographic subjects." Mimeographed paper presented
       at the Southwestern Anthropological Association meetings,
       Asilomar, California.
DANIEL, JACK L.
1970   The facilitation of white-black communication. *The Journal of Com-
       munication* 20 (2): 134–141.
GIFFORD, JAMES
1970   "Prehistory: perspectives from the past as trajectories to the future,"
       in *Symposium on Cultural Futuristics: Pre-Conference Volume.*
       Washington, D.C.: American Anthropological Association.
GOODALE, JANE C.
1970   *Tiwi wives: a study of the women of Melville Island, Australia.*
       Seattle: University of Washington Press.
HALL, EDWARD T.
1959   *The silent language.* Greenwich: Fawcett Publications.
1964   Adumbration as a feature of intercultural communication. *The eth-
       nography of communication.* Edited by J. J. Gumperz and Dell
       Hymes. *American Anthropologist* 66 (6, pt. 2): 154–163.
1966   *The hidden dimension.* Garden City: Doubleday.
HALL, EDWARD T., WILLIAM FOOTE-WHYTE
1960   Intercultural communication: a guide to men of action. *Human
       Organization* 19: 5–12.
HARE, PAUL
1952   *Handbook of small group research.* New York: Free Press.
1966   "The dimensions of social interaction," in *Communication and cul-
       ture: readings in the codes of human interaction.* Edited by Alfred G.
       Smith, 88–94. New York: Holt, Rinehart and Winston.
HYMES, DELL
1964   Introduction: toward ethnographies of communication. *The ethnog-
       raphy of communication.* Edited by J. J. Gumperz and Dell Hymes.
       American Anthropologist 66 (6, pt. 2): 1–34.
1967   "The anthropology of communication," in *Human communication
       theory: original essays.* Edited by F. E. X. Dance, 1–39. New York:
       Holt, Rinehart and Winston.
JACOBS, SUE-ELLEN
1970a "Social structures as communication: a formal methodology for
       analysis of social systems." Unpublished doctoral dissertation, Uni-
       versity of Colorado, Boulder, Colorado.

1970b "Analysis of social systems in terms of communication processes." Paper presented at the Society for Applied Anthropology meetings, Boulder, Colorado.

1970c "Clinical anthropology: techniques for problem analysis in urban systems." Paper presented at the Southwestern Anthropological Association meetings, Asilomar, California.

1974 *Women in perspective: a guide for cross-cultural studies.* Urbana: University of Illinois Press.

KAUFFMAN, LYNN E.

1970 "The value and utility of proxemics and proxetics in applied anthropology." Paper presented at the Society for Applied Anthropology meetings, Boulder, Colorado.

1971 Tactesics: the study of touch. A model for proxemic analysis. *Semiotica* 4(2): 149–161.

KIRA, ALEXANDER

1966 *The bathroom: criteria for design.* New York: Bantam Books.

LÉVI-STRAUSS, CLAUDE

1952 "Toward a general theory of communication." Mimeographed paper distributed for the Conference of Anthropologists and Linguists, at the Linguistic Institute, jointly sponsored by Indiana University and the Linguistic Society of America, July 21–31.

1970 We no longer know how to bring our children into the world we have built. *Mademoiselle* 77: 236–237.

MARTIN, M. KAY, BARBARA VOORHIES

1975 *Female of the species.* New York: Columbia University Press.

MARUYAMA, MAGOROH

1961 Communicational epistemology (in three parts). *The British Journal for the Philosophy of Science*, XI (44): 319–327; XII (45): 52–62; XII (46): 117–131.

1962 Awareness and unawareness of misunderstandings. *Methodos* 13: 255–275.

1963 Basic elements of misunderstandings (in two parts). *Dialectica* 16: 78–92; 99–110.

1970 "Epistemology of social science research: explorations in in-culture researchers." Mimeographed manuscript. Social Science Research Institute, University of Hawaii.

1978 "Endogenous research and polyocular anthropology," in *Perspectives on ethnicity.* Edited by Regina E. Holloman and Serghei Arutiunov. World Anthropology. The Hague, Mouton.

McLUHAN, MARSHALL, HARLEY PARKER

1969 *Through the vanishing point: space in poetry and painting.* New York: Harper Colophon Books, Harper and Row.

MEAD, MARGARET

1970 A conversation with Margaret Mead and T. George Harris on the anthropological age. *Psychology Today* 4 (2): 58–64, 74–76.

MEAD, MARGARET, RUDOLF MODLEY

1967 Communication among all people, everywhere. *Natural History* 1967: 56–63.

MEERLO, JOOST A. M.

1967 "Communication and mental contagion," in *Communication concepts and perspectives.* Edited by Lee Thayer, 1–24, Washington: Spartan Books.

REITER, RAYNA R., *editor*
   1975   *Toward an anthropology of women.* New York: Monthly Review Press.
ROSALDO, MICHELLE ZIMBALIST, LOUISE LAMPHERE, *editors*
   1974   *Women, culture and society.* Stanford: Stanford University Press.
SCHLEGEL, ALICE
   1972   *Male dominance and female autonomy.* Boston: HRAF Press.
SOMMER, ROBERT
   1969   *Personal space: the behavioral basis of design.* Englewood Cliffs: Prentice-Hall.
SOMMERVILLE, JOANNE
   1970   "Some ways of thinking about dance and body movement." Paper presented at the meetings of the Southwestern Anthropological Association, Asilomar, California.
WATSON, MICHAEL
   1968   "Proxemics and semiotics." Mimeographed paper presented at the 68th annual meetings of the American Anthropological Association, New Orleans.
WATSON, MICHAEL, T. D. GRAVES
   1966   Quantitative research in proxemic behavior. *American Anthropologist* 68: 971–985.
WEINER, ANNETTE B.
   1976   *Women of value, men of renown: new perspectives in Trobriand exchange.* Austin: University of Texas Press.
WESTERMAN, FLOYD, JIMMY CURTISS
   1970   "Here come the anthros." On the L.P. record *Custer died for your sins.* Perception Records.
WILLIAMS, FREDERICK, *editor*
   1970   *Language and poverty: perspectives on a theme.* Chicago: Markham.

Symbiotization of Cultural Heterogeneity: Scientific, Epistemological, and Aesthetic Bases

MAGOROH MARUYAMA

As several authors have pointed out (Boulding "Futuristics and the imaging capacity of the West," this volume; Harkins "Futurism in man: humanism, social technology, and survival," this volume; Gerlach "Fumbling freely into the future," this volume; and Maruyama "Toward human futuristics," this volume), during the past decade we have seen the emergence and increasing acceptance of a new type of logic in many segments of American society. The hippy movement of the affluent young, the ethnic movements of oppressed minority groups, and the ecology movement which finds supporters among both conservatives and liberals in the middle class, are all converging on a logic opposed to traditional mainstream Americal logic:

Traditional mainstream logic	Emerging logic
hierarchical	interactionist
nonreciprocal causality	reciprocal causality
uniformistic	heterogenistic
competitive	symbiotic
classificational	relational
quantitative	qualitative

The three segments of our society mentioned — affluent young people, oppressed minority groups, and the middle class — did not arrive at this new logic for the same reason, nor did they necessarily perceive one another to be converging on the same logic. The black ghetto residents who had to strive for material improvement of their lives tended to regard hippies as silly rich kids trying to go backward materially. They also tended to consider pollution as a rich people's problem. Conversely the hippies, though antiestablishment, did not necessarily have much insight into the nature of the oppression imposed upon black ghetto residents.

Therefore the convergence of these three segments of society on a common logic is a result of their mutually *independent* recognition of the inadequacy of traditional mainstream logic. As Gerlach (this volume) points out, even within each of the segments the movements began with small, independent groups, which only later became more and more coordinated. This recognition of the inadequacy of traditional mainstream logic by such widely independent sources is an indication, as Kuhn (1962) and McEachron (1971) have pointed out, that it is the total structure, not the component structures, of our society that has become obsolete. However, many of the proponents of the current social and cultural movements have fallen into the fallacies of the old logic, against which they are rebelling. For example, the do-your-own-thingism and the small-is-beautiful movement are often distorted into isolationism and regionalism instead of heterogenistic interactive symbiosis; the ecology movement into static harmonism instead of the morphogenetic harmonism of natural systems; the "consciousness" movement into the dichotomy of the mental and the physical, and into hierarchical rank-ordering of values; new mushrooming religions into universalistic homogenism; holism into abstractionism instead of relational study of specific contexts in real life situations. These instances indicate the unwitting persistence of the fallacies of the old logic even among the most avant-garde revolutionaries (Maruyama 1978b).

Given the obsolescence of traditional mainstream logic and the emergence of a new logic, the question can be raised as to whether the new logic is able to adequately meet the needs of the next stage of our civilization. The purpose of this paper is to demonstrate that this emerging logic is not only compatible with the most recent innovation in the logic of science, but has already stood the test of survival and growth in the epistemological as well as the aesthetic dimensions in many cultures. This emerging logic is both ultramodern and very ancient.

GENERAL ORIENTATION

In two ways that are relevant to our discussion, the Second World War has become a milestone in the application of mutualistic logic on a global scale. On the one hand, in the sciences the mathematical formulation of feedback systems as a result of the development of radar-guided, computer-controlled antiaircraft artillery elevated the concept of reciprocal causality to the level of scientific respectability. On the other hand, the fall of the colonial powers and the subsequent independence of many African and Asian countries marked the end of uniracial domination and the beginning of the ethnic and cultural heterogenization and dehierarchization of the world.

Many types of mutualistic and pluralistic logic have existed for centuries, mainly in Africa, East and Southeast Asia, among Eskimos and Aleuts, and in many of the original tribes of the Americas, but also from time to time in white cultures. To give some examples of the latter, there were the nominalists of medieval Europe, the existentialist philosophers of the post-Kantian age, and electronic engineers using oscillators since around 1910. But the mainstream logic of the Greco-European-American tradition had been unidirectional, universalistic (homogenistic), hierarchical, and classificational.

This paper first discusses that the reciprocal causal model is a very recent innovation in the logic of science and then discusses the epistemological and aesthetic aspects of mutualistic logics which have existed in many cultures.

THE SCIENTIFIC BASIS

During the Second World War, the application of radar and the computer to the control of antiaircraft artillery weapons prompted a rigorous and sophisticated study of feedback systems in order to reduce the error between the projectile and the target (Wiener 1949). This was the beginning of the study of many other types of feedback system (Von Foerster 1949–1953; Maruyama 1963a; Buckley 1968; Milsum 1968; Waddington 1969–1971). Feedback systems are reciprocal causal systems.

The development of the study of feedback systems can be roughly divided into two phases with the dividing line around 1960. In the 1940's and 1950's engineers and biological scientists focused their attention mainly on deviation-counteracting feedback systems (so-called negative feedback systems) which were useful for automatic control of various engineering devices and automatic regulation in biological systems. During the same period, however, a small number of thinkers, for example the Swedish economist Gunnar Myrdal and the cultural psychiatrist Gregory Bateson, began to formulate theories of deviation-amplifying, reciprocal causal processes (so-called positive feedback systems). During the Second World War Myrdal published his *American dilemma* (1943), a study of economic vicious circles in the American ghettos, and after the War his *Economic theory and underdeveloped regions* (1957), a study of economic vicious circles in materially poor countries and in international trade. He also emphasized the constructive use of deviation-amplifying, reciprocal causal processes. For example, if the economy of a poor country is given an initial kick in the right direction, this small initial change can be amplified to produce a disproportionally large measure of economic development compared to the size of the initial kick.

More detailed laboratory-type research on deviation-amplifying reciprocal causal processes lagged behind that on deviation-counteracting reciprocal causal processes, and became formalized around 1960 (Ulam 1962; Braverman and Schrandt 1966). Deviation-amplifying reciprocal causal processes can increase differentiation, and grow structure, and generate complexity (Maruyama 1962, 1963b; Waddington 1968, 1969, 1970, 1972). They are found in the interaction of cells during the growth of the embryo, in interspecific and intraspecific interaction in the evolutionary process, etc. The same principle can apply to the growth of a city, or to culture change (Buckley 1968).

For almost 2,500 years — since the time of Anaximandros, Xenophanes, and Anaxagoras, whom we will discuss later in this paper — the traditional mainstream principle of "scientific" thinking was based on nonreciprocal causality. Though there had been scientists from time to time (Darwin 1857; Wright 1931; Tinbergen 1937; Spemann 1938) who used reciprocal causal models, mutualistic logic did not enter the "mainstream" of Western science until the study of feedback systems. As late as the 1950's, Hans Reichenbach, a leading philosopher of science, declared that reciprocal causality was impossible (Reichenbach 1956: 39). Consequently he could not explain evolution or steady growth of complexity in causal terms. He had to attribute such processes to "finality," rather than to causality.

Ironically the information theory which Claude Shannon formulated soon after the Second World War (1949), and which contributed greatly to the development of the study of deviation-counteracting feedback systems, was trapped in the same dilemma as that of Reichenbach. Shannon's theory was formulated in classificational epistemology, which is a variation of hierarchical epistemology and sees the universe as consisting of disjointed categories, subcategories, and supercategories. In Shannon's theory, the amount of information is related to the degree of specificity and measured by the degree of improbability of the structure of the "message" or the "data" contrasted to the combination of random, independent events in the given context. Left to the influence of independent random events, it is highly probable that structures will decay. Independent random events are not likely to generate structures steadily and systematically. Therefore, in Shannon's formulation, information can only decrease. Evolution and growth of complexity are impossible in this formulation, or are at least so highly improbable that their common occurrence must be attributed to processes which are inexplicable in Shannon's theory. On the other hand, evolution, growth, and life have become causally explicable in mutualistic logic: deviation-amplifying, reciprocal causal processes can increase differentiation, complexity, and structure; and deviation-counteracting, reciprocal causal processes can maintain them. It is not without reason that some people designate reciprocal causal processes as "anti-entropic," "the love principle," "agape" (Boulding, "Futuristics and the imaging capacity of the West," this volume). In this context Shannon's theory may be called "the death principle" (unrelated to Freud).

Since the "discovery" of reciprocal causal logic in science ("unscientific" cultures had known it long before), it has become scientifically clear that *the basic rule of the biological and social universe is increase of diversification, heterogeneity, and symbiotization. What survives is not the strongest, but the most symbiotic.* We have been misled by the traditional mainstream "scientific" logic of nonreciprocal causality and by the model of classical physics into believing that generalizability, universality, homogenization, and competition are not only the rules of the universe but also *desirable* goals for our society.

There are several other ways in which we have been misled by the logic of nonreciprocal causality. For example, one of the sacred laws in traditional science stated that similar conditions produce similar results. Consequently, dissimilar results were attributed to dissimilar conditions. A great deal of scientific research was influenced by this philosophy. For example, when scientists tried to find out why some identical-twin brothers differed from each other they looked for a difference in their environment or in the influence of other people. It did not occur to them that neither environment nor other people might be responsible for the difference. They overlooked the possibility that the interaction between the brothers might have been deviation-amplifying, or that the two brothers (with identical amplifier circuitry within themselves) amplified some very small difference in their experience. Again, when historians or geographers tried to find out why one of two places with identical conditions had become a city and the other had not, they tried to find some large differences in an unknown variable in the initial conditions. They overlooked the possibility that some almost insignificant event, such as a traveler, getting stranded because of his horse's illness, might have acted as an initial stimulus, on which a system of deviation-amplification worked. In such cases, it is more meaningful to study the circuitry of deviation-amplification, and it would be a waste of time to look for nonexistent large differences in the initial conditions. I have applied the methodology of the reciprocal causal model in my analysis of Danish culture (Maruyama 1961).

The law of causality is now revised to state that similar conditions may produce dissimilar results if there is a deviation-amplifying, reciprocal causal network. It is important to note that this revision is possible without the introduction of indeterminism and probabilism. But if we combine this revision with indeterminism, we obtain the following: a small initial deviation, which is within the range of high probability, may develop into a large deviation of low probability (or, more precisely, into a large deviation which is very improbable within the framework of probabilistic unidirectional causality).

It has already been many decades since the theory of relativity challenged the notion of substance, and since quantum mechanics questioned the principle of identity. Reciprocal causal logic can challenge the notion of substance and the principle of identity from another angle and without the help of the theory of relativity or quantum mechanics. It shows precisely how differentiation, growth, and increase of complexity can take place; how heterogeneity can arise out of seeming homogeneity; and how new structures create themselves without a predesigned blueprint. This is a considerable challenge to the notion of permanence, homogeneity, and universal validity, which are some of the consequences of the notions of substance and identity.

THE EPISTEMOLOGICAL BASIS

Several types of mutualistic logic have existed in many cultures for several thousand years. Mutualistic thinking is therefore not just the unrealistic wishful dreaming of hippies, but is viable, as these cultures have shown. As examples of mutualistic logic, let us discuss three of the following four examples: (1) the multielement mutualism of the Navajos; (2) the complementarism of the Chinese; (3) the heterogenism of the Mandenka; and (4) the situationalism and contextualism of the Japanese.

Navajo Multielement Mutualism

The Navajo universe consists of mutual relations between different types of beings as well as between beings of the same type: humans, animals, supernaturals, ghosts, and natural forces (Kluckhohn 1949; Maruyama 1967). Humans can manipulate supernatural and natural forces by using appropriate formulae, and these forces can influence humans; animals can influence people, and people can influence animals. There is no hierarchy in terms of the direction of influence. Among humans, there were no hierarchical organizations until white government made the Navajos set up a tribal council and other organizational structures. There were no chiefs in the sense of political authority. Old men and women and people with experience were sought out as advisers when the occasion arose, but those who sought their advice did not have to follow it; they could ignore the advice or change advisers. White people often mistook these advisers for chiefs or leaders.

No one, either human or supernatural, is perfect, omnipotent, or omniscient. In fact, such concepts do not exist in Navajo epistemology. There are not even the concepts of "good" and "evil." The Navajo concept closest to our "good" is "nice." Each of the supernaturals can be both beneficial and dangerous to humans, depending on the circumstances and the way humans behave toward it. Each medicine man's ability has limits, and even respected medicine men "go dry" unless they know some harmful witchcraft. Talented speakers are pleasant to hear, but too much talking spoils its own beauty. Drinking is enjoyable. But too much drinking results in loss of reasoning power and in dangerous mistakes. There was no concept of punishment. The man who caused damage or killed someone was not punished but was made to repair the damage or take care of the dead man's family. If someone's behavior did not conform to the usual custom, no one would prohibit it, but people felt sorry for him because some misfortune would certainly result from the disturbed harmony in the universe.

The purpose of life is to maintain harmony and enjoy beauty and pleasure. The Navajos live scattered over a wide area. But when a family shears wool, plants vegetables, harvests crops, or builds a house, relatives and friends come from great distances to help, even though the concept of paid labor is gradually changing this traditional pattern. The cooperativeness of the Navajos is not based on belief in the unity of society, on obedience to a supreme order, or on centralized coordination. On the contrary, their cooperation stems from their respect for the individual. Their universe consists of informal interrelations between individuals and between clans. Even a child possesses his own livestock and is free to dispose of his own property in any way he wishes. Men and women are equal, and each person chooses his own way of doing things. For example, a husband may choose to own a horse and his wife may choose to own turquoise necklaces, or vice versa. When they travel together, one may ride the horse and the other may walk.

Epistemologically, Navajos may be considered to resemble the nominalists in some ways. Like Swedes and Danes, Navajos judge each situation in its specific circumstances and do not think in terms of general principles or absolutes. Yet Navajos are not atomistic as some nominalists were, because Navajos think in terms of harmony, relations, and contexts, not in terms of unrelated individuals.

To maintain harmony with other beings in the universe, one must know the complex workings of these beings and their forces. Ignorance causes mistakes, and mistakes bring misfortune and illness. Therefore knowledge is virtue. Since the purpose of Navajo religion is to maintain harmony, knowledge is religious. There is no separation of science, religion, ethics, and aesthetics in Navajo culture.

The ceremony called "sing" exemplifies the inseparability of science, religion, ethics, aesthetics, and even economics, fun, social activity, and psychological outlet. A sing is called for when someone is ill. An ordinary sing takes three days to perform, but some may last nine days. A sing is the occasion for a large, enjoyable social gathering. People who hear that there will be a sing come from considerable distances. They contribute whatever food they can: those whose crops were good bring more, others less. But everybody can eat as much as he wants. There are games, dances, and other activities, though recently these extra activities have been increasingly omitted.

For the patient, the feeling that so many people care for him is as much a part of the cure as the curing ceremony itself. The medicine man traces the source of illness to some mistakes in the maintenance of harmony, and he performs corrective actions which require highly complex and precise knowledge and formulae, as well as artistic skills in singing, sand painting, etc. An atmosphere of intense concentration dominates the ritual — not a concentration which can be called solemnity, supplication, or humility, but rather like the concentration of an engineer operating a complicated machine. Minutely detailed prescriptions have to be followed. But just as engineers take a break during their work, moments of relaxation and even joking often punctuate the Navajo rituals. If an apprentice medicine man is present, he may make mistakes in singing. This often causes good-natured laughter both on the part of the apprentice himself and on the part of the audience. Sings are frequent. During the summer there are one or two every week within reach of most Navajos who thus can find frequent sources of food, social contact, and psychological outlet.

Chinese Complementarism

While Navajo epistemology is one of multielement nonhierarchical mutualism, Chinese epistemology may be called complementarism of two aspects of every phenomenon. This epistemology has been most lucidly explained by Chang (1938). Chang sees Western logic as characterized by the law of identity, and consequently by the rule of exclusiveness and classification such as "A or not A," "A and non-A."

Chinese thought, in contrast, puts the emphasis on relational qualities. For example, buying and selling are seen, not as opposite activities, but as the same transaction viewed from the different standpoints of buyer and seller. Similarly, "the front and the rear are perceived as mutually accompanying," and "something and nothing are mutually generative." To rephrase this in today's jargon, what Chang pointed out was the polyocular perspective of Chinese epistemology which is interested in cross-perspective relations, and for which the typically Western question "which point of view is right and which is wrong" is irrelevant.

Though Chang did not make it explicit, in my view Westerners misinterpret some Chinese statements such as "the long and the short are mutually relative" or "the difficult and the easy are mutually supportive" as examples of "relativism," in the sense of comparability or displacement of a point of origin on a scale. But such an interpretation is a "dimension reduction" (Maruyama 1962) and dimension addition, missing the real dimension and adding an irrelevant dimension. I think the basic spirit of Chinese logic is that "the two are inseparable" and "you cannot have one without the other" in the same way that you cannot have a car with only the front and not the rear end. On the other hand, the spirit of Western relativism is "if there are two different things, one is higher (bigger, heavier, longer, etc.) than the other," and "a big thing will look smaller from the point of view of a still bigger thing," which does not indicate the inseparability or mutual need of one for the other. Neither is Chinese logic a dialectic logic in the Hegelian and Marxian sense. As Chang pointed out, the Hegelian and Marxian dialectic is a logic of opposition, while Chinese logic is a logic of complementarity.

According to Chang, Chinese religious life was not unlike that of the early Greeks before Xenophanes, who were polytheistic and whose gods were imperfect like humans. Yet religious ideas in China were not associated with the rituals of worship and the institution of official temples. It is not certain whether there were any deities before the concept of heaven arose. But even after this concept arose, the Chinese were never concerned with it as a being or an agent. When the Chinese speak of heaven, they have in mind only providence (intention of heaven) which is merely a manifestation of heaven. The Chinese are concerned with the will of heaven without being too particular about heaven itself, because, according to the Chinese view the will of heaven is heaven itself, and to inquire into heaven without paying attention to its will is logically inconceivable. There is not first heaven and later the manifestation of its will. The Chinese have never considered heaven as an entity, and, so long as it is not an entity, it is not a substance.

In today's jargon, Chinese epistemology is event-oriented, not substance-oriented. According to Chang, the later cognizance of the problem of substance by the Chinese is due to the influence of India. In Chang's own phrasing (1938), Western thought is characterized by a "what-priority attitude," while Chinese thought is characterized by a "how-priority attitude."

The Heterogenism of the Mandenka

Professor Camara's paper in this volume discusses in detail the heterogenistic logic of the Mandenka.

Japanese Situationalism and Contextualism

While Chinese epistemology is based on complementarity, Japanese epistemology can be characterized as situational, contextual, and non-cyclic ephemeral, with some components of vertical mutualism. I have discussed the three historical epistemological currents in Japan — the morphogenetic Jomon, the homeostatic Yayoi and the hierarchical Yamato — in another volume in this *World Anthropology* series (Maruyama 1978a). But now let me add here a description of the modern mixture of the three currents.

A very frequent comment made by Americans on arrival in Japan immediately after the Second World War was that the Japanese did not express their "real" opinions. This misinterpretation was based on Western epistemology, which assumes that opinions as well as individuals subsist like a material substance which has identity and some invariability in time and space. In Japanese epistemology, neither the individual nor any opinion subsist in that manner. The combination of individuals creates a situation, and the situation defines the opinion. Different combinations of individuals create different situations, which result in different expressions. Furthermore, a Japanese behaves in social, familial, and other contexts in ways which are more complex than appears to outsiders. However, Japanese situationalism and contextualism is not Machiavellian. In a way the Japanese are somewhat puritanical and stoic in their ethical attitude, while the Chinese are much more pragmatic. What the Americans interpreted as inconsistency and lack of integrity in the Japanese was behavior strictly regulated by situational and contextual logic. In fact, it indicated a high degree of integrity of a different type, based on a strong sense of obligations and duties.

Structurally, Japanese society is hierarchical. But epistemologically this may be called vertical mutualism, as compared to the usual

Western concept of social hierarchy with a unidirectional flow of authority. This vertical mutualism consists of a strong sense of obligation of the superordinate to the subordinate as well as of the subordinate to the superordinate. In a business company, for example, the superordinate feels a strong sense of obligation to care for the physical and mental welfare of his subordinates. Westerners call this paternalism. But it should be distinguished from paternalism in the "do-gooder" sense.

An example can illustrate the nature of this vertical mutualism more fully than theoretical discussion. A person I know very well, whom I shall call Mr. S, works for a company. Initially Mr. S was indebted to the president who hired him. Since Mr. S had no house, the president let him live in one section of his house. The president promised Mr. S that he would give him a part of his private land on which to build a house. Later the president made a serious miscalculation in business forecasting, and spent heavily in buying equipment for a processing method which soon became obsolete. He was removed from the position of president, his land was held in mortgage, and he could not give Mr. S the land he had promised. He now feels strongly obliged to Mr. S, and when occasion arises he makes onerous expenditures on his (Mr. S's) behalf in spite of his own financial difficulties and in spite of the fact that he has no reason to expect any profit from doing so. Mr. S, on the other hand, is no longer under an obligation to the expresident. The company is doing poorly, and Mr. S is underpaid and overworked even though he became a division chief several years ago. He could easily obtain a better-paying job elsewhere, but he does not leave because he feels responsible for his subordinates. To use a Western metaphor, he feels like the captain who does not abandon his ship until the last passenger has left it.

A Japanese company is like a huge extended family. I do not mean that the employees consist of members of the same family. That practice is largely obsolete in industrial Japan. On the contrary, what I mean is that a large company takes in many unrelated people and makes them "relatives" of a kind.

Another aspect of Japanese epistemology is its nonlegalism, which is shared with the Chinese. Though resort to law is increasing in Japan due to Westernization, the Japanese and Chinese prefer to avoid legal procedures. For example, the Japanese used to prefer to settle car accident damages from each other's pockets without making a claim on insurance companies. This is another indication of mutualism rather than hierarchism. The Japanese also share relational logic with the Chinese. One of the problems the children and grandchildren of Japanese immigrants in the United States suffer from is the influence of Western classificational logic on their thinking: "I am an Asian

American. I am not really an American. I am not really an Asian. Therefore I am nothing." This type of logic creates very serious mental health problems. But reasoning of this kind does not occur in the relational logic of the Japanese in Japan. People in Japan go to the Shinto shrine for marriage, to the Buddhist temple for funerals, and to a Christian church for Christmas, and they see no problem in doing this.

The four cultures we have discussed do not exhaust all the types of mutualistic logic which exist in many cultures of the world. Nevertheless, these four examples show the viability of mutualistic logic, and even some of its advantages. Generally speaking, mutualistic logic is more flexible than nonreciprocal logic, not only in itself but also in culture contact situations. For example, there was a missionary who brought his God to a polytheistic culture in Africa. The tribe had some 300 gods constituting the harmony of the universe. The tribe welcomed the missionary as the missionary's new god would surely fit into the harmonistic universe — as all gods are harmonious in this tribe's view. However, the missionary insisted on the rightness of his one God and the wrongness of the 300 gods. This certainly was very irreligious from the point of view of the tribe.

Another advantage of reciprocal logics is that their heterogenistic nature prepares people for culture change with much less culture shock and future shock than the nonreciprocal homogenistic logic which monopolarizes people (Maruyama 1966), as I will discuss shortly. In the world, there are more reciprocal logics than there are nonreciprocal logics. In this sense nonreciprocal logics are more like an abnormality, and it is interesting to trace their historical development.

Origins of Western Nonreciprocal Logic

The early Greeks had many gods who were more like human beings than crystallizations of perfection. However, in the sixth century B.C., a Greek scientist, Anaximandros, conceived the notion of "infinity" as the inexhaustible protosubstance of the universe. As no material knowable by human senses fulfilled his requirements for the infinity-substance, he thought that this substance must be beyond all human experience. Xenophanes applied Anaximandros's notion of the infinity-substance to religion. Proud of his "discovery" and scornful of the human-like gods of Greek mythology, Xenophanes declared that his infinite god was incomparable to humans and eternal. In the fifth century B.C., Anaxagoras invented the notion of a power-substance that penetrated things and caused them to move. He thought that the power-substance must be a soul, and must have order and purpose. He ascribed rationality to the power-substance. Thus, Western theology had its origin in Greek mathematics and science, and has been borrowing its epistemological structure from Western types of mathematics and science ever since, even though many religious Westerners believe that mathematics and science are derived from God.

What we know as "Aristotelian logic" had its origin in the teachings of Greek sophists who, shortly after Anaxagoras's invention of the notion of power-substance, formulated the principle of identity and the law of contradiction, and thus began the Westerners' tendency to think in black and white. A little later, Plato gave abstract ideas a higher reality than concrete things and advocated that true reality had no substance. Here was the beginning of the Western inclination toward abstract principles. The "reality" of abstract concepts such as "good" and "evil" took firm root. Plato also formulated the logical subordination of the particular to the general. And finally in the fourth century B.C., Aristotle established the logic of deduction of the particular from the general. Circular reasoning was forbidden. Thereafter, Western science relied mostly on the assumption of a nonreciprocal flow of causality and neglected the mutuality in natural and social events. The same logic was also applied to religion and ethics: God as omniscient, omnipotent, perfect creator, and prime mover of the universe; hierarchical social organization; a dichotomy between good and evil; disdain of "material things;" belief in the universal validity of one way of thinking and believing. When Christ arrived 300 years later, Western theologians fitted his teaching into the theology based on this logic. Inspired by Christian theology, Mohammedanism was born six centuries later.

There have been rebels within the Western cultures against this type of logic throughout history: Augustinus, the nominalists, Hamann, Kierkegaard, Nietzsche, Bergson, Heidegger, Sartre, to mention only some. But nonreciprocal logic retained its influence as the mainstream logic of the Western cultures. Even the rebellions tended toward individualism rather than toward reciprocal logics. They were mainly rebellions of faith and feelings against knowledge, of subjectivism against objectivism, of individual uniqueness against universalism, and of free will against determinism. Those who entertained mutualistic thoughts were mainly biologists, particularly since Darwin. But they did not formulate their mutualistic logic into a philosophy.

One of the factors contributing to the persistence of nonreciprocal logic in Western cultures seems to be the nuclear family system which encourages "monopolarization" in personality development (Maruyama 1966). Monopolarization is a psychological need to believe that there is one universal truth, and to seek out, depend on, find security in, and hang onto one authority, one theory, uniformity, homogeneity, and standardization. In cultures in which children have close relations with many adults — whether they are in extended families, in communal child rearing, in a system of frequent child exchange, or in a system in which a person's obligations to many specific individuals are emphasized — there seems to be less tendency toward monopolarization. It is not a coincidence that in the current epistemological revolution toward mutualistic logic in our society, many nonnuclear forms of family are experimented with.

THE AESTHETIC BASIS

Aesthetic principles vary from culture to culture. Some Islamic designs are characterized by intricate repetition of minute details. The European Vitruvius principle also achieves its design unity by repetition of similar elements. On the other hand, Japanese gardens and flower arrangements avoid repetitions and redundancies and create harmony from dissimilar elements. In Japan repetitiousness, whether in design, in poetry, or in human behavior, is considered *kudoi* [heavy, overdone, obnoxious] and is avoided. The contrary of *kudoi* is *sappari* [fresh, clear] which is a very important consideration in Japanese aesthetics.

In China, however, we find both the principle of repetition and the principle of *sappari*. Chinese architecture and decorations can be highly elaborate, repetitious, and strong in color, and some ancient Chinese poems are quite profuse in extravagant adjectives, while traditional Chinese paintings as a whole are nonrepetitious in composition. Neither principle is exclusively characteristic of either Western or Eastern cultures. Hopi design is elaborate, while much Swedish design is *sappari*.

There are different basic numbers in different cultures. In Navajo, the basic number seems to be four, particularly in songs. In Sioux, the basic numbers seem to be four, corresponding to the four directions, and six when sky and earth are sometimes included as additional directions. The Japanese Ikebana [flower arrangement] is usually based on various principles of making compositions out of three, five, seven, or nine different elements. Many Japanese designs use a triangle of unequal sides as the basic layout, often with secondary triangles added which should be dissimilar to the main triangle, unlike European architectural design in which the subdominant forms are expected to repeat the main form.

There are also cultural differences in the concept of a design object's relation to other objects. For example, in Japanese architecture there has been, and still is, a great concern to harmonize the building with its surroundings. On the other hand, many American architects, particularly urban architects, tend to regard the building mainly as an expression of the building's individuality.

The existence of these cultural differences in aesthetic principles indicates that even in aesthetics there are heterogenistic as well as homogenistic principles, and that harmony and beauty can be created from heterogeneity. These considerations make us ask ourselves further questions like: (1) can we apply aesthetic principles of heterogeneity to social hardware such as urban and regional planning? (2) can we devise interactive aesthetic metaprinciples capable of combining several designs, some of which are based on homogenistic and others on heterogenistic principles?

The answer to the first question cannot yet be given, because hardly any examples of such hardware have been produced yet. There are numerous urban designs which include buildings with different functions. But usually the philosophy of such designs has been to bring these buildings to unity by means of shared features, such as similar details or similar proportionality. An urban area with an overall design with components based on different principles, or a building consisting of suites or rooms with contrasting philosophies, have yet to be created. A shopping center built in such a way, or even a student dormitory consisting of rooms in different styles, would be very attractive and interesting.

The answer to the second question seems affirmative. Some examples of such metaprinciples already exist. Kenzo Tange's olympic sports building complex in Tokyo can be regarded as one. The overall design is heterogeneous, based on the principle of interactive and morphogenetic flow of lines (Maruyama 1978c). It is also asymmetrical and nonredundant. If you take the components separately, some are homogeneous and redundant within themselves, while others are heterogeneous.

Such metaprinciples have not yet been applied to urban planning. But in some cities there is an emergence of different cultural principles in architecture, which can be used later as components of an overall metadesign. For example, in San Francisco the residents of the Chinatown area have designed and proposed some housing projects with a high ratio of occupants per square foot, which will enable old persons to stay near the younger generations. This is all in accordance with Chinese culture. In another part of San Francisco black architects have designed houses with shower and bath facilities directly attached to the large living room. This is in keeping with the black tradition in the United States. Black families in cities often receive migrants from rural areas. These new arrivals sleep in the living room until they find a job and a place of their own to live. The host family is able to express its hospitality by having a bathroom attached to the living room.

At present, each community is acting independently in such endeavors. But as society becomes more heterogenistic, interactive urban designs to anticipate, accommodate, and symbiotize the heterogeneity become necessary and useful.

There are two ways that heterogenization may proceed: through localization and through interweaving. In localization, the heterogeneity between localities increases, while each locality may remain or become homogeneous. In interweaving, heterogeneity in each locality increases, while the differences between localities decrease. At present, localization is more conspicuous than interweaving. In the next stage of our social heterogenization, interweaving may increase.We need to develop aesthetic metaprinciples of heterogenization and symbiotization of heterogeneity for both localization and interweaving. For each of these two ways, there are three different principles of heterogenization: (a) independent-event; (b) homeostatic; (c) morphogenetic. These are discussed elsewhere (Maruyama 1978c).

INDUSTRIALIZATION AND HETEROGENIZATION

It is generally believed that industrialization and the use of technology will homogenize the world. This is a fallacy, as Jack Shuman elaborates in his paper in this volume. As technology advances, people's lives become more heterogenized. I need not duplicate Jack Shuman's discussion of heterogenization in technologically advanced countries. However, I would like to discuss whether or not the industrialization of nonindustrial countries will tend to make the world homogeneous.

Until recently, it was commonly assumed that the industrialization of the European and North American countries was closely related to the fact that these countries were Christian in religion and ethics. It was often proposed that Christianization was somehow necessary for the industrialization (or modernization) of non-Christian conutries. Studies of recent social change in the world have shown that this assumption is incorrect. Many countries in Africa, the Middle East, and Southeast Asia have become industrialized while retaining their religion, ethics, and traditional patterns of life. Japan and China are no longer exceptions as non-Christian industrial countries. Many cultures have even enhanced their traditions by new technological means. This indicates not only that industrialization can increase heterogenization, but also, more importantly, that *what technology does, depends on the philosophy with which it is used.* Once we realize this, it becomes clear that technology itself is not an evil. Whether or not technology becomes an evil depends on the kind of philosophy with which it is used. We must reexamine the philosophy with which we use technology, instead of putting the blame on technology itself.

At the same time, the technology-importing countries need to be able to distinguish technology from the religion, philosophy, and ideology of the countries from which they import it. Too often, the technology-importing countries are eager to imitate everything American, everything European, or everything Russian, regardless of whether it is useless, impractical, or destructive. Many Polynesians gave up their native foods for canned foods, to the detriment of their health. Many Japanese gave up their traditional, naturally ventilated houses for Western-style houses, which need to be air-conditioned. The Western-style toilet collects and breeds flies in hot countries. These are material examples. The mental and spiritual damage resulting from the indiscriminate and unnecessary importation of religion, philosophy, ideology and ways of life from industrialized countries can be much more harmful. If nothing else, they cause self-depreciation, feelings of inferiority, inadequacy, and self-hate.

Heterogenization of the world is beneficial to all countries. It enriches the cultural resources of the world, provides niches for individuals who want to migrate into them, and supplies a wide range of patterns for those social segments that want to practice interweaving. Furthermore, as Wright (1931) pointed out, it increases the speed of human cultural evolution by providing cultural subgroups among which interbreeding can take place.

HETEROGENIZATION AND ISOLATIONISM

There is one danger in heterogenization, though this is less harmful than homogenization. However contradictory it may seem, a heterogeneous system can create components which are different from one another but highly homogeneous within themselves. As I discussed in my paper at our first Symposium on Cultural Futuristics ("Toward human futuristics," this volume), this happens especially when there is high horizontal mobility. People seeking congenial groups subdivide into small cliques, which tend to become isolated and highly homogeneous. The do-your-own-thing movement can end in such an arrangement. In fact, I have met an organizer of encounter groups whose universe is limited to her own group members. She had very little interest in anything outside her little universe and she hated black people. Of course, this is not any worse than living in a fascist homogenistic country, but it comes very close to it. The danger comes not from the heterogenistic system itself but from some individuals' tendency to homogenize and avoid heterogeneity. Perhaps a heterogenistic system should allow for such homogenistic components. Similarly, the "small is beautiful" movement may be incorrectly based on isolationistic or homogenistic philosophies.

NEED FOR HEURISTICS IN IMPLEMENTING THE SYMBIOTIZATION OF HETEROGENEITY

Given heterogeneous elements, how do you symbiotize them? We have touched upon this problem a little in our discussion of aesthetic principles. In aesthetics, much depends on the insight and intuition of the artist. In biological processes, symbiotization is achieved simply because symbiotic individuals and species have more chances of surviving than nonsymbiotic individuals and species. But how would we do it in the social process? We still do not have adequate methods or even rules of thumb for increasing symbiotization. That is why we have oppression, exploitation, and war. I have only a very rudimentary guideline to offer, which goes as follows:

In a heterogenistic society symbiotic combinations of diverse individuals or groupings must be worked out. Suppose Individual A has Goal A, Individual B has Goal B, Individual C has Goal C, etc. Individual A has several alternative ways $a_1, a_2, a_3, \ldots$ of achieving his Goal A. Individual B has several alternative ways $b_1, b_2, b_3, \ldots$ of achieving his Goal B, and similarly for other individuals. Some combinations $a_i b_j c_k \ldots$ of these alternative ways may be symbiotic, while other combinations may not. Individuals for whom a symbiotic combination can be found among the alternative ways to their respective goals can be hooked up in a network of symbiosis. Individuals who cannot be combined symbiotically can be hooked up in separate networks. Each of these networks is heterogeneous.

On the other hand, individuals who share a similar goal may be combined in a grouping. A grouping is therefore homogeneous in goal and can be treated like an individual in the network analysis. A grouping does not have to be geographic or ethnic. It can be occupational, recreational, or otherwise. Groupings for which a symbiotic combination can be found among the alternative ways to their respective goals can be hooked up in a network of symbiosis.

The development of theories and methods for such symbiotization belongs to the future.

REFERENCES

BRAVERMAN, MAXWELL H., R. G. SCHRANDT
  1966   "Colony development of a polymorphic hydroid as a problem in pattern formation," in *The Cnidaria and their evolution*. London: Academic Press.
BUCKLEY, W.
  1968   *Modern systems research for the behavioral scientist*. Chicago: Aldine.

CHANG., T. S.
1938 A Chinese philosopher's theory of knowledge. *Yenching Journal of Social Studies* 1.

DARWIN, CHARLES
1857 *The origin of species.*

KLUCKHOHN, C.
1949 "The philosophy of Navaho Indians," in *Ideological differences and world order.* Edited by F. S. C. Northrop. New Haven: Yale University Press.

KUHN, T.
1962 *The structure of scientific revolutions.* Chicago: University of Chicago Press.

MARUYAMA, M.
1961 Multilateral mutual simultaneous causal relationships among the modes of communication, sociometric pattern, and intellectual orientation in the Danish culture. *Phylon* 22: 41–58.
1962 Awareness and unawareness of misunderstandings. *Methodos* 13: 255–275.
1963a The second cybernetics: deviation-amplifying mutual causal processes. *American Scientist* 51: 164–179; 250–256.
1963b Generating complex patterns by means of simple rules of interaction. *Methodos* 14: 17–26.
1966 Monopolarization, family and individuality. *Psychiatric Quarterly* 40: 133–149.
1967 The Navajo philosophy: an esthetic ethic of mutuality. *Mental Hygiene* 51: 242–249.
1978a "Psychotopology and its application to cross-disciplinary, cross-professional and cross-cultural communication," in *Perspectives on ethnicity.* Edited by Regina E. Holloman and Serghei Arutiunov. World Anthropology. The Hague: Mouton.
1978b "New theories in old epistemological traps." *Proceedings of 1978 Annual Meeting of Society for General Systems Research.* Washington, D.C.: Society for General Systems Research.
1978c Heterogenistics and morphogenetics: toward a new concept of the scientific. *Theory and Society.* 5: 75–96.

McEACHRON, N. B.
1971 "Theoretical framework," in *Forces for societal transformation in the United States 1950–2000*, volume one. Menlo Park, California: Educational Policy Research Center, Stanford Research Institute.

MILSUM, J.
1968 *Positive feedback.* Oxford and New York: Pergamon Press.

MYRDAL, GUNNAR
1943 *American dilemma.* New York: Harper and Row.
1957 *Economic theory and underdeveloped regions.* London: Duckworth.

REICHENBACH, HANS
1956 *Direction of time.* Berkeley: University of California Press.

SHANNON, CLAUDE, WARREN WEAVER
1949 *The mathematical theory of communication.* Urbana: University of Illinois Press.

SPEMANN, HANS
1938 *Embryonic development and induction.* New York: Hafner.

TINBERGEN, J.
1937 *An econometric approach to business cycle problems.* Paris.

ULAM, S.
   1962   "On some mathematical problems connected with patterns of growth figures." *Proceedings of Symposium on Applied Mathematics* 14: 215–224.
VON FOERSTER, H.
   1949–1953   *Transactions of the VIth to Xth Conferences on Cybernetics.* New York: Josiah Macy, Jr. Foundation.
WADDINGTON, C. H.
   1968–1972   *Towards a theoretical biology,* four volumes. Chicago: Aldine.
WIENER, N.
   1949   *Extrapolation, interpolation and smoothing of stationary time series with engineering applications.* Cambridge: M.I.T. Press.
WRIGHT, S.
   1931   Evolution in Mendelian populations. *Genetics* 16: 97–159.

Ways of Perceiving Oneself
in Urban Planning Interaction

EDMUND BACON

> Many are the things that man
> Seeing must understand.
> Not seeing, how shall he know
> What lies in the hand
> Of time to come?
>> Sophocles, *Ajax.*

> ... Beholding [seeing with understanding] is just not a mirror which always remains the same, but a living power of apprehension which has its own inward history and has passed through many stages.
>> Heinrich Wölfflin, *Principles of Art History*, 1915.

> A man of antiquity sailing a boat, quite content and enjoying the ingenious comfort of the contrivance. The ancients represents the scene accordingly. And now: What a modern man experiences as he walks across the deck of a steamer: (1) his own movement, (2) the movement of the ship which may be in the opposite direction. (3) the direction and velocity of the current, (4) the rotation of the earth, (5) its orbit (6) the orbits of the moons and planets around it. Result: an interplay of movements in the universe, at their the "I" on the ship.
>> Paul Klee, "Creative Credo", 1920
>> from *The Thinking Eye.*

From *Design of cities* Revised edition 1974: Viking Press. 1976: Penguin paperback.

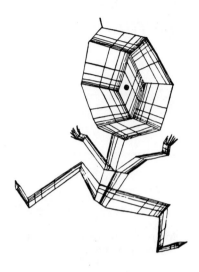

OUTGOING

In the two drawings on this page Klee presents two kinds of people. Here is the outgoing man, ebullient, involved, exposed in both his strengths and his frailities. He reaches for more than he has or knows; he leaps into space aware of the possible consequences of a fall; a man with the courage to be vulnerable.

INGROWN

Here is the opposite type of man, inward-looking, self-concerned, and safe, reducing contact with the outside to an absolute minimum, avoiding exposure and involvement. One's environment will surely determine the form of one's self and one's function in relation to one's environment will surely determine the form of one's self and one's work, whether the "one" be a person or an institution.

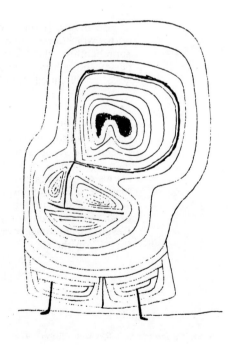

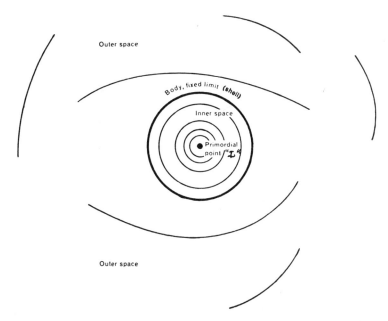

The application of the design process is greatly influenced by the way the designer and the client perceive themselves. The primordial point the "I" in the Klee diagram above, may be thought of as the individual, the artist, the creator, the organizer, the planner. It may also be an institution, a university, building proposal, an innovative concept. In each case, the "I" has a definite view of its own identity, its own function and purpose, and its own aspirations. These, in turn, will influence the form that its physical extensions will take, the influence it exerts on the space immediately around it, the "inner space" in the diagram above.

The primordial point, the "I," also has its "outer space," the broader milieu within which its inner, more intimately related spaces function. While in this diagram Klee has designated the divider between the two as a fixed limit, a shell, it can also be seen in more abstract terms as the fluid division between the inner, the intimate, the familiar, the inherited, the customary, and the outer, the unfamiliar, the untried, the challenging, the dangerous, the painful, and the potentially disastrous. Each person, social group, each institution has the inner and outer spaces. The dress and folkways of the newer generation provide a protective inner space for the group just as surely as do the country clubs and social registers of the older: each has its area outside, repugnant and terrifying. The way in which one's self relates to these two determines the nature of one's life and one's contribution to society, and, in physical terms, the nature and form of an institution.

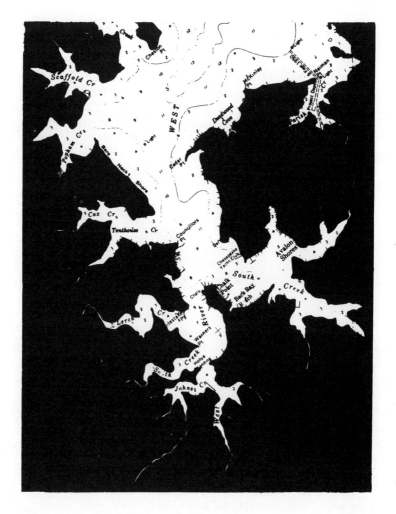

Favorable Environment

WAYS OF PERCEIVING ENVIRONMENT

From a Boat

Key to the form of one's self1image of one's projection into the space around one is whether one views his immediate and his more distant environment as hostile or favorable.

To demonstrate how the same thing may look to different people, these drawings were prepared showing favorable and hostile environments on the same terrain as seen by the boatman and the motorist. In the drawing on the left, the "I" on the boat sees danger as the land, the hazard increasing in intensity as the land rises in the bottom of the bay, and as it approaches laterally.

From an Automobile
The hostile environment for the motorist is the very environment that is safe for the boatman and vice versa (drawing on the right). This obvious definition of environmental hostility is paralleled by a much more subtle and insidious feeling of environmental hostility which bears great influence on architecture. Its impact is recorded in the forms of buildings at various points in history. When viewed in this light, these buildings become remarkably sensitive barometers of changes in degree of hostility or harmony between the structure and the environment in which it is located.

■ *Hostile Environment*

WAYS OF PERCEIVING SPACE

Key to the whole concept is the way in which one perceives the continuity of space within which the inner and outer spaces operate. The four squares (left) illustrate different ways in which such perception can take place. They should be thought of as planes of indefinite size, extending in all directions to the horizon and beyond.

The square at the top represents space as a boundless unit, the continuous interaction of opposites represented by black and white producing an unbroken extent of gray, as in systems of nature.

In the second square man enters and draws a line, whether physical or conceptual, dividing the system into two elements: love-hate, good-evil, indissolubly establishing duality.

In the third square the line is bent, creating an inequivalence. By the act of bending the line, the designer establishes the dominance of one element and the subdominance of the other.

In the fourth square the line is closed, creating a duality of a new sort: one (the darker square) a discrete object clearly defined which detaches itself from the other, the lighter gray plane of indefinite extent which surrounds it. The question then becomes whether because of exotopic blindness the designer sees only the discrete object, as he has been taught to do from infancy in the Western world, or whether he sees the situation as a plane of indefinite extent with a hole in it.

Paul Klee defines the inner square in relation to the line as endotopic, and the outer plane as exotopic, and illustrates ways in which these two intermesh when controlled by lines of differing character.

UNITY

DUALITY

DOMINANCE AND SUB-DOMINANCE

ENDOTOPIC AND EXOTOPIC

ENDOTOPIC

Shape — When viewed in endotopic terms the design process becomes that of making shapes. Architecture becomes the imposition of capricious shapes into the environment.

Mass — The third dimension is seen as the vertical projection of capricious shapes, and architecture becomes preoccupied with mass as geometrical form.

Object — The approach culminates in thinking of the building as a discrete object, created independently of its background, arbitrarily placed in anonymous space. The negative aspects are stressed because so many designers are heavily endotopic, but true design involves an interplay of endotopic and exotopic thinking.

EXOTOPIC

Space — When viewed in exotopic terms the design process becomes that of articulating for human purposes some portion of a space of indefinite extent.

Movement — Since the articulations of space can be experienced only through movement, the designer's function becomes that of providing channels of movement related to larger movement systems.

Form — In this approach form emerges naturally from the movement systems so that the step of creating capricious shapes doesn't exist in the design process.

A key test of design is whether the shapes are arbitrary or are derived from movement systems.

FAVORABLE ENVIRONMENT

In the medieval period, because of the limited effectiveness of the military missiles of the time, the degree of hositility of the environment varied markedly within horizontal layers. In the drawing of Castle of Saumur from *The book of hours of the Duke of Berry*, the architectural forms respond to this variation as it rises vertically. Here in the upper air, the architecture leaps outward into space, exposing itself in all directions, involving itself with the atmosphere to the point that the turrets, foliate projections, spires, and pinnacles seem almost to dissolve into space.

INTERMEDIATE ENVIRON-MENT

In this intermediate section of the castle, partly but not completely removed from the threat of military missiles, the architecture involves itself in space beyond the minimum. The vertical ridges deliberately extend the area, and so the vulnerability of the wall. The architectural express is of a single direction of thrust, up and away from the hostile environment of the ground.

HOSTILE ENVIRONMENT

Here the architectural forms are completely dominated by the need to resist the hostile environment outside. The inward-looking convex forms produce the minimum surface exposure for the maximum interior volume, and the curved mass tended to deflect such missiles as the military mind could produce.

The Klee diagrams in the center suggest the response of the primordial point to the three environmental conditions.

OUTREACH

In these three plans we see the struggle of the medieval structure to free itself from the oppressive demands of an environment seen as totally hostile.

In the upper plan, a late castle is beginning to break out of the rigid circular form of earlier fortifications, and to involve itself more richly in its environment, reaching out to significant points around, it, even at the cost and dangers of greater exposure.

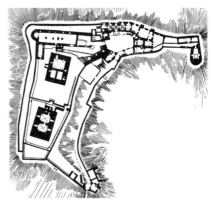

INTERMEDIATE

In this plan the internal structural discipline of the groin vault demands rectangular overall form. The need for protection from a hostile environment in turn suggests minimum exposure and so a circular form. In this design, created within the tension of these two conflicting demands, military considerations clearly outweighted structural logic.

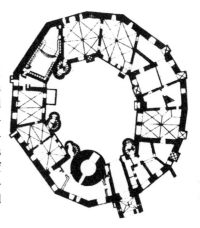

INWARD LOOKING

The medieval tower is the most efficient possible structure when protection from a hostile environment is seen as the dominant consideration. The resemblance between this plan and the Klee drawing on page (3) is striking. Here the "inner space" is that space around the tower which is controlled by armaments within it. The divider between this and the darker, uncontrolled "outer space" is not a "fixed shell" but an intangible line determined by the efficiency of the armaments.

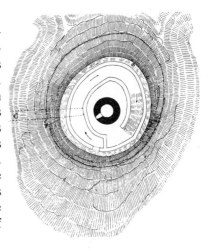

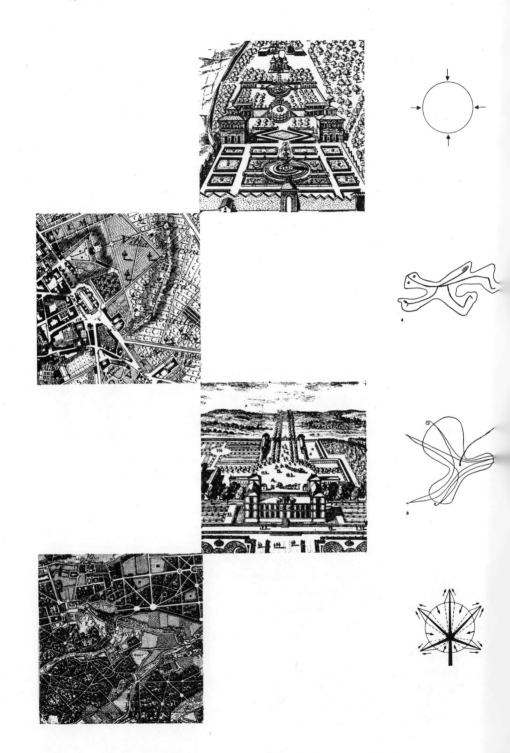

INWARD LOOKING

As we move into the Renaissance, we observe the outpush of architecture into an environment gradually freed of the most oppressive elements of medieval hostility. The fully developed Italian villa, such as the 1560 Villa Lante at Bagnaja shown on the left, contained the seeds of later work in its thrusts and counterthrusts, but all of these were totally contained within clearly defined bounding walls in the endotopic sense. The diagrams in the center are from Paul Klee's *The thinking eye* (1961).

OUTREACH

In 1585 Pope Sixtus V introduced a new design dimension into Italian thought by his plans for Rome. These burst the bounds of any clearly defined building project and utilized the entire city of Rome as the design field. While the thrusts and counterthrusts of his movement systems extended over great distances, they always reached out to definite objects, and finally came to rest at some terminal point, such as a church, a gate, or a square

OUTGOING

An entirely new dimension of design was introduced into France in the eighteenth century in the form of design thrusts that had no clear termination, that penetrated the boundaries of the inner space, that extended outward indefinitely, over the horizon seemingly to infinity. These concepts were developed at the time of the Encyclopedists and the mathematical explorations of infinity, and establish the idea of a design structure capable of indefinite extension over time.

INVOLVEMENT

The fourth design element, suggested by the Klee diagram to the left, involves not only the penetration of the inner space by an outward push, but concurrently a countermovement of outer space influences penetrating inwardly toward the source. While this is illustrated here by the remarkable interaction of design thrust in the Paris region, it might better be illustrated in the institutional sense by the kind of involvement that is tending to come about today when wide sectors of people invade what the professional designer previously had thought was his private inner space of design.

INVOLVEMENT TODAY

As I propose to indicate on the following pages, involvement encompasses much more than cerebral comprehension. It is a necessary ingredient for the creation of competent design.

Sigfried Giedion in his great book *Space, time, and architecture* stresses the importance of moving beyond the purely cerebral into the realm of feeling, of involving one's sensibilities and emotions. Rudolph Arnheim, in Gyorgy Kepes's *Education of vision*, quotes Albert Einstein's letter to Jacques Hadamard, "The words or the language as they are written or spoken do not seem to play any role in my mechanism of thought. The psychical entities which seem to serve as elements in thought are certain signs and more or less clear images which can be 'voluntarily' reproduced and combined." And further: "The above-mentioned elements are, in my case, of visual and some of muscular type. Conventional words or other signs have to be sought for laboriously only in a secondary stage, when the mentioned associative play is sufficiently established and can be reproduced at will." He adds his own comment "If Enstein's procedure is representative of intelligent reasoning, we may be strangling the potential of our brainpower systematically by forcing our youth to think primarily with verbal and numerical signs."(1965).

Leonard K. Eaton in his book *Two Chicago architects and their clients* says, "As long ago as 1919 Carl Seashore noted that musically talented students possessed high auditory imagery [the ability to re-create a tone image], and that this faculty was closely related to motor imagery and motor tendencies: *these motor images are perceived in terms of feelings, of effort and strain in the body.* This kinesthetic response plays a large part in the enjoyment derived from active participation in music, architecture and sport." (1969, emphasis mine).

The point here is not bodily movement as "exercise" or "recreation," separate and divorced from the act of design, but rather bodily response as a built-in ingredient of the design process. It relates to the range of the images or models that are used in design. Thus if one is bodily inert or incompetent, one tends to sit and contemplate. The forms that associate with this kind of bodily condition are crystalline shapes, spheres, cubes, or pyramids, discrete forms which can be comprehended without the need for bestirring oneself, for putting forth the muscular effort required for moving about. If one is physically and muscularly in such condition that it is a joy to move about, that one is impelled by an inner drive to leap forward to the next and the next experience, a very different range of perception of space and time is brought into play, and one is inclined to think in terms of linkages rather than discrete elements.

This may be illustrated by the problem of perceiving the basic design idea of two national capital cities: Washington, D. C., and Peking. If one stands at the foot of the Washington Monument at the intersection of the two main axes of the United States Capital, one has only to move around the basic elements of monumental Washington. In Peking there just is no way to perceive the design except by making the effort to move through the spaces over a two-mile track. One cannot see from one part to another because each part is totally enclosed, yet it is not any individual part, but rather the linkage, which is the design.

In the education of small children we have systematically suppressed the motor tendency by forcing them to sit still for long hours at a time. In advanced education we have systematically denigrated sensory, sensual, and muscular perception, and fostered the dichotomy between body and thought. A reintegration is called for, not to make the student "healthy," but to equip him with the basic faculties needed for his work. Training in muscular skill and muscular and sensory perception should be part of every architectural and planning school. I believe that anyone intending to practice architecture or planning should be able to run up three flights of stairs without noticeable loss of breath and take joy in doing it.

Inward Looking

THE INVOLVEMENT OF THE SQUARE

Above stands the square, the paradigm of architectural thought, compact, self-contained, the minimum exterior exposure for the maximum interior area if a minimum number of perpendicular straight lines is also an objective. The form was developed in earliest times when protection from a hostile environment was building's main purpose. While still efficient as an enclosure of space, and still relevant to parts of a larger whole, it remains all too often as the paradigm for the whole itself. Here the residual effect can be damaging indeed. If it is used by an institution, a university in a low-income area, for example, and each extension is designed as nearly as possible to reconstruct a square of larger dimension, the impression will be given that the institution regards the environment into which it is projecting itself as hostile. The physical form will have a minimum of exposure and so of environmental involvement. The shape of the edge and the nature of the edge are both important because of the way in which they communicate the institution's message to its neighbors, of favorableness or hostility, as when a neighborhood rose up in protest because a university put a chain link fence along one portion of its boundary.

What follows is a geometrical development of the square in an attempt to present a countermodel for the growth and extension of an entity, be it an institution or an idea. At the top of page 489 the square projects itself into a cross, substantially increasing its length of exposure to the environment while retaining its original area. This increases the degree of involvement, but the form continues to be an aggressive one.

In the lower diagram on page 489 the finest line designates the form produced when this same principle of exposure is applied to each of the nine sub-squares produced by the cross form. The two diagrams on page 490 show the forms produced by extending this principle in two more stages. The figure on page 491 shows the form taken to still one more stage of development.

It will be seen that the length of the line bounding the entity can be increased indefinitely while holding the diagram within definite bounds. As the bounding line approaches infinity, the degree of environmental involvement becomes greater and greater.

Outreach

Outgoing

Involvement A

Involvement B

TOWARD TOTAL INVOLVEMENT

We have now come full cycle from the simple circle of Paul Klee defining the limit between inner space and outer space through the square which, orthogonally, most nearly approximates Klee's circle, through the square extension on the three previous pages, to the diagram on p. 491. The systematic application of the principle produced a form with elements approaching the circle, related to each other in definite groupings and subgroupings. Yet the figure on page 491 is just as surely a single area with a single bounding line as is the Klee circle. It demonstrates that involvement tends to dissolve the distinction between the inner and the outer, and produces forms implicit in the first step of outreach, but difficult to anticipate in their entirety.

Of course this form is only a stage in a continuous progression to infinity. The line of exposure becomes longer and longer and the levels of foci become greater and greater with each stage of development, each of these approaching infinity. The point at which a form comes to rest along this progression is the point of equilibrium between the inner and environmental forces in terms of hostility and favorableness.

It should be restated that the geometrical form of this diagram has no symbolic significance beyond the principle it embodies. It should also be restated that, while this illustration was deliberately intended to suggest new ways of defining the boundaries of institutional site plans in cities, the ideas it engenders relate to a much wider range of issues, the form of urban extension within a metropolitan region, (with maximum exposure to open space), the form of implantation of a new idea in a social group or indeed of a new institution within society. It relates wherever there is an inner and an outer, and that is nearly everywhere.

MOVING INTO THE FUTURE

The Klee drawing opposite expresses the concept of movement, of tense lines of progression from one place to another, interwoven into a total fabric. To this have been added points of conjunction, of flowering and enrichment, places of repose. These are important too, and they also call upon the highest expression of architecture, but they can be understood only in relation to the movement to arrive there and anticipation of the movement away.

Together these two elements, the architecture of movement and architecture of repose, make up the city as a work of art, and this is the people's art. The product of city design can be experienced by anyone, without qualification, on an equal basis. It could become a great democratic statement of the life we share in common.

The test of our achievement is whether we are able to break away from our fragmented approach to this problem and begin to see the city as a whole, dealing with it as a complete organism. Here, again, we may listen to the words of Paul Klee:

Accordingly, a sense of totality has gradually entered into the artist's conception of the natural object, whether this object be a plant, animal, or man; whether it be situated in the space of the house, the landscape, or the world, and the first consequence is that a more spatial conception of the object as such is born.

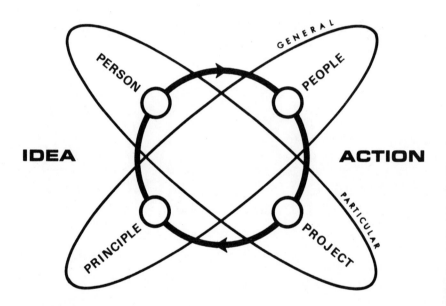

DECISION MAKING

The way in which decisions are made becomes a key element if one thinks of architectural form in terms of growth. On pp. 498 and 499 pages are portrayed the growth of the pedestrian systems in central Montreal, developed under the guidance of Vincent Ponte, and in central Philadelphia. On pp. 496 and 497 the growth of the Philadelphia system is portrayed as it exists simultaneously as an idea in the minds of the public, the idea insofar as it had been resolved into engineering plans, the idea as it existed in the mind of the most imaginative and forward-looking designer, and the idea insofar as it had manifested itself in terms of construction on the ground. Each of these four tracks has its own morphology, rate of change and history of evolution; each interacts with the other in varying degrees. The diagram on pp. 496 and 497 attempts to symbolize this process, showing horizontally the different states of the design idea in the interest of simplicity here including only two of the four simultaneous tracks.

The diagram opposite attempts to identify the focal elements in the interplay between idea and action just discussed. These are divided into the general and the particular. Thus the distinction is made between the project and the principle from which it was derived, and which its use will influence, and between the general prevailing opinions and attitudes of the people as against the points of view and proposals of those persons who make up, at any one time, the most active and articulate leadership. Here, again, there is continuous cyclical interaction, not just a one-way street. The leaders may influence the people and the people influence the leaders, or change them. The nature, competence, relevance and, hopefully, inspiring qualities of the design hypothesis that is fed into this process has a great influence on the direction that it takes, and on the relative position of the four focal elements. In the diagram on pp. 496 and 497 the circular movement illustrated above is stretched out to produce the spiral, the vertical dimension being time.

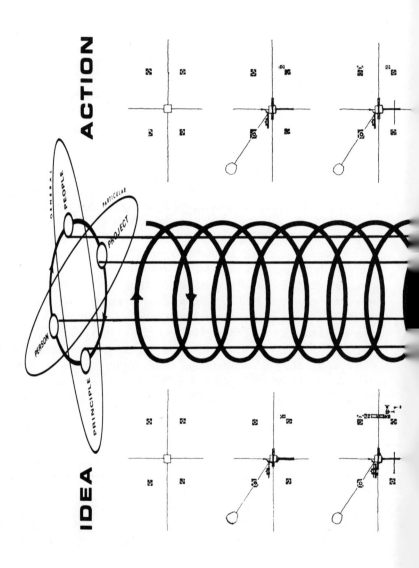

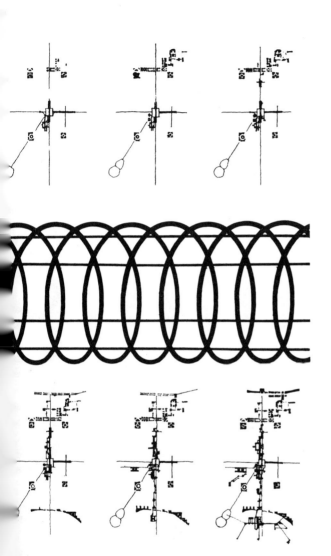

GROWTH OF FORM

PEDESTRIAN   SPACES

MONTREAL

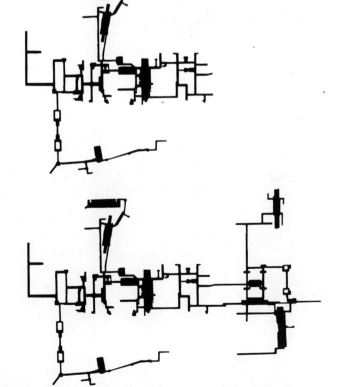

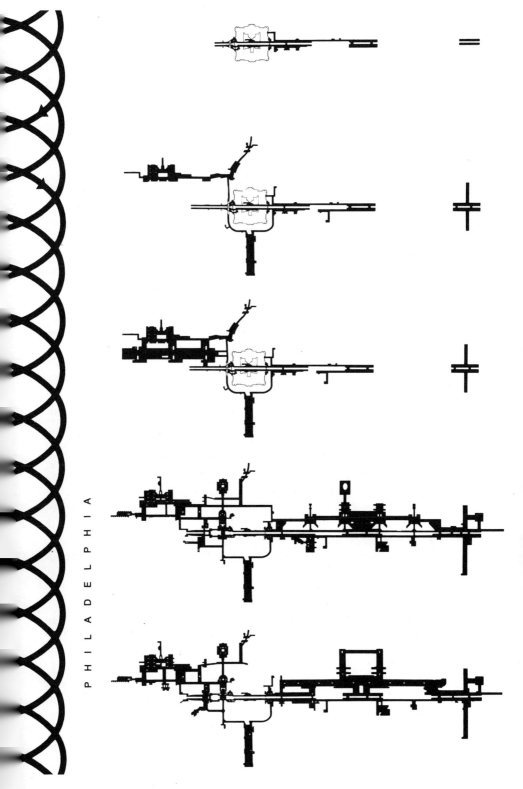

CYCLICAL FEEDBACK

In 1968 on the Aegean Sea, at the Sixth Delos Symposion conducted under the guidance of C. A. Doxiades, noted Greek city planner, a discussion took place on the parallel between biological processes and human institutions. British biologist C. H. Waddington asserted that technology must permit people to be involved in the evolution of their own environment. Robert A. Aldrich, United States pediatrician, developed the model of the DNA molecule containing the code for man, so arranging and organizing cellular growth in the body that an individual man is produced. Each man contains the code for an environment, and the DNA is selected to remain active in the future according to the quality of the environment which man has produced, in a never-ending cycle. He compared the process with a guided missile, the guidance system consisting of the interaction of internal and external controls. Jonas E. Salk, inventor of the Salk Vaccine, noted that the DNA molecule is getting longer and longer. He pointed out that man was implicit in the earliest DNA, but that to anticipate man at that time would have been impossible. Waddington presented the view that we should organize the process for shaping the future rather than deciding what the future ought to be.

The diagram on the opposite page and those on the following two pages present a model for such a process related to city building. The DNA function, so clearly present in the processes of nature, offers a useful parallel in considering the planning function in human institutions. Rather than imposing a rigid plan for the future, or, indeed, a series of rigid alternatives to choose from, it may be seen as a continuing process of hypothesis formation and reformation in response to feedback. On this basis it is seen as a continually changing system of order which is capable of influencing a multiplicity of individual actions to interrelate to such a degree that some sort of coherent organism is produced. In this sense it contains the code City in the same sense that, biologically, DNA contains the code Man and, in the same sense, it must reconstruct itself as it receives the impact of the ever-changing environment.

After extended communications some portion of the physical proposals that are contained in the initial hypothesis will be accepted and, through constructive technology, will be realized on the ground, and so become part of the living processes of people. By the very fact of their existence they will have a direct impact on some portion, large or small, of the lives of a varying number of people.

The tragedy of urban design today is that this effect on the quality of life of people of what is actually built is not given the emphasis it deserves, yet it is here that the vital element of feedback is generated.

If the designer cuts himself off from the impact of feedback, or if he imposes a filter under which he exposes himself only to that portion of feedback he wants to receive, the entire cyclical process is maimed or halted.

Just how the reality of the impact of concepts, ideas, institutions, processes, proposals, and built environment on people's lives can best be communicated to the persons and institutions responsible for formulating new proposals for city building is very much undetermined. The social sciences and particularly the behavioral sciences should be engaged. Unfortunately these sciences have, in the past, visualized their role as that of observers of social phenomena, and therefore of studying the social acts of the past. To be effective in terms of city building, the social sciences will have to recast their thinking to recognize the general speeding up of the pace of development, the phenomenon of simultaneity, and develop methods of measurement of social change in terms of people's states of mind, of the fundamentals of the quality of life, through social indicators which are sufficiently sensitive to respond to change quickly. These should be designed to provide the administrator with a continuous flow of insights so he may reformulate the hypothesis in the light of the reality of the impact of the program on people's lives. This may well be the major thrust of the innovative effort of the social sciences over the next several decades.

On the following two pages I have attempted to indicate diagrammatically the actual process of hypothesis formation and reformation within this system.

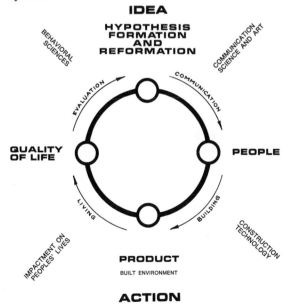

HYPOTHESIS FORMATION AND
REFORMATION

1. An hypothesis consists of some model for a system of order, for an interrelationship between several separate elements so as to create a new entity. If it is structured clearly and is communicated to the people involved, they will view its several parts, and, in accord with the binary system of the computer, accept some elements and reject others. The column on the immediate right presents four hypotheses developed in sequence. The column on the far right shows those parts of these hypotheses which are rejected by the community; the center column indicates the parts which are acceptable to the community.

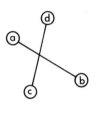

2. The result of the first go-round of the feedback cycle is the destruction of hypothesis number 1 by the community. The product which survived community review is not a system of order but rather several disconnected elements and relationships (top center column). It is (or should be) now the function of the planner to use these elements as the basis upon which to structure a new hypothesis. Additional elements and new connections must be added to reformulate a whole.

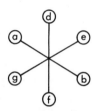

3. Hypothesis number 2 is acted upon by the community (which may be a neighborhood group, the members of a school board, the citizens of an entire city, or, indeed, the United States Congress), which rejects most of the new elements and relationships (middle diagram, per right column) but which accepts elements "e," and thereby establishes the new direction of thrust which becomes the crucial force in the further hypothesis formation. This, as seen on the right, grows more complex.

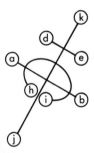

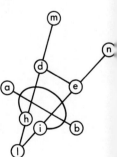

4. The community rejects the central line of authority in hypothesis number 3 but otherwise finds it acceptable. The hypothesis reformulator restructures it into the form shown to the right. Three new elements are added, the central line of authority is replaced by an open vector or direction of thrust, and this hypothesis is found acceptable by the community and so is built. Thus it becomes the subject of evaluation to determine whether, in life use, it actually fulfils its objective.

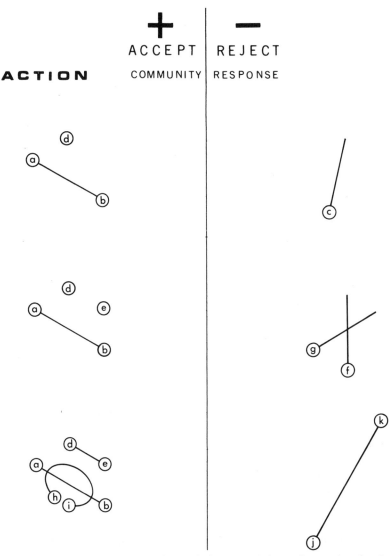

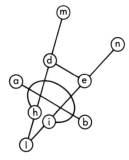

Note that several hypotheses in the left-hand column form no coherent sequence, nor do the elements of community rejection above. The portions of the disparate hypotheses acceptable to the community (center column) made a pattern of coherent growth. The form of the final system is implicit in each step of community acceptance, almost as though the community previewed the final product.

SYNTHESIS

The most noteworthy aspect of the process portrayed on the previous two pages is that the final hypothesis is the creation of neither the community nor the designer, but is the product of the interaction of each.

For such interaction to be productive, two conditions must be present:

1. An understanding on the part of both the designer and the community of the nature of the process and how it works.

2. A willingness on the part of each to plunge into it fully, to give of themselves, to submit to the discipline it entails, and to bring to it, fully, the creative input it demands.

Continued exposure to participation in this process will have a profound effect both on the individuals and on the institutions which surround them.

For the purposes of architecture it will require a rethinking of the fundamental relationship between the professional and the client, as well as who the client really is. Traditional habits of architectural arrogance will have to give way to an honest commitment to the principle that the client has a role. Traditional commitment to the interests of the individual client will have to give way to a more inclusive definition of client, under which concern for the immediate employer is extended to take into account the people and the community which surround him. For this to be fully incorporated into the rules, procedures, philosophy, and practice of architecture, landscape architecture, and urban and regional planning, a basic reshaping of the professions and their educational institutions is required.

For the individual designer, architect, or planner, nothing less than a revolution of this own self-image is necessary. However, if he proves to be capable of embarking on the process, if he is able and willing to expose himself fully to feedback, including the pain this implies, and in a valid sense, employ the feedback in hypothesis reformation, he will find that he himself is greatly changed by the interaction; that he is tempered by the heat of the confrontation, and that, after some time, he will not be able to tell in hypothesis formation how much is the product of his own internal drives and how much comes from his immersion in community values.

For the community this process means a new articulation of leadership and a new development of procedures, of delegated responsibility for negotiation, of quick review and decision making. It involves acceptance of the value of professional input (not necessarily from outside the community), and it involves abandonment of the simplistic notions that have grown up around the words "advocacy planning" under which it is assumed that those persons who, at any one time, purport to represent the community, actually do, and that they, of themselves, can do the whole job with no outside help.

For the individual in the community the fully effective operation of this feedback cycle involves some degree of self-restraint and self-discipline because it implies listening on both sides. However, when the individual in the community finds by doing that the process is really working, his view of himself and the society in which he is functioning will so radically alter that the changes will come about quite naturally.

Finally, it is important to stress again that hypothesis formation and reformation may occur anywhere, within the profession, within government, within the community, but without it the process will be meaningless.

REFERENCES

EATON, LEONARD K.
  1969   *Two Chicago architects and their clients: Frank Lloyd Wright and Howard Van Doren Shaw.* Cambridge: M.I.T. Press.
GIDEON, SIGFRIED
  1941   *Space, time and architecture.* Cambridge: Harvard University Press.
KEPES, GYORGY
  1965   *Education of vision.* New York: George Braziller.
KLEE, PAUL
  1961   *The thinking eye, the notebooks of Paul Klee.* Edited by Jürg Spiller. New York: George Wittenborn.
WÖLFFLIN, HEINRICH
  1915   *Principles of art history.* Translated by M. D. Hottlinger.

Education for the Future

"The Anthropology of the Future" as an Academic Discipline

ROGER W. WESCOTT

The phrase "anthropology of the future" here refers primarily to the study of the future by anthropologists rather than to anthropology in its anticipated future form. As time passes, however, these two kinds of anthropology may be expected increasingly to merge, so that distinctions between them become otiose. The phrase "academic discipline" exhibits a similar short-range ambiguity. It can refer either to research on the future, of the kind currently pursued most actively by such think tanks as the Hudson Institute and the Rand Corporation, or to offering courses on the future, as is now done by a number of American colleges and universities. Here again my leaning is toward a both-and rather than an either-or interpretation. For, while my primary responsibility is in the classroom, I am also engaged in research on the future on behalf of a New England foundation. And in the long term, both the classroom and the research institute as we know them may be transformed beyond recognition — or even merged in some new kind of center for the generation and dissemination of knowledge. Strictly speaking, moreover, "the anthropology of the future" should rather be characterized as a subdiscipline, since it represents only a portion of either the established discipline of anthropology or the emerging discipline of future study. Alternatively, it might be styled an "interdiscipline," since it is a hybrid of the two disciplines just named.

Because of its preoccupation with time, futuristics may be expected, as James Gifford observes (1970), to show from the outset a special concern for its own history. In this connection, it seems worth noting that the earliest explicitly futuristic research dates from 1923, when J. B. Haldane wrote *Daedalus, or the future of science* for the Kegan Paul book series *Today and Tomorrow*. As in the case of most other disciplines, exploratory investigation preceded curricular crystalization by several decades. So it will come as scant surprise that there were apparently no courses in futuristics until Alvin Toffler offered "The Sociology of the Future" at The New School for Social Research in 1966. Equally predictable, moreover, is the fact that futuristics tends to focus on modes or techniques of prediction. Albert and Donna Wilson (1970) recognize three major types of futuristic prediction: determinative, normative, and random. These types of prediction, if I understand them correctly, correspond roughly to the three types of diachronic projection which, in the syllabus of the Drew course on "Man's Future," I call forecasting, prophecy, and precognition respectively. Forecasting is extrapolation of currently observable trends; prophecy is helping to produce a preferred future by advocating it; and precognition is apprehension of the future by perceptual or conceptual means that are not yet elucidated.

Of recognized techniques for anticipating the future, two stand out as especially suitable to group situations such as that of the college classroom. The first is the anonymously generated tactic known as "brain-storming," whereby all participants give free rein to their imaginations and build on one another's imaginings as far as ingenuity can take them. The only restriction on the initial phase of their interaction is that all skeptical critiques must be held in abeyance until imagination has played itself out, whereupon the process of winnowing begins, and the hopefully copious grain is separated from the still more abundant chaff.

The second is Olaf Helmer's "Delphi technique" (1966), which is more restrictive and hence, inevitably, more expensive in terms of both time and effort. It is restrictive in two senses: first, it involves only such participants as are regarded as experts on the subject concerned; and second, it requires each participant to make several predictions rather than only one. The reason for the repeated predictions is that after each round of predictions, every participant is confronted with the collective prediction (formulated by averaging) of the group as a whole and asked to modify his prediction in accordance, not only with the substance of the group prediction, but also with the rationale accompanying it and the appended data on which the rationale was based. To avoid both ego-protecting stubbornness and its converse, the bandwagon effect, all predictions are made anonymously. Thus, no individual need be embarrassed by his deviation from the group norm, and none can browbeat his fellows by his prestige or force of personality alone.

In contrast to such head-on intellectual attacks on the world to come stands the indirect approach to the future favored by Elise Boulding ("Futuristics and the imaging capacity of the West," this volume). For her, the longest way round may be the shortest way home: that is, we are more likely to understand the nonpresent that lies before us in terms of the nonpresent that lies behind us than in terms of the present alone. Implicitly at least, she seems to be rephrasing Santayana's dictum "those ignorant of the past are doomed to repeat it" (1906) so as to read "those who understand the past are free to innovate." From this standpoint (which, as a former historian, I find persuasive), the most satisfactory term for the study of the future is probably Roderick Seidenberg's neologism "posthistory" (1950).

A second type of indirect approach to the future is that recommended, pursuant to earlier suggestions from Edmund Carpenter and Marshall McLuhan (1960), by the Wilsons (1970). They propose that futurists scan the arts — aural and plastic as well as graphic — for clues to those subliminal changes in outlook and attitude that generally precede overt changes in doctrine and behavior. In short, they view the arts as barometers of the future. In this connection, one is inevitably reminded of the pronouncements of two aestheticians from pre-Fascist Italy: sculptor Umberto Boccioni, who declared that "we are primitives of an unknown culture" (1910), and pamphleteer F. T. Marinetti, who wrote the first "Futurist Manifesto" (1909) asserting that only a Dionysian fusion of art and technology could save both from sterility.

However, even if futurists prove to be no more adept than others at predicting the shape of things to come, futuristics, it seems to me, has a major contribution to make both to formal education and to the general intellectual climate of our times. For futuristics is inherently mind-stretching: it prods us to consider possibilities which "the cake of custom" predisposes us to ignore. It can even be called therapeutic, in that it helps us avoid that peculiarly contemporary and increasingly endemic form of cultural trauma which Alvin Toffler has christened "future shock" (1970). And one of the most effective of those remedial means by which "the patient may minister to himself" is that of writing what Herman Kahn calls "alternative scenarios" of the future (1967). In this way the individual can prepare himself psychologically for such a broad spectrum of possible futures that the actual future, when it comes, is unlikely to prove traumatic to him. Needless to say, this principle has collective as well as individual applications. Just as many universities now have poets or artists in residence as regular members of their academic staffs, so in future they might have dreamers in residence, whose main job would be to expect the unexpected and articulate their anticipations in a manner readily interpretable by colleagues and students.

The term "dreamer," in this case, can be construed almost as literally as the reader may choose. For the most recent research from sleep laboratories indicates, first, that all viviparous mammals dream; second, that man dreams more than any other mammal; third, that the young dream more than the elderly; and fourth, that those deprived of dreams (by tranquilization or deliberate interruption of the rapid eye-movement phase of sleep) exhibit behavioral disturbances. What all of this suggests is that dreams are preadaptive mechanisms that help animals to cope with the unexpected. In this sense, ancient and preliterate peoples were quite justified in regarding dreams and other hypnoid visions as prophetic, as were artists and psychoanalysts in regarding them as creative. For dreams not only anticipate but also generate the future. If, then, it is true that mammals are, psychologically speaking, the only futuristic taxon on our planet, it follows that man is the most futuristic of earth's species. And professional futurists show themselves, by the nature of their concerns, to be at once the most mammalian of mammals and the most human of men.

Just, however, as men's dreams are far from being all pleasant, the task of the futurist is far from being an invariable joy. Futuristics has its built-in frustrations, not the least of which being, as Gifford points out (1970), that the futurist can never fully practice what he preaches. His lot is worse than that of the sinologist who is forbidden to visit China — for, if he is willing to face the risks, the sinologist can at least pay a sneak visit to the area of his interest. But, until and unless a workable time machine is actually invented, the futurist remains in the position of an area specialist who can never under any circumstances enjoy firsthand experience of his subject matter. On the other hand, it would be unfair to create the impression that futuristics is merely a sophisticated form of academic self-punishment. It is, on the contrary, an exciting new field of investigation which offers to its practitioners an almost unparalleled degree of disciplined intellectual freedom. For not only is futuristics, like any healthy science, a self-correcting discipline; it is also, as Gifford observes, a self-transforming discipline and even, in Dennis Gabor's words, a "self-inventing" discipline (1964).

Like most other new disciplines, moreover, futuristics clearly has a future, which contemporary futurists are still enviably free to choose. From an academic point of view, the most immediate and pressing problem is that of the institutional structure within which futuristics can best realize its own potential while making a maximal contribution to adjacent disciplines — especially, though not exclusively, the social and biological sciences. And here opinion is divided. While all participants in the American Anthropological Association's Symposium on Cultural Futuristics agreed that both courses and research projects on the future are desirable, they parted company on the question of departmentalization — Gifford advocating departments of futuristics (1970) and Robert McKnight opposing them (this volume). With regard to departments as such, I am inclined to follow McKnight. Like many generalists, I have too often found departmental boundaries acting as barriers both to discovery and to the dissemination of knowledge, and I have no wish to see such barriers erected either within or around futuristics. For departments too readily become miniature bureaucratic empires composed of individuals whose primary interest lies in outdistancing potential rivals within the empire and excluding potential rivals from outside it.

In the case of futuristics, such a development, I feel, would be doubly unfortunate. The first reason why I would be reluctant to see futuristics departmentalized is that, for the past decade at least, futurists have comprised a kind of intellectual freemasonry or "invisible college," whose members are exceptionally open to new ideas and almost wholly uncompetitive in their relations with one another. Since 1969, for example, when I joined the World Future Society, I have had more contact with futurists by mail and telephone than I have had with my fellow specialists in ethnolinguistics since 1956, when I joined the American Anthropological Association and the Linguistic Society of America. The second reason — which is ultimately, no doubt, the more compelling of the two — is that futuristics, being intrinsically interdisciplinary in nature, would probably suffer more from the kind of social and intellectual isolation fostered by departmentalism than do more monolithic fields of study. And either constriction of scope or failure of imagination among futurists would be a misfortune not only for them but also for those policy makers who consult them and all members of the public whose lives are dependent, for better or worse, on the decisions of others.

In place of college departments of futuristics, I recommend university programs involving most, if not all, existing departments. Such programs, if well administered, would give even more to subscribing departments in the form of fresh methods and concepts than they would draw from them in the form of individual talents and specialized techniques.

Thus far, however, we have adduced no reasons for a special relationship between anthropology and futuristics. What do they have in common? And what can they offer each other? First, as Steven Polgar notes (1970), both anthropology and futuristics are generalized rather than specialized disciplines. Both freely cross divisional lines between the humanities, the social sciences, and the natural sciences. Second, as Margaret Mead observes (this volume), both anthropology and futuristics have long-range perspectives. Unlike sociology, which confines itself to recent decades, or even history, which confines itself to recent millennia, anthropology and futuristics range freely over the span of both human and prehuman evolution and so provide a uniquely panoramic view of the progress of earthly intelligence. And third, as Gifford reiterates, one of the four major anthropological subdisciplines — prehistory — may be regarded as a mirror image of futuristics (a fact recognized, as we have seen, even by non-anthropologists, as witness the use of the term "posthistory" as a synonym for futuristics). The major factor, of course, linking prehistory with futuristics is the fact that both are compelled to make their diachronic generalizations in the absence of written documents and hence to fill in the long gaps in their knowledge by perilous extrapolation from a few points of relative certitude.

Another link between prehistory and futuristics is the fact that a number of prehistoric conditions seem now to be in process of reinstating themselves. Three such conditions are the absence of war, the absence of urbanism, and the absence of literacy. While none of these three institutions has yet disappeared and some are still spreading locally, signs appear to be unmistakable that war is approaching the stage of self-cancellation, that the world's largest cities are decaying at the center, and that telephony and sound recording increasingly compete with mail and print as means of long-distance communication. Such considerations, presumably, are the reason for the growing currency of terms such as Daniel Bell's "post-industrialism" (1973), Kenneth Boulding's "post-civilization" (1964) and Paul Tillich's "post-Christianity" (1966) to describe the new culture that may be emerging around us. What all of them have in common is a recognition of the fact that the city-centered order of the past five millennia seems to be giving way to a more diffuse social structure. (The term that I prefer for it is "globalization," since this draws attention primarily to the positive aspect of the process — namely, planetary unification — rather than to the negative aspect — that is, the decline of traditional civility.)

Yet another link between prehistory and futuristics is that the predictive techniques commonly associated only with the latter may in fact be employed in the former as well. When this occurs, the conjecture — at least insofar as it can be checked by subsequently discovered evidence — is sometimes referred to as "retrospective prediction." A good example is provided by the field of comparative philology. During the 1880's, German linguists like Kretschmer and Meyer "predicted" that, if inscriptions in Mycenean Greek were ever discovered, they would exhibit certain specific phonological characteristics of a type intermediate between proto-Indo-European and Homeric Greek. Such inscriptions, in syllabic script, were in fact discovered by Sir Arthur Evans in the 1900's and deciphered by Chadwick and Ventris in the 1950's. And they confirmed the linguistic predictions made of them even more fully than linguists would have dared to expect.

Ethnography, too, as McKnight points out (this volume), has more links with futuristics than most anthropologists seem inclined to con-

cede. For, despite their habitual warnings to laymen to avoid sterotyp-
ing preliterates as backward savages, anthropologists themselves, in
most cases, tend to view preliterates as being, in Riesman's terms,
wholly "tradition-directed" (1953) — that is, addicted to stability and
oriented exclusively toward the past. In fact, however, most simpler
societies devote at least as much time to the discovery of the future,
through consultation of oracles and diviners, as to the amplification of
the past, through storytelling and ancestral cults. And a few, such as
the Austronesians, may, in such otherwise bizarre activities as the
Kula-ring trade, actually be placing innovation ahead of either profit
making or the cementing of social ties as a collective goal.

Undoubtedly, then, anthropology, while hardly the queen of the
futuristic disciplines, does have much to offer to futuristics. Does
futuristics offer a comparable contribution to anthropology? I think it
does. What futuristics can contribute to anthropologists is a liberation
of the anthropological imagination. To anthropologists, who like to
think of themselves as free-ranging souls with a richly diverse and
exotic subject matter, this suggestion may come as an unwelcome
surprise. But I believe it is true that, partly as a result of a tacit division
of the time scale with sociologists (whereby sociologists received contemporary society as their domain), most anthropologists live in the
past. Even in those cases where anthropologists are investigating living
peoples and cultures, they tend to select those that have been least
Westernized — which generally means peoples who are themselves
living in the past. Whatever the reason, however, for the fossilization
of anthropological categories, futuristics bids fair to reverse the trend
and restore some degree of temporal balance between our attention to
the past and our concern for the future.

Yet, once it is agreed that a fruitful relation can and should exist
between anthropology and futuristics, it remains a question of how to
implement that relation in practical terms. For a teacher, of course, the
logical procedure is to work toward "futurizing" his curriculum. But
again, how? The least disturbing way to do this is probably to inject a
gradually increasing futuristic content into each anthropology course
offered, until, after a decade or so, the futuristic component of each
approaches fifty percent. Such a tactic, however, besides being slow, is
devious. And what is most needed, as far as the promotion of futuristic
anthropology is concerned, is a dramatization of the persistent failure
of most anthropologists to "face the future" in any systematic way. To
this end, introduction of a new course on the anthropology of the
future is likely to be most effective.

It is also likely, on the other hand, to provoke collegial opposition,
both within the department and without. Many anthropologists are
inclined to feel that the pre-Western world has more than enough

material to last for the lifetime of their discipline. And some practitioners of other social sciences are reluctant to see anthropology
introduce futuristics, when there are sister disciplines that have less
investment in the past and more experience in forecasting than anthropology has. (While it may seem surprising that little opposition
comes from natural scientists, the ironic reason for this intellectual
tolerance is apparently the unflattering one that, since they already
view most of the findings of the behavioral studies as "social science
fiction," they see little threat in a new social science which promises
what they perceive as merely more of the same.)

Here at Drew University, Anthropology 140, "Man's Future," had a
distinctly harder time than most new anthropology courses in winning
acceptance. In fact, in its initial form, it was rejected. Only after it had
been cross-listed and renamed Anthropology/Sociology 140, "Man's
Future Social and Cultural Development," was it finally accepted,
largely because it now partook of sociology's longer experience and
greater prestige in the field of futuristics. It was, moreover, accepted
only as an alternate year course and on condition that it be reviewed
by the college faculty before being reapproved for a second offering. In
short, the course has a uniquely probationary status — which, however,
may well be the status most appropriate to a course whose subject
matter is the precarious social order of a newly emerged species like
our own.

During the summer of 1970, the period between the official approval
of the course and its first test run, my own feeling about it was what
might be expected of any teacher contemplating a radically new
assignment: one of ambivalence. Being intellectually naked is at once a
liberating and an anxiety provoking experience. And if anything, the
divided feelings involved are stronger in anticipation than in realization. The academic experimenter is keenly aware of the raised eye-
brows of his colleagues and wonders whether student response will be
sufficiently positive to offset them. Even if he is sanguine enough to
assume popularity for this course, he still ponders the wisdom of
making any curricular presentation at a teaching institution that is not
conveniently close to a futuristically oriented research institute of the
sort recommended by Thornton Page (1970). Once fall arrived, however, and I found myself with a student enrollment more than four
times as large as that in most upper-level anthropology courses, my
concerns, I discovered, were of a different sort. The first was how to
sustain the sense of intellectual excitement with which most students
evidently had entered the course; and the second was how to adapt to
a lecture situation a course plan originally designed for a seminar
situation.

My response to the first challenge was to present the course as a kind of training ground for the future — more specifically, as a school for time travelers. Such a phrase, far from being an overdramatization of the facts, is, I think, merely a graphic recognition of the immensity of the cultural migration in which all of us are perforce engaged — from civilization to globalization. In this time travelers' school, we will also train explorers, not only of physical space (the outer space discussed by Page, the intermediate space of the oceans, and the inner space of earth's mantle), but also of biological space (the outer space of the biosphere, the intermediate space of animal societies, and the inner space of the endosomatic organs). Cultural space stands in equal need of exploration. And to make sure that it is well explored, we should, as Richard Jones suggests (1970), encourage both ethnogenesis, or the deliberate creation of new subcultures, and the description of these subcultures by ethnographers born and raised within them, as Sue-Ellen Jacobs suggests (this volume). Finally, psychic space itself must be explored, not only by all conventional means, but also biochemically, electromagnetically, and otherwise. The sense of adventure conveyed by these suggestions proved to be contagious; and while few students were actively engaged in every type of intellectual exploration, most responded positively to exploratory proposals. The second problem — overpopulation of the classroom — meant that we could not follow the procedure taken for granted in most advanced courses: having every student present at least one written or oral report to the entire group for discussion. Instead, about half of those enrolled agreed reluctantly to have their semester grades (required by college regulations) based on a final examination.

Most other procedural matters were handled without difficulty. None of us wanted classroom quizzes or midterm examinations. Group reports were considered but rejected because of grading difficulties. Guest lecturers, on the other hand, proved popular both in prospect and in practice. By the end of the term, we had heard an economist speaking on the cost of depollution, an administrator on educational planning, a botanist on resource management, a theologian on model communities, and a chaplain on the future of Christianity. Not only did these visits offer a refreshing variety of viewpoints, but their short-term focus on the decade of the 1970's provided a healthy counterweight to my own long-term emphasis on the twenty-first century.

At the outset of the course, I posed ten "entrance" questions to which all of us were to seek at least tentative answers before our collective exit. These were:

1. How predictable is the future?
2. Are there experts on the future?
3. Who is best prepared for the future?

4. Are we victims of our own technology?
5. Is space exploration escapist?
6. Is science fast becoming indistinguishable from science fiction?
7. Is civilization (as traditional literate urbanism) coming to an end?
8. Is utopianism useful?
9. Are experiments in human relations ethical?
10. Is futuristics diverting anthropologists from more appropriate pursuits?

To these questions, our eventual answers — heavily weighted no doubt in the direction of the instructor's views — were:

1. Perhaps a third of major future developments can be predicted by extrapolation, but a good two-thirds must be predicted by other means or else left unpredicted.

2. While there are no experts on the future, there are students of the future, and their skills may be expected to increase with experience and dedication.

3. Those best prepared for the future are those who are most open to innovation without being compulsive seekers after novelty.

4. We are victims of our own technology only to the degree that we victimize ourselves and each other in all areas of our lives.

5. Space exploration is no more escapist than, to use Robert Frost's word, it is "pursuitist." In either case, it is innovative; and, as such, it may be expected to give us, if nothing else, fresh perspectives on terrestrial problems.

6. Insofar as facts are not objects but generalizations about objects, all facts are fictitious — that is, creations by generalizers. Insofar, on the other hand, as facts are low-level generalizations while fictions are high-level generalizations, the "lead time" for conversion of fiction into fact is growing steadily shorter as our ability to generalize increases. In this sense, the two are now converging; and this convergence of fact and fiction will eventually become tantamount to merger.

7. Many signs suggest that we are currently experiencing a shift of cultural phase comparable to the agricultural and urban revolutions described by Gordon Childe (1970). The question of whether this "change of life" is menarchic or menopausal in nature is probably more emotive than substantive — though one may hope that it will prove at once intellectually menarchic and demographically menopausal. And other metaphors, such as the religious image of tranfiguration, the entomological concept of metamorphosis, or Earl Hubbard's birth model, may turn out to be more appropriate comparisons. In any case, the most crucial fact about our impending transformation is that it will almost certainly be, for most purposes, irrevers-

ible. Though we may change for the worse, rather than for the better, we cannot escape change.

8. If utopianism is the quest for a better society, a query about the utility of utopianism becomes a query about the utility of the good. In their broadest senses, the two, if not identical, are meaningless. In their narrower senses, to be sure, utility and goodness are discrete. But even here it seems appropriate to respond to the initial (and highly prejudicial) question with an equally rhetorical question. This is the response provided by Benjamin Franklin (1970) when a skeptic asked him, "Of what use is electricity?" Answering question with question, he replied, "Of what use is a baby?" In more declarative terms, however, we might say that utopia is best defined not as a situation in which good is guaranteed but rather as one in which it is maximally free to develop. In this sense, utopianism is indeed useful because it potentiates invention — not just technological invention but, as Dennis Gabor writes, every sort of invention, up to and including self-invention (1964).

9. In terms of the traditional Judeo-Christian dichotomy between man (who is moral) and nature (which is not), it is moral for men to experiment with other species but immoral for them to experiment with one another. Yet, as John Platt points out (1970), it is precisely such a discriminatory attitude that has, by degrading the biosphere as a whole, paradoxically threatened the survival of our own species. To redress the balance, however, we cannot turn back the cultural clock and abandon all experiment. What we must rather do is learn to experiment responsibly and compassionately rather than recklessly and unfeeling — and learn to be as sensitively experimental toward ourselves and our institutions as toward alien species and their habitats.

10. Futuristics has not as yet diverted many anthropologists from their habitual pursuits. But within a decade it will undoubtedly begin to do so; and at this point choices between alternative priorities will become necessary. To be sure, not all such choices need be invidious ones. For, as Margaret Mead reminds us (this volume), openness toward the computer as a research tool should enable each of us to explore many more lines of promising investigation than we now do, and so adopt a both-and in preference to an either-or approach to our varied interests. No amount of analytical automation, however, can eliminate all need for anthropological priorities. And my own preference, once we have agreed to put futuristics at or near the top of our priority list, is that we should put doctrinal and methodological polemics at the bottom; so that, when and if elimination becomes unavoidable, such crucial concerns as salvage anthropology (the preservation of vanishing societies or, failing that, of an exhaustive record of their cultures) may retain a solid footing on our ladder of concern.

Of the forty-seven students enrolled in Drew University's course on man's future, fourteen gave oral reports, eleven gave written reports, and twenty-two took the final written essay examination. Some representative report titles were: "Progress in Organ Transplantation," "The Communitarian Movement," and "Emerging Architectural Forms." The average grade of reports was B+ — substantially higher than the B— average that is usual in advanced courses and, of course, far higher than the C+ average of intermediate courses and the C average of introductory courses. While it is always possible that my zeal for futuristics blunted my critical faculties while evaluating these reports, I think rather that the chief reason for their exceptionally high grades was the exceptionally high motivation of the student expositors.

Of the twenty or so books placed on library reserve or designated as optional reading, only four were read by 20 percent or more of those enrolled in the course. These were, in order of readership demand: (1) *The second genesis* by Albert Rosenfeld; (2) *Toward the year 2000* by Daniel Bell; (3) *Profiles of the future* by Arthur Clarke; (4) *Man modified* by David Fishlock. What most surprised me about the results of this bibliographic "popularity poll" was that, although only one member of the class was a biological sciences major, a majority of the class showed more interest in the biological future than in the cultural future; and, although only one member of the class was a physical sciences major, a majority of the class found astronomical frontiers second in challenge only to social frontiers.

Most of the topics listed in the course syllabus were at least minimally covered either in class reports, visiting lectures, "lecturettes" by the instructor, or general classroom discussion. Four major topics, however, that were almost wholly neglected were: (1) group predictions; (2) futurist organizations; (3) the future of education; (4) science fiction. The reasons why it was possible to slight these important subjects are easy to give. First, because of heavy enrollment, classroom time was at such a premium that it was inevitable that many minor and even some major topics would go untreated. The only thing that was not clear was which topics would be singled out, so to speak, for inattention. But this question too was easily answered in terms of the pedagogic policy of nondirectiveness which I adopted and followed (though with decreasing enthusiasm) throughout the semester. Predictions, organizations, education, and fiction were deemphasized by the students themselves simply because they did not respond to them as positively as they did, for example, to topics such as pollution, urbanism, genetic engineering, and psychological reconditioning. Yet the underlying question remains why — if only by default — the students chose the topics that they did. My guess is that futurist organizations were passed over because of antibureaucratic sentiment; that group predictions were avoided because they are too demanding; that the future of education was overlooked because students felt too close to it to view it in perspective; and that science fiction was dismissed as trivial.

Shortly before the national anthropology convention in November, I received a telephone inquiry from economist-futurist Robert Theobald (who had perused my preliminary course materials) about the progress of the course. What he most wanted information on was student response to the syllabus topics and the reading material. I told him quite candidly that I was disappointed in overall student performance — not, of course, in comparison with that in other courses (for it was superior, at least gradewise) but rather in comparison with what I had expected of it before the course began. For during the late 1960's, I had been impressed by Margaret Mead's characterization of cold war youth as natives of the space age and of their elders, including most futurists, as immigrants into that age, whose only hope of genuine naturalization lay in internalizing the culture that was emerging around them (1970). In planning the course, therefore, I had worried primarily about my own susceptibility to the role of an uncomprehending alien in the nascent future and had leaned over backward to avoid those paternalistic attitudes which, however appropriate they might have been in more traditional courses, seemed likely to prove stifling in this one. To my surprise, however, most of the young "natives" in my course proved to be cautious, pedestrian, and patently vulnerable to future shock. So it was with some feeling of relief that I learned from Theobald that he and most other futuristics teachers whom he knew had had precisely the same experience.

In part, no doubt, this shyness of the future on the part of students must be put down to the type of long-term conditioning to academic conformity that they have undergone in school and college. And if so, our readiness, as teachers, to make sport of the intellectual timidity of our charges is on a par with the unconscious hypocrisy of those sophisticated but conventional parents who laugh at the naive prudery of their own children. If we fail to encourage imagination and initiative in most of our teaching, we can hardly expect students to exhibit these qualities on those rare occasions when we suddenly, and from the student point of view inexplicably, reward them. Nevertheless, there is, I think, at least one genuinely endogenous factor in the youth culture itself, which has the ironic effect of reinforcing the results of the academic lockstep. This factor is the intense teen-age focus on the knife-edged present, leading equally to rejection of the past (as moribund) and of the future (as threatening). To "the now generation," all planning seems futile, whether it is individual or collective. Their tendency is to drift as passively as possible through the System —

familial, educational, and military — and then "see what happens" when they come of age. Needless to say, such an attitude infects gifted students quite as much as mediocre ones and goes far to dim whatever vision they might have had of emergent opportunities.

On the last day of class, a poll was taken to ascertain student opinion on whether the course should be given again and, if so, how often. No one voted to drop the course or even, as the anthropology and sociology departments proposed, to have it offered once every two years. Instead, the votes were divided between a majority who wanted the course offered once each year and a minority who wanted it offered every semester. (At present, the only anthropology course offered every semester is Anthropology 1, "Introductory Anthropology.")

With the first semester's teaching over, it seemed time to make plans for the next offering of the course. As far as overall policy was concerned, I expected to shift to a more directive approach to the question of which topics should be covered in class and by what means they should be presented. During the final week of class, the students themselves had suggested that there should be fewer student reports presented and that those accepted should be more tightly tied, as regards subject matter, to the weekly topics listed in the syllabus. I have interpreted this and other expressions of student opinion as a mandate for me to assume more control over the direction of classroom discussion than I did at first. Next time I would be inclined to duplicate and distribute a list of prospective report topics, and while permitting considerable deviation from it in both wording and coverage, not allow this deviation to be capricious in motivation or indefinite in extent.

As far as extramural applications of the course and its contents are concerned, I feel strongly that, if anthropologists are to make as substantial a contribution to the growth of futuristics as their colleagues in literature, economics, and biology have already done, they must begin to write their own versions of what Kahn calls "scenarios" of the future rather than confining themselves to critical commentaries on nonanthropological scenarists. I also believe that, just as anthropologists like Paul Bohannan are now succeeding, after strenuous effort, in having anthropology courses introduced into secondary school curricula, futurists must make a comparable effort to inject futuristic elements into precollege teaching materials — as they have already done, in some cases, with graduate school programs.

Finally, and most important, I believe that we must heed Richard Jones' cautionary reminder that many short-term, and even some long-term, plans for our collective future are actually being made right now by corporate, government, and military authorities, without public knowledge or consent (1970). As long as such planning is kept secret, the futuristic labors of members of teaching and research institutions will remain academic in the most pejorative sense of that word. In recognizing this fact, I am not adopting the cynical view that all public policy is, in effect, the product of deliberate conspiracy. I believe rather that policy makers are busy men who feel — not, perhaps, without reason — that laymen are too short-sighted and scholars too preoccupied to care about the shaping of national and global destinies and who, consequently, try to make their weighty decisions as quickly, quietly, and pragmatically as possible. Yet even if we make the optimistic assumption that our leaders are, for the most part, men of good will, we are still unjustified in making the further assumption that good will is enough. The world is too complex and its evolutionary movement too opaque to be left to even the most skillful improvisation.

What, then, should futurists do? Whatever their disciplinary background, they should, I believe, do everything in their power not only to inform the general public of the existence and utility of futuristics but also make direct and effective contact with policy makers. For, when unwise policies are implemented, they are more often implemented in ignorance than in defiance of available information. Without what Buckminster Fuller calls an "operating manual" (1969), Spaceship Earth can hardly avoid ever more severe mishandling. But a usable manual cannot be written on the basis of pure speculation; it requires constant operating feedback. Such feedback can be obtained only from interaction between theory and practice, or to put it more concretely, from interaction between futurists and decision makers. And while futurists, true to their academic leanings, might prefer that administrators make pilgrimages to academia for enlightenment, they cannot expect such pilgrimages and should not wait for them. If, as they believe, futurists appreciate the opportunities and dangers of our turbulently transitional age better than anyone else, then it is their responsibility to reach those foci of power at which the opportunities can best be seized and the dangers most effectively avoided. By this I mean to suggest, not that futurists should stage *coups d'état*, but rather that they must discover vastly more effective channels of public communication than have as yet been devised. For, to repeat the warning of H. G. Wells, the race in which we are ever more crucially involved is that between education and catastrophe (1938).

APPENDIX 1: TERMS USED BY VARIOUS AUTHORS TO DESIGNATE THE STUDY OF FUTURE

Because it is a newly fledged discipline, the study of the future has not yet acquired a name that is accepted by all or even most of its practitioners.

Table I.   Alternative names for "The study of the future"

Type	Term	Proponent (when known)	Meaning (when not apparent))
words of Greek origin	1 alleotics 2 mellology 3 stochology	Wescott Jedrzejewski	study of change study of the future science of conjecture
words of Latin origin	4 futuribles	Jouvenel	possible futures
hybrid (Greco-Latin) words	5 futurism 6 futuristics 7 futurology 8 posthistory	 Flechtheim Seidenberg	
phrases	9 future studies 10 futures research 11 futures study 12 the science of the future	 Boucher Mead	

Despite the venerability of the tradition of giving new disciplines Greek names, none of the three Hellenic coinages for the study of the future has as yet received appreciable currency. These three are: Clement Jedrzejewski's "stochology" (the science of conjecture [1970]); the anonymously minted "mellology" (the science of the future); and my own "alleotics" (the study of change). The only purely Latin term for this field is Bertrand de Jouvenel's "futuribles" (possible futures [1967]), which though it has caught on in France and Italy, has made little headway in northern Europe or the United States.

We are left, then, with hybrid terms of Greco-Latin origin, such as the unattributable word "futurism," and phrases, such as Wayne Boucher's "futures research" (1974). Probably because phrases are clumsy, they too have gained little currency. In practice, the two leading terminological contenders are Ossip Flechtheim's "futurology" (1966) and the slightly less Hellenic word "futuristics," the term preferred (though probably not created) by James Dator (1970). My own preference is for "futuristics," partly because its Greek and Latin elements are less discordant with one another than in the case of "futurology," and partly because the term "futurology" is uncomfortably reminiscent of the still polemic anthropological term "culturology." Despite the negativity manifest in these arguments, I propose to confine myself to the term "futuristics" in all further references to the study of the future and to "futurists" in references to its practitioners.

Etymologically speaking, the term "futuristics" comes, of course, through the English word "future," from the Latin verbal adjective *futurus* [about to be] whose base is *fu*-(as in *fuit* [was]). This base, in turn, is derived from the proto-Indo-European root *bheu-* [to grow]. From this root we inherited, through Greek, the English nouns "phylum" (descent group), "physics" (the study of nature), and "phytoplankton" (marine flora). And from the same root, through Germanic, we inherited the English words "be," "big," and "bud."

If, in the tradition of Morris Swadesh (1970), I may be allowed to go beyond conventional Indo-European philology and recognize consonantal as well as vocalic apophony in the reconstructed parent language of English, Greek, and Latin, then other cognates of the word "futuristics" may be identified. From proto-Indo-European *beu-[to swell], we derive, through Latin, the English adjective "buccal" (pertaining to the mouth cavity), and through Germanic, the English words "pucker," "pudgy," and "pup." And finally, from proto-Indo-European *peu-[to procreate], we derive, through Greek, the English noun "pedagogy" (literally [child driving]); through Latin, the English words "pupil" (literally [infant]), "pupate" (to metamorphose) and "pullulate" (to blossom); and, through Germanic, the English noun "foal." The three proto-Indo-European roots *bheu-, *beu-, and *peu- then, would in turn be derived from a single pre-Indo-European root *PEu- [to germinate].

APPENDIX 2: FINAL EXAMINATION FOR ANTHRO-POLOGY/SOCIOLOGY 140, "MAN'S FUTURE SOCIAL AND CULTURAL DEVELOPMENT"

8:50–12 a.m., Wednesday, January 13   College of Liberal Arts
Mr. Wescott   Drew University

Write a one-hour essay on each of TWO of the following six questions:

1. Assess the strengths and weaknesses of your three required texts in relation to (a) one another, (b) the optional readings on library reserve, and (c) the required texts in other upper level courses you have taken.

2. Of the various new concepts and developments discussed in this course, which was most startling to you? The term that Toffler applies to being taken by surprise by the emergent culture is "future shock." Would you call such shock beneficial or harmful? Explain and justify your answer.

3. Is Utopianism useful? Is it ethical to experiment with human relations? Whatever your answers, present some emergent social problems and state how you would solve them. How utopian or experimental are your solutions?

4. How can we best prepare for a future in which the unexpected component seems to grow constantly larger? What arguments can you give for and against the training of professional futurists as a means of coping with the unexpected? Would you be willing to be such a futurist? If so, why; and if not, why not?

5. Is futuristics diverting social scientists from more appropriate pursuits? Those who say so usually maintain that, if we understand the past and cope with the present, the future will take care of itself. Evaluate this claim.

6. Write a brief autobiography of your own future. How did you arrive at its main features? Does it include your death? If so, at what age? If not, why not?

Quality is far more important than quantity in your answer. Think out or outline each essay before you write text.

When you hand in your answer booklet or booklets, you must also *sign and submit this question sheet.*

APPENDIX 3: PROBABLE BIBLIOGRAPHY FOR ANTH./ SOC. 140, "MAN'S FUTURE," DREW UNIVERSITY

Mr. Wescott

PRIMARY TEXT:

Maryjane Dunstan, *Worlds in the Making*

SUPPLEMENTARY TEXTS:
Kenneth Boulding, *The Meaning of the Twentieth Century*
Arthur Clarke, *Profiles of the Future*

CLOSED RESERVE:
Daniel Bell, *Toward the Year* 2000
Nigel Calder, *The World in* 1984
Dandridge Cole, *Beyond Tomorrow*
Olaf Helmer, *Social Technology*
Robert Jungk, *Mankind* 2000
Herman Kahn, *The Year* 2000
Edward Lindaman, *Space: A New Direction for Mankind*
Robert Prehoda, *Designing the Future*
Albert Rosenfeld, *The Second Genesis*
Alvin Toffler, *Future Shock*

OPEN SHELF:
Edward De Bono, *New Think*
David Fishlock, *Man Modified*
Theodore Gordon, *The Future*
Alan Harrington, *The Immortalist*
Thomas Kuhn, *The Structure of Scientific Revolutions*
Richard Landers, *Man's Place in the Dybosphere*
John McHale, *The Future of the Future*
Neil Ruzic, *The Case for Going to the Moon*
Henry Still, *Man: The Next* 30 *Years*
Roger Wescott, *The Divine Animal*

REFERENCES

BELL, DANIEL
    1973   *The coming of post-industrial society.* New York: Basic Books.
BOCCIONI, UMBERTO
    1910   *The technical Manifesto of the futurist painters.* Milan.
BOUCHER, WAYNE
    1974   "Futures research," an address to the first plenary meeting of the Governor's Advisory Council on the Future of New Jersey. Trenton, New Jersey, June, 1974.
BOULDING, KENNETH E.
    1964   *The meaning of the twentieth century.* New York: Harper.
CARPENTER, EDMUND, MARSHALL McLUHAN
    1960   *Explorations in communication.* Boston: Beacon Press.

CHADWICK, JOHN, MICHAEL VENTRIS
1958   *The decipherment of linear B.* London: Cambridge University Press.
CHILDE, V. GORDON
1928   *The most ancient East.* London: Kegan Paul.
DATOR, JAMES A.
1970   "The State of Hawaii Task Force on Political Decision Making in the year 2000," in *Symposium on cultural futuristics: pre-conference volume.* Edited by Magoroh Maruyama and Arthur Harkins. Washington, D.C.: American Anthropological Association.
DE JOUVENEL, BERTRAND
1967   *The art of conjecture.* New York: Basic Books.
FLECHTHEIM, OSSIP K.
1966   *History and futurology.* Meisenheim am Glan, West Germany: Hain.
FRANKLIN, BENJAMIN
1970   *The autobiography of Benjamin Franklin and other pieces.* London: Oxford University Press.
FULLER, R. BUCKMINSTER
1969   *An operating manual for spaceship earth.* Carbondale, Illinois: Southern Illinois University Press.
GABOR, DENNIS
1964   *Inventing the future.* New York: Knopf.
GIFFORD, JAMES C.
1970   "Prehistory: perspectives from the past as trajectories to the future," in *Symposium on cultural futuristics: pre-conference volume.* Edited by Magoroh Maruyama and Arthur Harkins. Washington, D.C.: American Anthropological Association.
HELMER, OLAF
1966   *Social technology.* New York: Basic Books.
JACOBS, SUE-ELLEN
1970   "Ethnocommunication: past, present, and future," in *Symposium on cultural futuristics: pre-conference volume.* Edited by Magoroh Maruyama and Arthur Harkins. Washington, D.C.: American Anthropological Association.
JEDRZEJEWSKI, CLEMENT S.
1970   Toward a new educational order. *The Dialogist,* Spring 1970.
JONES, RICHARD D.
1970   "Cultural futurology," in *Symposium on cultural futuristics: pre-conference volume.* Edited by Magoroh Maruyama and Arthur Harkins. Washington, D.C.: American Anthropological Association.
KAHN, HERMAN, A. J. WIENER
1967   *The year 2000.* London: MacMillan.
KRETSCHMER, PAUL
1896   *Einleitung in die Geschichte der griechischen Sprache.* Goettingen.
MARINETTI, FILIPPO TOMMASO EMILIO
1909   "Manifeste de futurisme." Article in *Le Figaro,* Paris, February 20.
MEAD, MARGARET
1970   *Culture and commitment: a study of the generation gap.* Garden City, New York: Natural History Press.
MEYER, GUSTAV
1896   *Eine griechische Grammatik.* Leipzig.
PAGE, THORNTON
1970   "Man in space," in *Symposium on cultural futuristics: pre-conference volume.* Edited by Magoroh Maruyama and Arthur Harkins. Washington, D.C.: American Anthropology Association.

PLATT, JOHN R.
　1970　*Perception and change: projections for survival.* Ann Arbor: University of Michigan Press.
POLGAR, STEVEN
　1970　"The possible and the desirable: cultural futurology and population," in *Symposium on cultural futuristics: pre-conference volume.* Edited by Magoroh Maruyama and Arthur Harkins. Washington, D.C.: American Anthropological Association.
RIESMAN, DAVID, *et al.*
　1953　*The lonely crowd: a study of the changing American character.* Garden City, New York: Doubleday.
SANTAYANA, GEORGE
　1906　*The life of reason.* New York: Scribner's.
SEIDENBERG, RODERICK
　1950　*Posthistoric man.* Chapel Hill: University of North Carolina Press.
SWADESH, MORRIS
　1970　The problems of consonantal doublets in Indo-European. *Word* 26 (1).
TILLICH, PAUL J.
　1966　*The future of religions.* New York: Harper.
TOFFLER, ALVIN
　1970　*Future shock.* New York: Random House.
WELLS, HERBERT GEORGE
　1938　*World brain.* Garden City, New York: Doubleday.
WILSON, ALBERT, DONNA WILSON
　1970　"Toward the institutionalization of change," in *Symposium on cultural futuristics: pre-conference volume.* Edited by Magoroh Maruyama and Arthur Harkins. Washington, D.C.: American Anthropological Association.

Futurizing the Power Industry

ARTHUR M. HARKINS, RICHARD G. WOODS, I. KAREN
SHERARTS, and DONALD O. IMSLAND

> ... any dollar earned to the detriment of mankind is a dollar
> stolen. Not only from the people but from yourself. There is no
> way of stealing from anyone else these days ... all theft is from
> yourself.
>
> ISAAC ASIMOV

> Today, many, many people see corporations as abstract, imper-
> sonal, distant, almost fictitious institutions whose products pour
> across their environment and whose advertising messages deluge
> them, but who have no real corporeal existence.
>
> I think that corporations simply to maintain the standards of the
> past are going to have to increase their self-consciousness as to
> their own social responsibility.
>
> CARL MADDEN

> (Quotations taken from a series of interviews with selected
> Washington, D.C. and New York City futurists by personnel of
> the ABC Power Company "pseudonym", September, 1971.)

In the summer of 1972 the authors, as consultants to the ABC Power
Company "pseudonym" in the central United States, cooperated with
employees of the company to design a unique nine-month program
called "Future Trends." Future Trends was developed as part of the
company's new emphasis on personnel education. We will describe
Future Trends in this paper, analyze it, and suggest in broad terms
some logical follow-up programs for private and public sector organizations. We will draw upon some of the ideas in the developing field of
cultural futuristics and upon other resources.

First, some background to the Program itself. In 1969 the research
biophysicist John Platt wrote an article for *Science* that is well known
to many persons. In that article, Platt warned that "social inventions"
must be used to prevent a number of crises that could overwhelm

mankind. Calling for the formation of new task forces which might begin the process of crisis intervention, Platt recommended six starting points for action: (1) peacekeeping mechanisms and feedback stabilization; (2) biotechnology; (3) game theory; (4) psychological and social theory; (5) social indicators; and (6) channels of effectiveness. Platt's challenge to us was not delivered in a lighthearted manner:

The task is clear. The task is huge. The time is horribly short. In the past, we have had science for intellectual pleasure, and science for the control of nature. We have had science for war. But today, the whole human experiment may hang on the question of how fast we now press the development of science for survival (1969: 1121).

John Platt is not the only scholar issuing dire warnings and offering upbeat suggestions for the success of mankind. In 1971 the *Futurist* magazine published the results of an MIT computer study that later appeared in a book entitled *The limits to growth* (1972). The study was carried out under the auspices of the Club of Rome. According to Dennis L. Meadows, author of the *Futurist* article and co-author of *The limits to growth*, three convictions united the members of the Club of Rome:

1. The long-term prospects of our global society are poor at the moment, and the situation appears to be deteriorating.
2. The only viable solutions to global problems will be those with a trans-national perspective and a planning time horizon much greater than those currently exhibited by any state.
3. Scientific attempts to identify the fundamental interactions which determine the rate and direction of global evolution, realistic assessments of our feasible options, and concerted efforts to achieve a more satisfactory global situation can lead to a substantial improvement over our current situation (1971: 137).

While many reviewers have heaped praise or criticism upon the Club of Rome study, one general conclusion seems warranted. Regardless of imperfections in the computer-based study (questionable programming assumptions, inadequate data base, unwarranted pessimism about technological breakthroughs, etc.), there is a need for this type of study. Such a study, despite the problems, can stimulate further research on the planetary systems that may be crucial to man's survival.

In January, 1972 the *Ecologist* published "A blueprint for survival," (Goldsmith, et al. 1972), a paper which supported the work done by the Club of Rome. It charged that planetary breakdowns were not only possible, but were inevitable. The paper declared that the British and other governments were "either refusing to face the relevant facts, or

[were] briefing their scientists in such a way that their seriousness [was] played down" (1972:1). The authors of "A blueprint for survival" called for nothing less than an international movement formulating ' a new philosophy of life, whose goals can be achieved without destroying the environment, and a precise and comprehensive programme for bringing about the sort of society in which it can be implemented" (1972: 1).

In April, 1971, the Institute for the Future (IFF) in Middletown, Connecticut published *A forecast of the interaction between business and society in the next five years* (Gordon et al. 1971). The report focused on the "potential interaction of business and society in the next five years ... [It dealt] primarily with problems, suspected and expected.... [It focused] on the forces of change which are pressing business to create new responses to real or imagined social issues" (1971: iii). The IFF study was based on the Delphi method, and the conclusion was that business organizations will increasingly interact with "action groups" with which they have had little or no previous contact. A number of groups would be included:

1. Consumer groups, which through various means exert pressure on business and government to improve the safety, durability, and efficiency of products.
2. "Women's liberation" groups, which are actively trying to bring about elimination of sexually discriminatory practices in society.
3. Radical student groups, which are trying to force institutions to behave in ways they consider "moral."
4. Conservative groups, which actively oppose radical action and demands and seek to preserve the status quo.
5. Government, which in this study comprises both federal and state bodies.
6. Racial interest groups, which seek to promote actions designed to enhance ethnic pride and eliminate social inequities related to race.
7. Labor unions, organized labor, in particular the largest unions in the country (1971: 4).

The major conclusions reached by Delphi panelists in the IFF study cannot be construed as comforting to business:

1. The turmoil in which business currently finds itself can be expected to continue at least through 1975.
2. Militant actions will be directed against business by radical groups in an effort to gain their ends.
3. Other means of protest or coercion will be used with increasing frequency in the next five years. These include litigation, sit-ins, and various forms of federal action designed to move business toward the solution of social problems.
4. Profitable operation of business is expected to continue, and profitable solutions to social problems will be generally welcome.

5. Public-relations and advertising campaigns publicizing minor business contributions to social issues will not, for the most part, significantly influence the events or goals which trigger them.

6. The students who contributed to this study were more skeptical than the businessmen about the possibility that most of the radical goals will be achieved by 1975.

7. Among the goals considered, those supported by business were viewed as more likely to be achieved, and those opposed by business less likely.

8. Some of the respondents indicated their belief that business should exert its significant influence over national domestic and foreign policy in order to instigate national policy changes that various groups would consider to be in the public interest; therefore, according to this view, an effective means of instigating national policy changes is to induce business to take the initiative in promulgating changes.

9. In the conceptual review which followed the Delphi study, specific actions were suggested by the Institute staff and several consultants for further business consideration. These actions fall under the following headings: new kinds of insurance and credit; new kinds of research and development; new internal corporate policies; the establishment of new types of businesses; actions by business associations; the creation of new incentives for business by government; and the petitioning of government by business for new kinds of legislation (1971: 4–5).

The change-focused findings of the IFF Delphi study can prompt various reactions, ranging from despair to a positive "seizing of the moment" as an opportunity for business. One of the authors of this paper chose to view the situation optimistically, and wrote the following about the IFF study in December 1971:

One privileged group of Americans which will have significant opportunities to invent new mechanisms for social adaptation, it seems to me, consists of the managers or decision-makers of large-scale, private, profit-making corporations. I would argue that management progress for the future largely would consist of active participation with other social forces in the design and implementation of socio-economic alternatives to the present. I would make that assertion on the basis that American managers have an opportunity to participate in social change and in their own metamorphosis because of their present advantageous position in terms of economic power, organizational capability to deal with change, and access to information. It seems to me that such an opportunity is about the best that is available to any of us these days in the mounting crisis of transformation. I would hold to such a definition of management progress for the future even though one must freely admit that the nature of *postcivilized society* is now unclear and uncertain and could just as easily become the anti-Utopias of Orwell and Huxley as it could become a society devoid of the major sources of human suffering and filled with opportunities for the realization of human potential. What *is* becoming clear is that institutions designed to function even a relatively few years ago no longer can cope with new complexities, mounting performance pressures, and changing expectations and values; to avoid substantive change and adaptation in such circumstances might be expected to lead to institutional decay and atrophy, and there is no reason to believe that American business is somehow mysteriously exempt from these forces. I would not argue that most business managers are any more aware of the "crisis of transformation" and the "Great Transition" [Boulding] than are others in our society, and I have no idea whether they would share the conception of management progress for the future outlined here.

Certainly, American managers may see alternatives for the future quite different from broad participation with others in developing adaptive socio-economic structures. They could simply opt for increased efforts to "make the system work," and to engineer slow, incremental change and improvement which would not be disruptive of accepted and rewarding business practices in the short-run. Of course, there is much talk along these lines. However, such a strategy might be difficult to bring off. The very rapidity, complexity, and pervasiveness of change today creates pressures on old structures to flex rapidly and the rising expectations of an alert and well-educated citizenry create forces that "the system" never before had to satisfy. When one considers that the system may never have worked as well as we thought it did (except for those of us who knew how to make it work), the addition of new pressures becomes even more significant (Woods 1971: 1–2, original emphasis).

From this basically optimistic point of view, the authors proposed the Future Trends Program to the ABC Power Company management. Several meetings were held during the summer of 1971 with the authors and ABC personnel. The intention was to develop a cooperative approach to the Program which would result in the best possible combination of resources from within the company as well as from the "outside." A proposal for the Program was written. In part, the proposal stressed a rationale for studying the future, the changes surrounding contemporary corporations, the necessity for adaptive organizational behavior, and the format within which the Program should be developed and criticized.

Why should the future be the focus for intensive study? It has been suggested that human expectations, hopes and anticipations are largely responsible for the sort of human futures which do occur. If humans can consciously strive to shape their own futures, then the study of future trends and alternatives is simply a means of coming to grips with the sort of information needed to make choices. Of course, it is not possible to predict the exact nature of the future, but it is possible to describe plausible alternative pathways for human societies and to assess the consequences of these options. Since man's potential for constructive and destructive behavior is ever widening because of burgeoning technology and sophistication, it is important for him to assess alternative futures.

In a sense, our current concern and dismay over ecological and environmental damage and our concern about involvement in foreign wars are belated recognitions that costly and perhaps, inappropriate human choices were made in the past. Such choices are often difficult to reverse, and seldom is it possible to recover the human and other costs associated with them, so the careful consideration of alternatives by all citizens becomes a matter of self-interested wisdom. At the same time, mankind must move ahead rather than hesitate in a defensive stance while the problems of living in a changing society mount. Choices and decisions cannot be deferred for too long without increasing social dissatisfaction and frustration.

Industrial executives and managers are people who are probably more accustomed to thinking about the future than most citizens, because planning and the anticipation of future change are so vital to competitive survival. However, it is no longer possible to depend upon the relatively simple device of projecting the technological and competitive developments for an industry to sketch the likely managerial decisions which will have to be made to ensure survival and success in the market place, since product innovation and maneuvering by competitors do not account for the basic changes underway in the larger society. The actions of a concerned electorate (witness the SST), changing values and life-styles (hippies, retirement villages, leisure), and the decline of some institutions (small farms, the church) at the same time that others (Common Cause, Nader's Raiders) ascend, and the adaptive efforts and agonies of other institutions (universities, welfare, the Congress, public employment) are only a few examples of basic structural changes in the existing order which must be considered for one to become an *informed* and *aware* decision-maker. Without doing so, the roles of managers and decision-makers are apt to become more and more those of *reacting* to change once it is well underway, and the consequences of the resulting adaptive lag could be disastrous — for society and for the firm. Further, as national priorities become established, the public's expectations of firms — especially quasi-public ones such as utilities — may be expected to take a sharper focus, particularly around the social and environmental consequences of managerial behavior.

Coping with the future requires that managers and decision-makers depend less upon extensions of the past and more upon an expanded awareness and knowledge of contemporary and potential developments in the *total* society.

Most effective organizations today have very little difficulty coping with the expected. It is the unexpected which throws them, and this means that anticipation of future developments is a crucial element in the survival and adaptation of economic organizations. Because we cannot predict the future with accuracy, it is necessary to look far ahead into areas where the immediate rewards are unclear and even doubtful. While "hard-nosed" managements may find such activity a "poor risk," they will, by adhering to the well-defined and familiar, stumble into the future rather than move confidently into it. Such an outlook places a premium upon innovation and experimentation, rather than stability and continuity; it accepts the ultimate necessity of re-defining the goals of the organization, its management "principles," the roles of employees and the relationships between them — if necessary the entire culture of the organization. All this, it must be remembered, is for the sake of ensuring organizational survival and health.

The final format of the program should not be established without extensive involvement of ABC representatives. While University persons can suggest possible alternatives, they are not in a position to adequately assess the impact of training format upon the operating requirements of ABC. It may be, for example, unreasonable to expect those enrolled to attend every session or to attend sessions scheduled at certain critical times. Much depends upon the emphasis ABC management wishes to place upon the program. If it is regarded simply as another sort of management "meeting," one might expect that other pressures would take priority with some frequency. If, on the other hand, the program is regarded as critical to the ABC operation, other pressures may be accorded a lesser priority, and regular adherence to the program's sessions would be more likely. It might be helpful if some of the persons who are likely to be enrollees are included as part of the planning process (Proposed ABC Future Trends Program, pp. 1–4; original emphasis).

The course was approved along the lines suggested in the proposal. Classes began on October 7, 1971, and continued until June 8, 1972. Thirty-four employees of ABC Power Company representing many professional backgrounds were invited into the program by management. The employees received a letter from a senior vice-president, which clearly indicated the seriousness of the business community's predicament. It said:

Dear Fellow Employee:

Charles F. Kettering once said, "We must all be concerned about the future because we will be spending the rest of our lives there." Dutch sociologist Frederick L. Polak has written, "Thinking about the future is not only the mightiest lever of progress, but also the condition of survival." Pierre Bertaux, a French historian, recently stated, "A people with a dynamic image of the future is like a car with a powerful engine. A weak or poor image of the future does not furnish the driving force necessary to propel a people through the challenge of history."

We at ABC are very much involved with the future. A fossil plant requires seventy-six months of careful planning, and a nuclear plant requires ninety months. Our planners in power supply must project the energy demand of our service area more than a decade in advance to the year 1990. And our financial planners must look carefully at economic trends so that adequate capitalization is available when we need it.

The past decade has brought vast changes in society, as well as at ABC. We know the coming decade will not be static; most experts predict that change will accelerate. We at ABC must learn to anticipate change and predict the future rather than simply respond to it. This will allow us to be a "dynamic" company and better serve our customers and employees.

The officers of the company have agreed that a serious study of the future by selected individuals is needed. A Future Trends Program has been planned, which will begin the first week in October and continue through the second week in June 1972. It will cover many aspects of our changing society, as indicated on the enclosed outline.

We have selected you to become a participant in this program. It will require a weekly, two-hour meeting in Section I of the auditorium in the General Office building. The program will include readings, tapes, films, speakers, and group discussion. There will be no papers or exams required. You will progress at your own pace relative to your time and interest.

We hope the design and content of the course will capture your interest. Michael Marien, a Research Fellow at the Syracuse University Research Corporation, who will speak at the December 9 session, has stated ". . . your Future Trends Program appears to be one of the best attempts to attain an overview of the future that I know of. It would therefore be quite valuable to others as a model of excellence in helping others to think productively about the future" (Invitational letter from a senior vice-president of the ABC Power Company to selected employees, 8 September, 1971).

We start our examination of the Program with the final presentation to the course itself. This presentation was made by one of the authors as a short but thorough overview of the major points made throughout the course:

We began this program by viewing a multi-media presentation concerning the future in which a number of futurists commented about the growing rate of change and what it means. William Ewald counseled utilities to play it "open and honest" during the forthcoming crisis of crises and noted that most large-scale institutions have a tendency to reinforce their members for doing things as they were done in the past, even when changes in the external socio-economic environment demand new adaptations. Carl Madden thought that we now place an excessive value upon material wealth and thought the price of energy should increase. (Apparently, the Edison Electric Institute agrees — its directors recently announced that the organization would try to raise $86.6 million for research in 1973 and $137.6 million in 1974 to be used for research of nuclear generation among other projects, and these sums would be raised by rate increases.) This appears to be a new development since the R&D task force report which we reviewed. Ian Wilson of General Electric told us that we are in an era of rapid, complex and pervasive change where many of the rules of the game are subject to revision. Among other pressures, he noted the pressure for a reexamination of the role of boards of directors and pressures for public representation on these boards. Ian stressed the need for a new kind of corporate planning which would acknowledge the new complexities of the real world.

This morning's newspaper carries an account of a proposal for corporate restructuring just made by James Summer, President of General Mills. Summer notes that public criticism of corporations is rising at the same time that public needs for social services are often unmet and sometimes poorly met. Despite management protestations of "public responsibility," carefully designed by public relations consultants, Summer maintains that corporations are even more single-mindedly devoted to pursuing profitability than before, due to the fact that the owner-manager has given way to the investor, who has no control over, or responsibility for, the actions of the corporation. "Social responsibility" today for many corporations means giving people and money to various non-profit organizations, but this means that the vital interests of the firm and its management are not really at stake. Summer proposes that the largest corporations staff and fund subsidiaries to operate at "minimal profit" and compete in such social service areas as health care, vocational training, child care, and management of housing programs. With boards divided evenly between investors, labor and "the market" (meaning consumer and community), he feels these corporations would exhibit greater sensitivity to the social costs of their actions. This arrangement, Summer believes, would allow corporations to organize low-profit subsidiaries in the public service area without fear of stockholder suits.

This is in contradiction to Tony Wiener's assertion last week that the corporation's role be a limited one. I agree that corporations can't do everything, but I have more faith than he in the malleability of the corporation. And it would be good to find out just what corporations *can* do. As R. Buckminster Fuller puts it — when you experiment, you always know more than you did before. Even where there is failure, you know what does not work.

These new complexities of the real world make a good many of the old, comfortable ways of looking at the world obsolete. A basic point made in *Beyond left and right* is that the real radical or change-oriented thought of our time is surprisingly free from conventional political and ideological labeling. Kenneth Boulding makes that point when he says that, if humans make it in the "Great Transition" from civilization to postcivilization, they will have to avoid the traps of war, population, technology and resource depletion and *ideology*. (How many of us — when we began the course — would have thought that — before it was finished — we would one morning turn on our TV sets and watch President Nixon exchanging toasts with the Chinese communist leaders and later signing an agreement in what seemed like every 15 minutes with Russian leaders. According to the dogmas of political and economic ideologies we've been living with, at least since the early part of this century, those events just should not have happened, but they did.) Mr. ————— [company president] asked you for help in establishing ABC as a leader in social change. He cautioned against doing things for the sole reason that you are directed to do them. He noted that most adults today do not understand young people, and he pointed out that it is very difficult to understand a changing society, especially when it is undergirded with changing values.

Some of us may have thought that mankind is surely in a totally new situation with respect to change today, but Weston LaBarre made us aware that it is human to adapt and evolve through culture and technology (rather than through physical changes). The different ways in which cultures have dealt with the environment and with survival is something we viewed in the film *A time for man*. Today we are just becoming aware of threats to survival which we did not understand before, and we will have to deal with those threats through culture change. The *rate* of change today *is* truly staggering, and that means stress upon cultural forms, such as institutions. One of these institutions is education, and Mike Marien contrasted *closed teaching systems* with *open learning systems* for us. While educational change is now quite commonly controversial — after all, who hasn't heard of busing and permissiveness? — Marien asserted that the real stimulus to educational change is yet to come. It will appear in the form of the discovery of ignorance in a society which prides itself on its massive educational expenditures. When we learn to admit our ignorance without loss of face, we will ignite a veritable explosion in learning (and much of that learning may take unconventional forms, such as the form of this class). After all, most people still really believe that learning should occur from age 6 to 18 or from 6 to 21 only, despite the fact that learning needs continue throughout life and are crucial when changes are underway.

The relationship of learning to culture and "the generation gap" is something we learned about from Margaret Mead. Charles Reich's *The greening of America* gave us some insight into the world view of young Americans, and the study by Daniel Yankelovich added insight about another dimension to the "counterculture" — something called the New Naturalism. Young people are the focal point of value change and much of what we've encountered in this course suggests there are structural shifts underway in values. Anthony Wiener flatly asserted that values haven't changed, based upon a Hudson Institute compilation of public opinion poll data. I had a look at the information last Monday while visiting the Futures Group in Connecticut, and I don't think his conclusion is at all warranted. There's very little public opinion data on a longitudinal basis, and what there is mostly allows only inferences about values. Values are difficult to identify and study, but it seems reasonable to conclude that, while many people retain so-called "traditional" values, there always has been in American an on-going renewal of values. That probably is an inevitable part of a country which is committed to technological and economic progress and which is the most future-oriented country in the world.

When we looked at the future of the family we had a chance to examine some forms of corporate families. As an update of that, you might want to look at a recent issue of *Life*, which contains a report of one corporate family largely composed of retired persons, many of whom (although they were all reasonably healthy and able to care for themselves) would otherwise have had no choice but to live in a nursing home in order to have companionship. Having a place in a family obviously was preferred by these people over the impersonal relationships so common in more formal institutions. If the corporate family arrangement catches on among senior citizens, what we will have seen is the innovation of a new living arrangement by the "radical fringe" which is then picked up, adapted somewhat, then appropriated by the part of society we most likely would call "conservative."

When we looked at the future of medicine, we saw serious consideration of "artificial" life in various forms and new forms of health service delivery (for which legislation is already proposed), the prospect of mind-altering drugs in the future, and some rather substantial local efforts in sophisticated medical testing and in the invention, design and manufacture of mechanical parts for humans (or should I say for cyborgs?).

We heard from the much-maligned Dennis Meadows about *The limits to growth*, easily the most controversial futures development during the past five years. The notion of policies limiting growth is now being hotly debated at the U.N. Conference on the Environment. The study was castigated by Brendan O'Regan and Tony Wiener, both of whom have more faith in technological solutions and both of whom stressed the needs of Third World people and the poor generally for economic growth. But it was H. Wentworth Eldredge, I believe, who pointed out that Dennis Meadows is one of the new B-school products from whom we shall hear a great deal more, and I think that *much* of the criticism directed toward the study is based not where it should be — on the model and toward its improvement — but rather on the fact that it has upset things. After all, from the point of view of the specialist, economists should be the ones doing such world modeling and that is partly why so much criticism has come from economists. But the fact is that economists have not been doing such modeling and, as far as we know, no one has undertaken to do it, not the U.N., not the American Economic Association, not even the Hudson Institute. I guess I agree with some members of the class in believing that the value of the study lies not in its specific projections but in its development of a model which can be further refined and improved. It is clear that Boulding is one who is concerned about *Limits*. He said, you will recall, that despite the study's shortcomings, there is a *real* wolf out there. Boulding put his finger on a major shortcoming of the model in its failure to include man himself — in terms of his undeveloped capacity. Natural resources, says Boulding, may be a function of human knowledge. Still, Boulding notes in a recent review of *Limits to growth* in *The New Republic* that our present sense of finitude is accentuated by the space enterprise where "we have seen our own beautiful blue and white planet and we suddenly come to realize that it is the only decent bit of real estate in a very long way."

We are, I think, just now feeling the effects of the knowledge revolution, and we are most impressed with its negative effects — the overload of new information and the problems associated with handling it, the alienation and apathy it may cause in people when they realize that simple goals may not be easily attained in a complicated world, the shaking and erosion which inevitably affects institutions and people who are firmly wedded to a single world view or to a single ideology. This tendency of Western man — called monopolarization by Maruyama — is something we may have to modify. Maybe we could learn from the Maruyamas in this world how to tolerate in our heads the notion that there are many truths in the world which are not just competing for the one single truth, but are different facets of a very comprehensive truth. If we can learn how to do that while retaining our ability to act in pursuit of single-purpose goals, as we must, then I think we might be happier about our human predicament and better able to shift goals and behavior as we need to do so. Right now there are some young people who can shift world views, but in doing so seem to lose their ability to act because of disorientation. They become unable to produce — to do their jobs — but this may be a transitory, developmental matter.

We are improving our means of communication — as you learned from a panel of local experts — and we are certainly becoming more planetary and less local in our communications. For this reason, and because knowledge continues to accelerate, I think it's safe to assume that our perceptions of who we are and what our environment is like will change in the years ahead. That will be disquieting to a lot of people, and there will be those who will argue for the management of communications and for the total design of societies so that much individuality, pluralism, freedom, human potentiality, and choice will be eliminated in favor of stable, predictable human behavior reinforced by cleverly designed reward systems *à la* B. F. Skinner. That will be very seductive to some people. There is a sort of attractiveness to immersing oneself in a kind of somnambulent tranquility, perhaps aided by drugs, when all the rules around you are changing. We *could have* a society something like *THX 1138*. But persons who opt for that way of life will forfeit the chance of choosing, in Buckminster Fuller's terms, between *utopia or oblivion*. They will have to put up with whatever the high priests of human programming decide is prudent and appropriate. Perhaps I'm too old-fashioned to accept such radical thought as social system engineering, but I'd prefer to see us devise our own solutions drawn from *social invention* and the change of people and institutions. Sometimes it seems our gravest enemy is our tendency to strive toward the building of eternal, unchanging monuments in the form of institutions. That precedent was so well established before us by the Egyptians and the Aztecs. We could be tomorrow's dinosaurs, but I think we shall not if we opt for more learning, more experimentation, more research, and more adaptation, while devising new ways to satisfy human physical, emotional, and security needs. In all of this corporations can have a part. In fact, they just might lead the way (Woods 1972; original emphasis).

The Future Trends Program resulted in "reuseable" materials for regular participants as well as newcomers to Future Trends content. Below is an outline of the course.

Course Outline

THE FUTURE FOR ABC

October 7	A preview of the course which stresses the unique traits
October 14	of man enabling him to adapt to the future and which
October 21	answers the questions, "Why study the future?" and "How to study the future?" Then, special attention by invited speakers to the future of the power industry and the future of ABC.

THE FUTURE OF MANAGEMENT

October 28	An examination of future needs for internal and external
November 4	management information which will enable cooperating
November 11	humans in working organizations to adapt their individual

and group efforts to various systems. The dilemmas posed by desires for individual and institutional privacy. Attention to the functions of future management by a guest speaker.

THE FUTURE OF LEARNING

November 18	An inquiry into traditional, contemporary, and possible
December 2	future social learning styles of the young. Youth counter-
December 9	cultures and the significance of gaps between generations
December 16	and between cultures. A guest speaker will describe

potential future modes of learning for all age groups. Finally, a review of the first three units, followed by an introduction and preview to forthcoming units.

THE FUTURE OF THE FAMILY

January 6	A look at the origins and functions of the family as a
January 13	fundamental social and economic unit. Present and po-
January 20	tential variations in family structure will be examined. A

guest expert will suggest alternative futures for the family and family living.

THE FUTURE OF HEALTH AND MEDICINE

January 27	A fresh look at human health and medicine as it relates to
February 3	the ecosystem. Future aspects of old medicine. The future
February 10	for health and medicine as viewed by an invited speaker.

THE FUTURE OF MATERIAL WEALTH AND SOCIAL FREEDOM

February 17	The development and significance of technology among
February 24	animals and humans. Variations in human technology as
March 2	they might affect the future. A view of the future of
March 9	material wealth and social freedom by a guest informant.

Then, review of previous units with a preview of material to come.

THE FUTURE OF COMMUNICATIONS

April 6	Animal signs and human language. Variations in human
April 13	communication and in the technology of communication.
April 20	An invited speaker suggests communications futures.

THE FUTURE OF DEMOCRATIC PARTICIPATION

April 27	The nature of human social life, including cooperation
May 4	and competition. Various human social styles and their
May 11	future determinants. An outside resource person offers

some conjecture about the future of democratic participation.

THE FUTURE OF NATURAL AND ARTIFICIAL ENVIRONMENTS

May 18	The biosphere and its influence upon human settlements.
May 25	Human settlements as shelter and amenity. Experiments
June 1	with cities and new towns. An invited specialist speaks
June 8	about the future of natural and artificial environments. Finally, conclusions for the course and general prospects for the future (ABC Future Trends Program, Course Outline).

Evaluation of the ABC Future Trends Program was conducted in several ways: through a "Participants' Log"; through a formal questionnaire; through private and group discussions with participants and faculty; and through other subjective means. A consultant to the ABC Power Company prepared an evaluation of the course based on several of the items contained in the questionnaire. Portions of his analysis follow:

The regular (monthly) meetings focus on futures for selected institutions, with additional information inputs from books, reprints, and tapes. The course outline includes: The Future for ABC, The Future of Management, The Future of Learning, The Future of the Family, The Future of Health and Medicine, The Future of Material Wealth and Social Freedom, The Future of Communications, The Future of Democratic Participation, and The Future of Natural and Artificial Environments.

The main contribution of this approach is to make the learner more conscious of what he believes about these institutions, why he believes it, how much he values his beliefs, and what new kinds of information will change them. Hopefully this approach also invites attention to personal and corporate renewal and regeneration.

Many questions were asked of course enrollees in the March 8, 1972, "Request for Observations." Those questions selected for discussion are presented below. Also included are the course enrollees' expressions of their interest in pursuing certain class projects.

Before presenting these selected findings, some preliminary remarks on method may be helpful. Measures of complex situations which do not lend themselves to scalar quantification — like the ABC Future Trends Program — are most often made by judgments of presumably competent observers, and some suitable statistical combination of these is then taken as the measure of the magnitude in question. Everything hinges on the sensitivity and reliability with which the discriminating judgments are made.

Question 1 Are you more, or less, confident that ABC can effectively plan for the future?

Of 25 respondents, 19 said more. (In quantitative idiom, when more = 1 and less = 0, the answer was mean = 0.76 with a standard deviation = 0.43.)

Question 2 Is study of the broad-gauged future an appropriate activity for employees of ABC?

Of 25 respondents, 24 said yes. (In quantative idiom, when yes = 1 and no = 0, the mean = 0.96 with a standard deviation = 0.19.)

Question 3   Are you better prepared to cope with change as a result of the course?

Of 25 respondents, 23 said yes. (In quantitative idiom, mean = 0.92 with a standard deviation = 0.27.)

Question 4   Should the Future Trends Program be expanded within the company? This question was designed to elicit a written reply.

Of 25 respondents, 11 replied with a simple "yes"; 10 said "yes, but..."; 4 said "no, because ..." The "qualified yes" respondents said: "... but with more emphasis on the future of business;" "first to all management to get them moving before it is too late and then to balance of all employees;" "select groups;" "but more time must be available than I have had for it;" "if top management is committed to change;" "We must start to constructively plan for the future. We must also realize that people's values may be changing rapidly;" "gradually;" "This course of study could and would be of great benefit to all;" "Definitely — perhaps offer to those interested for personal reasons and not because they might look better in the company's eyes. Would like more management to take it;" "If it is a valuable 'human' educational program, it should be available to as many as possible."

The "qualified no" respondents said:

"Not unless it is made more specific and shortened;" "Not a generalized course offered to all. Officers of the Company and *select* personnel (not necessarily high in organization);" "Only to selected individuals;" "This program is not for everybody! I think it should be offered to select managers who will have some responsibility in the planning of the ABC Company future."

The imputation of elitism to some respondents seems justified. Possibly this results from the way they entered the course — by invitation, with their consent. Or possibly this elite complex is part of the price to be paid for a program addressed to innovation and change with its appeals to imagination and creativity.

Question 5   In what way(s) do you feel the program as a whole will be of value to you? Perhaps the fact that 14 replies were returned (from 25 respondents) is important in interpreting the evidence. Apparently 11 respondents did not understand the question or, in any event, framed no reply to it.

Very few research instruments are available to assess the influence of a course of studies in the area of values. Even if the instruments were available now, only time would reveal what the actual consequences will be. Obviously we must do our own thinking on this elusive issue. Let us look at how some articulate respondents replied and in what ways the program as a whole is conceived as "valuable" by them:

"It has enforced my desire to work for a controlled future, a planned future, rather than just letting it happen;" "Increase in knowledge re: evaluations of the future by others. Hopefully will get insight on how to have some beneficial effect on the future;" "By seeing that the Company (and my job) must change to meet new trends by giving me new insight into how to study the future."

These replies are roughly representative of those provided by the learners. They feel that they have been informed about a number of courses of action that are available; they have not been instructed about the effectiveness of the choices, they have been motivated to change their valuations of outcomes, but cannot specify precisely how. In brief, they have a map of the future of sorts and what they want now are directions for map-making.

Class Projects Learners were asked: "How interested are you in any of the following projects as an outgrowth of the course?" All 25 respondents provided their estimates of their interest in the projects specified, and 5 respondents also suggested other projects.

Their replies are easiest to present in a quantitative idiom (where 5 = very interested, to 1 = disinterested).

Mean	S.D.	Item	Content
4.40	0.69	h.	Sharing information with other businesses
4.32	0.68	g.	Design of ABC Social Indicator System
4.12	0.91	e.	Design of Advanced ABC Course
4.04	0.82	b.	Delphi Study of ABC Employees
4.00	0.89	c.	Delphi Study of ABC Customers
3.76	1.07	d.	Class Presentation to Officers
3.68	0.97	f.	Design of Technological Forecasting System for ABC
3.56	1.02	a.	Delphi Study of Future Trends Class

Other projects suggested are:
"Just wish some sort of impartial survey of ABC employees could be taken to reflect the general employee *shock* at Company internal policies — so that the results might point out to officers the effects on employees and the need for an internal social action program;" "Delphi study of the future of Metro area development;" "Employee Delphi — explore questions of opportunity for job creativity; maximize one's individual talents' management decision . . . criteria; non-union wage benefit negotiations;" "Ghastly examination of long-term effects of radiation pollution. Study of employee reaction to Delphi of ABC customers;" "Delphi study of ABC employees re: specific subjects."

Apparently the learners have stabilized their social relationships and are opting for projects which will minimally stress their status or security within the group.

In summary, to meet the broad challenges, opportunities, and responsibilities for the total learning environment as typified by the movement of American business to more socially oriented purposes, ABC management will face four critical needs:

Modification of management practices, techniques, and philosophy to be in tune with *new personal and societal values.* For example, the top leadership group must create and implement new measurement, control, and *reward systems* that are capable of dealing with changing ideas about efficiency and about manpower as a corporate resource.

Specification of selection criteria for managerial manpower to meet requirements for managing in the *total learning environment,* rather than in the historic environment based on the eight traditional assumptions. For example, the current top leadership group may not be appropriate models for leaders in the future total learning environment, just as the top leadership group of the 30's or 40's or even 50's may not have been models for today's leaders.

Development of relatively unused *interpersonal skills* to new levels of understanding, acceptance, and application. For example, the top leadership group will learn how to deal more competently and comfortably with *conflict, widely diverse values,* and *man-manager dialogues.*

Development of new leadership styles appropriate to the *total learning environment.* For example, the top leadership group will necessarily be less directive in its management than now, more aware of social and political factors, more cognizant of the "new" and differing needs of employees as *"productive" learners*, users or customers as *"served" learners*, shareholders as *"investing" learners*, and the public-at-large as *"beneficiary" learners*.

[I recommend that] a goàl analysis of *"Future-directed mind-set"* be performed. This analysis must proceed to the point where the main elements (performances) are described. It is a way to discover what the essence of the goal means. If you know what it is that you want to achieve, and know what that achievement looks like when you have it, you can make better decisions about how to get there.

If the goal is too intangible to be specified in performances, no one must claim that the goal is being achieved . . . or that it is not.

Very little attention has been paid to reinforcing learners. Without specifying performances, no meaningful feedback can be provided to learners or to others whose support of the program is needed. Simply plying learners with information about future trends, or exhorting them to be alert and concerned about the future will change very little. What favorable consequences are provided for learners? How does attending to future trends make the learner's world any brighter?

In my judgment, the need the ABC Future Trends Program addresses is at least as compelling today as it was last year. "We at ABC must learn to anticipate change and predict the future rather than simply respond to it." —————'s expression of that need has been considerably (and possibly tediously) explicated in this report.

The evidence supporting this need is neither better nor worse than it was a year ago. However, the knowledges, skills, attitudes, and understandings of "future trends" are possessions which learners must acquire from themselves, not gifts which the company can bestow. The *process* of acquisition is a slow one, which is never quite certain nor complete (Jacobson 1972: 14–23, original emphasis).

The author of this evaluation detailed replies to several other questions. On the whole, the results of this questionnaire survey appear to indicate general acceptance of the Future Trends Program, along with indications of interest in expanded alternatives for the continuation of future studies.

Entries in the course logs by participants were maintained on a weekly basis. These entries were made over the course of the nine-month program by most, but not all, of the participants. In general, it appears that participants became more critically interested in the study of alternative futures as their general familiarity with literature and other resources increased. An area of particular concern to some participants was the future of the family. Reflected in questionnaire data, this concern is especially clear in the third set of participant log entries, as well as in the results of a second survey on the future of marriage and the family conducted within the class. This survey involved about half the participants.

One of the most interesting insights into ABC personnel was obtained through a classroom survey about the future drawn from a local newspaper. (Two authors of this report had contributed earlier to the development of the paper's questionnaire on the future.) Appendix 2 contains the results of the newspaper survey and the results of a similar ABC survey conducted through the Future Trends Program. Comparative data obtained from two University of Minnesota summer classes concerned with the future are also provided in Appendix 2. Perhaps the single most striking result of the data comparison is the very high percentages of ABC personnel, University of Minnesota students, and a random selection of Minnesota respondents who felt that planning would bring about a better future.

As corporate structures seek to define the dimensions of the shifting environment and the implications of change for business, mission redefinitions (planning) occur. The Conference Board of New York recently released a document which attempts to analyze changing sociocultural conditions in terms of information technology. In the section of this document which dealt with the effects on the business world of information technology, the authors came to these conclusions:

Information technology will affect business operations in the United States by increasing its range of choices, aiding in the determination and control of its structure, and improving its competitive position at home and abroad.

Multi-objective goals and programs are becoming absolute essentials for most large and medium-sized corporations; developments in information technology make possible their formulation and their management.

New policy-formulation centers will soon be considered essential within (and outside) the business community in order to help senior executives conduct more timely and effective multi-objective planning, determine the new interrelationships between business, government, and the rest of society, regulate the orderly introduction of new technologies, and identify the need for problem-formulation as well as decision-making information networks within business and between business and other sectors.

Corporations will require a new kind and quality of business management, which will be able to command the information process for purposes of formulating multi-objective goals and programs, identifying and analyzing complex new market challenges and opportunities, allocating scarce resources, and taking into account on a real time basis the growing significance of pressure groups.

The value of a company's contribution to society by the knowledge and information it creates and makes available will introduce a new concept of "profitability" beyond the usual cost accounting of corporate profits; information technology provides a tool to assess these environmental and social benefits.

Information technology offers business more effective means of identifying and developing new products and services to meet the skyrocketing national demands for solutions to "human systems" problems.

Consumers, utilizing developments in information technology will have increasingly instant and effective means for anticipating or reacting to corporate policies, decisions, products, and services, and will make their influence be felt on a continuous rather than ad hoc basis.

Employees not at the decision-making level will be required to be, by today's standards, highly skilled in certain aspects of information technology. This will require new criteria for hiring and new programs for training employees.

Unless business modifies, or even alters, its structure and operations so as to incorporate the latest information technology, it will lose out to domestic and foreign competition.

Multinational firms will need new kinds of decision-making models, data banks, and communications networks.

Information as a form of wealth and a national resource will require new definitions of "property" and considerable modification of existing antitrust regulations (The Conference Board 1972).

Earlier, Ian Wilson of the General Electric Company looked into the sociocultural changes which would bring about those shifts in business behavior listed above and in the Institute for the Future study. Wilson forecast the following changes, all of which will have their implications for the business community:

(1) An emphasis on the "quality of life," from the quality of products to the quality of our environment; (2) Some modification of the old Puritan work ethic, and a growing belief that leisure is a valid activity in its own right; (3) A new "self-image" that a rising level of education bestows on its graduates; (4) A rejection of authoritarianism as an acceptable style; (5) A growing belief in the values of pluralism, decentralization, participation, involvement; (6) A heightened respect for individual conscience and dignity; (7) An increased public impatience, a "lower frustration tolerance," with many forms of economic hardship (such as poverty and unemployment), and with social injustice in all its forms.

In sum, these (and other) changes would quite radically reorder our public and private values. Particularly among the young and the better-educated, we are likely to see a shift in emphasis:

(1) From considerations of quantity ("more"), toward considerations of quality ("better"); (2) From the concept of independence, toward the concept of interdependence; (3) From the satisfaction of private material needs, toward meeting public needs; (4) From the primacy of technical efficiency, toward considerations of social justice and equity; (5) From the dictates of organizational convenience, toward the aspirations of self-development of an organization's members; (6) From authoritarianism, toward participation; (7) From uniformity and centralization, toward pluralism and diversity; (8) From preservation of the systems' status quo and routine, toward promotion and acceptance of change (Wilson 1971: 106).

The authors of the Conference Board document and Ian Wilson seem to have suggested the changing sociocultural conditions and the changed business conditions which will interact in the next several decades. How might corporate individuals themselves react to these altered conditions? In the Conference Board report John McHale led another group of authors into an analysis of this problem. These authors have developed a simple but effective typology of individual responses to changing information environments:

ACCEPTANCE (I) ⟵————————⟶ INDIFFERENCE (III)

Those who accept, become skilled in, and make extensive use of the new information environment to pursue their individual and collective goals: will tend to be future oriented; open to a wide variety of intellectual inputs; their sources of reward and punishment may depend on traditional styles or derive from new role definitions of man.	Those "functionally" affluent through their own entrepreneurial or other skills and/or through subsidy able to remain indifferent to the demands of the new information environment may tend to be: unmotivated by commitment or ideology towards closer participation; undereducated in its potentials so as to be unresponsive to it or seek its use only where compatible with their specific desires and satisfactions; as consumption/play oriented, will measure public action only in terms of more immediate impacts on, or threats to, their security.
Those unable to use the new information environment because they are socially or culturally inadequate, i.e. as a result of inadequate education* or discrimination, will tend towards: values and life-styles oriented towards those now considered conventional as to right/wrong, worthy/unworthy, etc.; insulating themselves from information disturbing to such value systems; being ineffective in using the changing environment — and knowing it.	Those who reject the larger implications of the new information environment — including some who are occupationally skilled in the area: may be actively or passively alienated from the commitments of the larger society and tend to be ideologically separated from it; will live by different values and life-styles and either be reclusive in their personal orientation or activity-engaged in "outward" social movements.

INADEQUACY (IV) ⟵————————⟶ REJECTION (II)

Figure 1. Typology of individual responses to changing information environments

Thus do the Peter and Paul principles become clearer as we understand that business and other leaders may well fall within the three "low coping" cells in the two-by-two typology.

To achieve a measure of control over adaptation to changing sociocultural environments, corporations and other organizations need to pay much more attention to long-range goals and to recognize that the study of alternative futures is not irresponsible behavior, but

---

* Inadequate education is here meant to include the education provided most people who will populate the next twenty years — an education that leaves them incompetent in analytic and synthetic cognitive skills, in interpersonal relationships, and in self-understanding (The Conference Board of New York 1972b).

behavior necessary to prepare the present so that desirable futures may emerge. Gerald Feinberg (1969, 1971) has made an excellent case for the utility of long-range goals for humanity, and the National Goals research staff, created by President Nixon in 1969, has attempted the same task but with less flair (1970). In June, 1971 the electric utilities industry published *Electric utilities industry research and development goals through the year 2000*, a report of the Research and Development Goals Task Force to the Electric Research Council. (Interestingly enough, this document featured a cover quotation from Albert Einstein as follows: "The concern for man and his destiny must always be the chief interest of all technical effort.") F. D. Barrett (1971) asserting that the "new breed of worker" will *demand* the right to be heard and to share in organizational thought and decision making, puts a great deal of stock in "creativity" as a means of moving business organizations ahead. His principal mechanism seems to be an expanded suggestion system. H. Wentworth Eldredge (1970) has proposed six "pay-offs" for long-term operational goaling. We believe that Eldredge's points are directly applicable to the problems of business and provide an excellent justification for the Future Trends course:

Social change projection. Guidelines may here be glimpsed as to what "surprise-free projections" and the "standard world" of the future will be like.

Alternate possible futures. This forces creativity and can be coupled with hardheaded Plan-Program-Budget Systems (PPB). It most certainly upsets the trite acceptance of a given value system and a unilinear evolutionary process. It reaffirms the faith that all planners have in potential trend-bending and in building "desired states."

Process. Futurism consists of what will be, what might be, why and how to bend the trend. Process, as stated above, is implicit in this form of intellectual/operationally oriented exercise.

Value shifts (possible ones) are forced to a high level of attention. This is the most sensitive part of all macro-time-scale planning and perhaps the most thought provoking.

National economic and social accounting. The whole question of monitoring change and the sophisticating of our present inadequate and too shrewd monetary accounting, so ably presented by Bertram M. Gross and by Sheldon and Moore is brought to the fore. Mention should be made ... of immediate possibilities for the combination of information systems and sampling to amplify our hard data on "soft" (social, aesthetic, etc.) questions.

People planning. The best of macro-time-planning programs can founder on shoals of babies — not to mention nonmodern adults.

... each sub-system is not an end in itself; it is a portion of a whole. All thought and action must be holistic to work in the real world leading toward [an operationally useful policy] (Eldredge 1970: 14).

Using different language, Maruyama has called for the "de-monopolarization of epistemologies" to allow for "trans-epistemological process" ("true" education). The methods Maruyama proposes for the development of true learning are based on trans-epistemological experiences which were in many ways built into the Future Trends Program:

The methods I propose are: (1) exposure to various existing epistemologies such as non-Aristotelian logics, the nonhierarchical epistemology of the Nava-jos and Eskimos, the Chinese logic of complementarity, Einstein's cosmology, quantum versus wave theory of light, principle of mutual causality in cyberne-tics, measurement versus topology, etc.; (2) minimizing psychological depen-dence upon a single epistemology in order to minimize psychological defen-siveness toward other epistemologies; (3) developing the habit of questioning established theories and definitions; (4) open-minded examination of what is excluded from the present science; (5) use of imagination; and (6) discipline in experiments, data collection, and field experience ("Toward human futuris-tics," this volume).

Under the assumption that Maruyama is correct, the present authors are in the process of developing a new program for the ABC Power Company based upon more advanced hardware and software com-munications technologies. The Future Trends Program for 1972–73 has been redesigned. Several of the major handicaps of the first effort have been removed. One of these is the limitation of the program's "reach" to only about 35 people; at that rate it would take more than a dozen years to reach even 500 people. We have reduced the number of man-hours required for involvement in the course, we have reduced the quantity of materials required for reading and for listening, and we have considerably reduced the need for guest speakers. We have developed an instrument which can be used with equal success inside or outside the company. In effect, we have combined the concept of "Profiles of the Future" with the Future Trends Program and come up with a model which introduces novices to the future and serves as an update system for previous Future Trends participants and other relative sophisticates.

The new design might be called "The Futures Report." It includes a series of ten monthly multimedia presentations each about a half hour in length. Each presentation attempts to capsulize major events, ideas, or trends which relate to changing cultural conditions. The programs are designed to meet the needs of business and professional persons, as well as to inspire average citizens. The set of ten can be used in a series (as a course) or individually. The first in the series is entitled, "What About the Future?" It uses statements read by professional voices, parts of existing tapes, music, and slides from many sources. The second deals with earth as a total system. The remaining titles are: Human and Natural Systems; Varieties of Human Culture; Varieties of Technology; Levels and Types of Human Societies; Potentials in Human Organization; Images of the Future: World Culture; Images of the Future: The Individual.

The Futures Report is a "skeleton" around which many other things can be built. Our thought is to identify groupings of not more than twenty-five people each. These might include all the ABC division managers, all department heads, all officers, an entire department, or it could include a mix within the company or a mix of company and noncompany people. Each group could function on its own. One group simply chooses to view the presentation each month; if so, it cannot avoid a brief discussion about alternative futures with someone know-ledgeable such as the authors or someone from last year's Future Trends class. Other groups might choose to meet informally every two weeks. Each presentation will be introduced, viewed, and discussed during a ninety minute period. Reprints, tapes, books, references, media programs, and other resources will be available. A carefully prepared outline or digest of each of the presentations will be distrib-uted. In addition, a monthly newsletter will be circulated announcing the next showing and giving highlights of its contents and suggestions for reading and listening.

The Futures Report is being designed so that it will have a duration of up to three years. It can easily be updated as change occurs. It can be made available to other business groups, used at colleges or universities, and set up in large shopping centers or at conventions. The number of possible uses is immense and will grow as the program is developed.

APPENDIX 1; SURVEY FROM THE *MINNEAPOLIS TRIBUNE* (SUN. AUG. 8, 1971)

Most Minnesotans See Need to Plan Future: Minnesota Poll

There are good and bad situations in store 100 years from now if Minnesotans are right in what they see in the future.

First the good news. According to a majority of the men and women interviewed by the *Minneapolis Tribune*'s Minnesota Poll, the United States will be a leading world power in 2071, pollution will be under control, and Americans will have a strong religious faith. The bad news is that World War III cannot be avoided, hunger and poverty will still be present (according to 49 percent), and some of the world's resources will be completely used up.

After Minnesotans gave their predictions, 56 percent concluded the world of 2071 will be in better shape than it is now, while 37 percent said 1971 is equal to or better than what's in store 100 years from now. Seven percent were undecided. There is almost unanimous agreement in the survey that whatever the future, it will turn out better if we start planning for it now.

The first question asked of a cross-section of 600 adults in July was: "Would you say you are very curious, mildly curious, or not too curious about the future?" Fifty-three percent said very curious, 35 percent mildly curious and 12 percent not curious.

Interviewers next asked about six specific predictions on the future. The questions and answers obtained were:

	WILL	WILL NOT	OTHER OR NO OPINION
One hundred years from now, in 2071, do you think the United States will or will not be one of the leading nations of the world?	65%	28%	7%
Do you think hunger and poverty in the world will or will not be markedly reduced in 2071?	44	49	7
Do you think people will or will not have completely used up any of the world's supply of resources?	57	39	4
Do you think the countries of the world will or will not avoid having another war in the next 100 years?	41	56	3
Do you think pollution will or will not be under control in 2071?	64	33	3
Do you think Americans will or will not have a strong religious faith in 2071?	61	33	6

This is how different segments of Minnesotans are identified as to their optimism or pessimism on the world's condition 100 years from now:

MOOD OF DIFFERENT MINNESOTANS ON WHETHER
WORLD WILL BE IN BETTER SHAPE IN 2071
(All adults = Average)

Men	Average
Women	Average
18–29 years	Average
30–39 years	Optimistic
40–49 years	Optimistic
50–59 years	Pessimistic
60 and over	Pessimistic
Southern Minnesota	Average
Twin cities area	Optimistic
Northern Minnesota	Pessimistic
Adults with grade school education	Pessimistic
High school	Average
College	Optimistic
Catholics	Optimistic
Protestants	Average
Labor union members	Pessimistic

The next question: "Do you think the world could come to an end before 2071?" Fifty-one percent said that it could, 43 percent said it could not, and 6 percent had no opinion.

The last question in the series was: "Do you think we can provide for a better future by planning ahead?" Ninety-three percent said a better future can be had by planning ahead and 5 percent said planning would not help. Two percent had no opinion.

The types and methods of planning for a better future suggested by men and women in the survey include: better preservation of land and resources, urban planning, and housing (38 percent), moral and religious considerations, easing social tensions (20 percent), striving for world peace and cooperation with other nations (16 percent), preservation of freedom and democracy, good government (16 percent), economic planning, elimination of poverty and unemployment (14 percent), population control (13 percent), improving agriculture and food production practices (11 percent), and educational, scientific and technological advances (11 percent).

Men and women in the survey who feel the world generally will be in better shape in 2071 collectively are more confident about each of the specific aspects than are those who said the world will not be in better shape 100 years from now:

BELIEVE:	WORLD WILL BE IN BETTER SHAPE	WORLD WILL NOT BE IN BETTER SHAPE
U.S. will be a leading nation	73%	55%
Hunger and poverty will be markedly reduced	56	28
Some of resources will be used up	51	66
Countries will avoid another world war	45	34
Pollution will be under control	72	53
Americans will have strong religious faith	71	44

The results of the *Minneapolis Tribune*'s Minnesota Poll are based on personal in-the-home interviews with 600 men and women 18 years of age or older. Respondents are selected by probability sampling procedures and interviewed by a staff of 110 trained interviewers. The Minnesota Poll was established in 1944 as a public service.

APPENDIX 2: SURVEY RESULTS

In this report are the combined results of three surveys on the future. The most recent survey was made on October 14, 1971. It involved thirty-one employees of ABC Power Company who are currently participating in a "Future Trends" course. The other two surveys were made during July, 1971. The Minnesota Poll (see Appendix 1), a public service provided by the *Minneapolis Star and Tribune*, questioned Minnesotans about their ideas and attitudes concerning life in the year 2071. This poll was based on interviews with 600 men and women eighteen years of age and older. The respondents were selected by probability sampling procedures and questioned by a staff of 110 trained interviewers.

The second survey involved eighty-three undergraduates at the University of Minnesota. The students, fifty-one women and thirty-three men, were enrolled in one of two summer classes: "Societies of the Future" and "The School and Society." Both classes stressed materials on the future and were taught by Associate Professor Arthur M. Harkins. The survey was given during the first few days of school. Although this survey is not based on a representative sampling of university student opinion, it provides an interesting contrast to the Minnesota Poll which tends to reflect general public opinion.

1. Would you say you are very curious, mildly curious, or not too curious about the future?

	ABC	M	MN POLL
very curious	55	53	53
mildly curious	39	43	35
not too curious	3	2	12
Other or no opinion	3	1	0

2a. Do you think the United States will or will not be one of the leading nations of the world in 1980?

	ABC	UM
will	97	95
will not	3	2
No opinion or other	0	2

2b. In 2000?

	ABC	UM
will	84	75
will not	13	17
No opinion or other	3	8

2c. In 2071?

	ABC	UM	MN POLL
will	48	34	65
will not	16	41	28
No opinion or other	35	25	7

ABC COMMENTS:

Depends upon decisions and actions taken in interim, but believe that a more world-wide affiliation will develop.

By then I think more nations will have come to be on an equal basis — otherwise we will not have survived.

3a. Do you think hunger and poverty in the world will or will not be markedly reduced in 1980?

	ABC	UM
will	16	19
will not	84	72
No opinion or other	0	9

3b. In 2000?

	ABC	UM
will	42	56
will not	55	37
No opinion or other	3	6

ABC COMMENTS:
  Good start.

3c In 2071?

	ABC	UM	MN POLL
will	58	69	44
will not	29	14	49
No opinion or other	13	16	7

4a. Do you think people will or will not have completely used up any of the world's supply of resources such as oil, coal, and timber by the year 1980?

	ABC	UM
will	0	21
will not	100	73
No opinion or other	0	6

4b. In 2000?

	ABC	UM
will	26	63
will not	68	29
No opinion or other	6	8

4c. In 2071?

	ABC	UM	MN POLL
will	42	78	57
will not	39	8	39
No opinion or other	19	13	4

5a. Do you think the countries of the world will or will not avoid having another world war by 1980?

	ABC	UM
will	84	66
will not	16	24
No opinion or other	0	10

5b. By 2000?

	ABC	UM
will	55	56
will not	32	28
No opinion or other	13	16

ABC COMMENTS:
  If other than "a" we will have ceased to exist. ("a" refers to first response.)

5c. Do you think the countries of the world will or will not avoid having another war in the next 100 years?

	ABC	UM	MN POLL
will	45	56	41
will not	32	21	56
No opinion or other	23	23	3

ABC COMMENTS:
Hope so but cannot offer informed opinion.

6a. Do you think pollution will or will not be under control in 1980?

	ABC	UM
will	13	13
will not	87	82
No opinion or other	0	5

6b. In 2000?

	ABC	UM
will	68	58
will not	29	33
No opinion or other	3	10

ABC COMMENTS:
Possibly, but not completely. New forms of pollution will have been iden-tified.

6c. In 2071?

	ABC	UM	MN POLL
will	74	87	64
will not	10	7	33
No opinion or other	16	6	3

7a. Do you think Americans will or will not have a strong religious faith in 1980?

	ABC	UM
will	58	37
will not	39	48
No opinion or other	3	14

ABC COMMENTS:
Majority will not.

7b. In 2000?

	ABC	UM
will	58	22
will not	32	58
No opinion or other	10	21

7c. In 2071?

	ABC	UM	MN POLL
will	45	17	61
will not	29	56	33
No opinion or other	26	26	6

8a. Do you think the world will or will not be in better shape in 1980 than it is now?

	ABC	UM
will	65	35
will not	29	53
No opinion or other	6	12

ABC COMMENTS:
Not necessarily yet — but on the way.

8b. In 2000?

	ABC	UM
will	77	65
will not	10	18
No opinion or other	13	17

ABC COMMENTS:
This I feel will be a turning point in history and improvements will be made after this year.

8c. In 2071?

	ABC	UM	MN POLL
will	68	63	56
will not	10	11	37
No opinion or other	23	27	7

9a. Do you think the world could come to an end before 1980?

	ABC	UM
could	42	60
could not	42	31
No opinion or other	16	9

ABC COMMENTS:
But I don't believe it will; highly improbable.
It could by some natural event however I doubt it. I also doubt very much whether man will destroy it.
Armageddon could come at any time before 1980, not to destroy the earth, but to remove the wicked system of mankind.

9b. In 2000?

	ABC	UM
could	42	63
could not	42	24
No opinion or other	16	13

ABC COMMENTS:
Armageddon will have come before 2000.

9c. In 2071?

	ABC	UM	MN POLL
could	45	66	51
could not	39	18	43
No opinion or other	16	16	6

10. Do you think we can provide for a better future by planning ahead?

	ABC	UM	MN POLL
yes	97	93	93
no	3	4	5
No opinion or other	0	3	2

REFERENCES

BARRETT, F. D.
  1971 Tomorrow's management: creative and participative. *The Futurist* 5 (1): 12–13.
ELDREDGE, H. WENTWORTH
  1970 "Toward a national policy for planning the environment." Reprinted from *Urban planning in transition*. New York: Grossman.
FEINBERG, GERALD
  1969 Mankind's search for long-range goals. *The Futurist* 3 (3): 60–63.
  1971 Long-range goals and the environment. *The Futurist* 5 (6): 241–246.
GOLDSMITH, E., R. ALLEN, M. ALLABY, J. DAVOLL, S. LAWRENCE
  1972 A blueprint for survival. *The Ecologist* 2 (1).
GORDON, T., D. L. LITTLE, H. L. STRUDLER, D. D. LUSTGARTEN
  1971 "A forecast of the interaction between business and society in the next five years." Report R-21 for the Institute for the Future, April 1971. Middletown, Connecticut.
JACOBSON, REX
  1972 "An interim appraisal of the ABC Future Trends Program." Report to the ABC Power Company (April 10).
MEADOWS, DENNIS L.
  1971 The predicament of mankind. *The Futurist* (August): 137–144.
MEADOWS, D. H., D. L. MEADOWS, J. RANDERS, W. W. BEHRENS III
  1972 *The limits to growth.* New York: Universe Books.
NATIONAL GOALS RESEARCH STAFF
  1970 A nation seeks its goals. *The Futurist* 4(4): 113–118.

PLATT, JOHN
    1969   What we must do. *Science* 166 (November 28): 1115–1121.
RESEARCH AND DEVELOPMENT GOALS TASK FORCE
    1971   "Electric utilities industry research and development goals through the year 2000." Report to the Electric Research Council. Electric Research Council Publication No. 1–71.
THE CONFERENCE BOARD OF NEW YORK
    1972a "Executive digest," in *Information technology.* New York.
    1972b "Information technology, some critical implications for decision makers." Report No. 537
WILSON, IAN H.
    1971   The new Reformation, changing values and institutional goals. *The Futurist* 5 (3).
WOODS, RICHARD G.
    1971   "The management of private enterprise: progress for the future." Report for the Office for Applied Social Science and the Future. University of Minnesota.
    1972   "Future Trends in retrospect." Report presented at the final meeting of the ABC Future Trends Program, June 8.

SECTION EIGHT

*Future Cultural Alternatives:
Imaginative Use of
Anthropology*

A Future History

C. GEORGE BENELLO

In 2010 the scientist, Eskowitz, discovered the principle of time travel. At that time science was a state monopoly, since dwindling resources had made scientific research very costly. The United States of North America (into which Canada had some decades before been incorporated), the Soviet Union, China, and the United States of Europe were the only states that could afford major research. The space program had long since been given up, and thereafter research was devoted mainly to the development of food resources and the expansion of solar and other forms of nonextractive energy.

However, in North America one other project was given the highest priority. A small group of policy makers had become convinced that the only hope of maintaining even a minimum level of civilization was to go back and undo some of the havoc wrought in the twentieth century. This hope emerged after the accidental discovery that certain kinds of subatomic transformations seemed to have the capacity to warp time. At first the discovery led nowhere, but under the direction of Eskowitz, a nuclear physicist who had developed a theory of the reversibility of atomic transformations, hope rose that it might indeed be possible to create a means of reversing the flow of time under certain very limited conditions.

The North American Department of Research quickly set up the top-secret Iroquois Project, employing some of the most reputed physicists in the country. It was decided that even though the potential results of the project might be universally beneficial, the potential dangers were so great, that it was desirable to proceed with the greatest secrecy. Moreover, by that time the major governments had become highly centralized as a result of the imperative need to utilize most effectively the few resources left, and the possibility of any general policy consultation, either with citizens of North America or with those of any other country, simply never occurred to them.

By the year 2015 the project had had a limited degree of success. It was possible to transport objects and small animals backward in time through the creation of a localized time warp which, when its effects faded, brought the animal or object back to the present, relatively unchanged. Finally, using one of the larger solar fields to generate the necessary energy, a force field was created large enough to transport a man. At that point social scientists were invited to explore the possibilities of introducing a man, properly equipped with the necessary information and apparatus, into some critical juncture of the past, in the hope that this might skew the path of history sufficiently to halt the series of exponential growth rates, which by the twenty-first century had ruined the world economy, created mass starvation, and nearly sparked a nuclear war. This was averted only when North America and the Soviet Union accepted a World Resources Control Authority, for which other states had been pressing for some time.

The problem set before the social science group was a next-to-impossible one: to sufficiently skew the course of history to prevent the world resource crisis and the consequent social and political crises, by introducing one man into a temporally limited period of the past. It was calculated that by temporarily rerouting energy from some of the major solar fields in the southern part of North America, it might be possible to sustain one man for one week — and not more than two — before the time warp faded. This diversion of energy would not only be noticed but would cause severe consumer and industrial shortages. However, a technical emergency could be declared, and, given the power of the centralized government, little adverse reaction was anticipated.

The social science group at the Iroquois Project in the course of their deliberations soon rejected the possibility of changing history by any sort of rational argument with past authorities. The weak governments of pre-crisis states could not be expected, even if they had the will, to create the kind of socially responsive planning and overall control of population growth, resource expenditure, and industrial growth that would be necessary to avert the crisis that had occurred. Alternatives were discussed but all were clearly inadequate for the task. Then a sociologist named Lederson, whose brilliance had forced his inclusion in the group despite his political radicalism, made a suggestion which was at first rejected with horror, but, in the absence of any feasible alternative, was finally discussed seriously. Lederson proposed to assassinate President Roosevelt and the key industrial and political leaders responsible for the United States recovery from the Great Depression. To buttress his proposal, he stated that what had prevented the United States economy from complete collapse was the adroit response of Roosevelt and his New Deal assistants, but above all, Roosevelt's charisma and power as a political leader. These characteristics allowed him to initiate measures contrary to the existing capitalist ideology, despite opposition from the moneyed interests. Roosevelt's measures, however, did not so much change, as salvage the capitalist system. Lederson argued that it was the system of mature capitalism and growing corporate power which dictated the continuing need for unrestrained economic expansion, and population growth in order to provide the steady consumer demand needed by the productive apparatus.

Some of his fellow social scientists disagreed with Lederson, pointing to the inability of Russia to develop any ways to better contain either economic or population growth. But Lederson had an answer to that too. He pointed out that no other advanced industrial nation had gone through a crisis as extensive as that of the Great Depression, or one wherein the recovery had been so dependent on changes instigated essentially by one man. There was the possibility, he claimed, that if the recovery had not taken place, the United States might well have been induced to change the system radically. He agreed moreover that any change had to go beyond simply transforming the capitalist system into a centralized socialist system, which he said was really a form of state capitalism. It had to involve a fundamental transformation of values, leading to a rejection of the ideal of continued and unrestrained growth. And he claimed that he saw the way this could be done.

William Rapaport, a visiting fellow at the Institute of Advanced Behavioral Studies in Kingston, North Central Region, was originally a biologist. But his interests had led him into broad ecological studies of the relationship between social and cultural systems and the ways in which they utilize technology and the natural resources of the environment. Unlike many scientists given to a broad systems orientation, he had an active interest in history. And, at this point he thought he had a possible solution to a puzzle he had been aware of for some time. It was becoming increasingly evident that the world system was stabilizing itself at the time — 2018 — following a model that had been first developed in the United States of North America. For some sixty years the United States had been in a steady state with a stabilized population and economy. The Soviet Union shortly thereafter began to move in the same direction, and the consequent changes in the structure of world trade caused the developing nations to follow suit.

Moreover, cultural values had changed correspondingly. Out of the

chaos of the Great Depression and the almost total collapse of the
world trade system, there emerged a profound reaction to the happy-
go-lucky materialism which characterized early twentieth century development. In the United States, the prolonged social and cultural
breakdown that attended the economic collapse gave birth to various
religious movements. Predominant among these movements was a
fundamentalist messianism and a dormant utopianism such as had
flowered in the eighteenth and early nineteenth centuries and were
now revivified. The people of the United States, seeing their downfall
in predominantly moral terms, turned to religion with a vengeance.
Just as they had previously explained material success by seeing it as a
sign of religious redemption, so now they explained material failure as
a sign of God's wrath at their dissolute and materialistic ways.

Out of the chaos of exotic sects, importations from the Orient,
astrology, and magic, there emerged a strong counterculture movement in the 1940's characterized by a fundamental rejection of the
success ethic. It manifested itself initially in a back-to-nature reaction
and in communes, planned communities, a revival of the crafts, and an
ethic of love and brotherhood. But the extensive disenchantment with
the profit system meant that this movement was not simply an eddy in
the cultural mainstream. It was taken up by one of the Christian
congregations which combined religious revivalism with a sort of social
gospel concern for social reform. The leaders of this congregation,
having come across a set of documents by an unknown author and
addressed specifically to their congregation, were persuaded to consider seriously the implications of these documents. They managed in
the process to create a kind of socioreligious movement which had
certain similarities to the Soka Gakkai, a semi-religious movement
which by 1980 had become the major social and political force in
Japan.

It was here that Rapaport's historical studies had first begun to raise
some perplexing questions for him. The level of analysis in these
documents, which had come to be known as the Survival Code, was
clearly not within the tradition of reform Protestant theology, even
though the language seemed carefully — perhaps too carefully —
couched in such a fashion that it could not fail to appeal to the
theological concern of the congregation. In effect, the Code, if one
translated its theological language into a more sociological context,
constituted a thorough and detailed analysis of how the congregation
in question could become the vehicle for a thoroughgoing change in
the direction of American culture. The Code pointed to the resemblances between the counter culture and the early Christian
church, and indicated that what the movement needed most of all was
some culturally acceptable form which could translate its somewhat

esoteric insights into a language which the American man-in-the-street, profoundly disenchanted with what had happened to the American Dream, could understand and adopt as his own.

For Rapaport the matter rested there; the Code raised some interesting questions: its emphasis on the absolute necessity for a changed set of cultural values seemed to him prescient, and the sophistication of its discussion of positive feedback mechanisms, exponential growth, and runaway technology seemed to him to go far beyond the scope of the theological thinking of that time. But the Code was an isolated phenomenon, and the author remained unknown. Rapaport saw no way to clarify the mystery. However, his appointment as a visiting fellow to the Institute for Advanced Behavioral Studies in the year 2018 gave him the opportunity to pursue his historical researches. Rapaport then decided that any further clues would have to be sought elsewhere, and he determined to make a thorough study of the whole period in which the fundamental change in orientation in North American society had occurred.

He started by making a broad inventory of the major features of the present social system in North America. His focus had hitherto been on the ecological aspects of the system, and he now began to fill in the picture by applying the same broad systems approach to the social and cultural structure. The chaos and social breakdown of the great Depression had resulted in a fundamental break with the old system of uncontrolled production, consumption, and technological advance. But, while the resulting society was clearly following a different path, it was also clear that the notion of progress had not been lost, but rather transformed. The dynamism that characterized the previous period had been retained, but there had also developed an idea of limits — limited growth, limited technological advance, limited international involvement. The sense of endless physical and geographical vistas, which had characterized early American society with its continuous movement westward, had halted instead of being transformed into various forms of international expansionism, space races, endless productivity, and ever increasing GNP.

In its place the collapse of the previous system had first created a period of self-doubt and questioning. While chaos prevailed, during the thirties and early forties, social critics happily proclaimed the downfall of industrial society, and foresaw the fall of the American Empire in terms similar to that of the fall of the Roman Empire. Attempts to rebuild the industrial structure had all but failed because of the mass defection of youth and the confusion and social and political polarization of the older members of society. As with the Roman Empire, there had been a mass turning to mystery cults, apocalyptic forms, chiliastic visions of the Second Coming. But no

Messiah arrived to summon the faithful. However, an organization did emerge, which embraced the utopian vision of the counterculture and a Christian vision based on the early church and the tradition of radical Christianity that drew on Hus, the Quakers, the Hutterites, and other radical Christian sects.

Under the leadership of the Church of the New Reform — the congregation possessing the Survival Code — the growing religious impetus was organized and given direction. The organizational form was that of close-knit support groups whose members vowed to assist one another, while at the same time working to create a new society. As with the Soka Gakkai, the new movement, which called itself "The Brotherhood," was committed to creating the Heavenly City in this world rather than in the next. And, with Gramsci, it was committed to the idea of creating an overall social and cultural hegemony which left out nothing that was human. At first, it was linked to the counterculture in creating land-based communes. It then moved into the cities, creating living cooperatives and communes, then work cooperatives, and finally integrated cooperatives in which people worked and lived.

In doing this, it maintained its broad religious emphasis, which focused on the idea of *koinonia*, the ancient idea of brotherhood wherein salvation is not achieved individually but as an essentially communal act. This return to an ancient Christian concept constituted a major break with the individualism of Protestant Christianity. Another important break, which brought the Brotherhood into line with the growing counterculture movement, lay in its alignment with the Oriental view of man as part of nature. Rather than seeing man as the apex of all creation, the Brotherhood emphasized the ecological and spiritual unity of all things, seeing divinity as immanent in rocks and stones. This view coincided with the Code's doctrine that, unless man could see himself in a new relation to nature which respected all nature as part of the divine, he was in danger of destroying the ecological balance which alone made life on the planet possible. In short, the Brotherhood religion rejected the dualistic element in Christianity in favor of a more immanentist doctrine, congruent with Christian mystics such as Meister Eckhart and St. Francis of Assissi. The social manifestation of this doctrine lay in the notion of communal rather than individual salvation.

The manifestations of this Brotherhood religion were varied; it reintroduced the ancient idea of meditation, which had been largely lost in the Western religions. But it also reintroduced the idea of celebration, with large public festivals and ceremonies, and with the encouragement of art and drama having both religious and social emphasis. From these ideas annual religious rock-music festivals developed in various parts of the country, which drew together hundreds of thousands of young people and combined some of the features of rock festivals and revival meetings. These meetings were in fact membership drives out of which new cells, blocks, and regional units were formed so as to maintain and strengthen the impetus of the annual festivals.

The Brotherhood, although aware of political power, did not seek to create a political party. Its thinking, based on the Code, which reflected the thinking of theorists such as Buber and Landauer, led it to conclude that political power could only be contained and made functional if it was based on a healthy society, and in particular on institutions capable of successfully embodying the new value orientations. The Code had presented a vision in which the conquest of outer space was changed to the quest for mastery of inner space. The Promethean urge, which had hitherto characterized North America, was thus transformed into a dynamism which found expression in the cultivation of the world of the imagination and inner vision. Arts and crafts abounded, giving rise to new tastes in clothing and interior decoration. ESP became popular, and a large organization of telepathists was formed, with the avowed objective of seeking to supplement, if not replace, electronic communication with direct forms of extrasensory perception. Creativity was studied extensively, and curricula developed, starting in primary school, oriented toward the development of creativity rather than the mastery of facts.

The fact that the Brotherhood made no ostensible attempt to seek political power gave it a broad influence above sectarian political debate. The Code had outlined a strategy which emphasized cultural hegemony rather than political power, and broad geographic expansion which made no attempt to take over or confront the political and economic institutions surviving from the pre-Depression period. Instead the movement simply flowed around them, working largely in neighborhoods throughout the land, and building its own institutions in the interstices of the old system. As the movement grew, it coalesced, creating its own ecosystems of basic institutions embodying cultural and religious life, and education. It created community centers, and, as it developed further, work communities. In doing this, it moved into what was essentially a vacuum, since the old system had been so extensively discredited that people were eager to join a movement which promised a new way of life.

Around the last quarter of the twentieth century, the Brotherhood counted fifty million members, in a state of 200 millions which extended from the Arctic to the Rio Grande. Population was stabilized at that level, and industrial growth, under the pressure of selective boycotting by the Brotherhood, had come to a standstill. Although there had been a worldwide war in the forties which had split the

Brotherhood, a large part of which was anti-war and pacifist, anti-war pressures had seen to it that no continuing military establishment emerged from World War II. The Brotherhood reunited around the position that peace and world security could best be achieved by creating in the United States of North America a peaceful, nonexploitative society which could be the model for other states.

In the last decade of the twentieth century the Brotherhood started to consolidate its position as the dominant movement within the United States. Although it was still a minority of eighty millions, it possessed effective power, since no other organized sector of the nation claimed more than a fraction of such membership, much less a comparable level of commitment. The Code had indicated that the two remaining powers to be dealt with were the remaining corporations and the state. While the Brotherhood had grown in a period when the state, already weakened by the Depression, had then been forced to turn its energies to war, the corporations presented a different problem. At first the Brotherhood was not seen as a threat, and it was allowed to grow and develop its small producer cooperatives and communities of work. But with growth its implicit challenge to the economic system became evident. The primary industry sector which remained in the hands of the old industrialists attempted to crush the budding economic institutions of the Brotherhood by cutting off raw materials.

The Brotherhood responded with a series of boycotts. Members sold their cars and refused to buy new ones. They refused to buy consumer goods and made do with what they had. In addition they organized their membership among blue collar workers and threatened a series of wildcat strikes. At that point the government, haunted by the specter of another bout of economic chaos and collapse, stepped in with legislation to force industry to trade with the Brotherhood. The final result of this attempt to strangle the economic growth of the Brotherhood was to discredit the remaining pre-Depression industrialists, and revive all the suspicions of big business which had arisen during the Depression. The Brotherhood then went on the offensive, arguing that only under Brotherhood control would the country be safe from business interests which otherwise would continue to seek profit at the expense of others, and of the general social good.

A giant fund-raising drive netted three billion dollars, and with this and the leverage of its influence on the country's banks, the Brotherhood proceeded to buy out the majority of the old industrialists. Following the approach outlined in the Code, it set up a complex system involving work units within the factories, with delegates within the enterprise forming policy committees, which were in turn coordinated with committees of consumers and local community members.

These committees laid down policy guidelines on working conditions, production goals, personnel policies, pollution standards, and the use of surplus. A joint governing committee made up of delegates from the three groups of workers, consumers, and community members was set up to head the enterprise. Rather than restricting itself to the notion of profit, it considered the disposal of the total productive surplus of the enterprise, and decided how much to reinvest, how much to pay to workers, and how much to use for community enterprises and community betterment.

With control of the primary sector of industry in their hands, the Brotherhood began to turn its attention to the problem of government. Already many areas of local government were controlled by Brotherhood members, and at the local level the network of institutions created by the Brotherhood exercised actual control of local government. In effect, the political system, which recognized only the individual vote, and was thus susceptible to takeover by organized interests which could control voting blocks, began slowly to give way under pressure from the Brotherhood. Up to this point the Brotherhood had kept clear of national politics. But with the control of the economy in their hands, the need was evident for some form of sociopolitical coordination. Accordingly, it formed a political arm, the New Democracy Party, and proclaimed as its goal the total restructuring of political institutions in the state.

With the emerging social goals that were the result of the Brotherhood's efforts to create a decentralized, democratically controlled economy, the need for a more functional political system had become evident, and so there was nothing especially novel about the Brotherhood's platform. But with characteristic thoroughness, it had worked out its plan for restructuring in detail, and distributed widely a pamphlet describing the plan. The philosophical basis was that the group, not the individual, was the locus of the political process, since only in the group could ongoing decision making take place. Its plan thus resembled guild socialist models of the early twentieth century, but was expanded to include all basic organizations. In broad outline, it resembled the Yugoslav system of self-government, but with several differences. For one, in place of a single premier, it provided a Governing Committee, made up of five people chosen by a Congress elected as described below. This committee was made responsible for the ongoing administration of the government, but was strictly subject to congressional policy control. Congress was made up of four Assemblies: the Assembly of Nationalities, which represented racial and ethnic minorities; the Assembly of Services, which represented health, education, and other public services; the Assembly of Producers, which represented the industrial sector; and the Regional Assembly, which represented the twelve major geographic regions of the United States of North America. This structure was reproduced in the regions themselves, except that in place of the Regional Assembly there were Public Assemblies, of delegates from subregions — variously counties and cities.

Moreover, the plan was to create basic ecological-political units, although this was seen as a long-term task. These units, defined as the smallest ecological units capable of a full social and cultural life, with populations of from 10,000 to 300,000 were to be brought into being by decentralizing the cities and creating a variety of smaller centers so planned that they would be economically and culturally self-sufficient. These units, when developed, would then form the basic units of the political system. Following the principle of merging the political with the social, these units would to a large degree be autonomous, following their nature as basic ecological units. They would be governed by an assembly of delegates from all the major institutions, and social and ethnic groups within them. Enfranchisement would depend on recognition of the right of a new group to send a delegate to the assembly. Rather than operating through a political party apparatus with vested interests of its own, therefore, the political sphere was seen as nothing more than a forum for the coordination of society's existing institutional systems.

The development of this plan, especially at basic unit level, was to be through an iterative-evolutionary process in which the final shape of the units would result from initiatives taken within broadly defined boundaries, leading to a closer definition of the shape and makeup of those boundaries. The Brotherhood believed that little of the final economic, social, and cultural shape of society could be forecast or extrapolated from the existing system, dependent as it was upon a separation of the public and private sectors, and upon the proliferation of economic and social institutions which were national and even multinational in scope. Until this system was replaced by one in which all control was placed within the ecological unit — and this meant the creation of economic centers and population centers defined by these units — it was felt that defining the nature and makeup of the ultimate ecological units would be impossible.

The merging of the political and the social, combined with the granting of maximum autonomy to the basic units, gave rise to a principle of decentralization: that in a functional system, all power that could be exercised locally would be retained at local level. Only those services and activities that were by their nature regional or national would be administered on those levels. Since the economy was now almost entirely dependent on nonextractive forms of power — mainly solar energy — this meant a division between the amount of power that could be produced locally, which, in the case of the Southern Region, was most of it, and the power which had to be fed to the Northern Region from the gigantic solar fields in the South. Economic planning was to be divided between the regions, since it was on this level that variations in economic resources were most prominent, and it was on this level that the basic ecological units where production was organized were located.

The Brotherhood proceeded to campaign extensively for its plan to restructure the political system. Aware by then that its organized voting power meant that its essay into politics could brook no significant opposition, it concentrated its efforts on a program to convince nonmembers that it did not seek to take over political power, but to dissolve political institutions, as such, completely. It affirmed its intention of dissolving the New Democracy Party after the elections and argued that only by decentralizing and debureaucratizing the political system, as it had already done to a large degree with the economic system, could the political system be made to truly respond to people's needs.

As part of its program it carried on a series of local campaigns aimed at public service bureaucracies, exposing cases of irresponsible administration and misuse of public funds. Since this was the last holdout of bureaucratic and centralized administration within a culture already grown suspicious of centralization and bureaucracy, it was not difficult to persuade people that education and other public services should be totally reorganized. Welfare would be done away with, and a guaranteed income given to those unable to work and to apprentices, pupils and students. At the same time, work need not be alienating, as the Brotherhood had amply demonstrated, and it argued that everyone with the capacity to do so had the responsibility to make some form of productive contribution to society.

By then, with the collapse of the ethos that linked work with profit, work had been redefined to include all socially useful activity, including child care, housework, and cultural creation. Within its production cooperatives and communities of work, the Brotherhood had narrowed income level differentials to about 1 : 3. This difference in incomes functioned to reward skill and training as well as leadership, not so much out of a feeling that it was necessary to maintain incentive as out of the belief that income still represented an appropriate reward, although only a partial one, for the development of exceptional ability and commitment. Since members of the Brotherhood's work organizations did not care so much about income, which they tended increasingly to regard as a right, as they did about job satisfaction and the excitement of taking part in a nation-wide social experiment, income differences were of only minor importance.

The Brotherhood argued that public services should be brought into line with the values and organization principles expressed in its productive organizations, and pointed to the vastly greater efficiency and lower administrative overheads of its own organizations compared to those of the unwieldy government bureaucracies. This argument, probably more than any other, served to convince nonmembers that the Brotherhood program of political reform was in the interests of everyone. The New Democracy Party gained an overwhelming political victory, despite the small number of holdouts for the old order who came largely from the higher echelons of government, and who saw their positions and high salaries threatened. In a last effort to preserve their positions, they brought an action against the New Democracy Party, claiming that it was simply an agent and tool of the Brotherhood. The Brotherhood, they argued, was a sectarian religious organization, and because of the constitutional rule separating church and state, could not lawfully engage in political activity. Whatever the merits of the case, no judge was about to declare the election invalid in the face of the landslide that had occurred, and so the New Democracy Party, having won, was forthwith dissolved. The President, a certain Lester Hardy, not actually a member of the Brotherhood although sympathetic to its aims, supported by a majority in both houses of Congress, began the long task of overhauling the political system.

The new government structure took its form from the cultural values which had developed in the latter half of the twentieth century. Rejecting the old obsession with production and economic growth, the focus of government shifted to concern for cultural development which had already served to turn back the tide of increasing homogenization of culture and massification of society. Local and regional differences had begun to appear again and, encouraged by the Brotherhood, had taken the form of the development of indigenous architectural styles, craft industries, and cultural events. Already much of the consumer economy was organized for local distribution, studies undertaken by the Brotherhood having indicated that much consumer production was most efficiently undertaken on a subregional level. Moreover, with the spread of the Brotherhood's production cooperatives and communities of work, products increasingly took on a character of the locality from which they originated. Tastes changed accordingly, and it became a mark of discrimination to possess household articles and clothing which were locally procured and possessed a local character.

Following the principle of integrating the work place and the household, the Brotherhood encouraged the development of cottage industries and crafts, so that everything from the assembly of electrical components to weaving and pottery was carried on either in the household or in block or village factories within a few steps of where people lived. Also, in the interest of reintegrating institutions into the ongoing forms of local and neighborhood life, the Brotherhood had deinstitutionalized its schools, old people's homes, and mental asylums. The task of educating and caring for the infirm and mentally ill was taken over by the neighborhood as a whole, with the old and the infirm housed in the neighborhood. Education became a matter of apprenticeship in the different institutions of the neighborhood and locality, and all work, service, and cultural organizations were opened to apprenticeship-type learning.

To Rapaport, reviewing the history of the last eighty years, it was apparent that the society in which he lived had a coherence, validity, and broad acceptance by its members that made it appear natural and, in fact, inevitable. The Depression and pre-Depression world had the character of a bad dream from which society had ultimately awakened. But on the other hand, if one made the necessary effort at historical imagination, it became evident that the course of events was far from necessary. Indeed it seemed dependent on a particular set of historical circumstances which stood out by virtue of their uniqueness. Japan, having lost the war, had then developed a mass movement which within twenty years numbered twenty million members. But this movement, the Soka Gakkai, had lacked the historical prescience seemingly possessed by the Brotherhood, and its social analysis, although powerful, was flawed and incomplete.

The Brotherhood, on the contrary, combined in a quite unique fashion, a unifying vision, with a seemingly detailed insight into its execution. This insight seemed to spring from a single source, rather than being the product of collective wisdom. The Brotherhood had made no effort to maintain the Code as an esoteric document, and neither did they claim that it contained any sort of revealed truth, or was the basis of all doctrine. Yet it was clear to anyone who studied the Code carefully that the Brotherhood had used it as the blueprint for their plan of social transformation. The prescience that lay in the Code expressed itself, not so much in any particular prognosis of the course of events, as in a detailed plan for social reconstruction that evidently left nothing out. Moreover, it contained a deep and essentially accurate analysis of the contradictions within the pre-Depression social and economic system. Couched in theological language, it spoke of idolatry, and defined it as the domination of the whole by one part of the social project and human endeavor.

Its analysis of the pre-Depression system did not focus only on the material benefits derived from uncontrolled technological advance, but also brought out its Promethean character. Technology, it said, represented essentially an extension of human power. By linking powerful mechanisms as extensions of the senses, it gave the society operating such mechanisms an unparalleled, but ultimately specious, sense of control over its environment. It spoke of the cybernetic linkups of man and machine via the automobile, the airplane, the telephone, and mass media. With power over the machine, came power over men and the power to influence and sway men's minds. The intoxication with technological power, the Code said, could lead, and indeed was leading, to a crumbling of the relationship between man and nature, between man and man, and consequently between man and God.

If one turned to the Depression itself, at first glance it seemed to possess a character of historical inevitability. Marxism had predicted the downfall of the capitalist system, and the course of events in the United States appeared to be an almost classic fulfillment of that prediction — except that what had emerged was far more complex than the classless society. If one took a closer look, however, questions arose. At first, it looked as if the New Deal administration under Franklin Roosevelt would be capable of salvaging the capitalist system. Certainly the program pointed in the right direction, with a projected massive response by the government in the form of make-work programs, the pumping of government funds into critical sectors of the economy, and a degree of regulation of the excesses of free enterprise. But then, in the face of opposition from the big business interests, Roosevelt had suddenly backed off, and had ended by proclaiming the sacredness of the free enterprise system. He had, in short, abandoned his own program, leaving the economy to its own devices. Then, when a populist opposition movement with socialist leanings emerged, he had smashed it mercilessly, invoking the specter of a Communist conspiracy. His name became a synonym for reactionary and dogmatic anti-Communism, and the purges he instigated in the government guaranteed that none of the New Deal measures, which he himself had helped initiate, would come into effect.

By the end of his first term, the country lay in shambles around the feet of the by-then-discredited administration. The next administration was Republican, and adopted a program that was unabashedly pro-big business. It continued the repressive measures of the Roosevelt administration and succeeded in furthering the polarization of the country. But by that time people were beginning to lose faith in the power of government to solve their problems, and were turning instead to religion and the counterculture. This was the period of the rise of the Brotherhood, and Roosevelt himself, in the remaining years of his life, had turned his energies to the building of the Brotherhood — another seemingly inexplicable reversal of his previous convictions.

Supposing, thought Rapaport, that the response to the Depression was based on something more than the set of collective decisions which made up the usual course of history. Supposing some form of intervention had occurred, which was based on knowledge not available at the time. Leaving aside for the moment the modalities of this intervention, what would be its implications for the present? Assuming that the intervention was human and not divine — and Rapaport was not given to enlarging already implausible hypotheses beyond what was necessary to explain the present — then it would mean, if his suspicions were correct, that the present social system represented a process of conscious planning that had been going on at least since the Roosevelt administration. Rapaport felt intuitively that the chances were historically much more on the side of a recovery of the capitalist system than on the side of any basic change in that system occasioned by the Depression. Yet a deep change had occurred, resulting largely from the seemingly inexplicable behavior of one man, plus the fortuitous rise of an organization which had become, with the aid of some very special knowledge, a social movement. And that knowledge, contained in the Code, Rapaport was convinced was historically suspect.

However, in order to round out the understanding of the present, it was then necessary to fix the other limit in the process of intervention. If it had begun in the Roosevelt administration — presumably sometime in the early thirties — could it have originated in the future? One explanation was some remarkable form of prescience; but mere prescience was one thing, being able to change the course of history was another. It was far more likely that some form of intervention from the future had occurred. If so, since the physics of time-reversible particles had been developed only recently, one could assume that, in the alternate future, technology had not proceeded significantly faster; for while its impact on the social system was controlled, there was no limit to pure research in the present system, and the alternate system was not likely to be much in advance. But what of the limits ahead? Could not the intervention have been planned a century, or for that matter ten centuries ahead of now? However, analysis of the incremental growth processes inherent in the uncontrolled productivity and population growth of pre-Depression times indicated a cataclysm in about the first quarter of the twenty-first century. Moreover, the interlocking character of the positive feedback cycles causing incremental growth made it increasingly unlikely that a systems change would take place before the cataclysm.

This meant first, that unless the intervention had occurred, or rather was to occur in the relatively distant future, it would be most likely to originate in the precataclysm period, on the assumption that it would take a significant amount of time to rebuild the technological system to a point where time travel was possible. Moreover, if the technology of time travel was possible in the precataclysm period, there would be a maximum incentive to develop it then and to use it, before the cataclysm occurred. Hence the time period of the intervention which had altered history would in all probability be either in the alternate recent past, or the near future.

But back to the present, thought Rapaport. Assume that the present was the result of a consciously planned and fundamental change in the course of history. While it would be correct to assume that it was planned mainly to avert a cataclysm (the energy requirements for such an intervention, as Rapaport knew, were enormous, and could only be made available as a national policy decision) would the intervention be limited to trying to ensure the collapse of the industrial system? Presumably, there would also be an attempt to ensure that a sound alternative was created, and this jibed with the role of the Code, which, Rapaport suspected, was far more critical than was admitted. Where had it come from? How had it been planned? Was it mere chance that the policies of the Brotherhood coincided so completely with the teachings of the Code? And more broadly, to what extent was the present society explainable in terms of the Code, or indeed in terms of any consciously worked-out plan? Rapaport always saw this society as characterized by a particular genius — its capacity to transcend the demands of mere survival and move on to develop higher forms of culture. The genius of this society seemed to express itself in its creativity and variety: the imaginative flowering of the arts and sciences, but above all the richness of the very social fabric, the network of human relationships which had evolved in a unique fashion over the last fifty years.

Kingston where Rapaport lived was one of the towns created by the Brotherhood toward the end of the twentieth century, centered originally around a Brotherhood monastery. The Brotherhood had revived monasticism, and established a number of monasteries which embodied varying sets of purposes and life-styles. A few resembled the cloistered monasteries of the Middle Ages, devoted primarily to the contemplative life. But others closely resembled planned communities with a religious orientation, such as the Bruderhof. Most of them devoted themselves to some form of service — running hospitals, caring for the aged and infirm — which they integrated in varying degrees into their daily lives. Rather than poverty, chastity, and obedience, their ideals were brotherhood and service.

Other religious groups had then proceeded to set up their own monasteries, and a number of them ran different enterprises producing craft goods, toys, wine, furniture, and other items. The monastery in Kingston ran a small college primarily for the training of administrators and planners. In many Brotherhood institutions, administration was elective, and the elected were sent for three-month courses at

Brotherhood training institutions. With the rise of religious idealism after the Depression, the Brotherhood felt the need to reintroduce the monastic ideal, seeing it as fitting the needs of the large group of disenchanted young people who had turned their backs on money-making and wished to dedicate their lives to community service. Later, with the proliferation of Brotherhood schools, neighborhood centers, rural communes, and factories, the Brotherhood set up training programs to inculcate administrators in Brotherhood ideals and train them in the forms of elective administration which had evolved. The Kingston monastery was one of the first such centers.

The town had then developed somewhat in the fashion of a college town. The Institute of Advanced Behavioral Studies had been set up by the college, but had achieved a largely separate existence as a center for research into broad social and cultural questions. Social research had, during the latter part of the twentieth century, developed a theory of man which combined elements of a number of different, hitherto fragmented disciplines. From anthropology it took the notion of the primitive culture and refined and developed it into a generalized definition of a folk society applicable to industrialized societies. Anthropology, psychology, and ecology had been used to develop the science of behavioral ecology, which provided a criterion for evaluating the richness of the social environment in terms of significant settings for growth and learning. This then utilized the theory of organization and systems analysis to develop organization and community forms which were ecologically sound, and facilitated maximum human growth.

Behind it all lay progress in evolving a theory of man upon which an empirical development ethic could be based, oriented toward full utilization of human resources and potentialities. In broad terms, this was a humanistic psychology utilizing the notions of meta-needs and stages of development which had come to the fore in the middle and latter half of the twentieth century. In the twenty-first century, attention had been heavily focused on developing a social theory of limits, which would delineate broad outlines within which social construction, facilitative of human growth, could occur. In the early part of the twentieth century much social theory had concentrated on problems of socialization and social control, to offset the alienating character of the system. But after the Depression and consequent breakdown of the normative system, thought focused heavily on social construction and the psychology of liberatory organizations and institutions.

Part of the Institute's research was directed to the application of models developed within the United States, chiefly by the Brotherhood, to other societies which used different paths to cultural and industrial development. Much research went into studies of how economic growth-oriented societies could be changed into economic steady-state systems. This research was heavily occupied with the changes needed in cultural values. Necessarily, much of this research was based on the success of the Brotherhood in changing the whole thrust of culture from what could be described as external-growth orientation to internal-growth orientation.

In addition to the Institute and the monastery, Kingston had a lumber mill and furniture factory. These had been set up as a result of the feeling that the monastery-college and the Institute made Kingston somewhat too etherealized and specialized in intellectual work. Following the principle that the basic ecological and social units should seek to integrate the major social activities, members of the Kingston Assembly had pointed to the lack of space and facilities for manual work, and had decided to develop appropriate enterprises. The choice of woodworking was made because an enterprising cabinet maker had volunteered to set up a woodworking enterprise. Although he was aware that the rewards would not be primarily monetary, he knew that he would receive ample support as well as recognition from the community, so he organized the enterprise with the help of funds provided by the Assembly. When it became evident that a lumber mill would efficiently serve a furniture factory, it too was set up.

One debate that Rapaport had taken part in, had centered upon whether intellectuals in the community should work in the lumber mill and furniture factory. Two positions on the question evolved: the integrationist and the divisionist. While the monastery, reflecting the Brotherhood position, sided with the integrationists, the Institute, reflecting the intellectual tradition derived from pre-Brotherhood days, sided with the divisionists. For the integrationists, the principle that the basic divisions which had characterized the pre-Brotherhood and pre-Depression society should be discarded was seen as applying to the individual. They argued that just as a balance between work and leisure; private, family, and public life; individual and group activity all applied to the individual, so the balance between manual and mental work should also be integrated at the level of the individual.

The Institute agreed with the basic principle of integration, but maintained that it was unreal to apply it at the level of the individual. Rather, they argued, certain forms of integration took place within the basic ecological unit itself. For it was here that rural and urban life were integrated, especially in the new communities created by the Brotherhood. Kingston possessed a large farming sector, some of whose members engaged in other forms of work as well. The planned use of land meant that nobody was far from the countryside and its activities, and the members of the Institute also engaged in farming or craft work. To require that everybody engage in manual as well as intellectual work, would be to enforce a code that had hitherto been voluntary. Moreover, it would endanger the principle of voluntary social participation, which left people free to work alone or in groups. Since no one was required to engage in administrative or committee activity, either on an organizational or an Assembly level, the Institute argued that no one should be required to engage in any particular form of labor either.

But this did not convince the strict integrationists, who maintained (following the Chinese position of a century before) that to allow a group to engage in exclusively intellectual work would be implicitly to encourage the development of an elite. Admittedly, an ecological perspective indicated that all forms of human activity were equally necessary, but certain forms seemed to carry higher rewards than others. The divisionists countered this by arguing that differentiation of functions was acceptable so long as overall integration obtained within the basic social unit. In point of fact, they argued, there was little difference in life-styles or community activities between the members of the Institute and the workers at the furniture plant. Institute members traveled more, but this was because of their work. It was recognized that some work was more challenging.

Although Rapaport tended to side with the divisionists, he suspected that the solution to the argument required that the problem be posed differently. From his position as a sociologist, he saw the problem as demanding organizational rather than individual solutions. Perhaps the Institute as a whole should be required to engage in some specific service to the community. He felt also that the factory's demand that Institute members assist in some fashion was based on a misplaced perception of status difference. The leisure activities of factory workers and Institute members differed along predictable lines: Institute members preferred chess and classical music, while factory members preferred bocce ball and dominoes. Institute members had a leaning toward natural wood-finished bungalow-type houses, while factory members preferred to live in modern houses of synthetic materials. But both supported the local soccer team, and both groups used the local artificial lake and rivers.

It was clear that the Institute, not the college or the monastery, had been the focus of the debate. In many communities the debate had never been raised at all, and it was the existence of the Institute, with its orientation toward pure intellectual work, which had given rise to the differences. The basic problem of the division of labor had been solved, Rapaport felt, with the principle of elective administration, which rotated administrative posts while making policy decisions and also the organization of work matters for decision by the corporate body as a whole. Since the Institute seemed to be the locus of this particular problem, the Institute should probably deal with it as a problem in community relations between itself and the community. Moreover, it was important to notice that, while the debate existed, it was not an acrimonious one, and there was no hostility to individual Institute members.

Kingston, for Rapaport, was representative of the growth of the new society. Centered around the Brotherhood monastery, it lay close to the guiding light of that society. When the monastery institutionalized its outreach activities in the form of a college for planning and administration, Kingston had developed as a kind of laboratory town where student planners and administrators worked in various kinds of apprenticeship situations in local institutions. The monastery held periodic retreats for residents of the surrounding communities. During these an effort was made to engage in an intense group experience by living together closely for several weeks and discussing personal and social objectives and values. In some cases, when the retreat consisted of members of a single community there was a second phase in which the members formed themselves into a planning group, and with the help of college staff, engaged in a kind of buzz session to devise new settings for their community, or to solve community problems.

Physically, Kingston had developed into a town of gardens and assorted apartment houses and private dwellings. But with the founding of the college, studies had been made of the psycho-social development of individuals in Kingston. The development of the environmental settings for psycho-social advancement correlated well with studies of individual growth. The least changes were evident in the generation that had reached maturity during the Depression years, and in the fifties, the time of troubles. The next generation rated much higher on autonomy, self-reliance, altruism, emotional maturity, and openness than did the previous generation. The generation after it, born toward the end of the twentieth century, presented a different picture still. Whereas their fathers presented a composite picture of a generation primarily oriented toward inner and aesthetic values, and often suspicious of external forms of achievement, the new generation took for granted the nonexploitative values, sensitivity toward others, emphasis on affective rather than cognitive values, all of which their fathers had cherished in a rather protective fashion, and thus became a generation of joiners and institution builders, developing many of the extant social and cultural settings.

In a sense they were extroverts, inhabitants of a bright, sunlit world where freedoms were assumed, whereas their fathers and forefathers had fought for these freedoms. Their world had become socially stable, and the time of troubles was merely a distant memory. Stability derived from a shared set of assumptions about the meaning and purpose of life in society. Human growth was all-important, but it could only occur within a close-knit set of interrelationships. For many this framework was provided by the cells of the Brotherhood, but with its coming to power as the dominant institution in society, around the end of the twentieth century, the Brotherhood itself had sought to change that. At this point the Code was of no help, save to suggest that the nuclear family was not a divinely ordained institution.

For the Brotherhood, the problem of replacing the cell structure of its own organization with a working substitute was one of the most difficult it had tackled. It believed that its major function was to lead the way toward the creation of a new culture and a new integration of the social system around new cultural values. For this, new organizational forms were necessary, forms consonant with the new values. But it was believed that human associations should be allowed to form of themselves naturally under the stimulus of the new culture. The problem had to be faced, however, in the area describing the interface between the new formal structure of social institutions created by the Brotherhood and the informal association structure which was developing beneath it. Ideally, the Brotherhood theorists saw a continuation and blending of the formal and informal structures, but this did not solve all the problems of organization. In the case of control of community institutions, how should that control be defined? Should neighborhoods be defined as the minimal social and political units, or, as with the Brotherhood support groups, blocks? What was the role of families? What should the basic unit of representation be?

The answers were made difficult because in the immediate post-Depression period a variety of new close-knit associations had sprung up in response to the overall social breakdown. Families took to creating living communes of three or four families, young people took to communes, and the encounter-group movement took on the form of long-lasting units devoted to individual liberation. There were also women's groups, meditation groups, groups for the mentally disturbed, for addicts, and for alcoholics. Gradually, with the reorganization of society, people began to seek pluralistic attachments again, but even among nonmembers of the Brotherhood various forms of block association sprung up. The Brotherhood's solution was to some extent arbitrary, but successful. After a study of the size and behavior of its cells, which varied from ten to twenty-five or thirty members, it decided that the primary requisite was agglutination, and that groups tended to split of their own accord when they got unwieldy. It therefore proclaimed that any group consisting of twelve members or more could be formally enfranchised as a local unit.

The Brotherhood then proceeded to base all forms of delegation on this unit. In factories work units of twelve or more were set up, and in communities families and individuals formed groups which then developed autonomous functions such as forming commune units, day-care units, cooking or service units, and purchase units for cars, boats, and appliances. Those who chose not to join a group were free to do so. The law simply stated that if one wished to take part in public affairs, the group was the vehicle. This did not require much change in larger structures, and the impact of the system on the existing voluntary and associational structure was small, except to the extent that it normalized it. As this happened, the Brotherhood gradually phased out its own system of support groups, which in many cases simply meant that the group became attached to the local neighborhood social system directly rather than via the Brotherhood.

For Rapaport, the chief impact of the group system on the social structure was that it rendered it permeable, responsive to social initiatives, rather than opaque and unresponsive — the characteristic of pre-Brotherhood organizations. The new generation, as it took its place in society, was not faced with a *fait accompli*, formed, governed, and oriented to the wishes of the previous generation. Thus, rather than having a society whose chief function was to socialize new members to its preexisting purposes and forms, a society arose which was flexible, changing, innovative, and experimental. This was facilitated by having group membership open to all ages. New groups formed and were enfranchised, old groups that had outlived their usefulness ceased to exist or took on new goals. At the same time private goals and values were tempered by the social experience of the groups. No one could, by virtue of prior inheritance or position, dictate goals to others, and hence the stability of the social system was based on its permeability, and through this, its capacity to allow for testing, challenge, and growth on the part of its members.

Kingston was a small community, but the variety of its activities rivaled that of much larger and wealthier communities of pre-Depression times. These activities were open to all, and used by all. As a result of the social disposition of all resources, public settings came to the fore. Rather than the private castles of suburbia, with their own lawns, fences, and largely private life, the life of Kingston was far more public, taking place in squares, parks, playgrounds, plazas, and coffee houses. It was not simply that the settings were there; people were not isolated by their work nor by the ethos of a society given to manipulation and reification. With this change people had come out of their shells, sought contact with one another, and had begun to think of the many settings whereby life could be enriched. The image of the creative person as essentially solitary and estranged gave way to the image of creativity as a manifold activity, sometimes social, sometimes individual, sometimes artistic, but more often involved in the creation of social forms. It was recognized that certain forms of creativity, those involving little or no adverse effects for other people need not be limited. The arts and most crafts fell into this category. Technological invention, on the other hand, was controlled, although the control operated mainly as a general awareness of the need to scrutinize invention carefully so as to understand its social implications. There was no department of technology at any government level. Funds for research were scrutinized, and funding of technological development was subject to the approval of the Assemblies, and through them of the Brotherhood, which continued to exert a strong moral influence of public decision making. However, where creativity gave rise to new social forms, as it increasingly did, there was a concern that the freedom to advance, to achieve prestige and recognition for social innovation, should be balanced by clear limitations on the power of any one person to control the lives of others. Out of this came a system of functional status, open to anyone, but limited in its scope for the exercise of power.

At one point, when his interest in systems theory had been at its highest, Rapaport had helped formulate a systems model capable of being used to evaluate the fit between occupational structure and existing distribution of work interests. The latter had been changing, moving back toward job categories that were organizational and determined by objective standards of success, away from the intense personalism that had characterized the first years after the breakaway from the growth system. It was recognized that an important index of social satisfaction, and consequently a negative index of social pathology, was the fit between the available job categories and individual work interests. The model which Rapaport had helped construct was based on extensive interviewing of both adult workers and the young involved in education and apprentice-type activities, and on data from the Assemblies at different levels on work needs and work demands.

To his surprise, Rapaport had found that the young of both sexes showed an increasing preference for following the vocation of their parents, or a vocation characteristic of their community. The determining value seemed to be a feeling for having roots. Rather than an achieving society, based on neurotic success drives, what had emerged was a communal and rooted society, where achievement was linked to existing emotional ties, to family and community. This provided a built-in stabilizing mechanism, and it soon became evident that the determining criterion of occupation was not so much innate personal preferences as the actual occupational structure within the community where the individual had been born. With the removal of the constriction caused by the profit system, occupational variety had flourished, and the monotony of both work and living environments, characteristic of the pre-Depression culture, had given way to a flowering of individual style and manifold work activities. This had been channeled by the communal nature of the new society into individuation at the ecological community level. By the first decade of the twenty-first century, a wide span of communities, representing a variety of architectural and environmental styles could be found. Many derived their identity from a major activity: some were craft communities, some devoted to tourism and sports, and others were noted for a particular product.

When it became evident to Rapaport that little or no friction was likely to be engendered between the occupational structure and work interests — partly because every community possessed a wide variety of occupations even when a single activity was dominant — he dropped his researches. Since the society had solved the problem of how to admit the young to full membership in the community via apprenticeship situations, and to full involvement in community affairs via the primary-group unit, there seemed to be no further problem in achieving an occupational and interest fit.

Rapaport had then turned to history, because of his conviction that the system's break with the past seemed arbitrary and engineered. Rapaport had been born in 1976, and his childhood had been spent in the ferment of the shaping of the new society during the period when the Brotherhood was consolidating its power over the remaining institutions of the old system, and setting up the forms of government which were to characterize the new system. When he was ten, Rapaport's parents had moved to Kingston, and he had become deeply involved in the development of the new community. By that time, Rapaport was old enough to see the changes in social relationships which had come about as a result of the new social forms. Kingston, like many new commutities, was largely made up of people sick of the old ways and eager to create a society for themselves where exploitation, manipulation, and the general distrust, characteristic of the old society, were absent.

At first a carefulness almost to the point of puritanism had characterized human relationships. People were quick to speak out against others who seemed to retain vestiges of the old ways. There was a suspicion of leadership and elitism of any sort. Within the family the realignment of values caused some friction as well. There had been much discussion of male-female relations, and the women's liberation movement, which had developed so quickly, sometimes broke up marriages and families. But it was recognized that the oppressiveness of the previous system had weighed equally on men as on women, and the major thrust of the women's liberation movement was increasingly directed toward the enhancement of the community through the creation of cluster families and toward affirming the importance of maintaining generational continuity through rebuilding the extended family. Often the older generation, which had grown up in the old system, kept apart. Rapaport's parents had welcomed the change from the start, and for him there was no generation gap to contend with.

Most of the founders of Kingston, including Rapaport's parents, had been Brotherhood members. As such, they had become accustomed to the close, support-group atmosphere of Brotherhood cells, where people were encouraged to criticize themselves and their cell members. For them, the transition to the new social forms was thus facilitated by their cell experience, which these forms simply mirrored and institutionalized in various ways. Rapaport differed from his parents largely in the unselfconsciousness with which he accepted the new ethic of greater intimacy, openness, and honesty, which his parents had had to come to terms with. When Kingston was settled, a major question had been whether the discipline of the cell groups would be sufficient to prevent power-hungry leadership from arising, and along with that, elitism and class distinctions. The initial caution and puritanism based on this self-doubt gradually gave way as the institutional patterns of Kingston formed and evolved. By the turn of the century it was Rapaport's generation which was at the helm, and the focus had shifted from a cautious concern for honest human relationships to the new social vistas. Now that the basic social forms had been created, the new challenge was to apply a humanized technology in ways which could enhance life, without damaging the ecosystem or destroying the close relationship of man to nature.

Rapaport believed strongly in the potentiality of technology to enhance life when harnessed to a humane vision. He knew that it required a mature society, clear as to its fundamental values, to cope with the greatly enhanced opportunities for domination — of man over nature and man over man — afforded by technology. Pre-Depression man had allowed technology to dictate social forms. Made in the likeness of the machine, he thus, while freeing himself had, in a more fundamental way, enslaved himself by bowing to technological and organizational imperatives perceived as iron laws. Rapaport believed that, in contrast to what had happened, the Great Depression could have been avoided and the system salvaged. But at some point, the psychological and social costs of the system which would have evolved would have proved too terrible to be borne. At that point, the system would have collapsed slowly into chaos, dissolving the glue of social norms and giving rise in its place to randomness and increasing entropy.

Instead, the collapse had been mercifully hastened, and out of this had emerged a totally different set of directions. The key institution in the old society had been the joint-stock company, which had evolved into the multinational corporation and the conglomerate. These had grown until they had shaped the environment, deforming and warping the rest of human culture to their own ends. When it came to the origins of the new forms, instigated by the Brotherhood, the matter was much murkier. The Survival Code bore a publication date of 1933, and this coincided with the date of the founding of the Brotherhood. But the growth of the Brotherhood was characterized by a virtual passion for anonymity by its leaders. True, Roosevelt himself had joined the Brotherhood, but soon afterwards, he had dropped from sight, becoming part of a collectivity which almost totally de-emphasized individual leadership and charisma. There were various accounts, which purported to tell the internal story of the Brother-hood, but they were mostly lurid and unreliable. Rapaport soon came to a dead end in his research on this question, and decided instead to investigate the present, to see if he could pick up any clue as to the nature and origins of the intervention in the past which he increasingly believed had taken place.

Some form of time travel had been developed about five years previously, and after some research, Rapaport ended up in the office of a Professor Schwartz. Schwartz readily admitted that time travel had been developed, and spoke of the Iroquois Project, which had totally disappeared, leaving no record. Schwartz was cryptic, but indicated that a Dr. Lederson was the man to see. Lederson, was one of the few men from the time that was no more and, moreover, had been instrumental in the intervention itself. Lederson, it appeared, was probably more responsible for the present than any other man. Accordingly Rapaport wrote to Lederson, and got agreement to an interview at Saratoga in the Upper Hudson Region.

Rapaport set out for Saratoga with many questions in his mind. What would be the status of those people directly involved in the intervention? Would they be conscious of two pasts, the old and the revised? For the vast majority there was only the revised one. But beyond the problems involved in changing time, there was also the social question. The intervention had obviously been successful — but how? What had been changed, and where? Rapaport knew from his discussions with Professor Schwartz that time travel required enormous energy, and could only be sustained for a short time. Thus a minimal intervention could be assumed, directed at a maximum effect. It made the question of the nature of the intervention almost more challenging than how the time travel itself was executed, and it was an area which Rapaport felt himself equipped to deal with, unlike the physics under-lying time travel.

Lederson was cordial and friendly. He invited Rapaport to stay with him for several days, and over that period answered Rapaport's many questions. It was impossible to say, Lederson explained, how extensively the present duplicated the alternate time system. Some people had certainly been born into the new system who had also existed in the old; Lederson was living proof of this, and he himself was no older than Rapaport, and had not been alive at the time of the intervention. But it was clear that consciousness had been completely altered. The Iroquois project had taken the precaution of keeping detailed records of the now nonexistent time track, and these, fortunately, had survived. But Lederson himself had no memory — or at least no conscious memory — of his work in the alternate time track. And yet, he said, there were dreams — and also a kind of recognition when he studied the Survival Code, of which he knew from the records, that he himself was the main author.

The account that Lederson gave of the intervention in the past was roughly as follows: a single person, carefully selected for his intelligence, capability, and persuasiveness, had been shot into the past with the necessary equipment. The equipment consisted of some small electronic devices which represented the state of the art at that time; a manual describing other technological developments as well as developments in physics and medicine; a set of documents, carefully prepared, to be presented to the leadership of a carefully chosen religious group already concerned about the direction of events, and finally, a brief description of the world of the early twenty-first century, and of the collapse facing it. The traveler to the past was instructed to gain an audience with Roosevelt, and persuade him to allow the Depression to run its course. If that did not succeed, the religious sect was to be contacted and, after they had been persuaded to assume the leadership in creating an alternate future, Roosevelt was to be assassinated. But the belief was that this would not be necessary, and that proved to be the case.

Rapaport then came to the question which interested him most: what had been the analysis underlying the Survival Code, and in Lederson's view, had it produced what had been expected of it? Lederson replied that the concern had been mainly to ensure survival by creating a society which would have strong enough countervalues to guarantee its never again being dominated by the growth ethos. What had actually come about had totally exceeded his powers of imagination. He had been strongly politically oriented, he explained, and had seen the need to get rid of both corporate capitalism and, more generally, the fetishism of power and profit, whether controlled by the state or by private corporations. He had realized that this had deep value implications, and indeed had developed the Survival Code on this basis, but he felt there was an absolute discontinuity between what his thinking must have been in drawing up the Code, and how he saw things now. Here he verified Rapaport's insights, for the miracle which he had failed to predict was the quality of freedom that had come to be the central feature of the new society. It was not the freedom that went with power and mastery, but a subtler and more pervasive freedom that came from the liberation of all social forms, making for an unparalleled surge of creativity, as people found themselves freed from the iron laws of technological and economic necessity.

It was this experience that had been beyond Lederson's predictions. People were freed to feel, to trust, to build linkages, and everywhere there was the excitement of having embarked upon a joint experiment which created new social forms and forged close ties as well. Lederson had had a kind of conversion. It had come from being confronted with a totally new experience, requiring a wrenching of his attitudes and values — away from the hardheaded instrumentalism and political radicalism of his former consciousness toward a new psychological openness. It was one thing to believe intellectually in liberation, and another to be confronted with its consequences. There had been a period of floundering, a feeling of being out of tune with the new ethos — which, ironically, he had been instrumental in setting in motion. He had been suspicious of the new generation, of the young who took to the new ethos naturally, developing a kind of closeness and intimacy among themselves that he could not but mistrust.

But then he had come to that the new generation for whom the new ethos of joy and expression was natural also possessed a strength and sense of purpose, even though it was expressed in terms different from his own. Those who had grown up in the new society valued their freedom and joy, and invested a great deal of energy in developing it. But they would brook no opposition from the old order, and they were quite clear in their condemnation of the old society, with its unidimensional outlook, and emphasis on things and techniques at the expense of people. There was strength there, and Lederson was able to identify with this strength and hardheadedness himself, and, through this, to make the necessary transition from a purely intellectual grasp of the meaning of liberation to a personal confrontation with its implications for his life and relationships.

And so Lederson had changed. He had assumed the painful task of looking at himself, and by extension, at his relationships with others: his family, friends, and colleagues. He had seen the richness around him, in contrast to his own psychic impoverishment, and had forced himself to be more open, seeking to enrich his relationships with others by dropping the hard veneer of defensiveness and practicality behind which he had hidden his real feelings. After the initial sense of release, when the new ideas had finally clicked into place and he had come to understand them, there were periods of depression and isolation. The world seemed to be moving so much faster than he was, passing him by; sometimes it made him feel like retreating to the old ways which were at least safe. But as he persisted, coming to terms with the new ethos, he realized that everything had not changed after all, and there was still value in work, persistence, character — all the old virtues. Liberation had a dialectic of its own, and, following it through, he concentrated on how to continue to apply his knowledge as a sociologist to articulating the new insights and feelings that now formed part of his social experience.

Lederson explained to Rapaport, that, as he saw it, institutions were invented, and those that best expressed the direction of the society, the current ethos, were taken up and reproduced throughout society by a process resembling natural selection. This had happened in pre-Depression years with the joint-stock company, which was the carrier of industrialism. It had been an invention which capitalized on the current need, and society had at first been more than willing to pay the attendant social costs. But then it had come to dominate the social environment, warping other social forms to its purposes. If, therefore, each age was characterized by its own particular institution, what would be the happy inventions of today, that would survive and flourish because they embodied the genius of the new liberation? This was the problem as he saw it, and he had joined the Brotherhood in its work of creating these new institutions.

Part of the answer lay in the new monasticism, the communes for both men and women which combined an interior with a social vision. There was continuous movement between the inner world and the outer world, and a search was made for ways to objectify and externalize the inner vision into a way of life. The importance of the new monasticism for Lederson was that here were found the unusually dedicated, the new heroes, and it was out of this milieu that a new image of man could arise. The Middle Ages had had saints, and the Renaissance men "for all seasons." But the Industrial Age, with the discrediting of the Protestant ethic and the tycoon, had lost this sense of high achievement. A society needed to embody its ideals in hero-figures who could show the way to others, just as much as it needed institutions which could capture and embody the prevailing ethos. It needed ways, Taos, or doh-disciplines which could serve as signposts to growth and the heroic. The early twentieth century had sought its heroes among the ranks of athletes, movie stars, and media heroes who were the products of P.R. men using videotape. But an authentic society needed authentic heroes, and Lederson had worked with the Brotherhood to formulate and institutionalize new ways of creating new types of hero.

The new heroes were not yet clear, Lederson felt, and yet there were examples: the new Leonardos did not work in solitude, entrusting their insights to notebooks, nor did they express themselves in an exclusively aesthetic vision. Neither did they express themselves through self-abnegation and the other-worldliness of the saint. Typically, they were the young of either sex, fully human and fully involved, men and women of action, whose genius lay in their social imagination, their vision and creativity. They were the creators of the new social forms: architects, planners, organizers, art and drama producers, dreamers. Many of them were women, because with the relinquishing of the business ethos a softer, fuller, more aesthetic kind of social imagination came into its own, replacing the hardheaded manipulativeness and technical skills of the business ethos; and here women were equal with men. Once the one-sided masculinity and power focus of the old society were gone, women came to the fore as leaders, visionaries, and activists.

It was these people, then, who were central to the creation of the new variety and richness which characterized society. Around such leaders would cluster those who sought adventure and challenge, who saw themselves as the vanguard of the new society. Many of them joined the Brotherhood New Corps, created to channel the energies of the adventurous into projects that had been given some initial thought by the Brotherhood. (This caution resulted from a number of kibbutz-like communities of young people, which had failed from an excess of zeal and lack of realism.) Others took part in decentralizing the cities, either by organizing new neighborhoods within them, or by creating new communities which were built up in the knowledge that they were, in broad terms, the prototypes of the new communities. The less adventurous then followed. In this way urban land was freed to be cleared and rebuilt on a more rational basis.

For Lederson, the challenge now was to make the monasteries that had sprung up, often in conjunction with a new town or community, the guiding institutions of the new society. He championed the monasteries, not because they exemplified the genius of the Brotherhood leadership in creating the new society, for this they had already done, but because they embodied authentic ways. He believed that they must become places where those with special dedication and commitment could go for training and emerge as leaders from whom all traces of egoism had been shorn, authentic new heroes possessed of unusual strength of mind and will, combined with vision. But this was in keeping with the original role of the monasteries as envisaged in the Survival Code, in which Lederson had also had a hand. The blueprint for the Brotherhood had been based on the accurate prediction that the chaos, following the discrediting of the old order, would lead to a revival of community and religious feeling. An institution which could solidify and direct the powerful new forces which had been let loose, would dominate the social landscape and be capable of giving it direction. First through the cell groups, and then through the monasteries, the Brotherhood had defined the goals and marked the outlines of the new movement, giving it a language which connected it with the past. This exemplified Romer's Principle, derived from paleontological research: for beneficial changes to survive, they must embody critical continuities with the past.

And so the answer was given to Rapaport, verifying his own understanding of the changes that had been wrought. The new society had a degree of human freedom and realization perhaps unparalleled in human history. And yet at the same time, in its major outlines, it had been highly planned. But the planning had to do with a major institutional form, and even more with a definite conception of man, rather than with a plan for the overall coordination of the social system. Because there were common values and a commonly held image of man and of society, great variety had sprung up within this context. Local cultures had developed, based on geography and occupation, but often more on the unique social vision that had gone into making the community. This localism and variety were complemented by the enduring humanism and utopian vision exemplified by the Brotherhood which, under the leadership of its great monasteries, gave a concrete form to human aspirations and ideals.

Univaria

DOROTHY L. KEUR and RUSSELL LaDUE

TRANSCRIPT 1 *(Adapted from Tape Uss Z158–S121–8E–5/30/19)*

"You have to realize, class," the teacher was saying, "how bad conditions were in our country toward the end of the twentieth century. Cities were so large as to be ungovernable. Crime was raging. Leaders were, many of them, incapable. Graft in government was widespread. Cars choked the highways. Pollution threatened the air and the water. Hatred among races was rampant. So was prejudice among religions. The family was breaking up. The population was exploding. The generations were drifting apart. Morality was breaking down. Corporate greed was the order of the day. War, or what they called defense, took half the tax dollar. Education had largely withdrawn into its own shell. And technology, despite incredible advances, was no longer in the service of humanity."

The class grew quiet, save for the almost inaudible hum of the students' cassette recorders. Two girls turned around to glance at Mrs. Meerkamp who was almost old enough to remember those times, and she nodded slightly in agreement with the teacher. Mr. Naughton, from one of the automotive corporations, glanced at his notes, wondering what kind of questions these twelve- to fifteen-year-olds might ask. Dr. Alpert, the fourth adult in the room, although only nineteen herself, smiled at the class reaction.

"It sounds as bad as Rome at the time of Caesar," Ben began, remembering last year's work.

"More like Athens," his twin sister, Beth, suggested. "A once-democratic country growing too wealthy, turning to war to protect its business interests, and losing its morality."

"But there's a big difference," Kurt pointed out. "You're forgetting that the level of technology in our country even then was far higher than in Rome or Greece; and that in itself brought a whole host of new problems."

"The automobile alone," Mr. Naughton nodded. But he did not go on to lecture. The class, like all social studies classes in Univaria, was a discussion, with students and nonstudents participating on an equal footing under the direction of a teacher.

"All right then," the teacher took over the class again. "We had all these problems. Can anyone see how they related, one to another? If we could find some kind of interrelation, we might be able to get to the basic problem. And if we did that, we might then be able to point the way to a solution."

"You mean as if we were the people back in those days?" asked Maria. "We know there's a solution, because we don't have these problems any more in Univaria."

"Yes," said the teacher. "But we always review a subject by trying to put ourselves in the place of the people of that country or that time. That way we can begin to understand the process of finding a solution; and the process is more important than the solution because that can help us in the future."

"I think the basic problem was the same one we've always had," David said. "Man is individually motivated. I mean ants and bees work for the hive, but people work for their own self-interest. And yet we're only effective when we work in groups."

"But the way you say it," Beth interrupted, "sounds like all we have to do is to reeducate man not to go for his own self-interest. And you can't do that. You have to start with man's biology. The biological nature of this species. When I'm hungry it's my nature to eat — not go feed the needy family down the block."

"Does everbody agree?" asked the teacher.

"I think you're right in starting with the nature of man," Dr. Alpert suggested. "But don't you think you ought to consider his psychology as well as his biology?"

"Hey, that's great!" said David. "Because I could only list half the problems under this biology/self-interest heading, I could see wars and crime and corruption in government and prejudice as all part of self-interest. But I had no place to put the breakup of the family, the population explosion, the generation gap, and the loss of morality, until you brought up psychology. So the basic problem is the biological and psychological nature of man. . ."

"That's not the problem, Dave," Hiroko interrupted, laughing. "That's the nature of man. That's the starting point."

"Yes," David nodded. "But it's the nature of man, which is to be individually motivated, whether psychologically or biologically, against the fact that groups of these self-interested men have to work and live together to be effective, that causes the problem." He stopped, out of breath.

"That's pretty good," said the teacher. "But doesn't that statement of the problem point the way to a solution?" She waited a moment, then went on. "You've been talking only about the way man is motivated. Aren't there other things in the nature of man. . . ." Five hands shot up.

"His brain. His ability to use symbols. Books, tapes, computer libraries. So that one generation can learn from another and not have to start all over." Ben had to pause for breath, and the whole class started talking at once.

"Maria," the teacher raised her voice.

"The whole idea of Univaria is to enable man to develop muscle, mind, and emotional response to their greatest potential," she answered.

"That's straight out of the book," Ivan objected.

"Yes, but it applies," Maria countered. "The principle is that we start with man; and, as he has muscles, using his muscles is good; as he has a brain, using his brain is good; as he has feelings, using those feelings is good."

"And how did late-twentieth-century man use his brain to solve the problem of the self-interested individual in society?" the teacher asked.

"By interposing evidence, reason, and judgment between impulse and action," Maria answered.

"Explain it in your own words, Maria," the teacher said.

"When you're a baby and you want something you can't have right then, you cry." Maria began. "Then as you grow up, you learn that you have to wait or work for things you want, and the same with learning. Before we come to believe something, we try to look at the evidence, and then figure out a solution, and then test that solution. And this is pretty much what man did in changing the country to Univaria."

"Why did we change the name of the country?" asked the teacher.

"Because the old name didn't make sense any more," Kurt answered. "Because when we went to the area-and-function government, with the zones represented in one house and the branches of business and education represented in the other, it was no longer logical to use names like United States or Union of Republics. Because there were no states or republics any more."

"The sixty-fourth, sixty-fifth, and sixty-sixth amendments!" Ben added.

"True," said the teacher. "But we're going too fast. Now Kurt already mentioned one of the changes in government, in the legislative branch, to be specific. What others are there?"

"In the executive branch," said Ivan. "It's headed by a troika. . .

three men, instead of one. And one comes from each of the two legislative houses, while the third is elected at large."

"But the most important thing," Beth interjected, "is that they all come from the leadership group. Not only the president, premier, and chairman, but the entire federal and local government personnel, including the military and police and everybody."

"Not everybody," David objected. "Only those in authority. The workers come from either the teenagers, or the people without jobs, who used to be what they called welfare cases."

"That's right, David," the teacher nodded. "But who can tell me more about this leadership group? Who are they? How are they chosen? Where do they live? How are they trained? How are they advanced to higher positions?"

"They're people who choose the group," began Ben. "Something like people used to choose the priesthood. They're people who want to serve others more than anything else. Like teachers. Like people who are dedicated to the good of the whole. To service of the species."

"They live everywhere," Hiroko broke in. "In the towns and cities and villages and farms. In all the zones. And they work in all fields. . . business, science, medicine, education, commerce, military, everything."

"Yes," the teacher nodded. "And how are they trained?"

"The same as everybody else, to begin with," said Kurt. "But in addition, they have several years before high school, and again before college, and again after college, and some of them, the highest, again after job training, and even after government service, in leadership training."

"A president, or chairman, or premier, for example, must have a basic grounding in philosophy and psychology," Hiroko broke in. "Plus a good background in the social sciences. Plus experience in education, science, business, and diplomacy. And he or she must have spent several years abroad in each of the two hemispheres. And these are only the qualifications. They then have to be elected."

"I think the way they're paid is important, too," said Ben. "The fact that their income level is fixed by grades, and there is no way for them to gain or lose financially by any act or opinion."

"You're getting ahead of me again," the teacher smiled. "Before we get into economics, not only of the leadership group, but of everybody, let's consider two more questions about the leadership group. First, how are they promoted? Second, are they the most intelligent, or important, or powerful people in our country?"

"They advance by grades set up by their board of regents," Ivan answered. "Based on achievement either in leadership education, or on their jobs in leadership posts."

"But they're not necessarily the smartest, most powerful, or important people in the country," David insisted. "A great scientist could be much smarter in his field and make discoveries that mean more than... than... almost anything to humanity. But he might be incapable as a leader. Or an industrialist. It doesn't matter. The ideal of Univaria is to use people at what they're best at."

"And those who don't get to the top, work in government anyway," said Beth. "In the federal agencies, or military, or local government, depending on their grade."

"That's good," the teacher nodded. "You may not have all the details and distinctions worked out, but you do have the idea. And, of course students can start pointing toward the leadership group as early as the year's break between primary and secondary school. So that we have a picture now of the Univarian government: two houses in the legislature, one representing areas or zones, the other representing functions; a tripartite executive function and the old or traditional judicial system. With the same structure mirrored in areas and zones, replacing the old state, county and city governments, which once had a reason for being, but often got in each other's way. But next let me ask you, what sort of laws did this new government pass? And why? I'm talking about basic legislation... that which deals with what David posed as the basic problem of society: how can individually motivated people work together?"

"I think the choice," David said, "was whether to impose a way of life on everybody by law or to let people evolve their own ways of life and impose only such laws as would give everybody a fair chance."

"If we'd imposed a planned way of life on everybody," Beth said frowning, "I'm afraid we would have ended up with a static society that wouldn't be able to compete with other countries in today's world. Also I don't think the people would have stood for it," she added.

"Yes," nodded the teacher. "But what laws did we enact to give everbody a fair chance, as David puts it. And how well are they working?"

"The floors and ceilings on income," Kurt said. "Everyone in Univaria can be sure of a living wage. Those who lose their jobs, or are for any reason out of work, still get that basic unit of income. In the late twentieth century it would have been about $5000 a year."

"But not like what they used to call welfare," said Ruth, breaking into the discussion for the first time. "Everyone gets it, but they have to work for it. On whatever government project is in progress nearby."

"And if they refuse?" asked the teacher.

"No one has refused," Ruth answered. "But if they do, the law says they will be deported. We have this arrangement with several of the undeveloped countries to accept our citizens. Some have tried it. But they've come back."

"And the ceiling," Kurt continued, "is fifty times the base unit. Of course there have been years when nobody has made that much. Even the president only makes forty times the base unit. I think this year though, a man in your company will make fifty times the base." He looked at Mr. Naughton.

"Yes, our chairman of the board will come close to that figure," Mr. Naughton nodded. So will the man in charge of the space program. And, I believe the chancellor of one of the western universities."

"So will the Worms," said Beth, referring to a recording group.

"Why should that be?" asked Maria.

"It's a question of their record and tape sales and what they can command on television or at concerts," Mr. Naughton explained.

"And don't forget," Dr. Alpert reminded them, "singing, shows, films, theater, music, painting, books, all the arts do serve the function of bringing people together. . . letting us individually motivated members feel we're really part of something bigger, namely the species. Much like religion used to." She blushed suddenly. "Or still does for many people, I should say," she added. "And maybe those who perform this function best should get paid the most. If there weren't a need for it, people wouldn't buy the records, would they?"

"That's true," said the teacher. "But again we're getting ahead of ourselves. We had started with government; we were talking about the basic legislation. (We'll get into the family, the social mores, education, art, and religion in a minute.) But first let's finish up government and economics. Okay?"

"In addition to the floor and ceiling on salaries," Kurt continued, "and even more important, I think, were the laws ending inheritance. No matter how much money a person amasses, it cannot be passed on to the next generation. I mean to his or her own children."

"This was the hardest legislation, too," said David, "both to write and pass. Trusts, and estates and foundations and property and all kinds of legal loopholes had to be done away with. And then the people with all this wealth, and the political power that it gave them, had to be convinced or outvoted."

"But now that we've done it," Ivan nodded, "it pays for the whole government. We don't need any other taxes any more. At least we haven't up to now. Although now my father tells me they're considering an income tax again. Only it will be the same percentage for everybody."

"But the main thing about the inheritance laws," Hiroko broke in, "is that they really do give everybody a fair chance, or an equal start in life. At least economically. The old way, where a child of one family

would have far more money than he would ever need, while hundreds
of other children would be practically starving just wasn't fair."

"It wasn't making very good use of our basic resource, either," said
Ben.

"What is our basic resource, Ben?" smiled the teacher.

"Our people. Their ability to think. To contribute. The old way,
most people never had a chance to develop fully, because of the
economic handicap they started out with."

Ruth raised her hand again. The teacher nodded. "I don't understand," the girl began. "I mean, I see how money or stocks or bonds
can go to the government when a person dies. But what about her
house, or her farm. Or property?"

"It's the same thing," said David, answering for the teacher. "Your
house goes to the government, and someone else buys it from the
government. And you've had the use of it while you were alive."

"But what about my children?" asked Ruth. I mean if I had
children," she laughed. "And I died, what would happen to them?
Would they have to move, or what?"

"You're talking about accidental death or sickness resulting in
death," the teacher explained. "Because ordinarily, of course, children
are grown and have become parents themselves, before their parents
die. But in such cases, if the children are very young, relatives or
friends of the parents can take them, or the local children's center will
provide. But more on the children's centers in a moment. Let's stay
with the economics of Univaria for now. What about business?"

"It's still the free enterprise system," Kurt said. "And with the
ceiling on income and the no inheritance idea, it seems to be working.
The big problem in the past was with the big corporations. As I
understand it anyway," he glanced at Mr. Naughton who nodded.
"They had so much wealth and power that there were almost no
controls on them. And sometimes management would make short-
range instead of long-range decisions. Is that right?" Again he addressed Mr. Naughton.

"The car makers were a prime example," Mr. Naughton nodded.
"In the old days one of our top men could make a decision to take fifty
dollars out of the cost of a car, for instance. With the company
producing a million cars a year, that man's decision would have saved
the company fifty million dollars. Actually it would have been more,
because with the lower cost, the price would have been lower and the
company would have sold more than its million cars that year. And the
man who made that decision would be a hero in the company, and
would probably be promoted, for having made this short-range decision.

"But in the long run that decision to take fifty dollars out of the car, would cost the company money, because it would affect the quality or safety of the car. And the people who bought that car would never again buy from that company. So that while it might have gained over fifty million dollars in the one year, the company might lose five hundred millions over the next ten years.

"That was what was wrong with our old system. We were set up to reward the short-range view. The man who made that short-range decision might have made several million dollars personally, which was what impelled him to make it. With the ceiling on income and no inheritance, as we have it now, there's no benefit or incentive for any man to make that kind of decision, and the way we're set up now we reward the long-range view rather than the short one.

"For example, we've limited ourselves on the number of cars the industry will make in any year. It's based on the population and the need for travel. Since we've got the population under control, and with decentralization having brought cities down to manageable size, the need for cars has declined. So we're making fewer, but we're making them better. More expensive, too, of course, so our profits are about where they've always been. But since they last longer, an individual really pays no more per year for a car than he used to."

"What about competition between the companies?" asked Kurt.

"It's still tremendous," Mr. Naughton grinned. "But now we're all competing with the long-range view in mind. In the old days we used to feel that 'what was good for General Motors was good for America.' Now we feel that what's bad for Univaria is bad for any car maker. We're trying to serve the country's needs, rather than exploit them. The greed has gone out of it."

"How did the change in attitude come about?" asked the teacher.

"Partly the salary ceilings and no inheritance. Partly the influx of economists and social scientists from the colleges into business. Partly the whole change in social structure that has taken place in this country," Mr. Naughton answered. "I'm sure Dr. Alpert could tell you more about that than I," he added.

"We're coming to that," the teacher nodded. "But I was glad to hear you mention the role that social as well as physical scientists are now playing in business. There used to be such a gulf between the colleges and the corporations. And there is another change in the people corporations now employ, which is important, too, I think. It used to be that only males between thirty and fifty were considered good material. Now it's male and female, from twenty to seventy, with no weighting for race, religion, or anything of that sort."

"Yes," Mr. Naughton agreed. "Our board of directors is one-third women, includes a twenty-year-old and our chairman is seventy-five. But you know the universities have drawn just as heavily from the corporations for their personnel, and I think they've gained by it as much as we have. After all, both are essentially just groups of people working together. We've added some of the thoughtfulness of university people; the universities have added some of the practicality of corporations. And both are now structured so that it's the talented people who tend to rise, rather than the politically astute, or monied people. There's just not that much politics any more in either corporations or universities. Not that we're, either of us, perfect yet."

"I think we're both heading the right way, though," the teacher nodded. "Now I think the class should realize that Mr. Naughton is speaking for all the large corporations, not just the auto makers," she added. "And that he's talking broadly about the way management feels in general. Two other questions, before we leave economics: What about capital? And what about the small businessman?"

"Well, with no inheritance, the stock market which supplies major capital, had to turn to the small investor. And with the ceiling on incomes, there were no more "killings" to be made on Wall Street. But actually this put the emphasis where it should have been all along — on investing in well-run companies, corporations, or universities. So that a far larger number of people are now in the market. And banks and other financial institutions continue to invest both in the market and in smaller companies. But again the long-range view, rather than the short-term gain is the basis for decisions. This means, too, that it's easier than ever for a man to get into a business of his own, providing he's got a needed product or service and a market that needs it."

"How do you define need?" asked Beth. "I mean people often want things that they don't need, and sometimes need things that they don't want."

"Very good point, Beth!" The teacher positively beamed. "And that brings us to the profound change in social structure Mr. Naughton mentioned. Where do you think we should start?"

"Home and family," said Beth promptly.

"Family first," suggested Maria.

"Then school and education," Hiroko added.

"Then home and town and city," Ben put in.

"Then wants and needs and morality and religion and sports and the arts," suggested David.

"I think you need philosophy and psychology in that category," Dr. Alpert amended.

"Yes," said the teacher, nodding.

"Then conservation and crime and ecology," Ivan put in. "Then how Univaria works with other countries."

"One thing at a time," said the teacher. "But we've come to the end of the class period. Now, we'll pick up on Wednesday. I want to thank

Mr. Naughton and Dr. Alpert. I want to apologize to Mrs. Meerkamp. I thought we'd get into this social area today, but we didn't. Can you come Wednesday?"

"Oh yes," Mrs. Meerkamp nodded.

"I'm not sure," said Mr. Naughton. "But I'll try."

"I have to," said Dr. Alpert.

"Good," said the teacher. "Class dismissed."

TRANSCRIPT 2 (*Adapted from Tape Uss Z158–S124–8E–6/2/19*)

"All right, class," the teacher began. "Mr Naughton called to say he can't be here today. He's appearing before the zone industrial committee. But he will come back for as long as we need him toward the end of the course when we're working on economics. We're glad to have Mrs. Meerkamp and Dr. Alpert with us again. Let's get started."

The children left the tables clustered around the computer readout in the work center, came forward, and settled themselves around the teacher in the discussion center at the front of the classroom, ready to continue the introductory session on Univaria.

"Last time we talked about the laws, government, business, and leadership of Univaria," the teacher went on. "These are the highly visible configurations of a culture, like the skyline of some great city. Easily identifiable. However, to really understand the culture, we have to get down to life as it is lived on the streets of the city... to the personal and family and social relationships that form the fabric of society. And this, in a sense, is more important to investigate, for it is out of these relationships, out of the 'life in the streets,' that the skyline rises... that the laws, business, and government of a culture emerge." She paused, looking at the class, wondering if she'd made the concept clear.

Hiroko nodded. "Yes," she said. "Because the universities and corporations and laws and governments just reflect the society they spring from, as the architecture reflects the life-style of a city, as in Rome, for example."

"But the architecture also influences the life of the city," Kurt objected. "And the laws, government, and business of a country influence the life of a country."

"It doesn't matter," Beth said. "They influence one another. But we've already talked about the skyline. So let's get down to the... what did you call it?... life as it is lived on the streets."

"Where shall we start?" asked the teacher.

"At birth?" wondered Maria.

"Before," Ruth suggested. "With marriage."

"But everybody doesn't get married," David pointed out.

"But only those that do have children," Ruth answered him. "Or are supposed to," she added.

"That's right," said the teacher. "Young people coming out of school, going into work or service or business, live together in all kinds of groups. Two or three boys, two or three girls, or more, pool their resources and take a house or an apartment. Or larger groups of both sexes live together in communes of all kinds. Some based on interests. Mutual interests, I mean. Some based on geographical convenience. Some based on work, like farming or forestry or service or whatever. Some even choose to live with their parents during this period, although fewer and fewer children choose this alternative each year. I said children. I shouldn't have. I should have said young people. Because the next thing I wanted to ask you was about children."

"When two people fall in love and want to have children, they get married," Maria answered. The class nodded.

"Why?" asked Dr. Alpert.

"Because," Beth began, "the main thing in a baby's life is love. I mean the main thing for the baby's health. Psychological health, in particular. And two people who love each other are best able to give that kind of love to a child."

"In fact that's one of the signs of love," Hiroko added. "I mean you can have sexual relationships with anybody you want to without having children. But when you want to have a child with somebody it is a sign that you really love them."

"With anybody?" asked the teacher.

"Anybody," Ivan nodded. "Provided both partners are over fifteen. There are no laws against homosexual relationships. And no stigma either."

"Yet homosexual relationships are declining," Dr. Alpert pointed out. "At least according to statistics. Why do you think that is?" The class couldn't answer. "It's because under the old culture a lot of homosexuality was fostered by a psychological imbalance in the family." The class looked blank.

"Maybe you could give us an example," the teacher suggested.

"When I was a girl," Mrs. Meerkamp entered the discussion, "many marriages were not based on love, but on economic necessity, or the wishes of the parents, or the stigma, especially for a girl, of not being married. A lot of girls would marry just to be married. They wouldn't really love their husbands. And all this pent up love, that had no expression, would be lavished on the child."

"Yes," Dr. Alpert nodded. "And with the mother giving all her love to the son, the father would resent it and end up resenting the son, and often wouldn't love the son. So that the son would grow up seeking the

love that he had never had from a man, and afraid of the overabundance of love he'd had from the woman, and often would turn to
homosexual relationships."

"Well that's why it's declining," Ben said. "Because now, only
people who really love each other have children. And there is no
imbalance of love in the family. I mean no lack of love from the father
or overabundance of love from the mother. So that's why."

"That's right," said the teacher. "And it works the same way for
girls, too." Dr. Alpert started to object, but the teacher went on. "Not
exactly the same way, but the same kind of way. We'll go into it more
thoroughly as we come to that part of the course. But for this
introductory discussion, I want to move on just now. Is there anything
else different about love and marriage and having children from when
Mrs. Meerkamp was a girl?"

"Only two children per family," said Kurt promptly. "At least till we
get the population stabilized. And I think we're almost at that point
already."

"The way children are raised is different now," Beth added. "I think
it used to be that only the men went to work, and the problem of
raising the kids fell on the woman." Mrs. Meerkamp nodded. "Now
both men and women go to work," Beth continued. "And when a
family has a child, both continue working. But you only work half a
day... say the mother in the morning and the father in the
afternoon... so that both share equally in bringing up the child. Of
course there's an adjustment for nursing mothers. They don't even
have to work half a day until the child is weaned."

"But both parents still get full pay," Ivan added. "And actually the
money that the corporations used to contribute to welfare and ghettoes
and that kind of project now goes to the parental fund. And costs less,
and accomplishes more."

"That's right," David agreed. "In Univaria we realize that our most
precious raw material is our people."

"All right then," the teacher smiled, "how do we take care of the
child; or, as David might say, conserve this raw material?"

"Conserve is the wrong word," Beth said emphatically. "And so is
raw material, I think, anyway. The child lives with its mother and
father until it's fifteen or older. But it starts nursery school for two
hours a day between two and three...."

"She means two or three years old," David broke in "not two or
three in the afternoon." He sat back and glared at Beth, who made a
face at him, and they both started to laugh.

"They start preschool at four or five... years old..." she corrected
herself with a glance at David, "primary school at six, intermediate
school at eleven to thirteen, high school at fifteen or sixteen...."

"She's wrong again," said David. "You get a year of service, working between intermediate and high school!"

"I know it," Beth continued. "But the ages aren't important, because you move on when you finish the work, not at any given age. That's why I was saying. . . ."

"All right, you two," the teacher smiled. "I want someone else to continue now. It's not a question of who's right or wrong. It's a question of what happens."

"I think the difference between what we're doing in education, and what they did before," Ben took up the challenge, "is basically that we're bringing kids out of the family and into the world sooner and more often. The nursery schools, the preschool, the work clubs after school, the year away from school and in work or service between intermediate and high school, the year or two of work or service between high school and college. The years between college and graduate school. Our whole idea is to bring kids into society, and to break down the barriers between education in school and in the life of the community."

"I think the whole teaching profession has changed, too," Mrs. Meerkamp added. "Teachers in my day used to assign homework from text books and give lectures or try to drum the homework into you. Even in the higher grades . . . even in graduate school . . . it was a self-enclosed thing. The only people who took graduate courses in English, for example, were people who were going to end up teaching English. And the best of those would end up teaching graduate courses to another generation of would-be English teachers. That's what I mean by self-enclosed."

"That's true," the teacher smiled. "Teaching is not trying to get data into a student's mind anymore, teaching is trying to engage the mind of a student, to show him that learning is possible in his own case, that his own mind is valuable, that he counts as an individual in our society. And beyond that to interpose evidence and reason and judgment between a problem and the solution of it. Or between his own impulse and his own action, not only in education, but in all aspects of life."

"We need some data in our minds," David objected. "Just in order to know what evidence applies and how to reason about it. I admit the tape libraries can hold more data than anybody . . . any one mind, I mean. But, my gosh, I can reason better than a six-year-old, and Mrs. Meerkamp can reason better than I can. Or can she?"

"Well, I know more about older people and how they feel than you do, David," Mrs. Meerkamp answered, "but you know more about younger people. And the beautiful thing about Univaria today is that both young people and old people count. Not just the middle-aged who used to think that we, neither of us mattered. They used to segregate us, in fact."

"Yes," David nodded. "But I mean I hope to be smarter in ten years than I am now. And twenty years, and fifty years."

"It's not the years, David," Mrs. Meerkamp smiled. "It's what you do with them. You will know more. Facts and things. But you'll have lost some of the freshness and intensity. Maybe . . ." She trailed off, reflecting on what might have been.

"We'll do more on that, too," the teacher promised. But right now we've got to finish up our introductory discussion. Next class we're seeing films, so if we don't finish today it will be harder to pick up the pieces next week. We've talked about the ways we live together, and families and children and the first years and education. We haven't gone very deeply into any of the facets of any of these things, but we can't just now. So let's press on. The family has been formed because two people loved each other so much they wanted to have children together. The child has been born and raised, at first by the mother and father . . ."

"And grandparents and uncles and aunts, too," Maria added. The teacher nodded.

"That's right, and the mother and father have shared in that rearing a lot more equally than in the old days, too. But the child has moved into the world sooner, and more often, as David says, than he used to. So let's take the child at the end of intermediate school. What happens now?"

"He has the vocational year before high school," said Kurt. "It's planned between him and his parents and his vocational counsellor. They don't pick a direction for him. They narrow it down to three areas. And he works three months in each area. Plus a month to make the decision, a month to evaluate the experience and a month's vacation."

"What sort of areas?" asked the teacher.

"I don't know them all yet," Kurt told her. "It won't be till after next year for us. But as I understand it, there's teaching and working with kids, and working with the land, and working with machines, and the whole sports/art/performance area. We know a lot of people and we see the things they're doing, and we have sort of a hunch of what we're good at in school, and our aptitude scores, and we just kind of put it all together."

"That's right," the teacher nodded. "Only it's not final, by any means. Dr. Alpert, for instance, started out in a completely different field in her first vocational year. Chemistry, wasn't it?"

"I was a mess," Dr. Alpert laughed. "I was a lab technician my first vocational year. By the time I finished high school, I was sure I wanted to be a writer. I didn't get into psychology until after college, before graduate school."

"So the system tries to help you find your vocation. But it doesn't keep you from changing your mind," the teacher summed it up. "And the vocational period after high school works the same way, only more in depth. In fact some people decide not to go on to college, by their own choice, of course. Because there are funds for everyone to go to school to whatever level suits him. Although there are longer and longer vocational periods between each level of study."

"That's because we're trying to bring schools and business closer together," Ruth said. "There shouldn't be those sharp dividing lines between what you do in school and what your parents do in work and what you grandparents do in government." (Her grandmother was a senator of the performing arts.)

"All right," the teacher picked it up. "What do you do besides going to school? What does life consist of for a twelve-year-old in Univaria today?"

"School we have to go to," Ivan began. "Like my parents go to work. After school today we've got football practice. Then I'll go home to dinner. And we'll talk and everything. Dad's trying to teach me about money and property and everything. So he'll go into that when we do the dishes. My older sister's working in the day-care center and she's trying to get Mom interested. So they'll be going to the zone meeting. My Mom's a delegate. Dad and I will probably watch Monday night football till they get home. Then we'll go to bed. Saturday we're going to the aquarium. Sunday Mom and I are going to the Giants' game. Dad and Sis are going to the concert. And we're meeting at Grampa's for dinner."

"Ivan mentioned the zone meeting," said the teacher. "Who can tell me about the zones?"

"They're the basic political unit," David beat the rest of the class to the answer. "Zones represent about twenty thousand families. They're like the old town meeting where people come and discuss what has to be done. Schools, streets, officials, taxes . . . that kind of stuff."

"They're also the basic town unit," Hiroko broke in. "And the new towns around the country are adopting zone planning, with the auditorium and theaters and stores in the center and the residential area surrounding it. Most of them don't even allow cars in the center anymore," she added. "Everything's close enough to walk to."

"But then on one end of the town is the airport," Kurt added. "And beyond the airport the industrial area for plants and factories."

"Of course there are very few new towns in Univaria," Ivan added. "But the existing towns and cities are adapting themselves to the same principles, as much as possible."

"What about the bigger cities?" asked the teacher.

"Each zone is its own section of the city. Like boroughs or suburbs," Beth answered. With its own center. Besides cities aren't that much of a problem anymore. With the vision phone and the computers and. . . ."

"Beth, Beth, Beth, wait one minute, dear," the teacher interrupted. "What you're saying is terribly important, but I want to stay with the small town zones and areas first. I was asking about cities only in that light."

"Well there are fifty zones to an area," said Ben. And fifty areas in the whole country. And regardless of geography, wherever there are fifty zones there's an area. One city alone takes in seven areas. And out in the southwest one area stretches thousands of miles. But the power is in the zones and in the federal government. The areas are just assemblies of zone leaders where they meet twice a year and talk things over."

"And choose candidates for the election," David added. "For the House of Representatives."

"How do they choose them?" the teacher asked.

"Well there are two parties. One for more planning and one for less planning. . . ."

"Only two?" asked the teacher.

"Yup," David nodded. "Because, when you take the long-range view, everything breaks down into that. All issues, from birth control to the space program. Anyway the leaders of the zones try to pick the four best from each party in the area meeting and then every two years we vote."

"We talked about politics last session," Maria protested. "Aren't we supposed to be more down to earth this session?"

"You're right, Maria," the teacher nodded. "But the zones are not only political; they're towns and cities and geographical units as well. And where you live affects how you live so that's why we're talking about them. But let's go on to the cities now."

"The big cities aren't so big any more," Beth said. "Because with all the communications we have now — computers and tapes and television and phones — people don't have to cluster together so much. Everybody in one company used to work in one office. But now people work in their homes or local offices, and have meetings by conference television calls, and fly to in-person meetings . . . so you don't need to cram together. My father dictates a report in the study, the secretary types it in zone fifty-six, and the report appears in ten cities at once, if he wants it to.

"And with stores and theaters and offices in every zone, there's no real advantage to going to the bigger cities any more. And this has helped pollution and traffic and crime, too."

"What about crime?" the teacher picked it up.

"There's no real hardship poverty anymore," David answered. "So nobody has to steal. With the salary ceilings there's no point in being dishonest in government. But most important, I think, is that we've taken the profit out of organized crime. Drugs are free to any addict in the hospitals. With the communes and the way people live now . . . I mean the sexual freedom we were talking about before, there's no market for prostitution. And gambling is easier through the government than anywhere else . . . so the main sources of funding organized crime have dried up. And when you take the long-range view, it doesn't pay. So about the only crime left is from psychologically troubled people, and that's more a medical problem." The class nodded.

"It's not all that simple," said the teacher, "but you're on the right track. Without great wealth and great poverty, crime doesn't flourish. Now what about religion, which used to be a strong deterrent to crime and a way of enabling the very rich and the very poor to live side by side without bloodshed?"

"Well everyone's free to believe what they want," Hiroko began. "Only we don't think one religion's any better than any other anymore. I mean most people don't. We think one man may be a better Christian or Jew or Hindu than another, or even atheist. Better in that he understands more and is more considerate and loving of his fellow man. But we don't think being a Hindu is better than being an atheist or a Catholic, for instance."

"I think it's bigger than that," Ben said thoughtfully. "We're all alone in the world, each of us, and we all feel a need to be together . . . to belong . . . to be part of the family of man. And religion has always said this, but so has literature, and art, and music, and even sports, and rock concerts, and movies, and television. All bring people together. They're like the cement that bind grains of sand and gravel into concrete. Don't you think?" he asked the teacher.

"Now who's asking the questions here?" she laughed. "But yes, there's a lot in what you say and we'll go into that whole area next year. And actually you'll each of you be going into it all your lives, every time you read a book or see a play or hear a concert."

"Or go to church?" asked Maria.

"Yes. Or go to church," nodded the teacher. "Is there anything you'd like to add, Dr. Alpert?" Dr. Alpert shook her head. "Or you, Mrs. Meerkamp?"

"I think they're all part of the same thing . . . the cement, as Ben called it. But I do think there are levels. I think at one point you like comic books and at another you like Shakespeare. Or at one point you thrill to a basketball game, and at another point to a revival meeting. But I agree that it's something everyone finds for himself. His own level, I mean."

"And I don't think it has to be in a group, either. You can read a book alone, or kneel in a church alone, and yet come away with this feeling of belonging... of being part of a family with everyone else. Now it's beginning to sound a little as though we've solved all the problems here in Univaria. What about it, class?"

"No way," said Ivan. "We've got the rest of the world to contend with."

"And we've got survival on the planet to think of," Kurt added. "Let alone the space program."

"What are we doing about the rest of the world?" the teacher asked.

"We're trying to prevent war," said Ivan. "So far for the past twenty years we've been lucky."

"How?" asked the teacher.

"Basically the same way we're trying to prevent crime," David answered. "By taking the profit out of it. Wars used to be advantageous to some people. The rich people. The ones who didn't have to fight. The ones who could sell more goods in wartime. But with the bomb and the ICBMs that changed. A big world war was no longer to anybody's advantage."

"But then we went to smaller wars," Beth protested.

"Because they were still advantageous to somebody," David answered. "It wasn't till we realized that our people were our most important national resource that we realized that there was no advantage. To us anyway."

"But you're leaving out the whole power politics," Ivan objected. "We still maintain a tremendous strike capability. We still have warning systems. It's still the argument that convinces Congress every time the space appropriation bill comes up. Because a lot of people in other countries are still working on the old principle."

"But David's still right," Kurt answered. "Because now it's our space program that's running the military, not the other way around. And the strike capability we have takes the profit out of war for anybody else. And it's a technological army today, not a manpower army. And don't forget our generals come from the leadership group."

"But other countries aren't like us," Ivan argued. "Right now there are three trouble spots in the world that could erupt into wars."

"But we wouldn't get dragged in, even if they did," Beth said. "And with three trouble spots right now, that's still a lot fewer than twenty or fifty years ago. And with our corporations going into other countries with the long-range view of developing those countries, the level of existence is being raised. So you don't have so many masses of starving people for some rabble-rouser to stir up into a revolution."

"That still doesn't solve it," Ivan protested. "There are three big powers in the world, right? The other two don't think the way we do. They're still out to foment minor wars to gain power for themselves."

And we're out to foment industry in the same countries," David got back into the argument. "And the more we do, the less vulnerable those countries are to agitation. Provided we really help the country and not milk it. And I think we are helping."

"We're going to have to stop here on this point," the teacher interrupted. "I just want you to talk a moment about survival on the planet before I sum up. Kurt?"

"We're not doing too badly," he began. "Pollution is under control with the decline of the cities and the corporations really feeling that what's bad for the country is bad for them. We've got population under control. The energy crisis is less critical, again with the decline of the cities and the safe atomic plants. Water is still a problem in many areas even though we've got desalination plants along the coasts. The trouble, of course, is that coastal regions have plenty of rainfall. Where we need the water is inland, hundreds of miles from the plants. The other big problem is the coming ice age. We've got a working time-table on it now, but what a change something like that could mean."

"Somebody once described civilization as an interlude between ice ages," the teacher nodded. "We do want ours to be more than that. But I'm going to have to stop you now. We have only two minutes left.

"Some people see a very slight difference between Univaria and the state of the world I described for you at the beginning of the period last Monday. Others see a very profound difference. Perhaps both are right. Some times a very slight change can make a very profound difference.

"A slight change in the marriage and sex customs has led to children being loved during their earliest years, a little more perhaps than before. A slight change in the inheritance tax has led to a little more equal opportunity for all children. The floors and ceilings on income have taken away some of the greed in the world and led corporations to adopt more of a long-range or larger view. The area and function legislature has led to less corruption and waste in government. The establishment of the leadership group has given us better service all the way from sanitation to the state department. And none of these things work alone, all of them work together, each making the next step a little easier, a little more productive.

"Think too of the proliferation of technology. The computer library and the tape cassettes in this classroom alone. The incredible communications system that ties all of us together, yet lets us live apart, in small communities, closer to nature, rather than in increasingly concentrated cities with all the inherent problems. How did we suddenly take control of technology and make it serve human ends rather than letting technology shape the culture, as many thought it was doing in the past?

"Actually we have always been in control of technology. It has always served human ends. But too many of the humans in control of technology were not themselves serving the ends of humanity, but rather their own special interests. In Univaria we have tried, to use David's phrase, 'to take the profit out of that kind of special interest.'"

A Socialist Alternative for the Future

EUGENE E. RUYLE

A major intellectual triumph of the nineteenth century was Marx's analysis of bourgeois society and how it contained the seeds of its own destruction, seeds which would mature and blossom into a more humane, socialist order. This future socialist order would emerge, he said, when the proletariat seized power and built upon the achievements of the bourgeoisie — the development of society's productive forces to a high degree, political freedom, and democracy — to eliminate the wage slavery which Marx saw as the cause of the misery and dehumanization of the working class. Marx's view of the future was similar to that of the father of American anthropology, Lewis Henry Morgan:

The time which has passed away since civilization began is but a fragment of the past duration of man's existence; and but a fragment of the ages yet to come. The dissolution of society bids fair to become the termination of a career of which property is the end and aim; because such a career contains the elements of self-destruction. Democracy in government, brotherhood in society, equality in rights and privileges, and universal education, foreshadow the next higher plane of society to which experience, intelligence and knowledge are steadily tending. It will be a revival, in a higher form, of the liberty, equality and fraternity of the ancient gentes (Morgan 1964: 467).

Although in many respects the twentieth century has been unkind to the revolutionary optimism of the nineteenth, the Marxist vision of a future socialist society continues to be a powerful force in the revolutionary struggles of the Third World peoples who are major subjects of anthropological research. In view of the current feeling that anthropologists should act in the interests of "their" people (as, some would argue, defined by the people themselves), it seems appropriate for anthropologists to draw upon their inventory of hundreds of different cultural configurations and their time perspective of millions of years to explore anew the dialectical and revolutionary aspects of the Marxist synthesis: Is there a general direction to cultural evolution and human history? Have the wars, revolutions, pogroms, and concentration camps of the twentieth century disproved Marx, or merely made more imperative the implementation of the Marxist program? What sorts of institutions and cultural patterns will be needed to eliminate exploitation and oppression and guarantee the free development of the individual in the socialist society of the future?

I have discussed the first two of these questions elsewhere (Ruyle 1977); this essay is intended to stimulate thinking and discussion on the last.

THE SOCIAL ORDER OF THE FUTURE

Socialism may be described as a nonexploitative, post-capitalist world industrial system in which strategic resources and the means of production are socially owned, democratically controlled, and rationally managed in order to produce for use rather than for profit. More important than man's control of production, however, is man's control of himself and the social order he inhabits. As long as man does not control his own social order, it towers over him like a mighty force of nature. But the history of humanity has been the history of man's increasing control of the forces of nature, and man's final triumph will be to bring his own social order under control and manage it so as to ensure the free and full development of every individual. It is only within such a socialist society that the social tensions within and between national societies can be resolved and man can come to be in harmony with himself, his fellows, and with nature.

Before examining the kinds of cultural phenomena which would characterize a socialist society, it may be well to clarify a few points, since we have all been brainwashed to a certain extent into believing such a society to be utopian and contrary to the nature of man.

It is essential to realize that the socialist society of the future, like the primitive communism of the past, will be based upon enlightened self-interest, not altruism. As humanity comes to understand how social ills are generated by systems of exploitation, individuals will realize that it is in their interest not only to avoid being exploited themselves, but also to prevent the emergence of any kind of exploitation. As the Wobblies used to say, "An injury to one is an injury to all." Thus, even if some people may wish to exploit others, they will be prevented from doing so, not just by the resistance of those being exploited, but by society as a whole. Those not being directly exploited will see that their own liberty will ultimately be threatened by the existence and growth of any exploitive system.

It may be objected that nothing will prevent the exploitation of minorities by majorities. Closer examination, however, reveals that this would be unlikely. If the spoils of such exploitation were to be equally distributed among the majority, there would not be enough benefits to justify the effort of suppressing the minority, and there would be no real point to the exploitation. If, on the other hand, the spoils were unequally distributed, this would not be a case of a majority exploiting a minority, but rather of one minority exploiting another with the support and assistance of the majority. The majority, however, would gain nothing and in fact be threatened by this, since what is today a minority exploiting another with the help of the majority would tomorrow be transformed into a minority exploiting the majority.

The above analysis assumes enlightened self-interest, that all men will be aware of the operation of the social system and of their own interests within such a system. The teachings of class society, of course, tell us that this is impossible, that the masses are by nature unconcerned with the workings of society and are too stupid to realize what is good for them. Scientific socialism rejects this notion and instead places its faith in the ability of the working class to come to grips with the real conditions of its existence and to act accordingly.

That such faith is not misplaced is indicated, first of all, by the fact that the genetic material of the working class is essentially the same as that of the ruling class (neo-racists such as Jensen (1969), Herrnstein (1971), and Shockley (1972) have argued to the contrary, but their ideas are generally rejected by physical anthropologists and human geneticists — see Brace, Gamble, and Bond 1971; Mead, Dobzhansky, Tobach, and Light 1968; and Ashley Montagu 1975). Thus, if the ruling class has the innate ability to manage the affairs of mankind, so must the working class. Any observed differences are the result of differential enculturation.

Further, the history of the international working class indicates that it has again and again attempted to take control of its own destiny and improve its conditions of existence. Such attempts have failed solely because of ruthless oppression by the ruling class. Regrettably, the past struggles of the working class are not generally publicized, so that the American working class, in particular, has been cut off from its own history by the bourgeois-controlled education system and media. Thus, any apparent lack of revolutionary potential within the working class is the result of class rule and not its cause.

GUARANTEED EMPLOYMENT

The basic precondition for the emergence of capitalism is a class of "free laborers" (or wage slaves), people who are legally free but who lack access to the means of production and are therefore compelled (economically) to sell their labor in order to exist. The capitalist system ensures that there will always be an oversupply of labor and this competitive disadvantage of the seller of labor permits capitalist exploitation. As Marx put it:

"If," says Wakefield, "all the members of the society are supposed to possess equal portions of capital ... no man would have a motive for accumulating more capital than he could use with his own hands. This is to some extent the case in new American settlements, where a passion for owning land prevents the existence of a class of labourers for hire." So long, therefore, as the labourer can accumulate for himself — and this he can do so long as he remains possessor of his means of production — capitalist accumulation and the capitalistic mode of production are impossible. The class of wage-labourers, essential to these, is wanting (1965: 767).

The first task of a socialist revolution will be to free the class of wage slaves from their economic bondage and to guarantee employment and a decent income for all. This will prevent exploitation and oppression in the working place and give to the working man a new security and a new dignity.

It is important to understand that work is not something imposed on man, but rather that it is often a source of satisfaction in itself. Labor is the human essence; man realizes his own species nature only by imposing his will on the environment. Man, therefore, fulfills himself in labor. In bourgeois society labor is a stigma of the lower classes, and therefore disesteemed, but in socialist society this stigma will be removed and man's "labor instinct" will find expression. Even in bourgeois society there is evidence that man does find satisfaction in the labor process itself: (1) the bourgeois themselves work very hard in our society, even though they are not economically compelled to do so. True, this effort is directed toward maintaining an exploitive system, but in the minds of the bourgeois themselves, it is for the good of society; (2) members of the bourgeoisie and the proletariat engage in spare-time labor — gardening, home repair, hobbies, and so forth — trying to get the satisfaction here that they do not have in their vocation; (3) even alienated wage labor can be a source of satisfaction (workers on assembly lines and even garbage workers are sometimes reported as taking pride in their work); (4) feelings of uselessness and aimlessness are common among retired people who are no longer able to do any productive work. All these considerations indicate that just as exercise is necessary for the health of the body, so the satisfactions gained from productive labor are necessary for the health of the psyche.

Most individuals will find employment in what might be called free corporations. These corporations will be organized along the lines of Vanek's "participatory economy," (1971) with the workers electing and controlling management. The corporations will operate the factories, farms, schools, hospitals, and other productive facilities owned by society, for the benefit of society, while providing their workers with an income. Some individuals may be self-employed as entrepreneurs meeting economic needs which are not met by the free corporations.

In addition, there will be a socialist industrial army, composed of all those unable or unwilling to find employment in the non-governmental economy. In some ways, this socialist industrial army will be similar to the industrial reserve army (the reserve army of unemployed) of bourgeois society. Unlike the industrial reserve army, however, the socialist industrial army will be a productive part of the economy and will provide a decent living for those in it. The socialist industrial army will serve a variety of economic functions: (1) it will act as an auxiliary labor force for the agricultural and industrial corporations during times of peak manpower demand, such as planting or harvesting; (2) it will act as an emergency relief force during natural disasters such as floods or earthquakes; (3) it may be used to perform various essential, unskilled and perhaps unpleasant tasks, such as street cleaning, garbage collecting, etc. If these are insufficient to fully occupy the work force of the socialist industrial army, additional work can be created. Recruits for the socialist industrial army will come from three basic sources.

First, all those who are unable or unwilling to find employment in the free corporations. It will be an employer of last resort, so to speak. Second, all youth, upon completion of formal compulsory schooling. They will have to serve a few years in the socialist industrial army. The time thus spent will be an essential part of the education of all individuals. It will give them a few years of additional maturity and work experience before they continue their education or embark on a career of their own choosing. Although work assignments will be based primarily upon social need, every effort will be made to take individual preferences and aspirations into account. Third, all individuals who are employed in the free corporations or are self-employed. They will be obliged to spend a part of each year — about a month, for example — in the socialist industrial army. This practice will inhibit the emergence of elitism by ensuring that everyone in a responsible position continues to have contact with, and to identify with, the masses. (The practice has been instituted in China for party cadres to serve this purpose.)

The socialist industrial army will perform a variety of important tasks, but its social functions will be more important than its economic ones. Since it will guarantee employment and an income to everyone, it will give the individual the kind of economic security which is the prerogative of the very wealthy today, and create a new dignity which is totally lacking in class society.

SOCIALIST DISTRIBUTION

A major goal of socialism is economic equality. This concept requires some explanation since it is usually misinterpreted and misunderstood. It does not mean that everyone will receive an identical amount of money, nor that everyone's consumption habits will be the same. Rather, it means that everyone will receive a roughly equal return on his labor and have the freedom to determine both his hours of work and the nature of his income expenditure.

The idea that everyone should have a roughly equivalent return on his labor will perhaps seem unfair to people reared in bourgeois society, since it may be felt that a skilled worker, such as a doctor, should be rewarded more highly than an unskilled worker, such as a hospital porter. This argument may seem reasonable in bourgeois society, where the costs of acquiring skills are largely borne by the individual. It makes little sense, however, in a socialist society where the cost of education is borne by society. If a medical student is supported at a decent level throughout his years at medical school, there need be no monetary incentive to enter the profession. Certain differentials in labor time may be desirable, however. For example, the hours of labor may be less for a doctor since he must spend time keeping up with new developments in medicine. Similarly, some occupations which are undesirable may have fewer mandatory labor hours. Thus, for example, if the standard work week is twenty-five hours, doctors may spend only fifteen seeing patients so that the remainder may be spent in reading journals; garbage collectors may work only twenty hours to offset the disagreeable nature of the job.

Another point is that individuals vary in the amount of time they want to spend working and in the standard of living they desire to work for. For example, one person may wish to cut his working hours in half and reduce his living standard in order to give himself more time for fishing; another may wish to increase his working hours and spend his greater income in expensive restaurants and nightclubs. There is no reason why individual preferences of this sort cannot be accommodated within the framework of a socialist society, as long as they are indeed based on the free choices of individuals. What cannot be tolerated is that those individuals who work least should be able to spend more money on luxuries, and that people should go fishing because they cannot find employment. Differentials in access to luxuries cannot be allowed to become associated with differentials in power and prestige.

An important aspect of the socialist economy will be the abolition of bourgeois money and its replacement by socialist accounting through socialist credit cards serving as media of exchange and stores of value. The form of money in bourgeois society permits and encourages the concealment of fraud, embezzlement, theft, and other ill-gotten gains. This will be impossible with socialist credit cards.

The socialist credit card could be quite similar to bourgeois credit cards, although there will be only one card, bearing the individual's photograph, name, place of residence and occupation, next of kin, and other essential information. It would serve as an identity card, driver's license, library card, fishing license, etc. Misuse could be prevented by requiring fingerprints when the card is used.

The use of such credit cards would immediately remove all incentive for theft from individuals or stores, since there would be no money to steal and whatever the store sold could be acquired easily through a credit card purchase. There remains, it is true, the possibility of chronic overdrawing of accounts; some individuals might consistently spend more than they earn. Such individuals could be counseled by financial officers of the government and, if necessary, sanctions could be imposed. What is more likely, however, is that individuals who failed to respond to counseling would be regarded as untrustworthy deviants, much as thieves and liars were regarded in primitive communist societies. Unless such behavior became widespread, there would be no need for harsh punishment to make an example of such individuals in order to protect private property and ensure respect for essentially unjust laws. These harsh punishments are necessary, of course, in class societies because of widespread poverty and extreme differentials of wealth. With these removed, the incentive for crimes against property would be removed.

Another important aspect of socialist distribution will be that many goods and services will be freely distributed according to need or desire. The economic principle here is that goods or services, for which the demand is essentially inelastic, could be distributed free, with a saving in accounting costs (see Mandel 1970: Chapter 17). The demand for goods such as salt, staple grains, and work clothing does not increase with a decrease in price, so that eliminating price would decrease the cost of distribution without increasing the cost of production. The free distribution of some services could actually decrease social costs. This is the case in medical care, since individuals who receive free medical care are more likely to have checkups and to consult doctors early in their illnesses, so that disorders are detected and treated early and medical costs reduced. Preventive care would be substituted for curative care. To a certain extent this socialist principle is already operative in bourgeois society, for example in police protection, which, in theory at least, is available to all according to need, not ability to pay taxes.

WORLD GOVERNMENT

In order to get away from the popular misconception of socialism as a centralized system run by the state, it is necessary to draw a distinction between government, the management of the collective affairs of society; and the state, a special instrument which monopolizes legitimate violence. Marxists, in defining the state as the executive committee of the ruling class, tend to obscure this distinction while making an even more important point: in class societies, both the government and the state are controlled by the ruling class and are used as instruments of class rule. With the elimination of class rule, the state is expected to wither away. Yet society will continue to have concerns which must be handled collectively, and government will not disappear. One aspect of government is the management of violence, which is the ultimate means of enforcement of every social order. We shall discuss this special problem of controlling the police and military below.

Under socialism, society's collective affairs will be administered through institutions of parliamentary democracy remarkably similar to those of bourgeois democracy. The important differences are these: (1) there will be no privileged minority with interests antagonistic to the majority and with greater power to influence governmental decision making, and (2) there will be special mechanisms to prevent governmental officials and bureaucrats from acquiring entrenched power.

In order to prevent buildups of bureaucratic power, all legislative, judicial and higher administrative officials will be elected directly by popular vote at regular intervals, subject to instant recall by their constituencies, and paid on the same scale as ordinary workers. Special privileges such as multiple residences, private airplanes and yachts, fleets of limousines, and personal servants will be abolished.

The structure of socialist democracy is shown in Figure 1. Every individual has dual representation, electing officials in both his place of work and his place of residence. General decisions about allocation of resources — what and how much is to be produced — and about the labor process itself will be made at the appropriate level. Each of the levels may have a tripartite separation of powers into legislative, executive, and judicial similar to bourgeois democracies. At the top will be a bicameral World Congress which will regulate the use of resources of our "Spaceship Earth" and generally regulate the nature of relationships between lower level social groupings.

We may turn now to a consideration of the role of police and

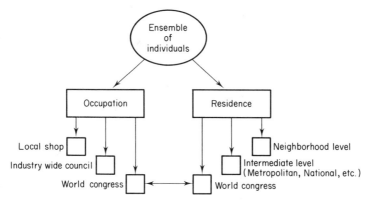

Figure 1. Structure of socialist democracy

military forces in socialist society. In bourgeois society, such specialists in violence protect the wealth and privileges of the ruling class by protecting the property structure on which bourgeois rule rests. As a result, they are continually called upon to intervene in fundamental class antagonisms between rich and poor.

Thus, the police have a dual appearance in class society, as friends of the rich and enemies of the poor. For example, in Westchester, a suburb of New York, where the inhabitants are wealthy and "respectable," one is likely to find that the police are truly public servants, with little antagonism between them and the people, and little "police brutality." The same police, however, in the ghettos of Harlem or Bedford-Stuyvesant, are a force standing above the people, an army of occupation so to speak.

With the replacement of class society by a classless, socialist society, the major sources of crime, conflict, and tension will disappear and with them the need for an oppressive instrument of social control. Nevertheless, it is unlikely that all crime and conflict will disappear, and some kind of police force will probably continue to be necessary. In their interaction with the people, however, these police will be more like the police in Westchester than the police in Harlem.

The structure of the socialist police force will include local police and higher level agencies, with a world police force at the top. All of these will be trained, professional police officers charged with law enforcement. In addition, there will be local volunteer forces recruited from the general population. Such local militias will serve a variety of functions.

First, they will discourage any attempts to dominate the community from outside. Ideally, of course, there should not be any need for this in a socialist order, but realistically, social systems are at best imperfect, and the best protection against outside domination is democratic control of the means of violence. This will be particularly true in the difficult transition period, while socialist institutions are still in the "shakedown" stage.

Even after the military need for local militias has passed, they will play other economic and psychological roles. It will give those members of the population who have a need to handle guns and use the instruments of violence a chance to do so without endangering society. It will provide a sense of local independence and freedom from outside domination. Finally, the local militia can be used in disaster relief, much as our own national guard is now used.

The question arises, of course, of whether there is a possibility that the police or militia might use their special access to the means of violence to set themselves up above society. To a large extent, this is a baseless worry. The problem of civilian control over the police and military has already been solved in bourgeois society. There may be corruption in the New York police force, for example, but there is no real fear that the police will take over New York City, or that the United States Army will take over the United States. Similarly, there is no real possibility that socialist police or militia will take over a socialist society.

THE FAMILY

As Engels suggested, socialism "will transform the relations between the sexes into a purely private matter which concerns only the persons involved and into which society has no occasion to intervene" (Marx and Engels 1968: 80). It will be up to the individual to freely enter into whatever kind of sexual and domestic relations with whatever like-minded individuals he chooses. Each individual, male and female, will have his own role in social production and his own independent income, so that the economic bases for sexual oppression and repression, "the dependence ... of the woman on the man and of the children on the parents," will be removed and the material base for sexual equality and freedom will be laid. The only role of the government will be to ensure that no one is either exploited, oppressed, or abused in a domestic relationship.

One anticipates that "the family" will persist, but that it will take a variety of forms, depending upon the personalities of the individuals concerned. Domestic arrangements will vary from independent individuals living alone with perhaps nonresident primary and accessory "spouses" similar to some Australian tribes, or perhaps the "visiting lover" arrangement of the Nayar, through nuclear and extended families (which will probably be most common), to communal domestic situations similar to some experimental communal living arrangements of today.

Society, of course, will have an interest in the raising of children and will ensure that all children are well cared for, well fed, well clothed, and well housed. The freedom of the growing child to develop his own potential will be protected, regardless of the domestic arrangements of his parents.

Both parents will have ample time off work to adequately care for the child throughout his early years. There will also be adequate nursery and child-care facilities which may be freely used so that parents are not unduly burdened by child care.

There may also be some sort of godparenthood or "big brother" institution in which a nonparental guardian is appointed or selected to generally look after the interests of the child from birth throughout his life.

RELIGION

When a primitive communist society worships its gods, it is in fact worshiping itself. Sacredness, in this Durkheimian view, is not a quality inherent in things, but rather a quality projected onto things by society. When an Australian aborigine worships his totemic ancestors, he is merely expressing in a different symbolic idiom the same truth about the interdependence and oneness of humanity and nature which ecologists express in the symbolic idiom of science. In addition to this sort of life-affirming religion, there are also magico-religious beliefs and practices which serve as an adjunct to social production and reproduction, coming into play when the force of rational social production is unable to control nature. Under conditions of primitive communism, then, religion is overwhelmingly a positive force.

In class society, religion takes on a new function, that of social control. With the emergence of the Church monopoly over access to the sacred and supernatural, religion comes under the control of the ruling class and is used to legitimize the differentials of wealth and power which emerge from class rule. As White (1959: 323) argued:

The function of the church in civil society is to preserve the integrity of the sociocultural system of which it is a part by (1) offensive-defensive relations with neighboring nations, (and) (2) keeping the subordinate class at home obedient and docile.

In addition to its role in legitimizing the status quo, religion also serves to divert the attention of the oppressed classes from the inequities of life and their own misery. As Marx put it:

Religious distress is at the same time the expression of real distress and the protest against real distress. Religion is the sigh of the oppressed creature, the heart of a heartless world, just as it is the spirit of a spiritless situation. It is the opium of the people (Selsam and Martel 1963: 227).

With the elimination of class rule, the forces which tend to warp and distort religion in class society will also be eliminated. As the roots of religion as a form of "false consciousness" disappear in a socialist society, religion itself will become transformed from an opiate into its original function, an affirmation of man's feeling that life itself is sacred. The criticism of religion by scientific socialism is not for the purpose of destroying but of liberating it. Marx continues:

The abolition of religion as the illusory happiness of the people is required for their real happiness. The demand to give up the illusions about its condition is the demand to give up a condition which needs illusions. The criticism of religion is therefore in embryo the criticism of the vale of woe, the halo of which is religion (Selsam and Martel 1963: 227).

As this "living flower" is cultivated, the feelings of sanctity, which free individuals feel with regard to nature and social products (art, music, cathedrals, etc.), will find expression in a variety of communal bodies of like-minded individuals; a return, in a sense, to the variety of pagan cults which characterized the ancient and primitive worlds, but on a newer and higher plane. When the wellsprings of religion are properly appreciated as lying within man, and cult members see that no one is going to prevent them from worshiping as they wish, they will also realize that their own worship can neither be enhanced by forcing it upon others nor diminished by others ignoring it. In the religious tolerance of the socialist society of the future, there will be no established church and none of the god-mongering of class society; neither will there be the militant atheism which characterizes the self-styled socialist states.

One function in which society as a whole may play a role is in affirming the sacredness of human labor. Sacredness, it should be emphasized again, is a quality bestowed on things and processes by humanity. The ensemble of individuals operating over generations determines what is sacred to the society. Since the human essence lies in social labor, it is entirely appropriate to bestow sanctity on certain forms of labor; service in the socialist industrial army may well take on the aspect of a sacred as well as a social duty, affirming the individual's obligation to work and his interdependence and brotherhood with his fellows. Further, the service of youth in the socialist industrial army may take on the aspect of a rite of passage, indicating the transition from childhood to responsible adulthood.

MISCELLANY

As an anthropologist, I have been concerned primarily with analyzing the social structural sources of dissatisfaction in class society and in designing a social structure which would eliminate this dissatisfaction. Since the sources of social discontent in bourgeois society lie in the wage slavery of the overwhelming majority of the population — and it is on this wage slavery that the wealth and privileges of the bourgeoisie are based — I have been most concerned with describing the institutions which would eliminate wage slavery and exploitation. I have been less concerned with other aspects of the future society, because I feel that once wage slavery has been eliminated and economic and political freedom and democracy have been established, it will be possible to apply a variety of proposals which, to the extent that they do not take into account the politico-economic realities of capitalism, are at present simply utopian. It may be well, however, to consider very briefly how certain specific problems could be solved under socialism.

Take the problem of automobiles. It is often said that the automobile dominates American life. In a sense this is true, but this sort of thinking is best considered as a variant of what Marx (1965: 72) called the "fetishism of commodities" in which the products of human labor "appear as independent beings endowed with life, and entering into relations with one another and the human race." It is not the automobile that dominates America; the automobile is simply a product of human labor. Rather it is those who profit from the sale of automobiles — the owners of the automobile, steel, oil, and rubber companies — that dominate American through the instrument of the automobile. Once this domination is understood and eliminated, we can begin to apply proposals to bring automobiles under human control, such as the proposal of Goodman (1964: 145–155) to ban private automobiles from Manhattan.

Or take the problem of urban planning. It is difficult to anticipate how urban the future population will be. I would imagine that it would be highly urbanized, to about the same degree as contemporary industrial societies. After all, cities are exciting places, centers of the arts and intellectual life, with an array of speciality shops, services, and restaurants which simply cannot exist without a large population. There is no reason why this would be any less true in a socialist society, and in a socialist society most of the reasons for not living in cities would be eliminated: pollution, crime, automobile congestion, high rents, and so forth.

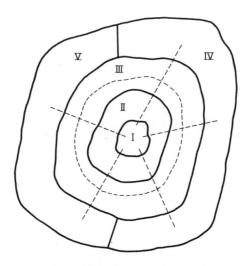

- - - - Rapid transit system
- I   Urban area: multiple unit and high density dwellings
- II   Green area: parkland and some farm corporations
- III   Suburbs: small farms and decentralized industry
- IV   Agricultural: farm corporations
- V   Miscellaneous: extractive industries, recreation, open
  areas for hermits and social discontents, wilderness

Figure 2.   Land use in a socialist metropolitan area

On the other hand, perhaps the urbanization trend would be reversed, and more people would choose to live on small, partially self-sufficient farms of one to ten acres. With a decentralized industrial base, imaginative programming in the mass media, and rapid transit, this would certainly be feasible without anyone suffering from rural isolation.

Any mixture of these two possibilities could be accommodated under a land-use plan such as that diagramed in Figure 2. The surburban area where farms and decentralized, nonpolluting factories would be intermingled, could be expanded or contracted according to the number of people who wished to live in a semirural atmosphere; so, too, could the urban area.

One thing which would be essential would be the regulation of the human population in order to maintain a stable rate of use of resources. It is clear that the population must stop growing at some point, and that point could only be decided after the revolution. I would imagine that the human population would decrease for a few centuries after the establishment of socialism, and then stabilize. My reasoning is based upon the doubt that the entire world population could use up resources at the rate the average American family does, so it will be necessary to either reduce living standards or decrease population, or both. But perhaps new energy sources will be developed which will enable a larger population to be sustained at an even higher level.

Finally, it should be noted that regional and international cultural diversity will continue. The basic institutions described above will everywhere be modified to fit existing cultural traditions. Existing diversity in language, music, art forms, literature, clothing, religious beliefs, and so forth will, of course, continue within a general international framework of liberty, equality, and fraternity.

CONCLUDING REMARKS

I have presented a number of proposals for a set of institutions which would enable humanity to manage its affairs in such a way as to eliminate exploitation and oppression and to permit the free development of the human potential. It is entirely appropriate for intellectuals to draft such rough plans for the future, but it must be kept in mind that the responsibility for building socialism lies with the working class, and it is they who will ultimately determine its form.

Finally, although I have suggested that socialism is inevitable barring some sort of catastrophe, this does not mean that it will come about automatically. Socialism must be built by the conscious activity of man, and it is hoped that the proposals in this essay will help create the kind of consciousness necessary for the construction of a socialist society. On this note, we may conclude by quoting Marx's XIth Thesis on Feuerbach: "The philosophers have only *interpreted* the world in various ways; the point, however, is to *change* it" (Selsam and Martel 1963: 318).

REFERENCES

ASHLEY MONTAGU, M. F., *editor*
    1975   *Race and IQ.* New York: Oxford University Press.
BRACE, C. LORING, GEORGE R. GAMBLE, JAMES T. BOND, *editors*
    1971   *Race and intelligence.* Anthropological Studies No. 8. Washington, D.C.: American Anthropological Association.
GOODMAN, PAUL
    1964   *Utopian essays and practical proposals.* New York: Vintage Books.
HERRNSTEIN, RICHARD
    1971   I.Q. *Atlantic Monthly.*
JENSEN, ARTHUR R.
    1969   How much can we boost IQ and scholastic achievement? *Harvard Educational Review* 39: 1–123.

MANDEL, ERNEST
1970   *Marxist economic theory*, two volumes. New York: Monthly Review Press.
MARX, KARL
1965   *Capital: a critical analysis of capitalist production*, volume one. Moscow: Progress Publishers.
MARX, KARL, FRIEDRICH ENGELS
1968   *The Communist manifesto.* New York: Monthly Review Press.
MEAD, M., T. DOBZHANSKY, E. TOBACH, R. E. LIGHT, *editors*
1968   *Science and the concept of race.* New York: Columbia University Press.
MORGAN, LEWIS HENRY
1964   *Ancient society.* Edited by Leslie A. White. Cambridge, Mass.: Harvard University Press.
RUYLE, EUGENE E.
1977   "The future as anthropology: socialism as a human ecological climax." Paper presented at the 21st Annual Meeting of the Kroeber Anthropological Society, Berkeley, May 7.
SELSAM, HOWARD, HARRY MARTEL
1963   *Readings in Marxist philosophy: from the writings of Marx, Engels and Lenin.* New York: International Publishers.
SHOCKLEY, WILLIAM
1972   Dysgenics, geneticity, raceology: a challenge to the intellectual responsibility of educators. *Phi Delta Kappan* 53: 297–312.
VANEK, JAROSLAV
1971   *The participatory economy: an evolutionary hypothesis and a strategy for development.* Ithaca, New York: Cornell University Press.
WHITE, LESLIE A.
1959   *The evolution of culture: the development of civilization to the fall of Rome.* New York: McGraw-Hill.

The State of Anthropology Today: A Comment

H. L. LEFFERTS, JR.

In considering material such as the articles by Benello, Keur and LaDue, and Ruyle depicting possible cultural alternatives in a future United States, we are apt to look at aspects such as the feasibility of their coming into being, the reasonableness of their continuing existence, and the depth of detail in illustrating potential for the satisfaction of what we consider to be human needs. This is a logical extension of the ethnographic approach which depicts how a people exists at a given time and it forms part of the basis of cultural anthropology. However, in this essay I will attempt to approach this on a different level and use these papers to view utopian ideas in the context of the system in which they were conceived.

It is right and eminently proper that anthropology should be concerned with the construction of cultural alternatives. To expand on Northrup Frye's analysis (1966), anthropology may be seen as the field of study which attempted, as a normal outcome of the growth of Western European Civilization, to subject the twin myths of that culture — the social contract and utopia — to rigorous, disciplined, investigation. Thus, anthropology is not only oriented to discovering man's nature, as implied in the studies of paleoanthropology, archaeology, and the pursuit of the primitive, but it must also, and has traditionally, considered the topic of future development. Anthropology also embodies the idea expressed by Montesquieu, when talking about cannibals, that no culture is so close to perfection that it cannot afford to examine other systems for possible insights into how it can better organize itself.

This leads, then, to an analysis of these papers not just in terms of themselves but, more importantly, in terms of what they have to offer for a consideration and understanding of ourselves. I have shown the papers by Benello, Keur and LaDue, and Ruyle to my students for comment. These students stated that what these papers presented to them was "old" and "dull." Their impressions may have been colored by the fact that they were used to reading science fiction as well as to putting their minds into different parallel and future orientations. They felt that the attitudes expressed were stereotyped and showed a fundamental lack of diversity. This expressed itself in two complementary positions:

First, the students felt that the papers were restricted by their dependence on the authors' views of Western civilization, or the United States, as having one basic flaw, be it population, energy, or social organization, and that this flaw would be exposed by a cataclysm, or near cataclysm, which acted as a trigger for the acceptance of the alternative. There was little recognition by the authors of the multiplicity and interplay of factors, and how these reinforce one another, in a real system — a recognition which is basic to the problem of taking hold of a system and revamping it.

Second, in the authors' formulation of alternatives, little was said about the interplay of forces, or the incorporation of what might be seen as exotic but relevant facets of "foreign" cultures into the new systems. Returning to Frye's analysis of literary utopias in the West, we find that he points to the pastoral mode as a basic countertheme to the overwhelming multiplicity of contrived needs with which we presently exist (Frye 1966: 47). But, in embracing pastoralism, must we remain so ethnocentric? A favorite tool of science fiction — and of ethnographers — is the incorporation of a touch of "foreignness," while at the same time making others believe in the reality of this new way of thinking, by using words or expressions from the constructed system. This criticism was not meant by the students to apply only to the literary style of the alternatives offered, but to point out that, inevitably, in the construction of a new system, different ideas and words would come into being (they are constantly coming into being as the "new" system evolves), and these would seem to require expression in their own terms.

While other comments were made by the students, I think that the above two would provide an excellent foundation for substantiating the hypothesis of this comment, that these works are better understood as a reflection of the state of anthropology today than as broadly based views of future alternatives. The impression arises that anthropology, in spite of its origin as the study of man's past and future, is limited in its conceptual orientation. Anthropology's view of man remains essentially Western, thus displaying an ethnocentrism which is rather difficult to understand, especially when one remembers that this field, as distinct from all others in the universe of academic discourse, has as a major part of its purpose the understanding of others in their own contexts. However, it is clear that, in spite of the idea of contextual legitimacy, when anthropologists talk about their field, the theoretical underpinnings of their observations remain tied to their own Western context.

Beyond this, however, several tenets of recent (and not so recent) Western derivation, such as conflict as part of an ongoing system, statistical norms as the basis of a culture beyond the comprehension of individuals involved in the system, mutual causality, etc. do provide modes for constructing future alternatives. Obviously, however, we have not assimilated these into our theoretical framework, any more than we have conceptualized the idea of molding a unified system utilizing the diverse customs we have seen and of which we have approved in our ethnographic travels.

This collection of designs for the future has been interesting. As a beginning it has its good as well as its bad points. A major good point illustrated here, is the initiation of a train of thought which leads to an examination of ourselves and our orientations. As the starting point of a "social planetarium," where we could begin to visualize alternative future constructions (Mead, cited in Plath 1971), much remains to be done. Let us continue the task.

REFERENCES

FRYE, NORTHRUP
    1966   "Varieties of literary utopias," in *Utopias and utopian thought.*
           Edited by F. E. Manuel, 25–49. Boston: Beacon Press.
PLATH, DAVID W., *editor*
    1971   *Aware of utopia.* Urbana: University of Illinois Press.

APPENDIX

Excerpts from the Transcription of the First Cultural Futuristics Symposium, Held at the American Anthropological Association 69th Annual Meeting

NOVEMBER 20, 1970.

Editor's Note: In 1970 a Symposium on Cultural Futuristics was held at the Annual Meeting of the American Anthropological Association. This symposium generated much interest among anthropologists, young and old. As a result, a futuristics symposium has become an annual event at American Anthropological Association meetings, with topics and focuses varying from year to year. The first three symposia, held in 1970, 1971, and 1972 respectively, dealt mainly with conceptualizations of cultural futuristics, the applications of anthropology to futuristics, conceptualizations of the future in various cultures, and some specific aspects and examples of cultural futuristics. The 1973 symposium was devoted to discussions of our future cultural alternatives, and the topic for 1974 was the cultures of communities beyond the surface of the Earth. In all these symposia we had virtually no participation from outside North America. The IXth International Congress of Anthropological and Ethnological Sciences provided a welcome occasion to include participants from the Third World and played an indispensable part in the development of cultural futuristics. On the other hand, the nature and rationale of the session on "The future of the human species seen by the entire species" at the ICAES was much influenced by our experience in previous cultural futuristics symposia. Since the 1970 symposium marked the beginning of the development of cultural futuristics, parts of the relevant discussions which took place there are reproduced here.

MARGARET MEAD: This is an anthropological meeting and the bulk of the people here are either anthropologists or would like to be, or are not quite sure but are considering it. And when I talk about what anthropology can contribute to a science of the future, I am not trying to stake out a claim for anthropologists. It is nonsense to have all these fragmented human sciences. The future is one of the places where we can all meet, because nobody owns a piece of the future. The future is the one place where countries at different levels of development can meet on equal terms. Whenever we discuss the past, people have a proprietary sense of their own past, so that if they speak a Latin-derived language they are better at Latin than anybody else, and if they are Chinese, they are better at Chinese history than anybody will ever be. But if the future is open, and therefore it provides a place for communication between the simplest society and the most advanced. I think this is tremendously important, especially for anthropologists who spend a lot of their time establishing communication with people at very different technological levels. It gives the same kind of release that I get in New Guinea, when I speak good Neo-Melanesian and so do the natives. I speak seven New Guinea languages, and there are over seven hundred. So I don't get very far with that, and I shall never speak them as well as they do. But I speak just as good Neo-Melanesian — that's pidgin English — as any New Guinean and they speak just as well as I do. And we suddenly meet and can talk on an equal-to-equal basis. And the future does the same for all the disciplines. The biologists don't know more about the future than the physicists, and the physicists admit that at present they know nothing. So we have a very good start.

Now for a general model of the way in which anthropologists can contribute — and I want to emphasize this over and over again — from the traditional disciplines that we have we can contribute the accumulated knowledge of various sources and various kinds of experience. If we can contribute to a whole — a shared whole — we can avoid perpetuating "ethnic social sciences" and instead all work together. I think "Spaceship Earth" is a very *bad* figure of speech for anthropologists because it deals entirely with a man-made situation and suggests a closed system. If we use instead the concept of an island and treat the planet as an island, only part of what happens there is man-made. A large proportion is part of our whole cosmic history and open to the solar system, the galaxy, and the universe. To study an island we need contributions from every known discipline if we are to make some sense of the whole and provide ourselves with a very small living model of the planet. We think at present that the tremendously aroused interest in the environment in recent years has been partly a by-product of looking at the Earth from the moon and seeing how small it really is — small and fragile instead of being something that we could exploit forever without fear of consequences. Professionally we deal with wholes: whole tribes, whole language groups, whole communities, and sometimes whole nations. To deal with the planet as a whole and then place it in the wider cosmic context is not difficult for us.

Taking up the point about antientropy that Elise Boulding has been making, you can place man as the antientropic force in the universe[1]

---

[1] See references for elaboration of this point. — *Editor.*

not just on this planet but in the entire universe — as the one part of biological evolution to date, which is able to deal consciously and planfully, perhaps too planfully, with antientropic forces. Now, as anthropologists we can enter this field and contribute to it at a great many levels, and I think it is important to realize this. The archaeologists can contribute; somebody who wants to sit on a small island and do blood types can contribute; and people who want to deal with larger fields can contribute. It is not necessary for everybody to think on a cosmic or planetary level, or even a national level, in order to make a contribution. What is important is to think at each turn, as we do it, what contribution it will make to the whole. In the symposium on fertility, reproduction, and population control, it was quite clear that anthropologists will work differently in the future, now that they know what is needed for the whole problem of population. And it is part of our tradition — a tradition I hope we will never lose — that we carry other people's needs in our heads when we go into the field. If we include contributions to an understanding of the future in the senses of building models for the future and accumulating more data about man in the past that can be relevant to the future, we can include the future in our fieldwork at a great number of different levels.

There are a great number of things that must be simulated because they are too dangerous to attempt, or because you can't get anybody to finance them. You know, this "build-a-little-model-nonnation-nation-and-see-how-it-works" idea would be fine if anybody was going to finance it, but they are not. I think that past experience shows that the chances of getting finance for studies or experiments of that sort are not very good. We may get a small city and that's about the limit. And we are not going (I hope) to have living experiments in plague or in wiping out one age-group in the population. We cannot have living experiments in what would happen if people lived to be 150, which is what everyone is prophesying at the moment. There are very large areas that are too dangerous, too bulky, or too incompatible with the current fabric of society to get financed and these could be handled by simulation. Anthropologists could make enormous contributions to simulation but they haven't done very much with it yet. The simulator will ask about special conditions: do you know about any society that ever did that? And we produce what we can out of the hat, and they produce something else, and you get a very good simulation. We ought to be participating in simulation actively and constructively so as to provide material that will be a kind of future data base for thinking about the future.

Now I shall list very briefly the fields in which I think anthropology can work. First, the nature of change and the historical background of today's world are all we have to base our thinking on as we move into the future. One thing that anthropologists know is that culture comes from culture, and art comes from art; they do not just come out of your gut, even with the help of LSD. Second, a comparative analysis of the nature of man, his innate characteristics and his capacity to learn to change will help correct the culture-bound theories of the behavioral sciences within the Western world. This is terribly important. To really integrate the thinking of other cultures into our culture-bound Western theories in psychology, political science, and sociology is one of the things that anthropologists ought to be able to do. Third, new theories can be generated by intensive research in small relatively closed societies in which intergenerational relationships can be closely examined. Today intergenerational relationships are fragmented almost everywhere. And in thinking about the future, one thing we need is a real understanding of intergenerational relationships. It was three generations that were working toward five, and we may be working toward six very rapidly. Fourth, we can become a source of new designs for living and for the extensive worldwide culture building which is needed in today's interconnected planetary system. Methodologically, one of the things that we anthropologists have is very, very long runs and this is one of the points that Wiener emphasized when we first began developing cybernetics. Most of the social sciences' runs are too short and the data are too problematic. But in paleontology, in prehistory, we have enormously long runs, and if we can learn how to arrange these we can do a great deal with them, with the kind of cybernetic mathematics that cannot be applied so well to things we have in our own society. Our disciplinary habits of dealing with wholes and of working with living people make it easier for anthropologists to relate to the "Now People" than for other social scientists: in most of the other social sciences, somebody collects the data which become little marks on paper, then somebody codes that, somebody does the statistics on the coding, and somebody else writes the book; he or she is a thousand miles from the living human beings that provided the data. It is this kind of social science that produces the kind of science fiction in which people are nothing but statistical cyphers. I think it's worth mentioning that on the whole, women have never been able to bear science fiction; it is mostly written by fifteen-year-old boys who have extraordinary technological imaginations but do not know a human being from a lamb, a goat, or a pig.

In a science of the future — I'm not using the word futurology, none of us like it; that is one thing we all agree on — we must accept responsibility in the same way that historians once accepted responsibility for giving us the best and most accurate information about the past that they could produce. We must try to provide the best information about the possibilities and alternatives for the future that can be produced at present. It is particularly important to keep track of nonsensical linear projections which leave out of account the fact that if any linear projection is made we immediately start doing something about it, and the projection becomes invalid. We need to deal with interconnected wholes. In this we should separate speculation from hard data as we have been taught to do in fieldwork. That is, a monograph about the future should include anything that we can now say about fossil fuels or the modifiability of the genes, or whatever, without evaluation in the same paragraph; the evaluation should be made in another paragraph. We need to make disciplined allowance for the extent to which the whole system of human culture is subject to feedback and unpredictable incursions of innovation or concatenations of events; we need to make allowance, too, for the dependence of this planet on wider cosmic systems. Probably nobody knows better than fieldworkers the unpredictability of the future and the extent to which unpredicted natural catastrophes, unpredicted biological events and unpredicted simple events like the collision of a ship with your canoe, are likely to upset everything that you have wanted.

At another level, we can scrutinize any planning, any prediction, any utopia, in the light of its being a part of the whole system. As a little exercise for fun, take Aldous Huxley's *Island* and try to work out the kinship system. He didn't take the trouble. It does not work. I would add something here that appeals, as a kind of cross-sectioning element running in a different direction from any of the approaches that Elise Boulding has suggested. And that is the relationship between conscious and unconscious purpose, because it has been suggested and particularly developed in the two Wenner-Gren conferences that Gregory Bateson ran. What is wrong with the world, at present, is conscious linear planning in which the rest of man's personality is not involved. We have to restore some kind of balance between the conscious and unconscious parts of the personality, the cosmic sense of the development of optima in complete systems instead of ramming through a freeway or some other technological change; it was the development of such partial, limited purposes that brought us to our present bad state.

One area in which we need to participate at once is the field of urban systems planning, which is developing very rapidly, and which could have all the bad technological results that have been predicted but could also have good ones if we can work on a sufficiently comprehensive plan. We could lay "utilitors," or corridors in which you put anything needed like wires, lasers, or pipelines. You make a grid, dig good-sized tunnels, and whatever anybody wants to wreck the surface of the world with goes through those tunnels. You could build small, self-sufficient, adequately serviced communities. I don't believe there's a community on this earth that isn't going to want electric light, and I've never seen one that lasted any length of time without it in the present-day world. But the whole technological framework could be put underground. Stop the building of roads that fragment systems; stop digging up every part of everything every week to fix something; put it underground where it can serve men; and then we could begin to design small, diversified communities which would be serviced in this sort of way. Like the island model, this model is one that it is possible to think with. Put technology where it belongs, as a servant of man, and then we can begin to work on the design of quite new and different kinds of societies. We have enough different cultures in our heads to provide a basis for developing new ones that nobody has ever thought of yet.

MICHAEL COHEN.   I am not an anthropologist, I am on a local planning board in New York City. We need anthropologists who can tell us how we can convince a community. We cannot change the fact that we are going to need electricity. One of the things that has been happening is that the scientists, particularly anthropologists of which we have supposedly many in New York City don't want any part of the political process, because politics is dirty and you get called names. If we don't go into the market place but stay in an ivory tower, all the sessions of futurologists here aren't going to do us any good at all in the practical day-in-day-out executing of the plans.

STEVEN POLGAR.   Anthropologists will not be used to convince people of something that we want done. If you are on the planning board, you should learn how to plan with people instead of trying to use anthropologists as your emissaries to missionize the heathen.

MARGARET MEAD.   Now I want to point out that futuristics conferences represent a hazard and an opportunity. At any moment in this country when one state does something, the other forty-nine may want to do the same. Suppose that every state in this union decided to do the same thing. We considered this when at one point in Hawaii there was a rumor that the state legislature was going to take a week off to think. That didn't happen, but that would have appealed to every state legislature in the United States at once, and then where would we have had the speakers to go to all of them? The same futurists turn up at every conference, they travel all the time, they have taken years off the ends of their lives by riding in jet planes. I don't get to one tenth of the ones I'm asked to. We can begin to develop, in each state, local groups of people whom anthropologists can help so that there will be a group of people locally that can take hold of the thing.

ANTHONY WILDEN.   I should like to look at the question of the relationship between entropy and negative entropy. When Elise Boulding mentioned antientropy and Margaret Mead mentioned man as the antientropic being, I did not understand what was meant, because it seems perfectly clear that if the physical world is entropic, the evolutionary world of man is negatively entropic in the sense that it increases in organization. Now antientropy must be something else that I do not understand, because hubris is one of the questions which has not really been dealt with. Gregory Bateson makes the point that hubris is what fuels the positive feedback in our relationship to our environment. Magoroh Maruyama has also written about this. If you get into a runaway relationship inside a communications system you have only three alternatives, depending on the level of the system concerned: either destruction, or evolution, or revolution. (What) I want to ask is: are we in a runaway relationship to our environment, to one another, both at the social and personal levels and at the biological level, and if so, how are we planning to introduce some negative feedback into the situation, so that instead of being faced with something like extinction, we can have something like a future?

MARGARET MEAD.   In the first place, I am not saying anything different, and you will notice I quoted from the Wenner-Gren Symposium; the whole idea of negative feedback came out of the original conferences on cybernetics which Gregory Bateson and Norbert Wiener and I all worked on. So there is nothing different or new here that is contradictory to anything that Elise Boulding or I have been saying. Both negative and positive feedback preserve and generate information in man and in life itself, and this concentrates energy in a more organized form, in a universe that is tending toward disorganization.[2] So what we mean by negative and positive feedback in this situation, or antientropic behavior, is the capacity of man to feel, to think, to organize, and to alter the system which is tending toward disorganization, but energy can be trapped and used in particular cases. Now, hubris would be the case where we did not recognize the nature of the whole system of which we are part, and if we do not recognize this then we create these runaways, consciously or unconsciously. I think

---

[2] *Editor's Note:* The first phase of the development of cybernetics primarily was focused on *negative feedback*. This was the period when the Josiah Macy, Jr. Foundation held annual conferences on cybernetics. The participants at these conferences included Heinz von Foerster, Arturo Rosenblueth, Norbert Wiener, Warren McCulloch, Johann von Neumann, Margaret Mead, Gregory Bateson, Kurt Lewin, and several others. Negative feedback is a process which counteracts deviation from goals or maintains equilibrium. Bateson and some others began exploring positive feedback.

The second phase of cybernetics, which began two decades ago, includes *positive* as well as negative feedback. Positive feedback is a change-amplifying process and can increase differentiation, complexity, and structuredness. The evolution and development of an embryo into an adult is an example of such processes. But positive feedback can also create runaway situations. Inflation is an example.

there is very little doubt that we are in a runaway situation, as you said, in relation to the environment and in terms of human relationships. But, as I see it, man himself, all life, all biological life represents a kind of antientropic behavior, and man with his consciousness of what is happening represents the highest degree of antientropic behavior that we know of at present in the universe. We don't know much about the universe but of the little we know, man represents this.

ELISE BOULDING.   Of the two aspects of the antientropic process, one is image learning, image creation, and feedback, and the other is the "agape," the loving. I think the only protection against hubris is love. The cognitive structure and image creation are no protection against hubris, but love is.

There is little difference between nonviolent and violent approaches to change. The more I look at both, and I have spent a lot of time with both, the more I realize that there is a vast shared reservoir of efforts to empathize with mankind. There is far more positive empathy in the violent revolutionary. As regards the unity of ends and means, I think the whole thing has to be redefined and I am no longer willing to accept the dichotomy between the violent and the nonviolent revolutionary.

MARGARET MEAD.   This is where we have to deal with the fact that the future is now! Any consequences of genetic research that matter are way in the future. What influences us is the belief that they might happen. If we think that they are likely to be terrible and that man is going to be engineered into a monstrosity, that becomes one more reason for not doing anything. If we think, on the other hand, that a greater understanding of the brain is likely to be achieved — which I believe is the next great breakthrough, not genetic engineering but a better understanding of the human brain — this is going to do for anthropology in the future what ethology did in the last decade, what learning theory has done, as we borrowed from one field or another and built it into our understanding of man. The understanding of the brain, which is just beginning, is going to be the next great field within which human consciousness can be raised to a different level by a cultural means.

REFERENCES

MARUYAMA, MAGOROH
   1978   Heterogenistics and morphogenistics: toward a new concept of the scientific. *Theory and Society* 5: 75–96.

MORIN, EDGAR
1977   *La méthode.* Paris: Seuil.
PRIGOGINE, ILYA, GREGOIRE NICOLIS
1977   *Self-organization in non-equilibrium systems.* New York: Wiley Interscience.

SUGGESTED READINGS

First Phase of Cybernetics

VON FOERSTER, HEINZ
1949–53 *Transactions of the Conferences on Cybernetics.* Josiah Macy, Jr. Foundation.
WIENER, NORBERT
1948   *Cybernetics.* New York: Wiley.

Second Phase of Cybernetics

MARUYAMA, MAGOROH
1961   Morphogenesis and morphoatasis. *Methodos* 12: 251–96.
MARUYAMA, MAGOROH
1963   The second cybernetics. Deviation-amplifying mutual causal processes. *American Scientist* 51: 164–79; 51: 250–56.
1977   Heterogenistics: an epistemological restructuring of biological and social sciences. *Cybernetica* 20: 69–86.
MILSUM, JOHN
1968   *Positive feedback.* Oxford: Pergamon.
POLGAR, STEVEN P.
1961   Evolution and the thermodynamic imperative. *Human Biology* 33: 99–109.

Biographical Notes

EDMUND BACON (1910–   ) was born in Philadelphia. After receiving a Bachelor of Architecture degree from Cornell University, he began his career in Shanghai. He returned to Philadelphia and held such positions as Executive Director, Philadelphia City Planning Commission; Co-designer, Better Philadelphia Exhibition; and Managing Director, Philadelphia Housing Association. Several major buildings in downtown Philadelphia were designed by him. At the moment he is Vice-President of Mondev Corporation Ltd. He has been a member of various United States government bodies including the Task Force Potomac River Basin Plan, the Urban Transportation Advisory Council, and the Citizens' Advisory Committee on Environmental Quality. Among the many awards he received are the Distinguished Service Award of the American Institute of Planners, the Brown Medal of the Franklin Institute and the Rockefeller Foundation Award. One of his numerous publications is his book *Design of cities.*

C. GEORGE BENELLO (1926–   ) was born in New York City. After receiving a B.A. in Philosophy from Harvard University, he did graduate work at the Université Laval and Brown University and obtained an M.A. in Literature and American Studies from San Francisco State College. He taught English in Japan — where he also studied Buddhism — and has been on the faculties of San Francisco State College, Goddard College and McGill University. Currently he teaches sociology at Sir George Williams University in Montreal and is President of Parallel Institute in that city, which has just received a grant from the Canadian government for a three-year research project to develop community-controlled enterprises. He has published extensively in national magazines and professional journals.

ELISE BOULDING received a B.A. from Douglas College and a Ph.D. from the University of Michigan. She is an Associate Professor of Sociology at the University of Colorado and Project Director of its Institute of Behavioral Science. She has done research on women's roles in Japan and the U.S.A. and has several publications on the sociology of the family. Her translation (from the Dutch) of Fred Polak's *Image of the future* was published by Oceana Publications. Her many functions include Secretary of the Inter-American Consortium on Peace Research, Education and Development; International Chairman of the Women's International League for Peace and Freedom; Secretary of the Ad Hoc International Work Group on Sociological Study of Sex Roles; member of the American Association for the Advancement of Science Commission on Science Education; and Editor of the *International Peace Research Newsletter.*

SORY CAMARA (1940–   ), a member of the Mandenka tribe, was born in Gueckédow, Republic of Guinea. His primary and secondary studies were carried out in his native country and his higher education was pursued at the Faculté des Lettres and the Faculté des Sciences at the University of Bordeaux where he received his Licence de Psychologie, Licence de Sociologie, and his Doctorat d'Ethnologie. He was a member of the technical staff at the Centre National de la Recherche Scientifique et de l'Éducation Nationale, and since 1971 he has been Maître-assistant d'Ethnologie at the University of Bordeaux II. He has carried out several research projects on the social organization, psychology, worldview and epistemology of the Mandenka.

LUTHER P. GERLACH (1930–   ) was born in Pennsylvania. He holds a B.A. degree from the University of Minnesota and a Ph.D. from the University of London. He has served on the faculties of Lafayette College and the California Institute of Technology and is currently a Professor of Anthropology at the University of Minnesota. He also has been Field Director of a U.S. State Department Refugee Investigation Program in West Germany. His field research was carried out in Kenya, Tanzania, and Uganda. A Fullbright Fellowship was one of the many research grants he received. He is the author of numerous publications on American social movements and the creator of films related to this area of study.

SAMIR GHABBOUR (1933–   ) was born in Cairo. He has a B.S. degree, a Diploma in Educational Psychology, an M.S. in Zoology, and a Ph.D. in Zoology/Ecology, all from the University of Cairo and now teaches biology and zoology in Cairo and Khartoum. He has more than thirty publications, has done research in ecology, physiology, zoogeography and soil ecology, and is planning research in the field of simulation of ecosystems of world nations.

JAMES C. GIFFORD (1927–1973) was born in New York City. He received his B.A. and M.A. in Anthropology from the University of Arizona and a Ph.D. from Harvard University. At the time of his death he was an Associate Professor of Anthropology at Temple University, Philadelphia. His major interests included archaeology of the American Southwest and Middle America, especially the "high" civilization of the ancient Maya. Within this speciality he concentrated on "the analysis of material culture in archaeological and ethnographic contexts in such ways as to illuminate the fundamental nature of man" and was instrumental in establishing type-variety ceramic analysis in the Maya area. Concomitantly he found and edited *Ceramica de Cultura Maya*. His publications include *Preclassic ceramics from Chalchuapa, El Salvador* (with R. J. Sharer); *Prehistoric Maya settlements in the Belize Valley* (with G. R. Willey, et. al.); *Prehistoric pottery analysis and the ceramics of Barton Ramie* and "Recent thought concerning the interpretation of Maya prehistory" (in *Mesoamerican archaeology: new approaches*).

ARTHUR M. HARKINS (1936–) was born in New York City and studied at the University of Massachusetts and University of Kansas where he earned a Ph.D. degree in 1968. He is an Associate Professor of Education and Sociology and Director of the Office for Applied Social Science and the Future at the University of Minnesota in Minneapolis. He has been a consultant to many business and industrial organizations, school systems, and colleges and has conducted research on contemporary Indian American migration patterns. His numerous publications mainly treat such topics as urban Native Americans, Native American education, and human futures and include a co-authored book *Indian Americans: the effects of urban migration* (Doubleday, forthcoming).

DONALD O. IMSLAND (1931–) was born in Iowa, U.S.A. After studying at Iowa State University, Luther College, and Luther Theological Seminary, he served as Executive Director of the Twin Cities Lay School of Theology and as Associate Director of the Minnesota Project in continuing adult education. He is owner and director of Human Design, a private consulting business concerned with human environment, and is a consultant on corporate planning of the Northern States Power Company. He has several publications covering such topics as ecology, environment, and futuristics.

SUE-ELLEN JACOBS received her Ph.D. in Anthropology from the University of Colorado and teaches at the Department of Urban and Regional Planning, University of Illinois. Her earlier experiences as a registered nurse in four southern states (U.S.A.) awakened her awareness of the discrepancies between the theories about "minority groups" and the actual life situation of these people. This, and her experience in the differential treatment of patients by various staff members in hospitals, led her to develop a new method of inquiry called "ethnocommunication." Her interests include women's liberation and she has conducted studies on women's roles in various subcultures, ethnic groups, and in urban-poverty environments.

DOROTHY L. KEUR (1904–   ) was born in New York. She obtained her Ph.D. degree from Columbia University, and has been Professor of Anthropology at Hunter College, from which she has retired. She has been President of the American Ethnological Society. Her publications include archaeological studies of Navajo acculturation, and contributions to the *Encyclopedie van de Nederlandse Antillen.*

RUSSELL LADUE (1924–   ) was born in Iowa. He attended the Universities of Wisconsin and Michigan and Columbia University, and obtained his M.A. degree at the University of Wisconsin. He has taught at the University of Michigan and Cornell University, and has gone into advertising, marketing and theater. He is Executive Director of the Ford Dealers Alliance, and has published a novel *No more with me* (Doubleday).

H. L. LEFFERTS, JR. (1939–   ) was born in Virginia, U.S.A. He studied at Colgate University and the University of Illinois and obtained his Ph.D. from the University of Colorado. After teaching anthropology at the University of Colorado and at the Air Force Academy, he is now in the Department of Anthropology of Drew University. He conducted research on the ecology and social organization in northeastern Thailand and on the anthropological aspects of negotiation and contracts.

ROBERT K. MCKNIGHT received his M.A. and Ph.D. degrees in Anthropology from Ohio State University and is Chairman of the Department of Geography-Anthropology at California State University at Hayward. He is exploring a method of research called "incultural anthropology" and is particularly interested in the concepts of progress, modernization, evolution, and development. With J. W. Bennett and H. Paswin he wrote *In search of identity: the Japanese overseas scholar in the United States.*

MAGOROH MARUYAMA (1929–   ) was born in Japan, and studied at the University of California at Berkeley, and the Universities of Munich, Heidelberg, Copenhagen and Lund. He received his B.A. in Mathematics and a Ph.D. in Philosophy. His sixty publications include "The second cybernetics" in *American Scientist*, 1963. He lived among Eskimos in Alaska and Navajo Indians in Arizona, and in San Quentin Prison he organized a team of inmates as researchers. This led him to the development of the "endogenous research" methodology which was later applied to research *by* ghetto residents and migrant farm workers. He has been on the faculties of the University of California at Berkeley, Stanford University, Brandeis University, Antioch College, and Portland State University in Oregon. He currently teaches at the University of Illinois Urbana.

MARGARET MEAD (1901–   ) was born in Philadelphia. She received her B.A. from Barnard College, and her M.A. in Psychology and Ph.D. in Anthropology from Columbia University. She is a member of the Department of Anthropology at the American Museum of Natural History, Adjunct Professor of Anthropology at Columbia University, Professor of Social Sciences and Chairman of the Department of Social Sciences at the College of the Liberal Arts at Lincoln Center of Fordham University, and Visiting Professor of Anthropology at the Department of Psychiatry, College of Medicine, University of Cincinnati. Between 1926 and 1967, she made twelve field trips to the South Seas. Among her books are: *Coming of age in Samoa, Growing up in New Guinea, Sex and temperament in three primitive societies, Male and female, Soviet attitudes towards authority*, and *Culture and commitment: a study of the generation gap.* Her publications specifically dealing with the future are: "Towards more vivid utopias," "The future as shared culture," "Education for humanity in a developing world," and "The life cycle and its variations: the division of roles." Presently she is President of the World Society for Ekistics and the Scientist's Institute for Public Information.

T. K. MOULIK (1936–   ) was born in India, attended the Indian Agricultural Research Institute, Calcutta University and obtained B.S., M.S. and Ph.D. degrees in Agriculture. He has been Agricultural Extension Officer in the Government of West Bengal, Research Associate at the Institute of Public Administration, Assistant Professor of Behavioral Science, communication behavior specialist at the Indian Agricultural Research Institute, and sociologist for USAID, all in Delhi. He has published extensively in international journals, particularly on diffusion of innovations and social change in developing countries. Currently he is a Research Fellow at the New Guinea

Research Unit, Research School of Pacific Studies, Australian National University and is planning research on the impact of mining on the farmers of Bougainville, New Guinea.

KIVUTO NDENTI is in the Department of Sociology, University of Nairobi, Kenya.

CHUDI C. NWA-CHIL was born in Nigeria, and received his B.A., M.Sc., and Ph.D. degrees in Sociology from the University of Lund, Sweden, where he taught until 1972. He then went to Tanzania to teach at the University of Dar Es Salaam. He has written several articles on education, social problems, manpower needs, and international assistance in Nigeria and Tanzania, and is currently conducting research on educational selectivity, opportunity, and performance in Tanzania.

STEVEN POLGAR is Associate Director of the Carolina Population Center and Associate Professor of Anthropology at the University of North Carolina. He received his Ph.D. in anthropology from the University of Chicago, and an M.P.H. degree in Public Health Practice from Harvard University. He taught at the University of Chicago and the University of California at Berkeley, was Director of Research at Planned Parenthood World Population in New York, and is currently a consultant to the Human Reproduction Unit of the World Health Organization in Geneva. He conducted researches in action anthropology among the Fox Indians of Iowa, on community development in Ghana, on schizophrenia among American soldiers, on medical care among the blacks in California, and on family planning in poverty areas of New York City.

EUGENE E. RUYLE (1936–   ) was born in California. He received a B.A. degree from the University of California at Berkeley, an M. A. from Yale University and a Ph.D. from Columbia University, all in anthropology. He served in the U.S. Marine Corps, was a correctional officer at San Quentin Prison in California, conducted research in Japan, and since 1970 he has been an Assistant Professor of Anthropology at the University of Virginia. He has published several articles on slavery, capitalism, caste, jails in Virginia, ghettos in Japan, and related subjects.

I. KAREN SHERARTS (1944–   ) was born in Minnesota, U.S.A. She studied at the College of St. Scholastica and the University of Minnesota, and received her M.A. degree in 1974. She has been a social worker, a research fellow, and a consultant to community programs and industry, and has several publications on Native Americans and education.

JACK N. SHUMAN (1938–   ) obtained his A.B. in Physical Sciences at Syracuse University, an M.A. in History of Science at Harvard University, and a Ph.D. in History of Social Systems at Georgetown University. He has been on the research staff at Georgetown and Syracuse Universities and at the Institute for Applied Technology. From 1963 to 1971 he was a Technical Information Specialist and Policy Analyst at the U.S. Department of Commerce and from 1971 to 1973 a Program Policy Analyst at the U.S. Department of Health, Education and Welfare. Recently he returned to the U.S. Department of Commerce as a Technical Information Specialist. His seventeen publications and presentations treat topics such as science policy, information and data systems, general systems models for the future, use and misuse of simulation models, scientific and technical communication, and technology transfer.

EVAN C. VLACHOS (1935–   ) was born in Greece, obtained his LL.B. degree in Law at the University of Athens and his M.A. and Ph.D. in Sociology at Indiana University. He has been on the faculties of Indiana University, Pierce College in Athens, and the University of Colorado, and has been a research specialist, principal investigator and a consultant with various United States government agencies including HUD, NSF, AID, OWRR, with the Army Corps of Engineers and the Utah State Highway Department, on the subjects of juvenile delinquency, community development, water resources and environmental design. He has published more than twenty books and articles, and has given numerous papers, addresses and speeches at professional meetings. Currently he teaches at Colorado State University.

ROGER W. WESCOTT (1925–   ) was born in Philadelphia and is Professor of Linguistics and Chairman of the Anthropology Department at Drew University. He received his B.A. degree in History, M.A. in Indology and Ph. D. in Linguistics, all at Princeton University. Later he obtained his B.Litt. at Oxford University. After fieldwork in Nigeria, he taught history and human relations at M.I.T. and Boston University, and English and Social Science at Michigan State University where he was also Director of the African Language Program. Before coming to Drew University, he was Professor of Anthropology and History at Southern Connecticut State College. He has been a Rhodes Scholar, an ACLS Scholar and a Ford Fellow. He has written seven books including *The divine animal*, numerous articles and five anthologized chapters. He is now working on a book tentatively entitled *Faces of the future*, and is teaching a course "Man's Future."

ANTHONY WILDEN (1935–   ) was born in London, studied at the Universities of Victoria and British Columbia and obtained his Ph.D.

degree at Johns Hopkins in 1968. He has taught literature and communications at the University of California, San Diego and has been Visiting Professor of Sociology at the Université du Bénin, Togo, West Africa, and at the École Pratique des Hautes Études, Sorbonne, Paris. Later he has been a Research Associate of the National Science Foundation on the project "Design and Management of Environmental Systems" at Michigan State University. Currently he is in the Department of Communication, Simon Fraser University, Burnaby, B.C., Canada. He also served as a consultant to the Research Division of the Radio-Télévision Française. He published three books and fifteen articles on the subjects of communication theory, information theory, epistemology, psychoanalysis, cybernetics, and ecosystems, and has been a Consulting Editor of *Psychology Today.*

RICHARD G. WOODS (1933–   ) was born in Oklahoma U.S.A. and studied at the Universities of Tulsa and Minnesota. He has been a consultant and Employee Relations Research Coordinator at the Whirlpool Corporation, Manpower Management Specialist in the U.S. Air Force, and Special Assistant to the Director of Personnel Services of General Mills, Inc. He has taught at the University of Minnesota, and has been Co-Director of the Office for Applied Social Science and the Future of that university. He has more than fifty publications on industrial relations, futures research, and American Indians.

Index of Names

Index of Subjects

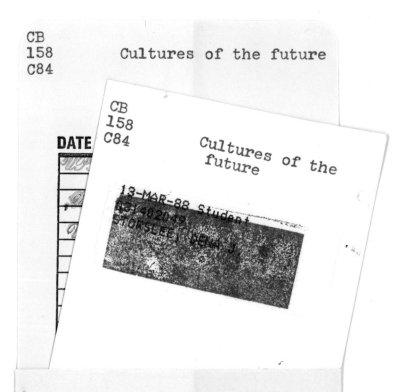